Ideas and Patterns in Literature

A series of literature anthologies accompanied by Student Guides

A Teacher's Edition of each Student Guide is available.

THE AUTHORS

John F. Sutton is Project Director of English in Darien, Connecticut, and Head of the English Department of the Darien Junior High Schools.

Annette Silverstone is Chairman of the English Department at Bedford Junior High School, Westport, Connecticut.

Martha L. Smith, an Assistant Director of the Education Service Center in Fort Worth, Texas, was formerly a teacher and supervisor in Texas schools.

GENERAL EDITORS

Edgar H. Knapp, Associate Professor of English and Education at The Pennsylvania State University, has taught in secondary schools and is author of Introduction to Poetry.

William G. Leary, Professor of English at California State College at Los Angeles, is author of Thought and Statement and other texts for high school and college.

CONSULTANT

Delores Minor is Supervisor of High School English, Detroit Public Schools.

JOHN F. SUTTON

ANNETTE SILVERSTONE

MARTHA L. SMITH

IDEAS and PATTERNS in Literature I

GENERAL EDITORS:

Edgar H. Knapp

William G. Leary

CONSULTANT: *Delores Minor*

Harcourt, Brace & World, Inc.
New York   Chicago   San Francisco   Atlanta   Dallas

Copyright © 1970 by Harcourt, Brace & World, Inc.
All rights reserved. No part of this publication may be reproduced or transmitted in any form or by any means, electronic or mechanical, including photocopy, recording, or any information storage and retrieval system, without permission in writing from the publisher.

Printed in the United States of America.

ACKNOWLEDGMENTS: *For permission to reprint copyrighted material, grateful acknowledgment is made to the following publishers, authors, and agents:*

Stewart Alsop and Dr. Ralph E. Lapp: "The Strange Death of Louis Slotin" by Stewart Alsop and Ralph E. Lapp.

Atheneum Publishers: The Miracle Worker, a play by William Gibson, copyright © 1956, 1957 by William Gibson; copyright © 1959, 1960 by Tamarack Productions, Ltd., and George S. Klein and Leo Garel as trustees under three separate deeds of trust. CAUTION: *The Miracle Worker* is the sole property of the above named copyright Owners and is fully protected by copyright. It may not be acted by professionals or amateurs without written permission and the payment of a royalty. All rights, including professional, amateur, stock, radio broadcasting, television, motion picture, recitation, lecturing, public reading and the rights of translation into foreign languages are reserved. All inquiries should be addressed to the Owners' agent, Leah Salisbury, Inc., 790 Madison Avenue, New York, New York 10021.

The Atlantic Monthly: "The Erne from the Coast" by T. O. Beachcroft, copyright © 1951 by The Atlantic Monthly Company, Boston, Massachusetts 02116.

The Master, Fellows and Scholars of Christ's College, Cambridge: "Orpheus and Eurydice" from *Gods, Heroes, and Men of Ancient Greece* by W. H. D. Rouse.

Collins-Knowlton-Wing, Inc.: "The Palace of Olympus" from *Greek Gods and Heroes* by Robert Graves, copyright © 1960 by Robert Graves.

Curtis Brown, Ltd.: "A Caution to Everybody" from *Private Dining Room and Other New Verses* by Ogden Nash, copyright © 1950 by Ogden Nash.

Dodd, Mead & Company, Inc.: "Trifles" from *Plays* by Susan Glaspell, copyright 1920 by Dodd, Mead & Company, Inc.; copyright renewed 1948 by Susan Glaspell. "The Ballad of Blasphemous Bill" from *The Complete Poems of Robert Service.*

Doubleday & Company, Inc.: From *An Introduction to Haiku* by Harold G. Henderson, copyright © 1958 by Harold G. Henderson. "the lesson of the moth" from *archy and mehitabel* by Don Marquis, copyright 1927 by Doubleday & Company, Inc. "Enemy Territory," copyright © 1964 by William Melvin Kelley, from *Dancers on the Shore* by William Melvin Kelley. *The Lilies of the Field* by William E. Barrett, copyright © 1962 by William E. Barrett.

The Estate of Sir Arthur Conan Doyle and Mary Yost Associates: "The Adventure of the Norwood Builder" from *Complete Sherlock Holmes* by Sir Arthur Conan Doyle.

Norma Millay Ellis: "The Courage That My Mother Had" and "Spring" from *Collected Poems* by Edna St. Vincent Millay, copyright 1954 by Norma Millay Ellis. Published by Harper & Row.

Farrar, Straus & Giroux, Inc.: "The Night of Kondén Diara" from *The Dark Child* by Camara Laye, copyright 1954 by Camara Laye.

Harcourt, Brace & World, Inc.: "Wind Song" from *Smoke and Steel* by Carl Sandburg, copyright 1920, by Harcourt, Brace & World, Inc.; renewed, 1948, by Carl Sandburg. "old age sticks" from *95 Poems* by E. E. Cummings, © 1958 by E. E. Cummings. "The Shepherd's Daughter" from *After Thirty Years: The Daring Young Man on the Flying Trapeze* by William Saroyan, copyright © 1934, 1962, 1964 by William Saroyan. "A Father Sees a Son Nearing Manhood" from *The People, Yes* by Carl Sandburg, copyright 1936, by Harcourt, Brace & World, Inc.; copyright 1964, by Carl Sandburg. "King Juke" from *Afternoon of a Pawnbroker and Other Poems,* copyright 1943, by Kenneth Fearing. "Abraham Lincoln" abridged from *A Lincoln Preface,* copyright 1953, by Carl Sandburg, and *Abraham Lincoln: The Prairie Years and the War Years* and *The Sandburg Range* by Carl Sandburg, copyright 1926, by Harcourt, Brace & World, Inc.; copyright 1939, 1954, 1957, 1967, by Carl Sandburg. "The Marriage Proposal" by Anton Chekhov, translated by George Kearns and Marina Liapunov, copyright © 1970 by Harcourt, Brace & World, Inc.

Harper & Row, Publishers, Incorporated: "At the Aquarium" from *Poems of Five Decades* by Max Eastman, copyright 1942, 1954 by Max Eastman. "The Crazy Woman" from *Selected Poems* by Gwendolyn Brooks, copyright © 1960 by Gwendolyn Brooks Blakely. From pp. 342–353 "Slang and Its Relatives" from *Understanding English* by Paul Roberts, copyright © 1958 by Paul Roberts.

M. Carl Holman: "Song" by M. Carl Holman from *The Poetry of the Negro 1746-1949*, edited by Langston Hughes and Arna Bontemps.

Holt, Rinehart and Winston, Inc.: "Limited" from *Chicago Poems* by Carl Sandburg, copyright 1916 by Holt, Rinehart and Winston, Inc., copyright 1944 by Carl Sandburg. "Christmas" from *Homecoming* by Floyd Dell, copyright 1933, © 1961 by Floyd Dell. "The Runaway" from *Complete Poems of Robert Frost*, copyright 1923 by Holt, Rinehart and Winston, Inc., copyright 1951 by Robert Frost. "Loveliest of Trees" from "A Shropshire Lad" — Authorised Edition — from *The Collected Poems of A. E. Housman*, copyright 1939, 1940, © 1959 by Holt, Rinehart and Winston, Inc., copyright © 1967 by Robert E. Symons. "Nathan Hale" by Nancy Hale, from *There Were Giants in the Land*, copyright 1942 by Holt, Rinehart and Winston, Inc. "'Out, Out —'" from *Complete Poems of Robert Frost*, copyright 1916 by Holt, Rinehart and Winston, Inc., copyright 1944 by Robert Frost.

Houghton Mifflin Company: "The Lover of Beauty" ("Pygmalion and Galatea") from *Greek Myths* by Olivia Coolidge. From *Words from the Myths* by Isaac Asimov.

Indiana University Press: "Homage" and "Any Man's Advice to His Son" from *New and Selected Poems* by Kenneth Fearing.

Alfred A. Knopf, Inc.: "Sonic Boom," © copyright 1959 by John Updike, from *Telephone Poles and Other Poems* by John Updike. "Early Marriage," copyright 1934 by The Curtis Publishing Company and renewed 1962 by Conrad Richter, from *Early Americana and Other Stories* by Conrad Richter. "Dunkirk," copyright 1941 by Robert Nathan, from *The Green Leaf* by Robert Nathan. "Survival," copyright 1944 by John Hersey, from *Here to Stay* by John Hersey. This article was first published in a slightly different form in *The New Yorker*. From *Down These Mean Streets* ("Puerto Rican Paradise") by Piri Thomas, copyright © 1967 by Piri Thomas.

J. B. Lippincott Company: "The Highwayman" from *Collected Poems* by Alfred Noyes, copyright 1906, 1934 by Alfred Noyes. "Words Began with Pictures" was originally "Painted Pebbles and Cave Pictures" and "Sign-for-a-Sound Writing" from *Painted Rock to Printed Page* by Frances Rogers, copyright © 1960 by Frances Rogers.

Little, Brown and Company: End from "The Man Who Liked Dickens" from *A Handful of Dust* by Evelyn Waugh, copyright 1944 by Evelyn Waugh.

The Macmillan Company of Canada, Ltd.: "Phaëthon" from *Four Ages of Man* by Jay MacPherson.

The Macmillan Company: "Landscape as Metal and Flowers" from *Collected Poems* by Winfield Townley Scott, copyright 1941 by Winfield Townley Scott. "Crystal Moment" from *The Yolk of Thunder* by Robert P. Tristram Coffin, copyright 1932 by The Macmillan Company; renewed 1960 by Margaret Halvosa. "The Dark Hills" from *Collected Poems* by Edwin Arlington Robinson, copyright 1920 by The Macmillan Company; renewed 1948 by Ruth Nivison. "How Much Is True?" and Afterword by Mary Renault from *Theseus: A Greek Legend Retold* by Charles Kingsley with an Afterword by Mary Renault, copyright © Mary Renault 1964. "The Real Message to García" from *Lost Men of American History* by Stewart Holbrook, copyright 1946 by Stewart H. Holbrook. From *Manchild in the Promised Land* ("A Goodbye Speech") by Claude Brown, copyright © by Claude Brown 1965.

Florence Ripley Mastin and The New York Times Company: "Eight-Cylinder Man" from *Lyric Verse* by Florence Ripley Mastin, copyright © 1960 by The New York Times Company, copyright 1962 by Florence Ripley Mastin.

Harold Matson Company, Inc.: "There Will Come Soft Rains" by Ray Bradbury, copyright 1950 by Ray Bradbury.

McGraw-Hill Book Company: "Land of Our Enemies" from *Clearing in the Sky* by Jesse Stuart, copyright 1950 by Jesse Stuart. "The King and the Peasant" by Saadi, from *Literature of the World* edited by Thelma G. James, et al.

Literary Executor of W. Somerset Maugham: "Appointment in Samarra" from *Sheppey* by W. Somerset Maugham.

Negro Digest and Roqua Wassam: "Tornado Threat" by Roqua Wassam from *Negro Digest* Magazine.

New Directions Publishing Corporation: "New Moon" by Tu Fu from *One Hundred Poems from the Chinese* by Kenneth Rexroth. All rights reserved.

Harold Ober Associates Inc.: "The Enemy" by Pearl S. Buck, copyright © 1942 by Pearl S. Buck. "Thank You, M'am" from *The Langston Hughes Reader* by Langston Hughes, copyright © 1958 by Langston Hughes. "Juke Box Love Song" from *Montage of a Dream Deferred* by Langston Hughes, copyright © 1951 by Langston Hughes.

October House Inc.: "Those Winter Sundays" by Robert Hayden from *Selected Poems*, copyright © 1966 by Robert Hayden.

Oxford University Press: "How the Animals Got Their Color" and "How the Animals Got Their Tails" from *The Bavenda* by H. A. Stayt. Published by Oxford University Press for the International African Institute.

A. D. Peters & Co. Literary Agents: "The Sniper" from *Spring Sowing* by Liam O'Flaherty. "The Man Who Liked Dickens" a TV adaptation by Robert Tallman of an Evelyn Waugh story.

Random House, Inc.: From *Act One* by Moss Hart, © copyright 1959 by Catherine Carlisle Hart and Joseph M. Hyman, Trustees.

Paul R. Reynolds, Inc., *599 Fifth Avenue, New York 10017:* "Four Haiku" from *American Negro Poetry* by Richard Wright, copyright © 1963 by Richard Wright.

Simon and Schuster, Inc.: "The Monster" from *Of Men and Music* by Deems Taylor, copyright 1937 by Deems Taylor. "My Mysterious Malady" from *Portrait of Myself* by Margaret Bourke-White, copyright © 1963 by Margaret Bourke-White.

The Society of Authors as the representative of the Literary Trustees of Walter de la Mare: "The Listeners" from *Collected Poems* by Walter de la Mare.

James Still: "A Ride on the Short Dog" by James Still, copyright 1951 by The Atlantic Monthly Company, Boston, Massachusetts 02116.

May Swenson: "Three Jet Planes" by May Swenson from *Another Animal: Poems (Poets of Today Vol. 1*, Charles Scribner's Sons, 1954).

Helen Thurber: "The Tiger Who Would Be King," copyright © 1956 James Thurber, from *Further Fables For Our Time.* Published by Simon and Schuster, Inc.

Twayne Publishers, Inc.: "The Tropics of New York" from *Selected Poems of Claude McKay.*

The Viking Press, Inc.: "All day I hear the noise of waters" from *Collected Poems* by James Joyce, copyright 1918 by B. W. Huebsch, Inc., 1946 by Nora Joyce. "The Seven Ages of a Newspaper Subscriber" from *Times Three* by Phyllis McGinley, copyright 1946 by Phyllis McGinley. Originally appeared in *The New Yorker. The Pearl* by John Steinbeck, copyright © 1945 by John Steinbeck.

PICTURE CREDITS: p. 72, Culver Pictures, Inc.; p. 112, National Gallery of Oslo, Norway; p. 166, Vatican Museum (Mansell Collection); p. 226, Arthor Cantor; p. 360, Inge Morath from Magnum; p. 444, Lincoln National Life Foundation, Fort Wayne, Indiana; p. 508, Mrs. Andrew Wyeth; p. 622, Bradley Smith, New York; p. 686, from *Aesop: Five Centuries of Illustrated Fables,* sel. by John J. McKendry, The Metropolitan Museum of Art; p. 698, Northern Natural Gas Company Collection, Joslyn Art Museum, Omaha, Nebraska; p. 732, The Cleveland Museum, John L. Severance Fund.

Contents

BOOK ONE

PART 1 *Homer* The Odyssey 1

PART 2 Greek Myths and Their Uses 73

Robert Graves	The Palace of Olympus 75
Jay Macpherson	Phaëthon 82
W. H. D. Rouse	Orpheus and Eurydice 85
Olivia Coolidge	Pygmalion and Galatea 89
Charles Kingsley	Theseus 91
Mary Renault	How Much Is True? 101
Isaac Asimov	Words from the Myths 107

PART 3 Coming of Age 113

Camara Laye	The Night of Kondén Diara 115
Conrad Richter	Early Marriage 127
T. O. Beachcroft	The Erne from the Coast 144
Floyd Dell	Christmas 157
Claude Brown	A Goodbye Speech 161
Kenneth Fearing	Any Man's Advice to His Son 163
Carl Sandburg	A Father Sees a Son Nearing Manhood 164

vii

PART 4	The Storyteller 167
Edgar Allan Poe	The Cask of Amontillado 171
Ray Bradbury	There Will Come Soft Rains 178
Sir Arthur Conan Doyle	The Adventure of the Norwood Builder 185
Jesse Stuart	Land of Our Enemies 208
Alfred Noyes	The Highwayman 216
Robert Frost	"Out, Out — " 220
Robert W. Service	The Ballad of Blasphemous Bill 222

BOOK TWO

PART 1	William Gibson
	The Miracle Worker 227

PART 2	Commitment to Others 317
Pearl S. Buck	The Enemy 319
Stewart Alsop and Ralph E. Lapp	The Strange Death of Louis Slotin 339
The Bible	The Good Samaritan 351
Björnsterne Björnson	A Father 352
Langston Hughes	Thank You, Ma'am 356

PART 3	The Playwright at Work 361
Anton Chekhov	The Marriage Proposal 363
Robert Tallman	The Man Who Liked Dickens 375 (Television version)
Evelyn Waugh	The Man Who Liked Dickens 391 (Original ending)

PART 4 Language and Comunication 395

Frances Rogers	Words Began with Pictures 397
Paul Roberts	Slang and Its Relatives 406
Lewis Carroll	Humpty Dumpty on the Meaning of Words 414
Anne Sullivan Macy	Everything Has a Name 418

PART 5 Sights and Sounds 425

THE SEA

James Joyce	All Day I Hear 428
Alfred, Lord Tennyson	Break, Break, Break 428
Henry Wadsworth Longfellow	The Tide Rises, The Tide Falls 429

THE SKY

Roqua Wassam	Tornado Threat 430
Tu Fu	New Moon 431
May Swenson	Three Jet Planes 431
Carl Sandburg	Wind Song 432

THE WORLD AROUND US

Robert P. Tristram Coffin	Crystal Moment 433
Claude McKay	The Tropics in New York 434
Winfield Townley Scott	Landscape as Metal and Flowers 435
Edwin Arlington Robinson	The Dark Hills 435
Robert Frost	The Runaway 436

	SOUNDS
Kenneth Fearing	King Juke 437
Langston Hughes	Juke Box Love Song 438
Walter de la Mare	The Listeners 438
	HAIKU
	Eight Japanese Haiku 440
Richard Wright	Four Haiku 442

BOOK THREE

PART 1	*Carl Sandburg*
	Abraham Lincoln 445
	FROM A Lincoln Preface 448
	FROM The Prairie Years 452
	FROM The War Years 499

PART 2	The Biographer's Art 509
John Hersey	Survival 511
Margaret Bourke-White	My Mysterious Malady 524
Deems Taylor	The Monster 540
Moss Hart	Act One 544
Piri Thomas	Puerto Rican Paradise 550

PART 3	The Common Man as Hero 555
William E. Barrett	The Lilies of the Field 557
Nancy Hale	Nathan Hale 605
William Melvin Kelley	Enemy Territory 610
Robert Nathan	Dunkirk 618

BOOK FOUR

PART 1 John Steinbeck
The Pearl   623

PART 2 Fables and Legends   687

Aesop	The Dog in the Manger 689
Aesop	The Mice and the Cat 689
African Folk Tale	How the Animals Got Their Color 690
African Folk Tale	How the Animals Got Their Tails 690
Jean de La Fontaine	The Old Cat and the Young Mouse 691
Saadi	The Legend of the King and the Peasant 692
James Thurber	The Tiger Who Would Be King 693
William Saroyan	The Shepherd's Daughter 695

PART 3 Twists of Fate   699

W. Somerset Maugham	Appointment in Samarra 699
Liam O'Flaherty	The Sniper 701
Susan Glaspell	Trifles 705
James Still	A Ride on the Short Dog 719
Stewart Holbrook	The Real Message to García 721

PART 4 The Poet's Search for Values 733

LIFE AND DEATH

William Shakespeare	The Hollow Crown	735
Carl Sandburg	Limited	735
Don Marquis	The Lesson of the Moth	736
John Updike	Sonic Boom	738

MAN AND NATURE

A. E. Housman	Loveliest of Trees	739
Walt Whitman	When I Heard the Learn'd Astronomer	740
Edna St. Vincent Millay	Spring	740
Florence Ripley Mastin	Eight-Cylinder Man	741
Max Eastman	At the Aquarium	741

YOUTH AND AGE

Robert Hayden	Those Winter Sundays	742
E. E. Cummings	old age sticks	743
William Shakespeare	The Seven Ages of Man	744
Phyllis McGinley	The Seven Ages of a Newspaper Subscriber	745

SUCCESS AND FAILURE

Percy Bysshe Shelley	Ozymandias	746
Kenneth Fearing	Homage	747
Ogden Nash	A Caution to Everybody	747
Edwin Arlington Robinson	Richard Cory	748
M. Carl Holman	Song	749

FAITH AND COURAGE

Edna St. Vincent Millay   The Courage That
                       My Mother Had   750
Gwendolyn Brooks   The Crazy Woman   751
Emily Dickinson   I Never Saw a Moor   751

Index   752

This bronze statue of a Greek warrior
dates from the 6th century B.C.

Wadsworth Atheneum, Hartford, J. P. Morgan Collection (Lee Boltin)

BOOK ONE | PART 1

THE ODYSSEY

Homer

More than three thousand years ago an invading Greek army burned and leveled the walled city of Troy on the coast of Asia Minor. Today, no one really knows the causes of this war. It may have been an attempt to control an important trade route, or it may have been a pirate raid. But the Trojan War did happen, and the Greeks thought of it as an important event in history. Over the years they came to regard the men who had fought on both sides as great heroes. Legends grew up about these heroes, and the legends were mingled with myths of gods and goddesses.

Hundreds of years after the Trojan War, the Greek poet Homer brought together many of these legends and myths and wove them into two long epic poems we call the Iliad (after Ilium, another name for Troy) and the Odyssey (after Odysseus, the hero). No one knows exactly when or where Homer was born. No one is even sure that he was able to read and write: the two poems began as oral literature and may not have been written down until years later.

At any rate, scholars tell us that Homer lived in the eighth century B.C. — perhaps a bit earlier, perhaps a bit later. According to tradition, he was a blind minstrel who wandered from court to court chanting his stories to the accompaniment of a lyre (a kind of harp). He did more than entertain his audiences: he sang about what it meant to be a man and what it meant to be a Greek, he reminded his listeners of how great their ancestors had been, and he provided them with models of bravery.

Odysseus was one of the Greek heroes who fought in the Trojan War, and the Odyssey is the tale of how he and his men endured many hardships on their long voyage home. It also tells of how Odysseus' son Telemachus went in search of his father and of the battle they had to fight to restore order in their country of Ithaca.

During the Trojan War, Odysseus was one of the leading Greek chiefs, but he is not a major figure in the Iliad. However, when he is on the scene, we can see that this is indeed the same character who is the hero of the Odyssey. He is a clever, crafty schemer. More often than not, he gets out of difficult scrapes by the use of a clever trick rather than through his physical strength.

Odysseus had a most ingenious idea that brought about the fall of Troy and the end of the war. He advised the Greeks to build a huge, hollow wooden horse and to leave it at the gates of Troy. The Trojans were tricked into thinking that the Greek army had sailed for home, leaving the wooden horse behind. They dragged the horse inside the walls of the city. But hiding inside the horse were Odysseus and his men. At night they crept out and opened the gates of the city. The Trojans were taken by surprise. The Greeks rushed into the city, burned it, and slaughtered most of the inhabitants.

Poseidon, the god of the sea, had sided with the Trojans. Because Odysseus had thought up the plan which brought Troy to defeat, Poseidon became his enemy. When the war was over and Odysseus set out for his own country, Ithaca. Poseidon did everything in his power to block his journey.

The Odyssey

Invocation to the Muse

Tell me, O Muse, of that ingenious hero who traveled far and wide after he had sacked the famous town of Troy. Many cities did he visit, and many were the nations with whose manners and customs he was acquainted; moreover, he suffered much by the sea while trying to save his own life and bring his men safely home, but do what he might, he could not save his men, for they perished through their own sheer folly in eating the cattle of the sun god, Hyperion, so the god prevented them from ever reaching home.

So now all the Greeks who escaped death in battle or by shipwreck had got safely home except Odysseus (ō·dis′ē·əs), and he, though he was longing to return to his wife and country, was detained by the goddess Calypso, who had got him into a large cave and wanted to marry him. But as years went by, there came a time when the gods settled that he should go back to Ithaca; all the gods had now begun to pity him except Poseidon (pō·sī′dən), who still persecuted him without ceasing and would not let him get home.

Now, when Poseidon had gone off to the Ethiopians, who are at the world's ends, the other gods met in the house of Olympian Zeus.

And Athena said, "Father, son of Cronus, king of kings, my heart bleeds for Odysseus, when I think of his sufferings in that lonely island, far away from all his friends. It is an island covered with forest, in the very middle of the sea, and a goddess lives there, daughter of the magician Atlas, who carries the great columns that keep heaven and earth apart. She has got hold of Odysseus, and has kept him there for seven years continuously to make him forget his home, so that he is tired of life, and thinks of nothing but how he may once more see the smoke of his own chimneys. You, sir, take no heed of this, and yet when Odysseus was before Troy, did he not offer you many a burnt sacrifice? Why then should you keep on being so angry with him?"

And Zeus said, "My child, what are you talking about? How can I forget Odysseus, than whom there is no more capable man on earth nor more liberal in his offerings to the immortal gods that live in heaven? Bear in mind, however, that Poseidon is still furious with Odysseus for having blinded the eye of Polyphemus (pol'i·fē'məs), his son and king of the Cyclopes (sī'klō·pēz). Therefore, though he does not kill Odysseus outright, he torments him by preventing him from getting home. Still, let us lay our heads together and see how we can help him to return; Poseidon will then be pacified, for if we all agree, he can hardly stand out against us."

BOOKS 1–4

[The Odyssey is divided into twenty-four books, or chapters. Odysseus, the hero, does not appear until the beginning of Book 5, and it is there that we begin the story. The central character of the first four books is Telemachus, the son of Odysseus. Telemachus has come of age while his father was fighting the Trojan War and struggling to get home to Ithaca. With Athena's help, Telemachus sets out in search of his father. Our story begins with the first appearance of Odysseus, shipwrecked on Calypso's island.]

BOOK 5

Zeus Decides to Help Odysseus

And now, as Dawn rose from her couch to bring light alike to mortals and immortals, the gods met in council and with them Zeus, the lord of thunder, who is their king. Thereon Athena began to tell them of the many sufferings of Odysseus, for she pitied him away there in the house of the nymph Calypso.

"Father Zeus," said she, "and all you other gods that live in everlasting bliss, may there never be such a thing as a kind and well disposed ruler any more nor one who will govern equitably. May they all henceforth be cruel and unjust, for there is not one of his subjects but has forgotten Odysseus, who ruled them as though he were their father. There he is, lying in great misery on an island where dwells the nymph Calypso, who will not let him go; and he cannot get back to his own country, for he can find neither ships nor sailors to take him over the sea. Furthermore, wicked people are now trying to murder his only son, Telemachus, who is coming home from Pylos and Sparta, where he has been to see if he can get news of his father."

"What, my dear, are you talking about?" replied her father. "Did you not make this plan yourself, that Odysseus will come home and punish the suitors? Besides, you are perfectly able to protect Telemachus and to see him safely home again."

When he had thus spoken, he said to his son Hermes, "Hermes, you are our messenger; go therefore and tell Calypso we have decreed that poor Odysseus is to return home. He is to be convoyed neither by gods nor by men, but after a perilous voyage of twenty days upon a raft, he is to reach the fertile land of the Phaeacians (fē·ā'shē·inz), who will honor him as though he were one of ourselves. They will send him in a ship to his own country and will give him more bronze and gold than he would have brought back from Troy if he had had all his prize money and had got home without disaster. This is how we have settled that he shall return to his country and his friends."

Thus he spoke, and Hermes did as he was told. He bound on his glittering golden sandals, with which he could fly like the wind over land and sea. He took the wand, with which he seals men's eyes in sleep or wakes them just as he pleases, and flew holding it in his hand. Then he swooped down through the sky till he reached the level of the sea, whose waves he skimmed like a cormorant[1] that flies fishing close down on the vast swell of the ocean and drenching its thick plumage in the spray. He flew and flew over many a wave, but when at last he got to the island which was his journey's end, he left the sea and went on by land till he came to the cave where the nymph Calypso lived.

Calypso's Island

Calypso knew him at once — for the gods all know each other, no matter how far they live from one another — but Odysseus was not there. He was on the seashore as usual, looking out upon the barren ocean with tears in his eyes, groaning and breaking his heart for sorrow. Calypso gave Hermes a seat and said, "Why have you come

---

[1] *cormorant:* a large webfooted sea bird.

to see me, Hermes — honored and ever welcome — for you do not visit me often?"

As she spoke, she drew a table loaded with ambrosia [2] beside him and mixed him some red nectar,[3] so Hermes ate and drank till he had enough and then said:

"We are speaking god and goddess to one another, and you ask me why I have come here, and I will tell you truly as you would have me do. Zeus sent me. He says that you have here the most unlucky of all those who fought nine years before the city of King Priam and sailed home in the tenth year after having sacked it. On their way home, they sinned against Athena, who raised both wind and waves against them, so that all his brave companions perished, and he alone was carried hither by wind and tide. Zeus says that you are to let this man go at once, for it is decreed that he shall not perish here, far from his own people, but shall return to his house and country and see his friends again."

Calypso trembled when she heard this. "You gods," she exclaimed, "ought to be ashamed of yourselves. You are always jealous and hate seeing a goddess take a fancy to a mortal man. I found the poor creature sitting all alone astride a keel, for Zeus had struck his ship with lightning and sunk it in mid-ocean, so that all his crew were drowned, while he himself was driven by wind and waves onto my island. I got fond of him and looked after him and had set my heart on making him immortal, so that he should never grow old all his days. Still I cannot cross Zeus nor bring his counsels to nothing; therefore, if he insists upon it, let the man go beyond the seas again."

"Then send him away," said Hermes, "or Zeus will be angry with you and punish you."

On this he took his leave, and Calypso went out to look for Odysseus. She found him sitting upon the beach with his eyes filled with tears and dying of sheer homesickness. Calypso then went close up to him and said:

"My poor fellow, you shall not stay here grieving your life out any longer. I am going to send you away of my own free will, so go, cut some planks of wood, and make yourself a large raft with an upper deck that it may carry you safely over the sea. I will put bread, wine, and water on board to save you from starving. I will also give

---

[2] *ambrosia*: the food of the gods, giving immortality.
[3] *nectar*: the drink of the gods.

you clothes and will send you a fair wind to take you home if the gods in heaven so will it — for they know more about these things and can settle them better than I can."

Odysseus shuddered as he heard her. "Now, goddess," he answered, "there is something behind all this; you cannot be really meaning to help me home when you bid me do such a dreadful thing as put to sea on a raft. Not even a well-equipped ship with a fair wind could venture on such a distant voyage. Nothing that you can say or do shall make me go on board a raft unless you first solemnly swear that you are plotting no mischief against me."

Calypso smiled at this and patted him with her hand. "You know a great deal," said she, "but you are quite wrong here. May heaven above and earth below be my witnesses, with the waters of the river Styx — and this is the most solemn oath which a blessed god can take — that I mean you no sort of harm and am only advising you to do exactly what I should do myself in your place. I am dealing with you quite straightforwardly; my heart is not made of iron, and I am very sorry for you. But if you could only know how much suffering is in store for you before you get back to your own country, you would stay where you are and let me make you immortal, no matter how anxious you may be to see this wife of yours, of whom you are thinking all the time day after day. Yet I flatter myself that I am no less tall or attractive-looking than she is, for it is not to be expected that a mortal woman should compare in beauty with an immortal."

"Goddess," replied Odysseus, "do not be angry with me about this. I am quite aware that my wife, Penelope, is nothing like so tall or so beautiful as yourself. Nevertheless, I want to get home and can think of nothing else. If some god wrecks me when I am on the sea, I will bear it and make the best of it. I have had infinite trouble both by land and by sea already, so let this go with the rest."

Presently the sun set and it became dark, and so the pair retired into the inner part of the cave.

Odysseus Builds the Raft

When the child of morning, rosy-fingered Dawn, appeared, the goddess at once set herself to think how she could speed Odysseus on his way. So she gave him a great bronze ax that suited his hands;

it was sharpened on both sides and had a beautiful olivewood handle fitted firmly onto it. She also gave him a sharp adz and then led the way to the far end of the island, where the largest trees grew — alder, poplar, and pine, that reached the sky — very dry and well seasoned, so as to sail light for him in the water. Then, when she had shown him where the best trees grew, Calypso went home, leaving him to cut them, which he soon finished doing. He cut down twenty trees in all and adzed them smooth, squaring them by rule in good workmanlike fashion. Meanwhile, Calypso came back with some augers, so he bored holes with them and fitted the timbers together with bolts and rivets. He made the raft as broad as a skilled shipwright makes the beam of a large vessel, and he fixed a deck on top of the ribs. He also made a mast with a yardarm and a rudder to steer with. Calypso brought him some linen to make sails, and he made these, too, excellently, making them fast with braces and sheets. Last of all, with the help of levers, he drew the raft down into the water.

In four days he had completed the whole work, and on the fifth Calypso sent him from the island after washing him and giving him some clean clothes. She gave him a goatskin full of deep red wine, and another, larger one of water; she also gave him a bag full of provisions, and put on board much good meat. She made the wind fair and warm for him, and Odysseus gladly spread his sail before it, while he sat and guided the raft skillfully by means of the rudder. He never closed his eyes but kept them fixed on the Pleiades,[4] on late-setting Boötes,[5] and on the Bear, which turns round and round where it is, facing Orion, and alone never dipping into the stream of Oceanus, for Calypso had told him to keep this to his left. Seventeen days did he sail over the sea, and on the eighteenth the dim outlines of the mountains on the nearest part of the Phaeacian coast appeared, rising like a shield on the horizon.

Poseidon's Anger

But King Poseidon, who was just returning from the Ethiopians, caught sight of Odysseus a long way off. He could see him sailing upon the sea, and it made him very angry. He shook his head and

---

[4] *Pleiades* (plē′ə·dēz): stars in the constellation Taurus.
[5] *Boötes* (bō·ō′tēz): a constellation, the Bear Keeper.

muttered to himself, "So the gods have been changing their minds about Odysseus while I was away in Ethiopia, and now he is close to the land of the Phaeacians, where it is decreed that he shall escape from the calamities that have befallen him. Still, he shall have plenty of hardship yet before he reaches it."

Then he gathered his clouds together, grasped his trident,[6] stirred it around in the sea, and roused the rage of every wind that blows, till earth, sea, and sky were hidden in cloud and night sprang forth out of the heavens. Winds from east, south, north, and west fell upon Odysseus all at the same time, and a tremendous sea got up, so that his heart began to fail him. "Alas," he said to himself in his dismay, "whatever will become of me? I am afraid Calypso was right when she said I should have trouble by sea before I got back home. It is all coming true. How black is Zeus making heaven with his clouds, and what a sea the winds are raising from every quarter at once. I am now sure to perish. Blessed and thrice blessed were those Greeks who fell before Troy. I wish I had been killed on the day when the Trojans were attacking me so fiercely around the dead body of Achilles, for then I should have had a proper burial and the Greeks would have honored my name; but now it seems that I shall come to a most pitiable end."

As he spoke, a sea broke over him with such terrific fury that the raft reeled, and he was carried overboard a long way off. He let go the helm, and the force of the hurricane was so great that it broke the mast halfway up, and both sail and yard went over into the sea. For a long time Odysseus was under water, and it was all he could do to rise to the surface again, for the clothes Calypso had given him weighed him down; but at last he got his head above water and spat out the bitter brine that was running down his face in streams. In spite of all this, however, he did not lose sight of his raft but swam as fast as he could toward it, got hold of it, and climbed on board again so as to escape drowning. The sea took the raft and tossed it about as autumn winds whirl thistledown round and round upon a road. It was as though the south, north, east, and west winds were all tossing it backward and forward between them.

Then Poseidon sent a terrible great wave that seemed to rear itself above his head till it broke right over the raft, which then went to pieces as though it were a heap of dry chaff tossed about by a whirl-

---

[6] *trident* (trīd'nt): a three-pronged fork, the emblem of Poseidon.

wind. Odysseus got astride of one plank and rode upon it as if he were on horseback. He then took off the clothes Calypso had given him and plunged into the sea, meaning to swim to shore. King Poseidon watched him as he did so and shook his head, muttering to himself, "There now, swim up and down as you best can till you come to those god-favored people. I do not think you will be able to say that I have let you off too lightly." On this he lashed his horses and drove to his palace.

Athena Brings the Raft to Shore

But Athena resolved to help Odysseus, so she bound the paths of all the winds except one and made them lie quite still; but she roused a good stiff breeze from the north that should calm the waters till Odysseus reached the land of the Phaeacians, where he would be safe.

He floated about for two nights and two days in the water, with a heavy swell on the sea and death staring him in the face; but when the third day broke, the wind fell and there was a dead calm. As he rose on the swell, he looked eagerly ahead and could see land quite near. Then, as children rejoice when their dear father begins to get better after having for a long time borne a disease sent him by some angry spirit, so was Odysseus thankful when he again saw land and trees and swam on with all his strength that he might once more set foot upon dry ground. When, however, he got within earshot, he began to hear the surf thundering up against the rocks, for the swell still broke against them with a terrific roar. Everything was enveloped in spray; there were no harbors where a ship might ride nor shelter of any kind but only headlands, low-lying rocks, and cliffs.

Here poor Odysseus would have certainly perished even in spite of his own destiny if Athena had not helped him to keep his wits about him. He swam seaward again, beyond reach of the surf that was beating against the land, and at the same time he kept looking toward the shore to see if he could find some bay or sloping beach. Soon, as he swam on, he came to the mouth of a river, and here he thought would be the best place, for there were no rocks and it afforded shelter from the wind. He felt that there was a current, so he prayed inwardly to the god of the river and said:

"Hear me, O king, whoever you may be, and save me from the anger of the sea god, Poseidon, for I approach you prayerfully. Any stranger who comes has at all times a claim even upon the gods, and so in my distress I draw near to your stream and beg your help. Have mercy upon me, O king, for I declare myself your suppliant."

Then the god stopped his stream and stilled the waves, making all calm before him and bringing him safely into the mouth of the river. Here at last Odysseus' knees and strong hands failed him, for the sea had completely broken him. His body was all swollen, and sea water ran out through his mouth and nostrils, so that he could neither breathe nor speak and lay swooning from sheer exhaustion. Presently, when he had got his breath again, he left the river, laid himself down among the rushes, and kissed the earth.

Then, as one who lives alone in the country, far from any neighbor, hides a glowing brand in the ashes, keeping the flame alight, to save himself from having to get a light elsewhere, even so did Odysseus cover himself up with leaves; and Athena shed a sweet sleep upon his eyes, closed his eyelids, and made him lose all memory of his sorrows.

BOOK 6

So here Odysseus slept, overcome by sleep and toil, but Athena went off to the country and city of the Phaeacians, where King Alcinous (al·sin'ō·əs) was now reigning. To his house did Athena go to further the return of Odysseus.

She went straight to the beautifully decorated bedroom in which there slept a girl who was as lovely as a goddess, Nausicaa (nô·sik'ā·ə), daughter of King Alcinous. Athena took the form of a friend of Nausicaa and, coming up to the girl's bedside like a breath of wind, she stood at her head and said:

"Nausicaa, what can your mother have been about, to have such a lazy daughter? Here are your clothes all lying in disorder, yet you are going to be married almost immediately. Suppose, then, that we make tomorrow a washing day and start at daybreak, for the washing pools are some way from the town." And when she had said this, Athena went away to Olympus.

Soon morning came and woke Nausicaa, who began wondering

about her dream; she therefore went to the other end of the house to tell her father and mother all about it, and she happened to catch her father just as he was going out to attend a meeting of the town council. She stopped him and said:

"Father dear, could you manage to let me have a good big wagon? I want to take all our dirty clothes to the river and wash them."

On this he gave his orders to the servants, who got the wagon out, harnessed the mules, and yoked them, while the girl brought the clothes down from the linen room and placed them on the wagon. Her mother prepared a basket of provisions. The girl now got into the wagon, and her mother gave her also a golden flask of oil, that she and her women might anoint themselves. Then she took the whip and reins and lashed the mules on, and they set off, their hoofs clattering on the road. They pulled without flagging and carried not only Nausicaa and her wash of clothes but also the maids who were with her.

When they reached the waterside, they went to the washing pools, through which there ran at all times enough pure water to wash any quantity of linen, no matter how dirty. They took the clothes out of the wagon, put them in the water, and vied with one another in treading them in the pits to get the dirt out. After they had washed them and got them quite clean, they laid them out by the seaside and set about washing themselves and anointing themselves with olive oil. Then they got their dinner by the side of the stream and waited for the sun to finish drying the clothes. When they had done dinner, they threw off the veils that covered their heads and began to play.

Nausicaa Finds Odysseus

When it was time for them to start home, and they were folding the clothes and putting them into the wagon, Athena began to consider how Odysseus should wake up and see the handsome girl who was to conduct him to the city of the Phaeacians. The girl, therefore, threw a ball at one of the maids, which missed her and fell into deep water. On this they all shouted, and the noise they made woke Odysseus, who sat up in his bed of leaves and began to wonder what it might all be.

"Alas," said he to himself, "what kind of people have I come among? Are they cruel, savage, and uncivilized, or hospitable and humane? I seem to hear the voices of young women. So at any rate I am among a race of men and women. Let me try if I cannot manage to get a look at them."

As he said this, he crept from under his bush. He looked like some lion of the wilderness that stalks about exulting in his strength and defying both wind and rain. On seeing one so unkempt and so begrimed with salt water, the other girls scampered off along the spits that jutted out into the sea, but Nausicaa stood firm, for Athena put courage into her heart. She stood right in front of Odysseus. He addressed her in honeyed and persuasive language.

"O queen," he said, "I implore your aid — but tell me, are you a goddess or are you a mortal woman? I never yet saw anyone so beautiful and am lost in admiration as I behold you.

"Have pity upon me, for you are the first person I have met, and I know no one else in this country. Show me the way to your town, and let me have anything that you may have brought hither to wrap your clothes in. May heaven grant you in all things your heart's desire — husband, house, and a happy, peaceful home, for there is nothing better in this world than that man and wife should be of one mind in a house."

To this Nausicaa answered, "Stranger, you appear to be a sensible, well-disposed person. There is no accounting for luck; Zeus gives prosperity to rich and poor just as he chooses, so you must take what he has seen fit to send you and make the best of it. Now, however, that you have come to our country, you shall not want for clothes nor for anything else that a foreigner in distress may reasonably look for. I will show you the way to the town and will tell you the name of our people; we are called Phaeacians, and I am the daughter of King Alcinous."

Then she called her maids and said, "Stay where you are, you girls. Can you not see a man without running away from him? Do you take him for a robber or a murderer? This is only some poor man who has lost his way, and we must be kind to him, for strangers and foreigners in distress are under Zeus's protection; so, girls, give the stranger something to eat and drink."

On this the maids left off running away and began calling one another back. They made Odysseus sit down in the shelter as Nausicaa had told them and brought him a tunic and a cloak. They also brought him the little golden flask of oil and told him to go and wash in the stream.

Then they stood on one side, while Odysseus washed himself in the stream and scrubbed the brine from his back and from his broad shoulders. When he had thoroughly washed himself and had got the brine out of his hair, he anointed himself with oil and put on the clothes which the girl had given him. Athena then made him look taller and stronger than before. She also made the hair grow thick on top of his head and flow down in curls like hyacinth blossoms. She glorified him about the head and shoulders as a skillful workman who has studied art enriches a piece of silver by gilding it, so that his work is full of beauty.

Odysseus then went and sat down a little way off upon the beach, looking young and handsome, and the girl gazed on him with admiration; then she said to her maids:

"Hush, my dears, for I want to say something. I believe the gods who live in heaven have sent this man to the Phaeacians. When I first saw him, I thought him unattractive, but now his appearance is like that of the gods who dwell in heaven. I should like my future husband to be just such a one as he is, if he would only stay here and not want to go away. However, give him something to eat and drink."

They did as they were told and set food before Odysseus, who ate and drank ravenously, for it was long since he had had food of any kind. Meanwhile, Nausicaa turned to other thoughts. She got the linen folded and placed in the wagon, she then yoked the mules, and as she took her seat, she called to Odysseus:

Nausicaa Brings Odysseus to Her Father's Palace

"Stranger, rise and let us be going back to the town; I will bring you to the house of my excellent father. But be sure and do as I bid you, for you seem to be a sensible person. As long as we are going past the fields and farmlands, follow briskly behind the wagon along with the maids and I will lead the way myself.

"Presently, however, we shall come near to the town. If, therefore, you want my father to give you an escort and to help you home, do as I bid you. You will see a beautiful grove of poplars by the roadside dedicated to Athena; it has a well in it and a meadow all round it. Sit down there and wait for a while till the rest of us can get into the town and reach my father's house. Then, when you think we must have done this, come into the town and ask the way to the house of my father, Alcinous. When you have got past the gates and through the outer court, go right across the hall till you come to my mother. You will find her sitting by the fire and spinning her purple wool by firelight. Close to her seat stands that of my father, on which he sits and drinks his wine like an immortal god. Never mind him, but go up to my mother, and lay your hands upon her knees if you would get home quickly. If you can gain her over, you may hope to see your own country again, no matter how distant it may be."

So saying, she lashed the mules with her whip and they left the river. The mules drew well, and their hoofs went up and down upon the road. As the sun was going down, they came to the sacred grove of Athena, and there Odysseus sat down and prayed to the mighty daughter of Zeus.

"Hear me," he cried, "untiring daughter of Zeus, hear me now, for you gave no heed to my prayers when Poseidon was wrecking me. Now, therefore, have pity upon me and grant that I may find friends and be hospitably received by the Phaeacians."

Thus did Odysseus pray, and Athena heard his prayer, but she would not show herself to him until he reached his own land, for she was afraid of her uncle Poseidon, who was still furious with him.

BOOKS 7 AND 8

[*Odysseus entered the town and found the magnificent palace of King Alcinous. He went straight to Queen Arete and begged her to help him get home. The Phaeacians promised to provide him with an escort. Odysseus did not reveal his identity but told how he had landed on Calypso's island, how Calypso had detained him for seven years, and how he had sailed away from her island. He described his arrival on Phaeacia and his meeting with Nausicaa. Odysseus impressed Alcinous greatly, and the king offered to make him his son-in-law. But the king also promised that he would not detain Odysseus against his will and would help him on his homeward journey.*

The next day Alcinous prepared a ship and crew for Odysseus and then gave a great feast in his honor. During the banquet, a bard sang of the feats of the heroes, of the quarrel between Odysseus and Achilles, and of the Trojan Horse. Odysseus wept when he heard these stories. Alcinous demanded that Odysseus reveal his identity, describe his travels, and explain why the tale of Troy had made him sad.

BOOK 9

Odysseus Begins His Story

Odysseus began his story, "I am Odysseus, son of Laertes, renowned among mankind for all manner of subtlety, so that my fame ascends to heaven. I live in Ithaca, which lies squat on the horizon, farthest off in the sea toward the sunset. It is a rugged island, but it breeds brave men, and my eyes know none that they better love to look upon. Now, however, I will tell you of the many hazardous adventures which by Zeus's will I met with on my return from Troy.

The City of the Cicones

"When I had set sail from there, the wind took me first to the city of the Cicones. There I sacked the town and put the people to the sword. We took much booty, which we divided fairly among us. I then said that we had better make off at once, but my men very foolishly would not obey me, so they stayed there drinking much wine and killing great numbers of sheep and oxen on the seashore. Meanwhile, the Cicones cried out for help to other Cicones who lived inland. These were more in number, and stronger, and they were more skilled in the art of war, for they could fight either from chariots or on foot. In the morning, therefore, they came as thick as leaves that blossom in summer, and the hand of heaven was against us, so that we were hard pressed. They set the battle in array near the ships, and the hosts aimed their bronze-shod spears at one another. So long as it was still morning, we held our own against them, though they were more in number than we; but as the sun went down, the Cicones got the better of us, and we lost six men from every ship we had. We got away with those that were left, and from there we sailed onward with sorrow in our hearts but glad to have escaped death though we had lost our comrades.

The Lotus Eaters

"I was driven by adverse winds for a space of nine days upon the sea, but on the tenth day we reached the land of the lotus eaters, who live on a food that comes from a kind of flower. Here we landed to take on fresh water, and our crews got their midday meal on the shore near the ships. When they had eaten and drunk, I sent two of my company to see what manner of men the people of the place might be. They started at once and went about among the lotus eaters, who did them no hurt but gave them to eat of the lotus, which was so delicious that those who ate it left off caring about home and did not even want to go back and say what had happened to them but were for staying and munching lotus with the lotus eaters without thinking further of their return. Nevertheless, though they wept bitterly, I forced them back to the ships and made them fast under the benches. Then I told the rest to go on board at once, lest any of them should taste of the lotus and leave off wanting to get home, so they took their places and smote the gray sea with their oars.

The Cyclopes

"We sailed on, always in much distress, till we came to the land of the lawless and inhuman Cyclopes. Now, the Cyclopes neither plant nor plough but trust in providence and live on the wheat, barley, and grapes which grow wild, and their wild grapes yield them wine as the sun and the rain make them grow. They have no laws nor assemblies of the people but live in caves on the tops of high mountains. Each is lord and master in his family, and they take no account of their neighbors.

"Now, off their harbor there lies a wooded and fertile island, not quite close to the land of the Cyclopes, but still not far. It is overrun with wild goats that breed there in great numbers and are never disturbed by foot of man. There we beached the ships, took down the sails, went ashore, and camped upon the beach till daybreak.

"When the child of morning, rosy-fingered Dawn, appeared, we admired the island and wandered all over it. We fetched our spears and bows and arrows from the ships and dividing ourselves into three bands, began to shoot the goats. Heaven sent us excellent hunting. While we were feasting, we kept turning our eyes toward the land of the Cyclopes, which was near by, and saw the smoke of their fires and heard their voices and the bleating of their sheep and goats, but when the sun went down and it became dark, we camped down upon the beach, and next morning I called a council.

" 'Stay here, my brave fellows,' said I, 'all the rest of you, while I go with my ship and investigate these people myself: I want to see if they are uncivilized savages, or a hospitable and humane race.'

"I went on board, bidding my men to do so also and loose the hawsers. So they took their places and smote the gray sea with their oars. When we got to the land, which was not far, there, on the face of a cliff near the sea, we saw a great cave overhung with laurels. It was a station for a great many sheep and goats, and outside there was a large yard, with a high wall around it made of stones sunk into the ground and of trees both pine and oak. This was the abode of a huge monster, with a single eye in the middle of his forehead, who used to pasture his flocks alone, away from the others. He would have nothing to do with other people but led the life of an outlaw. He was a horrid creature, not like a human being at all, but resembling rather some crag that stands out boldly against the sky on the top of a high mountain.

"I told my men to draw the ship ashore and stay where they were, all but the twelve best among them, who were to go with myself. I also took a goatskin of sweet red wine and a bag full of provisions with me, for I was afraid that I might have to deal with some savage who would be of great strength and would respect neither right nor law.

"We soon reached his cave, but he was out with his flocks, so we went inside and took stock of all that we could see. His cheese racks were loaded with cheeses, and he had more lambs and kids than his pens could hold. When they saw all this, my men begged me to let them first steal some cheeses and make off with them to the ship. They would then return, drive down the lambs and kids, put them on board, and sail away with them. It would have been indeed better if we had done so, but I would not listen to them, for I wanted to see the owner himself, in the hope that he might give me hospitality.

"We lit a fire and ate some of the cheese, having first made an offering of it to the gods, and then sat waiting till the Cyclops should come in with his sheep. When he came, he brought in with him a huge load of dry firewood to light the fire for his supper, and this he flung with such a noise onto the floor of his cave that we hid ourselves in fear at the far end of the cavern. Meanwhile, he drove in all the sheep and goats that he was going to milk. He rolled a huge stone to the mouth of the cave — so huge that two and twenty strong four-wheeled wagons would not be enough to draw it from its place against the doorway. When he had so done, he sat down and milked his sheep and goats, one after another. When he had got through with all his work, he lit the fire and then catching sight of us, he said:

" 'Strangers, who are you? Where do you sail from? Are you traders, or do you sail the sea as pirates, with your hands against every man and every man's hand against you?'

"We were frightened out of our senses by his loud voice and monstrous form, but I managed to say, 'We are Greeks on our way home from Troy, but by the will of Zeus and stress of weather, we have been driven far out of our course. We therefore humbly pray you to show us some hospitality and otherwise make us such presents as visitors may expect. May your excellency fear the wrath of heaven, for we are your suppliants, and Zeus takes all travelers under his protection, for he is the avenger of all suppliants and foreigners in distress.'

"To this he gave me a pitiless answer. 'Stranger,' said he, 'you are a fool, or else you know nothing of this country. You talk to me about fearing the gods or shunning their anger. We Cyclopes do not care about Zeus or any of your blessed gods, for we are much stronger than they. I shall not spare either yourself or your companions out of any regard for Zeus. And now tell me where you made your ship fast when you came on shore. Was it round the point, or is she lying straight off the land?'

"He said this to draw me out, but I was too cunning to be caught in that way, so I answered with a lie. 'Poseidon,' said I, 'sent my ship onto the rocks at the far end of your country, and wrecked it.'

"The cruel wretch made no answer, but with a sudden clutch he gripped up two of my men at once and dashed them down upon the ground as though they had been puppies. Their brains were shed upon the ground, and the earth was wet with their blood. Then he tore them limb from limb and supped upon them. He gobbled them up like a lion in the wilderness, flesh and bones, without leaving anything uneaten. As for us, we wept and lifted up our hands to heaven on seeing such a horrid sight, for we did not know what to do. But when the Cyclops had filled his huge paunch and had washed down his meal of human flesh with a drink of milk, he stretched himself full length upon the ground among his sheep and went to sleep. I was at first inclined to seize my sword, draw it, and drive it into his breast, but I reflected that if I did, we should all certainly be lost, for we should never be able to shift the stone which the monster had put in front of the door. So we stayed sobbing and sighing where we were till morning came.

"When the child of morning, rosy-fingered Dawn, appeared, he again lit his fire and milked his goats and sheep, one after another. As soon as he had got through with all his work, he snatched up two more of my men and began eating them for his morning meal. Presently, with the utmost ease, he rolled the stone away from the door and drove out his sheep, but he at once put it back again — as easily as though he were merely clapping the lid onto a quiver full of arrows. As soon as he had done so, he shouted after his sheep to drive them onto the mountain. So I was left to scheme some way of taking my revenge and covering myself with glory.

"In the end I thought it the best plan to do as follows: The Cyclops had a great club which was lying near one of the sheep pens. It was of green olive wood, and he had cut it intending to use it for a staff as soon as it should be dry. It was so huge that we could only compare it with the mast of a twenty-oared ship. I went up to this club and cut off about six feet of it. I then gave this piece to the men and told them to make it smooth at one end, which they proceeded to do, and lastly I brought it to a point myself, charring the end in the fire to make it harder. When I had done this, I hid it and told the men to cast lots which of them should venture along with myself to lift it and bore it into the monster's eye while he was asleep. The lot fell upon the very four whom I should have chosen, and I myself made five. In the evening the wretch came back from sheepherding and drove his flocks into the cave — this time driving them all inside and not leaving any in the yards. I suppose some fancy must have taken him, or a god must have prompted him to do so. As soon as he had put the stone back to its place against the door, he sat down and milked his sheep and his goats, one after another. When he had got through with all his work, he snatched up two more of my men and made his supper off them. So I went up to him with an ivy-wood bowl of deep red wine in my hands.

"'Look here, Cyclops,' said I, 'you have been eating a great deal of man's flesh, so take this and drink some wine, that you may see what kind of liquor we had on board my ship. I was bringing it to you as a drink offering, in the hope that you would take compassion upon me and help me on my way home. Instead all you do is to go on ramping[1] and raving most intolerably. You ought to be ashamed of yourself; how can you expect people to come and see you any more if you treat them in this way?'

"He then took the cup and drank. He was so delighted with the taste of the wine that he asked me for another bowlful. 'Be so kind,' he said, 'as to give me some more, and tell me your name at once. I want to make you a present that you will be glad to have.'

"I then gave him some more; three times I filled the bowl for him, and three times he drained it without thought or heed. Then, when I saw that the wine had got into his head, I said to him as plausibly as I could: 'Cyclops, you ask my name and I will tell it to you. Give me, therefore, the present you promised me. My name is Noman; this is what my father and mother and my friends have always called me.'

"But the cruel wretch said, 'Then I will eat all Noman's comrades, and will keep Noman for the last. This is the present that I will make him.'

"As he spoke, he reeled and fell back face upward on the ground. His great neck hung sideways, and a deep sleep took hold upon him. Then I thrust the beam of wood far into the embers to heat it and encouraged my men, lest any of them should turn fainthearted. When the wood, green though it was, was about to blaze, I drew it out of the fire glowing with heat, and my men gathered round me, for heaven had filled their hearts with courage. We drove the sharp end of the beam into the monster's eye, and bearing upon it with all my weight, I kept turning it round and round as though I were boring a hole in a ship's plank with an auger. Even thus did we bore the red-hot beam into his eye, till the boiling blood bubbled all over it as we worked it round and round, so that the steam from the burning eyeball scalded his eyelids and eyebrows and the roots of

---

[1] *ramp:* to act in a violent or threatening manner; storm; rampage.

the eye sputtered in the fire. As a blacksmith plunges an ax or hatchet into cold water to temper it — for it is this that gives strength to the iron — and it makes a great hiss as he does so, even thus did the Cyclops' eye hiss round the beam of olive wood, and his hideous yells made the cave ring again. We ran away in a fright, but he plucked the beam, all spattered with gore, from his eye and hurled it from him in a frenzy of rage and pain, shouting as he did so to the other Cyclopes who lived on the bleak headlands near him. So they gathered from all quarters around his cave when they heard him shouting and asked what was the matter with him.

" 'What ails you, Polyphemus,' said they, 'that you make such a noise, breaking the stillness of the night and preventing us from being able to sleep? Surely no man is carrying off your sheep? Surely no man is trying to kill you either by fraud or by force?'

"But Polyphemus shouted to them from inside the cave, 'Noman is killing me by fraud. Noman is killing me by force.'

" 'Then,' said they, 'if no man is attacking, you must be ill. When Zeus makes people ill, there is no help for it, and you had better pray to your father, Poseidon.'

"Then they went away, and I laughed inwardly at the success of my clever stratagem, but the Cyclops, groaning and in an agony of pain, felt about with his hand till he found the stone and took it from the door. Then he sat in the doorway and stretched his hands in front of it to catch anyone going out with the sheep, for he thought I might be foolish enough to attempt this.

"As for myself, I kept on puzzling how I could best save my own life and those of my companions. I schemed and schemed, as one who knows that his life depends upon it, for the danger was very great. In the end I decided that this plan would be the best: the male sheep were well grown and had a heavy black fleece, so I quietly bound them in threes together with some of the twigs on which the wicked monster used to sleep. There was a man under the middle sheep, and the two on either side were to cover him, so that there were three sheep to each man. As for myself, there was a ram finer than any of the others, so I caught hold of him by the back, slid down in the thick wool under his belly, and hung on patiently to his fleece, face upward, keeping a firm hold on it all the time.

"Thus, then, did we wait in great fear of mind till morning came, but when the child of morning, rosy-fingered Dawn, appeared, the male sheep hurried out to feed, while the ewes remained bleating about the pens waiting to be milked. Their master, in spite of all his pain, felt the backs of all the sheep as they passed by him, but without being sharp enough to find out that the men were underneath their bellies. As the ram was going out, last of all, heavy with its fleece and with the weight of my crafty self, Polyphemus laid hold of it and said:

" 'My good ram, what is it that makes you the last to leave my cave this morning? You do not usually let the others go before you but lead the mob with a run. But now you lag last of all. Is it because you know your master has lost his eye and are sorry because that wicked Noman and his horrid crew have overcome him with drink and blinded him? But I will have his life yet. If you could understand and talk, you would tell me where the wretch is hiding, and I would dash his brains upon the ground till they flew all over the cave. I should thus have some satisfaction for the harm this no-good Noman has done me.'

"As he spoke, he drove the ram outside, but when we were a little way out from the cave and yards, I first got from under the ram's belly and then freed my comrades. As for the sheep, which were very fat, by constantly heading them in the right direction, we managed to drive them down to the ship. The crew rejoiced greatly at seeing those of us who had escaped death but wept for the others whom the Cyclops had killed. However, I made signs to them by nodding and frowning that they were to hush their crying and told them to get all the sheep on board at once and put out to sea. So they went aboard, took their places, and smote the gray sea with their oars. Then, when I had got as far out as my voice would reach, I began to jeer at the Cyclops.

" 'Cyclops,' said I, 'you should have taken better measure of your man before eating up his comrades in your cave. You wretch, to eat up your visitors in your own house! You might have known that your sin would find you out, and now Zeus and the other gods have punished you.'

"He got more and more furious as he heard me, so he tore the top from off a high mountain and flung it just in front of my ship. The sea heaved as the rock fell into it, and the wash of the wave it raised carried us back toward the mainland and forced us toward the shore. But I snatched up a long pole and kept the ship off, making signs to my men, by nodding my head, that they must row for their lives, whereon they laid out with a will. When we had got twice as far as we were before, I was for jeering at the Cyclops again, but the men begged and prayed me to hold my tongue.

"But I would not listen to them and shouted out to him in my rage, 'Cyclops, if anyone asks you who it was that put your eye out and spoiled your beauty, say it was the valiant warrior Odysseus, son of Laertes, who lives in Ithaca.'

"On this he groaned and cried out, 'Alas, alas, then the old prophecy about me is coming true. There was a prophet here at one time, who told me that all this would happen to me someday and said I should lose my sight by the hand of Odysseus. I have been all along expecting someone of superhuman strength, whereas he turns out to be a little insignificant weakling, who has managed to blind my eye by taking advantage of me in my drink. Come here, then, Odysseus, that I may make you presents to show my hospitality and urge Poseidon to help you forward on your journey — for Poseidon and I are father and son. He, if he will, shall heal me, which no one else, neither god nor man, can do.'

"Then I said, 'I wish I could be as sure of killing you outright and sending you down to the house of Hades as I am that it will take more than Poseidon to cure that eye of yours.'

"On this he lifted up his hands to heaven and prayed, saying, 'Hear me, great Poseidon; if I am indeed your own son, grant that Odysseus may never reach his home alive. Or if he must get back to his friends at last, let him do so late and in sore plight after losing all his men. Let him reach his home in another man's ship and find trouble in his house.'

Poseidon's Anger

"Thus did he pray, and Poseidon heard his prayer. Then he picked up a rock much larger than the first, swung it aloft, and hurled it with prodigious force. It fell just short of the ship and was within a little of hitting the end of the rudder. The sea heaved as the rock fell into it, and the wash of the wave it raised drove us onward on our way toward the shore of the island.

"When at last we got to the island where we had left the rest of our ships, we found our comrades lamenting us and anxiously awaiting our return.

BOOK 10

The Island of the Winds

"Thence we went on to the island where Aeolus (ē'ə·ləs) lives. It is an island that floats upon the sea; all around it is an unbroken wall of bronze, and the cliffs drop sheer to the sea.

"Aeolus entertained me for a whole month, asking me questions all the time about Troy, the Greek fleet, and the return of the Greeks. I told him exactly how everything had happened, and when I said I must go and asked him to help me on my way, he set about doing so at once. He flayed me a prime oxhide to hold the roaring winds, which he shut up in the hide as in a sack — for Zeus had made him captain over the winds. He put the sack in the ship, and bound the mouth so tightly with a silver thread that not even a breath of a side wind could blow from any quarter. The west wind, which was fair for us, did he alone let blow as it chose; but it all came to nothing, for we were lost through our own folly.

"Nine days and nine nights we sailed, and on the tenth day our native land showed on the horizon. We got so close in that we could see the fires burning, and I, being then dead beat, fell into a light sleep, for I had never let the rudder out of my own hands, that we might get home the faster. On this the men fell to talking among themselves and said I was bringing back gold and silver in the sack that Aeolus had given me. One would turn to his neighbor and say, 'See what fine prizes he is taking home from Troy, while we, who have traveled just as far as he has, come back with hands as empty as we set out with — and now Aeolus has given him ever so much more. Quick — let us see what it all is, and how much gold and silver there is in the sack he gave him.'

"Thus they talked, and evil counsels prevailed. They loosed the sack, at which the winds flew howling forth and raised a storm that carried us weeping out to sea and away from our own country. Then I awoke and did not know whether to throw myself into the sea or to live on and make the best of it. But I bore it, covered myself up, and lay down in the ship, while the men lamented bitterly as the fierce winds bore our fleet back to the Aeolian island.

"When we reached it, we went ashore and I went straight to the house of Aeolus, where I found him feasting with his wife and family. They were astounded when they saw us and said, 'Odysseus, what brings you here? What god has been ill-treating you? We took great pains to help you on your way home to Ithaca or wherever it was that you wanted to go to.'

"I answered sorrowfully, 'My men have undone me. They and cruel sleep have ruined me. My friends, mend me this mischief, for you can if you will.'

"I spoke as movingly as I could, but they said nothing, till their father answered, 'Vilest of mankind, leave this island at once: I will not help anyone whom heaven hates. Be off, for you come here as one despised by heaven.' And with these words he sent me sorrowing from his door.

The Laestrygonians

"From there we sailed on till the men were worn out with long and fruitless rowing, for there was no longer any wind to help them. Six days, night and day, did we toil, and on the seventh day we reached the rocky stronghold of the Laestrygonians (les·tri·gŏ′nē·ənz).

"When we reached the harbor, we found it landlocked under steep cliffs, with a narrow entrance between two headlands. My captains took all their ships inside and made them fast close to one another, for there was never so much as a breath of wind inside, but it was always dead calm. I kept my own ship outside and moored it to a rock at the very end of the point; then I climbed a high rock to look around, but could see no sign either of man or of cattle, only some smoke rising from the ground. So I sent two of my company with an attendant to find out what sort of people the inhabitants were.

"The men when they got on shore followed a level road by which the people draw their firewood from the mountains into the town, till presently they met a young woman who had come outside to fetch water. They asked her who the king of that country might be and over what kind of people he ruled, so she directed them to her father's house, but when they got there, they found his wife to be a giantess as huge as a mountain, and they were horrified at the sight of her.

"She at once called her husband from the place of assembly, and immediately he set about killing my men. He snatched up one of them and began to make his dinner off him then and there, and so the other two men ran back to the ships as fast as ever they could. But he raised a hue and cry after them, and thousands of sturdy Laestrygonians sprang up from every quarter — ogres, not men. They threw vast rocks at us from the cliffs as though they had been mere stones, and I heard the horrid sound of the ships crunching up against one another and the death cries of my men as the Laestrygonians speared them like fishes and took them home to eat them. While they were thus killing my men inside the harbor, I drew my sword, cut the cable of my own ship, and told my men to row with all their might if they too would not suffer the same fate. So they rowed for their lives, and we were thankful when we got into open water out of reach of the rocks being hurled at us. As for the others, there was not one of them left.

Circe

"From there we sailed sadly on, glad to have escaped death, though we had lost our comrades, and came to the island where Circe (sûr'sē) lives — a great and cunning goddess. We brought our ship into a safe harbor silently, for some god guided us there, and having landed, we lay there for two days and two nights, worn out in body and mind. When the morning of the third day came, I took my spear and my sword and went away from the ship to look around and see if I could discover signs of human handiwork or hear the sound of voices. Climbing to the top of a high lookout, I saw the smoke of Circe's house rising upward amid a dense forest of trees, and when I saw this, I wondered whether, having seen the smoke, I should not go at once and find out more, but in the end I thought it best to go back to the ship and send some of my men instead of going myself.

"I called a council and said, 'My friends, we are in very great difficulties. Therefore listen to me. We have no idea where the sun either sets or rises, so that we do not even know east from west. I see no way out of it, but we must try and find one. We are certainly on an island, for I went as high as I could this morning and saw the sea reaching all around it to the horizon; it lies low but toward the middle I saw smoke rising out of a thick forest of trees.'

"Their hearts sank as they heard me, for they remembered how they had been treated by the Laestrygonians and by the savage ogre Polyphemus. They wept bitterly in their dismay, but there was nothing to be got by crying, so I divided them into two companies and set a captain over each. I gave one company to Eurylochus (yoo·ri·lō′kəs), while I took command of the other myself. Then we cast lots in a helmet, and the lot fell upon Eurylochus; so he set out with his twenty-two men, and they wept and so did we who were left behind.

"When they reached Circe's house, they found it built of cut stones, on a site that could be seen from afar, in the middle of the forest. There were wild mountain wolves and lions prowling all around it — poor bewitched creatures whom she had tamed by her enchantments and drugs. They did not attack my men but wagged their great tails, fawned upon them, and rubbed their noses lovingly against them. As hounds crowd around their master when they see him coming from dinner — for they know he will bring them something — even so did these wolves and lions with their great claws fawn upon my men, but the men were terribly frightened at seeing such strange creatures. Presently they reached the gates of the goddess's house, and as they stood there, they could hear Circe within, singing most beautifully as she worked at her loom.

"They called her, and she came down, unfastened the door, and bade them enter. They, thinking no evil, followed her, all except Eurylochus, who suspected mischief and stayed outside. When she had got them into her house, she set them upon benches and seats and mixed them a dish with cheese, honey, meal, and wine, but she drugged it with wicked poisons to make them forget their homes, and when they had drunk, she turned them into pigs by a stroke of her wand and shut them up in her pigsties. They were like pigs — head, hair, and all, and they grunted just as pigs do; but their senses were the same as before, and they remembered everything.

"Thus then were they shut up squealing, and Circe threw them some acorns and beechnuts such as pigs eat, but Eurylochus hurried back to tell me about the sad fate of our comrades.

"Then I took my sword of bronze and slung it over my shoulders; I also took my bow and told Eurylochus to come back with me and show me the way. But he threw his arms around me, saying, 'Sir, do not force me to go with you, but let me stay here, for I know you will not bring one of them back with you nor even return alive yourself; let us see if we cannot escape with the few that are left us, for we may still save our lives.'

" 'Stay where you are, then,' answered I, 'eating and drinking at the ship, but I must go.'

Hermes Helps Odysseus

"With this I left the ship and went up inland. When I got through the charmed grove and was near the great house of the enchantress Circe, I met Hermes, god of the golden wand, disguised as a young man. He came up to me and took my hand within his own, saying, 'My poor unhappy man, where are you going over these hills, alone and without knowing the way? Your men are shut up in Circe's pigsties. Are you coming to set them free? I fear that you yourself will not return either and will have to stay there with the rest of them. But never mind, I will protect you and get you out of your difficulty. Take this herb, which is one of great power, and keep it about you when you go to Circe's house. It will be a charm to you against every kind of mischief.

" 'And I will tell you of all the witchcraft that Circe will try to practice upon you. She will mix a drink for you, and she will drug the meal with which she makes it, but she will not be able to charm you, for the power of the herb that I shall give you will prevent her spells from working. I will tell you all about it. When Circe strikes you with her wand, draw your sword and spring upon her as though you were going to kill her. She will be frightened. Then you must make her swear solemnly by all the blessed gods that she will plot no further mischief against you.'

"As he spoke, he pulled the herb out of the ground and showed me what it was like. The root was black, while the flower was as white as milk.

"Then Hermes went back to high Olympus, passing over the wooded island; but I went onward to the house of Circe, and my heart was clouded with care as I walked along. When I got to the gates, I stood there and called the goddess; and as soon as she heard me, she came down, opened the door, and asked me to come in. So I followed her, much troubled in my mind. She set me on a richly decorated seat and mixed a drink for me in a golden goblet; but she drugged it, for she meant me mischief. When she had given it to me, and I had drunk it without its charming me, she struck me with her wand. 'There now,' she cried, 'be off to the pigsty with the rest of them.'

"But I rushed at her with my sword drawn as though I would kill her, at which she fell with a loud scream, clasped my knees, and spoke piteously, saying, 'Who are you? From what place and people have you come? How can it be that my drugs have no power to charm you? You must be spellproof; surely you can be none other than the bold hero Odysseus, who Hermes always said would come here someday with his ship while on his way home from Troy. So be it then; sheathe your sword, that we may make friends and learn to trust each other.'

"And I answered, 'Circe, how can you expect me to be friendly with you when you have just been turning all my men into pigs? And now that you have got me here myself, you mean me mischief too. You must take your solemn oath to plot no further harm against me.'

"So she swore at once as I told her. 'Now,' I said, 'you must free my men and bring them to me, that I may see them with my own eyes.'

"When I had said this, she went straight through the court with her wand in her hand and opened the pigsty doors. My men came out like so many prime hogs and stood looking at her, but she went about them and rubbed each with a second drug. Then the bristles fell off, and they became men again, younger than they were before and much taller and better-looking. They knew me at once, seized me each of them by the hand, and wept for joy till the whole house was filled with the sound, and Circe herself was so sorry for them that she came up to me and said, 'Odysseus, noble son of Laertes, go back at once to the sea where you have left your ship, and first draw it onto the land. Then hide all your ship's gear and property in some cave, and come back here with your men.' Thus did she speak, and we assented.

"We stayed with Circe for a whole year feasting upon an untold quantity of meat and wine. But when the year had passed, my men called me apart and said, 'Sir, it is time you began to think about going home, if you are to be spared to see your house and native country at all.'

"Thus did they speak and I agreed. Then through the whole day we feasted our fill on meat and wine, but when the sun went down and it became dark, the men laid themselves down to sleep in the dark hall. I, however, besought Circe by her knees, and the goddess listened to what I had to say. 'Circe,' said I, 'please keep the promise you made me about helping me on my homeward voyage. I want to get back and so do my men; they are always pestering me with their complaints as soon as your back is turned.'

"And the goddess answered, 'Odysseus, noble son of Laertes, none of you shall stay here any longer if you do not want to, but there is another journey which you have got to take before you can sail homeward. You must go to the house of Hades and of dread Persephone (pər·sef′ə·nē) to consult the ghost of the blind Theban prophet Teiresias (tī·rē′sē·əs).'

"I was dismayed when I heard this. I wept and would gladly have lived no longer to see the light of the sun, but presently I was tired of weeping.

" 'You will need no guide,' she answered. 'Raise your mast, set your white sails, sit quite still, and the north wind will blow you there of itself. When your ship has crossed the waters of Oceanus, you will reach the fertile shore of Persephone's country; here beach your ship upon the shore of Oceanus, and go straight on to the dark abode of Hades. You will find it near the place where you will see a rock, just where two roaring rivers run into one another.

" 'When you have reached this spot, as I now tell you, dig a trench a cubit or so in length and breadth, and pour into it as a drink offering to all the dead, first honey mixed with milk, then wine, and in the third place water — sprinkling white barley meal over the whole. Moreover, you must offer many prayers to the poor feeble ghosts and promise them that when you get back to Ithaca, you will offer a sacrifice to them. More particularly you must promise that Teiresias shall have a black sheep all to himself, the finest in all your flocks.

" 'When you shall have thus besought the ghosts with your prayers, offer them a ram and a black ewe. On this, many dead men's ghosts will come to you, and you must tell your men to skin the two sheep that you have just killed and offer them as a burnt sacrifice with prayers to Hades and to Persephone. Then draw your sword and sit there, so as to prevent any other poor ghost from coming near the spilled blood before Teiresias shall have answered your questions. The seer will presently come to you and will tell you about your voyage — what stages you are to make and how you are to sail the sea so as to reach your home.'

"It was daybreak by the time she had done speaking, so I went about among the men everywhere all over the house and spoke kindly to each of them. 'You must not lie sleeping here any longer,' said I to them. 'We must be going, for Circe has told me all about it.' And on this they did as I told them.

Odysseus Sets Out for the Land of the Dead

"I got the men together and said to them, 'You think you are about to start home again, but Circe has explained to me that instead of this, we have got to go to the house of Hades and Persephone to consult the ghost of the Theban prophet Teiresias.'

"The men were brokenhearted as they heard me and threw themselves on the ground, groaning and tearing their hair, but they did not mend matters by crying. When we reached the seashore, weeping and lamenting our fate, Circe brought a ram and a ewe as sacrifices for Teiresias and the other ghosts of Hades, and tied them near the ship. She passed through the midst of us without our knowing it, for who can see the comings and goings of a god, if the god does not wish to be seen?"

BOOK 11

[*Continuing his story, Odysseus told of his visit to the Land of the Dead. There he made offerings and sacrifices, and the dead appeared. The prophet Teiresias was one of the first to approach. He told Odysseus that Poseidon was angry at him because he had blinded his son Polyphemus. Teiresias warned Odysseus not to harm the cattle when he reached the sun god's island, or else his ship and all his men would be destroyed. Odysseus might escape, but he would* return home to find his house overrun by suitors. After predicting that Odysseus would kill the suitors and advising him to appease Poseidon, Teiresias departed. Odysseus met the ghost of his mother, who told him about his family's great sorrow for him, sorrow which had caused her death. Then Odysseus described the other ghosts he saw, the wives and daughters of famous men, his comrades in the war, and other heroes. He would have liked to see more, but was afraid that he would be trapped by a monster, and so he returned to his ship. Then Odysseus and his men sailed back to Circe's island.]

BOOK 12

Circe's Advice

"Circe took me by the hand and bade me be seated away from the others, while she reclined by my side and asked me all about our adventures.

" 'So far so good,' said she, when I had ended my story, 'and now pay attention to what I am about to tell you. First you will come to the Sirens, who enchant all who come near them. If anyone unwarily draws in too close and hears the singing of the Sirens, his wife and children will never welcome him home again, for they sit in a green field and bewitch him with the sweetness of their song. There is a great heap of dead men's bones lying all around. Therefore, pass these Sirens by, and stop your men's ears with wax that none of them may hear. But if you like, you can listen yourself, for you may get the men to bind you as you stand upright at the base of the mast, and they must lash the rope's ends to the mast itself, that you may have the pleasure of listening. If you beg the men to unloose you, then they must bind you faster.

" 'When your crew have taken you past these Sirens, I will not give you definite directions as to which of two courses you are to take. I will lay the two alternatives before you, and you must consider them for yourself. On the one hand, there are some overhanging rocks against which the deep blue waves beat with terrific fury. The blessed gods call these rocks the Wanderers. No ship that ever came to these rocks has got away again, but the waves and whirlwinds of fire carry the wreckage and the bodies of dead men.

" 'In the other direction are two rocks, of which the one reaches heaven and its peak is lost in a dark cloud. This never leaves it, so that the top is never clear, not even in summer and early autumn. No man, though he had twenty hands and twenty feet, could get a foothold on it and climb it, for it runs sheer up, as smooth as though it had been polished. In the middle of it there is a large cavern, looking west; you must take your ship this way, but the cave is so high up that not even the stoutest archer could send an arrow into it. Inside it Scylla (sil'ə) sits and yelps with a voice that you might take to be that of a young hound, but in truth she is a dreadful monster and no one — not even a god — could face her without being terror-struck. She has twelve misshapen feet and six necks of the most prodigious length; and at the end of each neck she has a frightful head with three rows of teeth in each, all set very close together, so that they would crunch anyone to death in a moment, and she sits deep within her shady cell thrusting out her heads and peering all round the rock, fishing for dolphins or dogfish or any larger monster that she can catch. No ship ever yet got past her without losing some men, for she shoots out all her heads at once, and carries off a man in each mouth.

" 'You will find the other rock lies lower, but they are so close together that there is not more than a bowshot between them. A large fig tree in full leaf grows upon it, and under it lies the sucking whirlpool of Charybdis (kə·rib'dis). Three times in the day does she vomit forth her waters, and three times she sucks them down again. See that you be not there at this dangerous time, for if you are, Poseidon himself could not save you. You must hug the Scylla side and drive your ship by as fast as you can, for you had better lose six men than your whole crew.

" 'You will now come to an island where you will see many cattle and sheep belonging to the sun god Hyperion — seven herds of cattle and seven flocks of sheep, with fifty head in each flock. They do not breed, nor do they become fewer in number, and they are tended by goddesses who are children of the sun god. If you leave these flocks unharmed and think of nothing but getting home, you may yet after much hardship reach Ithaca. But if you harm them, then I forewarn you of the destruction both of your ship and of your comrades; and even though you may yourself escape, you will return late, after losing all your men.'

"Here she ended, and dawn, enthroned in gold, began to show

in heaven, and so Circe returned inland. I then went on board and told my men to loose the ship from her moorings, so they at once got into her, took their places, and began to smite the gray sea with their oars. Presently the great and cunning goddess Circe befriended us with a fair wind that blew dead aft and stayed steadily with us, keeping our sails well filled, so we set in order the ship's gear and let her go as wind and helmsman headed her.

"Then, being much troubled in mind, I said to my men, 'My friends, it is not right that one or two of us alone should know the prophecies that Circe has made me. I will therefore tell you about them, so that whether we live or die, we may do so with our eyes open. First, she said, we were to keep clear of the Sirens, who sit and sing most beautifully in a field of flowers; but she said I might hear them myself so long as no one else did. Therefore, take me and bind me to the base of the mast. Bind me so tightly that I cannot possibly break away, and lash the rope's ends to the mast itself. If I beg you to set me free, then bind me more tightly still.'

The Sirens

"I had hardly finished telling everything to the men before we reached the island of the Sirens, for the wind had been very favorable. Then all of a sudden it fell dead calm. There was not a breath of wind nor a ripple upon the water, so the men furled the sails and stowed them. Then taking to their oars, they whitened the water with the foam they raised in rowing. Meanwhile, I took a large piece of wax and cut it up small with my sword. Then I kneaded the wax in my strong hands till it became soft, which it soon did between the kneading and the rays of the sun god. Then I stopped the ears of all my men, and they bound me hands and feet to the mast as I stood upright at its base, but they went on rowing themselves. When we had got within earshot of the land and the ship was going at a good rate, the Sirens saw that we were getting close inshore and began their singing.

" 'Come here,' they sang, 'renowned Odysseus, and listen to our voices. No one ever sailed past us without staying to hear the enchanting sweetness of our song — and he who listens will go on his way not only charmed but wiser, for we know all the ills that the gods laid upon the Greeks and Trojans before Troy and can tell you everything that happens over the whole world.'

"They sang these words most musically, and as I longed to hear them further, I made signs by frowning to my men that they should set me free. But they quickened their stroke and bound me with still stronger bonds till we had got out of hearing of the Sirens' voices. Then my men took the wax from their ears and unbound me.

"Immediately after we had got past the island, I saw a great wave from which spray was rising, and I heard a loud roaring sound. The men were so frightened that they let go of their oars, for the whole sea resounded with the rushing of the waters, but the ship stayed where it was, for the men had stopped rowing. I went round, therefore, and urged them not to lose heart.

" 'My friends,' said I, 'this is not the first time that we have been in danger, and we are in nothing like so bad a case as when the Cyclops shut us up in his cave. My courage and wise counsel saved us then, and we shall live to look back on all this as well. Now, therefore, let us all do as I say, trust in Zeus and row on with might and main.'

Scylla and Charybdis

"So they did as I told them, but I said nothing about the awful monster Scylla, for I knew the men would not go on rowing if I did but would huddle together in the hold. In one thing only did I disobey Circe's strict instructions — I put on my armor. Then seizing two strong spears, I took my stand on the ship's bows, for it was there that I expected first to see the monster of the rock, who was to do my men so much harm.

"Then we entered the straits in great fear of mind, for on the one hand was Scylla and on the other dread Charybdis kept sucking up the salt water. When she vomited it out, it was like the water in a cauldron when it is boiling over upon a great fire, and the spray reached the top of the rocks on either side. When she began to draw it in, we could see the water inside whirling round and round, and a frightening roar sounded all around the rock. We could see the bottom of the whirlpool all black with sand and mud, and the men were at their wits' ends for fear. While we were looking at this, and were expecting each moment to be our last, Scylla pounded down suddenly upon us and snatched up my six best men. I was looking at the ship and my men, and then I saw their hands and feet high above me, struggling in the air as Scylla was carrying them off, and I heard them call out my name in one last despairing cry. As a fisherman, seated with his long fishing rod upon some jutting rock, throws bait into the water to deceive the poor little fishes and casts his line into the sea and throws them gasping onto the land as he catches them one by one — even so did Scylla land these panting creatures on her rock and munch them up at the mouth of her den, while they screamed and stretched out their hands to me in their mortal agony. This was the most sickening sight that I saw throughout all my voyages.

The Island of the Sun God

"When we had passed the Wandering rocks, with Scylla and terrible Charybdis, we reached the noble island of the sun god, where were the cattle and sheep belonging to the sun, Hyperion. While still at sea in my ship, I could hear the cattle lowing as they came home to the stalls and the sheep bleating. Then I remembered what Teiresias had told me and how carefully Circe had warned me to shun the island of the blessed sun god. So, being much troubled, I said to the men, 'My men, I know you are hard pressed, but listen while I tell you the prophecy that Teiresias made me and how carefully Circe warned me to shun the island of the blessed sun god, for it was here, she said, that our worst danger would lie. Head the ship, therefore, away from the island.'

"The men were in despair at this, and Eurylochus at once gave me an insolent answer. 'Odysseus,' said he, 'you are hard. You are very strong yourself and never get worn out. You seem to be made of iron, and now, though your men are exhausted with toil and lack of sleep, you will not let them land and cook themselves a good supper, but order them to put out to sea and go blindly on through the night. Let us obey the night and prepare our supper here next to the ship; tomorrow morning we will go on board again and put out to sea.'

"Thus spoke Eurylochus, and the men approved his words. I saw that heaven meant us a mischief and said, 'You force me to yield, for you are many against one, but at any rate each one of you must take his solemn oath that if he meet with a herd of cattle or a large flock of sheep, he will not be so mad as to kill a single head of either but will be satisfied with the food that Circe has given us.'

"They all swore as I bade them, and when they had completed their oath, we made the ship fast in a harbor that was near a stream of fresh water, and the men went ashore and cooked their suppers.

" 'My friends,' said I, 'we have meat and drink in the ship; let us mind, therefore, and not touch the cattle, or we shall suffer for it, for these cattle and sheep belong to the mighty sun, who sees and hears everything.' And again they promised that they would obey.

'For a whole month the wind blew steadily from the south, and there was no other wind, but only south and east. As long as grain and wine held out, the men did not touch the cattle when they were hungry. When, however, they had eaten all there was in the ship, they were forced to go further afield, fishing with hook and line, catching birds, and taking whatever they could lay their hands on, for they were starving. One day, therefore, I went up inland that I might pray heaven to show me some means of getting away. When I had gone far enough to be clear of all my men and had found a place that was well sheltered from the wind, I washed my hands and prayed to all the gods in Olympus, till by and by they sent me off into a sweet sleep.

"Meanwhile, Eurylochus had been giving evil counsel to the men. 'Listen to me,' said he, 'my poor comrades. All deaths are bad enough, but there is none so bad as starving. Why should not we drive in the best of these cows and offer them in sacrifice to the immortal gods? If we ever get back to Ithaca, we can build a fine temple to the sun god and enrich it with every kind of ornament. If, however, he is determined to sink our ship out of revenge for these horned cattle, and the other gods are of the same mind, I for one would rather drink salt water once for all and have done with it, than be starved to death by inches on such a desert island as this is.'

"Thus spoke Eurylochus, and the men approved his words. Now, the cattle, so fair and goodly, were feeding not far from the ship. The men, therefore, drove in the best of them, and they all stood around them saying their prayers. When they had done praying, they killed the cows and skinned them. They cut out the thighbones, offering them as a sacrifice. Then they cut the rest up small and put the pieces upon the spits.

"By this time, my deep sleep had left me, and I turned back to the ship and to the seashore. As I drew near, I began to smell hot roast meat, so I groaned out a prayer to the immortal gods. 'Father Zeus,' I exclaimed, 'and all you other gods who live in everlasting bliss, you have done me a cruel mischief by the sleep into which you have sent me. See what fine work these men of mine have been making in my absence.'

"As soon as I got down to my ship and to the seashore, I rebuked each one of the men separately, but we could see no way out of it, for the cows were already dead. And indeed the gods began at once to show signs and wonders among us, for the hides of the cattle crawled about, and the joints upon the spits began to low like cows, and the meat kept on making a noise like the lowing of cattle.

Odysseus' Men Are Punished

"For six days my men kept driving in the best cows and feasting upon them, but on the seventh day, the fury of the gale subsided. We therefore went on board, raised our masts, spread sail, and put out to sea. As soon as we were well away from the island and could see nothing but sky and sea, Zeus set a black cloud over our ship, and the sea grew dark beneath it. We did not get on much farther, for in another moment we were caught by a terrific squall from the west that snapped the forestays of the mast so that it fell aft, while all the ship's gear tumbled about at the bottom of the vessel. The mast fell upon the head of the helmsman in the ship's stern, so that the bones of his head were crushed to pieces, and he fell overboard as though he were diving, with no more life left in him.

"Then Zeus let fly with his thunderbolts, and the ship went round and round, and was filled with fire and sulfur as the lightning struck it. The men all fell into the sea. They were carried about in the water around the ship, looking like so many sea gulls, but the god presently deprived them of all chance of getting home again.

"I lashed the mast and keel together, and getting astride of them, was carried wherever the winds chose to take me. I was carried along for nine days, till on the tenth night the gods brought me to the island where dwells the great and powerful goddess Calypso. She took me in and was kind to me, but I need say no more about this, for I told you and your noble wife all about it yesterday, and I hate telling again what has already been clearly told."

BOOKS 13–15

[Odysseus ended his story and then asked King Alcinous to lend him a ship that would take him home to Ithaca. And so, after his years of wandering, he arrived on the shores of Ithaca, alone, almost a stranger. Athena, as usual, was there to help him. Since Odysseus faced danger from the suitors, who wanted his property, the first thing the goddess did was to disguise him as an old beggar.

In his beggar's disguise, Odysseus went directly to the hut of Eumaeus (yōō·mē′əs), the swineherd, where he was hospitably welcomed and fed. Odysseus did not disclose his identity but made up a long story to explain who he was and how he had come to Ithaca. He swore that he had heard that Odysseus was nearby and would return home within a month, but Eumaeus would not believe him. After supper it began to storm, so Eumaeus made a bed for Odysseus near the fire but went out himself to watch over his pigs.

Meanwhile, Athena went to Sparta and told Telemachus that he must return home at once. She also told him how to avoid the suitors' ambush. She said that on arriving in Ithaca, he should go straight to the swineherd's hut.

In the swineherd's hut, Odysseus continued to test Eumaeus's hospitality. Eumaeus warned Odysseus against going into the town and advised him that having anything to do with the suitors would get him into trouble. He said that Odysseus should stay at the hut, where he was welcome, and await Telemachus's return.

At daybreak, Telemachus landed in Ithaca. As Athena had commanded, he set out for the swineherd's hut.]

BOOK 16

Telemachus Returns to Ithaca

Odysseus and the swineherd had lit a fire in the hut and were getting breakfast ready at daybreak. When Telemachus came up and stood at the door, Eumaeus sprang to his feet, and the bowls in which he was mixing wine fell from his hands, as he made his way toward his young master.

"So you are come, Telemachus," he said. "When I heard you had gone to Pylos, I was sure I was never going to see you any more. Come in, my dear child, and sit down, that I may have a good look at you now you are home again."

As he spoke, he took Telemachus's spear and Telemachus crossed the stone threshold and came inside. Odysseus rose from his seat to give him place as he entered, but Telemachus checked him. "Sit down, stranger," said he. "I can easily find another seat."

Odysseus went back to his own place, and Eumaeus spread some green brushwood on the floor and threw a sheepskin on top of it for Telemachus to sit upon. After they had eaten and drunk, Telemachus said to Eumaeus, "Old friend, where does this stranger come from? How did his crew bring him to Ithaca, and who were they? For assuredly he did not come here by land."

To this the swineherd Eumaeus answered, "My son, I will tell you the real truth. He says he is a Cretan and that he has been a great traveler. I will put him into your hands. Do whatever you like with him, only remember that he is your suppliant."

"I am very much distressed," said Telemachus, "by what you have just told me. How can I take this stranger into my house? I am as yet young and am not strong enough to hold my own if any man attacks me. Still, as the stranger has come to your house, I will find him a cloak and tunic of good wear, with a sword and sandals, and will send him wherever he wants to go. But I will not have him go near the suitors, for they are very insolent and are sure to ill-treat him in a way that would greatly grieve me."

Then Odysseus said, "Sir, I am much shocked by what you have said about the insolent way in which the suitors are behaving toward a gentleman like you. Tell me, do you submit to such treatment tamely, or has some god set your people against you? If I were the son of Odysseus or, indeed, if Odysseus himself came as a beggar — for there is still some hope of his return — if it were so, a stranger could cut off my head if I did not go to the house and attack every one of these men. If they were too many for me — I being single-handed — I would rather die fighting in my own house than see such disgraceful sights day after day."

And Telemachus answered, "I will tell you truly everything. I am the only son of Odysseus, who left me behind him when he went away, so that I have never been of any use to him. Thus it comes that my house is in the hands of numberless marauders, for the chiefs from all the neighboring islands, as also all the principal men of Ithaca itself, are eating up my house under the pretext of paying court to my mother, who will neither say that she will not marry nor yet bring matters to an end, so they are making havoc of my estate and before long will finish me too. The issue, however, rests with heaven."

Eumaeus, therefore, took his sandals, bound them to his feet, and started for the town. Athena watched him depart and then came up to the hut in the form of a woman, fair, stately, and wise. She stood against the side of the entry and revealed herself to Odysseus, but Telemachus could not see her. She nodded her head and motioned to Odysseus with her eyebrows, at which he left the hut and stood before her outside the main wall of the yard. Then she said to him:

"Odysseus, noble son of Laertes, it is now time for you to tell your son: do not keep him in the dark any longer but lay your plans for the destruction of the suitors and then make for the town. I will not be long in joining you, for I too am eager for the fray."

As she spoke, she touched him with her golden wand. First she threw a fair clean tunic and cloak about his shoulders; then she made him younger and of more imposing presence. She gave him back his color, filled out his cheeks, and let his beard become dark again. Then she went away, and Odysseus came back inside the hut. His son was astounded when he saw him and turned his eyes away for fear he might be looking upon a god.

"Stranger," said he, "how suddenly you have changed from what you were a moment or two ago. You are dressed differently, and your color is not the same. Are you some one or other of the gods that live in heaven?"

Telemachus Meets His Father

And Odysseus said, "I am no god; why should you take me for one? I am your father, on whose account you grieve and suffer so much at the hands of lawless men."

As he spoke, he kissed his son, and a tear fell from his cheek onto the ground, for he had restrained all tears till now. But Telemachus could not yet believe that he was his father and said:

"You are not my father, but some god flattering me with vain hopes that I may grieve all the more; no mortal man could of himself contrive to do as you have been doing and make yourself old and young at a moment's notice unless a god were with him. A second ago you were old and all in rags, and now you are like some god come down from heaven."

Odysseus answered, "Telemachus, you ought not to be too astonished at my being really here. There is no other Odysseus who will come home. Such as I am, it is I, who after long wandering and much hardship have got home in the twentieth year to my own country. What you wonder at is the work of the goddess Athena, who does with me whatever she will, for she can do what she pleases. At one moment she makes me like a beggar, and the next I am a young man with good clothes on my back; it is an easy matter for the gods who live in heaven to make any man look either rich or poor."

As he spoke, he sat down, and Telemachus threw his arms about his father and wept. They were both so much moved that they cried aloud like eagles or vultures with crooked talons that have been robbed of their half-fledged young by peasants. Then Telemachus suddenly said, "In what ship, my dear father, did your crew bring you to Ithaca? For you cannot have come by land."

"I will tell you the truth, my son," replied Odysseus. "It was the Phaeacians who brought me here. They are great sailors and are in the habit of giving escorts to anyone who reaches their coasts. They took me over the sea while I was fast asleep and landed me in Ithaca, after giving me many presents in bronze, gold, and clothing. These things by heaven's mercy are lying concealed in a cave, and I am now come here on the suggestion of Athena, that we may consult about killing our enemies. First, therefore, give me a list of the suitors, with their number, that I may learn who and how many they are. I can then turn the matter over in my mind and see whether we two can fight the whole body of them ourselves or whether we must find others to help us."

To this Telemachus answered, "Father, I have always heard of your renown both in the field and in council, but the task you talk of is a very great one. I am awed at the mere thought of it; two men cannot stand against many and brave ones. There are not ten suitors only, nor twice ten, but ten many times over. If we face such numbers as this, you may have bitter cause to regret your coming and your revenge. See whether you cannot think of someone who would be willing to come and help us."

"Listen to me," replied Odysseus, "and think whether Athena and her father, Zeus, may seem sufficient or whether I am to try and find someone else as well."

"Those whom you have named," answered Telemachus, "are a couple of good allies, for though they dwell high up among the clouds they have power over both gods and men."

Odysseus Forms a Plan

"These two," continued Odysseus, "will not keep long out of the fray when the suitors and we fight in my house. Now, therefore, return home early tomorrow morning, and go about among the suitors as before. Later on, the swineherd will bring me to the city disguised as a miserable old beggar. If you see them ill-treating me, steel your heart against my sufferings; even though they drag me feet foremost out of the house or throw things at me, look on and do nothing beyond gently trying to make them behave more reasonably; but they will not listen to you, for the day of their reckoning is at hand. Furthermore I say, and you remember my words: when Athena shall put it in my mind, I will nod my head to you, and on seeing me do this, you must collect all the armor that is in the house and hide it in the strong storeroom. Make some excuse when the suitors ask you why you are removing it; say that you have taken it to be out of the way of the smoke, as it is no longer what it was when Odysseus went away but has become soiled and begrimed with soot. Add to this more particularly that you are afraid Zeus may set them on to quarrel over their wine and that they may do each other some harm, for the sight of arms sometimes tempts people to use them. But leave a sword and a spear apiece for yourself and me and a couple of oxhide shields, so that we can snatch them up at any moment; Zeus and Athena will then soon bewitch these people. There is also another matter: if you are indeed my son and my blood runs in your veins, let no one know that Odysseus is within the house — neither Laertes nor yet the swineherd nor any of the servants nor even Penelope herself. Let you and me test the women alone, and let us also sound out some other of the menservants, to see who is on our side and whose hand is against us."

"Father," replied Telemachus, "you will find that I can keep your counsel. I do not think, however, the plan you propose will turn out well for either of us. Think it over. It will take us a long time to go the round of the farms and sound out the men, and all the time the suitors will be wasting your estate. Test the women by all means, to see who are disloyal and who innocent, but I am not in favor of going round and sounding the men. We can attend to that later on if you really have some sign from Zeus that he will support you."

Thus did they converse, and meanwhile the ship which had brought Telemachus and his crew from Pylos had reached the town of Ithaca.

The suitors were surprised and angry at what had happened, so they went outside the great wall that ran around the outer court and held a council near the man entrance. Eurymachus was the first to speak.

"My friends," said he, "this voyage of Telemachus's is a very serious matter; we were sure that it would come to nothing. Now, however, let us draw a ship into the water and get a crew together to send after the others and tell them to come back as fast as they can."

He had hardly done speaking when Amphinomus (am·fin′oo·məs) turned in his place and saw the ship they had sent to capture Telemachus inside the harbor, with the crew lowering her sails and putting by their oars, so he laughed, and said to the others, "We need not send them any message, for they are here. Some god must have told them, or else they saw the ship go by and could not overtake her."

On this, they rose and went to the waterside. The crew then drew the ship on shore, and they went up in a body to the place of assembly, but they would not let anyone old or young sit along with them, and Antinous spoke first.

The Suitors Plot Against Telemachus

"See how the gods have saved this man from destruction. We kept a succession of lookouts upon the headlands all day long, and when the sun was down, we never went on shore to sleep but waited in the ship all night till morning in the hope of capturing and killing him; but some god has convoyed him home in spite of us. Let us consider how we can make an end of him. He must not escape us. Our affair is never likely to come off while he is alive, for he is very shrewd, and public feeling is not all on our side. Let us try and lay hold of him either on his farm away from the town or on his road here. Then we can divide up his property among us, and let his mother and the man who marries her have the house."

They all held their peace until Amphinomus rose to speak. "My friends," said he, "I am not in favor of killing Telemachus. It is an evil thing to kill one who is of noble blood. Let us first take counsel of the gods, and if the oracles of Zeus advise it, I will both help to kill him myself and urge everyone else to do so; but if they dissuade us, I would have you hold your hands."

Thus did he speak, and his words pleased them well, so they rose and went to the house of Odysseus, where they took their accustomed seats.

Penelope Accuses the Suitors

Then Penelope decided that she would show herself to the suitors. She knew of the plot against Telemachus, for the servant Medon had overheard their counsels and had told her. She went down, therefore, to the court, holding a veil before her face, and rebuked Antinous, saying:

"Antinous, insolent and wicked schemer, they say you are the best speaker and councilor of any man your own age in Ithaca, but you are nothing of the kind. You plot the death of Telemachus, and devour Odysseus' property without paying for it, and you break my heart by wooing his wife and trying to kill his son. Leave off doing so, and stop the others also."

To this Eurymachus answered, "Take heart, Queen Penelope, and do not trouble yourself about these matters. The man is not yet born, nor ever will be, who shall lay hands upon your son, Telemachus, while I yet live to look upon the face of the earth. Telemachus is much the dearest friend I have and has nothing to fear from the hands of us suitors. Of course, if death comes to him from the gods, he cannot escape it." He said this to quiet her, but in reality he was plotting against Telemachus.

Then Penelope went upstairs again and mourned her husband till Athena shed sleep over her eyes.

BOOK 17

When the child of morning, rosy-fingered Dawn, appeared, Telemachus bound on his sandals and took a strong spear that suited his hands, for he wanted to go into the city. "Old friend," said he to the swineherd, "I will now go to the town and show myself to my mother, for she will never leave off weeping till she has seen me. As for this unfortunate stranger, take him to the town and let him beg there of anyone who will give him a drink and a piece of bread. I have trouble enough of my own and cannot be burdened with other people. If this makes him angry, so much the worse for him, but I like to say what I mean."

On this, Telemachus strode off through the yard, brooding his revenge upon the suitors. When he reached home, he stood his spear against a pillar, crossed the stone, and went inside.

Telemachus and Penelope

Nurse Eurycleia saw him long before anyone else did, and she burst out crying as she ran up to him. Penelope came out of her room looking like Artemis (är′tə·mis) or Aphrodite (af′rə·dī′tē), and wept as she flung her arms about her son. She kissed his forehead and both his eyes. "Light of my eyes," she spoke fondly to him, "so you are come home again; I thought I was never going to see you any more. To think of your having gone off to Pylos, without saying anything about it or obtaining my consent, to seek news of your father. But come, tell me what you saw."

"I will tell you the truth," replied her son. "We went to Pylos and saw Nestor, who took me to his house and treated me as though I were a son of his own who had just returned after a long absence; but he said he had not heard a word about Odysseus, whether he was alive or dead. He sent me, therefore, with a chariot and horses to Menelaus. There I saw Helen, for whose sake so many, both Greeks and Trojans, were in heaven's wisdom doomed to suffer.

Menelaus asked me what it was that had brought me to Sparta and I told him the whole truth, at which he said, 'So then, these cowards would take over a brave man's house? A deer might as well lay her newborn young in the lair of a lion and then go off to feed in the forest or in some grassy dell. The lion, when he comes back to his lair, will make short work of them, and so will Odysseus with these suitors. As regards your question, however, I will not deceive you, but what the old man of the sea told me, so much I will tell you in full. He said he could see Odysseus on an island sorrowing bitterly in the house of the nymph Calypso, who was keeping him prisoner, and he could not reach his home, for he had no ships nor sailors to take him over the sea.' This was what Menelaus told me, and when I had heard his story, I came away. The gods then gave me a fair wind and soon brought me safe home again." With these words he moved the heart of Penelope.

Odysseus Comes into the Town

Meanwhile the suitors were throwing the discus, or aiming with spears at a mark on the leveled ground in front of the house, and behaving with all their old insolence. But when it was time for dinner, they left their sports, and when they were within the house, they laid their cloaks on the benches and seats inside and then sacrificed some sheep, goats, pigs, and a heifer, all of them fat and well-grown. Thus they made ready for their meal.

In the meantime, Odysseus and the swineherd were starting for the town. Odysseus put his shabby old tattered wallet over his shoulders, and Eumaeus gave him a stick to his liking. The swineherd led the way, and his master followed after, looking like some broken-down old tramp as he leaned upon his staff, his clothes all in rags. When they had got over the rough, steep ground and were nearing the city, they reached the fountain from which the citizens drew their water. Above the fountain there was an altar to the nymphs, at which travelers used to sacrifice. Here Melanthius (mel·ən'thē·əs), the goatherd, overtook them as he was driving down some goats, the best in his flock, for the suitors' dinner. When he saw Eumaeus and Odysseus, he taunted them with foul language, which made Odysseus very angry.

"There you go," cried he, "and a precious pair you are. Where, threshold and eat what the suitors had given him, but he first went up to Antinous and said:

"Sir, give me something. You are not, surely, the poorest man here; you seem to be a chief, foremost among them all; therefore, you should be the better giver, and I will tell far and wide of your generosity. I, too, was a rich man once and had a fine house of my own; in those days I gave to many a tramp such as I now am, no matter who he might be or what he wanted. I had any number of servants and all the other things which people have who live well and are accounted wealthy, but it pleased Zeus to take all away from me."

Antinous Insults Odysseus

Then Antinous said, "What god can have sent such a pestilence to plague us during our dinner? Get away from my table, into the middle of the hall."

On this Odysseus began to move off and said, "Your looks, my fine sir, are better than your breeding. If you were in your own house, you would not spare a poor man so much as a pinch of salt, for though you are in another man's and surrounded with abundance, you cannot find it in you to give him even a piece of bread."

This made Antinous very angry, and he scowled at him, saying, "You shall pay for this before you get clear of the hall." With these words he threw a footstool at him and hit him on the right shoulder blade near the top of his back. Odysseus stood firm as a rock, and the blow did not even stagger him, but he shook his head in silence as he brooded on his revenge. Then he went back to the door and sat down there, laying his well-filled wallet at his feet.

"Listen to me," he cried, "you suitors of Queen Penelope, that I may speak as I am minded. Antinous has hit me while in the service of my miserable belly, which is always getting people into trouble. Still, if the poor have gods at all, I pray them that Antinous may come to a bad end before his marriage."

"Sit where you are, and eat your food in silence, or be off elsewhere," shouted Antinous. "If you say more I will have you dragged hand and foot through the courts, and the skin will be stripped from your body."

The other suitors were much displeased at this.

pray, master swineherd, are you taking this poor miserable object? It would make anyone sick to see such a creature at table. A fellow like this never won a prize for anything in his life but will go about rubbing his shoulders against every man's doorpost, begging for a few scraps of food. He will do nothing but beg food all the town over to feed his greedy belly. If he goes near Odysseus' house, he will get his head broken by the stools they will fling at him, till they turn him out."

On this, as he passed, he gave Odysseus a kick on the hip, but Odysseus stood firm, and did not budge from the path. For a moment he wondered whether or not to fly at the goatherd and kill him with his staff or fling him to the ground and beat his brains out. He decided, however, to endure it and kept himself in check.

The goatherd left them and went quickly forward and soon reached the house of his master. When he got there, he went in and took his seat among the suitors opposite Eurymachus, who liked him better than any of the others. The servants brought him a portion of meat, and a housekeeper set bread before him, that he might eat. Presently Odysseus and the swineherd came up to the house and stood by it, amid a sound of music, for Phemius was just beginning to sing to the suitors. Then Odysseus took hold of the swineherd's hand and said:

"Eumaeus, this house of Odysseus is a very fine place. No matter how far you go, you will find few like it. One building keeps following on after another. The outer court has a wall with battlements all around it. The doors are double-folding and of good workmanship; it would be a hard matter to take it by force of arms. I see, too, that there are many people banqueting inside, for there is a smell of roast meat, and I hear a sound of music."

Then Eumaeus said, "You have perceived aright, as indeed you generally do; but let us think what will be our best course. Will you go inside first and join the suitors, leaving me here behind you, or will you wait here and let me go in first? But do not wait long, or someone may see you loitering about outside and throw something at you. Consider this matter, I pray you."

And Odysseus answered, "I understand. Go in first and leave me here where I am. I am quite used to being beaten and having things thrown at me. I have been so much knocked about in war and by sea that I am case-hardened. But a man cannot hide away the cravings of a hungry belly; this is an enemy which gives much trouble to all men; it is because of this that ships are fitted out to sail the seas and to make war upon other people."

Odysseus Is Recognized by His Dog

As they were thus talking, a dog that had been lying asleep raised his head and pricked up his ears. This was Argus, whom Odysseus had bred before setting out for Troy. In the old days, he used to be taken out by the young men when they went hunting wild goats or deer or hares, but now, his master being gone, he was lying neglected and full of fleas in front of the stable doors. As soon as he saw Odysseus standing there, he dropped his ears and wagged his tail, but he could not get close up to his master. When Odysseus saw the dog on the other side of the yard, he dashed a tear from his eyes without Eumaeus seeing it and said:

"Eumaeus, what a noble hound that is over yonder; his build is splendid. Is he as fine a fellow as he looks, or is he only one of those dogs that come begging about a table and are kept merely for show?"

"This hound," answered Eumaeus, "belonged to him who has died in a far country. If he were what he was when Odysseus left for Troy, he would soon show you what he could do. There was not a wild beast in the forest that could get away from him when he was once on its tracks. But now he has fallen on evil times, for his master is dead and gone, and the women take no care of him."

As he spoke, he went inside the buildings to the hall where the suitors were, but Argus died as soon as he had recognized his master after twenty years.

Telemachus saw Eumaeus long before anyone else did, and beckoned him to come and sit beside him.

Immediately afterward Odysseus came inside, looking like a poor miserable old beggar, leaning on his staff, clothes all in rags, and sat down just inside the doors. Telemachus took a whole loaf from the breadbasket, with as much meat as he could hold in his two hands, and said to Eumaeus, "Take this to the stranger."

So Eumaeus went up to him and said, "Stranger, Telemachus sends you this."

Odysseus answered, "May King Zeus grant all happiness to

Telemachus and fulfill the desire of his heart."

Then with both hands he took what Telemachus had sent and laid it on the dirty old wallet at his feet. He went on eat while the bard was singing. And as the suitors applauded the Athena went up to Odysseus and prompted him to beg pie bread from each one of the suitors, that he might see what ki people they were and tell the good from the bad. Odysseus, fore, went on his round, going from left to right, and stretche his hands to beg as though he were a real beggar. Some of the ied him and were curious about him, asking one another w was and where he came from.

Then Antinous began to abuse the swineherd. "You idio cried, "what have you brought this man to town for? Have v tramps and beggars enough already to pester us as we sit at Do you think it a small thing that such people gather here to your master's property, that you must bring this man as well?

And Eumaeus answered, "Antinous, your birth is good bu words evil. It was no doing of mine that he came here. You ways harder on Odysseus' servants than any of the other suit and above all on me, but I do not care so long as Telemach Penelope are alive and here."

But Telemachus said, "Hush, do not answer him. Antino the bitterest tongue of all the suitors, and he makes the worse."

Then, turning to Antinous, he said, "Antinous, you take as care of my interests as though I were your son. Why shou want to see this stranger turned out of the house? Heaven Take something and give it to him yourself; I do not grudg bid you take it. Never mind my mother nor any of the other s in the house; but I know you will not do what I say, for y more fond of eating things yourself than of giving them t people."

"What do you mean, Telemachus," replied Antinous, "1 swaggering talk? If all the suitors were to give him as much a he would not come here again for another three months."

As he spoke, he drew the stool on which he rested his fee under the table and made as though he would throw it at Oc but the other suitors all gave him something and filled his with bread and meat. He was about, therefore, to go back

BOOK 18

[Penelope, hearing of the stranger's arrival, went down to the great hall to see him, but did not recognize the beggar as Odysseus. After more quarreling, the suitors ended the festivities and went to their own houses.

To prepare for the battle with the suitors, Odysseus and Telemachus hid all the armor in the house so that the suitors would have no protection.

Then Penelope talked with the "stranger," who told her that Odysseus was still alive and on his way home. Penelope found it hard to believe the beggar but honored him as a guest.]

BOOK 19

Penelope said: "Alas! I shall never welcome him home again. It was an ill fate that he ever set out for that detested city whose name I cannot bring myself even to mention."

Then Odysseus answered, "Madam, wife of Odysseus, do not disfigure yourself further by grieving for your loss, though I can hardly blame you for doing so. I have lately heard of Odysseus as being alive and on his way home. He is bringing back much valuable treasure; but his ship and all his crew were lost, for Zeus and the sun god were angry with him because his men had slaughtered the sun god's cattle, and they were all drowned. But Odysseus clung to the keel of the ship and drifted onto the land of the Phaeacians. There is no man living who is so wily as he is; there is no one can compare with him. Odysseus will return in this selfsame year; with the end of this moon and the beginning of the next he will be here."

"May it be even so," answered Penelope. "If your words come true, you shall have such gifts and such goodwill from me that all who see you shall congratulate you; but I know very well how it will all be. Odysseus will never return. And now, you maids, wash the stranger's feet for him, and make him a bed on a couch with rugs and blankets, that he may be warm and quiet till morning."

Odysseus answered, "Madam, I shall not let any of the young servants about your house wash my feet, but if you have any old and respectable woman who has gone through as much trouble as I have, I will allow her to wash them."

To this Penelope said, "My dear sir, of all the guests who ever yet came to my house there never was one who spoke as sensibly as you do. There happens to be in the house a most respectable old woman — the same who received my poor dear husband in her arms the night he was born and nursed him in infancy. She is very feeble now, but she shall wash your feet. Come here," said she, "Eurycleia, and wash a friend of your master; I suppose Odysseus' hands and feet are very much the same now as his are, for trouble ages all of us dreadfully fast."

Odysseus and His Old Nurse, Eurycleia

On these words, the old woman covered her face with her hands. She began to weep and made lamentation, saying, "I will wash your feet myself gladly enough, as Penelope has said that I am to do so. And let me say this, too: we have had all kinds of strangers in distress come here before now, but I make bold to say that no one ever yet came who was so like Odysseus in figure, voice, and feet as you are."

"Those who have seen us both," answered Odysseus, "have always said we were wonderfully like each other, and now you have noticed it, too."

Then the old woman took the basin in which she was going to wash his feet and poured plenty of cold water into it, adding hot till the bath was warm enough. Odysseus sat by the fire, but before long he turned away from the light, for it occurred to him that when the old woman had hold of his leg she would recognize a certain scar which it bore, and the whole truth would come out. And indeed, as soon as she began washing her master, she at once knew the scar as one that had been given him by a wild boar when he was hunting on Mount Parnassus with his grandfather. She dropped the foot at once. The leg fell into the bath, which rang out and was overturned, so that all the water was spilled on the ground. Eurycleia's eyes, between her joy and grief, filled with tears, and she could not speak, but she caught Odysseus by the beard and said,

"My dear child, you are Odysseus himself, only I did not know you till I had actually touched you."

As she spoke, she looked toward Penelope, as though wanting to tell her that her dear husband was in the house, but Penelope was unable to look in that direction and observe what was going on, for Athena had diverted her attention. Odysseus caught Eurycleia by the throat with his right hand and with his left drew her close to him and said, "Nurse, do you wish to destroy me now that after twenty years of wandering I am at last come to my own home again? Since it has been given you by heaven to recognize me, hold your tongue, and do not say a word about it to anyone else in the house, for if you do, I tell you — and it shall surely be — that if heaven grants me to take the lives of these suitors, I will not spare you, though you are my own nurse, when I am killing the other women."

"My child," answered Eurycleia, "what are you talking about? You know very well that nothing can either bend or break me. I will hold my tongue like a stone or a piece of iron"; and she left the hall to fetch some more water, for the first had been all spilled. When she had washed him and anointed him with oil, Odysseus drew his seat nearer to the fire to warm himself and hid the scar under his rags. Then Penelope began talking to him and said:

"Stranger, I should like to speak with you briefly about another matter. It is indeed nearly bedtime — for those, at least, who can sleep in spite of sorrow. The coming dawn will usher in the ill-omened day that is to part me from the house of Odysseus, for I am about to hold a tournament of axes. My husband used to set up twelve axes in the hall, one in front of the other, like the stays upon which a ship is built. He would then go back from them and shoot an arrow through the whole twelve. I shall make the suitors try to do the same thing, and whichever of them can string the bow most easily and send his arrow through all the twelves axes, him will I marry."

Then Odysseus answered, "Madam, wife of Odysseus, you need not put off your tournament, for Odysseus will return before they can string the bow and send their arrows through the iron."

She then went upstairs to her own room, not alone, but attended by her maidens, and when there, she lamented her dear husband till Athena shed sweet sleep over her eyelids.

BOOK 20

[Brooding over how he would kill the suitors, Odysseus could not sleep. Finally, he remembered how he had escaped from the Cyclops. Athena appeared and encouraged him, and then he slept.

As the feast began the next day, Telemachus boldly warned the suitors not to mistreat the beggar. But Athena would not let the suitors stop their insolence, and they continued to abuse Odysseus. One suitor suggested that Telemachus urge Penelope to remarry so that Telemachus could enjoy his house in peace. Telemachus replied that he favored his mother's remarrying but that he would never force her to do so. Then Athena filled the suitors' hearts with forebodings, but they did not guess the doom that had been prepared for them.]

BOOK 21

The Tournament of the Axes

Athena now put it in Penelope's mind to make the suitors try their skill with the bow and with the iron axes, in contest among themselves, as a means of bringing about their destruction. She went upstairs and got the storeroom key. She then went with her maidens into the storeroom at the end of the house, where her husband's treasures of gold, bronze, and wrought iron were kept, also his bow and quiver full of deadly arrows. She took down the bow with its bow case from the peg on which it hung. She sat down with it on her knees, weeping bitterly as she took the bow out of its case, and when her tears had relieved her, she went to the hall where the suitors were, carrying the bow and the quiver, with the many deadly arrows that were inside it. Along with her came her maids, bearing a chest that contained the axes which her husband had won as prizes. When she reached the suitors, she stood by one of the pillars supporting the room. Then she said:

Penelope Rebukes the Suitors

"Listen to me, you suitors, who persist in abusing the hospitality of this house because its owner has been long absent and without other pretext than that you want to marry me. This, then, being the prize that you are contending for, I will put before you the mighty bow of Odysseus, and whoever of you shall string it most easily and send his arrow through each one of twelve axes, him will I follow and leave my lawful husband's house, so fine and so abounding in wealth. But even so, I am sure that I shall remember it in my dreams."

So she spoke and told Eumaeus to set the bow and the axes before the suitors, and Eumaeus wept as he took them to do as she had bidden him.

Then Telemachus spoke. "Come on then, make no excuses for delay, but let us see whether you can string the bow or not. I too will try it, for if I can string it and shoot through the iron, I should not be so sorry if my mother were to leave this house to go with a stranger, knowing myself capable now of using the fine weapons that belonged to my father."

As he spoke, he sprang from his seat, threw his crimson cloak from him, and took his sword from his shoulder. First he set the axes in a row, in a long groove which he had dug for them and had made straight by line. Then he stamped the earth tight around them, and everyone was surprised when they saw him set them up so orderly, though he had never seen anything of the kind before. This done, he went on to the threshold to try the bow; three times he tugged at it; trying with all his might to draw the string, and three times he had to leave off. He was trying for the fourth time and would have strung it, had not Odysseus shaken his head to check him in spite of his eagerness. So he said:

"Alas! I shall either always be feeble, or I am too young and have not yet reached my full strength so as to be able to hold my own if anyone attacks me. You others, therefore, who are stronger than I, try the bow and get this contest settled."

On this, he put the bow down, letting it lean against the door, with the arrow standing against the top of the bow. Then he sat down on the seat from which he had risen, and Antinous said:

"Come on, each of you in turn."

The rest agreed, and Leiodes was the first to rise. He was the only man who hated their evil deeds and was indignant with the others. He was now the first to take the bow and arrow, but he could not string the bow, for his hands were weak and unused to hard work.

He said to the suitors, "My friends, I cannot string it; let another have it. This bow shall take the life and soul out of many a chief among us, for it is better to die than to live after having missed the prize that has brought us so long together."

On this he put the bow down, letting it lean against the door, with the arrow standing against the tip of the bow. Then he took his seat again on the seat from which he had risen, and Antinous rebuked him, saying:

"Leiodes, what are you talking about? Your words are nonsense. It makes me angry to listen to you. Shall, then, this bow take the life of many a chief among us, merely because you cannot bend it yourself? True, you were not born to be an archer, but there are others who will soon string it."

Then he said to Melanthius, the goatherd, "Look sharp, light a fire in the court, and set a seat nearby with a sheepskin on it. Bring us also a large ball of lard from what they have in the house. Let us warm the bow and grease it. We will then try it again and end the contest."

Melanthius lit the fire and set a seat covered with sheepskins beside it. He also brought a great ball of lard from what they had in the house, and the suitors warmed the bow and again tried it, but they were not nearly strong enough to string it. Nevertheless, there still remained Antinous and Eurymachus, who were the ringleaders among the suitors and the foremost among them all.

Then the swineherd and the stockman left the hall together, and Odysseus followed them. When they had got outside the gates and the outer yard, Odysseus said to them quietly:

"Stockman, and you, swineherd, I have something in my mind which I am in doubt whether to say or not, but I think I will say it. Would you stand by Odysseus if some god should bring him back here all of a sudden? Say which you would do — side with the suitors or with Odysseus?"

"If Father Zeus," answered the stockman, "were but to bring Odysseus back, you should see with what might I would fight for him."

In like words Eumaeus prayed to all the gods that Odysseus might return. When, therefore, he saw for certain what their feelings were, Odysseus said, "It is I, Odysseus, who am here. I have suffered much, but at last, in the twentieth year, I am come back to my own country. I find that you two alone of all my menservants are glad that I should do so, for I have not heard any of the others praying for my return. To you two, therefore, will I reveal the truth. If heaven shall deliver the suitors into my hands, I will find wives for both of you and will give you houses close to my own, and you shall be to me as though you were brothers and friends of Telemachus. I will now give you convincing proof, that you may know me for certain. See, here is the scar from the boar's tooth that ripped me when I was out hunting on Mount Parnassus."

As he spoke, he drew his rags aside from the great scar, and when they had examined it thoroughly, they both of them wept about Odysseus, threw their arms around him, and kissed his head and shoulders, while Odysseus kissed their hands and faces in return. But Odysseus checked them and said:

"Stop your weeping, or someone will come outside and see us and tell those who are inside. When you go in, do so separately, not both together. I will go first and you follow afterward. Let this, moreover, be the signal between us: the suitors will all try to prevent me from getting hold of the bow and quiver. Therefore, you, Eumaeus, bring it through the hall and place it in my hands, and tell the women to close the doors of their apartment. If they hear any groaning or uproar as of men fighting about the house, they must not come out. They must keep quiet and stay where they are at their work. And fasten the doors of the outer court and bind them securely at once."

When he had thus spoken, he went back to the house and took the seat that he had left. Presently his two servants followed him inside.

At this moment the bow was in the hands of Eurymachus, who was warming it by the fire, but even so he could not string it. He heaved a deep sigh and said, "I grieve for myself and for us all; I do not care nearly so much about the marriage, for there are plenty of other women in Ithaca and elsewhere. What I feel most is the fact of our being so inferior to Odysseus in strength that we cannot string his bow. This will disgrace us in the eyes of those who are yet unborn."

"It shall not be so, Eurymachus," said Antinous, "and you know it yourself. Today is the feast of Apollo throughout all the land. Who can string a bow on such a day as this? Put it on one side. As for the axes, they can stay where they are, for no one is likely to come to the house and take them away. Let the cupbearer go round the cups, that we may make our drink offerings and drop this matter of the bow. Tomorrow we can sacrifice to Apollo, the mighty archer, and again try the bow and end the contest."

The rest approved his words, and menservants poured water over the hands of the guests, while pages filled the mixing bowls with wine and water and handed it round. Then, when they had drunk as much as they desired, Odysseus craftily said:

"Suitors of the famous queen, may I speak? Give me the bow, that I may test the power of my hands among you all and see whether I still have as much strength as I used to have or whether travel and neglect have made an end of it."

This made them all very angry, for they feared he might string the bow. Antinous therefore rebuked him fiercely, saying, "Wretched creature, you have not so much as a grain of sense in your whole body. It will go hard with you if you string the bow: you will find no mercy from anyone here; you will never get away alive, so drink and keep quiet without getting into a quarrel with men younger than yourself."

Penelope then spoke to him. "Antinous," said she, "it is not right that you should ill-treat any guest of Telemachus who comes to this house. If the stranger should prove strong enough to string the mighty bow of Odysseus, can you suppose that he would take me home with him and make me his wife? Even the man himself can have no such idea in his mind."

Then Telemachus said, "Mother, I am the only man in Ithaca who has the right to let anyone have the bow or to refuse it. No one shall force me one way or the other, not even though I choose to make the stranger a present of the bow outright and let him take it away with him. Go, then, within the house and busy yourself with your daily duties, your loom, your distaff, and the ordering of your servants. This bow is a man's matter and mine above all others, for it is I who am master here."

She went wondering back into the house, impressed by her son's words. Then, going with her handmaids upstairs into her room, she mourned her dear husband till Athena sent sweet sleep over her eyelids.

The swineherd now took up the bow and was taking it to Odysseus, but the suitors shouted at him from all parts of the hall, and one of them said, "You idiot, where are you taking the bow? Are you out of your wits? If Apollo and the other gods will grant our prayer, your own hounds shall get you into some quiet place, and tear you to pieces."

Eumaeus was frightened at the outcry they all raised, so he put the bow down, but Telemachus shouted at him from the other side of the hall and threatened him, saying, "Father Eumaeus, bring the bow on in spite of them."

Thus he spoke, and they all laughed heartily, which put them in a better humor with Telemachus, so Eumaeus brought the bow down the hall and placed it in the hands of Odysseus. When he had done this, he called Eurycleia apart and said to her, "Eurycleia, Telemachus says you are to close the doors of the women's apartments. If they hear any groaning or uproar as of men fighting about the house, they are not to come out but are to keep quiet and stay where they are at their work."

Eurycleia did as she was told and closed the doors of the women's apartments.

Odysseus Strings the Bow

Meanwhile, the stockman slipped quietly out and fastened the gates of the outer court. There was a ship's cable lying in the gatehouse, so he made the gates fast with it and then came in again, resuming the seat that he had left, and kept an eye on Odysseus, who had now got the bow in his hands and was turning it every way about and testing it all over to see whether the worms had been eating into its two horns during his absence.

And when he had examined it all over, he strung it as easily as a skilled bard strings a new peg of his lyre and makes the twisted gut fast at both ends. Then he took it in his right hand to test the string, and it sang sweetly under his touch like the twittering of a swallow. The suitors were dismayed and turned color as they heard it. At that moment, moreover, Zeus thundered loudly as a sign, and the heart of Odysseus rejoiced as he heard the omen that Zeus had sent him.

He took an arrow that was lying upon the table — for those which the Greeks were so shortly about to taste were all inside the quiver

— he laid it on the center piece of the bow and drew the notch of the arrow and the string toward him. When he had taken aim, he let fly, and his arrow pierced every one of the handle holes of the axes from the first onward till it had gone right through them and into the outer courtyard. Then he said to Telemachus:

"Your guest has not disgraced you, Telemachus."

As he spoke, he made a sign with his eyebrows, and Telemachus girded on his sword, grasped his spear, and stood armed beside his father's seat.

BOOK 22

The Battle in the Great Hall

Then Odysseus tore off his rags and sprang onto the broad threshold with his bow and his quiver full of arrows. He poured the arrows onto the ground at his feet and said, "The mighty contest is at an end. I will now see whether Apollo will let me hit another mark which no man has yet hit."

On this, he aimed a deadly arrow at Antinous, who was about to take up a two-handled gold cup to drink his wine and already had it in his hands. He had no thought of death — who among all the revelers would think that one man, however brave, would stand alone among so many and kill him? The arrow struck Antinous in the throat, and the point went clean through his neck, so that he fell over and the cup dropped from his hand, while a thick stream of blood gushed from his nostrils. He kicked the table from him and upset the things on it, so that the bread and roasted meats all fell onto the ground. The suitors were in an uproar when they saw that a man had been hit. They sprang up from their seats and looked everywhere toward the walls, but there was neither shield nor spear, and they rebuked Odysseus very angrily. "Stranger," said they, "you shall pay for shooting people in this way: you shall see no other contest; you are a doomed man. He whom you have slain was the foremost youth in Ithaca, and the vultures shall devour you for having killed him."

Thus they spoke, for they thought that he had killed Antinous by mistake and did not perceive that death was hanging over every one of them. But Odysseus glared at them and said:

"Dogs, did you think that I should not come back from Troy? You have wasted my property and have wooed my wife while I was still living. You have feared neither god nor man, and now you shall die."

They turned pale with fear as he spoke, and every man looked round about to see where he might fly for safety, but Eurymachus alone spoke.

"If you are Odysseus," said he, "then what you have said is just. We have done much wrong on your lands and in your house. But Antinous, who was responsible for the offending, lies dead already. It was all his doing. It was not that he wanted to marry Penelope; what he wanted was to kill your son and to be chief man in Ithaca. Now, therefore, that he has met the death which was his due, spare the lives of your people. We will make everything good among ourselves and pay you in full for all that we have eaten and drunk. Each one of us shall pay you a fine worth twenty oxen, and we will keep on giving you gold and bronze till your heart is softened. Until we have done this, no one can complain of your being enraged against us."

Odysseus again glared at him and said, "Though you should give me all that you have in the world now and all that you ever shall have, I will not stay my hand till I have paid all of you in full. You must fight or run for your lives; not a man of you shall escape."

Their hearts sank as they heard him, but Eurymachus again spoke, saying:

"My friends, this man will give us no quarter. He will stand where he is and shoot us down till he has killed every man among us. Let us then show fight; draw your swords, and hold up the tables to shield you from his arrows."

As he spoke, he drew his keen blade of bronze, sharpened on both sides, and with a loud cry sprang toward Odysseus, but Odysseus instantly shot an arrow into his breast that fixed itself in his liver. He dropped his sword and fell doubled up over his table. The cup and all the meat went over onto the ground as he hit the earth with his forehead in the agonies of death, and he kicked the stool with his feet until his eyes were closed in darkness.

Then Amphinomus drew his sword and made straight at Odysseus to try and get him away from the door, but Telemachus was too quick for him and struck him from behind. The spear caught him between the shoulders and went right through his chest, so that he fell heavily to the ground and struck the earth with his forehead. Then Telemachus sprang away from him, leaving his spear still in the body, for he was afraid that if he stopped to pull it out, some one might come up and strike him with his sword or knock him down, so he set off at a run and immediately was at his father's side. Then he said:

"Father, let me bring you a shield, two spears, and a brass helmet. I will arm myself as well and will bring other armor for the swineherd and the stockman, for we had better be armed."

"Run and get them," answered Odysseus, "while my arrows hold out, or when I am alone, they may get me away from the door."

Telemachus did as his father said and went off to the storeroom where the armor was kept. He chose four shields, eight spears, and four brass helmets with horsehair plumes. He brought them with all speed to his father and armed himself first, while the stockman and the swineherd also put on their armor and took their places near Odysseus. Meanwhile, Odysseus, as long as his arrows lasted, had been shooting the suitors one by one, and they fell thick one on another. When his arrows gave out, he leaned the bow against the end wall of the house by the doorpost and hung a shield four hides thick about his shoulders. On his mighty head he set his helmet, well made, with a crest of horsehair that nodded menacingly above it, and he grasped two bronze-tipped spears.

The Punishment of the Suitors

Then the four men stood on the threshold, fierce and full of fury; nevertheless, those who were in the body of the hall were still both brave and many. Then Zeus's daughter Athena came up to them, having assumed the voice and form of Mentor. Odysseus was glad when he saw her and said, "Mentor, lend me your help, and do not forget your old comrade nor the many good turns he has done you."

But all the time he thought it was Athena, and the suitors from the other side raised an uproar when they saw her. Agelaus was the first to reproach her. "Mentor," he cried, "do not let Odysseus trick you into siding with him and fighting the suitors. This is what we will do: when we have killed these people, father and son, we will kill you, too. You shall pay for it with your head, and when we have killed you, we will take all you have and add it to Odysseus' property. We will not let your sons live in your house nor your daughters, nor shall your widow continue to live in the city of Ithaca."

This made Athena still more furious, so she scolded Odysseus angrily. "Odysseus," said she, "your strength and prowess are no longer what they were when you fought for nine long years among the Trojans about the noble lady Helen. You killed many a man in those days, and it was through your stratagem that Troy was taken. How is it that you are so much less valiant now when you are on your own ground, face to face with the suitors in your own house? Come on, my good fellow, stand by my side and see how Mentor shall fight your foes and repay your kindnesses."

But she would not give him full victory as yet, for she wished still further to test his own strength and courage and that of his brave son, so she flew up to one of the rafters in the roof of the hall and sat upon it in the form of a swallow.

Meanwhile, the suitors were still fighting for their lives. Many had already fallen under the arrows of Odysseus. Agelaus shouted to them and said, "My friends, he will soon have to leave off, for Mentor has gone away after having done nothing for him but brag. They are standing at the doors alone. Do not aim at him all at once, but six of you throw your spears first and see if you cannot cover yourselves with glory by killing him. When he has fallen, we need not worry about the others."

They threw their spears as he bade them, but Athena made them all of no effect. One hit a pillar of the hall; another went against the door; the pointed shaft of another struck the wall. And as soon as they had avoided all the spears of the suitors, Odysseus said to his own men, "My friends, we too had better drive into the middle of them, or they will crown all the harm they have done us by killing us outright."

They therefore aimed straight in front of them and threw their spears. Odysseus killed Demoptolemus, Telemachus Euryades, Eumaeus Elatus, while the stockman killed Pisander. These all bit the dust, and as the others drew back into a corner, Odysseus and his men rushed forward and regained their spears by drawing them from the bodies of the dead.

The suitors now aimed a second time, but again Athena made

their weapons for the most part without effect. Still, Amphimedon took a piece of the top skin from off Telemachus's wrist, and a spear managed to graze Eumaeus's shoulder above his shield. Then Odysseus and his men let drive again into the crowd of suitors.

Then Odysseus struck the son of Damastor with a spear in close fight, while Telemachus hit Leocritus in the belly, and the dart went clean through him, so that he fell forward full on his face upon the ground. Then Athena from her seat on the rafter held up her deadly shield, and the suitors panicked. They fled to the other end of the hall like a herd of cattle maddened by the gadfly in early summer, when the days are at their longest. As eagle-beaked, crook-taloned vultures from the mountains swoop down on the smaller birds that cower in flocks upon the ground and kill them, for they can neither fight nor fly, and onlookers enjoy the sport — even so did Odysseus and his men fall upon the suitors and strike them on every side. They made a horrible groaning as their brains were being battered in, and the ground ran with their blood.

Leiodes then caught the knees of Odysseus and said, "Odysseus, I beseech you, have mercy upon me and spare me. I never wronged anyone in your house either in word or in deed, and I tried to stop the others. I saw them, but they would not listen, and now they are paying for their folly. I was their sacrificing priest. If you kill me, I shall die without having done anything to deserve it and shall have got no thanks for all the good that I did."

Odysseus looked sternly at him and answered, "If you were their sacrificing priest, you must have prayed many a time that it might be long before I got home again and that you might marry my wife. Therefore, you shall die."

With these words, he picked up the sword that Agelaus had dropped when he was being killed and which was lying upon the ground. Then he struck Leiodes on the back of his neck, so that his head fell rolling in the dust while he was yet speaking.

The minstrel Phemius, who had been forced by the suitors to sing to them, now tried to save his life. Going up to Odysseus, he caught hold of his knees and said, "Odysseus, I beseech you, have mercy on me and spare me. You will be sorry for it afterward if you kill a bard who can sing both for gods and men as I can. I make all my songs myself, and heaven inspires me. I would sing to you as though you were a god; do not therefore be in such a hurry to cut my head off. Your own son, Telemachus, will tell you that I did not want to come to your house and sing to the suitors after their meals, but they were too many and too strong for me, so they made me."

Telemachus heard him, and at once went up to his father. "Stop!" he cried. "The man is innocent, do not hurt him; and we will spare Medon too, who was always good to me when I was a boy."

Medon caught these words of Telemachus, for he was crouching under a seat, beneath which he had hidden by covering himself up with an ox-hide; so he threw off the hide, went up to Telemachus, and grasped his knees.

"Here I am, my dear sir," said he. "Stay your hand, therefore, and tell your father, or he will kill me."

Odysseus smiled at him and answered, "Fear not; Telemachus has saved your life, that you may know in future and tell other people how much better good deeds prosper than evil ones. Go, therefore, outside the hall into the outer court, and be out of the way of the slaughter — you and the bard — while I finish my work here inside."

Then Odysseus looked the whole house carefully over, to see if anyone had managed to hide himself and was still living, but he found them all lying in the dust in their blood. They were like fishes which fishermen have netted out of the sea and thrown upon the beach to lie gasping for water till the heat of the sun makes an end of them. Even so were the suitors lying all huddled up, one against the other.

The Punishment of the Unfaithful Maids

Then Odysseus said to Telemachus, "Call nurse Eurycleia; I have something to say to her."

Telemachus went and knocked at the door of the women's room. "Make haste," said he, "you old woman who have been set over all the other women in the house. Come outside; my father wishes to speak to you."

When Eurycleia heard this, she unfastened the door of the women's room and came out, following Telemachus. She found Odysseus among the corpses, spattered with blood and filth like a lion that has just been devouring an ox, his breast and both his cheeks all bloody, smeared from head to foot with gore so that he was a fearful sight. When she saw all the corpses and such a quantity of blood, she was beginning to cry out for joy, for she saw that a great deed had been done; but Odysseus checked her. "Old woman," said he, "rejoice in silence; restrain yourself, and do not make any noise about it; it is an unholy thing to exult over dead men. Heaven's doom and their own evil deeds have brought these men to destruction, for they respected no man in the whole world, neither rich nor poor, who came near them, and they have come to a bad end as a punishment for their wickedness and folly. Now, however, tell me which of the women in the house have misconducted themselves and which are innocent."

"I will tell you the truth, my son," answered Eurycleia. "There are fifty women in the house whom we have taught to do things, such as carding wool and all kinds of household work. Of these, twelve in all have misbehaved and have been wanting in respect to me and also to Penelope. They showed no disrespect to Telemachus, for he has only lately grown up, and his mother never permitted him to give orders to the female servants; but let me go upstairs and tell your wife all that has happened, for some god has sent her to sleep."

"Do not wake her yet," answered Odysseus, "but tell the women who have misconducted themselves to come to me."

Eurycleia left the hall to tell the women and make them come to Odysseus. In the meantime he called Telemachus, the stockman, and the swineherd. "Begin," said he, "to remove the dead, and make the women help you. Then get sponges and clean water to wash down the tables and seats. When you have thoroughly cleansed the whole house, take the women into the space between the domed room and the wall of the outer court and run them through with your swords till they are quite dead."

On this, the women came down in a body, weeping and wailing bitterly. First they carried the dead bodies out and propped them up against one another in the gatehouse. Odysseus himself ordered them about and made them do their work quickly, so they had to carry the bodies out. When they had done this, they cleaned all the tables and seats with sponges and water, while Telemachus and the two others shoveled up the blood and dirt from the ground and the women carried it all away and put it out of doors. Then, when they had made the whole place quite clean and orderly, they took the women out and hemmed them in the narrow space between the wall of the domed room and that of the yard, so that they could not get away. And Telemachus said to the other two, "I shall not let these women die a clean death, for they were insolent to me and my mother."

So saying, he made a ship's cable fast to a great pillar and attached it to the top of the domed room, at a good height, so that none of the women's feet should touch the ground. As thrushes or doves beat against a net that has been set for them in a thicket just as they were getting to their nests and an unwished-for sleep awaits them, even so did the women have to put their heads in nooses one after the other and die most miserably. Their feet moved convulsively for a while but not for very long.

When they had done this, they washed their hands and feet and went back into the house, for all was now over; and Odysseus said to Eurycleia, "Bring me sulfur, which cleanses all pollution, and fetch fire also, that I may burn it and purify the hall. Go also and tell Penelope to come here with her attendants and also all the maidservants that are in the house."

"All that you have said is wise," answered Eurycleia, "but let me bring you some clean clothes — a tunic and cloak. Do not keep these rags on your back any longer. It is not right."

"First light me a fire," replied Odysseus.

She brought the fire and sulfur, as he had told her, and Odysseus thoroughly purified the hall and both the inner and outer courts. Then she went inside to call the women and tell them what had happened, and they came from their apartment with torches in their hands and pressed around Odysseus to embrace him, kissing his head and shoulders and taking hold of his hands. It made him feel like weeping, for he remembered every one of them.

BOOK 23

After the Battle

Eurycleia now went upstairs laughing to tell her mistress that her dear husband had come home. "Wake up, Penelope, my dear child," she exclaimed. "Odysseus has at last come home again, and has killed the suitors who were giving so much trouble in his house, eating up his estate and ill-treating his son."

Penelope came down to the great hall. She could hardly believe that this was really Odysseus, and so she tested him again with questions that only Odysseus could answer.

Penelope Recognizes Odysseus

When she heard the sure proofs Odysseus now gave her, she broke down. She flew weeping to his side, flung her arms about his neck, and kissed him. "Do not be angry with me, Odysseus," she cried, "you, who are the wisest of mankind. We have suffered, both of us. Heaven has denied us the happiness of spending our youth and growing old together. Do not then be angry or hurt when I did not embrace you as soon as I saw you. I have been shuddering all the time through fear that someone might come here and deceive me with a lying story."

Then Odysseus in his turn melted and wept as he clasped his dear and faithful wife to his bosom. As the sight of land is welcome to men who are swimming toward the shore, when Poseidon has wrecked their ship with the fury of his winds and waves; even so was her husband welcome to her and she looked upon him, and she could not tear her two fair arms from about his neck.

At last, however, Odysseus said, "Wife, we have not yet reached the end of our troubles. I have an unknown amount of toil still to undergo. It is long and difficult, but I must go through with it, for thus the ghost of Teiresias prophesied, on the day when I went down into Hades to ask about my return and that of my companions."

"Teiresias told me to travel far and wide, carrying an oar, till I came to a country where the people have never heard of the sea and do not even mix salt with their food, who know nothing about ships nor oars that are as the wings of a ship. He said that a traveler should meet me and ask me whether it was a winnowing shovel [1] that I had on my shoulder. On this, I was to fix my oar in the ground and sacrifice a ram, a bull, and a boar to Poseidon, after which I was to go home and offer sacrifices to all the gods in heaven, one after the other. As for myself, he said that death should come to me from the sea, a very gentle death when I was full of years and

---
[1] *winnowing shovel:* used to separate grain from chaff.

peace of mind and my people happy around me. All this, he said, should surely come to pass."

BOOK 24

[Odysseus found his father working in the vineyard, but the old man did not recognize him. They talked of Ithaca and its sad state, and Laertes asked for news of Odysseus. The "stranger" said that he had not seen Odysseus for five years. Laertes groaned at this, and Odysseus could hide his feelings no longer. He embraced his father, identifying himself by the scar on his leg. Odysseus told his father of the slaughter of the suitors, and then they went up to the house.

Meanwhile, news of the suitors' fate spread through the town. Their families took away and buried the bodies of their sons and brothers. Then they met in assembly and swore revenge against Odysseus. Some changed their minds when it was reported that a god had fought beside Odysseus. They were reminded that the suitors had brought their deaths on themselves. Others, however, armed themselves and went to fight with Odysseus and his men. On the advice of Zeus, Athena intervened and made peace in Ithaca.]

The movie Black Orpheus retold the Greek myth of the poet and musician who charmed the gods with his songs. In this modern version of the myth, the Greek hero became a young Brazilian, his lyre a guitar.

BOOK ONE | PART 2

GREEK MYTHS AND THEIR USES

Who can see the comings and goings of a god, if the god does not wish to be seen?
ODYSSEY, Book 10

Myths are stories about gods and goddesses. Ancient writers such as Homer gave the myths their present form, but the myths themselves go back far beyond Homer's time. They are the creations of primitive people who lived long before the invention of writing.

These primitive people had to be practical. Everything they did had a purpose, and the stories they invented were more than entertainment. Today we try to explain the world around us through science. Primitive man explained his world by means of stories, and he tried to control it by magic. We explain rain and lightning by saying that the atmospheric conditions are such and such. The ancient Greeks might have said that Zeus was pouring water from the skies and hurling his thunderbolts. Their myths answered such questions as: How was the earth created? What causes the seasons to change?

Cicero, a Roman writer, said, "Wherever we go we walk upon a story." He meant that the myths were not distant, made-up tales in books: they were a kind of reality; they were living truths. Today we often hear the word "myth" used in the sense of "something that is not true" as in: "They say he has a lot of money, but it's a myth." But for those who made them, the myths were a reasonable way of talking about nature and about patterns of human experience. For the ancient Greeks, every town, every river, every grove had its local gods and demons.

There were thousands of local myths and heroes. In time these stories came to revolve around the figure of Zeus, the father of the gods. The worship of Zeus and the other members of his Olympian family became the official religion of Greece. Later, as power and civilization shifted from Greece to Rome, the Romans took over the Greek myths. The gods were the same, but the Romans changed their names: Zeus became Jupiter, Aphrodite became Venus, and so forth.

Every people has its myths, but the myths of the Greeks and Romans are the most important for Americans to understand because they form such a central part of our tradition. We no longer believe in the Greek myths in the same way that men and women of Homer's time believed in them, but they still are a part of our lives.

The Greek myths as we know them have changed from their "primitive" forms. Our sources for the myths are poets such as Homer and Hesiod, who lived and wrote in times that were fairly civilized. Edith Hamilton writes: "In Greece man first realized what mankind was. . . . The Greeks made the gods in their own image. That had not entered the mind of man before."

In the Odyssey, *you have already met many of the Greek gods. Here Robert Graves tells the stories of the most important gods and goddesses. They quarrel, fall in love, have loyalties and jealousies much like mortals.*

The Palace of Olympus

ROBERT GRAVES

The twelve most important gods and goddesses of ancient Greece, called the Olympians, belonged to the same large, quarrelsome family. Though thinking little of the smaller, old-fashioned gods over whom they ruled, they thought even less of mortals. All the Olympians lived together in an enormous palace, set well above the usual level of clouds at the top of Mount Olympus, the highest mountain in Greece. Great walls, too steep for climbing, protected the Palace. The Olympians' masons, gigantic one-eyed Cyclopes, had built them on much the same plan as royal palaces on earth.

At the southern end, just behind the Council Hall, and looking toward the famous Greek cities of Athens, Thebes, Sparta, Corinth, Argos, and Mycenae, were the private apartments of King Zeus, the father-god, and Queen Hera, the mother-goddess. The northern end of the palace, looking across the valley of Tempe toward the wild hills of Macedonia, consisted of the kitchen, banqueting hall, armory, workshops, and servants' quarters. In between came a square court, open to the sky, with covered cloisters and private rooms on each side, belonging to the other five Olympian gods and the other five Olympian goddesses. Beyond the kitchen and servants' quarters stood cottages for smaller gods, sheds for chariots, stables for horses, kennels for hounds, and a sort of zoo where the Olympians kept their sacred animals. These included a bear, a lion, a peacock, an eagle, tigers, stags, a cow, a crane, snakes, a wild boar, white bulls, a wild cat, mice, swans, herons, an owl, a tortoise, and a tank full of fish.

In the Council Hall the Olympians met at times to discuss mortal affairs — such as which army on earth should be allowed to win a war and whether they ought to punish some king or queen who had been behaving proudly or disgustingly. But for the most part they were too busy with their own quarrels and lawsuits to take much notice of mortal affairs.

King Zeus had an enormous throne of polished black Egyptian marble, decorated in gold. Seven steps led up to it, each of them enameled with one of the seven colors of the rainbow. A bright blue covering above showed that the whole sky belonged to Zeus alone; and on the right arm of his throne perched a ruby-eyed golden eagle clutching jagged strips of pure tin, which meant that Zeus could kill whatever enemies he pleased by throwing a thunderbolt of forked lightning at them. A purple ram's fleece covered the cold seat. Zeus used it for magical rain-making in times of drought. He was a strong, brave, stupid, noisy, violent, conceited god and always on the watch lest his family should try to get rid of him, having once himself got rid of his wicked, idle, cannibalistic father Cronus, King of the Titans and Titanesses. The Olympians could not die, but Zeus, with the help of his two elder brothers, Hades and Poseidon, had banished Cronus to a distant island in the Atlantic — perhaps the Azores, perhaps Torrey Island, off the coast of Ireland. Zeus, Hades, and Poseidon then drew lots for the three parts of Cronus's kingdom. Zeus won the sky, Poseidon the sea, Hades the Underworld; they shared the earth among them. One of Zeus's emblems was the eagle; another was the woodpecker.

Cronus managed at last to escape from the island in a small boat and, changing his name to Saturn, settled quietly among the Italians, and behaved very well. In fact, until Zeus discovered his escape and banished him again, Saturn's reign was known as the Golden Age. Mortals in Italy lived without work or trouble, eating only acorns, wild fruit, honey, and nuts and drinking only milk or water. They never fought wars and spent their days dancing and singing.

Queen Hera had an ivory throne, with three crystal steps leading up to it. Golden cuckoos and willow leaves decorated the back, and a full moon hung above it. Hera sat on a white cowskin, which she sometimes used for rain-making magic if Zeus could not be bothered to stop a drought. She disliked being Zeus's wife, because he was frequently marrying mortal women and saying, with a sneer, that these marriages did not count — his brides would soon grow ugly and die, but she was his Queen and perpetually young and beautiful.

When first asked to marry him, Hera had refused and had gone on refusing every year for three hundred years. But one springtime Zeus disguised himself as a poor cuckoo caught in a thunderstorm and tapped at her window. Hera, not seeing through his disguise, let the cuckoo in, stroked his wet feathers, and whispered: "Poor bird, I love you." At once, Zeus changed back again into his true shape and said: "Now you must marry me!" After this, however badly Zeus behaved, Hera felt obliged to set a good example to gods and goddesses and mortals, as the mother of heaven. Her emblem was the cow, the most motherly of animals; but, not wishing to be thought as plain-looking and placid as a cow, she also used the peacock and the lion.

These two thrones faced down the Council Hall toward the door leading into the open courtyard. Along the sides of the hall stood ten other thrones — for five goddesses on Hera's side, for five gods on Zeus's.

Poseidon, god of the seas and rivers, had the second-largest throne. It was of gray-green, white-streaked marble, ornamented with coral, gold, and mother-of-pearl. The arms were carved in the shape of sea-beasts, and Poseidon sat on sealskin. For his help in banishing Cronus and the Titans, Zeus had married him to Amphitrite (am·fə·trī′tē), the former sea-goddess, and allowed him to take over all her titles. Though Poseidon hated to be less important than his younger brother and always went about scowling, he feared Zeus's thunderbolt. His only weapon was a trident, with which he could stir up the sea and so wreck ships, but Zeus never traveled by ship. When Poseidon felt even crosser than usual, he would drive away in his chariot to a palace under the waves and there let his rage cool. As his emblem, Poseidon chose the horse, an animal which he pretended to have created. Large waves are still called "white horses" because of this.

Opposite Poseidon sat his sister Demeter (di·mē′tər), goddess of all useful fruits, grasses, and grains. Her throne of bright green malachite [1] was ornamented with ears of barley in gold and little golden pigs for luck. Demeter seldom smiled, except when her daughter Per-

---
[1] *malachite* (mal′ə·kīt): a kind of copper ore.

sephone — unhappily married to the hateful Hades, god of the dead — came to visit her once a year. Demeter had been rather wild as a girl, and nobody could remember the name of Persephone's father, probably some country god married for a drunken joke at a harvest festival. Demeter's emblem was the poppy, which grows red as blood among the barley.

Next to Poseidon sat Hephaestus (hi·fes′təs), a son of Zeus and Hera. Being the god of goldsmiths, jewelers, blacksmiths, masons, and carpenters, he had built all these thrones himself and made his own a masterpiece of every different metal and precious stone to be found. The seat could swivel about, the arms could move up and down, and the whole throne rolled along automatically wherever he wished, like the three-legged golden tables in his workshop. Hephaestus had hobbled ever since birth, when Zeus roared at Hera: "A brat as weak as this is unworthy of me!" — and threw him far out over the walls of Olympus. In his fall Hephaestus broke a leg so badly that he had to wear a golden leg-iron. He kept a country house on Lemnos, the island where he had struck earth; and his emblem was the quail, a bird that does a hobbling dance in springtime.

Opposite Hephaestus sat Athena, goddess of wisdom, who first taught him how to handle tools and knew more than anyone else about pottery, weaving, and all useful arts. Her silver throne had golden basketwork at the back and sides and a crown of violets, made from blue lapis lazuli, set above it. Its arms ended in grinning Gorgons' heads. Athena, wise though she was, did not know the names of her parents. Poseidon claimed her as his daughter by a marriage with an African goddess called Libya. It is true that, as a child, she had been found wandering in a goatskin by the shores of a Libyan lake; but rather than admit herself the daughter of Poseidon, whom she thought very stupid, she allowed Zeus to pretend she was his. Zeus announced that one day, overcome by a fearful headache, he had howled aloud like a thousand wolves hunting in a pack. Hephaestus, he said, then ran up with an ax and kindly split open his skull, and out sprang Athena, dressed in full armor. Athena was also a battle-goddess yet never went to war unless forced — being too sensible to pick quarrels — and when she fought, always won. She chose the wise owl as her emblem and had a town house at Athens.

THE PALACE OF OLYMPUS

Next to Athena sat Aphrodite, goddess of love and beauty. Nobody knew who her parents were, either. The South Wind said that he had once seen her floating in a scallop shell off the island of Cythera and steered her gently ashore. She may have been a daughter of Amphitrite by a smaller god named Triton, who used to blow roaring blasts on a conch, or perhaps by old Cronus. Amphitrite refused to say a word on the subject. Aphrodite's throne was silver, the back shaped like a scallop shell, the seat made of swan's-down, and under her feet lay a golden mat — an embroidery of golden bees, apples, and sparrows. To keep Aphrodite out of mischief, Zeus decided that she needed a hard-working, decent husband and naturally chose his son Hephaestus. Hephaestus exclaimed: "Now I am the happiest god alive!" But she thought it disgraceful to be the wife of a sooty-faced, horny-handed, crippled smith. Aphrodite's emblem was the dove.

Opposite Aphrodite sat Ares (âr'ēz), Hephaestus' tall, handsome, boastful, cruel brother, who loved fighting for its own sake. Ares and Aphrodite were continually holding hands and giggling in corners, which made Hephaestus jealous. Yet if he ever complained to the Council, Zeus would laugh at him, saying: "Fool, why did you give your wife that magic belt? Can you blame your brother if he falls in love with her when she wears it?" Ares's throne was built of brass, strong and ugly — those huge brass knobs in the shape of skulls and that cushion-cover of human skin! Ares had no manners, no learning, and the worst of taste, yet Aphrodite thought him wonderful. His emblems were a wild boar and a bloodstained spear. He kept a country house among the rough woods of Thrace.

Next to Ares sat Apollo, the god of music, poetry, medicine, archery, and young unmarried men — Zeus's son by Leto, one of the smaller goddesses, whom he married to annoy Hera. Apollo rebelled against his father once or twice but got well punished each time and learned to behave more sensibly. His highly polished golden throne had magical inscriptions carved all over it, a back shaped like a lyre, and a python skin to sit on. Above hung a golden sundisk with twenty-one rays shaped like arrows because he pretended to manage the sun. Apollo's emblem was a mouse; mice were supposed to know the secrets of earth and tell them to him. (He preferred white mice to ordinary ones; most boys still do.) Apollo owned a splendid house at Delphi on the top of Mount Parnassus, built around the famous oracle [2] which he stole from Mother Earth, Zeus's grandmother.

Opposite Apollo sat his twin-sister Artemis, goddess of hunting and of unmarried girls, from whom he had learned medicine and archery. Her throne was of pure silver, with a wolfskin to sit on, and the back shaped like two date palms, one on each side of a new-moon boat. Apollo married several mortal wives at different times. Once he chased a girl named Daphne (daf'nē), who cried out for help to Mother Earth and got turned into a laurel tree before he could catch and kiss her. Artemis, however, hated the idea of marriage, although she kindly took care of mothers when their babies were born. She much preferred hunting, fishing, and swimming in moonlit mountain pools. If any mortal man happened to see her, she used to change him into a stag and hunt him to death. She chose as her emblem the she-bear, the most dangerous of all wild animals in Greece.

Last in the row of gods sat Hermes, the god of merchants, bankers, thieves, fortunetellers, and heralds, born in Arcadia. His throne was cut out of a single piece of solid gray rock, the arms shaped like rams' heads, and a goatskin for the seat. On its back he had carved a swastika, this being the shape of a fire-making machine invented by him — the firedrill. Until then, housewives used to borrow glowing pieces of charcoal from their neighbors. Hermes also invented the alphabet, and one of his emblems was the crane, because cranes fly in a V — the first letter he wrote. Another of Hermes's emblems was a peeled hazel stick, which he carried as the Messenger of the Olympians: white ribbons dangled from it, which foolish people often mistook for snakes.

Last in the row of goddesses sat Zeus's eldest sister, Hestia, goddess of the home: on a plain, uncarved wooden throne and a plain cushion woven of undyed wool. Hestia, the kindest and most peaceable of all the Olympians, hated the continual family quarrels and never troubled to choose any particular emblem of her own. She used to tend the charcoal hearth in the middle of the Council Hall.

That made six gods and six goddesses. But one day Zeus announced that Dionysus (dī'ə·nī'səs), his son by a mortal woman, had invented wine and must be given a seat in the Council. Thir-

---

[2] *oracle* (ôr'ə·kəl): a priest through whom the gods spoke; the oracle of Apollo at Delphi, who made pronouncements on matters of religion, politics, etc.

teen Olympians would have been an unlucky number, so Hestia offered him her seat, just to keep the peace. Now there were seven gods and five goddesses, an unjust state of affairs because, when questions about women had to be discussed, the gods outvoted the goddesses. Dionysus' throne was gold-plated fir wood, ornamented with bunches of grapes carved in amethyst (a violet-colored stone), snakes carved in serpentine (a stone with many markings), and various horned animals besides. He took the tiger for his emblem, having once visited India at the head of a drunken army and brought tigers back as souvenirs.

Of the other gods and goddesses living on Olympus, Heracles the porter slept in the gatehouse, and Poseidon's wife Amphitrite has already been mentioned. There were also Dionysus' mother Semele, whom he persuaded Zeus to turn into a goddess; Iris, Hera's messenger, who used to run along the rainbow; the goddess Nemesis, who kept a list for the Olympians of proud mortals due to be punished; Aphrodite's wicked little son Eros, god of love, who enjoyed shooting arrows at people to make them fall ridiculously in love; Ganymede, Zeus's handsome young cup-bearer; and the nine Muses, who sang in the Banqueting Hall.

In a room behind the kitchen sat the three Fates. They were the oldest goddesses in existence, too old for anybody to remember where they came from. The Fates decided how long each mortal should live by spinning a linen thread to measure exactly so many inches and feet for months and years and then snipping it off with a pair of shears. They also knew but seldom revealed what would be the fate of each Olympian god. Even Zeus feared them for that reason.

The Olympians drank nectar, a sweet drink made from fermented honey, and ate ambrosia, said to be an uncooked mixture of honey, water, fruit, olive oil, cheese, and barley — though this may be doubted. Some claim that certain speckled mushrooms were the true food of the Olympians, created whenever Zeus's thunderbolt struck the earth, and that this kept them immortal. Because the Olympians also loved the smell though not the taste of roast beef and mutton, mortals used to sacrifice sheep and cattle to them, afterward eating the meat themselves.

Phaëthon

JAY MAC PHERSON

The great sun-god Helios (Apollo) came down to earth to visit a mortal woman named Clymene (klī′mə·nē), the Queen of Ethiopia, a country especially dear to him, and when he went back to his palace in the sky, he left her with a child. Clymene called him Phaëthon (fā′ə·thon), "Shining." When he was still a young boy, being teased by his friends about having no father, Phaëthon persuaded Clymene to tell him the secret of his birth. "I swear to you," she said, "by the light above that sees me, that you are the child of that sun which you see, the sun that guides the world."

Phaëthon was eager to go immediately and seek out his great father, and Clymene instructed him how to get there. The way was not far, as the Sun's palace stood at the eastern edge of the world. By passing first through his own land of Ethiopia and then through the land of the Indians, Phaëthon was able to get there quite easily.

The palace of Helios was a wonderful structure, glittering from far off with gold and bronze that shone like fire. Inside Phaëthon discovered the great Sun sitting on his throne, in a blaze of light that made it hard to look at him. Phaëthon stood trembling and shielding his face until the Sun turned on him those eyes that see everything and said, "My son — for I am proud to call such a young hero my child — tell me why you have come all this way to find me." Phaëthon boldly asked for some proof that he was indeed the child of Helios, and the god replied, "Ask for any gift you desire, and I shall bestow it on you. Let that hidden underground river which alone of all things my eyes have never seen, and by which the gods take their oaths, be witness to my promise."

Then Phaëthon's pride was kindled, and he asked to be allowed for one day to drive the chariot of the Sun.

No sooner had these words been spoken than Helios repented of his oath. "My son," he said, "there is nothing I would not give to be released from my promise. You do not know what you are asking. Not one of the gods besides myself, not even mighty Zeus who hurls the thunderbolts from Mount Olympus, has the strength and skill to manage my chariot. Its fire-breathing horses are wild, and hard even for me to control. Be warned in time and ask a different gift."

Burning with eager ambition, Phaëthon stood firm; and his father, sad at heart, led him out to the chariot, the work of the smith-god Hephaestus. While he was still admiring it, the moment came: Eos the dawn-goddess opened the doors of her rosy house, the stars departed, led by their shepherd the Morning Star, and the fire-breathing immortal horses of the Sun stamped in their harness. There could be no delay. Setting his son in his place and advising him to be sure to keep to the broad middle path across the heavens, Helios let him go. Phaëthon seized the reins, gave them a shake, and was off.

As soon as they felt that an unskilled hand was guiding them and that the chariot carried less than its usual weight, the winged horses whinnied, tossed their heads, and plunged wildly about, forsaking the broad track and racing toward the highest heavens. The wretched Phaëthon was terrified when he saw how far the earth lay beneath him, and the cold stars of the northern constellations shuddered to feel the unaccustomed heat as the chariot hurtled past. Meanwhile, those on earth missed the sun's friendly warmth, usually so constant, and wondered what could have happened to cause such upheaval in the heavens. The great beasts of the upper sky, Scorpion and Crab and the rest, scared the frantic driver right out of his wits. In his fright he let the reins fall from his hands, and the horses now raged entirely without control. Shying away from the highest stars, they began to dash toward the earth. Their speed scorched even the cool clouds, and the Moon as they passed was astonished to see her brother's chariot dive lower than her own.

The earth began to catch fire, starting at the mountain tops. Where all moisture was dried out the ground split open, riven with great cracks and fissures. Meadows, crops, and forests were blasted; wooded hills flamed like torches. Libya became a desert. Many rivers plunged underground to escape, and some have not reappeared yet: the Nile fled to the ends of the earth to hide his head, which is still hidden, leaving empty the seven channels through which he used to meet the sea.

Beholding this universal destruction, Zeus called together all the gods. With one voice they agreed, even sorrowful Helios, that if the whole earth were not to perish, the desperate charioteer must be stopped. Then, mounting to the highest point of heaven, Zeus launched one of his powerful thunderbolts that always reach their mark. Cleaving the skies, it struck Phaëthon and tumbled him from the chariot. With his hair on fire, he fell like a comet, leaving a trail of light. At last the waters of the Italian river Po received him, far from his native land. The nymphs of Italy buried his body beside the river shore.

There was great lamentation in the palace of Ethiopia when Phaëthon's fate was known. His sisters, also children of the Sun, were especially wild in their sorrow, until the gods, pitying their distress, changed them into weeping trees — poplars, from whose bark drip tears of amber to this day.

The best versions of the next two stories come to us through Ovid, a Roman poet who lived in the years 43 B.C. to A.D. 18. To Ovid the ancient myths were nothing more than good stories. He collected and retold almost all of them.

The story of Orpheus and Eurydice is one of the most famous love stories in classical mythology. Versions of the story have been found in many countries.

Orpheus and Eurydice

W. H. D. ROUSE

Orpheus (ôr'fē-əs) was one of the heroes who went in quest of the Golden Fleece. To the sound of his harp, the ship *Argo* glided down into the sea. The sound of his harp made the Clashing Rocks stand still just one minute, when the *Argo* was passing through. The sound of his harp helped to send the sleepless dragon to sleep.

You see, he was a rare hand with the harp; and no wonder, for his father was Apollo, and Apollo taught him to play upon his own harp. He played so beautifully that all the wild beasts on Mount Olympus used to come and lie down all around him to listen. More than that, even the trees would pluck up their roots, if they were not too old and too deep, and hop along to listen. Even the rocks rolled out of their places and came to listen. All the country people were enchanted; the wild Satyrs (sat'ərs) used to dance around him, wagging their tails.

He married a wife named Eurydice (yōō·rid'ə·sē), whom he loved very much. One day Eurydice trod on a snake, which bit her foot, and she died.

Orpheus would not be comforted. He played on his harp no more; he wandered over the mountains and through the forests and mourned his lost wife. At last he determined that he would go down to the dark house of Hades and bring her back.

So he entered the dark cave and traversed the dark tunnel which led through the earth to the dark house of Hades. When he came to the gate, the three-headed dog Cerberus growled and would have bitten him; but Orpheus played a soft tune on his harp, and the dog dropped his three heads on his paws and gently wagged his tail and let Orpheus go by.

When he came to the great hall of Hades, what a sight met his eyes! There sat King Hades and Queen Persephone on their thrones. There sat the three Judges of the Dead — for there is justice in the house of Hades. Every soul, when it comes into that place, must give account for deeds done in the body: those who are good are dismissed to the Elysian Fields, to be at peace; those who are bad receive punishment proper to their deeds.

There Orpheus saw some of the great sinners enduring their punishment. He saw a family of nine-and-forty sisters, the Danaïdes (də·nā′·ə·dēz), who had all been married on one day and had murdered their husbands in the night. They were condemned to draw water and carry it in jars to a huge vessel with holes in the bottom, so as fast as they poured the water in, it ran out.

He saw the punishment of the cruel King Tantalus. In his life on earth, Tantalus once entertained the gods at a feast. Like the wicked King of Arcadia, he wanted to see if they really had more wisdom than men. So he killed his own son Pelops and cooked the body and offered it to the gods to eat. They all knew it at once and refused, except Demeter, who ate a bit of the shoulder, because she had just lost her daughter and did not know what she was doing. Pelops was brought back to life and made well again, all but the bit of his shoulder, which was missing; but Demeter put an ivory shoulder in its place. This Tantalus was punished by being hungry and thirsty forever. He stood in the middle of a lake of water: when he bent down his head to drink, the water all slid away; if he scooped up a handful, the water ran through his fingers. All around the water grew trees laden with fruit: apples and pears, figs and grapes, and oranges; when he stretched out his hand to pluck one, the tree whisked it away into the air above him. Did you ever hear something called tantalizing? If so, the word should remind you of Tantalus, who was always disappointed when he hoped for something good.

He saw Sisyphus (sis′·ə·fəs), the most cunning and deceitful of men, who had betrayed the secrets of the gods. His punishment was to roll a huge stone up to the top of a hill. He pushed with head and shoulders, panting and sweating and covered with dust; but whenever he got to the top, the stone would gently slide off on one side or the other and roll down to the bottom. Then he had to begin all over again.

He saw Ixion (ik·sī'ən), who also had committed an act of treachery to the gods. His punishment was the strangest of all. He was fastened to a wheel with four spokes, one for each leg and arm, and the wheel went around and around forever.

That was the scene which met the eye of Orpheus as he entered the dark house of Hades. The soul of Eurydice was there waiting, for her case had not yet been heard; there were so many waiting for judgment. But Orpheus pleaded with Hades that he might take her back to life.

Hades said, "Why should I treat her otherwise than I treat the other souls?"

Orpheus was silent; then his eyes flashed, and he said in a loud voice, "This is why!" and struck up a tune on his harp. The melody began soft, then rose and rang loudly through the dark hall; and as the melody sounded, Hades leaned forward on his throne and listened. Persephone turned her head and sat still and listened. The three Judges ceased their questions and listened. The Danaïdes stood still and listened and let the water do what it would — the water ceased to run out of the holes. Tantalus's lake stood still, and Tantalus had a good drink, then he listened too. The stone of Sisyphus rolled up to Orpheus and lay still. Ixion's wheel stood still and Ixion with it, to listen to the wonderful sounds. At last Hades said: "Your music is worth a life. Take her and go, but be very careful never to look back at her till you come to your own door."

Orpheus was glad enough to have her on any conditions; so he turned around and went toward the gate, still playing upon his harp, and Eurydice followed him. Out of the gate he went, still playing, past the three-headed Cerberus, along the dark tunnel, out of the dark cave, and then he thought to himself, "I wonder if Eurydice is following," for he could not hear her footsteps. Without thinking, he turned to look: there she was, close behind — but even as he looked, she uttered a cry. She began to fade, and in a few moments, like a wisp of smoke, she had vanished.

Now there was no hope for Orpheus. But he seems to have learned the wisdom of the gods by his journey to the house of Hades, for he no longer played on his harp, but he made wonderful poems, telling mankind what to do if they wished to please the gods and to be happy after death. Some say he also taught them to eat only vegetables and not to kill animals for food. Perhaps he remembered how sensible the animals were in listening to his music; but that can hardly be the reason, for the trees listened too, and no doubt the vegetables would have listened if they had been handy.

But Orpheus would not marry another wife. There were a number of wild women in Thrace, where he lived, and they used to hold feasts in honor of Dionysus every year and madden themselves with wine. Some say they were angry because Orpheus would not take one of them to wife. Whatever the reason may be, these women set on him and killed him and cut off his head and threw it into the river Hebrus. The river carried it into the sea, and it floated across to the island of Lesbos, by the town of Methymna, where it was washed ashore. And ever since that time, right down to our own day, the nightingales in the olive trees around Methymna sing more sweetly than any other nightingales in the world.

Here is another love story, in which an artist is in love with his work in an unusual way. This myth has been a favorite of storytellers right up to our own time. Shaw's play Pygmalion *and the musical* My Fair Lady *are modern versions of it.*

Pygmalion and Galatea

OLIVIA COOLIDGE

Pygmalion was a sculptor, a worker in marble, bronze, and ivory. He was so young and handsome that the girls as they went past his workshop used to look in and admire him, hoping that he would notice them. But Pygmalion was devoted only to his art. People seemed noisy and trivial to him, and ugly too, for he had an image of beauty in his mind which caused him to work over his statues from morning to night, smoothing, reworking, always in search of a loveliness beyond his powers of expression. In truth, the statues of Pygmalion were far more beautiful than human beings, and each statue was more nearly perfect than the last. Still, in every one Pygmalion felt that there was something lacking. While others would stand entranced before them, he never cared to look on anything he had finished but was immediately absorbed in the next attempt.

At last, however, he was working on an ivory statue of a girl in which he seemed to have expressed his ideal in every way. Even before it was done, he would lay down the chisel and stare at his work for an hour or so together, tracing in his mind the beauty that was as yet only half unfolded. By the time the statue was nearly finished, Pygmalion could think of nothing else. In his very dreams the statue haunted him. Then she seemed to wake up for him and come alive. The idea gave him exquisite pleasure, and he used to dwell on it. The dreams passed into daydreams until for many days Pygmalion made little progress on his almost finished statue. He would sit gazing at the maiden, whom he had christened Galatea (gal′ə·tē′ə), and imagining that perhaps he saw her move and the joy it would be if she actually were living. He became pale and exhausted; his dreams wore him out.

At last the statue was actually finished. The slightest touch of the chisel now would be a change for the worse. Half the night Pygmalion gazed at the beautiful image; then with a hopeless sigh he went to bed, pursued as ever by his dreams. The next day he arose early, for he had something to do. It was the festival of Aphrodite, the goddess of beauty, to whom Pygmalion, since he was a seeker after beauty, had always felt a special devotion. Never once had he failed to give Aphrodite every possible honor that was due to her. In truth, his whole life was lived in worship of the goddess. There were many splendid gifts being given her: snow-white bulls with their horns covered with gold; wine, oil, and incense; embroidered garments; carvings; offerings of gold and ivory. Both rich and poor came in turn to offer their gifts. As he approached the altar, Pygmalion prayed earnestly and saw the fire that burned there leap suddenly in flame. Tense excitement stirred him; he could stay no longer; he must get back to his statue, though he did not quite know what he expected there. Galatea was as he had left her. He looked at her longingly once more, and again, as he so often had, he seemed to see her stir. It was only a trick of imagination, he knew, because it had happened many times to him before. Nevertheless, on a sudden impulse he went over to Galatea and took her in his arms.

The statue really was moving! He felt the hard ivory grow soft and warm like wax in his clasp. He saw the lips grow red and the cheeks blush faintly pink. Unbelieving, he took her hand and lifted it. As he pressed it, he felt the fingers gently tighten in his own. Galatea opened her eyes and looked at him. There was understanding in her gaze. The red lips parted slightly, and as Pygmalion kissed them, they pressed against his own. Galatea stepped down from her pedestal into Pygmalion's arms a living girl. The next day two lovers went to pray at Aphrodite's shrine, the one thanking her for the gift of life, the other that his dreams and prayers had been answered and his lifelong devotion to the goddess thus rewarded.

The story of Theseus, like the Odyssey, *is a legend rather than a myth. In the* Odyssey, *however, the gods and goddesses took sides in the fortunes of the hero. "Theseus" takes place in a world that is full of magical and mysterious happenings, but the gods do not appear in it. The theme of the hero whose quest leads him to a dark labyrinth from which he must escape is a common one in literature.*

Theseus

CHARLES KINGSLEY

Once upon a time there was a princess in Troezen (trē′zən) who had one fair son named Theseus (thē′sē‑əs), the bravest lad in all the land; and she never smiled but when she looked at him, for her husband had forgotten her and lived far away. And she used to go up to the mountain above Troezen to the temple of Poseidon and sit there all day looking out across the bay to the purple peaks of the shore beyond. And when Theseus was fifteen years old, she took him up with her to the temple and into the temple yard. And she led him to a tall plane tree. And there she sighed and said, "Theseus, my son, go into that thicket, and you will find at the plane-tree foot a great flat stone. Lift it and bring me what lies underneath."

Then Theseus pushed his way in through the thick bushes and found a great flat stone all overgrown with ivy and moss. He tried to lift it, but he could not. And at last he came back to his mother and said, "I have found the stone, but I cannot lift it, nor do I think that any man could in all Troezen."

Then she sighed and said, "Let it be for another year. The day may come when you will be a stronger man than lives in all Troezen."

And when a full year was past, she led Theseus up again to the temple and bade him lift the stone, but he could not. Nor could Theseus lift the stone the next year, nor the year after; and he longed to ask his mother the meaning of that stone and what might lie underneath it, but her face was so sad that he had not the heart to ask.

So he said to himself, "The day shall surely come when I will lift that stone, though no man in Troezen can." And in order to grow strong, he spent all his days in wrestling and boxing and hurling and taming horses and hunting the boar and the bull and pursuing goats and deer among the rocks, till upon all the mountains there was no hunter so swift as Theseus.

And when his eighteenth year was past, his mother led him up again to the temple and said, "Theseus, lift the stone this day or never know who you are." And Theseus went into the thicket and stood over the stone and tugged at it, and it moved. Then his spirit swelled within him, and he said, "If I break my heart in my body, it shall up." And he tugged at it once more and lifted it and rolled it over with a shout.

And when he looked beneath it, on the ground lay a sword of bronze with a hilt of glittering gold and by it a pair of golden sandals, and he caught them up and burst through the bushes like a wild boar and leaped to his mother, holding them high above his head.

But when she saw them, she wept long in silence, hiding her fair face in her shawl; and Theseus stood by her wondering and wept also, he knew not why. And when she was tired of weeping, she lifted up her head and laid her finger on her lips and said, "Hide them, Theseus, my son, and come with me where we can look down upon the sea."

Then they went outside the sacred wall and looked down over the bright blue sea, and his mother said, "Do you see that land beyond?"

"Yes, that is Attica, where the Athenian people dwell."

"That is a fair land and large, Theseus, my son, and it looks toward the sunny south, a land of olive oil and honey, the joy of gods and men. What would you do, son Theseus, if you were king of such a land?"

Then his heart grew great within him, and he said, "If I were king of such a land, I would rule it wisely and well in wisdom and in might, so that when I died all men might weep over my tomb and cry, 'Alas for the shepherd of his people!'"

And Aithra smiled and said, "Take then the sword and the sandals, and go to your father, Aegeus (ē′jē-əs), king of Athens, and say to him, 'The stone is lifted, but whose is the pledge beneath it?' Then show him the sword and the sandals, and take what the gods shall send."

So Theseus stood there alone with his mind full of many hopes, and he longed for wings to fly across the sea and find his father. But after a while he sighed and said within himself, "What if my father will not receive me? And what have I done that he should?"

Then he thought a long while sadly, and at last he cried aloud, "Yes! I will make him love me, for I will prove myself worthy of his love. I will win honor and renown and do such deeds that Aegeus shall be proud of me. Did not Heracles win himself honor though he was oppressed and a slave? Where can I go to do as Heracles has done? Where can I find strange adventures, robbers, and monsters and the children of hell, the enemies of men? I will go by land into the mountains and around by the way of the Isthmus. Perhaps there I may hear of brave adventures and do something which shall win my father's love."

Theseus was tested in many trials and adventures. He overcame the monsters Periphetes, Sinis, Sciron, Kerkyon, and, finally, Procrustes.

Theseus Arrives in Athens

So Theseus went up through Athens, and all the people ran out to see him. But Theseus went on sadly and steadfastly, for his heart yearned after his father, and he went up the holy stairs and into the Acropolis, where Aegeus's palace stood.

Then Theseus called to the servants and said, "Go tell King Aegeus, your master, that Theseus of Troezen is here and asks to be his guest awhile."

A servant ran and told Aegeus, where he sat within his chamber beside Medea, the dark witch-woman. And when Aegeus heard of Troezen he turned pale and red again and rose from his seat trembling, while Medea watched him like a snake.

"What is Troezen to you?" she asked.

But he said hastily, "Do you not know who this Theseus is? The hero who has cleared the country of all monsters. But that he came from Troezen I never heard before. I must go and welcome him."

So Aegeus came out into the hall, and when Theseus saw him, his heart leaped into his mouth, and he longed to fall on his neck and welcome him. But he controlled himself and said, "My father may not wish for me after all. I will test him before I reveal myself." And he bowed before Aegeus and said, "I have delivered the king's realm from many monsters. Therefore, I am come to ask a reward of the king."

And old Aegeus looked on him and loved him. But he only sighed and said, "It is little that I can give you, noble lad, and nothing that is worthy of you, for surely you are no mortal man, or at least no mortal's son."

"All I ask," said Theseus, "is to eat and drink at your table."

"That I can give you," said Aegeus. Then he bade them put a seat for Theseus and set before him the best of the feast.

Medea's Plot

But Medea, the dark witch-woman, had been watching him all the while. She saw how Aegeus turned red and pale when the boy said that he came from Troezen. She saw too how his heart was opened toward Theseus and how Theseus bore himself. And she said to herself, "This youth will be master here. Perhaps he is nearer to Aegeus already than mere fancy." Then she went back into her chamber, while Theseus ate and drank.

But presently Medea came forth, decked in all her jewels and her rich Eastern robes. In her right hand she held a golden cup and in her left a flask of gold. And she came up to Theseus and spoke in a sweet, soft, winning voice.

"Hail to the hero, the conqueror, the unconquered, the destroyer of all evil things! Drink, hero, of my charmed cup, which gives rest after every toil, which heals all wounds and pours new life into the veins." And as she spoke, she poured from the flask into the cup, and the fragrance of the wine spread through the hall like the scent of thyme [1] and roses.

Theseus looked up in her fair face and into her deep dark eyes. And as he looked, he shrank and shuddered, for they were dry like the eyes of a snake. And he rose and said, "The wine is rich and fra-

---

[1] *thyme* (tīm): a small plant related to mint, with fragrant leaves used as a seasoning.

grant, and the wine-bearer as fair as the immortals. But let her pledge me first herself in the cup, that the wine may be the sweeter from her lips."

Then Medea turned pale and stammered, "Forgive me, fair hero, but I am ill and dare drink no wine." And Theseus looked again into her eyes and cried, "You shall pledge me in that cup or die." And he lifted up his bronze club, while all the guests looked on aghast.

Medea shrieked a fearful shriek and dashed the cup to the ground and fled. Where the wine flowed over the marble pavement the stone bubbled and crumbled and hissed under the fierce venom of the draught.

But Medea called her dragon chariot and sprang into it and fled aloft, away over land and sea, and no man saw her more.

And Aegeus cried, "What have you done?"

But Theseus pointed to the stone. "I have rid the land of an enchantment. Now I will rid it of one more." And he came close to Aegeus and drew from his bosom the sword and sandals and said the words which his mother had bade him.

Aegeus Recognizes His Son

And Aegeus stepped back a pace and looked at the boy till his eyes grew dim; and then he cast himself on his neck and wept, and Theseus wept on his neck till they had no strength left to weep more.

Then Aegeus turned to all the people and cried, "Behold my son, a better man than his father was before him."

So Theseus stayed with his father all the winter. And when the spring equinox drew near, all the Athenians grew sad and silent, and Theseus saw it and asked the reason. But no one would answer him a word. Then he went to his father and asked him. But Aegeus turned away his face and wept. "Do not ask, my son, beforehand about evils which must happen. It is enough to have to face them when they come."

And when the spring equinox came, a herald came to Athens and stood in the market and cried, "O people and king of Athens, where is your yearly tribute?" Then a great lamentation arose throughout the city. But Theseus stood up to the herald and cried, "I am a stranger here. Tell me, herald, why you come."

"To fetch the tribute which King Aegeus promised to Minos and confirmed his promise with an oath. For Minos conquered all this land and would not depart till this land had promised him tribute: seven youths and seven maidens every year, who go with me in a black-sailed ship till they come to hundred-citied Crete."

Then Theseus said, "I will go myself with these youths and maidens and kill Minos upon his royal throne."

But Aegeus shrieked and cried, "You shall not go, my son, the light of my old age, to whom alone I look to rule this people after I am dead and gone. You shall not go to die horribly, as those youths and maidens die. For Minos thrusts them into a labyrinth, which Daedalus (ded'ə·las) made for him among the rocks. From that labyrinth no one can escape, entangled in its winding ways, before they meet the Minotaur, the monster who feeds upon the flesh of men. There he devours them horribly, and they never see this land again."

Then Theseus grew red, and his ears tingled, and his heart beat loud in his bosom. And he stood awhile like a tall stone pillar on the cliffs above some hero's grave, and at last he spoke.

"Therefore, all the more I will go with them and slay the accursed beast. Have I not slain all evildoers and monsters that I might free this land? Where are Periphetes and Sinis and Kerkyon and Procrustes? This Minotaur shall go the road which they have gone, and Minos himself if he dare stay me."

"But how will you slay him, my son? For you must leave your club and your armor behind and be cast to the monster defenseless and naked like the rest."

And Theseus said, "Are there no stones in that labyrinth, and have I not fists and teeth? Did I need my club to kill Kerkyon, the terror of all mortal men?"

Then Aegeus clung to his knees, but he would not hear; and at last he let him go, weeping bitterly, and said only this: "Promise me but this, if you return in peace, though that may hardly be: take down the black sail of the ship and hoist instead a white sail, that I may know afar off that you are safe."

And Theseus promised and went out to the market place where the herald stood, while they drew lots for the youths and maidens who were to sail in that doleful crew. And the people stood wailing and weeping as the lot fell on this one and on that. But Theseus strode into their midst and cried, "Here is a youth who needs no lot. I myself will be one of the seven."

And the herald asked in wonder, "Fair youth, know you where you are going?"

And Theseus said, "I know. Let us go down to the black-sailed ship."

Theseus Sails for Crete

So they went down to the black-sailed ship, seven maidens and seven youths, and Theseus before them all, and the people following them, lamenting. But Theseus whispered to his companions, "Have hope, for the monster is not immortal. Where are Periphetes and Sinis and Sciron and all whom I have slain?" Then their hearts were comforted a little, but they wept as they went on board and as they sailed toward their deaths in Crete.

At last they came to Crete and to Cnossus and to the palace of Minos, the great king. He sat among the pillars of the hall upon his throne of beaten gold, and around him stood the speaking statues which Daedalus had made by his skill. For Daedalus was the most cunning of all Athenians, and he invented the plumb line and the auger and glue and many a tool with which wood is wrought. And he first set masts in ships, and yards, and his son made sails for them. But Perdix, his nephew, excelled him, for he invented the saw and its teeth, copying it from the backbone of a fish, and invented too the chisel and the compasses and the potter's wheel, which molds the clay. Therefore, Daedalus envied him and hurled him headlong from the temple of Athena. And Daedalus fled to Crete, to Minos, and worked for him many a year till he did a shameful deed, at which the sun hid his face on high.

Daedalus and Icarus

Then he fled the anger of Minos, he and Icarus (ik′ə·rəs), his son, having made themselves wings of feathers and fixed the feathers with wax. They flew over the sea toward Sicily. But Icarus flew too near the sun, and the wax of his wings was melted, and he fell into the Icarian Sea. But Daedalus came safely to Sicily and there wrought many a wondrous work.

So Theseus stood before Minos, and they looked each other in the face. And Minos bade servants take them to prison and cast them to the monster one by one. Then Theseus cried, "A favor, O Minos. Let me be thrown first to the beast. For I came for that very purpose, of my own will and not by lot."

"Who are you, then, brave youth?"

"I am the son of Aegeus, the king of Athens, and I am come here to end this matter."

And Minos pondered awhile, looking steadfastly at him, and he answered at last, mildly, "Go back in peace, my son. It is a pity that one so brave should die."

But Theseus said, "I have sworn that I will not go back till I have seen the monster face to face."

And at that Minos frowned and said, "Then you shall see him. Take the madman away." And they led Theseus away into the prison with the other youths and maidens.

Ariadne

But Ariadne (ar'ē·ad'nē), Minos's daughter, saw him as she came out of her white stone hall. And she loved him for his courage and his majesty and said, "Shame that such a youth should die!" And by night she went down to the prison and told him all her heart and said, "Flee down to your ship at once, for I have bribed the guards before the door. Flee, you and all your friends, and go back in peace to Greece, and take me with you, for my father will kill me miserably if he knows what I have done."

And Theseus stood silent awhile, for he was astonished by her beauty. But at last he said, "I cannot go home in peace till I have seen and slain this Minotaur and avenged the deaths of the youths and maidens and put an end to the terrors of my land."

"And will you kill the Minotaur? How, then?"

"I know not, nor do I care. But he must be strong if he is too strong for me." Then she loved him all the more and said, "But when you have killed him, how will you find your way out of the labyrinth?"

"I know not, neither do I care. But it must be a strange road, if I do not find it out before I have eaten up the monster's carcass."

Then she loved him all the more and said, "Fair youth, you are too bold, but I can help you, weak as I am. I will give you a sword, and with that perhaps you may slay the beast, and a clue of thread, and by that perhaps you may find your way out again. Only promise me that if you escape safe, you will take me home with you to Greece, for my father will surely kill me if he knows what I have done."

Then Theseus laughed and said, "Am I not safe enough now?" And he hid the sword and rolled up the thread in his hand. And then he swore to Ariadne and fell down before her and kissed her hands and her feet, and she wept over him a long while and then went away. And Theseus lay down and slept sweetly.

The Labyrinth and the Minotaur

And when the morning came, the guards came in and led him away to the labyrinth. And he went down into that doleful gulf through winding paths among the rocks, under caverns and arches and galleries, and over heaps of fallen stone. And he turned on the left hand and on the right hand and went up and down till his head was dizzy, but all the while he held his thread. For when he went in he had fastened it to a stone and left it to unroll out of his hand as he went on, and it lasted him till he met the Minotaur in a narrow chasm between black cliffs.

And when he saw him he stopped awhile, for he had never seen so strange a beast. His body was a man's, but his head was the head of a bull, his teeth were the teeth of a lion, and with them he tore his prey. And when he saw Theseus he roared and put his head down and rushed right at him.

But Theseus stepped aside nimbly and, as the Minotaur passed, cut him in the knee; and before he could turn in the narrow path, he followed him and stabbed him again and again from behind till the monster fled, bellowing wildly, for he had never before felt a wound. And Theseus followed him at full speed, holding the clue of thread in his left hand. Then on, through cavern after cavern, went they, the hunter and the hunted, while the hills bellowed to the monster's bellow. And at last Theseus came up with him where he lay panting and caught him by the horns and forced his head back and drove the keen sword through his throat.

Then he turned and went back, limping and weary, feeling his way by the clue of thread till he came to the mouth of that doleful place and saw waiting for him, whom but Ariadne! And he whispered, "It is done!" and showed her the sword. And she laid her finger on her lips and led him to the prison and opened the doors and set all the prisoners free, while the guards lay sleeping heavily, for she had silenced them with wine.

Then they fled to their ship together and leaped on board and hoisted the sail; and the night lay dark around them, so that they passed through Minos's ships and escaped all safe to Naxos; and there Ariadne became Theseus's wife.

But fair Ariadne never came to Athens with her husband. Some say that Theseus left her sleeping on Naxos and that Dionysus, the wine king, found her and took her up into the sky. And some say that Dionysus drove away Theseus and took Ariadne from him by force; but, however that may be, in his haste or in his grief, Theseus forgot to put up the white sail. Now Aegeus, his father, sat and watched day after day and strained his old eyes across the sea to see the ship afar. And when he saw the black sail and not the white one, he gave up Theseus for dead, and in his grief he fell into the sea and died; so it is called the Aegean Sea to this day.

And now Theseus was king of Athens, and he guarded it and ruled it well.

The exact origins of the Greek myths and legends will never be known. Archeologists have shown that some of the old legends have a basis in history. A most exciting archeological discovery was that of Heinrich Schliemann. Working from clues in Homer's epics, he was able to find the site of the city of Troy and establish that there really had been a Trojan War.

Mary Renault, who has written several novels about ancient Greece, including two about Theseus, explains in this essay why she calls the story of Theseus a legend rather than a fairy tale.

How Much Is True?

MARY RENAULT

So the story of Theseus ends. But where did it come from, and how much of it is true?

It is only about a hundred years since Charles Kingsley wrote this version of it for his children; but the tale itself is immensely older, as much as three thousand years. Its beginning is so lost in the darkness of forgotten time that Kingsley called it a fairy tale. So it may be. But in our day, things have come to light that he did not know, and I would rather call it a legend: a marvelous rumor that grew up about something real.

Kingsley got the story from old Greek books, two thousand years old or so, and turned it into English. But how did it live for the first thousand years? In songs and tales, not written down but learned by heart and told by the old to the young, age after age. During that time, in Greece, there were no books at all, and very few people could even write. This was not because the Greeks were stupid — they had some of the best minds in history — but because there had been terrible wars, in which the kings' palaces and the great houses were all plundered and burned. With them went the ancient records and the pictures of the past, of gods and heroes; and the learned men, who were too old to fight for their lives, were killed.

101

After the wars, times were so hard that men had all they could do to defend their homes from enemies and find enough food to live on. No one could make a living by teaching or by writing books. But the poets and the singers were still at work. For while a man is all alone, hunting in the woods, or driving a plow, or pruning vines, and singing an old song to himself for company, new words will come to him, and he will work on the song and make it better.

Some of these singers grew so good that they became bards, men who could make a living by their songs alone; and some were the sons of bards who had escaped the killing and taught them the songs. (When people cannot read, they have good memories for what they hear.) These singing storytellers would go from village to village, singing for food and bed; they would make, if they could, for the house of a chief or king, where there was more to spare and they would often get a gift as well. Suppertime there was the best time of the day. The lords would come back from war or hunting; the ladies would stop their work (for the greatest ladies did housework then) and put on what jewels they had: wreaths of gold flowers, belts embroidered with golden thread, and long twinkling earrings. They did not eat much all day; at night they wanted a good big meal, to be sat over and enjoyed. Then they liked to hear the wandering bard and made him welcome for a while; only the richest kings could afford to keep one all the year. They would give him a place of honor, with a share of the best meat and wine; and when they had eaten, he would sing of the old times, when the land was rich and life was splendid. Those days seemed wonderful, now, to think of, and they called them the Age of Gold. It seemed that kings and princes and heroes of those days must have been bigger, braver, stronger and more beautiful, which, if they were better fed while they were growing, was very likely true.

While the harper sang of those lavish times, the listeners forgot their hardships. They loved to hear of the ancient riches: gold cups so heavy that the king, to drink, must lift them with both hands; exquisite armor inlaid with battle scenes; chariots adorned with ivory and silver, drawn by horses that talked to their masters. For everything, they thought, had been marvelous then. If one of the old heroes had been great in his day, winning battles, and killing fierce beasts to save his people, the bard would build up the story till he was slaying a hundred warriors single-handed or fighting dragons and monsters like the Minotaur.

No man was ever born with a bull's head. But priests and sorcerers of old savage rites have worn the masks of animals and sacrificed human beings in secret caves. Perhaps it was one of these that Theseus killed. But *Minotaur*, in Greek, means only "the Bull of Minos"; and *Labyrinth*, in old Cretan, means just "the Place of the Ax." We know, now, that both these things were real.

Charles Kingsley had no chance of knowing. In his time, there was a great fashion for not believing anything you could not see under your nose. People who thought like this called themselves Rationalists, meaning "those who reason" — which was conceited, the truth being that when they had made up their minds to disbelieve in something, they could be as blind and pigheaded as anyone else. So, if they found in an old Greek tale one thing larger than life, which clearly could not have happened, they said it proved that none of the rest was true.

But a few men thought otherwise. Somewhere in the tales they found a smell of truth. They too could reason, and they thought that stories with so much life in them had not come out of nothing. They were few, but in the end they were proved right.

In Germany, less than a century and a half ago, lived a boy called Heinrich Schliemann.[1] His parents were so poor that he had to leave school when he was fourteen to go to work. But one day he heard an old man, who had been a scholar before he took to drink, recite a piece from the *Iliad* of Homer, the greatest Greek bard. This is the tale of the heroes who fought at Troy to win back Helen the Beautiful, whom Prince Paris had stolen away. (A son of Theseus fought among them.) It was in Greek, so of course the boy did not understand a word, yet the mere sound of it seemed to him so thrilling that, in his time off from work, he learned the language so as to read it all and know the story. Ever after that, it haunted his mind. He did not believe it was all a fairy tale; he felt in it something true. But how was he to prove it? The only way that he could see was to find Troy.

Schliemann had not the fare-money to travel twenty miles, yet he never gave up his dream. First he ran errands in a shop. Then he shipped as a cabin boy — a hard, tough job in those sailing days, but he hoped, no doubt, to find a ship that would take him to Troy.

---

[1] *Heinrich Schliemann* (hīn'rik shlē'män).

His ship was wrecked, and he had to work on land again. All this while he was reading Greek and learning about the past, but there was no proving from books that Troy was real. Most people would have been content to pity themselves and to think about what they might have done if they had had better luck. Not Schliemann. He worked his way up in a business house till he had saved enough money to become a merchant; and, having learned not only Greek but his job, too, he did so well that at last he was very rich. More than half his life had gone, but never a day had he forgotten Troy. And now he went to look for it.

In Turkey he found the windy plain that Homer wrote of and on it a great mound that did not look like nature's work. Something, he thought, was hidden under it. He bought the land from the Turks who owned it, hired a troop of workmen, and set them digging. There under the grass were the ruins of a huge city surrounded by walls, which had been burned after a siege, just as Homer said; and in the ruins was a crown of golden flowers, with golden chains hanging from it to twine in a lady's hair, just such a crown as Helen might have worn.

Now Schliemann was famous and honored everywhere. He had plenty of money left, and he began to think of other Greek tales that might have truth in them. Then he remembered mighty King Minos of Crete, who forced the lesser kings to send him tribute of youths and maidens to feed the Minotaur, till Theseus slew it. Schliemann went to Crete; and where the ancient city of Cnossus had stood was another mound, which might hide anything. He offered to buy the land, but the man who owned it and the olive trees that grew there asked far too much. Being a business man, he held off buying and left the island; but it was bad business this time, for before he could go back he died.

But other men had heard about the Cnossus mound; one of them was Sir Arthur Evans. He, unlike Schliemann, was a scholar and expert archeologist; he had been born rich besides and had no need to spend long years in raising money. He bought the Cnossus fields; and when he dug there, what he found was even more wonderful than what Schliemann had found at Troy.

He found not a walled city — for Crete, just as the old tales said, had ruled the seas and had not feared invaders — but a magnificent palace, so vast and rambling that it was like a maze. It had been thrown down in an earthquake and burned as well, either by enemies or when the earthquake had spilled the lamps. But enough was left of it to show its splendors.

Among the ruins were jeweled ornaments so finely made that few men today could copy them; rich swords with delicate inlay on the blades; gold-and-crystal necklaces; finely carved seals; even a board to play some game on — all made of gold. In this palace of three thousand years ago were water pipes and drains and painted pottery more tasteful than most that we make today. Carved in the walls, and set up as an emblem, were two-headed axes, called *Labrys* in the Cretan tongue, which shows how the palace got its name: the Labyrinth. But most important of all, the walls had been covered with pictures.

The plaster they were painted on had flaked off the stone walls, but the flakes were there and much could be pieced together, like bits of a jigsaw puzzle. The pictures showed the luxury of the Cretans, their beauty and graceful clothes — ladies with flounced skirts and pretty made-up faces, men wearing rich necklaces like the ones Evans had found in the ruins. But the thing that startled him most were the bulls. Not only pictures, but sculptures in clay as well, showed these great beasts with long horns curved forward. And swinging on their horns, riding on their heads, dancing around them, even vaulting and turning somersaults over their backs, there were slender boys and girls.

No one can prove that one of these boys was Theseus, and perhaps we shall never know. But playing with the bulls must have been a perilous sport, in which many must have died; and if the Cretans did not want their children to run the risk, they may well have taken captives from lands they ruled to learn the dangerous skill. Some think it was a rite of sacrifice to please Poseidon, the god of bulls and earthquakes, so that he would spare the island; earthquakes come often there and are greatly feared. To this day, in Crete, there is sometimes heard at such times, from some deep place underground, a sound like the bellowing of a tremendous bull. Perhaps the Minotaur was the priest of this fearful bull-god, wearing a bull-head mask; or perhaps it was the bulls themselves who chose, from the boys and girls who danced with them, the victims for the god. So it may be true that there was a real Theseus, a brave prince who offered to share the danger with his people. Perhaps he grew so skillful in the bull-play that he helped to save the rest. Perhaps Ariadne saw his courage and his grace and loved him (for they found at Cnossus a tablet of clay with a name written on it: "Ariadne, Mistress of the Labyrinth"). It may be that after he had escaped with all his comrades, he came back with an army and conquered Crete and saved all Greece from the hated tribute.

All the Greek tales say he was a good king to his people, a man who would not allow even a slave to be oppressed. Centuries later, when written history had begun, there was a shrine to his memory in Athens; if a slave or poor man flying from a cruel master took refuge there, no one dared seize him, for fear of Theseus' anger reaching from the grave; so they would set the man free. Memories are long in Greece; even the churches there are built on places that were already holy a thousand years before Christ was born. I do not think the Greeks would have honored Theseus for so many generations if he had not once lived and ruled them justly, fought their battles, saved them from peril, and won their love.

The English language contains words which have their origins in languages from all parts of the world, mostly European, but also African, Asian, and American Indian. In this essay, Isaac Asimov shows how many English words are related to the myths of ancient Greece and Rome.

Words from the Myths

ISAAC ASIMOV

After Christianity was established, the old religion died out and Europeans no longer believed in the old Greek and Roman gods. Those gods, and the myths about them, lived on in memory, however. The old literature did not die; it was too great to be allowed to die. In fact, the old Greek stories were so fascinating that men did not consider themselves really educated unless and until they had learned those stories. Educated men introduced words from the myths into their speaking, and some of those words remained in the language. For that reason, traces of the Greek myths are to be found today in every European tongue, including English.

For instance, a police car's signal is a *siren*, and a sea cow is a *sirenian*. A circus organ is a *calliope*, a jellyfish is a *medusa*, and an Australian anteater is an *echnida*. We call out in a *stentorian* voice, listen to a kindly *mentor* or a bearded *nestor*, despise a *hectoring* bully.

In every case mentioned, we are drawing upon the Greek stories, where a Siren was a death trap, Calliope a goddess, Medusa and Echnida horrible monsters, and Stentor, Mentor, Nestor, and Hector were men.

Scientists, particularly, drew upon the old myths. Until quite recently, Latin and Greek were the common languages of learned men of all nations. When some new animal or planet or chemical or phenomenon needed to be named, it would have been inconvenient if scientists of each nationality had used names drawn from their own language. The habit arose of giving a Latin or Greek name which all nationalities could use.

Since the Greek myths are so well known, it was natural to take words from those myths whenever they seemed to fit the situation. For instance, when uranium [1] was first broken down by fission during World War II, a new element was found amid the deadly radioactive heat. It was named *promethium* after Prometheus, who dared the deadly radioactive heat of the sun to bring fire to mankind.

Most of us are introduced to Greek myths in childhood but are taught to think of them only as interesting fairy tales and adventure stories. However, as you see, they are more than that. They are part of our culture, and much of our language is derived from them.

Some of the traces these myths have left are very familiar indeed. The sixth month was sacred to Juno and is called *June* to this day. Juno (Hera) is the goddess of marriage, and June is still considered the traditional month for marriage. Many girls dream of being not just a bride but a "June bride."

Ceres (Demeter) is the goddess of agriculture and particularly of grains, such as wheat, corn, rice, barley, and oats. These are the most important foods in a farming society and they are called *cereals* after Ceres.

The Greeks considered Aphrodite the most beautiful of the goddesses. She was the goddess of beauty and love. The Romans identified their own goddess of beauty, Venus, with Aphrodite, and the name Venus is more familiar to us. Under either name, the goddess is the prototype of beauty, that is, the original model with which everything since then must be compared. That is why, when we wish to pay a high compliment to the good looks of some girl, we call her a *Venus*. The Romans paid such honor to Venus that *venerate* has come to mean to honor and respect. Then, since age is respected, or should be, old men are said to be *venerable*.

Venus is the one goddess whose name was given to an important planet. This is the planet commonly called the "evening star" or the "morning star" (depending on which side of the sun it happens to be). It is the brightest and most beautiful object in the heavens next to the sun and moon and is far brighter than any star.

One of the sons of Zeus was Hermes. He was considered the messenger of the gods and so was naturally imagined as very swift. He is usually pictured with wings on his sandals and on his cap. He was

---

[1] *uranium:* based on the name of Uranus, Greek god of the sky.

also the god of commerce, cunning, and invention. Now of all the planets in the sky, the one that moves most quickly against the background of the stars was naturally named after the swift-footed Hermes. The Romans identified their own god of commerce, Mercury, with Hermes, and so we know the planet as *Mercury*.

Ares was the son of Zeus and Hera. He is the cruel and bloody god of war, who delighted in battle. When he went into battle, his sons, Phobos and Deimos, prepared his chariot. Since *phobos* is the Greek word for *fear* and *deimos* for *terror*, this is just a way of saying that war is attended by fear and terror.

Phobos leaves his mark in modern psychology,[2] for a *phobia* is an abnormal fear. *Claustrophobia* is the abnormal fear of closed places, for instance, and *agoraphobia* is the abnormal fear of wide open spaces. A certain disease affects the nerves so that the sufferer falls into convulsions if he tries to drink. It is therefore called *hydrophobia* ("fear of water") because the Greeks thought the convulsions were due to a fear of water instead of to a virus, as we now know they are.

It seems natural that the Greeks named the fourth planet after Ares, since the fourth planet shines with a ruddy color, resembling blood. That is fit for the god of war. The Romans identified their god of war, Mars, with Ares, so we know the planet as *Mars*. Originally Mars was one of the most important of the Roman gods, and an entire month of the year was dedicated to him. We still call the third month *March* in his honor.

Another child of Hera was Hephaestus. He was the god of smiths and was always pictured working at his forge. He was the only god shown working with his hands. The Romans had a god of fire and forge themselves, whom they pictured as working in the depths of Mount Etna, the Sicilian volcano. The Romans called this god Vulcan and identified him with Hephaestus. Vulcan is much the more familiar name to us. For one thing, all mountains that, like Mount Etna, belch fire and flame are now called *volcanoes*.

Another trace of the name is to be found in a matter concerning rubber. In the first part of the 1800's, attempts were made to use rubber in waterproof clothing. Unfortunately, the rubber got soft and sticky in warm weather and hard and leathery in cold weather.

---

[2] *psychology*: related to the name of Psyche, a beautiful maiden with whom Cupid fell in love; *psyche* means *soul* in Greek.

Chemists tried to find ways to prevent this. In 1839, an American inventor named Charles Goodyear discovered by accident that if rubber and sulfur were heated together, the rubber became dry and flexible in both hot and cold weather. In this way, rubber could finally be put to many practical uses. The process by which this was done involved the use of heat. Consequently, such rubber was said to be *vulcanized*.

The Romans had a nature god, Faunus. Faunus was a god of animal life in particular. He had a sister named Flora, who was the goddess of flowers and plant life in general. These names are now applied to animal and plant life, so that biologists speak of the *fauna* (animal life) and *flora* (plant life) of a particular region.

An example of a minor goddess is Iris, who, like Hermes, but on a lower level, served as a messenger of the gods. She specialized in bearing messages from the gods to human beings, and to do this she had frequently to descend from heaven to earth. The logical stairway by which this might be done was the rainbow, and, indeed, *iris* is the Greek word for rainbow.

The most remarkable thing about the rainbow is, of course, its many colors, so the word *iris* has come to be applied to other many-colored objects. For instance, as we all know, human eyes come in different shades of color. In 1721 a Danish naturalist, Jacob Benignus Winslow, called the colored part of the eye the *iris*, and the name has been kept. It is also applied to the flag, a plant with large flowers that come in a variety of colors.

The Roman goddess of health was Salus. For this reason, the word *salutary* means *healthful*. Furthermore, when we greet someone, we usually wish him or her good health, or imply that we do by asking after their well-being. "How are you?" we usually say. Therefore, a greeting is a *salutation* or a *salute*.

A minor Roman god should also be mentioned in connection with the name of one of the months, which are all Latin in origin.

I have already mentioned March (Mars) and June (Juno). But then there is a month involving Janus, who was the Roman god of doors, to begin with. He therefore became the god who presided over beginnings (entrance through a door) and endings (exit by a door). He was usually pictured with two faces, one looking forward and one backward.

The first month of the year is a time for beginning a new year and ending the old. We still celebrate it as a time for looking sentimentally at the past and hopefully toward the future. So it is named for Janus and called *January*. And, of course, a man who is in charge of the doors in a building, and of other parts of it as well, is a *janitor*.

The imaginative Greeks did not confine themselves to gods and demigods. They also dreamed up a variety of monsters of all types. Gaea,[3] the goddess of the earth, brought forth the most terrible monster of all and the largest giant who ever existed. He was named Typhon. He was hundreds of miles high and wide, and his arms and legs ended in serpents. For a while, the Olympians were completely terrified of him. Zeus was finally goaded into fighting Typhon. For a while it looked as though Zeus might actually be beaten and destroyed, but after a terrible fight, Zeus managed to use his thunderbolts and win.

The word Typhon was picked up from this myth (which became rather famous because of the excitement of the great fight) by the Arabs of the Middle Ages, who carried it to southeast Asia, where it is now used in the form of *typhoon* as a word for the hurricane.

[So the age of the ancient Greeks and Romans] did not die altogether, for it left behind it a never-to-be-forgotten heritage of stories, which remain part of our literature and life. Even if it ever happened that no one read the stories, our English language would still contain within its words the memory of those days of gods and heroes.

---

[3] *Gaea* (jē·ə): whose name gives us *geography, geology, geometry*.

"Albert's Son,"
painting by Andrew Wyeth.

BOOK ONE | PART 3

COMING OF AGE

You are too old to claim that you are a child any longer.
          ODYSSEY, Book 1

Much great literature is devoted to the theme of the coming of age. The Biblical story of Joseph and his brothers, for instance, is in the main a story of a young man's coming into his own. In recent centuries, novels based on this theme have become very popular. More often than not, these novels represent a young author's first work and reflect his own experience in achieving maturity. Several of Charles Dickens's best works, for example David Copperfield and Great Expectations, are such novels.

In the Odyssey, the story of Telemachus is a good example of the theme. When we meet him for the first time in Book 1, we see a young man who is just on the verge of coming of age. He is twenty years old and physically mature. But he has lived virtually all his life without his father's example and guidance, and he is not yet a man. We find him moody and brooding, helpless against the suitors, and quick to tears. Only at Athena's urging does he take any action: the voyage to Pylos and Sparta, which proves to be the big step in his coming of age.

What happens on that trip? Telemachus finds out who he is. In contrast to the scornful treatment of the suitors, kings and queens welcome him, remark on his resemblance to his father, and make him feel important. He is flattered and gains confidence. On his return to Ithaca, he is much surer of his own worth and now has a clearer view of who he is. His ordeal is yet to come, but his journey has prepared him for it. In the fight against the suitors at his father's side, he is not alone, as in most rites of passage, but he is acting like a man and a prince.

Thus, a series of events, rather than a single incident, brings about Telemachus's coming of age. He seems to achieve manhood in a short time, but actually no one comes of age all at once. No single experience in itself can bring maturity to a young person. But one such experience can be the first step on — or the climax to — what has been called "the adventure of discovering life."

Some sort of initiation ceremony is a part of the culture of all the peoples of the world. Anthropologists use the term "rite of passage" to refer to ceremonies which mark a youth's being granted full membership in a tribe or society. In these ceremonies the young candidate's worth is first tested, and then certain secrets and rituals of the tribe are revealed to him.

One such rite of passage is described in the following section from the Autobiography of a Young African, *by Camara Laye. The author, who was later educated in France, shows how tradition and custom were all-important in the life of his tribe.*

The Night of Kondén Diara

CAMARA LAYE

I was growing up. The time had come for me to join the society of the uninitiated. This rather mysterious society — and at that age it was very mysterious to me, though not very secret — comprised all the young boys of twelve, thirteen, and fourteen years of age, and it was run by our elders, whom we called the big *Kondéns*. I joined it one evening before the feast of Ramadan.[1]

As soon as the sun had gone down, the tom-tom had begun to beat. Even though it was being played in a remote part of the concession,[2] its notes had roused me at once, had struck my breast, had struck right at my heart, just as if Kodoké, our best player, had been playing for me alone. A little later I had heard the shrill voices of boys accompanying the tom-tom with their cries and singing. Yes, the time had come for me.

It was the first time I had spent the feast of Ramadan at Kou-

---

[1] *Ramadan:* Like many African tribes, Camara's had connections with the Moslem faith. The feast of Ramadan followed a thirty-day fast.
[2] *concession:* land used by Camara's people but owned by the government.

roussa. Until this year, my grandmother had always insisted on my spending it with her at Tindican. All that morning, and even more so in the afternoon, I had been in a state of great agitation, with everyone busy preparing for the festival, bumping into and pushing each other and asking me to help. Outside, the uproar was just as bad. Kouroussa is the chief town of our region, and all the canton chiefs, attended by their musicians, make it a custom to gather here for the festival. From the gateway to the concession I had watched them pass by, with their companies of praise-singers, balaphonists [3] and guitarists, drum and tom-tom players. Until now I had only been thinking of the festival and of the sumptuous feast that awaited me — but now there was something quite different in the wind.

The screaming crowd that surrounded Kodoké and his famous tom-tom was getting nearer. Going from one concession to another, the crowd would stop where there was a boy of an age to join the society and take him away. That is why it was so slow in coming, yet so sure, so ineluctable. As sure, as ineluctable as the fate that awaited me.

What fate? My meeting with Kondén Diara!

Now I was not unaware of who Kondén Diara was. My mother had often talked of him, and so at times had my uncles and whoever else had authority over me. They had threatened me only too often with Kondén Diara, that terrible bogeyman, that "lion that eats up little boys." And here was Kondén Diara — but was he a man? Was he an animal? Was he not rather half-man, half-animal? My friend Kouyaté believed he was more man than beast — here was Kondén Diara leaving the dim world of hearsay, here he was taking on flesh and blood, yes, and roused by Kodoké's tom-tom was prowling around the town! This night was to be the night of Kondén Diara.

Now I could hear the beating of the tom-tom very plainly — Kodoké was much nearer — I could hear perfectly the chanting and the shouts that rose into the dark. I could make out almost as distinctly the rather hollow, crisp, well-marked beats of the *coros* that are a kind of miniature canoe and are beaten with a bit of wood. I was standing at the entrance to the concession, waiting. I, too,

---

[3] *balaphonists* (bal·ə·fōn′ists): players on a West African xylophone with gourd resonators.

was holding my *coro*, ready to play it with the stick clutched nervously in my hand. I was waiting, hidden by the shadow of the hut. I was waiting, filled with a dreadful anxiety, my eyes searching the blackness.

"Well?" asked my father.

He had crossed the workshop without my hearing him.

"Are you afraid?"

"A little," I replied.

He laid his hand on my shoulder.

"It's all right. Don't worry."

He drew me to him, and I could feel his warmth; it warmed me, too, and I began to feel less frightened; my heart did not beat so fast.

"You mustn't be afraid."

"No."

I knew that whatever my fear might be I must be brave. I wasn't to show fright or to run off and hide. Still less was I to resist or cry out when my elders carried me off.

"I, too, went through this test," said my father.

"What happens to you?" I asked.

"Nothing you need really be afraid of, nothing you can not overcome by your own will power. Remember: you have to control your fear; you have to control yourself. Kondén Diara will not take you away. He will roar. But he won't do more than roar. You won't be frightened, now, will you?"

"I'll try not to be."

"Even if you are frightened, do not show it."

He went away, and I began waiting again, and the disturbing uproar came nearer and nearer. Suddenly I saw the crowd emerging from the dark and rushing toward me. Kodoké, his tom-tom slung over one shoulder, was marching at their head, followed by the drummers.

I ran back quickly into the yard, and, standing in the middle of it, I awaited the awful invasion with as much courage as I could manage. I did not have long to wait. The crowd was upon me. It was spreading tumultuously all around me, overwhelming me with shouts and cries and beating tom-toms, beating drums. It formed a circle, and I found myself in the center, alone, curiously isolated, still free and yet already captive. Inside the circle, I recognized

Kouyaté and others, many of them friends of mine who had been collected as the crowd moved on, collected as I was to be, as I already was; and it seemed to me they were none of them looking very happy — but was I any more happy than they? I began to beat my *coro*, as they were doing. Perhaps I was beating it with less confidence than they.

At this point young girls and women joined the circle and began to dance. Young men and adolescents, stepping out of the crowd, moved into the circle too and began to dance facing the women. The men sang, the women clapped their hands. Soon the only ones left to form the circle were the boys. They too began to sing — they were not allowed to dance — and, as they sang, sang in unison, they forgot their anxiety. I too sang with them. When, having formed a circle again, the crowd left our concession, I went with it almost willingly, beating my *coro* with great enthusiasm. Kouyaté was on my right.

Toward the middle of the night our tour of the town and the collection of boys were finished. We had arrived at the farthest outskirts of the concessions, and in front of us lay only the brush. Here the women and young girls left us. Then the grown men left. We were alone with the older boys, or should I say "delivered over" to them — for I remember the often rather disagreeable natures and rarely pleasant manners of those older ones.

The women and young girls now hurried back to their dwellings. Actually, they can not have been any more at ease than we were. I know for a fact that not one of them would have ventured to leave town on this night. Already they found the town and the night sinister. I am certain that more than one who went back to her concession alone was to regret having joined the crowd. They took courage only after they had shut the gates of their concessions and the doors of their huts. Meanwhile, they hurried on and from time to time cast unquiet looks behind them. In a short while, when Kondén Diara would begin to roar, they would not be able to stop shaking with fright. They would all shake uncontrollably. Then they would run to make sure the doors were all properly barred. For them, as for us, though in a much less significant way, this night would be the night of Kondén Diara.

As soon as our elders had made sure that no intruder was present to disturb the mysteriousness of the ceremony, we left the town behind and entered the bush by a path which leads to a sacred place where each year the initiation takes place. The place is well known: it is situated under an enormous bombax tree, a hollow at the junction of the river Komoni and the river Niger. At normal times it is not forbidden to go there; but certainly it has not always been so, and some emanation from the past I never knew still seems to hover around the huge trunk of the bombax tree. I think that a night such as the one we were going through must certainly have resurrected a part of that past.

We were walking in silence, closely hemmed in by our elders. Perhaps they were afraid we might escape? It looked like it. I do not think, however, that the idea of escape had occurred to any of us. The night, and that particular night, seemed impenetrable. Who knew where Kondén Diara had his lair? Who knew where he was prowling? But was it not right here, near the hollow? Yes, it must be here. And if we had to face him— and certainly we had to face him — it would surely be better to do so in a crowd, in this jostling group that seemed to make us all one, and seemed like a last refuge from the peril that was approaching.

Yet for all our nearness to one another and for all the vigilance of our elders, our march — so silent after the recent uproar — through the wan moonlight, far from the town, frightened us. And we were filled with terror at the thought of the sacred place toward which we were going, and the hidden presence of Kondén Diara.

Were our elders marching so closely beside us only to keep watch over us? Perhaps. But it is likely that they too felt something of the terror which had seized us. They too found the night and the silence disturbing. And for them, as for us, marching close together was a means of putting down terror.

Just before we reached the hollow, we saw flames leap from a huge wood fire previously hidden by bushes. Kouyaté squeezed my arm, and I knew he was referring to the fire. Yes, there was a fire. There too was Kondén Diara, the hidden presence of Kondén Diara. But there was also a reassuring presence in the depth of the night: a great fire! My spirits rose — at least they rose a little — and I squeezed Kouyaté's arm in return. I quickened my steps — we all quickened our steps — and the crimson radiance of the fire enveloped us. We had a harbor now, this kind of haven from the night: a huge blaze and, at our backs, the enormous trunk of the bombax tree. Oh! It was a precarious haven! But, however poor, it was infinitely better than the silence and the dark, the sullen silence of the dark. We assembled beneath the bombax tree. The ground beneath had been cleared of reeds and tall grasses.

Our elders suddenly shouted: "Kneel!"

We at once fell to our knees.

"Heads down!"

We lowered our heads.

"Lower than that!"

We bent our heads right to the ground, as if in prayer.

"Now hide your eyes!"

We didn't have to be told twice. We shut our eyes tight and pressed our hands over them. For would we not die of fright and horror if we should see, or so much as catch a glimpse of, Kondén Diara? Our elders walked up and down, behind us and in front of us, to make sure that we had all obeyed their orders to the letter. Woe to him who would have the audacity to disobey! He would be cruelly whipped. It would be a whipping all the more cruel because he would have no hope of redress, for he would find no one to listen to his complaint, no one to transgress against custom. But who would have the audacity to disobey?

Now that we were on our knees with our foreheads to the ground and our hands pressed over our eyes, Kondén Diara's roaring suddenly burst out.

We were expecting to hear this hoarse roar, we were not expecting any other sound, but it took us by surprise and shattered us, froze our hearts with its unexpectedness. And it was not only a lion, it was not only Kondén Diara roaring: there were ten, twenty, perhaps thirty lions that took their lead from him, uttering their terrible roars and surrounding the hollow; ten or twenty lions separated from us by a few yards only and whom the great wood fire would perhaps not always keep at bay; lions of every size and every age — we could tell that by the way they roared — from the very oldest ones to the very youngest cubs. No, not one of us would dream of venturing to open an eye, not one! Not one of us would dare to lift his head from the ground; he would rather bury it in the earth. And I bent down as far as I could; we all bent down further; we bent our knees as much as we could; we kept our backs as low as possible. I made myself — we all made ourselves — as small as we could.

"You mustn't be afraid!" I said to myself. "You must master your fear! Your father has commanded you to!"

But how was I to master it? Even in the town, far away from this clearing, women and children trembled and hid themselves in their huts. They heard the growling of Kondén Diara, and many of them stopped their ears to keep it out. The braver arose — that night it took courage to leave one's bed — and went again and again to check the doors and see that they were shut tight. How was I to stave off fear when I was within range of the dread monster? If he pleased, Kondén Diara could leap the fire in one bound and sink his claws in my back!

I did not doubt the presence of the monster, not for a single instant. Who could assemble such a numerous herd, hold such a nocturnal revel, if not Kondén Diara?

"He alone," I said to myself, "he alone has such power over lions. . . . Keep away, Kondén Diara! Keep away! Go back into the bush! . . ." But Kondén Diara went on with his revels, and sometimes it seemed to me that he roared right over my head, right into my own ears. "Keep away, I implore you, Kondén Diara!"

What was it my father had said? "Kondén Diara roars; but he won't do more than roar; he will not take you away. . . ." Yes, something like that. But was it true, really true?

There was also a rumor that Kondén Diara sometimes pounced with fearsome claws on someone or other and carried him far away, far, far away into the depths of the bush; and then, days and days afterward, months or even years later, quite by chance a huntsman might discover some whitened bones.

And do not people also die of fright? Ah! how I wished this roaring would stop! How I wished I was far away from this clearing, back in the concession, in the warm security of the hut! Would this roaring never cease?

"Go away, Kondén Diara! Go away! Stop roaring." Oh! those roars! I felt as if I could bear them no longer.

Whereupon, suddenly, they stopped! They stopped just as they had begun, so suddenly, in fact, that I felt only reluctant relief. Was it over? Really over? Was it not just a temporary interruption? No, I dared not feel relieved just yet. And then suddenly the voice of one of the older boys rang out: "Get up!"

I heaved a sigh of relief. This time it was really over. We looked at one another: I looked at Kouyaté and the others. If there were only a little more light. . . . But the light from the fire was sufficient: great drops of sweat were still beading our foreheads; yet the night was chill. . . . Yes, we were afraid. We were not able to conceal our fear.

A new command rang out, and we sat down in front of the fire. Now our elders began our initiation. For the rest of the night they taught us the chants. We never moved. We learned the words and tunes as we heard them. We were as attentive as if we had been at school, entirely attentive and docile.

When dawn came, our instruction was at an end. My legs and arms were numb. I worked my joints and rubbed my legs for a while, but my blood still flowed slowly. I was worn out, and I was cold. Looking around me, I could not understand why I had shaken with fear during the night: the first rays of dawn were falling so gently, so reassuringly, on the bombax tree, on the clearing. The sky looked so pure! Who would have believed that a few hours earlier a pack of lions led by Kondén Diara in person had been raging fiercely in the high grass and among the reeds and that they had been separated from us only by a wood fire which had just now gone out as dawn came? No one. I would have doubted my own senses and set it all down as a nightmare if I had not noticed more than one of my companions casting an occasional fearful glance in the direction of the highest grass.

But what were those long white threads which hung from, or, rather, waved from the top of the bombax tree and which appeared to write on the sky the direction in which the town lay? I had not time to wonder very long at this: our elders were regrouping us; and, because most of us were almost sleepwalking, the operation was carried out with difficulty, with shouts, and with some rough treatment. Finally we started off back to the town, singing our new songs, and we sang them with unbelievably carefree abandon: as the steed that scents the approaching stable suddenly quickens his step, however weary he may be.

When we reached the first concessions, the presence of the long white threads struck me once more: all the principal huts had these threads on the very tops of their roofs.

"Do you see the white threads?" I asked Kouyaté.

"I can see them. They are always there after the ceremony in the clearing."

"Who puts them there?"

Kouyaté shrugged his shoulders.

"That's where they come from," I said, pointing to the distant bombax tree.

"Someone must have climbed up."

"Who could possibly climb a bombax tree?"

"I don't know."

"Could anyone possibly get his arms around such a huge trunk?" I said. "And even if he could, how could he hoist himself on bark all covered with all those thorns? You're talking nonsense. Can't you imagine what a job it would be just to reach the first branches?"

"Why do you expect me to know more about this than you do?" asked Kouyaté.

"Because this is the first time I have taken part in the ceremony, while you — "

I didn't finish my sentence. We had reached the main square of the town. I stared in amazement at the bombax trees in the market place. They too were ornamented with the same white threads. All but the humblest huts, indeed, and all the big trees were tied to one another by these white threads whose focal point was the enormous bombax tree in the clearing, the sacred place marked by the bombax tree.

"The swallows tie them on," said Kouyaté suddenly.

"Swallows? Are you crazy?" I said. "Swallows don't fly by night."

I questioned one of the older boys who was walking beside me.

"It is our great chief who does it," he said. "Our chief turns himself into a swallow during the night. He flies from tree to tree and from hut to hut, and all these threads are tied on in less time than it takes to tell."

"He flies from tree to tree like a swallow?"

"Yes. He's a real swallow and as swift. Everyone knows that."

"Isn't that what I told you?" asked Kouyaté.

I did not say another word. The night of Kondén Diara was a strange night, a terrible and miraculous night, a night that passed all understanding.

As on the previous evening, we went from one concession to another, preceded by tom-toms and drums, and our companions left us one after another as they reached their homes. Whenever we passed a concession where someone whose courage had failed him had refused to join us, a mocking chant rose from our ranks.

I arrived at our concession completely exhausted but very satisfied with myself: I had taken part in the ceremony of the lions! Even if I had not put up much of a show when Kondén Diara was roaring, that was my own affair; I could keep that to myself. I passed triumphantly over the threshold of our concession.

The festival of Ramadan was beginning. In the yard, I saw my parents, who were dressed to go to the mosque.

"Here you are at last," said my mother.

"Here I am," I said proudly.

"What kind of time is this to come home?" she said, pressing me to her bosom. "The night is over, and you haven't had a bit of sleep."

"The ceremony did not finish until break of day," I said.

"I know, I know," she said. "All you men are mad."

"What about the lions?" asked my father. "What about Kondén Diara?"

"I heard them," I replied. "They were very close; they were as near to me as I am to you now. There was only the fire between us."

"It's crazy," said my mother. "Go to bed, you're dropping with sleep." She turned toward my father: "Now, where's the sense in all that?"

"Well, it's the custom," said my father.

"I don't like such customs," she said. "Young boys should not have to stay awake all night."

"Were you afraid?" asked my father.

Should I admit that I was very frightened?

"Of course he was afraid," said my mother.

"Only a little," said my father.

"Go to bed," ordered my mother. "If you don't get some sleep now you'll fall asleep during the feast."

I went inside to lie down. Outside I heard my mother quarreling with my father. She thought it stupid to take unnecessary risks.

Later I got to know who Kondén Diara was, and I learned these things when the time had come for me to learn them. As long as we are not initiated, as long as we have not attained that second life that is our true existence, we are told nothing, and we can find out nothing.

We begin to have a vague understanding of the ceremony of the lions after we have taken part in it many times. But even then, we are careful to share our knowledge only with those companions who have had the same experience. And the real secret lies hidden until the day when we are initiated into our life as men.

No, they were not real lions that roared in the clearing, for it was the older boys, simply the older boys. They created the roaring sound with small boards, thick at the center, sharp at the edges: the edges were all sharper from having such a thick center. The board was ellipsoidal [4] in shape and very small. There was a hole on one side that permitted it to be tied to a string. The older boys swung it around like a sling, and, to increase the speed of the gyrations, they too turned with it. The board cut through the air and produced a sound like a lion's roar. The smallest boards imitated the roaring of the lion cubs; the biggest ones the roaring of full-grown lions.

It was childishly simple. What was not so childish was the effect produced at night on someone who did not expect it: the heart froze! If it had not been for the far greater fear of finding themselves lost in the bush, the terror it created would have made the boys run away. The bombax tree and the fire which had been kindled near it made a kind of haven which kept the uninitiated from running away.

But if Kondén Diara's roaring is easily explained, the presence of the long white threads binding the great bombax tree in the sacred clearing to the tallest trees and the principal houses of the town is less easily explained. For my own part, I never succeeded in obtaining an explanation: at the time when I might have obtained it — that is, when I should have taken my place among the older boys who conducted the ceremony — I was no longer living at Kouroussa. All I know is that these threads were spun from cotton and that bamboo poles were used to tie them to the tops of the huts. What I don't know is how they were attached to the tops of the bombax trees.

---

[4] *ellipsoidal* (ē'lip·soid'l): oval.

Our bombax trees are very big, and it is difficult to imagine poles sixty feet high. Such structures would certainly collapse, no matter how carefully they had been put together. Moreover, I do not see how the summit of these thorny trees could be reached by climbing. There is, of course, a kind of belt which tree-climbers use. It is tied around the tree and the climber gets inside it, placing the belt against the small of his back, then climbs by a series of jerks, pressing against the trunk with his feet. But such a procedure is quite preposterous given the enormous size of the trunks of our bombax trees.

Or why not plainly and simply use a sling? I do not know. A good slinger can work miracles. Perhaps it is this sort of miracle which would most easily explain the inexplicable presence of white threads at the summit of the bombax trees. But I can come to no final decision about it.

I do know that the men who tie the threads to the rooftops have to take great care not to mislay the bamboo poles. Things must not be revealed in that fashion. For it would take only one mislaid pole to start the women and children on the way to discovering the secret. That is why, as soon as the threads are tied, the poles and boards are removed. The usual hideouts are thatched roofs and secret places in the bush. And so nothing escapes about these manifestations of the power of Kondén Diara.

But what about the men? What about those who *do* know?

They won't breathe a single word about it. They keep their knowledge a close secret. Not only do they keep women and children in a state of uncertainty and terror, they also warn them to keep the doors of their huts firmly barred.

I know that such conduct must appear strange, but it is absolutely true. If the ceremony of the lions has the character of a game, if it is for the most part pure mystification, yet it has one important feature: it is a test, a training in hardship, a rite; the prelude to a tribal rite, and for the present that is all one can say. . . . It is obvious that if the secret were to be given away, the ceremony would lose much of its power. Certainly the teaching which follows the roaring of Kondén Diara would remain the same. But nothing would remain of the trial by fear, that occasion when every boy has the opportunity to overcome his fear and his own baser nature.

The American frontier was a great testing ground for young people. It offered many occasions when (in Camara Laye's words) "every boy has the opportunity to overcome his fear and his own baser nature." Often, young people had to think and act like adults, and they had to have an adult's endurance and courage. Here, a brother and sister make a journey to maturity through the Apache country of the American Southwest.

Early Marriage

CONRAD RICHTER

For two days the leathery face of Asa Putnam had been a document in cipher to anyone who could read the code. Since Saturday but one traveler had passed his solitary post, a speck of adobe and picket corrals lost on the vast, sandy stretch of the Santa Ana plain. Far as the eye could see from his doorway, the rutted El Paso trail — unfenced, gutterless, innocent of grading, gravel, culverts, or telephone poles, imprinted only by iron tires, the hoofs of horses and oxen, sheep and cattle, and the paw of the loping lobo wolf — lay with dust unraised.

Ordinarily, there were freighters with cracking whips and trailers rumbling on behind. Army trains to and from the forts set up their tents for the night beyond the springs. The private coaches of Santa Fe and Colorado merchants, of cattle kings and government officials, stopped long enough for the Putnam children to admire the ladies, the magnificent woodwork, and the luxurious cushions inside. Trail herds of gaunt red steers bawled for the water in the earthen tank, and pairs and companies of horsemen rode up and down.

But since Saturday not even a solitary buckboard[1] from the far settlements in the Cedar country had called for supplies or letters. Only a girl from the Blue Mesa had ridden in for her and her

---
[1] *buckboard:* a light, open carriage.

neighbors' mail. She had eaten dinner with the Putnams, refused to stay overnight, and started her long ride home.

A stranger from the East would have spoken about the stillness, the deadly waiting, and asked uneasily why Uncle Gideon hadn't come as promised. But in the Putnam household it was not mentioned.

Asa deliberately busied himself about the post, filling the bin beneath the counter with navy beans and green coffee, leafing through the packet of letters in the drawer, and making a long rite out of feeding the occupants of the picket corrals — four horses of which were fresh for the next stage.

Rife, just turned fifteen, carried water and gathered cow chips in an old hide dragged by a rope to his saddle horn. Ignacita, the Mexican housekeeper, spat sharply on her heavy irons in the torrid kitchen and kept glancing over her shoulder and out of the open door and windows.

And Nancy Belle, going on seventeen, packed and repacked the high, ironbound trunk that her father had bought for her at Santa Fe and sang softly to herself in the way that women sang fifty and sixty years ago.

Saturday she was being married at Gunstock, two hundred miles away — five days' journey in a wagon, four in a saddle or buckboard.

For six months she had thought of little else. The almanac fell apart at June as naturally as her mother's Bible did at the Twenty-third Psalm. So often had she run her finger down the page that anyone might tell from the worn line of type the very day she and Stephen Dewee would be man and wife. The Dewees lived four hundred miles west across the territory in the Beaverhead country. She and Stephen were taking a mountain ranch near his people, and for the wedding they had compromised on Gunstock, nearly equidistant from both families and convenient to friends scattered up and down the Rio Grande.

She had lighted a candle in the dusk, when a figure appeared reluctantly in her doorway. Asa Putnam had never been at ease in his daughter's bedroom. A tall, rawhide man in an unbuttoned, sagging vest, he was visibly embarrassed by any furnishings that suggested refinement. Invariably he kept his hat on in the house. He had it on now, a flat top and a flat brim, not so much like the

Western hats you see now. Nancy Belle knew that her mother's people had never forgiven him for bringing his young wife and their two small children to this lonely post, at the mercy of outlaws and the worse Apaches.

Tonight she could see that something bothered him. He gave her a sidewise glance, so sharp and characteristic.

"I don't expect, Nancy Belle, you could put off your weddin'?"

The girl stood quietly gazing at him with a face like the tintype [2] of her mother. But under her sedate gray dress, with tight waist and full skirts to the instep, she had frozen. She looked much older than her years. Her air of gentlefolk and her wide-apart gray eyes came from her mother. But the chin, tipped up with resolute fearlessness, was her father's.

"No, Papa!" Her two clear words held all the steady insistence of the desert.

"I figured how you'd feel," he nodded, avoiding her eyes. "I just wanted to put it up to you. I'd a' covered the *jornada* [3] on foot to be on time at my own weddin', but I didn't have to count on Gideon to hold me up."

"Are you telling me, Papa, that you can't go to Gunstock tomorrow?" Her voice remained quiet, but a coldness had seized her. Of all the people she had visualized at her wedding, the one next to Stephen she could least spare was the tall, grave figure of her father.

"I reckon I kind of can't, Nancy Belle," he said soberly. "Rife could tend to the stage all right and do the feedin'. But they's men come to this post no boy can handle." He shifted his position. "I figured once on closin' up the post till I got back. But the stage is comin' and the mail. And the freighters count on me for feed and grub. Then I got to protect my own property and the mail and freight for the Cedar country that's in the storage room."

"I know," Nancy Belle said steadily. "I can get to Gunstock all right."

Far back in her father's assaying eyes, she fancied she saw a glint of pride.

"You're pretty nigh a woman now, Nancy Belle. And Rife's a

---

[2] *tintype:* a photograph on metal.
[3] *jornada* (hôr:nä′dä): journey.

good slice of a man. It's a straight trail to the Rio Grande, once you turn at the old post. Both you and Rife's been over it before. Of course, I'd like to be at the weddin', but the boy can tell me about it." He went to the window. "Rife!" he called.

Nancy Belle's brother came in presently. A slight boy, with his father's blue eyes, he seldom made a fuss over anything, even when he shot a stray duck on the tank or when they braked down the last cedar hill into Santa Fe with all the open doors of the plaza shops in sight. And when his father told him now, he showed neither enthusiasm nor regret — merely straightened.

"Sure. I can take you, Nancy Belle," he said.

Something pulled under his sister's tight basque.[4] She remembered the long miles they would have in the wagon, the camps at lonely places, the ugly shadow ever hovering over the outposts of this frontier country, and the blight that, since Saturday, seemed to have fallen on the trail. Her eyes swam. Now, at the last minute, she yielded.

"If you'll let me ride, Papa, I'll wait another day for Uncle Gideon," she promised.

Her father's eyes moved to the ruffled red calico curtains at the shadeless windows.

"I don't hardly count on Gideon comin' any more, Nancy Belle. Besides, it's too long in the saddle to Gunstock — especially for a girl to get married. You'd be plumb wore out, and you wouldn't have your trunk. You couldn't get dressed for your weddin'."

He turned thoughtfully and went out, Rife close behind. Nancy Belle could hear her father's tones, slow and grave, coming from near one of the picket corrals.

It was too far to catch the words; but when they came in, she saw that her brother's features looked a little pale under the tan.

"You better get some sleep, Nancy Belle," her father said. "You and Rife are startin' before daylight. If Gideon comes, I'll ride after."

They had scarcely gone from the room when Ignacita came in from the kitchen, her black eyes glittering over a pile of freshly starched white in her arms.

"Nancy Belle, *chinita* — "[5] she whispered, plucking at the girl's

---

[4] *basque* (bask): a fitted garment, laced in the front and worn over a blouse.
[5] *chinita* (chē-nē'tä): a term of affection.

sleeve. "You don't say to your *papacito* ⁶ I talk to you! I have promise I don't scare you. But I can't see you go so far in the wilderness alone, *pobrecita!* ⁷ Sometimes people go safe from one place to the other, oh, *sí!* But sometimes, *chinita*, they don't come back! You have not the oldness like Ignacita. Ay, I tell you these old eyes have seen men and women quartered from a tree like sheep or maybe tied over a stove like I don't have the words to say to you."

Nancy Belle did not answer except to lay, one by one, the ironed pieces in her trunk — a bride's muslin underwear trimmed with red and blue featherstitching; long petticoats stiffly flounced with ruffles, and nightgowns long in the sleeve and high in the neck, with ruffles at wrist and throat. The Mexican woman went on hoarsely. The girl folded away her winter's cashmere dress, buttoned up the front and with a white fichu.⁸ She unwrapped and wrapped again in crumpled white tissue the red slippers the old gentleman on the stage had sent her as a wedding present from Philadelphia.

When Ignacita had left, she opened her keepsake box covered with colored shells. The mirror on the inside lid turned back a face as calm as the little golden clouds that hung of an evening over the east to catch the desert sunset. But after she had undressed and put on her nightdress, for a long time she was aware of the soft pound of her heart faintly swaying the bed on its rawhide springs.

At the first sound of Ignacita's hand on the kitchen stove, Nancy Belle sprang out of bed. She dressed on the brown pool of burro skin, the only carpet on her adobe floor. Through the west window she could see the morning star burning like a brilliant candle. It hung, she told herself, over Gunstock and the Beaverhead, where Stephen, at this moment, in their new log ranch house, lay thinking about her.

They ate in the kitchen by lamplight. She had never been so conscious of every detail — the great white cups and saucers, the familiar steel knives, the homey smell of the scorched paper lampshade, the unreadable eyes of her father, Rife, and Ignacita.

---

⁶ *papacito* (pä·pä·sē′tō) : little papa.
⁷ *pobrecita* (pō′brə·sē′tä) : poor little one.
⁸ *fichu* (fish′ōō) : a triangular piece of light material or lace worn about the neck and shoulders like a cape.

Asa Putnam himself carried out the trunk. There was already hay in the wagon, a gunnysack of oats, food in a canned-tomato box and utensils in another, a water keg, a bedroll tied in a wagon sheet, an ax, a bridle, and her own sidesaddle, made to order over a man's tree.[9] Her eyes caught the gleam of a rifle leaning up against the seat in the lantern light. Tethered to the rear of the wagon stood her saddle mare, Fancy, with pricked-up ears. She was going along to their new ranch home. Nancy Belle felt that she was still among intimate things, but outside the little circle of light lay darkness and the unknown.

When she said good-by to her father, he kissed her — something he had not done for years.

"You haven't changed your mind, Nancy Belle?" he asked.

She climbed quickly up over the wheel to the spring seat of the wagon before he might see that she was crying. Rife swung up like a monkey on the other side and pushed the rifle into the crevice behind the seat cushion. The lines tautened and the wagon lurched.

"*Dios* go with you safe to your husband, Nancy Belle!" she heard Ignacita cry after her.

The morning star had set. They moved into a world of silent blackness. Nancy Belle could not see how the horses remained on the trail. When she looked back, the only light in all these square miles of black, unfriendly earth was the yellow window of her father's post.

It was almost a vision, golden and faraway, like all beautiful things. She didn't trust herself to look again.

Two hours later the wagon was a lonely speck of boat rocking in an illimitable sage-green sea beneath the sun. The canvas wagon sheet fastened over the bows was a kind of sail, and eastward the sandy water did not stop rolling till it washed up at the foot of the faintly blue ramparts of the distant Espiritu Range.

Just before they turned west on the cross trail to the Rio Grande, a heavy wagon with a yoke of oxen in front and a cow behind toiled around the crumbling adobe walls of the old, abandoned posthouse. A bearded man and a thin woman with a white face sat on the seat. She held a baby in her arms, and three black-eyed children peered from under the wagon sheet.

The bearded man saluted and stopped his willing team. Rife did

---

[9] *tree*: saddletree, the frame of a saddle.

likewise. The woman spoke first. Her tongue was swift and slightly acid.

"You better turn around and follow us if you want to save your hair!" she called. "Yesterday a sheepherder told us he saw — "

A sharp word from the bearded man caused her to relapse into sullen silence. He asked Rife where he might be going, then climbed down to the trail and said he wanted to talk to him a little. The boy followed reluctantly behind his wagon. Nancy Belle could hear the bearded man's tones coming slow and grave like her father's, while the woman made silent and horribly expressive lip language.

Rife came back, walking stiffly. The bearded man climbed up beside the woman.

"They got to go on," he told her in a low tone, then saluted with his whip. "Good luck, boy! And you, miss!"

Rife raised his whip in stiff acknowledgment. The wagons creaked apart. Nancy Belle saw in front of her the trail to the Rio Grande, little more than a pair of wheel tracks that lost itself on the lonely plain. Rife seemed relieved that she did not ask what the bearded man had said. But it was enough for her not to be able to forget the woman's fearful signs and mouthings and the horror in the curious eyes of the staring children.

Sister and brother talked very little. Nancy Belle saw her brother's eyes keep sweeping the country, scanning the horizon. Bunches of bear grass that might have been feathers pinioned his blue gaze, and clumps of cane cactus that seemed to hold pointed gun barrels. At arroyos [10] thick with *chamiso* [11] and Apache plume she could see his feet tighten on the footboard. Once he pulled out the rifle, but it was only a herd of antelopes moving across the desert sage.

They camped for the night when the sun was still high. Nancy Belle asked no questions as the boy drove far off the trail into a grassy *cañada*.[12] She sang softly to herself as she fried the salt side bacon and put the black coffeepot to boil.

Rife hobbled Anton Chico and the Bar X horse and staked out Fancy close to the wagon.

She pretended not to notice when, before dark, he poured earth

---

[10] *arroyos* (ä·roi′ōs): deep, dry gullies.
[11] *chamiso* (shə·mē′sō) and *Apache plume:* desert shrubs.
[12] *cañada* (kä·nyä′də): glade.

on the fire till not a spark or wisp of smoke remained. Out of one eye she watched him climb the side of the *cañada* and stand long minutes sweeping the country from the ridge, a slight, tense figure against the sullen glow of the sunset.

"It's all right," he said when he came down. "You can go to bed."

"What's all right?" she asked him.

"The horses," he said, turning away, and Nancy Belle felt a stab of pain that so soon this boy must bear a man's responsibilities and tell a man's lies.

She prayed silently on her blankets spread on the hay in the wagon box, and lay down with her head on the sidesaddle, her unread Testament in her hand. She heard Rife unroll his camp bed on the ground beneath the wagon. It was all very strange and hushed without her father. Just to feel the Testament in her hand helped to calm her and to remember the day at the post when she had first met Stephen.

Her father had never let her come in contact with the men of the trail. Always, at the first sign of dust cloud on the horizon, he would tell both children to heap up the chip box, fill the water buckets, and carry saddles and bridles into the house. But this day Asa Putnam and Rife had gone to Fort Sumner. And to Nancy Belle, Uncle Gideon could seldom say no.

It had been a very hot day. She had been sitting in the shade of the earthen bank of the tank, moving her bare feet in the cool water, watching the ripples in the hot south wind. The leaves of the cottonwoods clashed overhead, and she heard nothing until she looked up, and there was a young man on a blue-gray horse, with dust clinging to his hat brim and mustache. His eyes were direct as an eagle's. Firm lines modeled his lean face. But what she noticed most at the time was the little bow tie on his dark shirt.

Instantly she had tucked her bare, wet legs under her red dress. Her face burned with shame, but the young stranger talked to her about her father coolly, as if she, a girl of fifteen, had not been caught barefooted. Then he did what in her mind was a noble thing. When Uncle Gideon came out, he magnificently turned his back for her to run into the house and pull on shoes and stockings.

She thought of Stephen constantly next day and the next. She had grown a little used to the journey without her father now — the still, uncertain nights under the wagon sheet, sitting, lying, listening, waiting; the less uncertain days with the sun on the endless spaces; her never-quiet perch on the high spring seat under the slanted bow; the bumps, creaks, and lumberings of the wagon; the sand sifting softly over the red, turning wheels; all afternoon the sun in their faces; ahead the far haze and heat waves in which were still lost Gunstock and the Rio Grande. Almost she had forgotten the bearded man with the oxen and the curious, detached horror in the eyes of his children.

Since morning of the third day, their progress had been slower. The trail seemed level, except for the heavy breathing of the horses. But when Nancy Belle glanced back, she could see the steady grade they had been climbing. Abruptly, in midafternoon, she found that the long, blue Espiritu Range had disappeared, vanished behind a high pine-clad hill which was its southernmost beginning. It was like the lizard that swallowed itself, a very real lizard. At this moment they were climbing over the lizard's tail.

"Cedars!" Rife said briefly, pointing with the whip to dark sprawling growths ahead.

"You breathe deep up here!" Nancy Belle drank in the light air.

Rife took a sniff, but his blue eyes never ceased to scan the high, black-thatched hill under whose frowning cliff they must pass.

"Soon we can see the Gunstock Mountains," Nancy Belle said.

"And Martin Cross's cabin," Rife nodded. "It's the last water to the Rio Grande."

"He's a nice old man," Nancy Belle ventured casually. "It would be nice to camp by his cabin tonight and talk."

The boy inclined his head. After a few moments he started to whistle softly. At the first cedar Nancy Belle leaped off the moving wagon and climbed back with an evergreen branch. The twig, crushed in her hand, smelled like some store in Santa Fe.

They gained the summit. A breeze was sweeping here from the southwest, and the horses freshened. But Rife had suddenly stopped whistling, and Nancy Belle's sprig of cedar lay on her lap. The frowning cliff of the pine-clad hill was still there. But Martin Cross's cabin had turned to a desolate mound of ashes. As they stared, a gust of wind sent wisps of smoke scurrying from the mound, and a red eye opened to watch them from the embers.

Nancy Belle felt an uncontrollable twitching in the hair roots at the base of her scalp.

Where Martin Cross's eastbound wheel tracks met the trail, Rife reluctantly halted the horses and wet his air-dried lips.

"The water keg's dry, and the horses. If Papa was here, he'd drive over."

"I'm the oldest." Nancy Belle found her voice steady. "I'll ride over. There might be something we can do."

The boy rose quickly. His eyes seemed to remember something his father had said.

"You can drive the wagon over if I wave."

He had thrown her the lines and slipped back through the canvas-covered tunnel of wagon box, picking up Fancy's bridle and the rifle. Barebacked he rode toward the smoldering ashes at the foot of that frowning hill. The chestnut mare's tail and mane streamed like something gold in the wind.

When she looked back to the trail, her eyes were pinioned by a light object in the wheel track ahead of the Bar X horse. It was a long gray feather. Instantly she told herself that it had come from some wild turkey Martin Cross had shot, and yet never had air anywhere become so suddenly horrible and choking as in this canyon.

Rife did not signal her to drive over. She saw him come riding back at full speed. The mare was snorting. As he stopped her at the wagon, her chestnut head kept turning back toward what had once been a cabin. Rife slipped the lead rope about her neck and climbed into the seat with the rifle in his hands.

"The water — you wouldn't want it!" he said thickly. His cheeks, she noticed, were the color of *yeso*.[13]

"Rife" — Nancy Belle touched his arm when she had driven down the canyon — "what did you see at the cabin?"

The boy sat deaf and rigid beside her, eyes staring straight ahead. She saw that his young hands were still tortured around the barrel of his rifle.

Far down on the pitch-dark mesa [14] she stopped the horses in the trail and listened. There were no stars, not a sound but the

---

[13] *yeso* (yā′sō): whitewash.
[14] *mesa* (mā′sə): a flat-topped hill with steeply sloping sides.

flapping of the wagon sheet in the wind and the clank of coffeepot and water bucket under the wagon. Half standing on the footboard, she guided the team off the trail in the intense blackness. Her swift hands helped the trembling boy stake out the mare and hobble the team. They did not light a lantern. Rife declined to eat. Nancy Belle chewed a few dry mouthfuls.

The wind came drawing out of the blackness with a great draft. It hissed through the grass, sucked and tore at the wagon sheet, and whistled through the spokes and brake rigging. Rife did not take his bedroll under the wagon tonight. He drew the ends of the wagon sheet together and lay down in the wagon box near his sister. For a long time they were silent. When she heard his heavy breathing, she lifted the rifle from his chest.

The storm grew. Sand began pelting against the canvas and sifted into the wagon box. An invisible cloud of choking dust found its way into eyes, mouth, ears, and lungs. Nancy Belle laid down the rifle a moment to pull a blanket over the face of the boy. He tossed and muttered pitifully, but he slept on.

Magically the rain, when it came, stopped the sand and dust. The girl drank in the clean-washed air. At daylight she slipped out to the ground. The mesa stretching away in the early light, touched here and there with feathers of mist, would have been beautiful except for a sharp new loneliness. The horses were gone!

At her exclamation, Rife appeared from the wagon box. His shame at having slept through the night was quickly overshadowed by their misfortune.

Together they found where Fancy's stake had been pulled out and dragged. Yards farther on they could tell by Anton Chico's tracks that his hobbles had parted.

Nancy Belle made her brother come back to the wagon and stuff his pockets with cold biscuits and antelope jerky.[15] She said she would have a hot breakfast ready when he returned. The horses, perhaps, were just down in some draw where they had drifted with the wind.

When he had gone with the rifle, she filled the coffeepot from a clearing water hole in the nearest arroyo. She fried potatoes and onions in the long-handled skillet. And when he did not come, she set fresh biscuits in the Dutch oven. Each biscuit held a square of

---

[15] *jerky*: meat cut into strips and dried.

salt side bacon in its top, and as it baked, the fat oozed down and incased it in a kind of glazed tastiness.

At noon she thought she heard a shot. Nowhere could she see him on the endless sweep of mesa. By late afternoon she was still alone. She read her Testament and wondered how many women over the world had read it in hours like this. Sitting in the shadow of the wagon, facing the direction in which he had gone, she looked up every few minutes. But all her eyes could find were cloud shadows racing across the lonely face of the mesa. All she could hear were the desolate cries from the unseen lark sparrows.

Darkness, stillness settled down on the empty land. She climbed back into the wagon and sat on the chuck box, hands rigid on her knees. Again and again she convinced herself that the horses could not have been driven off, or she would have seen the drivers' tracks. When wild, sharp barks shattered the stillness and set wires jerking in her limbs, she talked to herself steadily, but a little meaninglessly, of the post — on and on as the darkness was filled with the ringing and counter-ringing of shrill, cracked yappings — not long tones like a dog's, but incredibly short syllables rising, rising in a mad eternal scale and discord.

"I wish Papa had given me two of the chairs," she repeated. "Mamma said they were post oak from Texas. She said they had got white from scrubbing. I liked the laced rawhide seats with the hair left on. It made them soft to sit on. The seats in the parlor were black. And the ones in the kitchen were red. But I liked the brockle [16] one in my room best."

The insane din around the wagon had become terrific. There were only two or three of the animals, Nancy Belle guessed, but they threw their voices and echoes together to make a score.

"When I was little, I liked to go in the storage room," her voice went on, scarcely intelligible to her own ears. "It was dark and cool, and smelled of burlap and kerosene and whisky, and sweetish with brown sugar. I can see the fat sacks of green coffee. And the round tins of kerosene had boards on the side. The flour sacks were printed: 'Rough and Ready' in red letters. Mamma once used

---

[16] *brockle:* white with black or brown markings.

to make our underwear out of the sacking. I can smell the salt side bacon in the gunny sacks."

She could tell from the sounds that one of the animals was running insanely back and forth near the wagon tongue. She had never noticed before that they yelped both when breathing in and out. Suddenly came silence. It warned her. Instinctively she felt for the ax.

"Nancy Belle!" a boy's far, anxious voice called from the darkness.

She hallooed and leaned out over the tailboard. Three shadowy forms were coming across the mesa in the starlight. Never had horses looked so good.

"Were you scared?" Rife greeted. "Anything bother you?"

"Nothing," Nancy Belle said. "Just coyotes."

"I had to give Fancy her head after it got dark." He slid wearily to the ground. "She brought us straight back to the wagon."

Nancy Belle had wanted to put her arms around her brother. Now she hugged the mare instead. Rife ate fresh biscuits and a tin plate of cold potatoes. He drank several tin cups of coffee. Nancy Belle had slipped the oats-laden, gunnysack *morrals* [17] over the horses' heads.

"I had to walk halfway to the mountain," Rife said.

"Just help hitch up; then you can sleep all night," she promised.

It rained again heavily toward midnight. Flashes of lightning lit the drenched plain. For minutes at a time, quivering fingers of blue phosphorescence stood on the ears of the toiling horses. At dawn Nancy Belle still held the reins as the mud-splashed wagon crawled through a world bathed in early purple splendor.

Four days they had been crossing a hundred and seventy miles of desolate plain. Now the end waited in sight. To the west lay a land broken and tumbled by a mighty hand. Hill shouldered hill and range peered over range, all indescribably violet except where peaks tipped by the unseen sun were far-off flaming towers of copper.

It was a new land, her promised land, Stephen's land, Nancy Belle told herself, where nobody burned cow chips, but snapping cedar and pine, where cold water ran in the wooded canyons, and

---

[17] *morrals* (mō·rals') : feedbags.

the eye, weary of one flat circle the horizon around, had endless geometric designs to refresh the retina.

She sang softly as the wagon lumbered to the edge of a long, shallow valley, brown and uninhabited, running north and south, and desolate except for a winding ribbon that was white with sky and narrowly bordered with green.

"Rife!" Nancy Belle cried. "The Rio Grande!"

An hour afterward they pulled out of the sun into the shade of the long cottonwood *bosque*.[18] Nancy Belle wasn't singing now. Where she remembered wide sandbars glistening with sky and tracked by waterfowl, a chocolate-red flood rolled. Where had been the island, tops of tule and scrub willow swung to and fro with the current.

Anton Chico and the Bar X horse stopped of their own accord in the trail, ears pricked forward at the swirling brown wash. While Rife turned the three horses loose to graze, Nancy Belle silently fried bacon and made coffee. When she had washed skillet and tin dishes in the river, the boy had wired the wagon box to the brake rigging. Now he was tying securely one end of his rope to the center of the coupling pole under the wagon. The other end she knew he would fasten to the inadequate upper horn of the sidesaddle.

"I wouldn't mind the river if I just had my own saddle," he mourned.

They hitched up the team silently. Rife cinched the sidesaddle on Fancy and straddled it, the single stirrup useless to a man. Nancy Belle climbed into the wagon and picked up the lines. The other bank looked as far away as the Espiritu Range from the post. She wanted to say something to her brother — some last word, in case they didn't make it. But all she did was cluck her tongue to the horses.

Gingerly, one slow foot at a time, the team moved down the trail into the water.

"Give 'em their heads!" Rife called from the right rear.

Nancy Belle held a rein in each hand. The red channel water came to the wagon tongue, covered it, reached the horses' bellies. The team wanted to stop. Nancy Belle swung her whip, a stick tipped with a long rawhide lash. The wagon went on. The collars

---

[18] *bosque* (bos′kā): grove of trees.

of both horses kept dipping, but never entirely out of sight. Still barely wading, the slow team reached the firmer footing of the island.

Two thirds of the river still rolled in front of the wagon. The west bank did not seem to have grown much closer, but the east bank behind them had moved far away. The team had to be whipped into the violent current. The water churned white through the wagon wheels. Suddenly both horses appeared to stumble and drop out of sight. Their heads came up wildly, spray blowing from their nostrils. The muddy water hid their legs, but by their bobbing motions Nancy Belle knew that they were swimming.

"Keep 'em pointed up the river!" Rife shouted.

Already she felt the wagon floating. It swung downstream with the current; then Rife's rope from Fancy's saddle snubbed it. The team was snorting with every breath. The Bar X horse swam high in the water, his withers and part of his back out of the chocolate current. But all she could see of Anton Chico were his nose and ears.

Down between her ankles she saw water in the wagon box. She thought of the hemstitched sheets at the bottom of her trunk, the towels and pillowcases crocheted with shell lace. Her blue velvet corduroy dress was probably wet already, and all the cunning print aprons with dust caps to match. River water couldn't hurt the little yellow creamer, sugar bowl, and covered butter dish that had been her mother's. And the gingham dresses could be washed. What worried her were her wedding dress and the keepsake box, especially the tintypes, one of which was Rife in a child's suit edged with black braid, his brand-new hat on his knee.

An older Rife was shouting something behind her now. She couldn't catch the words. Then she found what it was. The neck and withers of Anton Chico raised suddenly out of the water and both horses were scrambling up the steep bank below the ford. Only quick work with the lines saved the wagon from turning over. Safe and blowing on the high bank, the dripping horses shook themselves like puppies.

Nancy Belle couldn't go on until she had opened the trunk and appraised the damage. Rife unsaddled Fancy and drove on with the refreshed team. Behind his slight back in the wagon box, the girl changed to her blue velvet corduroy, which was hardly wet at all.

Then she combed her hair and rolled into a cranny of her trunk the old felt hat that had been too large for her father.

A half-dozen riders met the wagon some miles down the Gunstock Canyon. All of them, Nancy Belle noticed, carried guns. Stephen wore a new white shirt and a gray hat with curled brim she had not seen before. He stood in his stirrups and swung her down in front of him on the saddle, where he kissed her. She had never felt his lips press into such a straight line.

"Papa couldn't come," she said. "So Rife brought me."

She felt Stephen's rigid arm around her.

"We just got in from the Beaverhead ourselves."

"He means they never get any news out in the Beaverhead or he'd 'a' come further east to meet you!" Uncle Billy Williams put in. He had a lovable, squeaky voice. "The Apaches been breakin' loose again. Funny you didn't hear anything over in your country."

Nancy Belle gave him an inscrutable look with her gray eyes. Uncle Billy pulled out his bandanna and blew his nose.

"They got my old friend Judge Hower and his wife and kid in a buggy on the Upper Espiritu. The man that found what they did to 'em, they say, cried like a baby."

"That's all right, Uncle Billy," Stephen said in a gentle voice.

Nancy Belle glanced at Rife. Her brother's face looked gray, the eyes staring as when he had ridden in the late afternoon sunlight from the smoking ashes of Martin Cross's cabin.

Nearly fifty people, gathered in the big parlor upstairs at the hotel, greeted Nancy Belle. An old man whose young black eyes twinkled out of a bearded face said he was glad to see that she had her "hair on straight." Rife stopped with the trunk before driving to the livery, and Stephen's mother showed Nancy Belle to a room to dress.

The guests stopped talking when she came into the parlor in her white wedding dress. Her basque came to a point in the front and back. It fitted like a glove. The silk underskirt came to her instep, and the ruffled overskirt to her knees. She had parted her hair from side to side and brushed the bangs down on her forehead. She felt very lightheaded. The wagon still seemed to be jerking under her.

She glimpsed Rife gazing at her, a rapt expression in his reticent blue eyes. She was glad to see that he had brushed his hair. The brass swinging lamp had been lighted and the dark woodwork of the parlor festooned with evergreen branches. White streamers from the wall met in a papier-mâché bell in one corner. She noticed two children peering eagerly from the dark hall.

Stephen came to her, very straight in a long coat and stand-up collar with a black tie. He led her up beneath the papier-mâché bell. In a sibilant, churchlike whisper, the Gunstock preacher made sure of her full name. Then he coughed and began the ceremony. He had a deep voice, but Nancy Belle didn't hear all of the service. Her mind kept going back to a tall, grave man in a lonely adobe post on the wide Santa Ana plain. And after she had said "I do," her lips moved, but she was not praying for Stephen, her husband.

Camara Laye's initiation into manhood brought with it no conflict between the boy and his parents or between the boy and his society. Such initiations are fixed by time and custom and are accepted without question. In European and American societies, the change from boyhood into manhood is often filled with conflict. Fathers may seem always to be looking for proof that their sons are ready to be men, and the sons may resent the demand that they prove themselves. In the story that follows, an English boy's coming of age is made difficult by his father's attitudes.

The Erne from the Coast

T. O. BEACHCROFT

1

"Where's Harry?" Mr. Thorburn came out of the back of the farmhouse. He stood in the middle of the well-kept farmyard. "Here, Harry!" he shouted. "Hi, Harry!"

He stood leaning on a stick and holding a letter in his hand, as he looked around the farmyard.

Mr. Thorburn was a red-faced, powerful man; he wore knee breeches and black leather gaiters. His face and well-fleshed body told you at a glance that Thorburn's Farm had not done too badly during the twenty years of his married life.

Harry, a fair-haired boy, came running across the yard.

"Harry," said the farmer to his son, "here's a letter come for old Michael. It will be about this visit he's to pay to his sick brother. Nice time of year for this to happen, I must say. You'd better take the letter to him at once."

"Where to?" said Harry.

"He's up on the hill, of course," said the farmer. "In his hut, or with the sheep somewhere. Your own brains could have told you that. Can't you ever use them? Go on, now."

"Right," said Harry. He turned to go.

"Don't take all day," said his father.

Mr. Thorburn stood looking after his son. He leaned heavily on the thorn stick which he always carried. Harry went through the gate in the low gray wall which ran around one side of the yard, where there were no buildings. Directly he left the farmyard, he began to climb. Thorburn's Farm was at the end of a valley. Green fields lay in front of it, and a wide road sloped gently down to the village a mile away; behind, the hill soared up, and high on the ridge of the hill was Michael's hut, three miles off, and climbing all the way.

Harry was thirteen, very yellow-haired and blue-eyed. He was a slip of a boy. It seemed unlikely that he could ever grow into such a stolid, heavy man as his father. Mr. Thorburn was every pound of fourteen stone,[1] as the men on the farm could have told you the day he broke his leg and they had to carry him back to the farmhouse on a hurdle.

Harry started off far too fast, taking the lower slopes almost at a run. His body was loose in its movements, and coltish, and by the time the real work began he was already tiring. However, the April day was fresh and rainy, and the cold of it kept him going. Gray gusts and showers swept over the hillside, and between them, with changing light, came faint gleams of sunshine, so that the shadows of the clouds raced along the hill beside him. Presently he cleared the gorse and heather, and came out on to the open hillside, which was bare except for short, tussocky grass. His home began to look far off beneath him. He could see his mother walking down toward the village with one of the dogs, and the baker's cart coming up from the village toward her. The fields were brown and green around the farmhouse, and the buildings were gray, with low stone walls.

He stopped several times to look back on the small distant farm. It took him well over an hour to reach the small hut where Michael lived by day and slept during most nights throughout the lambing season. He was not in his hut, but after a few minutes' search Harry found him. Michael was sitting without movement, watching the sheep and talking to his gray and white dog. He had a sack across his shoulders, which made him look rather like a rock with gray lichen on it. He looked up at Harry without moving.

"It's a hildy wildy day," he said, "but there'll be a glent of sunsheen yet."

---

[1] *stone:* a stone equals fourteen pounds, British weight.

Harry handed Michael the letter. Michael looked at it, and opened it very slowly, and spread the crackling paper out on his knee with brown hands. Harry watched him for some minutes as he studied the letter in silence.

"Letter'll be aboot my brother," said Michael at length. "I'm to goa and see him." He handed the letter to Harry. "Read it, Harry," he said. Harry read the letter to him twice.

"Tell thy dad," said Michael, "I'll be doon at farm i' the morn. Happen I'll be away three days. And tell him new lamb was born last neet, but it's sickly."

They looked at the small white bundle that lay on the grass beside its mother, hardly moving.

" 'T'll pick up," said Michael. He slowly stood and looked around at the distance.

Michael had rather long hair; it was between gray and white in color, and it blew in the wind. It was about the hue of an old sheep's skull that has lain out on the bare mountain. Michael's clothes and face and hair made Harry feel that he had slowly faded out on the hillside. He was all the color of rain on the stones and last year's bracken.

"It'll make a change," said Michael, "going off and sleeping in a bed."

"Goodbye," said Harry. "You'll be down at the farm tomorrow, then?"

"Aw reet," said Michael.

"Aw reet," said Harry.

Harry went slowly back to the farm. The rain had cleared off, and the evening was sunny, with a watery light, by the time he was home. Michael had been right. Harry gave his father the message, and told him about the lamb.

"It's a funny thing," said Harry, "that old Michael can't even read."

"Don't you be so smart," said Mr. Thorburn. "Michael knows a thing or two you don't. You don't want to go muckering about with an old fellow like Michael — best shepherd I've ever known."

Harry went away feeling somewhat abashed. Lately it seemed his father was always down on him, telling him he showed no sign of sense; telling him he ought to grow up a bit; telling him he was more like seven than thirteen.

He went to the kitchen. This was a big, stone-floored room with a huge plain table, where the whole household and several of the farm hands could sit down to dinner or tea at the same time. His mother and his aunt from the village were still lingering over their teacups, but there was no one else in the room except a small tortoise-shell cat, which was pacing around them asking for milk in a loud voice. The yellow evening light filled the room. His mother gave him tea and ham and bread and butter, and he ate it in silence, playing with the cat as he did so.

2

Next morning at nine o'clock there was a loud rap with a stick at the kitchen door, and there by the pump, with the hens running around his legs, stood Michael.

"Good morning, Mrs. Thorburn," he said. "Is Measter about?"

"Come on in with you," said Mrs. Thorburn, "and have a good hot cup o' tea. Have you eaten this morning?"

Michael clanked into the kitchen, his hobnails striking the flags, and he sat down at one end of the table.

"Aye," he said, "I've eaten, Missus. I had a good thoom-bit [2] when I rose up, but a cup of tea would be welcome."

As he drank the tea, Mr. Thorburn came in, bringing Harry with him. Michael, thought Harry, always looked rather strange when he was down in the village or in the farmhouse; rather as a pile of bracken or an armful of leaves would look if it were emptied out onto the parlor floor.

Michael talked to Mr. Thorburn about the sheep; about the new lamb; about young Bob, his nephew, who was coming over from another farm to look after the sheep while he was away.

"Tell en to watch new lamb," said Michael; "it's creachy.[3] I've put en in my little hut, and owd sheep is looking roun' t' doorway."

After his cup of tea Michael shook hands all around. Then he set off down to the village, where he was going to fall in with a lift.

Soon after he had gone, Bob arrived at the farm. He was a tall young man with a freckled face and red hair, big-boned and very

---
[2] *thoom-bit:* thumb-sized amount.
[3] *creachy:* sickly.

gentle in his voice and movements. He listened to all Mr. Thorburn's instructions and then set out for the shepherd's hut.

However, it seemed that Mr. Thorburn's luck with his shepherds was dead out. For the next evening, just as it was turning dark, Bob walked into the farmhouse kitchen. His face was tense with pain, and he was nursing his left arm with his right hand. Harry saw the ugly distorted shape and swelling at the wrist. Bob had fallen and broken the wrist earlier in the day, and by evening the pain had driven him back.

"I'm sorry, Mr. Thorburn," he kept on saying. "I'm a big fule."

The sheep had to be left for that night. Next morning it was again a cold, windy day, and clouds the color of gunmetal raced over the hill. The sun broke through fitfully, filling the valley with a steel-blue light in which the green grass looked vivid. Mr. Thorburn decided to send Harry out to the shepherd's hut for the day and night.

"Happen old Michael will be back some time tomorrow," he said. "You can look to the sheep, Harry, and see to that sick lamb for us. It's a good chance to make yourself useful."

Harry nodded.

"You can feed the lamb. Bob said it didn't seem to suck enough, and you can let me know if anything else happens. And you can keep an eye on the other lambs and see they don't get over the edges. There's no need to fold them at night; just let the dog round them up and see the flock is near the hut."

"There's blankets and everything in the hut, Harry," said Mrs. Thorburn, "and a spirit lamp to make tea. You can't come to harm."

Harry set off up the hill and began to climb. Out on the hilltop it was very lonely, and the wind was loud and gusty, with sudden snatches of rain. The sheep kept near the wooden hut most of the time; it was built in the lee of the ridge, and the best shelter was to be found near it. Harry looked after the sick lamb and brewed himself tea. He had Tassie, the gray and white sheepdog, for company. Time did not hang heavy. When evening came he rounded up the sheep and counted them, and, true to advice that Michael had given him, he slept in his boots as a true shepherd does, warmly wrapped up in the rugs.

He was awakened as soon as it was light by the dog barking. He went out in the gray dawn light, and found a rustle and agitation among the sheep. Tassie ran to him and back toward the sheep. The sheep were starting up alert, and showed a tendency to scatter. Harry looked around, wondering what the trouble was. Then he saw. A bird was hovering over the flock, and it was this that had attracted the sheep's attention. But what bird was it? It hovered like a hawk, soaring on outstretched wings; yet it was much too big for a hawk. As the bird came nearer Harry was astonished at its size. Once or twice it approached and then went soaring and floating away again. It was larger than any bird he had ever seen before — brownish in color, with a gray head and a hawk's beak.

Suddenly the bird began to drop as a hawk drops. A knot of sheep dashed apart. Tassie rushed toward the bird, his head down and his tail streaming out behind him. Harry followed. This must be an eagle, he thought. He saw it, looking larger still now it was on the ground, standing with outstretched wings over a lamb.

Tassie attacked, snarling in rage. The eagle rose at him. It struck at him with its feet and a flurry of beating wings. The dog was thrown back. He retreated slowly, snarling savagely as he went, his tail between his legs. He was frightened now, and uncertain what to do.

The eagle turned back to the lamb, took it in its talons again, and began to rise. It could not move quickly near the ground, and Harry came up with it. At once the eagle put the lamb on a rock and turned on him. He saw its talons driving toward his face, claws and spurs of steel — a stroke could tear your eyes out. He put up his arms in fear, and he felt the rush of wings around his face. With his arm above his head, he sank on one knee.

When he looked up again, the eagle was back on the lamb. It began to fly with long slow wingbeats. At first it scarcely rose, and flew with the lamb almost on the ground.

Harry ran, throwing a stone. He shouted. Tassie gave chase, snapping at the eagle as it went. But the eagle was working toward a chasm, a sheer drop in the hillside where no one could follow it. In another moment it was floating in the air, clear and away. Then it rose higher, and headed toward the coast, which was a few miles away over the hill.

Harry stood and watched it till it was out of sight. When it was gone, he turned and walked slowly back to the hut. There was not a sound to be heard now except the sudden rushes of wind. The hillside was bare and coverless except for the scattered black rocks. Tassie walked beside him. The dog was very subdued and hardly glanced to right or left.

It took some time to round the sheep up, or to find, at least, where the various parts of the flock had scattered themselves. The sick lamb and its mother had been enclosed all this time in a small fold near the hut. The ewe was still terrified.

An hour later Harry set off down the mountain side to the farm. Tassie looked after him doubtfully. He ran several times after him, but Harry sent him back to the hut.

It was the middle of the morning when Harry came back to the farmyard again. His father was standing in the middle of the yard, leaning on his stick, and giving advice to one of his cowmen. He broke off when he saw Harry come in through the gate, and walk toward him across the farmyard.

"Well," he said, "anything wrong, Harry? I thought you were going to stay till Michael came back."

"We've lost a lamb," said Harry, breathlessly. "It's been carried off by an eagle. It must have been an eagle."

"An eagle?" said Mr. Thorburn. He gave a laugh which mocked Harry. "Why didn't you stop it?"

"I tried," said Harry. "But I . . ."

Mr. Thorburn was in a bad mood. He had sold some heifers the day before at a disappointing price. He had had that morning a letter from the builders about repairs to some of the farm buildings, and there was work to be done which he could hardly afford. He was worried about Michael's absence. He felt as if the world were bearing down on him, and he had too many burdens to support.

He suddenly shouted at Harry, and his red face turned darker red.

"That's a lie!" he said. "There's been no eagle here in my lifetime. What's happened? Go on — tell me."

Harry stood before him. He looked at his father, but said nothing.

"You've lost that lamb," said Thorburn. "Let it fall down a hole or something. Any child from the village could have watched those sheep for a day. Then you're frightened, and come back here and lie to me."

Harry still said nothing.

"Come here," said Thorburn suddenly. He caught him by the arm and turned him around. "I'll teach you not to lie to me," he said. He raised his stick and hit Harry as hard as he could; then again and again.

"It's true," began Harry, and then cried out with pain at the blows.

At the third or fourth blow he wrenched himself away. Thorburn let him go. Harry walked away as fast as he could, through the gate and out of the yard, without looking around.

"Next time it will be a real beating," his father shouted after him. "Bring the eagle back, and then I'll believe you."

3

As soon as Harry was through the gate, he turned behind one of the barns where he was out of sight from the yard. He stood trembling and clenching his fists. He found there were tears on his face, and he forced himself not to cry. The blows hurt, yet they did not hurt very seriously. He would never have cried for that. But it had been done in front of another man. The other man had looked on, and he and his father had been laughing as he had almost run away. Harry clenched his fists; even now they were still talking about him.

He began to walk and then run up the hillside toward the hut. When he reached it, he was exhausted. He flung himself on the mattress and punched it again and again and clenched his teeth.

The day passed and nobody came from the farm. He began to feel better, and presently a new idea struck him, and with it a new hope. He prayed now that old Michael would not return today; that he would be able to spend another night alone in the hut; and that the eagle would come back next morning and attack the sheep again, and give him one more chance.

Harry went out and scanned the gray sky, and then knelt down on the grass and prayed for the eagle to come. Tassie, the gray and white sheepdog, looked at him questioningly. Soon it was getting dark, and he walked about the hill and rounded up the sheep. He counted the flock, and all was well. Then he looked around for a weapon. There was no gun in the hut, but he found a thick stave tipped with metal, part of some broken tool that had been thrown aside. He poised the stave in his hand and swung it; it was just a good weight to hit with. He would have to go straight at the eagle without hesitation and break its skull. After thinking about this for some time, he made himself tea, and ate some bread and butter and cold meat.

Down at the farm Mr. Thorburn in the evening told his wife what had happened. He was quite sure there had been no eagle. Mrs. Thorburn did not say much, but she said it was an extraordinary thing for Harry to have said. She told her husband that he ought not to have beaten the boy, but should have found out what the trouble really was.

"But I dare say there is no great harm done," she ended, philosophically.

Harry spent a restless night. He slept and lay awake by turns, but, sleeping or waking, he was tortured by the same images. He saw all the events of the day before. He saw how the eagle had first appeared above him; how it had attacked; how it had driven off Tassie and then him. He remembered his fear, and he planned again just how he could attack the eagle when it came back. Then he thought of himself going down toward the farm and he saw again the scene with his father.

All night long he saw these pictures and other scenes from his life. In every one of them he had made some mistake; he had made himself look ridiculous, and grown men had laughed at him. He had failed in strength or in common sense; he was always disappointing himself and his father. He was too young for his age. He was still a baby.

So the night passed. Early in the morning he heard Tassie barking.

He jumped up, fully clothed, and ran outside the hut. The cold air made him shiver; but he saw at once that his prayer had been answered. There was the eagle, above him, and already dropping down toward the sheep. It floated, poised on huge wings. The flock stood nervously huddled. Suddenly, as before, the attacker plunged toward them. They scattered, running in every direction. The eagle followed, and swooped on one weakly running lamb. At once it tried to rise again, but its heavy wingbeats took it along the earth. Near the ground it seemed cumbersome and awkward. Tassie was after it like a flash; Harry seized his weapon, the stave tipped with iron, and followed. When Tassie caught up with the eagle it turned and faced him, standing over the lamb.

Harry, as he ran, could see blood staining the white wool of the lamb's body; the eagle's wings were half spread out over it, and moving slowly. The huge bird was grayish-brown with a white head and tail. The beak was yellow, and the legs yellow and scaly.

It lowered its head, and with a fierce movement threatened Tassie; then, as the dog approached, it began to rock and stamp from foot to foot in a menacing dance; then it opened its beak and gave its fierce, yelping cry. Tassie hung back, his ears flattened against his head, snarling, creeping by inches toward the eagle; he was frightened, but he was brave. Then he ran in to attack.

The eagle left the lamb. With a lunging spring it aimed heavily at Tassie. It just cleared the ground and beat about Tassie with its wings, hovering over him. Tassie flattened out his body to the earth and turned his head upward with snapping jaws. But the eagle was over him and on him, its talons plunged into his side, and a piercing scream rang out. The eagle struck deliberately at the dog's skull three times; the beak's point hammered on his head, striking downward and sideways. Tassie lay limp on the ground, and, where his head had been, a red mixture of blood and brains flowed on the grass. When Harry took his eyes away from the blood, the eagle was standing on the lamb again.

Harry approached the eagle slowly, step by step. He gripped his stick firmly as he came. The eagle put its head down. It rocked on its feet as if preparing to leap. Behind the terrific beak, sharp as metal, was a shallow head, flat and broad as a snake's, glaring with light yellow un-animal eyes. The head and neck made weaving movements toward him.

At a pace or two from the eagle Harry stood still. In a second he would make a rush. He could break the eagle's skull, he told himself, with one good blow; then he could avenge Tassie and stand up to his father.

But he waited too long. The eagle tried to rise, and with its heavy sweeping beats was beginning to gain speed along the ground. Harry ran, stumbling over the uneven ground, among boulders and outcroppings of rock, trying to strike at the eagle as he went. But as soon as the eagle was in the air it was no longer heavy and clumsy. There was a sudden rush of wings and buffeting about his head as the eagle turned to drive him off. For a second he saw the talons sharp as metal, backed by the metal strength of the legs, striking at his face. He put up his arm. At once it was seared with a red-hot pain, and he could see the blood rush out.

He stepped back, and back again. The eagle, after this one fierce swoop at him, went around in a wide, low circle, and returned to the lamb. Harry saw that his coat sleeve was in ribbons, and that blood was running off the ends of his fingers and falling to the ground.

He stood panting; the wind blew across the empty high ground. The sheep had vanished from sight. Tassie lay dead near by, and he was utterly alone on the hills. There was nobody to watch what he did. The eagle might hurt him, but it could not jeer at him. He attacked it again, but already the eagle with its heavy wingbeats had cleared the ground; this time it took the lamb with it. Harry saw that it meant to fly, as it had flown yesterday, to an edge; and then out into the free air over the chasm, and over the valley far below.

Harry gave chase, stumbling over the broken ground and between the boulders — striking at the eagle as he went, trying to beat it down before it could escape. The eagle was hampered by his attack; and suddenly it swooped onto a projection of rock and turned again to drive him off. Harry was now in a bad position. The eagle stood on a rock at the height of his own shoulders, with the lamb beside it. It struck at his chest with its talons, beating its wings as it did so. Harry felt clothes and flesh being torn; buffeting blows began about his head; but he kept close to the eagle and struck at it again. He did not want simply to frighten it away, but to kill it. The eagle fought at first simply to drive Harry off; then, as he continued to attack, it became ferocious.

Harry saw his only chance was to keep close to the eagle and beat it down; but already it was at the height of his face. It struck at him from above, driving its steel claws at him, beating its wings about him. He was dazed by the buffeting which went on and on all around him; then with an agonizing stab he felt the claws seize and pierce his shoulder and neck. He struck upward desperately and blindly. As the eagle drove its beak at his head, his stick just turned the blow aside. The beak struck a glancing blow off the stick, and tore away his eyebrow.

Harry found that something was blinding him, and he felt a new sickening fear that already one of his eyes was gone. The outspread beating wings and weight of the eagle dragged him about, and he nearly lost his footing. He had forgotten, now, that he was proving anything to his father; he was fighting for his eyes. Three times he fended off the hammer stroke of the beak, and at these close quarters the blows of his club found their mark. He caught the eagle's head each time, and the bird was half-stunned.

Harry, reeling and staggering, felt the grip of the claws gradually loosen, and almost unbelievably the body of his enemy sagged, half fluttering to the ground. With a sudden spurt of new strength, Harry attacked, and rained blows on the bird's skull. The eagle struggled, and he followed, beating it down among the rocks. At last the eagle's movements stopped. He saw its skull was broken, and that it lay dead.

He stood for many minutes panting and unmoving, filled with a tremendous excitement; then he sat on a boulder. The fight had taken him near a steep edge a long way from the body of Tassie.

His wounds began to ache and burn. The sky and the horizon spun around him, but he forced himself to be firm and collected. After a while he stooped down and hoisted the eagle onto his shoulder. The wings dropped loosely down in front and behind. He set off toward the farm.

4

When he reached his home, the low gray walls, the plowed fields, and the green pasture fields were swimming before his eyes in a dizzy pattern. It was still the early part of the morning, but there was plenty of life in the farmyard, as usual. Some cows were being driven out. One of the carthorses was standing harnessed to a heavy wagon. Harry's father was talking to the carter and looking at the horse's leg.

When they saw Harry come toward them they waited, unmoving. They could hardly see at first who or what it was. Harry came up and dropped the bird at his father's feet. His coat was gone. His shirt hung in bloodstained rags about him; one arm was caked in blood; his right eyebrow hung in a loose flap, with the blood still oozing stickily down his cheek.

"Harry!" said Thorburn, catching him by the arm as he reeled.

He led the boy into the kitchen. There they gave him a glass of brandy and sponged him with warm water. There was a deep long wound in his left forearm. His chest was crisscrossed with cuts. The flesh was torn away from his neck where the talons had sunk in.

Presently the doctor came. Harry's wounds began to hurt like fire, but he talked excitedly. He was happier than he had ever been in his life. Everybody on the farm came in to see him and to see the eagle's body.

All day his father hung about him, looking into the kitchen every half hour. He said very little, but asked Harry several times how he felt. "Are you aw reet?" he kept saying. Once he took a cup of tea from his wife and carried it across the kitchen in order to give it to Harry with his own hands.

Later in the day old Michael came back, and Harry told him the whole story. Michael turned the bird over. He said it was an erne, a white-tailed sea eagle from the coast. He measured the wing span, and it was seven and a half feet. Michael had seen two or three when he was a boy — always near the coast — but this one, he said, was easily the largest.

Three days later Mr. Thorburn took Harry, still stiff and bandaged, down to the village inn. There he set him before a blazing fire all the evening, and in the presence of men from every cottage and farm Thorburn praised his son. He bought him a glass of beer and made Harry tell the story of his fight to everyone.

As he told it, Thorburn sat by him, hearing the story himself each time, making certain that Harry missed nothing about his struggle. Afterward every man drank Harry's health, and clapped Thorburn on the back and told him he ought to be proud of his son.

Later, in the silent darkness, they walked back to the farm again, and neither of them could find anything to say. Harry wondered if his father might not refer to the beating and apologize. Thorburn moved around the house, raking out fires and locking up. Then he picked up the lamp and, holding it above his head, led the way upstairs.

"Good night, Harry," said his father at last, as he took him to his bedroom door. "Are you aw reet?"

His father held the lamp up and looked into Harry's face. As the lamplight fell on it, he nodded. He said nothing more.

"Aye," said Harry, as he turned into his bedroom door, "I'm aw reet."

In the previous selections in "Coming of Age," young people entered adulthood either in a public ceremony or by meeting an important challenge. In each case the initiation was a kind of trial, accompanied by intense action. Sometimes, however, the achievement of maturity is a quiet change, a new awareness of the adult world.

Christmas

FLOYD DELL

That fall, before it was discovered that the soles of both my shoes were worn clear through, I still went to Sunday school. And one time the Sunday-school superintendent made a speech to all the classes. He said that these were hard times and that many poor children weren't getting enough to eat. It was the first time that I had heard about it. He asked everybody to bring some food for the poor children next Sunday. I felt very sorry for the poor children.

Also little envelopes were distributed to all the classes. Each little boy and girl was to bring money for the poor, next Sunday. The pretty Sunday-school teacher explained that we were to write our names, or have our parents write them, up in the left-hand corner of the little envelopes. . . . I told my mother all about it when I came home. And my mother gave me, the next Sunday, a small bag of potatoes to carry to Sunday school. I supposed the poor children's mothers would make potato soup out of them. . . . Potato soup was good. My father, who was quite a joker, would always say, as if he were surprised, "Ah! I see we have some nourishing soup today!" It was so good that we had it every day. My father was at home all day long and every day, now; and I liked that, even if he was grumpy as he sat reading General Grant's *Memoirs*. I had my parents all to myself, too; the others were away. My oldest brother was in Quincy, and memory does not reveal where the others were: perhaps with relatives in the country.

Taking my small bag of potatoes to Sunday school, I looked

around for the poor children; I was disappointed not to see them. I had heard about poor children in stories. But I was told just to put my contribution with the others on the big table in the side room.

I had brought with me the little yellow envelope, with some money in it and sealed up. My mother wouldn't tell me how much money she had put in it, but it felt like several dimes. Only she wouldn't let me write my name on the envelope. I had learned to write my name, and I was proud of being able to do it. But my mother said firmly, *no*, I must *not* write my name on the envelope; she didn't tell me why. On the way to Sunday school I had pressed the envelope against the coins until I could tell what they were; they weren't dimes but pennies.

When I handed in my envelope, my Sunday-school teacher noticed that my name wasn't on it, and she gave me a pencil; I could write my own name, she said. So I did. But I was confused because my mother had said not to; and when I came home, I confessed what I had done. She looked distressed. "I told you not to!" she said. But she didn't explain why. . . .

I didn't go back to school that fall. My mother said it was because I was sick. I did have a cold the week that school opened; I had been playing in the gutters and had got my feet wet because there were holes in my shoes. My father cut insoles out of cardboard, and I wore those in my shoes. As long as I had to stay in the house anyway, they were all right.

I stayed cooped up in the house, without any companionship. We didn't take a Sunday paper any more, but the *Barry Adage* came every week in the mails; and though I did not read small print, I could see the Santa Clauses and holly wreaths in the advertisements.

There was a calendar in the kitchen. The red days were Sundays and holidays; and that red 25 was Christmas. (It was on a Monday, and the two red figures would come right together in 1893; but this represents research in the *World Almanac*, not memory.) I knew when Sunday was because I could look out of the window and see the neighbor's children, all dressed up, going to Sunday school. I knew just when Christmas was going to be.

But there was something queer! My father and mother didn't say a word about Christmas. And once, when I spoke of it, there was a strange silence, so I didn't say anything more about it. But I wondered and was troubled. Why didn't they say anything about it? Was what I had said I wanted (memory refuses to supply that detail) too expensive?

I wasn't arrogant and talkative now. I was silent and frightened. What was the matter? Why didn't my father and mother say anything about Christmas? As the day approached, my chest grew tighter with anxiety.

Now it was the day before Christmas. I couldn't be mistaken. But not a word about it from my father and mother. I waited in painful bewilderment all day. I had supper with them, and was allowed to sit up for an hour. I was waiting for them to say something. "It's time for you to go to bed," my mother said gently. I *had* to say something.

"This is Christmas Eve, isn't it?" I asked, as if I didn't know. My father and mother looked at one another. Then my mother looked away. Her face was pale and stony. My father cleared his throat, and his face took on a joking look. He pretended he hadn't known it was Christmas Eve, because he hadn't been reading the papers. He said he would go downtown and find out.

My mother got up and walked out of the room. I didn't want my father to have to keep on being funny about it, so I got up and went to bed. I went by myself without having a light. I undressed in the dark and crawled into bed.

I was numb. As if I had been hit by something. It was hard to breathe. I ached all through. I was stunned — with finding out the truth.

My body knew before my mind quite did. In a minute, when I could think, my mind would know. And as the pain in my body ebbed, the pain in my mind began. I *knew*. I couldn't put it into words yet. But I knew why I had taken only a little bag of potatoes to Sunday school that fall. I knew why there had been only pennies in my little yellow envelope. I knew why I hadn't gone to school that fall — why I hadn't any new shoes — why we had been living on potato soup all winter. All these things, and others, many others, fitted themselves together in my mind, and meant something.

Then the words came into my mind and I whispered them into the darkness:

"*We're poor!*"

That was it. I was one of those poor children I had been sorry for, when I heard about them in Sunday school. My mother hadn't told me. My father was out of work, and we hadn't any money. That was why there wasn't going to be any Christmas at our house.

Then I remembered something that made me squirm with shame — a boast. (Memory will not yield this up. Had I said to some nice little boy, "I'm going to be President of the United States"? Or to a nice little girl: "I'll marry you when I grow up"? It was some boast as horribly shameful to remember.)

"*We're poor.*" There in bed in the dark, I whispered it over and over to myself. I was making myself get used to it. (Or — just torturing myself, as one pressed the tongue against a sore tooth? No, memory says not like that — but to keep myself from ever being such a fool again: suffering now, to keep this awful thing from ever happening again. Memory is clear on that; it was more like pulling the tooth, to get it over with — never mind the pain, this will be the end!)

It wasn't so bad, now that I knew. *I just hadn't known!* I had thought all sorts of foolish things; that I was going to Ann Arbor [1] — going to be a lawyer — going to make speeches in the Square, going to be President! Now I knew better.

I had wanted (something) for Christmas. I didn't want it, now. I didn't want anything.

I lay there in the dark, feeling the cold emotion of renunciation. (The tendrils of desire unfold their clasp on the outer world of objects, withdraw, shrivel up. Wishes shrivel up, turn black, die. It is like that.)

It hurt. But nothing would ever hurt again. I would never let myself want anything again.

I lay there stretched out straight and stiff in the dark, my fists clenched hard upon Nothing. . . .

In the morning it had been like a nightmare that is not clearly remembered — that one wishes to forget. Though I hadn't hung up any stocking, there was one hanging at the foot of my bed. A bag of popcorn and a lead pencil, for me. They had done the best they could, now they realized that I knew about Christmas. But they needn't have thought they had to. I didn't want anything.

---

[1] *Ann Arbor:* that is, to the University of Michigan.

By the time Claude Brown was eleven years old he had been in trouble with the law and been in and out of reform schools several times. This brief episode is from his autobiography, Manchild in the Promised Land. *It takes place just before Claude, convicted of petty thefts, is to leave for the Wiltwyck School for Boys, a school for difficult children in New York State. Knoxie is his friend.*

A Goodbye Speech

CLAUDE BROWN

It was snowing real hard outside. Mama was so nervous she tied my tie about six times before getting it right. I was all set to go downtown to an office to meet somebody who was going to take me upstate. Mama had locked my shoes in the closet the night before to make sure I didn't get out of the house while she was getting the other kids ready for school. Even though I couldn't get my shoes, Mama made me stay in the front room till we were ready to go. And every chance she got, Mama would come in the front room to check on me. She knew that if I had enough time, I would get my shoes out of that closet somehow. When Mama couldn't come out of the kitchen, she would call to me and ask me what I was doing. Every time she asked, I told her the real truth, that I wasn't doing anything.

It seemed like I had already started serving my time that morning, sitting there all dressed up, with everything on but my shoes and hat, in the room farthest away from the door. I was just sitting there at the window watching all that snow falling and feeling kind of sad. The snow just kept on falling, and I knew it was covering more than just the sidewalk. I knew Knoxie was waiting for me to come to his house, and I knew I wasn't going to make it, but I didn't care. Maybe it was because I knew what I would be doing for the next few days if I went to Knoxie's house. And I was wondering what would happen if I went to that office. Who would I meet there? Would there be something to steal there? Maybe I didn't care about not meeting Knoxie because I knew I couldn't get my shoes out of the closet.

Watching the snow fall made me think about a lot of things. I thought about what Dad had said the night before. He knew he would already have left for work when I got up that morning, so he gave me his goodbye speech the night before. I never used to listen to Dad when he talked to me — I never thought he had anything to say worth listening to — but I always used to make believe I was listening to him. But that night, I didn't even pretend I was thinking about what he said.

Dad started telling me that it would be a long time before I would see the streets of New York City again. And that maybe when I got back, I would appreciate them enough to stop all that damn stealing and stay home like somebody with some sense. He talked on and on like that. Then he said something. Dad asked me if I remembered when I used to get up every Sunday morning to go out and watch Mr. Jimmy win money from people who were dumb enough to go hunting for a pea that wasn't there. I told him I remembered. Then he asked me if I knew what a fool was. I said a fool was somebody stupid. Dad said I was right, but there was more to it than that. He said it takes a stupid person to keep looking for something that is never there. Dad told me to go into the kitchen and get a black-eyed pea.

When I came back with the pea, Dad had set up the card table and was sitting at it with three half-nutshells in front of him. I gave him the pea, and Dad started switching the shells around the way Mr. Jimmy used to do. It looked like Dad was doing it real slow, and I was sure I knew where the pea was all the time. I never knew Dad could do that trick, and even then I was sure he was doing it too slow. When Dad stopped sliding the nutshells around, he told me to pick up the one I thought the pea was under. We did this ten times. Each time, I was sure the pea was under the shell I picked up. Ten times I picked the wrong shell. After I made that last wrong pick, Dad looked at me and just kept shaking his head for a little while. Then he said, "That's jis what you been doin' all your life, lookin' for a pea that ain't there. And I'm mighty 'fraid that's how you gon end your whole life, lookin' for that pea."

As a child comes of age, his relationship with his father is crucial. He needs the kind of love and sympathetic support that Camara Laye and Rife Putnam received from their fathers and that Harry Thorburn and Telemachus received almost too late. How can a father best advise a son who is growing up? Here is how two poets answer that question.

Any Man's Advice to His Son

KENNETH FEARING

If you have lost the radio beam, then guide yourself by the sun or the stars.
(By the North Star at night, and in daytime by the compass and the sun.)
Should the sky be overcast and there are neither stars nor a sun, then steer by dead reckoning.
If the wind and direction and speed are not known, then trust to your wits and your luck.

Do you follow me? Do you understand? Or is this too difficult to learn?
But you must and you will, it is important that you do,
Because there may be troubles even greater than these that I have said.

Because, remember this: Trust no man fully.
Remember: If you must shoot at another man squeeze, do not jerk the trigger. Otherwise you may miss and die, yourself, at the hand of some other man's son.
And remember: In all this world there is nothing so easily squandered, or once gone, so completely lost as life.

I tell you this because I remember you when you were small,
And because I remember all your monstrous infant boasts and lies,
And the way you smiled, and how you ran and climbed, as no one else quite did, and how you fell and were bruised,
And because there is no other person, anywhere on earth, who remembers these things as clearly as I do now.

A Father Sees a Son Nearing Manhood

CARL SANDBURG

A father sees a son nearing manhood.
What shall he tell that son?
"Life is hard; be steel; be a rock."
And this might stand him for the storms
and serve him for humdrum and monotony
and guide him amid sudden betrayals
and tighten him for slack moments.
"Life is a soft loam; be gentle; go easy."
And this too might serve him.
Brutes have been gentled where lashes failed. 10
The growth of a frail flower in a path up
has sometimes shattered and split a rock.
A tough will counts. So does desire.
So does a rich soft wanting.
Without rich wanting nothing arrives.
Tell him too much money has killed men
and left them dead years before burial:
the quest of lucre° beyond a few easy needs
has twisted good enough men
sometimes into dry thwarted worms. 20
Tell him time as a stuff can be wasted.
Tell him to be a fool every so often
and to have no shame over having been a fool
yet learning something out of every folly
hoping to repeat none of the cheap follies
thus arriving at intimate understanding
of a world numbering many fools.
Tell him to be alone often and get at himself
and above all tell himself no lies about himself,
whatever the white lies and protective fronts 30
he may use amongst other people.

---

18. *lucre* (lōō′kər): money or riches.

Tell him solitude is creative if he is strong
and the final decisions are made in silent rooms.
Tell him to be different from other people
if it comes natural and easy being different.
Let him have lazy days seeking his deeper motives.
Let him seek deep for where he is a born natural.
    Then he may understand Shakespeare
    and the Wright brothers, Pasteur, Pavlov,
    Michael Faraday° and free imaginations   40
bringing changes into a world resenting change.
    He will be lonely enough
    to have time for the work
    he knows as his own.

---

40. *Wright brothers, Pasteur, Pavlov, Michael Faraday:* inventors and scientists.

The fox tells a story to Aesop, in this drawing on a Greek cup made in the 5th century B.C. The drawing is based on a tradition that Aesop took his fables from the animals themselves.

BOOK ONE | PART 4

THE STORYTELLER

Thus did he speak, and they all held their peace throughout the dark hall, enthralled by the charm of his story.
ODYSSEY, *Book 13*

A story can be as simple as a child's tale about an imaginary playmate or as complex as Homer's long epic, the Odyssey, which gives shape to the history and culture of his people. Different as these two storytellers are, Homer and the child have a great deal in common. They are both trying to entertain themselves and their audience. They are trying to find meaning in complex human experience. They invent characters and happenings that express their meaning. Stories are an important part of our lives. They introduce us to people and places we could never hope to meet or see. Through stories, our own experiences and feelings take on meaning and shape. Tales are one way we make sense of the world around us.

ORAL LITERATURE

Most of the stories in this book were written down. But some, such as the Odyssey and the fables and legends that appear later in this volume, began as oral literature. That is, they were told aloud and only written down many years later. There are some important differences between oral literature and written literature. For one thing, the old bards and minstrels often used verse (as Homer did) because the rhythm of the verse made the stories easier to sing and remember. Even after the invention of writing, stories were passed on by word of mouth because until modern times most people could not read and books were too expensive to own. Even today there are reports of tribes in Central Asia whose storytellers have memorized many thousands of lines of epic poetry and still recite their tales to attentive audiences.

THE PLOT

One thing is necessary to any narrative: a plot. The plot is simply the order of events, the "what happens" in the story. The plot may be very simple; it may not even be very interesting or original in itself. It is the storyteller who makes a good story or a bad one. The way in which he tells it, the language he uses, the characters and incidents he invents are of crucial importance. Still, as one writer puts it, the plot is the "indispensable skeleton" of any narrative.

The ancient Greek philosopher Aristotle said something about plot which may seem obvious but which is worth pointing out: a plot has a beginning, a middle, and an end. That is, an event begins, complications follow, and some sort of conclusion is reached. The simplest plot is the life of a man or woman: he or she is born, lives through a life filled with problems and events, and dies. The plot of the Odyssey might be simplified like this:

Beginning
  The Trojan war is over, and Odysseus sets out for his home in Ithaca.

Middle
  Odysseus encounters many delays and adventures on his way home: the Cyclopes, the Sirens, Circe, etc. Meanwhile, in Ithaca, the suitors are trying to woo Odysseus' wife, Penelope, and take his property. His son, Telemachus, goes in search of his father.

End
  Odysseus, with the help of his son, defeats the suitors and regains his kingdom.

Some plots are repeated over and over again. One of the most basic of all plots is at the center of the Odyssey: the hero's journey away from home on a quest or mission, his adventures, and his return.

You will find this basic plot in the story of Harry Thorburn in "The Erne from the Coast" on page 144.

CHARACTER AND SETTING

The stories in the following section have been chosen for the most part because of their interest as narratives. In reading them, you will probably be mainly concerned with the action, the plot; nevertheless, you should not neglect the characters or the setting in which the plot takes place. It is important to distinguish among the different elements in a story and to see how they interact. Some writers are very good at drawing lifelike characters but are weak at constructing plots. Others are good at evoking a setting — a town, an age, a forest — but not so good at making their characters vital and interesting. Obviously, the best stories are those in which the plot, characters, and setting all contribute their share to the effect of the narrative.

POINT OF VIEW

The elements of plot, character, and setting are not hard to recognize, but there is another element of narrative which is more complicated: point of view. Since every story has a storyteller, there must be some point of view from which he observes the characters and tells about what happens to them. Point of view sometimes is used to describe the writer's attitude, but in this section it will be used in its more precise sense: the point from which the reader views the story, or the character through whose eyes the action is seen.

The author may let one of his characters tell the story in his own voice. He becomes the "I" of the story. This point of view is called "first-person narration." An excellent example is Poe's "The Cask of Amontillado," in which the principal character tells his own story.

Perhaps the most common narrative technique is what may be called "third-person omniscient." (Omniscient means knowing everything.) The teller of the tale is not a character in the action but observes it from without. He knows everything that happens — or as much as he wants to know — even what the characters are thinking and what their motives are. The Odyssey is a good example: the "bard" who tells the tale takes us from Earth to Olympus, from

Ithaca to the Underworld, and from the thoughts and deeds of Odysseus to those of Penelope, Telemachus, and many other men and gods.

Another way to tell a tale is to have it narrated by a minor character, one who observes the action but is not central to it. This results in a combination of first- and third-person points of view. You will find this technique used by Conan Doyle (page 185), whose Sherlock Holmes stories are all told by Holmes's friend, Dr. Watson.

Some stories, like Alice in Wonderland and the Odyssey, we can hear and read over and over again. They continue to interest us even though we know how they are going to come out. Or, as a poet put it, "Literature is news that stays news." A strange thing about stories is that even though we know they are not "true," we expect them to be believable. The storyteller must construct a "real" world for his reader, leading him to say to himself: "I know this isn't really happening, but I can't help believing that it is."

To be believable, then, a story must be in some way true to life. In some way — because it is not the reality of the photograph or tape recording we look for from storytellers. As you will see in the stories and narrative poems that follow, each storyteller gives us back the world through his own imagination.

Edgar Allan Poe is one of the master storytellers of all time. He helped to establish the short story as a form of literature, and he invented the modern detective story. He is known particularly for his tales of horror, in which he creates nightmare worlds which seize the reader's imagination. Such a story is "The Cask of Amontillado" — about an Italian prince, Montresor, whose revenge on his enemy Fortunato is executed with deadly coolness.

The Cask of Amontillado

EDGAR ALLAN POE

The thousand injuries of Fortunato I had borne as I best could, but when he ventured upon insult, I vowed revenge. You, who so well know the nature of my soul, will not suppose, however, that I gave utterance to a threat. *At length* I would be avenged; this was a point definitely settled — but the very definitiveness with which it was resolved precluded the idea of risk. I must not only punish, but punish with impunity. A wrong is unredressed when retribution overtakes its redresser. It is equally unredressed when the avenger fails to make himself felt as such to him who had done the wrong.

It must be understood that neither by word nor deed had I given Fortunato cause to doubt my good will. I continued, as was my wont, to smile in his face, and he did not perceive that my smile *now* was at the thought of his immolation.

He had a weak point — this Fortunato — although in other regards he was a man to be respected and even feared. He prided himself on his connoisseurship in wine. Few Italians have the true virtuoso spirit. For the most part their enthusiasm is adapted to suit the time and opportunity — to practice imposture upon the British and Austrian millionaires. In painting and gemmary Fortunato, like his countrymen, was a quack — but in the matter of old wines he was sincere. In this respect I did not differ from him materially: I was skillful in the Italian vintages myself, and bought largely whenever I could.

It was about dusk, one evening during the supreme madness of the carnival season, that I encountered my friend. He accosted me with excessive warmth, for he had been drinking much. The man wore motley.[1] He had on a tight-fitting, parti-striped dress, and his head was surmounted by the conical cap and bells. I was so pleased to see him that I thought I should never have done wringing his hand.

I said to him: "My dear Fortunato, you are luckily met. How remarkably well you are looking today! But I have received a pipe [2] of what passes for Amontillado,[3] and I have my doubts."

"How?" said he. "Amontillado? A pipe? Impossible! And in the middle of the carnival!"

"I have my doubts," I replied; "and I was silly enough to pay the full Amontillado price without consulting you in the matter. You were not to be found, and I was fearful of losing a bargain."

"Amontillado!"

"I have my doubts."

"Amontillado!"

"And I must satisfy them."

"Amontillado!"

"As you are engaged, I am on my way to Luchesi. If anyone has a critical turn, it is he. He will tell me — "

"Luchesi cannot tell Amontillado from Sherry."

"And yet some fools will have it that his taste is a match for your own."

"Come, let us go."

"Whither?"

"To your vaults."

"My friend, no; I will not impose upon your good nature. I perceive you have an engagement. Luchesi — "

"I have no engagement; come."

"My friend, no. It is not the engagement, but the severe cold with

---

[1] *motley*: a garment of many colors, formerly worn by court jesters; here, a carnival costume.
[2] *pipe*: a large cask.
[3] *Amontillado* (ə·mon'tə·lä'dō): a dry Spanish wine.

which I perceive you are afflicted. The vaults are insufferably damp. They are encrusted with niter." [4]

"Let us go, nevertheless. The cold is merely nothing. Amontillado! You have been imposed upon. And as for Luchesi, he cannot distinguish Sherry from Amontillado."

Thus speaking, Fortunato possessed himself of my arm. Putting on a mask of black silk, and drawing a *roquelaire* [5] closely about my person, I suffered him to hurry me to my palazzo.[6]

There were no attendants at home; they had absconded to make merry in honor of the time. I had told them that I should not return until the morning, and had given them explicit orders not to stir from the house. These orders were sufficient, I well knew, to insure their immediate disappearance, one and all, as soon as my back was turned.

I took from their sconces [7] two flambeaux,[8] and giving one to Fortunato, bowed him through several suites of rooms to the archway that led into the vaults. I passed down a long and winding staircase, requesting him to be cautious as he followed. We came at length to the foot of the descent, and stood together on the damp ground of the catacombs of the Montresors.

The gait of my friend was unsteady, and the bells upon his cap jingled as he strode.

"The pipe?" said he.

"It is farther on," said I; "but observe the white webwork which gleams from these cavern walls."

He turned toward me, and looked into my eyes with two filmy orbs that distilled the rheum [9] of intoxication.

"Niter?" he asked, at length.

"Niter!" I replied. "How long have you had that cough?"

"Ugh! ugh! ugh! — ugh! ugh! ugh! — ugh! ugh! ugh! — ugh! ugh! ugh — ugh! ugh! ugh!"

My poor friend found it impossible to reply for many minutes.

"It is nothing," he said, at last.

"Come," I said, with decision, "we will go back; your health is

---

[4] *niter:* a damp salt deposit.
[5] *roquelaire* (rŏk'ə·lâr): a cloak.
[6] *palazzo* (pä·lät'sō): in Italy, a palace.
[7] *sconces:* wall brackets.
[8] *flambeaux* (flam'bōz): flaming torches.
[9] *rheum:* wateriness.

precious. You are rich, respected, admired, beloved; you are happy, as once I was. You are a man to be missed. For me it is no matter. We will go back; you will be ill, and I cannot be responsible. Besides, there is Luchesi — "

"Enough," he said; "the cough is a mere nothing; it will not kill me. I shall not die of a cough."

"True — true," I replied; "and, indeed, I had no intention of alarming you unnecessarily — but you should use all proper precautions. A draft of this Medoc will defend us from the damps."

Here I knocked off the neck of a bottle which I drew from a long row of its fellows that lay upon the mold.

"Drink," I said, presenting him the wine.

He raised it to his lips with a leer. He paused and nodded to me familiarly, while his bells jingled.

"I drink," he said, "to the buried that repose around us."

"And I to your long life."

He again took my arm, and we proceeded.

"These vaults," he said, "are extensive."

"The Montresors," I replied, "were a great and numerous family."

"I forget your arms." [10]

"A huge human foot d'or, in a field azure; the foot crushes a serpent rampant [11] whose fangs are embedded in the heel."

"And the motto?"

"*Nemo me impune lacessit.*" [12]

"Good!" he said.

The wine sparkled in his eyes and the bells jingled. My own fancy grew warm with the Medoc. We passed through walls of piled bones, with casks and puncheons [13] intermingling, into the inmost recesses of the catacombs. I paused again, and this time I made bold to seize Fortunato by an arm above the elbow.

"The niter," I said; "see, it increases. It hangs like moss upon the vaults. We are below the river's bed. The drops of moisture trickle among the bones. Come, we will go back ere it is too late. Your cough — "

"It is nothing," he said; "let us go on. But first, another draft of

---

[10] *arms*: the official insignia of a family.
[11] *d'or . . . rampant*: a gold foot in a blue field crushing a raised serpent.
[12] *Nemo me impune lacessit*: no one attacks me without punishment (Latin).
[13] *puncheons*: upright supporting timbers.

the Medoc."

I broke and reached him a flagon of De Grave. He emptied it at a breath. His eyes flashed with a fierce light. He laughed and threw the bottle upward with a gesticulation I did not understand.

I looked at him in surprise. He repeated the movement — a grotesque one.

"You do not comprehend?" he said.

"Not I," I replied.

"Then you are not of the brotherhood."

"How?"

"You are not of the masons."

"Yes, yes," I said; "yes, yes."

"You? Impossible! A mason?"

"A mason," I replied.

"A sign," he said.

"It is this," I answered, producing a trowel from beneath the folds of my *roquelaire*.

"You jest," he exclaimed, recoiling a few paces. "But let us proceed to the Amontillado."

"Be it so," I said, replacing the tool beneath the cloak, and again offering him my arm. He leaned upon it heavily. We continued our route in search of the Amontillado. We passed through a range of low arches, descended, passed on, and descending again, arrived at a deep crypt, in which the foulness of the air caused our flambeaux rather to glow than flame.

At the most remote end of the crypt there appeared another, less spacious. Its walls had been lined with human remains, piled to the vault overhead, in the fashion of the great catacombs of Paris. Three sides of this interior crypt were still ornamented in this manner. From the fourth the bones had been thrown down, and lay promiscuously upon the earth, forming at one point a mound of some size. Within the wall thus exposed by the displacing of the bones, we perceived a still interior recess, in depth about four feet, in width three, in height six or seven. It seemed to have been constructed for no special use within itself, but formed merely the interval between two of the colossal supports of the roof of the catacombs, and was backed by one of their circumscribing walls of solid granite.

It was in vain that Fortunato, uplifting his dull torch, endeavored to pry into the depth of the recess. Its termination the feeble light did not enable us to see.

"Proceed," I said; "herein is the Amontillado. As for Luchesi — "

"He is an ignoramus," interrupted my friend, as he stepped unsteadily forward, while I followed immediately at his heels. In an instant he had reached the extremity of the niche, and finding his progress arrested by the rock, stood stupidly bewildered. A moment more and I had fettered him to the granite. In its surface were two iron staples, distant from each other about two feet, horizontally. From one of these depended a short chain, from the other a padlock. Throwing the links about his waist, it was but the work of a few seconds to secure it. He was too much astounded to resist. Withdrawing the key, I stepped back from the recess.

"Pass your hand," I said, "over the wall; you cannot help feeling the niter. Indeed it is *very* damp. Once more let me *implore* you to return. No? Then I must positively leave you. But I must first render you all the little attentions in my power."

"The Amontillado!" ejaculated my friend, not yet recovered from his astonishment.

"True," I replied; "the Amontillado."

As I said these words I busied myself among the pile of bones of which I have before spoken. Throwing them aside, I soon uncovered a quantity of building stones and mortar. With these materials and with the aid of my trowel, I began vigorously to wall up the entrance of the niche.

I had scarcely laid the first tier of the masonry when I discovered that the intoxication of Fortunato had in a great measure worn off. The earliest indication I had of this was a low, moaning cry from the depth of the recess. It was *not* the cry of a drunken man. There was then a long and obstinate silence. I laid the second tier, and the third, and the fourth; and then I heard the furious vibrations of the chain. The noise lasted for several minutes, during which, that I might hearken to it with the more satisfaction, I ceased my labors and sat down upon the bones. When at last the clanking subsided, I resumed the trowel, and finished without interruption the fifth, the sixth, and the seventh tier. The wall was now nearly upon a level with my breast. I again paused, and holding the flambeaux over the masonwork, threw a few feeble rays upon the figure within.

A succession of loud and shrill screams, bursting suddenly from the throat of the chained form, seemed to thrust me violently back. For a brief moment I hesitated — I trembled. Unsheathing my rapier, I began to grope with it about the recess; but the thought of an instant reassured me. I placed my hand upon the solid fabric of the catacombs, and felt satisfied. I reapproached the wall. I replied to the yells of him who clamored. I re-echoed — I aided — I surpassed them in volume and in strength. I did this, and the clamorer grew still.

It was now midnight, and my task was drawing to a close. I had completed the eighth, the ninth, and the tenth tier. I had finished a portion of the last and the eleventh; there remained but a single stone to be fitted and plastered in. I struggled with its weight; I placed it partially in its destined position. But now there came from out the niche a low laugh that erected the hairs upon my head. It was succeeded by a sad voice, which I had difficulty in recognizing as that of the noble Fortunato. The voice said —

"Ha! ha! ha! — he! he! — a very good joke indeed — an excellent jest. We will have many a rich laugh about it at the palazzo — he! he! he! — over our wine — he! he! he!"

"The Amontillado!" I said.

"He! he! he! — he! he! he! — yes, the Amontillado. But is it not getting late? Will not they be awaiting us at the palazzo, the Lady Fortunato and the rest? Let us be gone."

"Yes," I said, "let us be gone."

"*For the love of God, Montresor!*"

"Yes," I said, "for the love of God!"

But to these words I hearkened in vain for a reply. I grew impatient. I called aloud.

"Fortunato!"

No answer. I called again:

"Fortunato!"

No answer still. I thrust a torch through the remaining aperture and let it fall within. There came forth in return only a jingling of the bells. My heart grew sick — on account of the dampness of the catacombs. I hastened to make an end of my labor. I forced the last stone into its position; I plastered it up. Against the new masonry I re-erected the old rampart of bones. For the half of a century no mortal has disturbed them. *In pace requiescat!* [14]

---

[14] *In pace requiescat:* May he rest in peace (Latin).

Science fiction became firmly established as a literary form in the nineteenth century with the tales of Jules Verne, which continue to be popular. Stories of this kind, set in a fantastic future or in other worlds, are often meant to be comments on or warnings to present-day society. Ray Bradbury places the following story on Earth in the year 2026. It is an unusual story in which the setting is the main character.

There Will Come Soft Rains

RAY BRADBURY

In the living room the voice-clock sang, *Ticktock, seven o'clock, time to get up, time to get up, seven o'clock!* as if it were afraid that nobody would. The morning house lay empty. The clock ticked on, repeating and repeating its sounds into the emptiness. *Seven-nine, breakfast time, seven-nine!*

In the kitchen the breakfast stove gave a hissing sigh and ejected from its warm interior eight pieces of perfectly browned toast, eight eggs sunnyside up, sixteen slices of bacon, two coffees, and two cool glasses of milk.

"Today is August 4, 2026," said a second voice from the kitchen ceiling, "in the city of Allendale, California." It repeated the date three times for memory's sake. "Today is Mr. Featherstone's birthday. Today is the anniversary of Tilita's marriage. Insurance is payable, as are the water, gas, and light bills."

Somewhere in the walls, relays clicked, memory tapes glided under electric eyes.

Eight-one, ticktock, eight-one o'clock, off to school, off to work, run, run, eight-one! But no doors slammed, no carpets took the soft tread of rubber heels. It was raining outside. The weather box on the front door sang quietly: "Rain, rain, go away; rubbers, raincoats for today . . ." And the rain tapped on the empty house, echoing.

Outside, the garage chimed and lifted its door to reveal the waiting car. After a long wait the door swung down again.

At eight-thirty the eggs were shriveled and the toast was like stone. An aluminum wedge scraped them into the sink, where hot water whirled them down a metal throat which digested and flushed them away to the distant sea. The dirty dishes were dropped into a hot washer and emerged twinkling dry.

Nine-fifteen, sang the clock, *time to clean.*

Out of warrens in the wall, tiny robot mice darted. The rooms were acrawl with the small cleaning animals, all rubber and metal. They thudded against chairs, whirling their mustached runners, kneading the rug nap, sucking gently at hidden dust. Then, like mysterious invaders, they popped into their burrows. Their pink electric eyes faded. The house was clean.

Ten o'clock. The sun came out from behind the rain. The house stood alone in a city of rubble and ashes. This was the one house left standing. At night the ruined city gave off a radioactive glow which could be seen for miles.

Ten-fifteen. The garden sprinklers whirled up in golden founts, filling the soft morning air with scatterings of brightness. The water pelted windowpanes, running down the charred west side where the house had been burned evenly free of its white paint. The entire west face of the house was black, save for five places. Here the silhouette in paint of a man mowing a lawn. Here, as in a photograph, a woman bent to pick flowers. Still farther over, their images burned on wood in one titanic instant, a small boy, hands flung into the air; higher up, the image of a thrown ball, and opposite him a girl, hands raised to catch a ball which never came down.

The five spots of paint — the man, the woman, the children, the ball — remained. The rest was a thin charcoaled layer.

The gentle sprinkler rain filled the garden with falling light.

Until this day, how well the house had kept its peace. How carefully it had inquired, "Who goes there? What's the password?" and, getting no answer from lonely foxes and whining cats, it had shut up its windows and drawn shades in an old-maidenly preoccupation with self-protection which bordered on a mechanical paranoia.[1]

It quivered at each sound, the house did. If a sparrow brushed a

---

[1] *paranoia:* a mental disorder in which a person often imagines others are persecuting him.

window, the shade snapped up. The bird, startled, flew off! No, not even a bird must touch the house!

The house was an altar with ten thousand attendants, big, small, servicing, attending, in choirs. But the gods had gone away, and the ritual of the religion continued senselessly, uselessly.

Twelve noon.

A dog whined, shivering, on the front porch.

The front door recognized the dog voice and opened. The dog, once huge and fleshy, but now gone to bone and covered with sores, moved in and through the house, tracking mud. Behind it whirred angry mice, angry at having to pick up mud, angry at inconvenience.

For not a leaf fragment blew under the door but what the wall panels flipped open and the copper scrap rats flashed swiftly out. The offending dust, hair, or paper, seized in miniature steel jaws, was raced back to the burrows. There, down tubes which fed into the cellar, it was dropped into the sighing vent of an incinerator which sat like evil Baal [2] in a dark corner.

The dog ran upstairs, hysterically yelping to each door, at last realizing, as the house realized, that only silence was here.

It sniffed the air and scratched the kitchen door. Behind the door, the stove was making pancakes which filled the house with a rich baked odor and the scent of maple syrup.

The dog frothed at the mouth, lying at the door, sniffing, its eyes turned to fire. It ran wildly in circles, biting at its tail, spun in a frenzy, and died. It lay in the parlor for an hour.

Two o'clock, sang a voice.

Delicately sensing decay at last, the regiments of mice hummed out as softly as blown gray leaves in an electrical wind.

Two-fifteen.

The dog was gone.

In the cellar, the incinerator glowed suddenly and a whirl of sparks leaped up the chimney.

Two thirty-five.

Bridge tables sprouted from patio walls. Playing cards fluttered onto pads in a shower of pips.[3] Martinis manifested on an oaken bench with egg-salad sandwiches. Music played.

---

[2] *Baal* (bā'əl): an ancient sun god, whose name in time took on evil connotations.

[3] *pips:* the markings on playing cards.

But the tables were silent and the cards untouched.

At four o'clock the tables folded like great butterflies back through the paneled walls.

Four-thirty.

The nursery walls glowed.

Animals took shape: yellow giraffes, blue lions, pink antelopes, lilac panthers cavorting in crystal substance. The walls were glass. They looked out upon color and fantasy. Hidden films clocked through well-oiled sprockets, and the walls lived. The nursery floor was woven to resemble a crisp, cereal meadow. Over this ran aluminum roaches and iron crickets, and in the hot still air butterflies of delicate red tissue wavered among the sharp aroma of animal spoors! There was a sound like a great matted yellow hive of bees within a dark bellows, the lazy bumble of a purring lion. And there was the patter of okapi[4] feet and the murmur of a fresh jungle rain, like other hoofs, falling upon the summer-starched grass. Now the walls dissolved into distances of parched weed, mile on mile, and warm endless sky. The animals drew away into thorn brakes and water holes.

It was the children's hour.

Five o'clock. The bath filled with clear hot water.

Six, seven, eight o'clock. The dinner dishes manipulated like magic tricks, and in the study a *click.* In the metal stand opposite the hearth, where a fire now blazed up warmly, a cigar popped out, half an inch of soft gray ash on it, smoking, waiting.

Nine o'clock. The beds warmed their hidden circuits, for nights were cool here.

Nine-five. A voice spoke from the study ceiling:

"Mrs. McClellan, which poem would you like this evening?"

The house was silent.

The voice said at last, "Since you express no preference, I shall select a poem at random." Quiet music rose to back the voice. "Sara Teasdale. As I recall, your favorite. . . .

> There will come soft rains and the smell of the ground,
> And swallows circling with their shimmering sound;

---

[4] *okapi* (ō·kä′pē): an animal related to the giraffe.

> And frogs in the pools singing at night,
> And wild plum trees in tremulous white;
>
> Robins will wear their feathery fire,
> Whistling their whims on a low fence-wire;
>
> And not one will know of the war, not one
> Will care at last when it is done.
>
> Not one would mind, neither bird nor tree,
> If mankind perished utterly;
>
> And Spring herself, when she woke at dawn
> Would scarcely know that we were gone.

The fire burned on the stone hearth and the cigar fell away into a mound of quiet ash on its tray. The empty chairs faced each other between the silent walls, and the music played.

At ten o'clock the house began to die.

The wind blew. A falling tree bough crashed through the kitchen window. Cleaning solvent, bottled, shattered over the stove. The room was ablaze in an instant!

"Fire!" screamed a voice. The house lights flashed, water pumps shot water from the ceilings. But the solvent spread on the linoleum, licking, eating, under the kitchen door, while the voices took it up in chorus: "Fire, fire, fire!"

The house tried to save itself. Doors sprang tightly shut, but the windows were broken by the heat and the wind blew and sucked upon the fire.

The house gave ground as the fire in ten billion angry sparks moved with flaming ease from room to room and then up the stairs. While scurrying water rats squeaked from the walls, pistoled their water, and ran for more. And the wall sprays let down showers of mechanical rain.

But too late. Somewhere, sighing, a pump shrugged to a stop. The quenching rain ceased. The reserve water supply which had filled baths and washed dishes for many quiet days was gone.

The fire crackled up the stairs. It fed upon Picassos and Matisses[5] in the upper halls, like delicacies, baking off the oily flesh, tenderly crisping the canvases into black shavings.

---

[5] *Picassos and Matisses:* paintings by the modern artists Pablo Picasso and Henri Matisse.

Now the fire lay in beds, stood in windows, changed the colors of drapes!

And then, reinforcements.

From attic trapdoors, blind robot faces peered down with faucet mouths gushing green chemical.

The fire backed off, as even an elephant must at the sight of a dead snake. Now there were twenty snakes whipping over the floor, killing the fire with a clear cold venom of green froth.

But the fire was clever. It had sent flames outside the house, up through the attic to the pumps there. An explosion! The attic brain which directed the pumps was shattered into bronze shrapnel on the beams.

The fire rushed back into every closet and felt of the clothes hung there.

The house shuddered, oak bone on bone, its bared skeleton cringing from the heat, its wire, its nerves revealed as if a surgeon had torn the skin off to let the red veins and capillaries quiver in the scalded air. Help, help! Fire! Run, run! Heat snapped mirrors like the brittle winter ice. And the voices wailed Fire, fire, run, run, like a tragic nursery rhyme, a dozen voices, high, low, like children dying in a forest, alone, alone. And the voices fading as the wires popped their sheathings like hot chestnuts. One, two, three, four, five voices died.

In the nursery the jungle burned. Blue lions roared, purple giraffes bounded off. The panthers ran in circles, changing color, and ten million animals, running before the fire, vanished off toward a distant steaming river. . . .

Ten more voices died. In the last instant under the fire avalanche, other choruses, oblivious, could be heard announcing the time, playing music, cutting the lawn by remote-control mower, or setting an umbrella frantically out and in the slamming and opening front door, a thousand things happening, like a clock shop when each clock strikes the hour insanely before or after the other, a scene of maniac confusion, yet unity; singing, screaming, a few last cleaning mice darting bravely out to carry the horrid ashes away! And one voice, with sublime disregard for the situation, read poetry aloud in the fiery study, until all the film spools burned, until all the wires withered and the circuits cracked.

The fire burst the house and let it slam flat down, puffing out skirts of spark and smoke.

In the kitchen, an instant before the rain of fire and timber, the stove could be seen making breakfasts at a psychopathic rate, ten dozen eggs, six loaves of toast, twenty dozen bacon strips, which, eaten by fire, started the stove working again, hysterically hissing!

The crash. The attic smashing into kitchen and parlor. The parlor into cellar, cellar into subcellar. Deep freeze, armchair, film tapes, circuits, beds, and all like skeletons thrown in a cluttered mound deep under.

Smoke and silence. A great quantity of smoke.

Dawn showed faintly in the east. Among the ruins, one wall stood alone. Within the wall, a last voice said, over and over again and again, even as the sun rose to shine upon the heaped rubble and steam:

"Today is August 5, 2026, today is August 5, 2026, today is . . ."

The shelves of any public library in England or America will testify to the enormous popularity of detective stories. Most detective stories can hardly be ranked among the greatest literature. For the most part, they are a form of pure entertainment, in which character is not examined too deeply and in which the writers do not explore the major concerns of humanity. But the tales of Sherlock Holmes certainly belong to English literature because of their unforgettable hero. Holmes has become almost a mythic figure.

The Adventure of the Norwood Builder

SIR ARTHUR CONAN DOYLE

"From the point of view of the criminal expert," said Mr. Sherlock Holmes, "London has become a singularly uninteresting city since the death of the late lamented Professor Moriarty."

"I can hardly think that you would find many decent citizens to agree with you," I answered.

"Well, well, I must not be selfish," said he, with a smile, as he pushed back his chair from the breakfast table. "The community is certainly the gainer, and no one the loser, save the poor out-of-work specialist, whose occupation has gone. With that man in the field, one's morning paper presented infinite possibilities. Often it was only the smallest trace, Watson, the faintest indication, and yet it was enough to tell me that the great malignant brain was there, as the gentlest tremors of the edges of the web remind one of the foul spider which lurks in the center. Petty thefts, wanton assaults, purposeless outrage — to the man who held the clue all could be worked into one connected whole. To the scientific student of the higher criminal world, no capital in Europe offered the advantages which London then possessed. But now —— " He shrugged his shoulders in humorous deprecation of the state of things which he had himself done so much to produce.

At the time of which I speak, Holmes had been back for some months, and I at his request had sold my practice and returned to share the old quarters in Baker Street. A young doctor, named Verner, had purchased my small Kensington practice, and given with astonishingly little demur the highest price that I ventured to ask — an incident which only explained itself some years later, when I found that Verner was a distant relation of Holmes, and that it was my friend who had really found the money.

Our months of partnership had not been so uneventful as he had stated, for I find, on looking over my notes, that this period includes the case of the papers of ex-President Murillo, and also the shocking affair of the Dutch steamship *Friesland*, which so nearly cost us both our lives. His cold and proud nature was always averse, however, from anything in the shape of public applause, and he bound me in the most stringent terms to say no further word of himself, his methods, or his successes — a prohibition which, as I have explained, has only now been removed.

Mr. Sherlock Holmes was leaning back in his chair after his whimsical protest, and was unfolding his morning paper in a leisurely fashion, when our attention was arrested by a tremendous ring at the bell, followed immediately by a hollow drumming sound, as if someone were beating on the outer door with his fist. As it opened there came a tumultuous rush into the hall, rapid feet clattered up the stair, and an instant later a wild-eyed and frantic young man, pale, disheveled, and palpitating, burst into the room. He looked from one to the other of us, and under our gaze of inquiry he became conscious that some apology was needed for this unceremonious entry.

"I'm sorry, Mr. Holmes," he cried. "You mustn't blame me. I am nearly mad. Mr. Holmes, I am the unhappy John Hector McFarlane."

He made the announcement as if the name alone would explain both his visit and its manner, but I could see, by my companion's unresponsive face, that it meant no more to him than to me.

"Have a cigarette, Mr. McFarlane," said he, pushing his case across. "I am sure that, with your symptoms, my friend Dr. Watson here would prescribe a sedative. The weather has been so very warm these last few days. Now, if you feel a little more composed, I should be glad if you would sit down in that chair, and tell us very slowly and quietly who you are, and what it is that you want. You mentioned your name as if I should recognize it, but I assure you that, beyond the obvious facts that you are a bachelor, a solicitor, a Freemason,[1] and an asthmatic, I know nothing whatever about you."

Familiar as I was with my friend's methods, it was not difficult for me to follow his deductions, and to observe the untidiness of attire, the sheaf of legal papers, the watch-charm, and the breathing which had prompted them. Our client, however, stared in amazement.

"Yes, I am all that, Mr. Holmes; and, in addition, I am the most unfortunate man at this moment in London. For heaven's sake, don't abandon me, Mr. Holmes! If they come to arrest me before I have finished my story, make them give me time, so that I may tell you the whole truth. I could go to jail happy if I knew that you were working for me outside."

"Arrest you!" said Holmes. "This is really most grati — most interesting. On what charge do you expect to be arrested?"

"Upon the charge of murdering Mr. Jonas Oldacre, of Lower Norwood."

My companion's expressive face showed a sympathy which was not, I am afraid, entirely unmixed with satisfaction.

"Dear me," said he, "it was only this moment at breakfast that I was saying to my friend, Dr. Watson, that sensational cases had disappeared out of our papers."

Our visitor stretched forward a quivering hand and picked up the *Daily Telegraph*, which still lay upon Holmes's knee.

"If you had looked at it, sir, you would have seen at a glance what the errand is on which I have come to you this morning. I feel as if my name and my misfortune must be in every man's mouth." He turned it over to expose the central page. "Here it is, and with your permission I will read it to you. Listen to this, Mr. Holmes. The headlines are: 'Mysterious Affair at Lower Norwood. Disappearance of a Well-Known Builder. Suspicion of Murder and Arson. A Clue to the Criminal.' That is the clue which they are already following, Mr. Holmes, and I know that it leads infallibly to me. I have been followed from London Bridge Station, and I am sure that they are

---

[1] *a solicitor, a Freemason:* a lawyer and a member of a secret order (Free and Accepted Masons).

only waiting for the warrant to arrest me. It will break my mother's heart — it will break her heart!" He wrung his hands in an agony of apprehension, and swayed backward and forward in his chair.

I looked with interest upon this man, who was accused of being the perpetrator of a crime of violence. He was flaxen-haired and handsome, in a washed-out negative fashion, with frightened blue eyes, and a clean-shaven face with a weak, sensitive mouth. His age may have been about twenty-seven, his dress and bearing that of a gentleman. From the pocket of his light summer overcoat protruded the bundle of endorsed papers which proclaimed his profession.

"We must use what time we have," said Holmes. "Watson, would you have the kindness to take the paper and to read the paragraph in question?"

Underneath the vigorous headlines which our client had quoted, I read the following suggestive narrative:

> "Late last night, or early this morning, an incident occurred at Lower Norwood which points, it is feared, to a serious crime. Mr. Jonas Oldacre is a well-known resident of that suburb, where he has carried on his business as a builder for many years. Mr. Oldacre is a bachelor, fifty-two years of age, and lives in Deep Dene House, at the Sydenham end of the road of that name. He has had the reputation of being a man of eccentric habits, secretive and retiring. For some years he has practically withdrawn from the business, in which is he said to have amassed considerable wealth. A small timber yard still exists, however, at the back of the house, and last night, about twelve o'clock, an alarm was given that one of the stacks was on fire. The engines were soon upon the spot, but the dry wood burned with great fury, and it was impossible to arrest the conflagration until the stack had been entirely consumed. Up to this point the incident bore the appearance of an ordinary accident, but fresh indications seem to point to serious crime. Surprise was expressed at the absence of the master of the establishment from the scene of the fire, and an inquiry followed, which showed that he had disappeared from the house. An examination of his room revealed that the bed had not been slept in, that a safe which stood in it was open, that a number of important papers were scattered about the room, and finally, that there were signs of a murderous struggle, slight traces of blood being found within the room, and an oaken walking stick, which also showed stains of blood upon

the handle. It is known that Mr. Jonas Oldacre had received a late visitor in his bedroom upon that night, and the stick found has been identified as the property of this person, who is a young London solicitor named John Hector McFarlane, junior partner of Graham and McFarlane, of 426 Gresham Buildings, E. C. The police believe that they have evidence in their possession which supplies a very convincing motive for the crime, and altogether it cannot be doubted that sensational developments will follow.

"LATER. — It is rumored as we go to press that Mr. John Hector McFarlane has actually been arrested on the charge of the murder of Mr. Jonas Oldacre. It is at least certain that a warrant has been issued. There have been further and sinister developments in the investigation at Norwood. Besides the signs of a struggle in the room of the unfortunate builder, it is now known that the French windows of his bedroom (which is on the ground floor) were found to be open, that there were marks as if some bulky object had been dragged across to the woodpile, and, finally, it is asserted that charred remains have been found among the charcoal ashes of the fire. The police theory is that a most sensational crime has been committed, that the victim was clubbed to death in his own bedroom, his papers rifled, and his dead body dragged across to the woodstack, which was then ignited so as to hide all traces of the crime. The conduct of the criminal investigation has been left in the experienced hands of Inspector Lestrade, of Scotland Yard, who is following up the clues with his accustomed energy and sagacity."

Sherlock Holmes listened with closed eyes and fingertips together to this remarkable account.

"The case has certainly some points of interest," said he, in his languid fashion. "May I ask, in the first place, Mr. McFarlane, how it is that you are still at liberty, since there appears to be enough evidence to justify your arrest?"

"I live at Torrington Lodge, Blackheath, with my parents, Mr. Holmes, but last night, having to do business very late with Mr. Jonas Oldacre, I stayed at a hotel in Norwood, and came to my business from there. I knew nothing of this affair until I was in the train, when I read what you have just heard. I at once saw the horrible danger of my position, and I hurried to put the case into your hands. I have no doubt that I should have been arrested either at my city office or at my home. A man followed me from London

Bridge Station, and I have no doubt —— Great heaven! what is that?"

It was a clang of the bell, followed instantly by heavy steps upon the stair. A moment later, our old friend Lestrade appeared in the doorway. Over his shoulder I caught a glimpse of one or two uniformed policemen outside.

"Mr. John Hector McFarlane?" said Lestrade.

Our unfortunate client rose with a ghastly face.

"I arrest you for the willful murder of Mr. Jonas Oldacre, of Lower Norwood."

McFarlane turned to us with a gesture of despair, and sank into his chair once more like one who is crushed.

"One moment, Lestrade," said Holmes. "Half an hour more or less can make no difference to you, and the gentleman was about to give us an account of this very interesting affair, which might aid us in clearing it up."

"I think there will be no difficulty in clearing it up," said Lestrade, grimly.

"None the less, with your permission, I should be much interested to hear his account."

"Well, Mr. Holmes, it is difficult for me to refuse you anything, for you have been of use to the force once or twice in the past, and we owe you a good turn at Scotland Yard," said Lestrade. "At the same time I must remain with my prisoner, and I am bound to warn him that anything he may say will appear in evidence against him."

"I wish nothing better," said our client. "All I ask is that you should hear and recognize the absolute truth."

Lestrade looked at his watch. "I'll give you half an hour," said he.

"I must explain first," said McFarlane, "that I knew nothing of Mr. Jonas Oldacre. His name was familiar to me, for many years ago my parents were acquainted with him, but they drifted apart. I was very much surprised, therefore, when yesterday, about three o'clock in the afternoon, he walked into my office in the city. But I was still more astonished when he told me the object of his visit. He had in his hand several sheets of a notebook, covered with scribbled writing — here they are — and he laid them on my table.

"'Here is my will,' said he. 'I want you, Mr. McFarlane, to cast it into proper legal shape. I will sit here while you do so.'

"I set myself to copy it, and you can imagine my astonishment when I found that, with some reservations, he had left all his property to me. He was a strange little ferret-like man, with white eyelashes, and when I looked up at him I found his keen gray eyes fixed upon me with an amused expression. I could hardly believe my own senses as I read the terms of the will; but he explained that he was a bachelor with hardly any living relation, that he had known my parents in his youth, and that he had always heard of me as a very deserving young man, and was assured that his money would be in worthy hands. Of course, I could only stammer out my thanks. The will was duly finished, signed, and witnessed by my clerk. This is it on the blue paper, and these slips, as I have explained, are the rough draft. Mr. Jonas Oldacre then informed me that there were a number of documents — building leases, title deeds, mortgages, scrip, and so forth — which it was necessary that I should see and understand. He said that his mind would not be easy until the whole thing was settled, and he begged me to come out to his house at Norwood that night, bringing the will with me, to arrange matters. 'Remember, my boy, not one word to your parents about the affair until everything is settled. We will keep it as a little surprise for them.' He was very insistent upon this point, and made me promise it faithfully.

"You can imagine, Mr. Holmes, that I was not in a humor to refuse him anything that he might ask. He was my benefactor, and all my desire was to carry out his wishes in every particular. I sent a telegram home, therefore, to say that I had important business on hand, and that it was impossible for me to say how late I might be. Mr. Oldacre had told me that he would like me to have supper with him at nine, as he might not be home before that hour. I had some difficulty in finding his house, however, and it was nearly half-past before I reached it. I found him —— "

"One moment!" said Holmes. "Who opened the door?"

"A middle-aged woman, who was, I suppose, his housekeeper."

"And it was she, I presume, who mentioned your name?"

"Exactly," said McFarlane.

"Pray proceed."

McFarlane wiped his damp brow, and then continued his narrative:

"I was shown by this woman into a sitting room, where a frugal supper was laid out. Afterwards, Mr. Jonas Oldacre led me into his bedroom, in which there stood a heavy safe. This he opened and took out a mass of documents, which we went over together. It was between eleven and twelve when we finished. He remarked that we must not disturb the housekeeper. He showed me out through his own French window, which had been open all this time."

"Was the blind down?" asked Holmes.

"I will not be sure, but I believe that it was only half down. Yes, I remember how he pulled it up in order to swing open the window. I could not find my stick, and he said, 'Never mind, my boy, I shall see a good deal of you now, I hope, and I will keep your stick until you come back to claim it.' I left him there, the safe open, and the papers made up in packets upon the table. It was so late that I could not get back to Blackheath, so I spent the night at the Anerley Arms, and I knew nothing more until I read of this horrible affair in the morning."

"Anything more that you would like to ask, Mr. Holmes?" said Lestrade, whose eyebrows had gone up once or twice during this remarkable explanation.

"Not until I have been to Blackheath."

"You mean to Norwood," said Lestrade.

"Oh, yes, no doubt that is what I must have meant," said Holmes, with his enigmatical smile. Lestrade had learned by more experiences than he would care to acknowledge that that razor-like brain could cut through that which was impenetrable to him. I saw him look curiously at my companion.

"I think I should like to have a word with you presently, Mr. Sherlock Holmes," said he. "Now, Mr. McFarlane, two of my constables are at the door, and there is a four-wheeler waiting." The wretched young man arose, and with a last beseeching glance at us walked from the room. The officers conducted him to the cab, but Lestrade remained.

Holmes had picked up the pages which formed the rough draft of the will, and was looking at them with the keenest interest upon his face.

"There are some points about that document, Lestrade, are there not?" said he, pushing them over.

The official looked at them with a puzzled expression.

"I can read the first few lines, and these in the middle of the second page, and one or two at the end. Those are as clear as print," said he, "but the writing in between is very bad, and there are three places where I cannot read it at all."

"What do you make of that?" said Holmes.

"Well, what do *you* make of it?"

"That it was written in a train. The good writing represents stations, the bad writing movement, and the very bad writing passing over points.[2] A scientific expert would pronounce at once that this was drawn up on a suburban line, since nowhere save in the immediate vicinity of a great city could there be so quick a succession of points. Granting that his whole journey was occupied in drawing up the will, then the train was an express, only stopping once between Norwood and London Bridge."

Lestrade began to laugh.

"You are too many for me when you begin to get on your theories, Mr. Holmes," said he. "How does this bear on the case?"

"Well, it corroborates the young man's story to the extent that the will was drawn up by Jonas Oldacre in his journey yesterday. It is curious — is it not? — that a man should draw up so important a document in so haphazard a fashion. It suggests that he did not think it was going to be of much practical importance. If a man drew up a will which he did not intend ever to be effective, he might do it so."

"Well, he drew up his own death warrant at the same time," said Lestrade.

"Oh, you think so?"

"Don't you?"

"Well, it is quite possible, but the case is not clear to me yet."

"Not clear? Well, if that isn't clear, what *could* be clear? Here is a young man who learns suddenly that, if a certain older man dies, he will succeed to a fortune. What does he do? He says nothing to anyone, but he arranges that he shall go out on some pretext to see his client that night. He waits until the only other person in the house is in bed, and then in the solitude of a man's room he murders him, burns his body in the woodpile, and departs to a neighboring hotel. The bloodstains in the room and also on the stick are very slight. It is probable that he imagined his crime to be a bloodless one, and hoped that if the body were consumed it would hide

---

[2] *points:* where tracks cross other tracks and cause trains to joggle.

all traces of the method of his death — traces which, for some reason, must have pointed to him. Is not all this obvious?"

"It strikes me, my good Lestrade, as being just a trifle too obvious," said Holmes. "You do not add imagination to your other great qualities, but if you could for one moment put yourself in the place of this young man, would you choose the very night after the will had been made to commit your crime? Would it not seem dangerous to you to make so very close a relation between the two incidents? Again, would you choose an occasion when you are known to be in the house, when a servant has let you in? And, finally, would you take the great pains to conceal the body, and yet leave your own stick as a sign that you were the criminal? Confess, Lestrade, that all this is very unlikely."

"As to the stick, Mr. Holmes, you know as well as I do that a criminal is often flurried, and does such things, which a cool man would avoid. He was very likely afraid to go back to the room. Give me another theory that would fit the facts."

"I could very easily give you half a dozen," said Holmes. "Here, for example, is a very possible and even probable one. I make you a free present of it. The older man is showing documents which are of evident value. A passing tramp sees them through the window, the blind of which is only half down. Exit the solicitor. Enter the tramp! He seizes a stick, which he observes there, kills Oldacre, and departs after burning the body."

"Why should the tramp burn the body?"

"For the matter of that, why should McFarlane?"

"To hide some evidence."

"Possibly the tramp wanted to hide that any murder at all had been committed."

"And why did the tramp take nothing?"

"Because they were papers that he could not negotiate."

Lestrade shook his head, though it seemed to me that his manner was less absolutely assured than before.

"Well, Mr. Sherlock Holmes, you may look for your tramp, and while you are finding him we will hold on to our man. The future will show which is right. Just notice this point, Mr. Holmes: that so far as we know, none of the papers were removed, and that the prisoner is the one man in the world who had no reason for removing them, since he was heir-at-law, and would come into them in any case."

My friend seemed struck by this remark.

"I don't mean to deny that the evidence is in some ways very strongly in favor of your theory," said he. "I only wish to point out that there are other theories possible. As you say, the future will decide. Good morning! I dare say that in the course of the day I shall drop in at Norwood and see how you are getting on."

When the detective departed, my friend rose and made his preparations for the day's work with the alert air of a man who has a congenial task before him.

"My first movement, Watson," said he, as he bustled into his frockcoat, "must, as I said, be in the direction of Blackheath."

"And why not Norwood?"

"Because we have in this case one singular incident coming close to the heels of another singular incident. The police are making the mistake of concentrating their attention upon the second, because it happens to be the one which is actually criminal. But it is evident to me that the logical way to approach the case is to begin by trying to throw some light upon the first incident — the curious will, so suddenly made, and to so unexpected an heir. It may do something to simplify what followed. No, my dear fellow, I don't think you can help me. There is no prospect of danger, or I should not dream of stirring out without you. I trust that when I see you in the evening, I will be able to report that I have been able to do something for this unfortunate youngster, who has thrown himself upon my protection."

It was late when my friend returned, and I could see, by a glance at his haggard and anxious face, that the high hopes with which he had started had not been fulfilled. For an hour he droned away upon his violin, endeavoring to soothe his own ruffled spirits. At last he flung down the instrument, and plunged into a detailed account of his misadventures.

"It's all going wrong, Watson — all as wrong as it can go. I kept a bold face before Lestrade, but, upon my soul, I believe that for once the fellow is on the right track and we are on the wrong. All my instincts are one way, and all the facts are the other, and I much fear that British juries have not yet attained that pitch of intelligence when they will give the preference to my theories over Lestrade's facts."

"Did you go to Blackheath?"

"Yes, Watson, I went there, and I found very quickly that the late lamented Oldacre was a pretty considerable blackguard. The father was away in search of his son. The mother was at home — a little, fluffy, blue-eyed person, in a tremor of fear and indignation. Of course, she would not admit even the possibility of his guilt. But she would not express either surprise or regret over the fate of Oldacre. On the contrary, she spoke of him with such bitterness that she was unconsciously considerably strengthening the case of the police, for of course, if her son had heard her speak of the man in this fashion, it would predispose him toward hatred and violence. 'He was more like a malignant and cunning ape than a human being,' said she, 'and he always was, ever since he was a young man.'

" 'You knew him at that time?' said I.

" 'Yes, I knew him well. In fact, he was an old suitor of mine. Thank heaven that I had the sense to turn away from him and to marry a better, if poorer, man. I was engaged to him, Mr. Holmes, when I heard a shocking story of how he had turned a cat loose in an aviary, and I was so horrified at his brutal cruelty that I would have nothing more to do with him.' She rummaged in a bureau, and presently she produced a photograph of a woman, shamefully defaced and mutilated with a knife. 'That is my own photograph,' she said. 'He sent it to me in that state, with his curse, upon my wedding morning.'

" 'Well,' said I, 'at least he has forgiven you now, since he has left all his property to your son.'

" 'Neither my son nor I want anything from Jonas Oldacre, dead or alive!' she cried, with a proper spirit. 'There is a God in heaven, Mr. Holmes, and that same God who has punished that wicked man will show, in His own good time, that my son's hands are guiltless of his blood.'

"Well, I tried one or two leads, but could get at nothing which would help our hypothesis, and several points which would make against it. I gave it up at last, and off I went to Norwood.

"This place, Deep Dene House, is a big modern villa of staring brick, standing back in its own grounds, with a laurel-clumped lawn in front of it. To the right and some distance back from the road was the timber yard which had been the scene of the fire. Here's a rough plan on a leaf of my notebook. This window on the left is the one which opens into Oldacre's room. You can look into it from the road, you see. That is about the only bit of consolation I have had today. Lestrade was not there, but his head constable did the honors. They had just found a great treasure-trove. They had spent the morning raking among the ashes of the burned woodpile, and besides the charred organic remains they had secured several discolored metal discs. I examined them with care, and there was no doubt that they were trouser buttons. I even distinguished that one of them was marked with the name of 'Hyams,' who was Oldacre's tailor. I then worked the lawn very carefully for signs and traces, but this drought has made everything as hard as iron. Nothing was to be seen save that some body or bundle had been dragged through a low privet hedge which is in a line with the woodpile. All that, of course, fits in with the official theory. I crawled about the lawn with an August sun on my back, but I got up at the end of an hour no wiser than before.

"Well, after this fiasco I went into the bedroom and examined that also. The bloodstains were very slight, mere smears and discolorations, but undoubtedly fresh. The stick had been removed, but there also the marks were slight. There is no doubt about the stick belonging to our client. He admits it. Footmarks of both men could be made out on the carpet, but none of any third person, which again is a trick for the other side. They were piling up their score all the time and we were at a standstill.

"Only one little gleam of hope did I get — and yet it amounted to nothing. I examined the contents of the safe, most of which had been taken out and left on the table. The papers had been made up into sealed envelopes, one or two of which had been opened by the police. They were not, so far as I could judge, of any great value, nor did the bankbook show that Mr. Oldacre was in such very affluent circumstances. But it seemed to me that all the papers were not there. There were allusions to some deeds — possibly the more valuable — which I could not find. This, of course, if we could definitely prove it, would turn Lestrade's argument against himself; for who would steal a thing if he knew that he would shortly inherit it?

"Finally, having drawn every other cover and picked up no scent, I tried my luck with the housekeeper. Mrs. Lexington is her name

— a little, dark, silent person, with suspicious and sidelong eyes. She could tell us something if she would — I am convinced of it. But she was as close as wax. Yes, she had let Mr. McFarlane in at half-past nine. She wished her hand had withered before she had done so. She had gone to bed at half-past ten. Her room was at the other end of the house, and she could hear nothing of what passed. Mr. McFarlane had left his hat, and to the best of her belief his stick, in the hall. She had been awakened by the alarm of fire. Her poor, dear master had certainly been murdered. Had he any enemies? Well, every man had enemies, but Mr. Oldacre kept himself very much to himself, and only met people in the way of business. She had seen the buttons, and was sure that they belonged to the clothes which he had worn last night. The woodpile was very dry, for it had not rained for a month. It burned like tinder, and by the time she reached the spot, nothing could be seen but flames. She and all the firemen smelled the burned flesh from inside it. She knew nothing of the papers, nor of Mr. Oldacre's private affairs.

"So, my dear Watson, there's my report of a failure. And yet — and yet — " he clenched his thin hands in a paroxysm of conviction — "I *know* it's all wrong. I feel it in my bones. There is something that has not come out, and that housekeeper knows it. There was a sort of sulky defiance in her eyes, which only goes with guilty knowledge. However, there's no good talking any more about it, Watson; but unless some lucky chance comes our way I fear that the Norwood Disappearance Case will not figure in that chronicle of our successes which I foresee that a patient public will sooner or later have to endure."

"Surely," said I, "the man's appearance would go far with any jury?"

"That is a dangerous argument, my dear Watson. You remember that terrible murderer, Bert Stevens, who wanted us to get him off in '87? Was there ever a more mild-mannered, Sunday-school young man?"

"It is true."

"Unless we succeed in establishing an alternative theory, this man is lost. You can hardly find a flaw in the case which can now be presented against him, and all further investigation has served to strengthen it. By the way, there is one curious little point about those papers which may serve us as the starting point for an inquiry. On looking over the bankbook I found that the low state of the balance was principally due to large checks which have been made out during the last year to Mr. Cornelius. I confess that I should be interested to know who this Mr. Cornelius may be with whom a retired builder has had such very large transactions. Is it possible that he has had a hand in the affair? Cornelius might be a broker, but we have found no scrip to correspond with these large payments. Failing any other indication, my researches must now take the direction of an inquiry at the bank for the gentleman who has cashed these checks. But I fear, my dear fellow, that our case will end ingloriously by Lestrade hanging our client, which will certainly be a triumph for Scotland Yard."

I do not know how far Sherlock Holmes took any sleep that night, but when I came down to breakfast I found him pale and harassed, his bright eyes the brighter for the dark shadows around them. The carpet around his chair was littered with cigarette ends and with the early editions of the morning papers. An open telegram lay upon the table.

"What do you think of this, Watson?" he asked, tossing it across. It was from Norwood, and ran as follows:

> Important fresh evidence to hand. McFarlane's guilt definitely established. Advise you to abandon case.
> LESTRADE.

"This sounds serious," said I.

"It is Lestrade's little cock-a-doodle of victory," Holmes answered, with a bitter smile. "And yet it may be premature to abandon the case. After all, important fresh evidence is a two-edged thing, and may possibly cut in a very different direction to that which Lestrade imagines. Take your breakfast, Watson, and we will go out together and see what we can do. I feel as if I shall need your company and your moral support today."

My friend had no breakfast himself, for it was one of his peculiarities that in his more intense moments he would permit himself no food, and I have known him to presume upon his iron strength until he has fainted from pure inanition. "At present I cannot spare energy and nerve force for digestion," he would say in answer to my medical remonstrances. I was not surprised, therefore, when this morning he left his untouched meal behind him, and started with me for Norwood. A crowd of morbid sightseers were still gathered around Deep Dene House, which was just such a suburban villa as I had pictured. Within the gates Lestrade met us, his face flushed with victory, his manner grossly triumphant.

"Well, Mr. Holmes, have you proved us to be wrong yet? Have you found your tramp?" he cried.

"I have formed no conclusion whatever," my companion answered.

"But we formed ours yesterday, and now it proves to be correct, so you must acknowledge that we have been a little in front of you this time, Mr. Holmes."

"You certainly have the air of something unusual having occurred," said Holmes.

Lestrade laughed loudly.

"You don't like being beaten any more than the rest of us do," said he. "A man can't expect always to have it his own way, can he, Dr. Watson? Step this way, if you please, gentlemen, and I think I can convince you once for all that it was John McFarlane who did this crime."

He led us through the passage and out into a dark hall beyond.

"This is where young McFarlane must have come out to get his hat after the crime was done," said he. "Now look at this." With dramatic suddenness he struck a match, and by its light exposed a stain of blood upon the whitewashed wall. As he held the match nearer, I saw that it was more than a stain. It was the well-marked print of a thumb.

"Look at that with your magnifying glass, Mr. Holmes."

"Yes, I am doing so."

"You are aware that no two thumb marks are alike?"

"I have heard something of the kind."

"Well, then, will you please compare that print with this wax impression of young McFarlane's right thumb, taken by my orders this morning?"

As he held the waxen print close to the bloodstain, it did not take a magnifying glass to see that the two were undoubtedly from the same thumb. It was evident to me that our unfortunate client was lost.

"That is final," said Lestrade.

"Yes, that is final," I involuntarily echoed.

"It is final," said Holmes.

Something in his tone caught my ear, and I turned to look at him. An extraordinary change had come over his face. It was writhing with inward merriment. His two eyes were shining like stars. It seemed to me that he was making desperate efforts to restrain a convulsive attack of laughter.

"Dear me! Dear me!" he said at last. "Well, now, who would have thought it? And how deceptive appearances may be, to be sure! Such a nice young man to look at! It is a lesson to us not to trust our own judgment, is it not, Lestrade?"

"Yes, some of us are a little too much inclined to be cocksure, Mr. Holmes," said Lestrade. The man's insolence was maddening, but we could not resent it.

"What a providential thing that this young man should press his right thumb against the wall in taking his hat from the peg! Such a very natural action, too, if you come to think of it." Holmes was outwardly calm, but his whole body gave a wriggle of suppressed excitement as he spoke.

"By the way, Lestrade, who made this remarkable discovery?"

"It was the housekeeper, Mrs. Lexington, who drew the night constable's attention to it."

"Where was the night constable?"

"He remained on guard in the bedroom where the crime was committed, so as to see that nothing was touched."

"But why didn't the police see this mark yesterday?"

"Well, we had no particular reason to make a careful examination of the hall. Besides, it's not in a very prominent place, as you see."

"No, no — of course not. I suppose there is no doubt that the mark was there yesterday?"

Lestrade looked at Holmes as if he thought he was going out of his mind. I confess that I was myself surprised both at his hilarious manner and at his rather wild observation.

"I don't know whether you think that McFarlane came out of jail in the dead of the night in order to strengthen the evidence against himself," said Lestrade. "I leave it to any expert in the world whether that is not the mark of his thumb."

"It is unquestionably the mark of his thumb."

"There, that's enough," said Lestrade. "I am a practical man, Mr. Holmes, and when I have got my evidence I come to my conclusions. If you have anything to say, you will find me writing my report in the sitting room."

Holmes had recovered his equanimity, though I still seemed to detect gleams of amusement in his expression.

"Dear me, this is a very sad development, Watson, is it not?" said he. "And yet there are singular points about it which hold out some hopes for our client."

"I am delighted to hear it," said I, heartily. "I was afraid it was all up with him."

"I would hardly go so far as to say that, my dear Watson. The fact is that there is one really serious flaw in this evidence to which our friend attaches so much importance."

"Indeed, Holmes! What is it?"

"Only this: that I *know* that that mark was not there when I examined the hall yesterday. And now, Watson, let us have a little stroll around in the sunshine."

With a confused brain, but with a heart into which some warmth of hope was returning, I accompanied my friend in a walk around the garden. Holmes took each face of the house in turn, and examined it with great interest. He then led the way inside, and went over the whole building from basement to attic. Most of the rooms were unfurnished, but none the less Holmes inspected them all minutely. Finally, on the top corridor, which ran outside three untenanted bedrooms, he again was seized with a spasm of merriment.

"There are really some very unique features about this case, Watson," said he. "I think it is time now that we took our friend Lestrade into our confidence. He has had his little smile at our expense, and perhaps we may do as much by him, if my reading of this problem proves to be correct. Yes, yes, I think I see how we should approach it."

The Scotland Yard inspector was still writing in the parlor when Holmes interrupted him.

"I understood that you were writing a report of this case," said he.

"So I am."

"Don't you think it may be a little premature? I can't help thinking that your evidence is not complete."

Lestrade knew my friend too well to disregard his words. He laid down his pen and looked curiously at him.

"What do you mean, Mr. Holmes?"

"Only that there is an important witness whom you have not seen."

"Can you produce him?"

"I think I can."

"Then do so."

"I will do my best. How many constables have you?"

"There are three within call."

"Excellent!" said Holmes. "May I ask if they are all large, able-bodied men with powerful voices?"

"I have no doubt they are, though I fail to see what their voices have to do with it."

"Perhaps I can help you to see that and one or two other things as well," said Holmes. "Kindly summon your men, and I will try."

Five minutes later, three policemen had assembled in the hall.

"In the outhouse you will find a considerable quantity of straw," said Holmes. "I will ask you to carry in two bundles of it. I think it will be of the greatest assistance in producing the witness whom I require. Thank you very much. I believe you have some matches in your pocket, Watson. Now, Mr. Lestrade, I will ask you all to accompany me to the top landing."

As I have said, there was a broad corridor there, which ran outside three empty bedrooms. At one end of the corridor we were all marshaled by Sherlock Holmes, the constables grinning and Lestrade staring at my friend with amazement, expectation, and derision chasing each other across his features. Holmes stood before us with the air of a conjurer who is performing a trick.

"Would you kindly send one of your constables for two buckets of water? Put the straw on the floor here, free from the wall on either side. Now I think that we are all ready."

Lestrade's face had begun to grow red and angry.

"I don't know whether you are playing a game with us, Mr. Sherlock Holmes," said he. "If you know anything, you can surely say it without all this tomfoolery."

"I assure you, my good Lestrade, that I have an excellent reason for everything that I do. You may possibly remember that you chaffed me a little, some hours ago, when the sun seemed on your side of the hedge, so you must not grudge me a little pomp and ceremony now. Might I ask you, Watson, to open that window, and then to put a match to the edge of the straw?"

I did so, and, driven by the draft, a coil of gray smoke swirled down the corridor, while the dry straw crackled and flamed.

"Now we must see if we can find this witness for you, Lestrade. Might I ask you all to join in the cry of 'Fire!'? Now then; one, two, three ——"

"Fire!" we all yelled.

"Thank you. I will trouble you once again."

"Fire!"

"Just once more, gentlemen, and all together."

"Fire!" The shout must have rung over Norwood.

It had hardly died away when an amazing thing happened. A door suddenly flew open out of what appeared to be solid wall at the end of the corridor, and a little, wizened man darted out of it, like a rabbit out of its burrow.

"Capital!" said Holmes, calmly. "Watson, a bucket of water over the straw. That will do! Lestrade, allow me to present you with your principal missing witness, Mr. Jonas Oldacre."

The detective stared at the newcomer with blank amazement. The latter was blinking in the bright light of the corridor, and peering at us and at the smoldering fire. It was an odious face — crafty, vicious, malignant, with shifty, light-gray eyes and white lashes.

"What's this, then?" said Lestrade, at last. "What have you been doing all this time, eh?"

Oldacre gave an uneasy laugh, shrinking back from the furious red face of the angry detective.

"I have done no harm."

"No harm? You've done your best to get an innocent man hanged. If it wasn't for this gentleman here, I am not sure that you would not have succeeded."

The wretched creature began to whimper.

"I am sure, sir, it was only my practical joke."

"Oh! a joke, was it? You won't find the laugh on your side, I promise you. Take him down, and keep him in the sitting room until I come. Mr. Holmes," he continued, when they had gone, "I could not speak before the constables, but I don't mind saying, in the presence of Dr. Watson, that this is the brightest thing that you have done yet, though it is a mystery to me how you did it. You have saved an innocent man's life, and you have prevented a very grave scandal, which would have ruined my reputation in the Force."

Holmes smiled, and clapped Lestrade upon the shoulder.

"Instead of being ruined, my good sir, you will find that your reputation has been enormously enhanced. Just make a few alterations in that report which you were writing, and they will understand how hard it is to throw dust in the eyes of Inspector Lestrade."

"And you don't want your name to appear?"

"Not at all. The work is its own reward. Perhaps I shall get the credit also at some distant day, when I permit my zealous historian to lay out his foolscap once more — eh, Watson? Well, now, let us see where this rat has been lurking."

A lath-and-plaster partition had been run across the passage six feet from the end, with a door cunningly concealed in it. It was lit within by slits under the eaves. A few articles of furniture and a supply of food and water were within, together with a number of books and papers.

"There's the advantage of being a builder," said Holmes, as we came out. "He was able to fix up his own little hiding place without any confederate — save, of course, that precious housekeeper of his, whom I should lose no time in adding to your bag, Lestrade."

"I'll take your advice. But how did you know of this place, Mr. Holmes?"

"I made up my mind that the fellow was in hiding in the house. When I paced one corridor and found it six feet shorter than the corresponding one below, it was pretty clear where he was. I thought he had not the nerve to lie quiet before an alarm of fire. We could, of course, have gone in and taken him, but it amused me to make him reveal himself. Besides, I owed you a little mystification, Lestrade, for your chaff in the morning."

"Well, sir, you certainly got equal with me on that. But how in the world did you know that he was in the house at all?"

"The thumb mark, Lestrade. You said it was final; and so it was, in a very different sense. I knew it had not been there the day before. I pay a good deal of attention to matters of detail, as you may have observed, and I had examined the hall, and was sure that the wall was clear. Therefore, it had been put on during the night."

"But how?"

"Very simply. When those packets were sealed up, Jonas Oldacre got McFarlane to secure one of the seals by putting his thumb upon the soft wax. It would be done so quickly and so naturally, that I daresay the young man himself has no recollection of it. Very likely it just so happened, and Oldacre had himself no notion of the use he would put it to. Brooding over the case in that den of his, it suddenly struck him what absolutely damning evidence he could make against McFarlane by using that thumb mark. It was the simplest thing in the world for him to take a wax impression from the seal, to moisten it in as much blood as he could get from a pin prick, and to put the mark upon the wall during the night, either with his own hand or with that of his housekeeper. If you examine among those documents which he took with him into his retreat, I will lay you a wager that you find the seal with the thumb mark upon it."

"Wonderful!" said Lestrade. "Wonderful! It's all as clear as crystal, as you put it. But what is the object of this deep deception, Mr. Holmes?"

It was amusing to me to see how the detective's overbearing manner had changed suddenly to that of a child asking questions of its teacher.

"Well, I don't think that is very hard to explain. A very deep, malicious, vindictive person is the gentleman who is now awaiting us downstairs. You know that he was once refused by McFarlane's mother? You don't! I told you that you should go to Blackheath first and Norwood afterward. Well, this injury, as he would consider it, has rankled in his wicked, scheming brain, and all his life he has longed for vengeance, but never seen his chance. During the last year or two, things have gone against him — secret speculation, I think — and he finds himself in a bad way. He determines to swindle his creditors, and for this purpose he pays large checks to a certain Mr. Cornelius, who is, I imagine, himself under another name. I have not traced these checks yet, but I have no doubt that they were banked under that name at some provincial town where Oldacre from time to time led a double existence. He intended to change his name altogether, draw this money, and vanish, starting life again elsewhere."

"Well, that's likely enough."

"It would strike him that in disappearing he might throw all pursuit off his track, and at the same time have an ample and crushing revenge upon his old sweetheart, if he could give the impression that he had been murdered by her only child. It was a masterpiece of villainy, and he carried it out like a master. The idea of the will, which would give an obvious motive for the crime, the secret visit unknown to his own parents, the retention of the stick, the blood, and the animal remains and buttons in the woodpile, all were admirable. It was a net from which it seemed to me, a few hours ago, that there was no possible escape. But he had not that supreme gift of the artist, the knowledge of when to stop. He wished to improve that which was already perfect — to draw the rope tighter yet around the neck of his unfortunate victim — and so he ruined all. Let us descend, Lestrade. There are just one or two questions that I would ask him."

The malignant creature was seated in his own parlor, with a policeman upon each side of him.

"It was a joke, my good sir — a practical joke, nothing more," he whined incessantly. "I assure you, sir, that I simply concealed myself in order to see the effect of my disappearance, and I am sure that you would not be so unjust as to imagine that I would have allowed any harm to befall poor young Mr. McFarlane."

"That's for a jury to decide," said Lestrade. "Anyhow, we shall have you on a charge of conspiracy, if not for attempted murder."

"And you'll probably find that your creditors will impound the banking account of Mr. Cornelius," said Holmes.

The little man started, and turned his malignant eyes upon my friend.

"I have to thank you for a good deal," said he. "Perhaps I'll pay my debt some day."

Holmes smiled indulgently.

"I fancy that, for some few years, you will find your time very fully occupied," said he. "By the way, what was it you put into the woodpile besides your old trousers? A dead dog, or rabbits, or what? You won't tell? Dear me, how very unkind of you! Well, well, I daresay that a couple of rabbits would account both for the blood and for the charred ashes. If ever you write an account, Watson, you can make rabbits serve your turn."

A storyteller works with his imagination and his experience. Some stories are very close to the author's own experience; others spring almost completely from his imagination. For example, although "The Cask of Amontillado" was written in America in the nineteenth century, it is set in Italy hundreds of years before. The narrator of the story does not resemble the author, Poe. The following story, however, is very close to a real event in the author's life. From Jesse Stuart's other writings we would discover that the boy in the story is similar to young Jesse himself.

The storyteller must use his imagination. He has to select details and arrange them in some order. He has to tell the story from a certain point of view. More than likely he wants to give his story a purpose or find a theme for it. He chooses a certain style for his story, a tone of voice. All of these things add up to the fact that every story is a work of the imagination, even when it is close to "what really happened." The fact that Jesse Stuart changed the name of the family in this story from "Stuart" to "Powderjay" is one indication that he wants the reader to see it as fiction, not as autobiography.

Land of Our Enemies

JESSE STUART

"Pap will never ride another log raft down this river," Pa said, as he looked from the train window at the Big Sandy River. "I've gone down this river to Gate City with 'im many a time when I was a little shaver. I've seen a big poplar log break loose from the raft and I've seen Pap jump from the raft onto it and the spikes in his boot heels wouldn't ketch and the log would dump 'im in the icy water. Pap would come up a-spittin' water and a-cussin'. But he'd get his log back to the raft. It makes a body have a funny feelin' to remember all of these things."

Our train was lumberin' and creakin' around the curves farther up the twisting Big Sandy. The sun had gone down and twilight was settling over the deep valley. Here and there we could see a light in a shack beside the railroad tracks. Soon the thin-leafed mountain slopes faded into twilight and gradually into darkness, until we could no longer see the outlines of the mountains and the white streams of water. We were riding into darkness, a darkness so thick that it looked like from the train window one could reach out and slice it into black ribbons with a pocketknife.

"Lindsay, Lindsay," the conductor said as he entered our coach. "All out for Lindsay!"

"Do you reckon anybody will be at the station to meet us?" I asked Pa.

"Somebody'll be here," he said. "Somebody'll be at this station to meet every train. Powderjays will be a-comin' back here on every train."

"When will they bury Grandpa?" I asked Pa.

"Shhh! Not so loud," he whispered, as he glanced over his shoulder.

I looked around to see two beardy-faced men with mean-lookin' eyes listening to what we said.

"You never know whether you're a-talkin' before a friend 'r an enemy here," Pa whispered to me.

The two beardy-faced men got up from their seats and followed us from the train.

"Air ye a-goin' to Cousin Mick Powderjay's funeral?" one of the men asked Pa soon as we had stepped off the train.

"That's where we're a-goin'," Pa said. "Is he akin to you?"

"We're brother's children," the man said. "I'm Zack Powderjay. And this is my brother, Dave Powderjay! We're Zack Powderjay's boys."

"I'm Mick Powderjay," Pa told them. "Pap's eleventh child by his first wife!"

"We've heard of ye," Zack Powderjay said. "See, we had to leave the Big Sandy a long time ago."

"When did you leave?" Pa asked.

"In President Hayes's administration," Dave Powderjay said.

"I left in Grover Cleveland's second administration," Pa said.

"Why did you leave?" Dave Powderjay asked Pa.

"Trouble with the Hornbuckles," he said.

"Trouble with th' Hornbuckles and Dangerfields caused us to leave," Dave said.

"Did Cousin Mick die a natural death?" Zack Powderjay asked Pa.

"I ain't heard yet but I know Pap didn't die a natural death," Pa said. "He had more enemies than he had ailments of the body."

"Ye're right, brother," a husky voice sounded in the darkness now that the train had gone. "I'm Keith Powderjay, son of Jimmie Powderjay, oldest son of Mick Powderjay. I've come to meet this train to direct any and all Powderjays and their bloodkin to the right spot."

"Then Pap was killed?" Pa asked Keith Powderjay, who had come close enough for Pa to recognize him.

Keith was a mountain of a man towering above us.

"He was beaten to death with a club," Keith told us. "Wait until you see 'im."

"Who kilt Cousin Mick?" Dave Powderjay asked.

"We know but we ain't a-sayin' now," Keith said. "Two men done it. And we got men out atter 'em tonight. Ye may hear of two deaths before mornin'."

"It makes my blood bile," Pa said. "But I've been expectin' somethin' to happen to Pap fer many years. He's been a-fightin' a long war."

"We're all riled a-plenty," Keith said. "We'd better git goin'."

"Do you have a lantern?" Pa asked. "I can't see well in the dark."

"But ye can't have a lantern, Uncle Mick," Keith said. "Lanterns air good targets at night."

"I've been away a long time," Pa said. "I jist fergot. Hit's all a-comin' back to me now."

And as we followed Keith Powderjay through the darkness, Pa's words came back to me. I remembered when we used to sit around the fire on winter nights at home how Pa would tell about going to the railroad station or to church and how he would walk in the darkness because he was afraid to carry a lantern. He would tell us how men had waited for him because he was a son of old Mick Powderjay and how he had been shot at many times. Once a bullet came so close he felt the wind from it on the tip of his nose.

"No talkin' here," Cousin Keith told us. "Quiet until I tell ye when to talk."

Everybody got quiet and we had to walk hand in hand with Cousin Keith leadin' us. But he had been over this path so many times, he could feel the path with his feet.

I'm glad Grandpa Powderjay moved to the Little Sandy River in Cleveland's administration, I thought. I'm glad Pa didn't go back with Grandpa when he got homesick for the Big Sandy and moved back to fight with his enemies. I'm glad Pa stayed on the Little Sandy and I was born there.

Grandpa had been a soldier; he had fought in Pennsylvania, Maryland, and Virginia. Gettysburg was a name to him that he would never forget; Antietam, Bull Run, Cold Harbor, Fredericksburg, Richmond [1] were names that I had heard him talk about since I could remember. He had fought through the war from beginning to end and the only scars he had were around his wrists where he had been hanged by the arms to the joist of an old house. Captured twice and hanged once, he had come out of the war a living man.

But this was not the war that got Grandpa into trouble. When he came home he fought a long war. It was a war that never ended. He waged war on the guerrilla bands, who had captured, killed, and plundered while he and other mountain men were away fighting in Northern and Southern armies. These guerrilla bands didn't belong to either army. Grandpa had fought them since eighteen sixty-five, all but the three years he had lived on the Little Sandy. Now they had gotten 'im in the end as they said they would.

"We're a-past the dangerous places," Cousin Keith said. "We're a-past the Hornbuckles and Dangerfields."

"How much fudder do we haf to go?" Dave Powderjay asked.

"About three miles," Cousin Keith said.

"When will they bury Pap?" Pa asked.

"Two o'clock in the mornin'," Cousin Keith said.

"It's too bad to haf to bury Pap at night," Pa sighed.

"But this is a land of our enemies," Cousin Keith said. "Grandpa died a-fightin' his enemies. He told me two days before he's kilt that if all his bloodkin had stayed with 'im he'd a-winned this war in the end."

"But brother Zack and I were glad to get out'n it," Dave Powderjay said. "Glad to get into the mountains of West Virginia. We left soon as Pap and brother Tom were kilt, and we have lived in West Virginia and raised our famblies in peace."

---

[1] *Gettysburg . . . Richmond:* scenes of Civil War battles.

I had never heard of a funeral at night but I had read in my history book in school where General Braddock[2] was buried at night so the Indians wouldn't find his grave. I guess the reason that we buried Grandpa at night wasn't that his enemies would bother his grave but that his enemies would bother his bloodkin that had gathered to see him buried. I knew if we couldn't walk from the railroad to the shack where Grandpa lived and carry a light we couldn't have a funeral in the daytime. I knew that we were among our enemies. Though we had killed many of their people, there wasn't a family among us but Pa's where one, two, or three men had not fallen from the ambush shots of our enemies.

Why are we such hated people? I thought.

"I'll tell you where Pap made his mistake," Pa said. "He made it when he married his second wife, Mattie Henson. She's a first cousin of Anse Dangerfield and Tobbie Hornbuckle! I can't understand what made Pap marry an en'my!"

"That's right, Uncle Mick," Cousin Keith said. "Ye hit the nail on the head. If our men air lucky tonight, ye'll know tomorrow that this is the truth."

I couldn't tell when we reached Grandpa's shack. There wasn't a light from any window. Cousin Keith knocked three times on the door; it was opened by Pa's oldest brother, Uncle Cief. "Come in," he said softly.

And we followed him into the crowd of our people — beardy-faced men, and women with deep-lined faces. There was silence in the room, and everybody's face was clouded.

"Where's Mattie?" Pa asked.

"She's not here anymore," Aunt Arabella said. "Pap and her's been separated fer some time."

And now I saw assembled for the first time Pa's people — my bloodkin from the East Kentucky mountains. They were my bloodkin that I had heard about but didn't know very well; many of the men had scars on their faces and hands and many of them limped. I was glad, after I looked at them, that I had not been through a long guerrilla war.

"Come this way," Cousin Keith said, beckoning to us.

---

[2] *General Braddock*: Edward Braddock, British general during the French and Indian War (1754–63).

We followed him into the room where Grandpa was in his homemade coffin.

"Look at this, won't ye!"

Cousin Keith pointed to the wide blue marks across Grandpa's battered face where he had been beaten to death. And then he bent over and opened his coat and shirt and showed us the pulp-beats on his chest. I had never seen a man beaten as he had been beaten — this mountain of a man who had died in the battle he had been fighting forty-six years. His face was clean shaven and his mustache neatly trimmed and his gray hair parted on the side. His mouth was set firmly. I had seen him in life when his mouth was set as it was now. His mouth was like this in life when he spoke of his enemies.

Pa turned and walked away. He couldn't stand to look at Grandpa. He went back into the room where the old crippled soldiers sat, wearing their tattered uniforms and holding their rifles in their hands. They had fought with Grandpa. Now they had come for his funeral. Pa called them by their names and shook their hands. They were white-haired, white-bearded, and grisly old warriors who had seen their best days and had come to see an old comrade buried. They seemed to have risen from a dim and distant past.

"Your pap wuz as good a soldier as ever lived," one spoke feebly to Pa. "But one war wuz not enough fer 'im. He oughta quit then. No use fightin' all his life."

"He was the best wrestler in Grant's army," another said. "I never saw him rode in all the bouts he had."

There were low whispers among my people in the small, crowded, three-room shack. Heavy quilts were hangin' over the windows so not a ray of light could be seen from the outside. Wind came between the log-cracks, and the flames of oil lamps sputtered and smoked the lamp globes. I remembered while I stood here among my people and these old soldiers in their faded uniforms what Pa had told Mom. He had told her how Grandpa wouldn't sleep in a room unless a lamp was burning. Said he put quilts over the windows so they wouldn't be a target for his enemies shooting with rifles from the thickets on the mountain slopes.

We were quiet enough in the shack to hear the roosters crow for midnight. And as soon as they had finished crowing from their roosts outside the shack, Uncle Jason came into the room.

"It's about time fer us to start," he announced.

Six of my cousins, sons of Pa's older brothers, picked up Grandpa's coffin and stepped out into the darkness. They were tall, beardy men with broad shoulders. The muscles in their forearms bulged as they carried the big coffin and the big warrior in it from his shack out into the darkness. Aunt Emerine blew out the lamps, and the crowd of Powderjays, their in-laws and friends, followed the coffin into the darkness. Cousin Keith led the way up the mountain path and we followed. A moon came from behind a dark breadloaf-shaped mountain where jutted rocks were outlined against the misty sky. There were whispers among us as we walked along slowly. Twice my cousins had to let six more cousins carry the coffin, since it was such a load in the darkness to carry up a mountain slope.

"Not one of Pap's eight young'ins by Mattie air here," Uncle Cief told Pa. "And hit's good they ain't here. Thar's too much en'my blood in 'em to suit us."

I didn't know the part-guerrilla Powderjays from the real Powderjays. But I knew that the real Powderjays didn't have any use for them even if the same blood did flow through their veins. I heard Pa and Uncle Cief talking about them as the crowd moved slowly along. I was with my people and it seemed like a dream. I didn't know there was a world like the one I was in.

Suddenly our stumbling, whispering funeral crowd stopped on a lonely mountaintop. I could see rows of brown sandstones that had been chiseled with pickaxes and broadaxes marking the rows of graves. And I saw men standing by a fresh-dug grave holding their picks, adzes, and long-handled shovels. An owl flew over us on outspread wings we could hear fanning the night wind. And on a distant mountaintop we heard a whippoorwill. But there was not a light nor a sound among us while my cousins placed Grandpa's coffin beside his grave. "Tonight, we're a-buryin' a soldier who has had many fights," an old soldier said after Grandpa's coffin had been placed beside the grave. "He has fit through a long war in the land of his enemies and he has fit well."

From among men and women of our silent funeral crowd two men walked toward the old soldier. As they walked toward him, Uncle Cief put his hand on his pistol until he recognized them. One whispered something to the old soldier in charge of Grandpa's funeral.

"And I'm glad to tell you Mick Powderjay's death has been avenged," the old soldier announced. "Eif Dangerfield and Battle Henson 've paid fer thar crime!"

That was all that was said for Grandpa. There wasn't a preacher to preach his funeral and there weren't any songs. The old soldiers fired a farewell volley across his grave, and the fire from their rifles was the only light we had seen except the moonlight shining dimly through the sheets of white mist rising from the valley below us. Grandpa's coffin was lowered into his grave with leather checklines on a mountaintop where only Powderjays, their bloodkin, and in-laws were buried — a mountain high enough to overlook the rugged land of our people and our enemies.

A dashing hero, a beautiful and brave heroine, a jealous villain — these are the ingredients of many romantic tales.

"The Highwayman" is a "literary ballad," one written by a modern author in imitation of the old folk ballads. Notice that it has a strong rhythm and repeats many sounds and words.

The Highwayman

ALFRED NOYES

PART 1

The wind was a torrent of darkness among the gusty trees,
The moon was a ghostly galleon tossed upon cloudy seas,
The road was a ribbon of moonlight over the purple moor,
And the highwayman came riding —
    Riding — riding —
The highwayman came riding, up to the old inn door.

He'd a French cocked hat on his forehead, a bunch of lace at his chin,
A coat of the claret velvet, and breeches of brown doeskin;
They fitted with never a wrinkle; his boots were up to the thigh!
And he rode with a jeweled twinkle, 10
    His pistol butts a-twinkle,
His rapier hilt a-twinkle, under the jeweled sky.

Over the cobbles he clattered and clashed in the dark inn yard,
And he tapped with his whip on the shutters, but all was locked and barred:
He whistled a tune to the window, and who should be waiting there
But the landlord's black-eyed daughter,
    Bess, the landlord's daughter,
Plaiting a dark red love knot into her long black hair.

And dark in the dark old inn yard a stable wicket creaked
Where Tim the ostler° listened; his face was white and peaked; 20

---

20. *ostler:* stableman, usually spelled *hostler.*

216

His eyes were hollows of madness, his hair like moldy hay,
But he loved the landlord's daughter,
    The landlord's red-lipped daughter,
Dumb as a dog he listened, and he heard the robber say —

"One kiss, my bonny sweetheart, I'm after a prize tonight,
But I shall be back with the yellow gold before the morning light;
Yet, if they press me sharply, and harry me through the day,
Then look for me by moonlight,
    Watch for me by moonlight,
I'll come to thee by moonlight, though hell should bar the way."

He rose upright in the stirrups; he scarce could reach her hand,   31
But she loosened her hair i' the casement!° His face burned like a brand
As the black cascade of perfume came tumbling over his breast;
And he kissed its waves in the moonlight,
    (Oh, sweet black waves in the moonlight!)
Then he tugged at his rein in the moonlight, and galloped away to the West.

PART 2

He did not come in the dawning; he did not come at noon;
And out o' the tawny sunset, before the rise o' the moon,
When the road was a gipsy's ribbon, looping the purple moor,
A red-coat troop came marching —   40
    Marching — marching —
King George's men came marching, up to the old inn door.

They said no word to the landlord, they drank his ale instead,
But they gagged his daughter and bound her to the foot of her narrow bed;
Two of them knelt at her casement, with muskets at their side!
There was death at every window;
    And hell at one dark window;
For Bess could see, through her casement, the road that *he* would ride.

---
32. *casement*: a window that opens out with hinges at the side.

They had tied her up to attention, with many a sniggering jest;
They had bound a musket beside her, with the barrel beneath her breast! 50
"Now keep good watch!" and they kissed her. She heard the dead man say —
Look for me by moonlight;
 Watch for me by moonlight;
I'll come to thee by moonlight, though hell should bar the way!

She twisted her hands behind her; but all the knots held good!
She writhed her hands till her fingers were wet with sweat or blood!
They stretched and strained in the darkness, and the hours crawled by like years,
Till now, on the stroke of midnight,
 Cold, on the stroke of midnight,
The tip of one finger touched it! The trigger at least was hers! 60

The tip of one finger touched it; she strove no more for the rest!
Up, she stood up to attention, with the barrel beneath her breast,
She would not risk their hearing: she would not strive again;
For the road lay bare in the moonlight;
 Blank and bare in the moonlight;
And the blood of her veins in the moonlight throbbed to her love's refrain.

Tlot-tlot; tlot-tlot! Had they heard it? The horse-hoofs ringing clear;
Tlot-tlot, tlot-tlot, in the distance? Were they deaf that they did not hear?
Down the ribbon of moonlight, over the brow of the hill,
The highwayman came riding, 70
 Riding, riding!
The red coats looked to their priming! She stood up, straight and still!

Tlot-tlot, in the frosty silence! *Tlot-tlot,* in the echoing night!
Nearer he came and nearer! Her face was like a light!
Her eyes grew wide for a moment; she drew one last deep breath,
Then her finger moved in the moonlight,
 Her musket shattered the moonlight,
Shattered her breast in the moonlight and warned him — with her death.

He turned; he spurred to the westward; he did not know who stood
Bowed, with her head o'er the musket, drenched with her own red
    blood! 80
Not till the dawn he heard it; his face grew gray to hear
How Bess, the landlord's daughter,
    The landlord's black-eyed daughter,
Had watched for her love in the moonlight, and died in the darkness there.

Back he spurred like a madman, shrieking a curse to the sky,
With the white road smoking behind him, and his rapier brandished
    high!
Blood red were his spurs in the golden moon; wine red was his velvet coat,
When they shot him down on the highway,
    Down like a dog on the highway,
And he lay in his blood on the highway, with a bunch of lace at his
    throat. 90

And still of a winter's night, they say, when the wind is in the trees,
When the moon is a ghostly galleon tossed upon cloudy seas,
When the road is a ribbon of moonlight over the purple moor,
A highwayman comes riding —
    Riding — riding —
A highwayman comes riding, up to the old inn door.

Over the cobbles he clatters and clangs in the dark inn yard;
And he taps with his whip on the shutters, but all is locked and
    barred;
He whistles a tune to the window, and who should be waiting there
    But the landlord's black-eyed daughter,   100
    Bess, the landlord's daughter,
    Plaiting a dark red love knot into her long black hair.

Frost based this poem on an incident that he read about in a newspaper. The event moved Frost so deeply, in fact, that although he often recited his poems, he never read " 'Out, Out — '." "That's a poem I never read in public — too cruel," he once said. The scene is a New Hampshire farmyard.

"Out, Out — "

ROBERT FROST

The buzz saw snarled and rattled in the yard
And made dust and dropped stove-length sticks of wood,
Sweet-scented stuff when the breeze drew across it.
And from there those that lifted eyes could count
Five mountain ranges one behind the other
Under the sunset far into Vermont.
And the saw snarled and rattled, snarled and rattled,
As it ran light, or had to bear a load.
And nothing happened: day was all but done.
Call it a day, I wish they might have said
To please the boy by giving him the half-hour
That a boy counts so much when saved from work.
His sister stood beside them in her apron
To tell them "Supper." At the word, the saw,
As if to prove saws knew what supper meant,
Leaped out at the boy's hand, or seemed to leap —
He must have given the hand. However it was,
Neither refused the meeting. But the hand!
The boy's first outcry was a rueful laugh,
As he swung toward them holding up the hand
Half in appeal, but half as if to keep
The life from spilling. Then the boy saw all —
Since he was old enough to know, big boy
Doing a man's work, though a child at heart —
He saw all spoiled. "Don't let him cut my hand off —
The doctor, when he comes. Don't let him, sister!"
So. But the hand was gone already.

The doctor put him in the dark of ether.
He lay and puffed his lips out with his breath.
And then — the watcher at his pulse took fright.
No one believed. They listened at his heart.
Little — less — nothing! — and that ended it.
No more to build on there. And they, since they
Were not the one dead, turned to their affairs.

Here is another literary ballad, this time a comic one. Service's poem is in the tradition of the tall tale or yarn. Setting: The Yukon during the Gold Rush.

The Ballad of Blasphemous Bill

ROBERT W. SERVICE

I took a contract to bury the body of blasphemous Bill MacKie,
Whenever, wherever, or whatsoever the manner of death he die —
Whether he die in the light o' day or under the peak-faced moon;
In cabin or dance hall, camp or dive, mucklucks or patent shoon;°
On velvet tundra° or virgin peak, by glacier, drift, or draw;
In muskeg hollow or canyon gloom, by avalanche, fang, or claw;
By battle, murder, or sudden wealth, by pestilence, hooch,° or lead —
I swore on the Book I would follow and look till I found my tombless dead.

For Bill was a dainty kind of cuss, and his mind was mighty sot
On a dinky patch with flowers and grass in a civilized bone-yard lot.   10
And where he died or how he died, it didn't matter a dram
So long as he had a grave with frills and a tombstone "epigram."
So I promised him, and he paid the price in good cheechako° coin
(Which the same I blowed in that very night down in the Tenderloin).°
Then I painted a three-foot slab of pine: "Here lies poor Bill MacKie,"
And I hung it up on my cabin wall and I waited for Bill to die.

---

4. *mucklucks* or *patent shoon:* sealskin boots or patent leather shoes.
5. *tundra:* treeless plain.
7. *hooch:* slang for liquor.
13. *cheechako:* in Alaska, a person newly arrived from the United States.
14. *Tenderloin:* the district in a town or city known for its vice and corruption.

THE BALLAD OF BLASPHEMOUS BILL 223

Years passed away, and at last one day came a squaw with a story strange,
Of a long-deserted line of traps 'way back of the Bighorn range;
Of a little hut by the great divide, and a white man stiff and still,
Lying there by his lonesome self, and I figured it must be Bill.   20
So I thought of the contract I'd made with him, and I took down from the shelf
The swell black box with the silver plate he'd picked out for hisself;
And I packed it full of grub and "hooch," and I slung it on the sleigh;
Then I harnessed up my team of dogs and was off at dawn of day.

You know what it's like in the Yukon wild when it's sixty-nine below;
When the ice worms wriggle their purple heads through the crust of the pale-blue snow;
When the pine trees crack like little guns in the silence of the wood,
And the icicles hang down like tusks under the parka hood;
When the stovepipe smoke breaks sudden off, and the sky is weirdly lit,
And the careless feel of a bit of steel burns like a red-hot spit;   30
When the mercury is a frozen ball, and the frostfiend stalks to kill —
Well, it was just like that that day when I set out to look for Bill.

Oh, the awful hush that seemed to crush me down on every hand,
As I blundered blind with a trail to find through that blank and bitter land;
Half-dazed, half-crazed in the winter wild, with its grim heartbreaking woes,
And the ruthless strife for a grip on life that only the sourdough° knows!
North by the compass, North I pressed; river and peak and plain
Passed like a dream I slept to lose and I waked to dream again.

River and plain and mighty peak — and who could stand unawed?
As their summits blazed, he could stand undazed at the foot of the throne of God.   40
North, aye, North, through a land accurst, shunned by the scouring brutes,

---

36. *sourdough*: slang for a pioneer or prospector.

And all I heard was my own harsh word and the whine of the mala-
mutes,°
Till at last I came to a cabin squat, built in the side of a hill,
And I burst in the door, and there on the floor, frozen to death, lay
Bill.

Ice, white ice, like a winding sheet, sheathing each smoke-grimed
wall;
Ice on the stovepipe, ice on the bed, ice gleaming over all;
Sparkling ice on the dead man's chest, glittering ice in his hair,
Ice on his fingers, ice in his heart, ice in his glassy stare;
Hard as a log and trussed like a frog, with his arms and legs out-
spread.
I gazed at the coffin I'd brought for him, and I gazed at the grue-
some dead, 50
And at last I spoke: "Bill liked his joke; but still, goldarn his eyes,
A man had ought to consider his mates in the way he goes and dies."

Have you ever stood in an Arctic hut in the shadow of the Pole,
With a little coffin six by three and a grief you can't control?
Have you ever sat by a frozen corpse that looks at you with a grin,
And that seems to say: "You may try all day, but you'll never jam
me in"?
I'm not a man of the quitting kind, but I never felt so blue
As I sat there gazing at that stiff and studying what I'd do.
Then I rose and I kicked off the husky dogs that were nosing round
about,
And I lit a roaring fire in the stove, and I started to thaw Bill out.

Well, I thawed and thawed for thirteen days, but it didn't seem no
good; 61
His arms and legs stuck out like pegs, as if they was made of wood.
Till at last I said: "It ain't no use — he's froze too hard to thaw:
He's obstinate, and he won't lie straight, so I guess I got to — *saw*."
So I sawed off poor Bill's arms and legs, and I laid him snug and
straight
In the little coffin he picked hisself, with the dinky silver plate;
And I came nigh near to shedding a tear as I nailed him safely
down;

---

42. *malamutes*: large Alaskan sled dogs.

Then I stowed him away in my Yukon sleigh, and I started back to town.

So I buried him as the contract was in a narrow grave and deep,
And there he's waiting the Great Cleanup, when the Judgment sluiceheads° sweep; 70
And I smoke my pipe and I meditate in the light of the Midnight Sun,
And sometimes I wonder if they *was*, the awful things I done.
And as I sit and the parson talks, expounding of the Law,
I often think of poor old Bill — *and how hard he was to saw.*

---

70. *sluiceheads:* openings of artificial channels for water.

From the original stage production
of The Miracle Worker:
Anne Bancroft as Annie,
Patty Duke as Helen.

BOOK TWO | PART 1

THE MIRACLE WORKER

William Gibson

The Miracle Worker has just begun. The theater is darkened; lights are bright on the stage. Most of the audience are in their seats, just settling down to watch the play. Three actors are on stage: a mother, a father, a doctor. The clothes they are wearing and the set which is their house tell the audience that the play takes place almost a hundred years ago. A few latecomers distract the audience's attention. The doctor leaves. The mother picks up a child from its crib and begins to sing to it. Suddenly the mother screams.

Now the attention of the entire audience is focused on the stage. A few minutes ago the audience was several hundred individuals. Now it is like a single person, sharing this dramatic moment. Only in the theater is this electrifying experience possible.

True, a play is literature because it has a script which has been written or printed. But it is very different from a novel, a story, or a poem, because it is not complete on the printed page. It is meant to be brought to life by actors moving and speaking on a stage. The stage itself can be in a magnificent auditorium or opera house, or it can be a few square feet of space at the front of a classroom. It doesn't matter: the important thing is that a play is an action — it is meant to be acted out before an audience.

For this reason, reading a play is quite different from reading other forms of literature, for one's imagination is even more important. In reading a play, you must create a whole theater in your mind. You must become the director, the designer, and all the actors. You must see the action, and hear the characters speak.

It is your task, then, to bring the play to life as you read it. You are actor and audience at the same time. To help you, the playwright usually supplies stage directions. He tells you how the set looks and what the characters are like. He also tells you things about the characters which they do not express directly in words. Thus, at the beginning of The Miracle Worker, William Gibson writes this stage direction:

> ". . . three adults in the bedroom are grouped around a crib. . . . They have been through a long vigil, and it shows in their tired bearing. . . ."

He also tells you from time to time what the characters are thinking and feeling so that you — or the actors — will know how to speak the lines. Notice in Scene One of The Miracle Worker that we are told that the Doctor speaks "amiably," and a bit later on that Kate is "puzzled."

The Miracle Worker has more stage directions than most plays for the simple reason that much of its action takes place in pantomime, that is, action without words. But no matter how complete the directions, they cannot perform the final task of bringing the play to life. That remains for the reader to do.

The Miracle Worker

The playing space is divided into two areas by a more or less diagonal line, which runs from downstage right to upstage left.

The area behind this diagonal is on platforms and represents the Keller house; inside we see, down right, a family room, and up center, elevated, a bedroom. On stage level near center, outside a porch, there is a water pump.

The other area, in front of the diagonal, is neutral ground; it accommodates various places as designated at various times — the yard before the Keller home, the Perkins Institution for the Blind, the garden house, and so forth.

The convention of the staging is one of cutting through time and place. To this end, the less set there is, the better. The stage therefore should be free, airy, unencumbered by walls. Apart from certain practical items — such as the pump, a window to climb out of, doors to be locked — locales should be only skeletal suggestions, and the movement from one to another should be accomplishable by little more than lights.

TIME *The 1880's.*
PLACE *In and around the Keller homestead in Tuscumbia, Alabama; also, briefly, the Perkins Institution for the Blind, in Boston.*

CHARACTERS

A DOCTOR
KATE KELLER, Helen's mother
CAPTAIN ARTHUR KELLER, Helen's father
HELEN
MARTHA and PERCY, neighborhood children
AUNT EV

JAMES KELLER, Helen's half-brother
ANAGNOS, the director of the Perkins Institution
ANNIE SULLIVAN
VINEY, the Kellers' maid
BLIND GIRLS
THE GARDENER

ACT 1

SCENE 1

It is night over the Keller homestead.

Inside, three adults in the bedroom are grouped around a crib, in lamplight. They have been through a long vigil, and it shows in their tired bearing and disarranged clothing. One is a young gentlewoman with a sweet, girlish face, KATE KELLER; *the second is an elderly* DOCTOR, *stethoscope at neck, thermometer in fingers; the third is a hearty gentleman in his forties with chin whiskers,* CAPTAIN ARTHUR KELLER.

DOCTOR She'll live.
KATE Thank God.

[*The* DOCTOR *leaves them together over the crib, packs his bag.*]

DOCTOR You're a pair of lucky parents. I can tell you now, I thought she wouldn't.
KELLER Nonsense, the child's a Keller; she has the constitution of a goat. She'll outive us all.
DOCTOR (*amiably*) Yes, especially if some of you Kellers don't get a night's sleep. I mean you, Mrs. Keller.
KELLER You hear, Katie?
KATE I hear.
KELLER (*indulgent*) I've brought up two of them, but this is my wife's first; she isn't battle-scarred yet.
KATE Doctor, don't be merely considerate; will my girl be all right?
DOCTOR Oh, by morning she'll be knocking down Captain Keller's fences again.
KATE And isn't there anything we should do?
KELLER (*jovial*) Put up stronger fencing, ha?
DOCTOR Just let her get well; she knows how to do it better than we do. (*He is packed, ready to leave.*) Main thing is the fever's gone; these things come and go in infants, never know why. Call it acute congestion of the stomach and brain.
KELLER I'll see you to your buggy, Doctor.
DOCTOR I've never seen a baby with more vitality, that's the truth.

[*He beams a good night at the baby and* KATE, *and* KELLER *leads him downstairs with a lamp. They go down the porch steps and across the yard, where the* DOCTOR *goes off left;* KELLER *stands with the lamp aloft.* KATE *meanwhile is bent lovingly over the crib, which emits a bleat; her finger is playful with the baby's face.*]

KATE Hush. Don't you cry now; you've been trouble enough. Call it acute congestion, indeed; I don't see what's so cute about a congestion, just because it's yours. We'll have your father run an editorial in his paper — the wonders of modern medicine — they don't know what they're curing even when they cure it. Men, men and their battle scars, we women will have to — (*But she breaks off, puzzled, moves her finger before the baby's eyes.*) Will have to — Helen? (*Now she moves her hand, quickly.*) Helen. (*She snaps her fingers at the baby's eyes twice, and her hand falters; after a moment she calls out, loudly.*) Captain. Captain, will you come — (*But she stares at the baby, and her next call is directly at her ears.*) Captain!

[*And now, still staring,* KATE *screams.* KELLER, *in the yard, hears it and runs with the lamp back to the house.* KATE *screams again, her look intent on the baby, and terrible.* KELLER *hurries in and up.*]

KELLER Katie? What's wrong?
KATE Look. (*She makes a pass with her hand in the crib, at the baby's eyes.*)
KELLER What, Katie? She's well; she needs only time to —
KATE She can't see. Look at her eyes. (*She takes the lamp from him, moves it before the child's face.*) She can't *see!*
KELLER (*hoarsely*) Helen.
KATE Or hear. When I screamed, she didn't blink. Not an eyelash —
KELLER Helen. Helen!
KATE She can't *hear* you!
KELLER *Helen!*

[*His face has something like fury in it, crying the child's name;* KATE, *almost fainting, presses her knuckles to her mouth to stop her own cry. The room dims out quickly.*]

SCENE 2

Time, in the form of a slow tune of distant belfry chimes which approaches in a crescendo and then fades, passes; the light comes up again on a day five years later, on three kneeling children and an old dog outside around the pump.

The dog is a setter named BELLE, *and she is sleeping. Two of the children are Negroes,* MARTHA *and* PERCY. *The third child is* HELEN, *six and a half years old, quite unkempt, in body a vivacious little person with a fine head, attractive, but noticeably blind, one eye larger and protruding; her gestures are abrupt, insistent, lacking in human restraint, and her face never smiles. She is flanked by the other two, in a litter of paper-doll cutouts, and while they speak,* HELEN's *hands thrust at their faces in turn, feeling baffledly at the movements of their lips.*

MARTHA (*snipping*) First I'm gonna cut off this doctor's legs — one, two, now then —

PERCY Why you cuttin' off that doctor's legs?

MARTHA I'm gonna give him an operation. Now I'm gonna cut off his arms — one, two. Now I'm gonna fix up — (*She pushes* HELEN's *hand away from her mouth.*) You stop that.

PERCY Cut off his stomach; that's a good operation.

MARTHA No, I'm gonna cut off his head first; he's got a bad cold.

PERCY Ain't gonna be much of that doctor left to fix up, when you finish all them opera —

[*But* HELEN *is poking her fingers inside his mouth, to feel his tongue; he bites at them, annoyed, and she jerks them away.* HELEN *now fingers her own lips, moving them in imitation, but soundlessly.*]

MARTHA What did you do, bite her hand?

PERCY That's how I do; she keeps pokin' her fingers in my mouth; I just bite 'em off.

MARTHA What's she tryin' to do now?

PERCY She's tryin' to *talk*. She's gonna get mad. Look at her tryin' to talk.

[HELEN *is scowling, the lips under her fingertips moving in ghostly silence, growing more and more frantic, until in a bizarre rage she bites at her own fingers. This sends* PERCY *off into laughter but alarms* MARTHA.]

MARTHA Hey, you stop now. (*She pulls* HELEN's *hand down.*) You just sit quiet and—

[*But at once* HELEN *topples* MARTHA *on her back, knees pinning her shoulders down, and grabs the scissors.* MARTHA *screams.* PERCY *darts to the bell string on the porch, yanks it, and the bell rings. Inside, the lights have been gradually coming up on the main room, where we see the family informally gathered, talking, but in pantomime.* KATE *sits darning socks near a cradle, occasionally rocking it;* CAPTAIN KELLER, *in spectacles, is working over newspaper pages at a table; a benign visitor in a hat,* AUNT EV, *is sharing the sewing basket, putting the finishing touches on a big, shapeless doll made out of towels; an indolent young man,* JAMES KELLER, *is at the window watching the children.*

With the ring of the bell KATE *is instantly on her feet and out the door onto the porch, to take in the scene; now we see what these five years have done to her—the girlish playfulness is gone; she is a woman steeled in grief.*]

KATE (*for the thousandth time*) Helen.

[*She is down the steps at once to them, seizing* HELEN's *wrists and lifting her off* MARTHA; MARTHA *runs off in tears and screams for momma, with* PERCY *after her.*]

Let me have those scissors.

[*Meanwhile the family inside is alerted,* AUNT EV *joining* JAMES *at the window;* CAPTAIN KELLER *resumes work.*]

JAMES (*blandly*) She only dug Martha's eyes out. Almost dug. It's always almost, no point worrying till it happens, is there?

[*They gaze out, while* KATE *reaches for the scissors in* HELEN's *hand. But* HELEN *pulls the scissors back; they struggle for them a moment; then* KATE *gives up, lets* HELEN *keep them. She tries to draw* HELEN *into the house.* HELEN *jerks away.* KATE *next goes down on her knees, takes* HELEN's *hands gently, and using the scissors like a doll, makes* HELEN *caress and cradle them; she points* HELEN's *finger houseward.* HELEN's *whole body now becomes eager; she surrenders the scissors,* KATE *turns her toward the door and gives her a little push.* HELEN *scrambles up and toward the house, and* KATE, *rising, follows her.*]

AUNT EV How does she stand it? Why haven't you seen this Baltimore man? It's not a thing you can let go on and on, like the weather.

JAMES The weather here doesn't ask permission of me, Aunt Ev. Speak to my father.

AUNT EV Arthur. Something ought to be done for that child.

KELLER A refreshing suggestion. What?

[KATE, *entering, turns* HELEN *to* AUNT EV, *who gives her the towel doll.*]

AUNT EV Why, this very famous oculist in Baltimore I wrote you about, what was his name?

KATE Dr. Chisholm.

AUNT EV Yes, I heard lots of cases of blindness people thought couldn't be cured he's cured; he just does wonders. Why don't you write to him?

KELLER I've stopped believing in wonders.

KATE (*rocks the cradle*) I think the Captain will write to him soon. Won't you, Captain?

KELLER No.

JAMES (*lightly*) Good money after bad, or bad after good. Or bad after bad —

AUNT EV Well, if it's just a question of money, Arthur, now you're marshal, you have this Yankee money. Might as well —

KELLER Not money. The child's been to specialists all over Alabama and Tennessee; if I thought it would do good, I'd have her to every fool doctor in the country.

KATE I think the Captain will write to him soon.

KELLER Katie. How many times can you let them break your heart?

KATE Any number of times.

[HELEN *meanwhile sits on the floor to explore the doll with her fingers, and her hand pauses over the face: this is no face, a blank area of towel, and it troubles her. Her hand searches for features, and taps questioningly for eyes, but no one notices. She then yanks at her* AUNT's *dress, and taps again vigorously for eyes.*]

AUNT EV What, child?

[*Obviously not hearing,* HELEN *commences to go around, from person to person, tapping for eyes, but no one attends or understands.*]

KATE (*no break*) As long as there's the least chance. For her to see. Or hear, or —
KELLER There isn't. Now I must finish here.
KATE I think, with your permission, Captain, I'd like to write.
KELLER I said no, Katie.
AUNT EV Why, writing does no harm, Arthur, only a little bitty letter. To see if he can help her.
KELLER He can't.
KATE We won't know that to be a fact, Captain, until after you write.
KELLER (*rising, emphatic*) Katie, he can't. (*He collects his papers.*)
JAMES (*facetiously*) Father stands up; that makes it a fact.
KELLER You be quiet! I'm badgered enough here by females, without your impudence.

[JAMES *shuts up, makes himself scarce.* HELEN *now is groping among things on* KELLER's *desk and paws his papers to the floor.* KELLER *is exasperated.*]

Katie.

[KATE *quickly turns* HELEN *away and retrieves the papers.*]

I might as well try to work in a henyard as in this house —

JAMES (*placating*) You really ought to put her away, Father.
KATE (*staring up*) What?
JAMES Some asylum. It's the kindest thing.
AUNT EV Why, she's your sister, James, not a nobody —
JAMES Half sister, and half — mentally defective; she can't even keep herself clean. It's not pleasant to see her about all the time.
KATE Do you dare? Complain of what you *can* see?
KELLER (*very annoyed*) This discussion is at an end! I'll thank you not to broach it again, Ev.

[*Silence descends at once.* HELEN *gropes her way with the doll, and* KELLER *turns back for a final word, explosive.*]

I've done as much as I can bear; I can't give my whole life to it! The house is at sixes and sevens from morning till night over the child; it's time some attention was paid to Mildred here instead!
KATE (*gently dry*) You'll wake her up, Captain.
KELLER I want some peace in the house; I don't care how, but one way we won't have it is by rushing up and down the country every time someone hears of a new quack. I'm as sensible to this affliction as anyone else; it hurts me to look at the girl.
KATE It was not our affliction I meant you to write about, Captain.

[HELEN *is back at* AUNT EV, *fingering her dress, and yanks two buttons from it.*]

AUNT EV Helen! My buttons.

[HELEN *pushes the buttons into the doll's face.* KATE *now sees, comes swiftly to kneel, lifts* HELEN's *hand to her own eyes in question.*]

KATE Eyes? (HELEN *nods energetically.*) She wants the doll to have eyes.

[*Another kind of silence now while* KATE *takes pins and buttons from the sewing basket and attaches them to the doll as eyes.* KELLER *stands, caught, and watches morosely.* AUNT EV *blinks, and conceals her emotion by inspecting her dress.*]

AUNT EV My goodness me, I'm not decent.
KATE She doesn't know better, Aunt Ev. I'll sew them on again.
JAMES Never learn with everyone letting her do anything she takes it into her mind to —
KELLER You be quiet!
JAMES What did I say now?
KELLER You talk too much.
JAMES I was agreeing with you!
KELLER Whatever it was. Deprived child, the least she can have are the little things she wants.

[JAMES, *very wounded, stalks out of the room onto the porch; he remains there, sulking.*]

AUNT EV (*indulgently*) It's worth a couple of buttons, Kate, look.

[HELEN *now has the doll with eyes, and cannot contain herself for joy; she rocks the doll, pats it vigorously, kisses it.*]

This child has more sense than all these men Kellers, if there's ever any way to reach that mind of hers.

[*But* HELEN *suddenly has come upon the cradle and unhesitatingly overturns it; the swaddled baby tumbles out, and* CAPTAIN KELLER *barely manages to dive and catch it in time.*]

KELLER Helen!

[*All are in commotion; the baby screams, but* HELEN, *unperturbed, is laying her doll in its place.* KATE, *on her knees, pulls her hands off the cradle, wringing them;* HELEN *is bewildered.*]

KATE Helen, Helen, you're not to do such things, how can I make you understand —

KELLER (*hoarsely*) Katie.

KATE How can I get it into your head, my darling, my poor —

KELLER Katie, some way of teaching her an iota of discipline has to be —

KATE (*flaring*) How can you discipline an afflicted child? Is it her fault?

[HELEN'S *fingers have fluttered to her* MOTHER'S *lips, vainly trying to comprehend their movements.*]

KELLER I didn't say it was her fault.

KATE Then, whose? I don't know what to do! How can I teach her — beat her until she's black and blue?

KELLER It's not safe to let her run around loose. Now there must be a way of confining her, somehow, so she can't —

KATE Where, in a cage? She's a growing child; she has to use her limbs!

KELLER Answer me one thing: is it fair to Mildred here?

KATE (*inexorably*) Are you willing to put her away?

[*Now* HELEN'S *face darkens in the same rage as at herself earlier, and her hand strikes at* KATE'S *lips.* KATE *catches her hand again, and* HELEN *begins to kick, struggle, twist.*]

KELLER Now what?

KATE She wants to talk, like — *be* like you and me.

[*She holds* HELEN, *struggling, until we hear from the child her first sound so far, an inarticulate weird noise in her throat, such as an animal in a trap might make; and* KATE *releases her. The second she is free,* HELEN *blunders away, collides violently with a chair, falls, and sits weeping.* KATE *comes to her, embraces, caresses, soothes her, and buries her own face in her hair until she can control her voice.*]

Every day she slips further away. And I don't know how to call her back.

AUNT EV Oh, I've a mind to take her up to Baltimore myself. If that doctor can't help her, maybe he'll know who can.

KELLER (*presently, heavily*) I'll write the man, Katie. (*He stands with the baby in his clasp, staring at* HELEN's *head hanging down on* KATE's *arm.*)

[*The lights dim out, except the one on* KATE *and* HELEN. *In the twilight* JAMES, AUNT EV, *and* KELLER *move off slowly, formally, in separate directions;* KATE *with* HELEN *in her arms remains, motionless, in an image which overlaps into the next scene and fades only when it is well under way.*]

SCENE 3

Without pause, from the dark, down left, we hear a man's voice with a Greek accent speaking.

ANAGNOS . . . who could do nothing for the girl, of course. It was Dr. Bell[1] who thought she might somehow be taught. I have written the family only that a suitable governess, Miss Annie Sullivan, has been found here in Boston. . . .

[*The lights begin to come up, down left, on a long table and chair. The table contains equipment for teaching the blind by touch — a small replica of the human skeleton, stuffed animals, models of flowers and plants, piles of books. The chair contains a girl of twenty,* ANNIE SULLIVAN, *with a face which in repose is grave and rather obstinate, and when active is impudent, combative, twinkling with all the life that is lacking in* HELEN's, *and handsome; there is a crude vitality to her. Her suitcase is at her*

---

[1] *Dr. Bell:* Alexander Graham Bell developed ways of teaching the deaf to speak.

knee. ANAGNOS, *a stocky, bearded man, comes into the light only toward the end of his speech.*]

... and will come. It will no doubt be difficult for you there, Annie. But it has been difficult for you at our school, too, hm? Gratifying, yes, when you came to us and could not spell your name, to accomplish so much here in a few years, but always an Irish battle. For independence. (*He studies* ANNIE, *humorously; she does not open her eyes.*) This is my last time to counsel you, Annie, and you do lack some — by some I mean *all* — what? — tact or talent to bend. To others. And what has saved you on more than one occasion here at Perkins is that there was nowhere to expel you to. Your eyes hurt?

ANNIE My ears, Mr. Anagnos. (*And now she has opened her eyes; they are inflamed, vague, slightly crossed, clouded by the granular growth of trachoma, and she often keeps them closed to shut out the pain of light.*)

ANAGNOS (*severely*) Nowhere but back to Tewksbury,[2] where children learn to be saucy. Annie, I know how dreadful it was there, but that battle is dead and done with; why not let it stay buried?

ANNIE (*cheerily*) I think God must owe me a resurrection.

ANAGNOS (*a bit shocked*) What?

ANNIE (*taps her brow*) Well, he keeps digging up that battle!

ANAGNOS That is not a proper thing to say, Annie. It is what I mean.

ANNIE (*meekly*) Yes. But I know what I'm like; what's this child like?

ANAGNOS Like?

ANNIE Well — bright or dull, to start off.

ANAGNOS No one knows. And if she is dull, you have no patience with this?

ANNIE Oh, in grownups you have to, Mr. Anagnos. I mean in children it just seems a little — precocious; can I use that word?

ANAGNOS Only if you can spell it.

ANNIE Premature. So I hope at least she's a bright one.

ANAGNOS Deaf, blind, mute — who knows? She is like a little safe, locked, that no one can open. Perhaps there is a treasure inside.

ANNIE Maybe it's empty, too?

---

[2] *Tewksbury:* the poorhouse where Annie Sullivan lived before coming to the Perkins Institution.

ANAGNOS Possible. I should warn you, she is much given to tantrums.

ANNIE Means something is inside. Well, so am I, if I believe all I hear. Maybe you should warn *them*.

ANAGNOS (*frowns*) Annie. I wrote them no word of your history. You will find yourself among strangers now, who know nothing of it.

ANNIE Well, we'll keep them in a state of blessed ignorance.

ANAGNOS Perhaps *you* should tell it?

ANNIE (*bristling*) Why? I have enough trouble with people who don't know.

ANAGNOS So they will understand. When you have trouble.

ANNIE The only time I have trouble is when I'm right. (*But she is amused at herself, as is* ANAGNOS.) Is it my fault it's so often? I won't give them trouble, Mr. Anagnos; I'll be so ladylike they won't notice I've come.

ANAGNOS Annie, be . . . humble. It is not as if you have so many offers to pick and choose. You will need their affection, working with this child.

ANNIE (*humorously*) I hope I won't need their pity.

ANAGNOS Oh, we can all use some pity. (*Crisply*) So. You are no longer our pupil; we throw you into the world, a teacher. *If the child can be taught.* No one expects you to work miracles, even for twenty-five dollars a month. Now, in this envelope a loan, for the railroad, which you will repay me when you have a bank account. But in this box, a gift. With our love.

[ANNIE *opens the small box he extends, and sees a garnet ring. She looks up, blinking, and down.*]

I think other friends are ready to say goodbye. (*He moves as though to open doors.*)

ANNIE Mr. Anagnos. (*Her voice is trembling.*) Dear Mr. Anagnos, I — (*But she swallows over getting the ring on her finger and cannot continue until she finds a woebegone joke.*) Well, what should I say, I'm an ignorant, opinionated girl, and everything I am I owe to you?

ANAGNOS (*smiles*) That is only half true, Annie.

ANNIE Which half? I crawled in here like a drowned rat; I thought I died when Jimmie died, that I'd never again — come alive. Well, you say "with love" so easy, and I haven't *loved* a soul since, and I never will, I suppose, but this place gave me more than my eyes back. Or taught me how to spell, which I'll never learn anyway; but with all the fights and the trouble I've been here, it taught me what help is and how to live again, and I don't want to say goodbye. Don't open the door, I'm crying.

ANAGNOS *(gently)* They will not see.

[*He moves again as though opening doors, and in comes a group of girls, eight-year-olds to seventeen-year-olds; as they walk, we see they are blind.* ANAGNOS *shepherds them in with a hand.*]

A CHILD Annie?
ANNIE *(her voice cheerful)* Here, Beatrice.

[*As soon as they locate her voice they throng joyfully to her, speaking all at once;* ANNIE *is down on her knees to the smallest, and the following are the more intelligible fragments in the general hubbub.*]

CHILDREN There's a present. We brought you a going-away present, Annie!
ANNIE Oh, now you shouldn't have —
CHILDREN We did, we did, where's the present?
SMALLEST CHILD *(mournfully)* Don't go, Annie, away.
CHILDREN Alice has it! Alice! Where's Alice? Here I am! Where? Here!

[*An arm is aloft out of the group, waving a present;* ANNIE *reaches for it.*]

ANNIE I have it. I have it, everybody, should I open it?
CHILDREN Open it! Everyone be quiet! Do, Annie! She's opening it. Ssh!

[*A settling of silence while* ANNIE *unwraps it. The present is a pair of smoked glasses, and she stands still.*]

Is it open, Annie?
ANNIE It's open.
CHILDREN It's for your eyes, Annie. Put them on, Annie! 'Cause Mrs. Hopkins said your eyes hurt since the operation. And she said you're going where the sun is *fierce*.
ANNIE I'm putting them on now.

SMALLEST CHILD (*mournfully*) Don't go, Annie, where the sun is fierce.
CHILDREN Do they fit all right?
ANNIE Oh, they fit just fine.
CHILDREN Did you put them on? Are they pretty, Annie?
ANNIE Oh, my eyes feel hundreds of percent better already, and pretty; why, do you know how I look in them? Splendiloquent. Like a race horse!
CHILDREN (*delighted*) There's another present! Beatrice! We have a present for Helen too! Give it to her, Beatrice. Here, Annie! (*This present is an elegant doll, with movable eyelids and a "momma" sound.*) It's for Helen. And we took up a collection to buy it. And Laura dressed it.
ANNIE It's beautiful!
CHILDREN So don't forget, you be sure to give it to Helen from us, Annie!
ANNIE I promise it will be the first thing I give her. If I don't keep it for myself, that is; you know I can't be trusted with dolls!
SMALLEST CHILD (*mournfully*) Don't go, Annie, to her.
ANNIE (*her arm around her*) Sarah, dear. I don't *want* to go.
SMALLEST CHILD Then why are you going?
ANNIE (*gently*) Because I'm a big girl now, and big girls have to earn a living. It's the only way I can. But if you don't smile for me first, what I'll just have to do is . . . (*She pauses, inviting it.*)
SMALLEST CHILD What?
ANNIE Put *you* in my suitcase, instead of this doll. And take *you* to Helen in Alabama!

[*This strikes the children as very funny, and they begin to laugh and tease the smallest child, who after a moment does smile for* ANNIE.]

ANAGNOS (*then*) Come, children. We must get the trunk into the carriage and Annie into her train, or no one will go to Alabama. Come, come.

[*He shepherds them out, and* ANNIE *is left alone on her knees with the doll in her lap. She reaches for her suitcase, and by a subtle change in the color of the light we go with her thoughts into another time. We hear a boy's voice whispering; perhaps we see shadowy intimations of these speakers in the background.*]

BOY'S VOICE Where we goin', Annie?
ANNIE (*in dread*) Jimmie.
BOY'S VOICE Where we goin'?
ANNIE I said — I'm takin' care of you —
BOY'S VOICE Forever and ever?
MAN'S VOICE (*impersonal*) Annie Sullivan, aged nine, virtually blind. James Sullivan, aged seven — What's the matter with your leg, Sonny?
ANNIE Forever and ever.
MAN'S VOICE Can't he walk without that crutch?

[ANNIE *shakes her head, and does not stop shaking it.*]

Girl goes to the women's ward. Boy to the men's.
BOY'S VOICE (*in terror*) Annie! Annie, don't let them take me — Annie!
ANAGNOS (*offstage*) Annie! Annie?

[*But this voice is real, in the present, and* ANNIE *comes up out of her horror, clearing her head with a final shake; the lights begin to pick out* KATE *in the* KELLER *house as* ANNIE, *in a bright tone, calls back.*]

ANNIE Coming!

[*The word catches* KATE, *who stands half-turned and attentive to it, almost as though hearing it. Meanwhile,* ANNIE *turns and hurries out, lugging the suitcase.*]

SCENE 4

The room dims out; the sound of railroad wheels begins from off left and maintains itself in a constant rhythm underneath the following scene; the remaining lights have come up on the KELLER *homestead.* JAMES *is lounging on the porch, waiting. In the upper bedroom which is to be* ANNIE'S, HELEN *is alone, puzzledly exploring, fingering, and smelling things: the curtains, empty drawers in the bureau, water in the pitcher by the washbasin, fresh towels on the bedstead. Downstairs in the family room* KATE, *turning to a mirror, hastily adjusts her bonnet, watched by* VINEY.

VINEY Let Mr. Jimmy go by himself; you been pokin' that garden

all day; you ought to rest your feet.
KATE I can't wait to see her, Viney.
VINEY Maybe she isn't gonna be on this train neither.
KATE Maybe she is.
VINEY And maybe she isn't.
KATE And maybe she is. Where's Helen?
VINEY She's upstairs, smellin' around. She knows somethin' funny's goin' on.
KATE Let her have her supper as soon as Mildred's in bed, and tell Captain Keller when he comes that we'll be delayed tonight.
VINEY Again.
KATE I don't think we need say "again." Simply "delayed" will do.

[*She runs upstairs to* ANNIE's *room*, VINEY *speaking after her.*]

VINEY I mean that's what he's gonna say: "What, again?"

[VINEY *works at setting the table. Upstairs* KATE *stands in the doorway, watching* HELEN's *groping explorations.*]

KATE Yes, we're expecting someone. Someone for my Helen.

[HELEN *happens upon her skirt, clutches her leg;* KATE, *in a tired dismay, kneels to tidy her hair and soiled pinafore.*]

Oh dear, this was clean not an hour ago.

[HELEN *feels her bonnet, shakes her head darkly, and tugs to get it off.* KATE *retains it with one hand, diverts* HELEN *by opening her other hand under her nose.*]

Here. For while I'm gone.

[HELEN *sniffs, reaches, and pops something into her mouth, while* KATE *speaks a bit guiltily.*]

I don't think one peppermint drop will spoil your supper.

[*She gives* HELEN *a quick kiss, evades her hands, and hurries downstairs again. Meanwhile,* CAPTAIN KELLER *has entered the yard from around the rear of the house, newspaper under arm, cleaning off and munching on some radishes; he sees* JAMES *lounging at the porch post.*]

KELLER Jimmie?

JAMES (*unmoving*) Sir?
KELLER (*eyes him*) You don't look dressed for anything useful, boy.
JAMES I'm not. It's for Miss Sullivan.
KELLER Needn't keep holding up that porch; we have wooden posts for that. I asked you to see that those strawberry plants were moved this evening.
JAMES I'm moving your — Mrs. Keller, instead. To the station.
KELLER (*heavily*) Mrs. Keller. Must you always speak of her as though you haven't met the lady?

[KATE *comes out on the porch, and* JAMES *inclines his head.*]

JAMES (*ironic*) Mother. (*He starts off the porch but sidesteps* KELLER'S *glare like a blow.*) I said "mother"!
KATE Captain.
KELLER Evening, my dear.
KATE We're off to meet the train, Captain. Supper will be a trifle delayed tonight.
KELLER What, again?
KATE (*backing out*) With your permission, Captain?

[*And they are gone.* KELLER *watches them offstage, morosely.*

Upstairs HELEN *meanwhile has groped for her mother, touched her cheek in a meaningful gesture, waited, touched her cheek, waited, then found the open door, and made her way down. Now she comes into the family room, touches her cheek again;* VINEY *regards her.*]

VINEY What you want, honey, your momma?

[HELEN *touches her cheek again.* VINEY *goes to the sideboard, gets a tea cake, gives it into* HELEN'S *hand;* HELEN *pops it into her mouth.*]

Guess one little tea cake won't ruin your appetite.

[*She turns* HELEN *toward the door.* HELEN *wanders out onto the porch as* KELLER *comes up the steps. Her hands encounter him, and she touches her cheek again, waits.*]

KELLER She's gone.

[*He is awkward with her; when he puts his hand on her head, she pulls away.* KELLER *stands regarding her, heavily.*]

She's gone, my son and I don't get along, you don't know I'm your father, no one likes me, and supper's delayed.

[HELEN *touches her cheek, waits.* KELLER *fishes in his pocket.*]

Here. I brought you some stick candy; one nibble of sweets can't do any harm.

[*He gives her a large stick of candy;* HELEN *falls to it.* VINEY *peers out the window.*]

VINEY (*reproachfully*) Cap'n Keller, now how'm I gonna get her to eat her supper when you fill her up with that trash?
KELLER (*roars*) Tend to your work!

[VINEY *beats a rapid retreat.* KELLER *thinks better of it and tries to get the candy away from* HELEN, *but* HELEN *hangs on to it; and when* KELLER *pulls, she gives his leg a kick.* KELLER *hops about.* HELEN *takes refuge with the candy down behind the pump, and* KELLER *then irately flings his newspaper on the porch floor, stamps into the house past* VINEY, *and disappears.*]

SCENE 5

The lights half dim on the homestead, where VINEY *and* HELEN, *going about their business, soon find their way off. Meanwhile, the railroad sounds off left have mounted in a crescendo to a climax typical of a depot at arrival time, the lights come up on stage left, and we see a suggestion of a station. Here* ANNIE, *in her smoked glasses and disarrayed by travel, is waiting with her suitcase while* JAMES *walks to meet her; she has a battered paperbound book, which is a Perkins report, under her arm.*

JAMES (*coolly*) Miss Sullivan?
ANNIE (*cheerily*) Here! At last! I've been on trains so many days I thought they must be backing up every time I dozed off —
JAMES I'm James Keller.
ANNIE James? (*The name stops her.*) I had a brother Jimmie. Are you Helen's?
JAMES I'm only half a brother. You're to be her governess?

ANNIE (*lightly*) Well. Try!
JAMES (*eyeing her*) You look like half a governess.

[KATE *enters.* ANNIE *stands moveless while* JAMES *takes her suitcase.* KATE's *gaze on her is doubtful, troubled.*]

Mrs. Keller, Miss Sullivan.

[KATE *takes her hand.*]

KATE (*simply*) We've met every train for two days.

[ANNIE *looks at* KATE's *face, and her good humor comes back.*]

ANNIE I changed trains every time they stopped; the man who sold me that ticket ought to be tied to the tracks —
JAMES You have a trunk, Miss Sullivan?
ANNIE Yes.

[*She passes* JAMES *a claim check, and he bears the suitcase out behind them.* ANNIE *holds the battered book.* KATE *is studying her face, and* ANNIE *returns the gaze; this is a mutual appraisal, Southern gentlewoman and working-class Irish girl, and* ANNIE *is not quite comfortable under it.*]

You didn't bring Helen; I was hoping you would.
KATE No, she's home.

[*A pause.* ANNIE *tries to make ladylike small talk, though her energy now and then erupts; she catches herself up whenever she hears it.*]

ANNIE You — live far from town, Mrs. Keller?
KATE Only a mile.
ANNIE Well. I suppose I can wait one more mile. But don't be surprised if I get out to push the horse!
KATE Helen's waiting for you too. There's been such a bustle in the house she expects something, heaven knows what.

[*Now she voices part of her doubt, not as such, but* ANNIE *understands it.*]

I expected — a desiccated spinster. You're very young.
ANNIE (*resolutely*) Oh, you should have seen me when I left Boston. I got much older on this trip.

KATE I mean, to teach anyone as difficult as Helen.
ANNIE I mean to try. They can't put you in jail for trying!
KATE Is it possible, even? To teach a deaf-blind child *half* of what an ordinary child learns — has that ever been done?
ANNIE Half?
KATE A tenth.
ANNIE (*reluctantly*) No.

[KATE's *face loses its remaining hope, still appraising her youth.*]

Dr. Howe [3] did wonders, but — an ordinary child? No, never. But then I thought when I was going over his reports — (*She indicates the one in her hand.*) — he never treated them like ordinary children. More like — eggs everyone was afraid would break.

KATE (*a pause*) May I ask how old you are?
ANNIE Well, I'm not in my teens, you know! I'm twenty.
KATE All of twenty.

[ANNIE *takes the bull by the horns, valiantly.*]

ANNIE Mrs. Keller, don't lose heart just because I'm not on my last legs. I have three big advantages over Dr. Howe that money couldn't buy for you. One is his work behind me; I've read every word he wrote about it, and he wasn't exactly what you'd call a man of few words. Another is to *be* young; why, I've got energy to do anything. The third is, I've been blind. (*But it costs her something to say this.*)
KATE (*quietly*) Advantages.
ANNIE (*wry*) Well, some have the luck of the Irish; some do not.

[KATE *smiles; she likes her.*]

KATE What will you try to teach her first?
ANNIE First, last, and in between — language.
KATE Language.
ANNIE Language is to the mind more than light is to the eye. Dr. Howe said that.
KATE Language. (*She shakes her head.*) *We* can't get through to teach her to sit still. You *are* young, despite your years, to have such — confidence. Do you, inside?

---

[3] *Dr. Howe:* S. G. Howe, who founded the Perkins Institution.

[ANNIE *studies her face; she likes her, too.*]

ANNIE No, to tell you the truth, I'm as shaky inside as a baby's rattle!

[*They smile at each other, and* KATE *pats her hand.*]

KATE Don't be.

[JAMES *returns to usher them off.*]

We'll do all we can to help, and to make you feel at home. Don't think of us as strangers, Miss Annie.

ANNIE (*cheerily*) Oh, strangers aren't so strange to me. I've known them all my life!

[KATE *smiles again,* ANNIE *smiles back, and they precede* JAMES *offstage.*]

SCENE 6

The lights dim on them, having simultaneously risen full on the house; VINEY *has already entered the family room, taken a water pitcher, and come out and down to the pump. She pumps real water. As she looks offstage, we hear the clop of hoofs, a carriage stopping, and voices.*

VINEY Cap'n Keller! Cap'n Keller, they're comin'!

[*She goes back into the house as* KELLER *comes out on the porch to gaze.*]

She sure came, Cap'n.

[KELLER *descends and crosses toward the carriage; this conversation begins offstage and moves on.*]

KELLER (*very courtly*) Welcome to Ivy Green, Miss Sullivan. I take it you are Miss Sullivan —
KATE My husband, Miss Annie, Captain Keller.
ANNIE (*her best behavior*) Captain, how do you do.
KELLER A pleasure to see you, at last. I trust you had an agreeable journey?
ANNIE Oh, I had several! When did this country get so big?

JAMES Where would you like the trunk, Father?
KELLER Where Miss Sullivan can get at it, I imagine.
ANNIE Yes, please. Where's Helen?
KELLER In the hall, Jimmie —
KATE We've put you in the upstairs corner room, Miss Annie; if there's any breeze at all this summer, you'll feel it —

[*In the house the setter* BELLE *flees into the family room, pursued by* HELEN *with groping hands; the dog doubles back out the same door, and* HELEN, *still groping for her, makes her way out to the porch; she is messy, her hair tumbled, her pinafore now ripped, her shoelaces untied.* KELLER *acquires the suitcase, and* ANNIE *gets her hands on it too, though still endeavoring to live up to the general air of propertied manners.*]

KELLER And the suitcase —
ANNIE (*pleasantly*) I'll take the suitcase, thanks.
KELLER Not at all, I have it, Miss Sullivan.
ANNIE I'd like it.
KELLER (*gallantly*) I couldn't think of it, Miss Sullivan. You'll find in the South we —
ANNIE Let me.
KELLER — view women as the flowers of civiliza —
ANNIE (*impatiently*) I've got something in it for Helen!

[*She tugs it free;* KELLER *stares.*]

Thank you. When do I see her?
KATE There. There is Helen.

[ANNIE *turns and sees* HELEN *on the porch. A moment of silence. Then* ANNIE *begins across the yard to her, lugging her suitcase.*]

KELLER (*sotto voce*[4]) Katie —

[KATE *silences him with a hand on his arm. When* ANNIE *finally reaches the porch steps, she stops, contemplating* HELEN *for a last moment before entering her world. Then she drops the suitcase on the porch with intentional heaviness;* HELEN *starts with the jar and comes to grope over it.* ANNIE *puts forth her hand and touches* HELEN'S. HELEN *at once grasps it and commences to*

---

[4] *sotto voce* (sot′ō vō′chē): softly, under the breath.

explore it, like reading a face. She moves her hand onto ANNIE'S *forearm and dress; and* ANNIE *brings her face within reach of* HELEN'S *fingers, which travel over it, quite without timidity, until they encounter and push aside the smoked glasses.* ANNIE'S *gaze is grave, unpitying, very attentive. She puts her hands on* HELEN'S *arms, but* HELEN *at once pulls away, and they confront each other with a distance between. Then* HELEN *returns to the suitcase, tries to open it, cannot.* ANNIE *points* HELEN'S *hand overhead.* HELEN *pulls away, tries to open the suitcase again;* ANNIE *points her hand overhead again.* HELEN *points overhead, a question; and* ANNIE, *drawing* HELEN'S *hand to her own face, nods.* HELEN *now begins tugging the suitcase toward the door; when* ANNIE *tries to take it from her, she fights her off and backs through the doorway with it.* ANNIE *stands a moment, then follows her in, and together they get the suitcase up the steps into* ANNIE'S *room.*]

KATE Well?
KELLER She's very rough, Katie.
KATE I like her, Captain.
KELLER Certainly rear a peculiar kind of young woman in the North. How old is she?
KATE (*vaguely*) Ohh — Well, she's not in her teens, you know.
KELLER She's only a child. What's her family like, shipping her off alone this far?
KATE I couldn't learn. She's very close-mouthed about some things.
KELLER Why does she wear those glasses? I like to see a person's eyes when I talk to —
KATE For the sun. She was blind.
KELLER Blind?
KATE She's had nine operations on her eyes. One just before she left.
KELLER Blind! Good heavens, do they expect one blind child to teach another? Has she experience at least? How long did she teach there?
KATE She was a pupil.
KELLER (*heavily*) Katie, Katie. This is her first position?
KATE (*bright voice*) She was valedictorian —
KELLER Here's a houseful of grownups can't cope with the child; how can an inexperienced, half-blind Yankee schoolgirl manage her?

[JAMES *moves in with the trunk on his shoulder.*]

JAMES (*easily*) Great improvement. Now we have two of them to look after.

KELLER You look after those strawberry plants!

[JAMES *stops with the trunk.* KELLER *turns from him without another word, and marches off.*]

JAMES Nothing I say is right.

KATE Why say anything? (*She calls.*) Don't be long, Captain, we'll have supper right away —

[*She goes into the house and through the rear door of the family room.* JAMES *trudges in with the trunk, takes it up the steps to* ANNIE'S *room, and sets it down outside the door. The lights elsewhere dim somewhat.*

Meanwhile, inside, ANNIE *has given* HELEN *a key; while* ANNIE *removes her bonnet,* HELEN *unlocks and opens the suitcase. The first thing she pulls out is a voluminous shawl. She fingers it until she perceives what it is; then she wraps it around her, and acquiring* ANNIE'S *bonnet and smoked glasses as well, dons the lot: the shawl swamps her, and the bonnet settles down upon the glasses, but she stands before a mirror cocking her head to one side, then to the other, in a mockery of adult action.* ANNIE *is amused and talks to her as one might to a kitten, with no trace of company manners.*]

ANNIE All the trouble I went to and that's how I look?

[HELEN *then comes back to the suitcase, gropes for more, lifts out a pair of female drawers.*]

Oh, no. Not the drawers!

[*But* HELEN, *discarding them, comes to the elegant doll. Her fingers explore its features, and when she raises it and finds its eyes open and close, she is at first startled, then delighted. She picks it up, taps its head vigorously, taps her own chest, and nods questioningly.* ANNIE *takes her finger, points it to the doll, points it to* HELEN, *and touching it to her own face, also nods.* HELEN *sits back on her heels, clasps the doll to herself, and rocks it.* ANNIE *studies her, still in bonnet and smoked glasses, like a caricature of herself, and addresses her humorously.*]

All right, Miss O'Sullivan. Let's begin with *doll*. (*She takes* HELEN's *hand; in her palm* ANNIE's *forefinger points, thumb holding her other fingers clenched.*) D. (*Her thumb next holds all her fingers clenched, touching* HELEN's *palm.*) O. (*Her thumb and forefinger extend.*) L. (*Same contact repeated.*) L. (*She puts* HELEN's *hand to the doll.*) Doll.

JAMES You spell pretty well.

[ANNIE, *in one hurried move, gets the drawers swiftly back into the suitcase, the lid banged shut, and her head turned, to see* JAMES *leaning in the doorway.*]

Finding out if she's ticklish? She is.

[ANNIE *regards him stonily, but* HELEN *after a scowling moment tugs at her hand again, imperious.* ANNIE *repeats the letters, and* HELEN *interrupts her fingers in the middle, feeling each of them, puzzled.* ANNIE *touches* HELEN's *hand to the doll and begins spelling into it again.*]

JAMES What is it, a game?
ANNIE (*curtly*) An alphabet.
JAMES Alphabet?
ANNIE For the deaf.

[HELEN *now repeats the finger movements in air, exactly, her head cocked to her own hand, and* ANNIE's *eyes suddenly gleam.*]

Ho. How *bright* she is!
JAMES You think she knows what she's doing?

[*He takes* HELEN's *hand, to throw a meaningless gesture into it; she repeats this one too.*]

She imitates everything; she's a monkey.
ANNIE (*very pleased*) Yes, she's a bright little monkey, all right.

[*She takes the doll from* HELEN *and reaches for her hand;* HELEN *instantly grabs the doll back.* ANNIE *takes it again, and* HELEN's *hand next, but* HELEN *is incensed now; when* ANNIE *draws her hand to her face to shake her head no, then tries to spell to her,*

[HELEN *slaps at* ANNIE's *face.* ANNIE *grasps* HELEN *by both arms and swings her into a chair, holding her pinned there, kicking, while glasses, doll, bonnet fly in various directions.* JAMES *laughs.*]

JAMES She wants her doll back.
ANNIE When she spells it.
JAMES Spell, she doesn't know the thing has a name, even.
ANNIE Of course not, who expects her to, now? All I want is her fingers to learn the letters.
JAMES Won't mean anything to her.

[ANNIE *gives him a look. She then tries to form* HELEN's *fingers into the letters, but* HELEN *swings a haymaker instead, which* ANNIE *barely ducks, at once pinning her down again.*]

Doesn't like that alphabet, Miss Sullivan. You invent it yourself?

[HELEN *is now in a rage, fighting tooth and nail to get out of the chair, and* ANNIE *answers while struggling and dodging her kicks.*]

ANNIE Spanish monks under a — vow of silence. Which I wish *you'd* take!

[*And suddenly releasing* HELEN's *hands, she comes and shuts the door in* JAMES's *face.* HELEN *drops to the floor, groping around for the doll.* ANNIE *looks around desperately, sees her purse on the bed, rummages in it, and comes up with a battered piece of cake wrapped in newspaper; with her foot she moves the doll deftly out of the way of* HELEN's *groping, and going on her knee, she lets* HELEN *smell the cake. When* HELEN *grabs for it,* ANNIE *removes the cake and spells quickly into the reaching hand.*]

Cake. From Washington, up north; it's the best I can do.

[HELEN's *hand waits, baffled.* ANNIE *repeats it.*]

C, a, k, e. Do what my fingers do; never mind what it means.

[*She touches the cake briefly to* HELEN's *nose, pats her hand, presents her own hand.* HELEN *spells the letters rapidly back.* ANNIE *pats her hand enthusiastically and gives her the cake;* HELEN *crams it into her mouth with both hands.* ANNIE *watches her, with humor.*]

Get it down fast; maybe I'll steal that back too. Now. (*She takes the doll, touches it to* HELEN's *nose, and spells again into her hand.*) D, o, l, l. Think it over.

[HELEN *thinks it over while* ANNIE *presents her own hand. Then* HELEN *spells three letters.* ANNIE *waits a second, then completes the word for* HELEN *in her palm.*]

L.

[*She hands over the doll, and* HELEN *gets a good grip on its leg.*]

Imitate now, understand later. End of the first les —

[*She never finishes, because* HELEN *swings the doll with a furious energy; it hits* ANNIE *squarely in the face, and she falls back with a cry of pain, her knuckles up to her mouth.* HELEN *waits, tensed for further combat. When* ANNIE *lowers her knuckles, she looks at blood on them; she works her lips, gets to her feet, finds the mirror, and bares her teeth at herself. Now she is furious herself.*]

You little wretch, no one's taught you *any* manners? I'll —

[*But rounding from the mirror, she sees the door slam;* HELEN *and the doll are on the outside, and* HELEN *is turning the key in the lock.* ANNIE *darts over, to pull the knob; the door is locked fast. She yanks it again.*]

Helen! Helen, let me out of —

[*She bats her brow at the folly of speaking, but* JAMES, *now downstairs, hears her and turns to see* HELEN *with the key and doll groping her way down the steps;* JAMES *takes in the whole situation, makes a move to intercept* HELEN, *but then changes his mind, lets her pass, and amusedly follows her out onto the porch. Upstairs,* ANNIE *meanwhile rattles the knob, kneels, peers through the keyhole, gets up. She goes to the window, looks down, frowns.* JAMES, *from the yard, sings gaily up to her.*]

JAMES "Buffalo girl, are you coming out tonight,
    Coming out tonight,
    Coming out — "

[*He drifts back into the house.* ANNIE *takes a handkerchief, nurses her mouth, stands in the middle of the room, staring at door and window in turn, and so catches sight of herself in the mirror —*

her cheek scratched, her hair disheveled, her handkerchief bloody, her face disgusted with herself. She addresses the mirror, with some irony.]

ANNIE Don't worry. They'll find you; you're not lost. Only out of place. (*But she coughs, spits something into her palm, and stares at it, outraged.*) And toothless. (*She winces.*) Oo! It hurts.

[*She pours some water into the basin, dips the handkerchief, and presses it to her mouth. Standing there, bent over the basin in pain — with the rest of the set dim and unreal, and the lights upon her taking on the subtle color of the past — she hears again, as do we, the faraway voices, and slowly she lifts her head to them; the boy's voice is the same; the others are cracked old crones in a nightmare, and perhaps we see their shadows.*]

BOY'S VOICE It hurts. Annie, it hurts.
FIRST CRONE'S VOICE Keep that brat shut up, can't you, girlie; how's a body to get any sleep in this damn ward?
BOY'S VOICE It hurts. It hurts.
SECOND CRONE'S VOICE Shut up, you!
BOY'S VOICE Annie, when are we goin' home? You promised!
ANNIE Jimmie —
BOY'S VOICE Forever and ever, you said forever —

[ANNIE *drops the handkerchief, averts to the window, and is arrested there by the next cry.*]

Annie? Annie, you there? Annie! It *hurts!*
THIRD CRONE'S VOICE Grab him, he's fallin'!
BOY'S VOICE *Annie!*
DOCTOR'S VOICE (*a pause, slowly*) Little girl. Little girl, I must tell you your brother will be going on a —

[*But* ANNIE *claps her hands to her ears, to shut this out; there is instant silence.*]

SCENE 7

As *the lights bring the other areas in again,* JAMES *goes to the steps to listen for any sound from upstairs.* KELLER, *re-entering from the left, crosses toward the house; he passes* HELEN *en route to her re-*

treat under the pump. KATE *re-enters the rear door of the family room, with flowers for the table.*

KATE Supper is ready, Jimmie, will you call your father?
JAMES Certainly. (*But he calls up the stairs, for* ANNIE's *benefit.*) Father! Supper!
KELLER (*at the door*) No need to shout, I've been cooling my heels for an hour. Sit down.
JAMES Certainly.
KELLER Viney!

[VINEY *backs in with a roast while they get settled around the table.*]

VINEY Yes, Cap'n, right here.
KATE Mildred went directly to sleep, Viney?
VINEY Oh, yes, that babe's an angel.
KATE And Helen had a good supper?
VINEY (*vaguely*) I dunno, Miss Kate, somehow she didn't have much of an appetite tonight —
KATE (*a bit guilty*) Oh. Dear.
KELLER (*hastily*) Well, now. Couldn't say the same for my part; I'm famished. Katie, your plate.
KATE (*looking*) But where is Miss Annie?

[A *silence*]

JAMES (*pleasantly*) In her room.
KELLER In her room? Doesn't she know hot food must be eaten hot? Go bring her down at once, Jimmie.
JAMES (*rises*) Certainly. I'll get a ladder.
KELLER (*stares*) What?
JAMES I'll need a ladder. Shouldn't take me long.
KATE (*stares*) What shouldn't take you —
KELLER Jimmie, do as I say! Go upstairs at once and tell Miss Sullivan supper is getting cold —
JAMES She's locked in her room.
KELLER Locked in her —
KATE What on earth are you —
JAMES Helen locked her in and made off with the key.
KATE (*rising*) And you sit here and say nothing?

JAMES Well, everyone's been telling me not to say anything.

[*He goes serenely out and across the yard, whistling.* KELLER, *thrusting up from his chair, makes for the stairs.*]

KATE Viney, look out in back for Helen. See if she has that key.
VINEY Yes, Miss Kate. (VINEY *goes out the rear door.*)
KELLER (*calling down*) She's out by the pump!

[KATE *goes out on the porch after* HELEN, *while* KELLER *knocks on* ANNIE's *door, then rattles the knob, imperiously.*]

Miss Sullivan! Are you in there?
ANNIE Oh, I'm in here, all right.
KELLER Is there no key on your side?
ANNIE (*with some asperity*) Well, if there was a key in here, I wouldn't be in here. Helen took it; the only thing on my side is me.
KELLER Miss Sullivan. I — (*He tries but cannot hold it back.*) Not in the house ten minutes — I don't see *how* you managed it!

[*He stomps downstairs again while* ANNIE *mutters to herself.*]

ANNIE And even I'm not on my side.
KELLER (*roaring*) Viney!
VINEY (*reappearing*) Yes, Cap'n?
KELLER Put that meat back in the oven!

[VINEY *bears the roast off again while* KELLER *strides out onto the porch.* KATE *is with* HELEN *at the pump, opening her hands.*]

KATE She has no key.
KELLER Nonsense, she must have the key. Have you searched in her pockets?
KATE Yes. She doesn't have it.
KELLER Katie, she must have the key.
KATE Would you prefer to search her yourself, Captain?
KELLER No, I would not prefer to search her! She almost took my kneecap off this evening, when I tried merely to —

[JAMES *reappears carrying a long ladder, with* PERCY *running after him to be in on things.*]

Take that ladder back!

JAMES Certainly.

[*He turns around with it.* MARTHA *comes skipping around the upstage corner of the house to be in on things, accompanied by the setter* BELLE.]

KATE She could have hidden the key.
KELLER Where?
KATE Anywhere. Under a stone. In the flower beds. In the grass —
KELLER Well, I can't plow up the entire grounds to find a missing key! Jimmie!
JAMES Sir?
KELLER Bring me a ladder!
JAMES Certainly.

[VINEY *comes around the downstage side of the house to be in on things; she has* MILDRED *over her shoulder, bleating.* KELLER *places the ladder against* ANNIE'S *window and mounts.* ANNIE *meanwhile is running about making herself presentable, washing the blood off her mouth, straightening her clothes, tidying her hair. The gardener enters to gaze in wonder, increasing the gathering ring of spectators.*]

KATE (*sharply*) What is Mildred doing up?
VINEY Cap'n woke her, ma'am, all that hollerin'.
KELLER Miss Sullivan!

[ANNIE *comes to the window, with as much air of gracious normality as she can manage;* KELLER *is at the window.*]

ANNIE (*brightly*) Yes, Captain Keller?
KELLER Come out!
ANNIE I don't see how I can. There isn't room.
KELLER I intend to carry you. Climb onto my shoulder and hold tight.
ANNIE Oh, no. It's — very chivalrous of you, but I'd really prefer to —
KELLER Miss Sullivan, follow instructions! I will not have you also tumbling out of our windows.

[ANNIE *obeys, with some misgivings.*]

I hope this is not a sample of what we may expect from you. In

the way of simplifying the work of looking after Helen.
ANNIE Captain Keller, I'm perfectly able to go down a ladder under my own —
KELLER I doubt it, Miss Sullivan. Simply hold onto my neck.

[*He begins down with her, while the spectators stand in a wide and somewhat awestricken circle, watching.* KELLER *half misses a rung, and* ANNIE *grabs at his whiskers.*]

My *neck*, Miss Sullivan!
ANNIE I'm sorry to inconvenience you this way —
KELLER No inconvenience, other than having that door taken down and the lock replaced if we fail to find that key.
ANNIE Oh, I'll look everywhere for it.
KELLER Thank you. Do not look in any room that can be locked. There.

[*He stands her on the ground.* JAMES *applauds.*]

ANNIE Thank you very much.

[*She smooths her skirt, looking as composed and ladylike as possible.* KELLER *stares around at the spectators.*]

KELLER Go, go, back to your work. What are you looking at here? There's nothing here to look at.

[*They break up, move off.*]

Now would it be possible for us to have supper, like other people? (*He marches into the house.*)
KATE Viney, serve supper. I'll put Mildred to sleep.

[*They all go in.* JAMES *is the last to leave, murmuring to* ANNIE *with a gesture.*]

JAMES Might as well leave the l, a, d, d, e, r, hm?

[ANNIE *ignores him, looking at* HELEN; JAMES *goes in too. Imperceptibly, the lights commence to narrow down.* ANNIE *and* HELEN *are now alone in the yard —* HELEN *seated at the pump, where she has been oblivious to it all, a battered little savage, playing with the doll in a picture of innocent contentment.* ANNIE *comes near, leans against the house, and taking off her smoked glasses, studies her, not without awe. Presently* HELEN *rises, gropes around to see if anyone is present;* ANNIE *evades her hand, and when* HELEN *is satisfied she is alone, the key suddenly protrudes out of her mouth. She takes it in her fingers, stands thinking, gropes to the pump, lifts a loose board, drops the key into the well, and hugs herself gleefully.* ANNIE *stares. But after a moment she shakes her head to herself; she cannot keep the smile from her lips.*]

ANNIE You devil. (*Her tone is one of great respect, humor, and acceptance of challenge.*) You think I'm so easily gotten rid of? You have a thing or two to learn, first. I have nothing else to do. (*She goes up the steps to the porch, but turns for a final word, almost of warning.*) And nowhere to go.

[*And presently she moves into the house to the others as the lights dim down and out, except for the small circle upon* HELEN, *solitary at the pump, which ends the act.*]

ACT 2

SCENE 1

It is evening.

The only room visible in the KELLER *house is* ANNIE'S, *where by lamplight* ANNIE *in a shawl is at a desk writing a letter; at her bureau* HELEN, *in her customary unkempt state, is tucking her doll in the bottom drawer as a cradle, the contents of which she has dumped out, creating as usual a fine disorder.*

ANNIE *mutters each word as she writes her letter, slowly, her eyes close to and almost touching the page, to follow with difficulty her penwork.*

ANNIE ". . . and, nobody, here, has, attempted, to, control, her. The, greatest, problem, I, have, is, how, to, discipline, her, without, breaking, her, spirit." (*Resolute voice*) "But, I, shall, insist, on, reasonable, obedience, from, the, start —"

[*At which point* HELEN, *groping about on the desk, knocks over the inkwell.* ANNIE *jumps up, rescues her letter, rights the inkwell, grabs a towel to stem the spillage, and then wipes at* HEL-

EN's *hands;* HELEN *as always pulls free, but not until* ANNIE *first gets three letters into her palm.*]

Ink.

[HELEN *is enough interested in and puzzled by this spelling that she proffers her hand again; so* ANNIE *spells and impassively dunks it back in the spillage.*]

Ink. It has a name.

[*She wipes the hand clean and leads* HELEN *to her bureau, where she looks for something to engage her. She finds a sewing card, with needle and thread, and going to her knees, shows* HELEN'S *hand how to connect one row of holes.*]

Down. Under. Up. And be careful of the needle —

[HELEN *gets it, and* ANNIE *rises.*]

Fine. You keep out of the ink and perhaps I can keep out of — the soup. (*She returns to the desk, tidies it, and resumes writing her letter, bent close to the page.*) "These, blots, are, her, handiwork. I — "

[*She is interrupted by a gasp:* HELEN *has stuck her finger, and sits sucking at it, darkly. Then with vengeful resolve she seizes her doll and is about to dash its brains out on the floor when* ANNIE, *diving, catches it in one hand, which she at once shakes with hopping pain but otherwise ignores, patiently.*]

All right, let's try temperance.

[*Taking the doll, she kneels, goes through the motion of knocking its head on the floor, spells into* HELEN'S *hand.*]

Bad, girl.

[*She lets* HELEN *feel the grieved expression on her face.* HELEN *imitates it. Next she makes* HELEN *caress the doll and kiss the hurt spot and hold it gently in her arms, then spells into her hand.*]

Good, girl.

[*She lets* HELEN *feel the smile on her face.* HELEN *sits with a scowl, which suddenly clears; she pats the doll, kisses it, wreathes her face in a large artificial smile, and bears the doll to the washstand, where she carefully sits it.* ANNIE *watches, pleased.*]

Very good girl —

[*Whereupon* HELEN *elevates the pitcher and dashes it on the floor instead.* ANNIE *leaps to her feet and stands inarticulate;* HELEN *calmly gropes back to sit to the sewing card and needle.*

ANNIE *manages to achieve self-control. She picks up a fragment or two of the pitcher, sees* HELEN *is puzzling over the card and resolutely kneels to demonstrate it again. She spells into* HELEN's *hand.* KATE *meanwhile coming around the corner with folded sheets on her arm, halts at the doorway and watches them for a moment in silence; she is moved, but level.*]

KATE (*presently*) What are you saying to her?

[ANNIE, *glancing up, is a bit embarrassed, and rises from the spelling, to find her company manners.*]

ANNIE Oh, I was just making conversation. Saying it was a sewing card.

KATE But does that — (*She imitates with her fingers.*) — mean that to her?

ANNIE No. No, she won't know what spelling is till she knows what a word is.

KATE Yet you keep spelling to her. Why?

ANNIE (*cheerily*) I like to hear myself talk!

KATE The Captain says it's like spelling to the fence post.

ANNIE (*a pause*) Does he, now?

KATE Is it?

ANNIE No, it's how I watch you talk to Mildred.

KATE Mildred?

ANNIE Any baby. Gibberish, grown-up gibberish, baby-talk gibberish; do they understand one word of it to start? Somehow they begin to. If they hear it, I'm letting Helen hear it.

KATE Other children are not — impaired.

ANNIE Ho, there's nothing impaired in that head; it works like a mousetrap!

KATE (*smiles*) But after a child hears how many words, Miss Annie, a million?

ANNIE I guess no mother's ever minded enough to count.

[*She drops her eyes to spell into* HELEN's *hand, again indicating the card;* HELEN *spells back, and* ANNIE *is amused.*]

KATE (*too quickly*) What did she spell?
ANNIE I spelt *card*. She spelt *cake!* (*She takes in* KATE's *quickness, and shakes her head, gently.*) No, it's only a finger game to her, Mrs. Keller. What she has to learn first is that things have names.
KATE And when will she learn?
ANNIE Maybe after a million and one words.

[*They hold each other's gaze;* KATE *then speaks quietly.*]

KATE I should like to learn those letters, Miss Annie.
ANNIE (*pleased*) I'll teach you tomorrow morning. That makes only half a million each!
KATE (*then*) It's her bedtime.

[ANNIE *reaches for the sewing card,* HELEN *objects,* ANNIE *insists, and* HELEN *gets rid of* ANNIE's *hand by jabbing it with the needle.* ANNIE *gasps and moves to grip* HELEN's *wrist; but* KATE *intervenes with a proffered sweet, and* HELEN *drops the card, crams the sweet into her mouth, and scrambles up to search her mother's hands for more.* ANNIE *nurses her wound, staring after the sweet.*]

I'm sorry, Miss Annie.
ANNIE (*indignantly*) Why does she get a reward? For stabbing me?
KATE Well — (*Then, tiredly*) We catch our flies with honey, I'm afraid. We haven't the heart for much else, and so many times she simply cannot be compelled.
ANNIE (*ominous*) Yes. I'm the same way myself.

[KATE *smiles, and leads* HELEN *off around the corner.* ANNIE, *alone in her room, picks up things and in the act of removing* HELEN's *doll gives way to unmannerly temptation: she throttles it. She drops it on her bed, and stands pondering. Then she turns back, sits decisively, and writes again, as the lights dim on her.*]

(*Grimly*) "The, more, I, think, the, more, certain, I, am, that, obedience, is, the, gateway, through, which, knowledge, enters, the, mind, of, the, child — "

[*On the word* obedience *a shaft of sunlight hits the water pump outside, while* ANNIE'S *voice ends in the dark, followed by a distant cockcrow; daylight comes up over another corner of the sky, with* VINEY'S *voice heard at once.*]

SCENE 2

VINEY Breakfast ready!

[VINEY *comes down into the sunlight beam and pumps a pitcherful of water. While the pitcher is brimming, we hear conversation from the dark; the light grows to the family room of the house, where all are either entering or already seated at breakfast, with* KELLER *and* JAMES *arguing the war.* HELEN *is wandering around the table to explore the contents of the other plates. When* ANNIE *is in her chair, she watches* HELEN. VINEY *re-enters, sets the pitcher on the table;* KATE *lifts the almost empty biscuit plate with an inquiring look;* VINEY *nods and bears it off back, neither of them interrupting the men.* ANNIE *meanwhile sits with fork quiet, watching* HELEN, *who at her mother's plate pokes her hand among some scrambled eggs.* KATE *catches* ANNIE'S *eyes on her, smiles with a wry gesture.* HELEN *moves on to* JAMES'S *plate, the male talk continuing,* JAMES *deferential and* KELLER *overriding.*]

JAMES . . . no, but shouldn't we give the devil his due, Father? The fact is we lost the South two years earlier when he outthought us behind Vicksburg.

KELLER *Outthought* is a peculiar word for a butcher.

JAMES Harness maker, wasn't he?

KELLER I said *butcher*; his only virtue as a soldier was numbers, and he led them to slaughter with no more regard than for so many sheep.

JAMES But even if in that sense he was a butcher, the fact is he —

KELLER And a drunken one, half the war.

JAMES Agreed, Father. If his own people said he was, I can't argue he —

KELLER Well, what is it you find to admire in such a man, Jimmie, the butchery or the drunkenness?

JAMES Neither, Father, only the fact that he beat us.

KELLER He didn't.

JAMES Is it your contention we won the war, sir?
KELLER He didn't beat us at Vicksburg. We lost Vicksburg because Pemberton gave Bragg five thousand of his cavalry, and Loring, whom I knew personally for a nincompoop before you were born, marched away from Champion's Hill with enough men to have held them; we lost Vicksburg by stupidity verging on treason.
JAMES I would have said we lost Vicksburg because Grant was one thing no Yankee general was before him —
KELLER Drunk? I doubt it.
JAMES Obstinate.
KELLER Obstinate. Could any of them compare even in that with old Stonewall? If he'd been there, we would still have Vicksburg.
JAMES Well, the butcher simply wouldn't give up; he tried four ways of getting around Vicksburg, and on the fifth try he got around. Anyone else would have pulled north and —
KELLER He wouldn't have got around if we'd had a Southerner in command, instead of a half-breed Yankee traitor like Pemberton. . . .

[*While this background talk is in progress,* HELEN *is working around the table, ultimately toward* ANNIE's *plate. She messes with her hands in* JAMES's *plate, then in* KELLER's, *both men taking it so for granted they hardly notice. Then* HELEN *comes groping with soiled hands past her own plate to* ANNIE's; *her hand goes to it, and* ANNIE, *who has been waiting, deliberately lifts and removes her hand.* HELEN *gropes again;* ANNIE *firmly pins her by the wrist, and removes her hand from the table.* HELEN *thrusts her hands again,* ANNIE *catches them, and* HELEN *begins to flail and make noises; the interruption brings* KELLER's *gaze upon them.*]

What's the matter there?
KATE Miss Annie. You see, she's accustomed to helping herself from our plates to anything she —
ANNIE (*evenly*) Yes, but *I'm* not accustomed to it.
KELLER No, of course not. Viney!
KATE Give her something, Jimmie, to quiet her.
JAMES (*blandly*) But her table manners are the best she has. Well.

[*He pokes across with a chunk of bacon at* HELEN's *hand, which* ANNIE *releases, but* HELEN *knocks the bacon away and stubbornly thrusts at* ANNIE's *plate;* ANNIE *grips her wrists again; the struggle mounts.*]

KELLER Let her this time, Miss Sullivan; it's the only way we get any adult conversation. If my son's half merits that description. (*He rises.*) I'll get you another plate.
ANNIE (*gripping* HELEN) I have a plate, thank you.
KATE (*calling*) Viney! I'm afraid what Captain Keller says is only too true; she'll persist in this until she gets her own way.
KELLER (*at the door*) Viney, bring Miss Sullivan another plate —
ANNIE (*stonily*) I have a plate, nothing's wrong with the *plate*, I intend to keep it.

[*Silence for a moment, except for* HELEN's *noises as she struggles to get loose; the* KELLERS *are a bit nonplussed, and* ANNIE *is too darkly intent on* HELEN's *manners to have any thoughts now of her own.*]

JAMES Ha. You see why they took Vicksburg?
KELLER (*uncertainly*) Miss Sullivan. One plate or another is hardly a matter to struggle with a deprived child about.
ANNIE Oh, I'd sooner have a more —

[HELEN *begins to kick;* ANNIE *moves her ankles to the opposite side of the chair.*]

— heroic issue myself, I —
KELLER No, I really must insist you —

[HELEN *bangs her toe on the chair and sinks to the floor, crying with rage and feigned injury;* ANNIE *keeps hold of her wrists, gazing down, while* KATE *rises.*]

Now she's hurt herself.
ANNIE (*grimly*) No, she hasn't.
KELLER Will you please let her hands go?
KATE Miss Annie, you don't know the child well enough yet; she'll keep —
ANNIE I know an ordinary tantrum well enough, when I see one, and a badly spoiled child —
JAMES Hear, hear.
KELLER (*very annoyed*) Miss Sullivan! You would have more un-

derstanding of your pupil if you had some pity in you. Now kindly do as I —
ANNIE Pity?

[*She releases* HELEN *to turn equally annoyed on* KELLER *across the table; instantly* HELEN *scrambles up and dives at* ANNIE'S *plate. This time* ANNIE *intercepts her by pouncing on her wrists like a hawk, and her temper boils.*]

For this *tyrant?* The whole house turns on her whims; is there anything she wants she doesn't get? I'll tell you what I pity: that the sun won't rise and set for her all her life, and every day you're telling her it will; what good will your pity do her when you're under the strawberries, Captain Keller?
KELLER (*outraged*) Kate, for the love of heaven, will you —
KATE Miss Annie, please, I don't think it serves to lose our —
ANNIE It does you good, that's all. It's less trouble to feel sorry for her than to teach her anything better, isn't it?
KELLER I fail to see where you have taught her anything yet, Miss Sullivan!
ANNIE I'll begin this minute if you'll leave the room, Captain Keller!
KELLER (*astonished*) Leave the —
ANNIE Everyone, please.

[*She struggles with* HELEN, *while* KELLER *endeavors to control his voice.*]

KELLER Miss Sullivan, you are here only as a paid teacher. Nothing more, and not to lecture —
ANNIE I can't *un*teach her six years of pity if you can't stand up to one tantrum! Old Stonewall, indeed. Mrs. Keller, you promised me help.
KATE Indeed I did, we truly want to —
ANNIE Then leave me alone with her. Now!
KELLER (*in a wrath*) Katie, will you come outside with me? At once, please.

[*He marches to the front door.* KATE *and* JAMES *follow him. Simultaneously* ANNIE *releases* HELEN'S *wrists, and the child again sinks to the floor, kicking and crying her weird noises;* ANNIE *steps over her to meet* VINEY *coming in the rear doorway with biscuits and a clean plate, surprised at the general commotion.*]

VINEY Heaven sakes —
ANNIE Out, please.

[*She backs* VINEY *out with one hand, closes the door on her astonished mouth, locks it, and removes the key.* KELLER *meanwhile snatches his hat from a rack, and* KATE *follows him down the porch steps.* JAMES *lingers in the doorway to address* ANNIE *across the room with a bow.*]

JAMES If it takes all summer, general.

[ANNIE *comes over to his door in turn, removing her glasses grimly; as* KELLER, *outside, begins speaking,* ANNIE *closes the door on* JAMES, *locks it, removes the key, and turns with her back against the door to stare ominously at* HELEN, *kicking on the floor.*

JAMES *takes his hat from the rack and, going down the porch steps, joins* KATE *and* KELLER *talking in the yard,* KELLER *in a sputter of ire.*]

KELLER This girl, this — cub of a girl — *presumes!* I tell you, I'm of half a mind to ship her back to Boston before the week is out. You can inform her so from me!
KATE (*eyebrows up*) I, Captain?
KELLER She's a *hireling!* Now I want it clear — unless there's an apology and a complete change of manner, she goes back on the next train! Will you make that quite clear?
KATE Where will you be, Captain, while I am making it quite —
KELLER At the office!

[*He begins off left, finds his napkin still in his irate hand, is uncertain with it, dabs his lips with dignity, gets rid of it in a toss to* JAMES, *and marches off.* JAMES *turns to eye* KATE.]

JAMES Will you?

[KATE'S *mouth is set, and* JAMES *studies it lightly.*]

I thought what she said was exceptionally intelligent. I've been saying it for years.
KATE (*not without scorn*) To his face? (*She comes to relieve him of the white napkin, but reverts again with it.*) Or will you take it, Jimmie? As a flag?

[JAMES *stalks out, much offended, and* KATE, *turning, stares across the yard at the house; the lights narrowing down to the following pantomime in the family room leave her motionless in the dark.*

ANNIE *meanwhile has begun by slapping both keys down on a shelf out of* HELEN'S *reach; she returns to the table upstage.* HELEN'S *kicking has subsided, and when from the floor her hand finds* ANNIE'S *chair empty, she pauses.* ANNIE *clears the table of* KATE'S, JAMES'S, *and* KELLER'S *plates; she gets back to her own across the table just in time to slide it deftly away from* HELEN'S *pouncing hand. She lifts the hand and moves it to* HELEN'S *plate, and after an instant's exploration* HELEN *again sits on the floor and drums her heels.* ANNIE *comes around the table and resumes her chair. When* HELEN *feels her skirt again, she ceases kicking, waits for whatever is to come, renews some kicking, waits again.* ANNIE, *retrieving her plate, takes up a forkful of food, stops it halfway to her mouth, gazes at it devoid of appetite, and half lowers it; but after a look at* HELEN *she sighs, dips the forkful toward* HELEN *in a for-your-sake toast, and puts it in her own mouth to chew, not without an effort.*

HELEN *now gets hold of the chair leg, and half succeeds in pulling the chair out from under her.* ANNIE *bangs it down with her rear, heavily, and sits with all her weight.* HELEN'S *next attempt to topple it is unavailing, so her fingers dive in a pinch at* ANNIE'S *flank.* ANNIE *in the middle of her mouthful almost loses it with startle, and she slaps down her fork to round on* HELEN. *The child comes up with curiosity to feel what* ANNIE *is doing, so* ANNIE *resumes eating, letting* HELEN'S *hand follow the movement of her fork to her mouth; whereupon* HELEN *at once reaches into* ANNIE'S *plate.* ANNIE *firmly removes her hand to her own plate.* HELEN *in reply pinches* ANNIE'S *thigh, a good mean pinchful that makes* ANNIE *jump.* ANNIE *sets the fork down and sits with her mouth tight.* HELEN *digs another pinch into her thigh, and this time* ANNIE *slaps her hand smartly away;* HELEN *retaliates with a roundhouse fist that catches* ANNIE *on the ear, and* ANNIE'S *hand leaps at once in a forceful slap across* HELEN'S *cheek;* HELEN *is the startled one now.* ANNIE'S *hand in compunction falters to her own face, but when* HELEN *hits at her again,* ANNIE *deliberately slaps her again.* HELEN *lifts her fist, irresolute, for another round-*

house, ANNIE *lifts her hand for another slap, and they freeze in this posture, while* HELEN *mulls it over. She thinks better of it, drops her fist, and giving* ANNIE *a wide berth, gropes around to her mother's chair, to find it empty; she blunders her way along the table, upstage, and encountering the empty chairs and missing plates, she looks bewildered; she gropes back to her mother's chair, again touches her cheek and indicates the chair, and waits for the world to answer.*

ANNIE *now reaches over to spell into her hand, but* HELEN *yanks it away; she gropes to the front door, tries the knob, and finds the door locked, with no key. She gropes to the rear door and finds it locked, with no key. She commences to bang on it.* ANNIE *rises, crosses, takes her wrists, draws her resisting back to the table, seats her, and releases her hands upon her plate; as* ANNIE *herself begins to sit,* HELEN *writhes out of her chair, runs to the front door, and tugs and kicks at it.* ANNIE *rises again, crosses, draws her by one wrist back to the table, seats her, and sits;* HELEN *escapes back to the door, knocking over her mother's chair en route.* ANNIE *rises again in pursuit, and this time lifts* HELEN *bodily from behind and bears her kicking to her chair. She deposits her, and once more turns to sit.* HELEN *scrambles out, but as she passes,* ANNIE *catches her up again from behind and deposits her in the chair;* HELEN *scrambles out on the other side for the rear door, but* ANNIE *at her heels catches her up and deposits her again in the chair. She stands behind it.* HELEN *scrambles out to her right, and the instant her feet hit the floor* ANNIE *lifts and deposits her back; she scrambles out to her left, and is at once lifted and deposited back. She tries right again and is deposited back, and tries left again and is deposited back, and now feints* ANNIE *to the right but is off to her left, and is promptly deposited back. She sits a moment, and then starts straight over the tabletop, dishware notwithstanding;* ANNIE *hauls her in and deposits her back, with her plate spilling in her lap, and she melts to the floor and crawls under the table, laborious among its legs and chairs; but* ANNIE *is swift around the table and waiting on the other side when she surfaces, immediately bearing her aloft;* HELEN *clutches at* JAMES's *chair for anchorage, but it comes with her, and halfway back she abandons it to the floor.* ANNIE *depos-*

its her in her chair, and waits. HELEN *sits tensed, motionless. Then she tentatively puts out her left foot and hand,* ANNIE *interposes her own hand, and at the contact* HELEN *jerks hers in. She tries her right foot,* ANNIE *blocks it with her own, and* HELEN *jerks hers in. Finally, leaning back, she slumps down in her chair, in a sullen biding.*

ANNIE *backs off a step and watches;* HELEN *offers no move.* ANNIE *takes a deep breath. Both of them and the room are in considerable disorder, two chairs down and the table a mess, but* ANNIE *makes no effort to tidy it; she only sits on her own chair and lets her energy refill. Then she takes up knife and fork, and resolutely addresses her food.* HELEN's *hand comes out to explore, and seeing it,* ANNIE *sits without moving; the child's hand goes over her hand and fork, pauses —* ANNIE *still does not move — and withdraws. Presently it moves for her own plate, slaps about for it, and stops, thwarted. At this,* ANNIE *again rises, recovers* HELEN's *plate from the floor and a handful of scattered food from the deranged tablecloth, drops it on the plate, and pushes the plate into contact with* HELEN's *fist. Neither of them now moves for a pregnant moment — until* HELEN *suddenly takes a grab of food and wolfs it down.* ANNIE *permits herself the humor of a minor bow and warming of her hands together; she wanders off a step or two, watching.* HELEN *cleans up the plate.*

After a glower of indecision, she holds the empty plate out for more. ANNIE *accepts it and, crossing to the removed plates, spoons food from them onto it; she stands debating the spoon, tapping it a few times on* HELEN's *plate; and when she returns with the plate, she brings the spoon too. She puts the spoon first into* HELEN's *hand, then sets the plate down.* HELEN, *discarding the spoon, reaches with her hand, and* ANNIE *stops it by the wrist; she replaces the spoon in it.* HELEN *impatiently discards it again, and again* ANNIE *stops her hand, to replace the spoon in it. This time* HELEN *throws the spoon on the floor.* ANNIE, *after considering it, lifts* HELEN *bodily out of the chair, and in a wrestling match on the floor closes her fingers upon the spoon, and returns her with it to the chair.* HELEN *again throws the spoon on the floor.* ANNIE *lifts her out of the chair again; but in the struggle over the spoon* HELEN, *with* ANNIE *on her back, sends her sliding over her head;* HELEN *flees back to her chair and scrambles into it. When* ANNIE *comes after her, she clutches it for dear life;* ANNIE *pries one hand loose, then the other, then the first again, then the other again, and then lifts* HELEN *by the waist, chair and all, and shakes the chair loose.* HELEN *wrestles to get free, but* ANNIE *pins her to the floor, closes her fingers upon the spoon, and lifts her kicking under one arm; with her other hand she gets the chair in place again and plunks* HELEN *back on it. When she releases her hand,* HELEN *throws the spoon at her.*

ANNIE *now removes the plate of food.* HELEN, *grabbing, finds it missing and commences to bang with her fists on the table.* ANNIE *collects a fistful of spoons and descends with them and the plate on* HELEN; *she lets her smell the plate, at which* HELEN *ceases banging, and* ANNIE *puts the plate down and a spoon in* HELEN's *hand.* HELEN *throws it on the floor.* ANNIE *puts another spoon in her hand.* HELEN *throws it on the floor.* ANNIE *puts another spoon in her hand.* HELEN *throws it on the floor. When* ANNIE *comes to her last spoon, she sits next to* HELEN *and, gripping the spoon in* HELEN's *hand, compels her to take food in it up to her mouth.* HELEN *sits with lips shut.* ANNIE *waits a stolid moment, then lowers* HELEN's *hand. She tries again;* HELEN's *lips remain shut.* ANNIE *waits, lowers* HELEN's *hand. She tries again; this time* HELEN *suddenly opens her mouth and accepts the food.* ANNIE *lowers the spoon with a sigh of relief, and* HELEN *spews the mouthful out at her face.* ANNIE *sits a moment with eyes closed, then takes the pitcher and dashes its water into* HELEN's *face, who gasps astonished.* ANNIE *with* HELEN's *hand takes up another spoonful and shoves it into her open mouth.* HELEN *swallows involuntarily, and while she is catching her breath,* ANNIE *forces her palm open, throws four swift letters into it, then another four, and bows toward her with devastating pleasantness.*]

ANNIE Good girl.

[ANNIE *lifts* HELEN's *hand to feel her face nodding;* HELEN *grabs a fistful of her hair, and yanks. The pain brings* ANNIE *to her knees, and* HELEN *pummels her; they roll under the table, and the lights commence to dim out on them.*]

SCENE 3

Simultaneously the light at left has been rising, slowly, so slowly that it seems at first we only imagine what is intimated in the yard: a few ghostlike figures, in silence, motionless, waiting. Now the distant belfry chimes commence to toll the hour, also very slowly, almost — it is twelve — interminably; the sense is that of a long time passing. We can identify the figures before the twelfth stroke, all facing the house in a kind of watch: KATE *is standing exactly as before, but now with the baby* MILDRED *sleeping in her arms; and placed here and there, unmoving, are* AUNT EV *in her hat, with a hanky to her nose; and the two children,* PERCY *and* MARTHA, *with necks outstretched eagerly; and* VINEY, *with a feather duster in her hand.*

The chimes cease, and there is silence. For a long moment none of the group moves.

VINEY (*presently*) What am I gonna do, Miss Kate? It's noontime, dinner's comin', I didn't get the breakfast dishes out of there yet.

[KATE *says nothing, stares at the house.* MARTHA *shifts* HELEN'S *doll in her clutch, and it plaintively says "momma."*]

KATE (*presently*) You run along, Martha.

[AUNT EV *blows her nose.*]

AUNT EV (*wretchedly*) I can't wait out here a minute longer, Kate; why, this could go on all afternoon, too.

KATE I'll tell the Captain you called.

VINEY (*to the children*) You hear what Miss Kate says? Never you mind what's going on here.

[*Still no one moves.*]

You run along and tend your own business. (*Finally* VINEY *turns on the children with the feather duster.*) Shoo!

[*The two children divide before her. She chases them off.* AUNT EV *comes to* KATE, *on her dignity.*]

AUNT EV Say what you like, Kate, but that child is a *Keller*. (*She opens her parasol, preparatory to leaving.*) I needn't remind you that all the Kellers are cousins to General Robert E. Lee. I don't know *who* that girl is.

[*She waits; but* KATE, *staring at the house, is without response.*]

The only Sullivan I've heard of — from Boston too, and I'd think twice before locking her up with that kind — is that man John L.[1]

[*And* AUNT EV *departs, with head high. Presently* VINEY *comes to* KATE, *her arms out for the baby.*]

VINEY You give me her, Miss Kate; I'll sneak her in back, to her crib.

[*But* KATE *is moveless until* VINEY *starts to take the baby;* KATE *looks down at her before relinquishing her.*]

KATE (*slowly*) This child never gives me a minute's worry.
VINEY Oh, yes, this one's the angel of the family, no question about that.

[*She begins off rear with the baby, heading around the house; and* KATE *now turns her back on it, her hand to her eyes. At this moment there is the slamming of a door, and when* KATE *wheels,* HELEN *is blundering down the porch steps into the light.* VINEY *halts, and* KATE *runs in;* HELEN *collides with her mother's knees and reels off and back to clutch them as her savior.* ANNIE, *with smoked glasses in hand, stands on the porch, also much undone, looking as though she had indeed just taken Vicksburg.* KATE, *taking in* HELEN'S *ravaged state, becomes steely in her gaze up at* ANNIE.]

KATE What happened?

[ANNIE *meets* KATE'S *gaze and gives a factual report, too exhausted for anything but a flat voice.*]

ANNIE She ate from her own plate. (*She thinks a moment.*) She ate with a spoon. Herself.

[KATE *frowns, uncertain with thought, and glances down at* HELEN.]

And she folded her napkin.

[KATE'S *gaze now wavers from* HELEN *to* ANNIE *and back.*]

---
[1] *John L.*: John L. Sullivan, a boxing champion of the late nineteenth century.

KATE (*softly*) Folded — her napkin?

ANNIE The room's a wreck, but her napkin is folded. (*She pauses, then*) I'll be in my room, Mrs. Keller.

[*She moves to re-enter the house, but she stops at* VINEY's *voice.*]

VINEY (*cheery*) Don't be long, Miss Annie. Dinner be ready right away!

[VINEY *carries* MILDRED *around the back of the house.* ANNIE *stands unmoving, takes a deep breath, stares over her shoulder at* KATE *and* HELEN, *then inclines her head graciously, and goes with a slight stagger into the house. The lights in her room above steal up in readiness for her.* KATE *remains alone with* HELEN *in the yard, standing protectively over her in a kind of wonder.*]

KATE (*slowly*) Folded her napkin.

[*She contemplates the wild head in her thighs and moves her fingertips over it, with such a tenderness, and something like a fear of its strangeness, that her own eyes close; she whispers, bending to it.*]

My Helen — folded her napkin —

[*And still erect, with only her head in surrender,* KATE, *for the first time that we see, loses her protracted war with grief, but she will not let a sound escape her; only the grimace of tears comes, and sobs that shake her in a grip of silence. But* HELEN *feels them, and her hand comes up in its own, wondering, to interrogate her mother's face, until* KATE *buries her lips in the child's palm.*]

Upstairs, ANNIE *enters her room, closes the door, and stands back against it; the lights, growing on her with their special color, commence to fade on* KATE *and* HELEN. *Then* ANNIE *goes wearily to her suitcase and lifts it to take it toward the bed. But it knocks an object to the floor, and she turns back to regard it. A new voice comes in a cultured murmur, hesitant, as with the effort of remembering a text.*]

MAN'S VOICE This — soul —

[ANNIE *puts the suitcase down and kneels to the object: it is the battered Perkins report, and she stands with it in her hand, letting memory try to speak.*]

This — blind, deaf, mute — woman —

[ANNIE *sits on her bed, opens the book, and finding the passage, brings it up an inch from her eyes to read, her face and lips following the overheard words, the voice quite factual now.*]

Can nothing be done to disinter this human soul? The whole neighborhood would rush to save this woman if she were buried alive by the caving in of a pit, and labor with zeal until she were dug out. Now if there were one who had as much patience as zeal, he might awaken her to a consciousness of her immortal —

[*When the boy's voice comes,* ANNIE *closes her eyes in pain.*]

BOY'S VOICE Annie? Annie, you there?
ANNIE Hush.
BOY'S VOICE Annie, what's that noise?

[ANNIE *tries not to answer; her own voice is drawn out of her, unwilling.*]

ANNIE Just a cot, Jimmie.
BOY'S VOICE Where they pushin' it?
ANNIE To the deadhouse.
BOY'S VOICE Annie. Does it hurt, to be dead?

[ANNIE *escapes by opening her eyes; her hand works restlessly over her cheek; she retreats into the book again, but the cracked old crones interrupt, whispering.* ANNIE *slowly lowers the book.*]

FIRST CRONE'S VOICE There is schools.
SECOND CRONE'S VOICE There is schools outside —
THIRD CRONE'S VOICE — schools where they teach blind ones, worse'n you —
FIRST CRONE'S VOICE To read —
SECOND CRONE'S VOICE To read and write —
THIRD CRONE'S VOICE There is schools outside where they —
FIRST CRONE'S VOICE There is schools —

[*Silence.* ANNIE *sits with her eyes shining, her hand almost in a caress over the book. Then*]

BOY'S VOICE You ain't goin' to school, are you, Annie?
ANNIE (*whispering*) When I grow up.

BOY'S VOICE You ain't either, Annie. You're goin' to stay here and take care of me.
ANNIE I'm goin' to school when I grow up.
BOY'S VOICE You said we'll be together, forever and ever and ever —
ANNIE (*fierce*) I'm goin' to school when I grow up!
DOCTOR'S VOICE (*slowly*) Little girl. Little girl, I must tell you. Your brother will be going on a journey, soon.

[ANNIE *sits rigid, in silence. Then the boy's voice pierces it, a shriek of terror.*]

BOY'S VOICE Annie!

[*It goes into* ANNIE *like a sword; she doubles onto it; the book falls to the floor. It takes her a racked moment to find herself and what she was engaged in here; when she sees the suitcase, she remembers, and lifts it once again toward the bed. But the voices are with her as she halts with suitcase in hand.*]

FIRST CRONE'S VOICE Goodbye, Annie.
DOCTOR'S VOICE Write me when you learn how.
SECOND CRONE'S VOICE Don't tell anyone you came from here. Don't tell anyone —
THIRD CRONE'S VOICE Yeah, don't tell anyone you came from —
FIRST CRONE'S VOICE Yeah, don't tell anyone —
SECOND CRONE'S VOICE Don't tell any —

[*The echoing voices fade. After a moment* ANNIE *lays the suitcase on the bed; and the last voice comes faintly, from far away.*]

BOY'S VOICE Annie. It hurts, to be dead. Forever.

[ANNIE *falls to her knees by the bed, stifling her mouth in it. When at last she rolls blindly away from it, her palm comes down on the open report; she opens her eyes, regards it dully, and then, still on her knees, takes in the print.*]

MAN'S VOICE (*factual*) — might awaken her to a consciousness of her immortal nature. The chance is small indeed; but with a smaller chance they would have dug desperately for her in the pit; and is the life of the soul of less import than that of the body?

[ANNIE *gets to her feet. She drops the book on the bed and pauses* over her suitcase; after a moment she unclasps and opens it. Standing before it, she comes to her decision; she at once turns to the bureau and, taking her things out of its drawers, commences to throw them into the open suitcase.]

SCENE 4

In the darkness down left a hand strikes a match and lights a hanging oil lamp. It is KELLER'S *hand, and his voice accompanies it, very angry; the lights rising here before they fade on* ANNIE *show* KELLER *and* KATE *inside a suggestion of a garden house, with a bay-window seat toward center and a door at back.*

KELLER Katie, I will not *have* it! Now you did not see when that girl after supper tonight went to look for Helen in her room —
KATE No.
KELLER The child practically climbed out of her window to escape from her! What kind of teacher *is* she? I thought I had seen her at her worst this morning, shouting at me, but I come home to find the entire house disorganized by her — Helen won't stay one second in the same room, won't come to the table with her, won't let herself be bathed or undressed or put to bed by her, or even by Viney now, and the end result is that *you* have to do more for the child than before we hired this girl's services! From the moment she stepped off the train, she's been nothing but a burden: incompetent, impertinent, ineffectual, immodest —
KATE She folded her napkin, Captain.
KELLER What?
KATE Not ineffectual. Helen did fold her napkin.
KELLER What in heaven's name is so extraordinary about folding a napkin?
KATE (*with some humor*) Well. It's more than you did, Captain.
KELLER Katie. I did not bring you all the way out here to the garden house to be frivolous. Now, how does Miss Sullivan propose to teach a deaf-blind pupil who won't let her even touch her?
KATE (*a pause*) I don't know.
KELLER The fact is, today she scuttled any chance she ever had of getting along with the child. If you can see any point or purpose to her staying on here longer, it's more than —

KATE What do you wish me to do?
KELLER I want you to give her notice.
KATE I can't.
KELLER Then if you won't, I must. I simply will not —

[*He is interrupted by a knock at the back door.* KELLER, *after a glance at* KATE, *moves to open the door;* ANNIE *in her smoked glasses is standing outside.* KELLER *contemplates her, heavily.*]

Miss Sullivan.
ANNIE Captain Keller.

[*She is nervous, keyed up to seizing the bull by the horns again, and she assumes a cheeriness which is not unshaky.*]

Viney said I'd find you both over here in the garden house. I thought we should — have a talk?
KELLER (*reluctantly*) Yes, I — Well, come in.

[ANNIE *enters, and is interested in this room; she rounds on her heel, anxiously, studying it.* KELLER *turns the matter over to* KATE, *sotto voce.*]

KATE (*turning it back, courteously*) Captain.

[KELLER *clears his throat, makes ready.*]

KELLER I, ah — wanted first to make my position clear to Mrs. Keller, in private. I have decided I — am not satisfied — in fact, am deeply dissatisfied — with the manner in which —
ANNIE (*intent*) Excuse me, is this little house ever in use?
KELLER (*with patience*) In the hunting season. If you will give me your attention, Miss Sullivan.

[ANNIE *turns her smoked glasses upon him; they hold his unwilling stare.*]

I have tried to make allowances for you because you come from a part of the country where people are — women, I should say — come from who — well, for whom — (*It begins to elude him.*) — allowances must — be made. I have decided, nevertheless, to — that is, decided I — (*Vexedly*) Miss Sullivan, I find it difficult to talk through those glasses.
ANNIE (*eagerly, removing them*) Oh, of course.

KELLER (*dourly*) Why do you wear them? The sun has been down for an hour.
ANNIE (*pleasantly, at the lamp*) Any kind of light hurts my eyes.

[*A silence;* KELLER *ponders her, heavily.*]

KELLER Put them on. Miss Sullivan, I have decided to — give you another chance.
ANNIE (*cheerfully*) To do what?
KELLER To — remain in our employ.

[ANNIE'S *eyes widen.*]

But on two conditions. I am not accustomed to rudeness in servants or women, and that is the first. If you are to stay, there must be a radical change of manner.
ANNIE (*a pause*) Whose?
KELLER (*exploding*) Yours, young lady; isn't it obvious? And the second is that you persuade me there's the slightest hope of your teaching a child who flees from you now like the plague, to anyone else she can find in this house.
ANNIE (*a pause*) There isn't.

[KATE *stops sewing, and fixes her eyes upon* ANNIE.]

KATE What, Miss Annie?
ANNIE It's hopeless here. I can't teach a child who runs away.
KELLER (*nonplussed*) Then — do I understand — you propose —
ANNIE Well, if we all agree it's hopeless, the next question is what —
KATE Miss Annie.

[*She is leaning toward* ANNIE *in deadly earnest; it commands both* ANNIE *and* KELLER.]

I am not agreed. I think perhaps you — underestimate Helen.
ANNIE I think everybody else here does.
KATE She did fold her napkin. She learns, she learns; do you know she began talking when she was six months old? She could say "water." Not really — "wahwah." "Wahwah," but she meant water; she knew what it meant, and only six months old. I never saw a child so — bright, or outgoing — (*Her voice is unsteady, but she gets it level.*) It's still in her, somewhere, isn't it? You should have seen her before her illness, such a good-tempered child —

ANNIE (*agreeably*) She's changed.

[*A pause,* KATE *not letting her eyes go; her appeal at last is unconditional and very quiet.*]

KATE Miss Annie, put up with it. And with us.

KELLER Us!

KATE Please? Like the lost lamb in the parable,[2] I love her all the more.

ANNIE Mrs. Keller, I don't think Helen's worst handicap is deafness or blindness. I think it's your love. And pity.

KELLER Now what does that mean?

ANNIE All of you here are so sorry for her you've kept her — like a pet; why, even a dog you housebreak. No wonder she won't let me come near her. It's useless for me to try to teach her language or anything else here. I might as well —

KATE (*cuts in*) Miss Annie, before you came, we spoke of putting her in an asylum.

[ANNIE *turns back to regard her. A pause.*]

ANNIE What kind of asylum?

KELLER For mental defectives.

KATE I visited there. I can't tell you what I saw, people like — animals, with — rats, in the halls, and — (*She shakes her head on her vision.*) What else are we to do, if you give up?

ANNIE Give up?

KATE You said it was hopeless.

ANNIE Here. Give up, why, I only today saw what has to be done, to begin! (*She glances from* KATE *to* KELLER, *who stare, waiting; and she makes it as plain and simple as her nervousness permits.*) I — want complete charge of her.

KELLER You already have that. It has resulted in —

ANNIE No, I mean day and night. She has to be dependent on me.

KATE For what?

ANNIE Everything. The food she eats, the clothes she wears, fresh — (*She is amused at herself, though very serious.*) — air, yes, the air she breathes; whatever her body needs is a — primer, to teach her out of. It's the only way; the one who lets her have it should be her teacher.

---

[2] *parable*: St. Luke, Chapter 15.

[*She considers them in turn; they digest it,* KELLER *frowning,* KATE *perplexed.*]

Not anyone who *loves* her — you have so many feelings they fall over each other like feet; you won't use your chances, and you won't let me.
KATE But if she runs from you — to us —
ANNIE Yes, that's the point. I'll have to live with her somewhere else.
KELLER What!
ANNIE Till she learns to depend on and listen to me.
KATE (*not without alarm*) For how long?
ANNIE As long as it takes. (*A pause. She takes a breath.*) I packed half my things already.
KELLER Miss — Sullivan!

[*But when* ANNIE *attends upon him, he is speechless, and she is merely earnest.*]

ANNIE Captain Keller, it meets both your conditions. It's the one way I can get back in touch with Helen, and I don't see how I can be rude to you again if you're not around to interfere with me.
KELLER (*red-faced*) And what is your intention if I say no? Pack the other half, for home, and abandon your charge to — to —
ANNIE The asylum? (*She waits, appraises* KELLER'S *glare and* KATE'S *uncertainty, and decides to use her weapons.*) I grew up in such an asylum. The state almshouse.

[KATE'S *head comes up on this, and* KELLER *stares hard;* ANNIE'S *tone is cheerful enough, albeit level as gunfire.*]

Rats — why, my brother Jimmie and I used to play with the rats because we didn't have toys. Maybe you'd like to know what Helen will find there, not on visiting days? One ward was full of the — old women, crippled, blind, most of them dying, but even if what they had was catching, there was nowhere else to move them, and that's where they put us. There were younger ones across the hall with T.B., and epileptic fits, and some insane. Some just had the D.T.'s.[3] The room Jimmie and I played in was the deadhouse, where they kept the bodies till they could dig —

---

[3] *D.T.'s*: delirium tremens, tremblings and hallucinations caused by excessive use of alcoholic liquors.

KATE (*closes her eyes*) Oh, my dear—

ANNIE —the graves. (*She is immune to* KATE's *compassion.*) No, it made me strong. But I don't think you need send Helen there. She's strong enough. (*She waits again; but when neither offers her a word, she simply concludes.*) No, I have no conditions, Captain Keller.

KATE (*not looking up*) Miss Annie.

ANNIE Yes.

KATE (*a pause*) Where would you—take Helen?

ANNIE Ohh—(*Brightly*) Italy?

KELLER (*wheeling*) What?

ANNIE Can't have everything, how would this garden house do? Furnish it, bring Helen here after a long ride so she won't recognize it, and you can see her every day. If she doesn't know. Well?

KATE (*a sigh of relief*) Is that all?

ANNIE That's all.

KATE Captain.

[KELLER *turns his head; and* KATE's *request is quiet but firm.*]

With your permission?

KELLER (*teeth in cigar*) Why must she depend on you for the food she eats?

ANNIE (*a pause*) I want control of it.

KELLER Why?

ANNIE It's a way to reach her.

KELLER (*stares*) You intend to *starve* her into letting you touch her?

ANNIE She won't starve, she'll learn. All's fair in love and war, Captain Keller. You never cut supplies?

KELLER This is hardly a war!

ANNIE Well, it's not love. A siege is a siege.

KELLER (*heavily*) Miss Sullivan. Do you *like* the child?

ANNIE (*straight in his eyes*) Do you?

[*A long pause*]

KATE You could have a servant here—

ANNIE (*amused*) I'll have enough work without looking after a servant! But that boy Percy could sleep here, run errands—

KATE (*also amused*) We can let Percy sleep here, I think, Captain?

ANNIE (*eagerly*) And some old furniture, all our own—

KATE (*also eager*) Captain? Do you think that walnut bedstead in the barn would be too —
KELLER I have not yet consented to Percy! Or to the house, or to the proposal! Or to Miss Sullivan's — staying on when I — (*But he erupts in an irate surrender.*) Very well, I consent to everything! (*He shakes the cigar at* ANNIE.) For two weeks. I'll give you two weeks in this place, and it will be a miracle if you get the child to tolerate you.
KATE Two weeks? Miss Annie, can you accomplish anything in two weeks?
KELLER Anything or not, two weeks, then the child comes back to us. Make up your mind, Miss Sullivan: yes or no?
ANNIE Two weeks. For only one miracle? (*She nods at him, nervously.*) I'll get her to tolerate me.

[KELLER *marches out and slams the door.* KATE *on her feet regards* ANNIE, *who is facing the door.*]

KATE (*then*) You can't think as little of love as you said.

[ANNIE *glances questioning.*]

Or you wouldn't stay.
ANNIE (*a pause*) I didn't come her for love. I came for money!

[KATE *shakes her head to this, with a smile; after a moment she extends her open hand.* ANNIE *looks at it, but when she puts hers out, it is not to shake hands, it is to set her fist in* KATE's *palm.*]

KATE (*puzzled*) Hm?
ANNIE A. It's the first of many. Twenty-six!

[KATE *squeezes her fist, squeezes it hard, and hastens out after* KELLER. ANNIE *stands as the door closes behind her, her manner so apprehensive that finally she slaps her brow, holds it, sighs, and, with her eyes closed, crosses herself for luck.*]

SCENE 5

The lights dim into a cool silhouette scene around her, the lamp paling out, and now, in formal entrances, persons appear around ANNIE *with furniture for the room:* PERCY *crosses the stage with a rocking chair and waits;* MARTHA, *from another direction, bears in a stool;* VINEY *bears in a small table; and the gardener rolls in a bed partway from left; and* ANNIE, *opening her eyes to put her glasses back on, sees them. She turns around in the room once and goes into action, pointing out locations for each article; the servants place them and leave, and* ANNIE *then darts around, interchanging them. In the midst of this — while* PERCY *and* MARTHA *reappear with a tray of food and a chair, respectively —* JAMES *comes down from the house with* ANNIE'S *suitcase, and stands viewing the room and her quizzically;* ANNIE *halts abruptly under his eye, embarrassed, then seizes the suitcase from his hand, explaining herself brightly.*

ANNIE I always wanted to live in a doll's house!

[*She sets the suitcase out of the way and continues;* VINEY, *at left, appears to position a rod with drapes for a doorway, and the gardener at center pushes in a wheelbarrow loaded with a couple of boxes of* HELEN'S *toys and clothes.* ANNIE *helps lift them into the room, and the gardener pushes the wheelbarrow off. In none of this is any heed taken of the imaginary walls of the garden house; the furniture is moved in from every side and itself defines the walls.*

ANNIE *now drags the box of toys into center, props up the doll conspicuously on top; with the people melted away, except for* JAMES, *all is again still. The lights turn again without pause, rising warmer.*]

JAMES You don't let go of things easily, do you? How will you — win her hand now, in this place?
ANNIE (*curtly*) Do I know? I lost my temper, and here we are!
JAMES (*lightly*) No touching, no teaching. Of course, you *are* bigger —
ANNIE I'm not counting on force; I'm counting on her. That little imp is dying to know.
JAMES Know what?
ANNIE Anything. Any and every crumb in God's creation. I'll have to use that appetite too. (*She gives the room a final survey, straightens the bed, arranges the curtains.*)
JAMES (*a pause*) Maybe she'll teach you.
ANNIE Of course.
JAMES That she isn't. That there's such a thing as — dullness of

heart. Acceptance. And letting go. Sooner or later we all give up, don't we?
ANNIE Maybe you all do. It's my idea of the original sin.
JAMES What is?
ANNIE (*witheringly*) Giving up.
JAMES (*nettled*) You won't open her. Why can't you let her be? Have some — pity on her, for being what she is —
ANNIE If I'd ever once thought like that, I'd be dead!
JAMES (*pleasantly*) You will be. Why trouble?

[ANNIE *turns to glare at him; he is mocking.*]

Or will you teach me? (*And with a bow, he drifts off.*)

[Now *in the distance there comes the clopping of hoofs, drawing near, and nearer, up to the door; and they halt.* ANNIE *wheels to face the door. When it opens this time, the* KELLERS — KATE *in traveling bonnet,* KELLER *also hatted — are standing there with* HELEN *between them; she is in a cloak.* KATE *gently cues her into the room.* HELEN *comes in groping, baffled, but interested in the new surroundings;* ANNIE *evades her exploring hand, her gaze not leaving the child.*]

ANNIE Does she know where she is?
KATE (*shakes her head*) We rode her out in the country for two hours.
KELLER For all she knows, she could be in another town —

[HELEN *stumbles over the box on the floor and in it discovers her doll and other battered toys, is pleased, sits to them, then becomes puzzled and suddenly very wary. She scrambles up and back to her mother's thighs, but* ANNIE *steps in, and it is hers that* HELEN *embraces.* HELEN *recoils, gropes, and touches her cheek instantly.*]

KATE That's her sign for me.
ANNIE I know.

[HELEN *waits, then recommences her groping, more urgently.* KATE *stands indecisive and takes an abrupt step toward her, but* ANNIE'S *hand is a barrier.*]

In two weeks.

KATE Miss Annie, I — Please be good to her. These two weeks, try to be very good to her —
ANNIE I will.

[KATE, *turning then, hurries out. The* KELLERS *cross back of the main house.*

ANNIE *closes the door.* HELEN *starts at the door jar and rushes it.* ANNIE *holds her off.* HELEN *kicks her, breaks free, and careens around the room like an imprisoned bird, colliding with furniture, groping wildly, repeatedly touching her cheek in a growing panic. When she has covered the room, she commences her weird screaming.* ANNIE *moves to comfort her, but her touch sends* HELEN *into a paroxysm of rage: she tears away, falls over her box of toys, flings its contents in handfuls in* ANNIE's *direction, flings the box too, reels to her feet, rips curtains from the window, bangs and kicks at the door, sweeps objects off the mantelpiece and shelf — a little tornado incarnate, all destruction, until she comes upon her doll and, in the act of hurling it, freezes. Then she clutches it to herself and in exhaustion sinks sobbing to the floor.* ANNIE *stands contemplating her, in some awe.*]

Two weeks. (*She shakes her head, not without a touch of disgusted bewilderment.*) What did I get into now?

[*The lights have been dimming throughout, and the garden house is lit only by moonlight now, with* ANNIE *lost in the patches of dark.*

KATE, *now hatless and coatless, enters the family room by the rear door, carrying a lamp.* KELLER, *also hatless, wanders simultaneously around the back of the main house to where* JAMES *has been waiting, in the rising moonlight, on the porch.*]

KELLER I can't understand it. I had every intention of dismissing that girl, not setting her up like an empress.
JAMES Yes, what's her secret, sir?
KELLER Secret?
JAMES (*pleasantly*) That enables her to get anything she wants out of you? When I can't.

[JAMES *turns to go into the house, but* KELLER *grasps his wrist, twisting him half to his knees.* KATE *comes from the porch.*]

KELLER (*angrily*) She does *not* get anything she —
JAMES (*in pain*) Don't — don't —
KATE Captain.
KELLER He's afraid. (*He throws* JAMES *away from him, with contempt.*) What *does* he want out of me?
JAMES (*an outcry*) My God, don't you know? (*He gazes from* KELLER *to* KATE.) Everything you forgot, when you forgot my mother.
KELLER What!

[JAMES *wheels into the house.* KELLER *takes a stride to the porch, to roar after him.*]

One thing that girl's secret is not: she doesn't fire one shot and disappear!

[KATE *stands rigid, and* KELLER *comes back to her.*]

Katie. Don't mind what he —
KATE Captain, I am proud of you.
KELLER For what?
KATE For letting this girl have what she needs.
KELLER Why can't my son be? He can't bear me; you'd think I treat him as hard as this girl does Helen — (*He breaks off, as it dawns in him.*)
KATE (*gently*) Perhaps you do.
KELLER But he has to learn some respect!
KATE (*a pause, wryly*) Do you like the child? (*She turns again to the porch, but pauses, reluctant.*) How empty the house is, tonight.

[*After a moment she continues on in.* KELLER *stands moveless, as the moonlight dies on him.*]

SCENE 6

The distant belfry chimes toll two o'clock, and with them, a moment later, comes the boy's voice on the wind, in a whisper.

BOY'S VOICE Annie. Annie.

[*In her patch of dark* ANNIE, *now in her nightgown, hurls a cup into a corner as though it were her grief, getting rid of its taste through her teeth.*]

ANNIE No! No pity, I won't have it. (*She comes to* HELEN, *prone on the floor.*) On either of us.

[*She goes to her knees, but when she touches* HELEN's *hand, the child starts up awake, recoils, and scrambles away from her under the bed.* ANNIE *stares after her. She strikes her palm on the floor, with passion.*]

I *will* touch you! (*She gets to her feet and paces in a kind of anger around the bed, her hand in her hair, and confronting* HELEN *at each turn.*) How, how? How do I — (ANNIE *stops. Then she calls out urgently, loudly.*) Percy! Percy! (*She moves swiftly to the drapes, at left.*) Percy, wake up!

[PERCY's *voice comes in a thick, sleepy mumble, unintelligible.*]

Get out of bed and come in here. I need you.

[ANNIE *darts away, finds and strikes a match and touches it to the hanging lamp; the lights come up dimly in the room, and* PERCY *stands bare to the waist in torn overalls between the drapes, with eyes closed, swaying.* ANNIE *goes to him, pats his cheeks vigorously.*]

Percy. You awake?
PERCY No'm.
ANNIE How would you like to play a nice game?
PERCY Whah?
ANNIE With Helen. She's under the bed. Touch her hand.

[*She kneels* PERCY *down at the bed, thrusting his hand under it to contact* HELEN's; HELEN *emits an animal sound and crawls to the opposite side, but commences sniffing.* ANNIE *rounds the bed with* PERCY *and thrusts his hand again at* HELEN; *this time* HELEN *clutches it, sniffs in recognition, and comes scrambling out after* PERCY, *to hug him with delight.* PERCY, *alarmed, struggles, and* HELEN's *fingers go to his mouth.*]

PERCY Lemme go. Lemme go —

[HELEN *fingers her own lips, as before, moving them in dumb imitation.*]

She's tryin' to talk. She's gonna hit me —

ANNIE (*grimly*) She *can* talk, if she only knew. I'll show you how. She makes letters. (*She opens* PERCY's *other hand and spells into it.*) This one is C. C.

[*She hits his palm with it a couple of times, her eyes upon* HELEN *across him;* HELEN *gropes to feel what* PERCY's *hand is doing, and when she encounters* ANNIE's, *she falls back from them.*]

She's mad at me now, though; she won't play. But she knows lots of letters. Here's another: A. C, a. C, a.

[*But she is watching* HELEN, *who comes groping, consumed with curiosity;* ANNIE *makes the letters in* PERCY's *hand, and* HELEN *pokes to question what they are up to. Then* HELEN *snatches* PERCY's *other hand and quickly spells four letters into it.* ANNIE *follows them aloud.*]

C, a, k, e! She spells *cake*; she gets cake. (*She is swiftly over to the tray of food to fetch cake and a jug of milk.*) She doesn't know yet it means this. Isn't it funny she knows how to spell it and doesn't *know* she knows?

[*She breaks the cake in two pieces and extends one to each;* HELEN *rolls away from her offer.*]

Well, if she won't play it with me, I'll play it with you. Would you like to learn one she doesn't know?
PERCY No'm.

[*But* ANNIE *seizes his wrist, and spells to him.*]

ANNIE M, i, l, k. M is this. I, that's an easy one, just the little finger. L is this —

[*And* HELEN *comes back with her hand, to feel the new word.* ANNIE *brushes her away and continues spelling aloud to* PERCY. HELEN's *hand comes back again and tries to get in;* ANNIE *brushes it away again.* HELEN's *hand insists, and* ANNIE *puts it away rudely.*]

No, why should I talk to you? I'm teaching Percy a new word. L. K is this —

[HELEN *now yanks their hands apart; she butts* PERCY *away, and thrusts her palm out insistently.* ANNIE's *eyes are bright with glee.*]

Ho, you're *jealous*, are you!

[HELEN's *hand waits, intractably waits.*]

All *right*.

[ANNIE *spells into it* "*milk*"; *and* HELEN *after a moment spells it back to* ANNIE. ANNIE *takes her hand, with her whole face shining. She gives a great sigh.*]

Good! So I'm finally back to where I can touch you, hm? Touch and go! No love lost, but here we go. (*She puts the jug of milk into* HELEN's *hand and squeezes* PERCY's *shoulder.*) You can go to bed now; you've earned your sleep. Thank you.

[PERCY, *stumbling up, weaves his way out through the drapes.* HELEN *finishes drinking and holds the jug out for* ANNIE; *when* ANNIE *takes it,* HELEN *crawls onto the bed and makes for sleep.* ANNIE *stands, looks down at her.*]

Now all I have to teach you is — one word. Everything.

[*She sets the jug down. On the floor now* ANNIE *spies the doll, stoops to pick it up, and with it dangling in her hand, turns off the lamp. A shaft of moonlight is left on* HELEN *in the bed and a second shaft on the rocking chair; and* ANNIE, *after putting off her smoked glasses, sits in the rocker with the doll. She is rather happy and dangles the doll on her knee, and it makes its "momma" sound.* ANNIE *whispers to it in mock solicitude.*]

Hush, little baby. Don't — say a word —

[*She lays it against her shoulder and begins rocking with it, patting its diminutive behind; she talks the lullaby to it, humorously at first.*]

"Momma's gonna buy you — a mockingbird:
If that — mockingbird don't sing —

[*The rhythm of the rocking takes her into the tune, softly, and more tenderly.*]

"Momma's gonna buy you a diamond ring:
If that diamond ring turns to brass —

[*A third shaft of moonlight outside now rises to pick out* JAMES *at the main house, with one foot on the porch step; he turns his body as if hearing the song.*]

"Momma's gonna buy you a looking glass:
If that looking glass gets broke —

[*In the family room a fourth shaft picks out* KELLER, *seated at the table, in thought; and he, too, lifts his head as if hearing.*]

"Momma's gonna buy you a billy goat:
If that billy goat won't pull —

[*The fifth shaft is upstairs in* ANNIE'S *room and picks out* KATE, *pacing there; and she halts, turning her head, too, as if hearing.*]

"Momma's gonna buy you a cart and bull:
If that cart and bull turns over,
Momma's gonna buy you a dog named Rover;
If that dog named Rover won't bark — "

[*With the shafts of moonlight on* HELEN *and* JAMES *and* KELLER *and* KATE, *all moveless, and* ANNIE *rocking the doll, the curtain ends the act.*]

ACT 3

SCENE 1

The stage is totally dark, until we see ANNIE *and* HELEN *silhouetted on the bed in the garden house.* ANNIE'S *voice is audible, very patient, and worn; it has been saying this for a long time.*

ANNIE Water, Helen. This is water. W, a, t, e, r. It has a *name.* (*A silence. Then*) Egg, e, g, g. It has a *name,* the name stands for the thing. Oh, it's so simple, simple as birth, to explain.

[*The lights have commenced to rise, not on the garden house but on the homestead. Then*]

Helen, Helen, the chick *has* to come out of its shell, sometime. You come out, too.

[*In the bedroom upstairs we see* VINEY *unhurriedly washing the window, dusting, turning the mattress, readying the room for use again; then in the family room a diminished group at one end of the table —* KATE, KELLER, JAMES *— finishing up a quiet breakfast; then outside, down right, the gardener on his knees, assisted by* MARTHA, *working with a trowel around a new trellis and wheelbarrow. The scene is one of everyday calm, and all are oblivious to* ANNIE's *voice.*]

There's only one way out, for you, and it's language. To learn that your fingers can talk. And say anything, anything you can name. This is mug. Mug, m, u, g. Helen, it has a *name*. It — has — a — *name —*

[KATE *rises from the table.*]

KELLER (*gently*) You haven't eaten, Katie.
KATE (*smiles, shakes her head*) I haven't the appetite. I'm too — restless, I can't sit to it.
KELLER You should eat, my dear. It will be a long day, waiting.
JAMES (*lightly*) But it's been a short two weeks. I never thought life could be so — noiseless, went much too quickly for me.

[KATE *and* KELLER *gaze at him, in silence.* JAMES *becomes uncomfortable.*]

ANNIE C, a, r, d. Card. C, a —
JAMES Well, the house has been practically normal, hasn't it?
KELLER (*harshly*) Jimmie.
JAMES Is it wrong to enjoy a quiet breakfast, after five years? And you two even seem to enjoy each other —
KELLER It could be even more noiseless, Jimmie, without your tongue running every minute. Haven't you enough feeling to imagine what Katie has been undergoing, ever since —

[KATE *stops him, with her hand on his arm.*]

KATE Captain. (*To* JAMES) It's true. The two weeks have been normal, quiet, all you say. But not short. Interminable. (*She rises and wanders out; she pauses on the porch steps, gazing toward the garden house.*)
ANNIE (*fading*) W, a, t, e, r. But it means *this*. W, a, t, e, r. *This*. W, a, t —
JAMES I only meant that Miss Sullivan is a boon. Of contention, though, it seems.

KELLER (*heavily*) If and when you're a parent, Jimmie, you will understand what separation means. A mother loses a — protector.
JAMES (*baffled*) Hm?
KELLER You'll learn, we don't just keep our children safe. They keep us safe. (*He rises, with his empty coffee cup and saucer.*) There are of course all kinds of separation; Katie has lived with one kind for five years. And another is disappointment. In a child.

[*He goes with the cup out the rear door.* JAMES *sits for a long moment of stillness. In the garden house the lights commence to come up;* ANNIE, *haggard at the table, is writing a letter, her face again almost in contact with the stationery;* HELEN, *apart on the stool, and for the first time as clean and neat as a button, is quietly crocheting an endless chain of wool, which snakes all around the room.*]

ANNIE "I, feel, every, day, more, and, more, in — " (*She pauses, and turns the pages of a dictionary open before her; her finger descends the words to a full stop. She elevates her eyebrows, then copies the word.*) " — adequate."

[*In the main house* JAMES *pushes up and goes to the front doorway after* KATE.]

JAMES Kate?

[KATE *turns her glance.* JAMES *is rather weary.*]

I'm sorry. Open my mouth — like that fairy tale, frogs jump out.
KATE No. It has been better. For everyone. (*She starts away, up center.*)
ANNIE (*writing*) "If, only, there, were, someone, to, help, me, I, need, a, teacher, as, much, as, Helen — "
JAMES Kate.

[KATE *halts, waits.*]

What does he want from me?
KATE That's not the question. Stand up to the world, Jimmie, that comes first.
JAMES (*a pause, wryly*) But the world is him.
KATE Yes. And no one can do it for you.

JAMES Kate. (*His voice is humble.*) At least we — Could you — be my friend?

KATE I am.

[KATE *turns to wander up back of the garden house.* ANNIE'S *murmur comes at once; the lights begin to die on the main house.*]

ANNIE " — my, mind, is, undisciplined, full, of, skips, and, jumps, and —" (*She halts, rereads, frowns.*) Hm.

[ANNIE *puts her nose again in the dictionary, flips back to an earlier page, and fingers down the words;* KATE *presently comes down toward the bay window with a trayful of food.*]

Disinter — disinterested — disjoin — dis — (*She backtracks, indignant.*) Disinterested, disjoin — Where's disipline? (*She goes a page or two back, searching with her finger, muttering.*) What a dictionary, have to know how to spell it before you can look up how to spell it — disciple, *discipline!* Diskipline. (*She corrects the word in her letter.*) Undisciplined.

[*But her eyes are bothering her; she closes them in exhaustion and gently fingers the eyelids.* KATE *watches her through the window.*]

KATE What are you doing to your eyes?

[ANNIE *glances around; she puts her smoked glasses on, and gets up to come over, assuming a cheerful energy.*]

ANNIE It's worse on my vanity! I'm learning to spell. It's like a surprise party — the most unexpected characters turn up.

KATE You're not to overwork your eyes, Miss Annie.

ANNIE Well. (*She takes the tray, sets it on her chair, and carries chair and tray to* HELEN.) Whatever I spell to Helen I'd better spell right.

KATE (*almost wistful*) How — serene she is.

ANNIE She learned this stitch yesterday. Now I can't get her to stop!

[*She disentangles one foot from the wool chain, and sets the chair before* HELEN. HELEN, *at its contact with her knee, feels the plate, promptly sets her crocheting down, and tucks the napkin in at her neck, but* ANNIE *withholds the spoon; when* HELEN *finds it missing, she folds her hands in her lap and quietly waits.* ANNIE *twinkles at* KATE *with mock devoutness.*]

Such a little lady, she'd sooner starve than eat with her fingers.

[*She gives* HELEN *the spoon, and* HELEN *begins to eat, neatly.*]

KATE You've taught her so much, these two weeks. I would never have —
ANNIE Not enough. (*She is suddenly gloomy, shakes her head.*) Obedience isn't enough. Well, she learned two nouns this morning, *key* and *water*, brings her up to eighteen nouns and three verbs.
KATE (*hesitant*) But — not —
ANNIE No. Not that they mean things. It's still a finger game, no meaning. (*She turns to* KATE, *abruptly.*) Mrs. Keller — (*But she defers it; she comes back, to sit in the bay and lift her hand.*) Shall we play our finger game?
KATE How will she learn it?
ANNIE It will come.

[*She spells a word;* KATE *does not respond.*]

KATE How?
ANNIE (*a pause*) How does a bird learn to fly? (*She spells again.*) We're born to use words, like wings; it has to come.
KATE How?
ANNIE (*another pause, wearily*) All right, I don't know how. (*She pushes up her glasses, to rub her eyes.*) I've done everything I could think of. Whatever she's learned here — keeping herself clean, knitting, stringing beads, meals, setting-up exercises each morning; we climb trees, hunt eggs, yesterday a chick was born in her hands — all of it I spell, everything we do, we never stop spelling. I go to bed with — writer's cramp from talking so much!
KATE I worry about you, Miss Annie. You must rest.
ANNIE Now? She spells back in her *sleep*, her fingers make letters when she doesn't know! In her bones those five fingers know, that hand aches to — speak out; and something in her mind is asleep; how do I — nudge that awake? That's the one question.
KATE With no answer.
ANNIE (*long pause*) Except keep at it. Like this.

[*She again begins spelling —* I, need — *and* KATE'S *brows gather, following the words.*]

KATE More — time?

[*She glances at* ANNIE, *who looks her in the eyes, silent.*]

Here?

ANNIE Spell it.

[KATE *spells a word* — no — *shaking her head;* ANNIE *spells two words* — why, not — *back, with an impatient question in her eyes; and* KATE *moves her head in pain to answer it.*]

KATE Because I can't —

ANNIE Spell it! If she ever learns, you'll have a lot to tell each other; start now.

[KATE *painstakingly spells in air. In the midst of this the rear door opens, and* KELLER *enters with the setter* BELLE *in tow.*]

KELLER Miss Sullivan? On my way to the office, I brought Helen a playmate —

ANNIE Outside please, Captain Keller.

KELLER My dear child, the two weeks are up today; surely you don't object to —

ANNIE (*rising*) They're not up till six o'clock.

KELLER (*indulgent*) Oh, now. What difference can a fraction of one day —

ANNIE An agreement is an agreement. Now you've been very good; I'm sure you can keep it up for a few more hours.

[*She escorts* KELLER *by the arm over the threshold; he obeys, leaving* BELLE.]

KELLER Miss Sullivan, you are a tyrant.

ANNIE Likewise, I'm sure. You can stand there, and close the door if she comes.

KATE I don't think you know how eager we are to have her back in our arms —

ANNIE I do know; it's my main worry.

KELLER It's like expecting a new child in the house. Well, she *is* — so composed, so — (*Gently*) Attractive. You've done wonders for her, Miss Sullivan.

ANNIE (*not a question*) Have I.
KELLER If there's anything you want from us in repayment, tell us; it will be a privilege to —
ANNIE I just told Mrs. Keller. I want more time.
KATE Miss Annie —
ANNIE Another week.

[HELEN *lifts her head, and begins to sniff.*]

KELLER We miss the child. *I* miss her, I'm glad to say; that's a different debt I owe you —
ANNIE Pay it to Helen. Give *her* another week.
KATE (*gently*) Doesn't she miss us?
KELLER Of course she does. What a wrench this unexplainable — exile must be to her, can you say it's not?
ANNIE No. But I —

[HELEN *is off the stool, to grope about the room; when she encounters* BELLE, *she throws her arms around the dog's neck in delight.*]

KATE Doesn't she need affection too, Miss Annie?
ANNIE (*wavering*) She — never shows me she needs it; she won't have any — caressing or —
KATE But you're not her mother.
KELLER And what would another week accomplish? We are more than satisfied; you've done more than we ever thought possible, taught her constructive —
ANNIE I can't promise anything. All I can —
KELLER (*no break*) — things to do, to behave like — even look like — a human child, so manageable, contented, cleaner, more —
ANNIE (*withering*) Cleaner.
KELLER Well. We say cleanliness is next to godliness, Miss —
ANNIE Cleanliness is next to nothing; she has to learn that everything has its name! That words can be her *eyes*, to everything in the world outside her, and inside too; what is she without words? With them she can think, have ideas, be reached; there's not a thought or fact in the world that can't be hers. You publish a newspaper, Captain Keller; do I have to tell you what words are? And she has them already —

KELLER Miss Sullivan.

ANNIE — eighteen nouns and three verbs; they're in her fingers now, I need only time to push *one* of them into her mind! One, and everything under the sun will follow. Don't you see what she's learned here is only clearing the way for that? I can't risk her unlearning it; give me more time alone with her, another week to —

KELLER Look.

[*He points, and* ANNIE *turns.* HELEN *is playing with* BELLE's *claws; she makes letters with her fingers, shows them to* BELLE, *waits with her palm, then manipulates the dog's claws.*]

What is she spelling?

[*A silence*]

KATE Water?

[ANNIE *nods.*]

KELLER Teaching a dog to spell. (*A pause*) The dog doesn't know what she means, any more than she knows what you mean, Miss Sullivan. I think you ask too much, of her and yourself. God may not have meant Helen to have the — eyes you speak of.

ANNIE (*toneless*) I mean her to.

KELLER (*curiously*) What is it to you?

[ANNIE's *head comes slowly up.*]

You make us see how we indulge her for our sake. Is the opposite true, for you?

ANNIE (*then*) Half a week?

KELLER An agreement *is* an agreement.

ANNIE Mrs. Keller?

KATE (*simply*) I want her back.

[*A wait;* ANNIE *then lets her hands drop in surrender, and nods.*]

KELLER I'll send Viney over to help you pack.

ANNIE Not until six o'clock. I have till six o'clock.

KELLER (*consenting*) Six o'clock. Come, Katie.

[KATE, *leaving the window, joins him around back while* KELLER *closes the door; they are shut out.*]

SCENE 2

Only the garden house is daylit now, and the light on it is narrowing down. ANNIE *stands watching* HELEN *work* BELLE's *claws. Then she settles beside them on her knees, and stops* HELEN's *hand.*

ANNIE (*gently*) No.

[*She shakes her head, with* HELEN's *hand to her face, then spells.*]

Dog. D, o, g. Dog.

[*She touches* HELEN's *hand to* BELLE. HELEN *dutifully pats the dog's head, and resumes spelling to its paw.*]

Not water.

[ANNIE *rolls to her feet, brings a tumbler of water back from the tray, and kneels with it, to seize* HELEN's *hand and spell.*]

Here. Water. Water.

[*She thrusts* HELEN's *hand into the tumbler.* HELEN *lifts her hand out dripping, wipes it daintily on* BELLE's *hide, and taking the tumbler from* ANNIE, *endeavors to thrust* BELLE's *paw into it.* ANNIE *sits watching, wearily.*]

I don't know how to tell you. Not a soul in the world knows how to tell you. Helen, Helen.

[*She bends in compassion to touch her lips to* HELEN's *temple, and instantly* HELEN *pauses, her hands off the dog, her head slightly averted. The lights are still narrowing, and* BELLE *slinks off. After a moment* ANNIE *sits back.*]

Yes, what's it to me? They're satisfied. Give them back their child and dog, both housebroken, everyone's satisfied. But me, and you.

[HELEN's *hand comes out into the light, groping.*]

Reach. *Reach!*

[ANNIE *extending her own hand, grips* HELEN's; *the two hands are clasped, tense in the light, the rest of the room changing in shadow.*]

I wanted to teach you — oh, everything the earth is full of, Helen, everything on it that's ours for a wink and it's gone, and what we are on it, the — light we bring to it and leave behind in — words, why, you can see five thousand years back in a light of words, everything we feel, think, know — and share, in words, so not a soul is in darkness, or done with, even in the grave. And I know, I *know*, one word and I can — put the world in your hand — and whatever it is to me, I won't take less! How, how, how do I tell you that *this* — (*She spells.*) — means a *word*, and the word means this *thing*, wool?

[*She thrusts the wool at* HELEN's *hand;* HELEN *sits, puzzled.* ANNIE *puts the crocheting aside.*]

Or this — s, t, o, o, l — means this *thing*, stool?

[*She claps* HELEN's *palm to the stool.* HELEN *waits, uncomprehending.* ANNIE *snatches up her napkin, spells.*]

Napkin! (*She forces it on* HELEN's *hand, waits, discards it, lifts a fold of the child's dress, spells.*) Dress! (*She lets it drop, spells.*) F, a, c, e, face!

[*She draws* HELEN's *hand to her cheek, and pressing it there, staring into the child's responseless eyes, hears the distant belfry begin to toll, slowly: one, two, three, four, five, six.*

On the third stroke the lights, stealing in around the garden house, show us figures waiting: VINEY, *the gardener,* MARTHA, PERCY *at the drapes, and* JAMES *on the dim porch.* ANNIE *and* HELEN *remain, frozen. The chimes die away. Silently* PERCY *moves the drape-rod back out of sight;* VINEY *steps into the room — not using the door — and unmakes the bed; the gardener brings the wheelbarrow over, leaves it handy, rolls the bed off;* VINEY *puts the bed linens on top of a waiting boxful of* HELEN's *toys, and loads the box on the wheelbarrow;* MARTHA *and* PERCY *take out the chairs, with the trayful, then the table; and* JAMES, *coming down and into the room, lifts* ANNIE's *suitcase from its corner.* VINEY *and the man load the remaining odds and ends on the wheelbarrow, and the man wheels it off.* VINEY *and the children, departing, leave only* JAMES *in the room with* ANNIE *and* HELEN. JAMES *studies the two of them, without mockery, and then, quietly going to the door and opening it, bears the suitcase out and houseward. He leaves the door open.*

KATE *steps into the doorway, and stands.* ANNIE, *lifting her gaze from* HELEN, *sees her; she takes* HELEN'S *hand from her cheek and returns it to the child's own, stroking it there twice, in her mother-sign, before spelling slowly into it.*]

M, o, t, h, e, r. Mother.

[HELEN, *with her hand free, strokes her cheek, suddenly forlorn.* ANNIE *takes her hand again.*]

M, o, t, h —

[*But* KATE *is trembling with such impatience that her voice breaks from her, harsh.*]

KATE Let her *come!*

[ANNIE *lifts* HELEN *to her feet, with a turn, and gives her a little push. Now* HELEN *begins groping, sensing something, trembling herself; and* KATE, *falling one step in onto her knees, clasps her, kissing her.* HELEN *clutches her as tight as she can.* KATE *is inarticulate, choked, repeating* HELEN'S *name again and again. She wheels with her in her arms, to stumble away out the doorway;* ANNIE *stands unmoving while* KATE, *in a blind walk, carries* HELEN *like a baby behind the main house, out of view.* ANNIE *is now alone on the stage. She turns, gazing around at the stripped room, bidding it silently farewell, impassively, like a defeated general on the deserted battlefield. All that remains is a stand with a basin of water; and here* ANNIE *takes up an eyecup, bathes each of her eyes, empties the eyecup, drops it in her purse, and tiredly locates her smoked glasses on the floor. The lights alter subtly; in the act of putting on her glasses,* ANNIE *hears something that stops her, with head lifted. We hear it too: the voices out of the past, including her own now, in a whisper.*]

BOY'S VOICE You said we'd be together forever — You promised, forever and — Annie!

ANAGNOS'S VOICE But that battle is dead and done with; why not let it stay buried?

ANNIE'S VOICE (*whispering*) I think God must owe me a resurrection.

ANAGNOS'S VOICE What?

[*A pause, and* ANNIE *answers it herself, heavily.*]

ANNIE And I owe God one.

BOY'S VOICE Forever and ever —

[ANNIE *shakes her head.*]

— forever, and ever, and —

[ANNIE *covers her ears.*]

— forever, and ever, and ever —

[*It pursues* ANNIE; *she flees to snatch up her purse, wheels to the doorway — and* KELLER *is standing in it. The lights have lost their special color.*]

KELLER Miss — Annie. (*He has an envelope in his fingers.*) I've been waiting to give you this.

ANNIE (*after a breath*) What?

KELLER Your first month's salary. (*He puts it in her hand.*) With many more to come, I trust. It doesn't express what we feel; it doesn't pay our debt. For what you've done.

ANNIE What have I done?

KELLER Taken a wild thing and given us back a child.

ANNIE (*presently*) I taught her one thing, *no*. Don't do this, don't do that —

KELLER It's more than all of us could, in all the years we —

ANNIE I wanted to teach her what language is. I wanted to teach her *yes*.

KELLER You will have time.

ANNIE I don't know how. I know without it, to do nothing but obey is — no gift; obedience without understanding is a — blindness too. Is that all I've wished on her?

KELLER (*gently*) No, no —

ANNIE Maybe. I don't know what else to do. Simply go on, keep doing what I've done, and have — faith that inside she's — That inside it's waiting. Like water, underground. All I can do is keep on.

KELLER It's enough. For us.

ANNIE You can help, Captain Keller.

KELLER How?

ANNIE Even learning *no* has been at a cost. Of much trouble and pain. Don't undo it.

KELLER Why should we wish to —

ANNIE (*abruptly*) The world isn't an easy place for anyone; I don't want her just to obey but to let her have her way in everything is a lie, to *her*, I can't — (*Her eyes fill; it takes her by surprise, and she laughs through it.*) And I don't even love her, she's not my child! Well. You've got to stand between that lie and her.

KELLER We'll try.

ANNIE Because *I* will. As long as you let me stay, that's one promise I'll keep.

KELLER Agreed. We've learned something too, I hope. (*A pause*) Won't you come now, to supper?

ANNIE Yes. (*She wags the envelope, ruefully.*) Why doesn't God pay his debts each month?

KELLER I beg your pardon?

ANNIE Nothing. I used to wonder how I could —

[*The lights are fading on them, simultaneously rising on the family room of the main house, where* VINEY *is polishing glassware at the table set for dinner.*]

— earn a living.

KELLER Oh, you do.

ANNIE I really do. Now the question is, can I survive it!

[KELLER *smiles, offers his arm.*]

KELLER May I?

[ANNIE *takes it, and the lights lose them as he escorts her out.*]

SCENE 3

Now in the family room the rear door opens, and HELEN *steps in. She stands a moment, then sniffs in one deep grateful breath, and her hands go out vigorously to familiar things — over the door panels, and to the chairs around the table, and over the silverware on the table — until she meets* VINEY; *she pats her flank approvingly.*

VINEY Oh, we're glad to have you back, too, prob'ly.

[HELEN *hurries, groping, to the front door, opens and closes it, removes its key, opens and closes it again to be sure it is unlocked, gropes back to the rear door and repeats the procedure, removing its key and hugging herself gleefully.*

AUNT EV *is next in by the rear door, with a relish tray; she bends to kiss* HELEN'S *cheek.* HELEN *finds* KATE *behind her, and thrusts the keys at her.*]

KATE What? Oh. (*To* EV) Keys.

[*She pockets them, lets* HELEN *feel them.*]

Yes, I'll keep the keys. I think we've had enough of locked doors, too.

[JAMES, *having earlier put* ANNIE'S *suitcase inside her door upstairs and taken himself out of view around the corner, now reappears and comes down the stairs as* ANNIE *and* KELLER *mount the porch steps. Following them into the family room, he pats* ANNIE'S *hair in passing, rather to her surprise.*]

JAMES Evening, general.

[*He takes his own chair opposite.*

VINEY *bears the empty water pitcher out to the porch. The remaining suggestion of garden house is gone now, and the water pump is unobstructed;* VINEY *pumps water into the pitcher.* KATE, *surveying the table, breaks the silence.*]

KATE Will you say the grace, Jimmie?

[*They bow their heads, except for* HELEN, *who palms her empty plate and then reaches to be sure her mother is there.* JAMES *considers a moment, glances across at* ANNIE, *lowers his head again, and obliges.*]

JAMES (*lightly*) And Jacob was left alone, and wrestled with an angel until the breaking of the day; and the hollow of Jacob's thigh was out of joint, as he wrestled with him; and the angel said, Let me go, for the day breaketh. And Jacob said, I will not let thee go, except thou bless me. Amen.

[ANNIE *has lifted her eyes suspiciously at* JAMES, *who winks expressionlessly and inclines his head to* HELEN.]

Oh, you angel.

[*The others lift their faces;* VINEY *returns with the pitcher, setting it down near* KATE, *then goes out the rear door; and* ANNIE *puts a napkin around* HELEN.]

AUNT EV That's a very strange grace, James.
KELLER Will you start the muffins, Ev?
JAMES It's from the Good Book, isn't it?
AUNT EV (*passing a plate*) Well, of course it is. Didn't you know?
JAMES Yes. I knew.
KELLER (*serving*) Ham, Miss Annie?
ANNIE Please.
AUNT EV Then, why ask?
JAMES I meant it *is* from the Good Book, and therefore a fitting grace.
AUNT EV Well, I don't know about *that*.
KATE (*with the pitcher*) Miss Annie?
ANNIE Thank you.
AUNT EV There's an awful *lot* of things in the Good Book that I wouldn't care to hear just before eating.

[*When* ANNIE *reaches for the pitcher,* HELEN *removes her napkin and drops it to the floor.* ANNIE *is filling* HELEN's *glass when she notices it; she considers* HELEN's *bland expression a moment, then bends, retrieves it, and tucks it around* HELEN's *neck again.*]

JAMES Well, fitting in the sense that Jacob's thigh was out of joint, and so is this piggie's.
AUNT EV I declare, James —
KATE Pickles, Aunt Ev?
AUNT EV Oh, I should say so, you know my opinion of your pickles —
KATE This is the end of them, I'm afraid. I didn't put up nearly enough last summer; this year I intend to —

[*She interrupts herself, seeing* HELEN *deliberately lift off her napkin and drop it again to the floor. She bends to retrieve it, but* ANNIE *stops her arm.*]

KELLER (*not noticing*) Reverend looked in at the office today to complain his hens have stopped laying. Poor fellow, *he* was out of joint; all he could —

[*He stops, too, to frown down the table at* KATE, HELEN, *and* ANNIE *in turn, all suspended in mid-motion.*]

JAMES (*not noticing*) I've always suspected those hens.
AUNT EV Of what?
JAMES I think they're Papists.[1] Has he tried —

[*He stops, too, following* KELLER's *eyes.* ANNIE *now stoops to pick the napkin up.*]

AUNT EV James, now you're pulling my — lower extremity; the first thing you know we'll be —

[*She stops, too, hearing herself in the silence.* ANNIE, *with everyone now watching, for the third time puts the napkin on* HELEN. HELEN *yanks it off and throws it down.* ANNIE *rises, lifts* HELEN's *plate, and bears it away.* HELEN, *feeling it gone, slides down and commences to kick up under the table; the dishes jump.* ANNIE *contemplates this for a moment, then coming back, takes* HELEN's *wrists firmly and swings her off the chair.* HELEN, *struggling, gets one hand free and catches at her mother's skirt; when* KATE *takes her by the shoulders,* HELEN *hangs quiet.*]

KATE Miss Annie.
ANNIE No.
KATE (*a pause*) It's a very special day.
ANNIE (*grimly*) It will be, when I give in to that.

[*She tries to disengage* HELEN's *hand;* KATE *lays hers on* ANNIE's.]

KATE Please. I've hardly had a chance to welcome her home —
ANNIE Captain Keller.
KELLER (*embarrassed*) Oh. Katie, we — had a little talk, Miss Annie feels that if we indulge Helen in these —
AUNT EV But what's the child done?
ANNIE She's learned not to throw things on the floor and kick. It took us the best part of two weeks and —
AUNT EV But only a napkin, it's not as if it were breakable!
ANNIE And everything she's learned *is?* Mrs. Keller, I don't think we should — play tug of war for her; either give her to me or you keep her from kicking.

---

[1] *Papists:* Roman Catholics.

KATE What do you wish to do?

ANNIE Let me take her from the table.

AUNT EV Oh, let her stay, my goodness, she's only a child; she doesn't have to wear a napkin if she doesn't want to her first evening —

ANNIE (*level*) And ask outsiders not to interfere.

AUNT EV (*astonished*) Out — outsi — I'm the child's *aunt!*

KATE (*distressed*) Will once hurt so much, Miss Annie? I've — made all Helen's favorite foods, tonight.

[*A pause*]

KELLER (*gently*) It's a homecoming party, Miss Annie.

[ANNIE *after a moment releases* HELEN. *But she cannot accept it; at her own chair she shakes her head and turns back, intent on* KATE.]

ANNIE She's testing you. You realize?

JAMES (*to* ANNIE) She's testing you.

KELLER Jimmie, be quiet.

[JAMES *sits, tense.*]

Now she's home, naturally she —

ANNIE And wants to see what will happen. At your hands. I said it was my main worry; is this what you promised me not half an hour ago?

KELLER (*reasonably*) But she's *not* kicking, now —

ANNIE And not learning not to. Mrs. Keller, teaching her is bound to be painful to everyone. I know it hurts to watch but she'll live up to just what you demand of her, and no more.

JAMES (*palely*) She's testing *you*.

KELLER (*testily*) Jimmie.

JAMES I have an opinion, I think I should —

KELLER No one's interested in hearing your opinion.

ANNIE *I'm* interested; of course she's testing me. Let me keep her to what she's learned, and she'll go on learning from me. Take her out of my hands, and it all comes apart.

[KATE *closes her eyes, digesting it;* ANNIE *sits again, with a brief comment for her.*]

Be bountiful, it's at her expense. (*She turns to* JAMES, *flatly.*)

Please pass me more of — her favorite foods.

[*Then* KATE *lifts* HELEN'S *hand, and turning her toward* ANNIE, *surrenders her;* HELEN *makes for her own chair.*]

KATE (*low*) Take her, Miss Annie.

ANNIE (*then*) Thank you.

[*But the moment* ANNIE, *rising, reaches for her hand,* HELEN *begins to fight and kick, clutching to the tablecloth and uttering laments.* ANNIE *again tries to loosen her hand, and* KELLER *rises.*]

KELLER (*tolerant*) I'm afraid you're the difficulty, Miss Annie. Now I'll keep her to what she's learned; you're quite right there —

[*He takes* HELEN'S *hands from* ANNIE, *pats them;* HELEN *quiets down.*]

— but I don't see that we need send her from the table; after all, she's the guest of honor. Bring her plate back.

ANNIE If she was a seeing child, none of you would tolerate one —

KELLER Well, she's not. I think some compromise is called for. Bring her plate, please.

[ANNIE'S *jaw sets, but she restores the plate while* KELLER *fastens the napkin around* HELEN'S *neck; she permits it.*]

There. It's not unnatural, most of us take some aversion to our teachers, and occasionally another hand can smooth things out.

[*He puts a fork in* HELEN'S *hand;* HELEN *takes it. Genially*]

Now. Shall we start all over?

[*He goes back around the table, and sits.* ANNIE *stands watching.* HELEN *is motionless, thinking things through, until with a wicked glee she deliberately flings the fork on the floor. After another moment she plunges her hand into her food and crams a fistful into her mouth.*]

JAMES (*wearily*) I think we've started all over —

[KELLER *shoots a glare at him as* HELEN *plunges her other hand into* ANNIE'S *plate.* ANNIE *at once moves in, to grasp her wrist; and* HELEN, *flinging out a hand, encounters the pitcher; she swings with it at* ANNIE; ANNIE, *falling back, blocks it with an elbow, but the water flies over her dress.* ANNIE *gets her breath, then snatches the pitcher away in one hand, hoists* HELEN *up bodily under the other arm, and starts to carry her out, kicking.* KELLER *stands.*]

ANNIE (*savagely polite*) Don't get up!
KELLER Where are you going?
ANNIE Don't smooth anything else out for me; don't interfere in any way! I treat her like a seeing child because I *ask* her to see, I *expect* her to see; don't undo what I do!
KELLER Where are you taking her?
ANNIE To make her fill this pitcher again!

[*She thrusts out with* HELEN *under her arm, but* HELEN *escapes up the stairs, and* ANNIE *runs after her.* KELLER *stands rigid.* AUNT EV *is astounded.*]

AUNT EV You let her speak to you like that, Arthur? A creature who *works* for you?
KELLER (*angrily*) No, I don't.

[*He is starting after* ANNIE *when* JAMES, *on his feet with shaky resolve, interposes his chair between them in* KELLER'S *path.*]

JAMES Let her go.
KELLER What!
JAMES (*a swallow*) I said — let her go. She's right. She's right, Kate's right, I'm right, and you're wrong. If you drive her away from here, it will be over my dead — chair; has it never occurred to you that on one occasion you might be consummately wrong?

[KELLER'S *stare is unbelieving, even a little fascinated.* KATE *rises in trepidation, to mediate.*]

KATE Captain.

[KELLER *stops her with his raised hand; his eyes stay on* JAMES'S *pale face for a long hold. When he finally finds his voice, it is gruff.*]

KELLER Sit down, everyone. Please sit down, Jimmie.

[JAMES *sits, and a moveless silence prevails;* KELLER'S *eyes do not leave him.*

ANNIE *has pulled* HELEN *downstairs again by one hand, the pitcher in her other hand, down the porch steps and across the yard to the pump. She puts* HELEN'S *hand on the pump handle, grimly.*]

ANNIE All right. Pump.

[HELEN *touches her cheek, waits uncertainly.*]

No, she's not here. Pump!

[*She forces* HELEN'S *hand to work the handle, then lets go. And* HELEN *obeys. She pumps till the water comes; then* ANNIE *puts the pitcher in her other hand and guides it under the spout, and the water tumbling half into and half around the pitcher douses* HELEN'S *hand.* ANNIE *takes over the handle to keep water coming and does automatically what she has done so many times before: spells into* HELEN'S *free palm.*]

Water. W, a, t, e, r. *Water.* It has a — *name* —

[*And now the miracle happens.* HELEN *drops the pitcher on the slab under the spout; it shatters. She stands transfixed.* ANNIE *freezes on the pump handle; there is a change in the sundown light and with it a change in* HELEN'S *face, some light coming into it we have never seen there, some struggle in the depths behind it; and her lips tremble, trying to remember something the muscles around them once knew, till at last it finds its way out, painfully, a baby sound buried under years of dumbness.*]

HELEN Wah. Wah. (*And again, with great effort*) Wah. Wah.

[HELEN *plunges her hand into the dwindling water, spells into her own palm. Then she gropes frantically;* ANNIE *reaches for her hand, and* HELEN *spells into* ANNIE'S *hand.*]

ANNIE (*whispering*) Yes.

[HELEN *spells into it again.*]

Yes!

[HELEN *grabs at the handle, pumps for more water, plunges her hand into its spurt and grabs* ANNIE'S *to spell it again.*]

Yes! Oh, my dear —

[*She falls to her knees to clasp* HELEN's *hand, but* HELEN *pulls it free, stands almost bewildered, then drops to the ground, pats it swiftly, holds up her palm, imperious.* ANNIE *spells into it.*]

Ground.

[HELEN *spells it back.*]

Yes!

[HELEN *whirls to the pump, pats it, holds up her palm, and* ANNIE *spells into it.*]

Pump.

[HELEN *spells it back.*]

Yes! Yes!

[*Now* HELEN *is in such an excitement she is possessed, wild, trembling, cannot be still, turns, runs, falls on the porch step, claps it, reaches out her palm, and* ANNIE *is at it instantly to spell.*]

Step.

[HELEN *has no time to spell back now; she whirls, groping, to touch anything, encounters the trellis, shakes it, thrusts out her palm, and* ANNIE *while spelling to her, cries wildly at the house.*]

Trellis. Mrs. Keller! Mrs. Keller!

[*Inside,* KATE *starts to her feet.* HELEN *scrambles back onto the porch, groping, and finds the bell string, tugs it; the bell rings, the distant chimes begin tolling the hour, all the bells in town seem to break into speech while* HELEN *reaches out and* ANNIE *spells feverishly into her hand.* KATE *hurries out, with* KELLER *after her;* AUNT EV *is on her feet to peer out the window; only* JAMES *remains at the table, and with a napkin wipes his damp brow. From up right and left the servants —* VINEY, *the two children, the gardener — run in and stand watching from a distance as* HELEN, *ringing the bell, with her other hand encounters her mother's skirt; when she throws a hand out,* ANNIE *spells into it.*]

Mother.

[KELLER *now seizes* HELEN's *hand; she touches him, gestures a hand, and* ANNIE *again spells.*]

Papa — she *knows!*

[KATE *and* KELLER *go to their knees, stammering, clutching* HELEN *to them, and* ANNIE *steps unsteadily back to watch the threesome,* HELEN *spelling wildly into* KATE's *hand, then into* KELLER's, KATE *spelling back into* HELEN's; *they cannot keep their hands off her and rock her in their clasp.*

Then HELEN *gropes, feels nothing, turns all around, pulls free, and comes with both hands groping, to find* ANNIE. *She encounters* ANNIE's *thighs;* ANNIE *kneels to her;* HELEN's *hand pats* ANNIE's *cheek impatiently, points a finger.* ANNIE *spells into it.*]

Teacher.

[HELEN *spells it back, slowly;* ANNIE *nods.*]

Teacher.

[*She holds* HELEN's *hand to her cheek. Presently* HELEN *withdraws it, not jerkily, only with reserve, and retreats a step. She stands thinking it over, then turns again and stumbles back to her parents. They try to embrace her, but she has something else in mind; it is to get the keys, and she hits* KATE's *pocket until* KATE *digs them out for her.*

ANNIE, *with her own load of emotion, has retreated, her back turned, toward the pump, to sit;* KATE *moves to* HELEN, *touches her hand questioningly, and* HELEN *spells a word to her.* KATE *comprehends it — their first act of verbal communication — and she can hardly utter the word aloud, in wonder, gratitude, and deprivation; it is a moment in which she simultaneously finds and loses a child.*]

KATE Teacher?

[ANNIE *turns; and* KATE, *facing* HELEN *in her direction by the shoulders, holds her back and then relinquishes her.* HELEN *feels her way across the yard, rather shyly, and when her moving hands touch* ANNIE's *skirt, she stops. Then she holds out the keys and places them in* ANNIE's *hand. For a moment neither of them moves. Then* HELEN *slides into* ANNIE'S *arms and, lifting away her smoked glasses, kisses her on the cheek.* ANNIE *gathers her in.* KATE, *torn both ways, turns from this, gestures the servants off, and makes her way into the house, on* KELLER'S *arm. The servants go, in separate directions. The lights are half down now, except over the pump.* ANNIE *and* HELEN *are alone in the yard.* ANNIE *has found* HELEN'S *hand, almost without knowing it, and she spells slowly into it, her voice unsteady, whispering.*]

ANNIE I, love, Helen. (*She clutches the child to her, tight this time, not spelling, whispering into her hair.*)

Forever, and —

[*She stops. The lights over the pump are taking on the color of the past, and it brings* ANNIE'S *head up, her eyes opening, in fear; and as slowly as though drawn she rises, to listen, with her hands on* HELEN'S *shoulders. She waits, waits, listening with ears and eyes both, slowly here, slowly there, and hears only silence. There are no voices. The color passes on, and when her eyes come back to* HELEN, *she can breathe the end of her phrase without fear.*]

— ever.

[*In the family room* KATE *has stood over the table, staring at* HELEN'S *plate, with* KELLER *at her shoulder; now* JAMES *takes a step to move her chair in, and* KATE *sits, with head erect, and* KELLER *inclines his head to* JAMES; *so it is* AUNT EV, *hesitant, and rather humble, who moves to the door.*

Outside, HELEN *tugs at* ANNIE'S *hand, and* ANNIE *comes with it.* HELEN *pulls her toward the house; and hand in hand, they cross the yard and ascend the porch steps, in the rising lights, to where* AUNT EV *is holding the door open for them.*

The curtain ends the play.]

"Mother and Child,"
painting by Mary Cassatt.

Witchita Art Museum, Roland P. Murdock Collection.

BOOK TWO | PART 2

COMMITMENT TO OTHERS

I wanted to teach you — oh, everything the earth is full of.
   THE MIRACLE WORKER, Act 3

In the heat of her concern for Helen Keller, Annie Sullivan makes a remarkable statement: "I didn't come here for love. I came for money!" But Helen's mother, and the audience, understand Annie's motives better than she does herself. She masks her devotion to Helen for many reasons, including a fear of failure and a refusal to be thought soft-hearted. Annie's defensiveness barely conceals the real core of her personality. She is a deeply committed person. Having suffered herself from an affliction similar to Helen's, she is relentless in her efforts to bring Helen out of the darkness and to restore her to life. But Annie is not soft and sentimental; she shows that simple kindness and moralizing can sometimes do more harm than good. The Miracle Worker, the story of a woman who was both unselfish and practical, is not a sermon, however, but a play. It dramatizes some of the basic questions which men continue to ask themselves.

Some of these questions are: How should a man behave? What is a man's responsibility to others? The selections in this section are concerned directly with the question of duty to others. Love, unselfishness, and devotion are values which almost no one would deny. If we ask: Is commitment to others a good thing? the answer will always come back: yes. But literature is concerned with testing general propositions against specific situations. The writers of the following selections show that the question is seldom a simple one. Men, in literature as in life, often find themselves having to decide between conflicting loyalties and values.

Commitment takes many shapes: it may heal, redeem, or save another from death. The committed person may know clearly what he is doing, or he may act instinctively. Society may oppose or support his deed. One thing is common to all forms of commitment: it requires sacrifice, it calls on the individual to go beyond himself for the sake of another. Sometimes, of course, the person showing devotion may be rewarded in a material way. Penelope in the Odyssey is a classic instance of devotion, and at the end of the epic we see her rewarded by the return of her husband and the establishment of order in her household. But often the rewards must be sought within the committed person himself. His need to serve may have been deeply felt. Service usually brings about an enlargement, an enrichment of character. In The Miracle Worker, Annie's success as a teacher releases her from her own tortured past and promises a future free from the hideous voices that haunted her. In the selections that follow, the reward for commitment to others may not always be as dramatically clear as in the play you have just read, but it is there nevertheless.

Commitment is not always a matter of miracle-working. Ordinary people can demonstrate it in ordinary ways, and history and literature record many such instances. The principal characters in the following stories and articles all accept the value of commitment to others. They examine in specific situations its rewards, dangers, and difficulties.

Now that the United States and Japan are friends and allies, it may be difficult to recall the deep animosity that once brought the two nations into conflict in World War II. Pearl Buck, a Nobel Prize winner who lived and worked in the Orient for many years, understood this animosity, but she was also aware of the possibilities of reconciliation between the two peoples. In this story she examines the difficult decisions faced by a Japanese doctor who found himself with conflicting loyalties.

The Enemy

PEARL S. BUCK

Dr. Sadao Hoki's house was built on a spot of the Japanese coast where as a little boy he had often played. The low, square stone house was set upon rocks well above a narrow beach that was outlined with bent pines. As a boy Sadao had climbed the pines, supporting himself on his bare feet, as he had seen men do in the South Seas when they climbed for coconuts. His father had taken him often to the islands of those seas, and never had he failed to say to the little grave boy at his side, "Those islands yonder, they are the steppingstones to the future for Japan."

"Where shall we step from them?" Sadao had asked seriously.

"Who knows?" his father had answered. "Who can limit our future? It depends on what we make it."

Sadao had taken this into his mind as he did everything his father said, his father who never joked or played with him, but who spent infinite pains upon him who was his only son. Sadao knew that his education was his father's chief concern. For this reason he had been sent at twenty-two to America to learn all that could be learned of surgery and medicine. He had come back at thirty, and before his father died, he had seen Sadao become famous not only as a surgeon but as a scientist. Because he was now perfecting a discovery which would render wounds entirely clean, he had not been sent abroad with the troops. Also, he knew, there was some slight danger that the old General might need an operation for a condition for which he was now being treated medically, and for this possibility Sadao was being kept in Japan.

Clouds were rising from the ocean now. The unexpected warmth of the past few days had at night drawn heavy fog from the cold waves. Sadao watched these mists hide outlines of a little island near the shore and then come creeping up the beach below the house, wreathing around the pines. In a few minutes fog would be wrapped about the house too. Then he would go into the room where Hana, his wife, would be waiting for him with the two children.

But at this moment the door opened and she looked out, a dark-blue woolen haori over her kimono. She came to him affectionately and put her arm through his as he stood, smiled, and said nothing. He had met Hana in America, but he had waited to fall in love with her until he was sure she was Japanese. His father would never have received her unless she had been pure in her race. He wondered often whom he would have married if he had not met Hana, and by what luck he had found her in the most casual way, by chance literally, at an American professor's house. The professor and his wife had been kind people, anxious to do something for their few foreign students, and the students, though bored, had accepted this kindness. Sadao had often told Hana how nearly he had not gone to Professor Harley's house that night — the rooms were so small, the food so bad, the professor's wife so voluble. But he had gone, and there he had found Hana, a new student, and had felt he would love her if it were at all possible.

Now he felt her hand on his arm and was aware of the pleasure it gave him, even though they had been married years enough to have the two children. For they had not married heedlessly in America. They had finished their work at school and had come home to Japan, and when his father had seen her, the marriage had been arranged in the old Japanese way, although Sadao and Hana had talked everything over beforehand. They were perfectly happy. She laid her cheek against his arm.

It was at this moment that both of them saw something black come out of the mists. It was a man. He was flung up out of the ocean — flung, it seemed, to his feet by a breaker. He staggered a few steps, his body outlined against the mist, his arms above his head. Then the curled mists hid him again.

"Who is that?" Hana cried. She dropped Sadao's arm and they both leaned over the railing of the veranda. Now they saw him again. The man was on his hands and knees, crawling. Then they saw him fall on his face and lie there.

"A fisherman perhaps," Sadao said, "washed from his boat." He ran quickly down the steps and behind him Hana came, her wide sleeves flying. A mile or two away on either side there were fishing villages, but here was only the bare and lonely coast, dangerous with rocks. The surf beyond the beach was spiked with rocks. Somehow the man had managed to come through them — he must be badly torn.

They saw when they came toward him that indeed it was so. The sand on one side of him had already a stain of red soaking through.

"He is wounded," Sadao exclaimed. He made haste to the man, who lay motionless, his face in the sand. An old cap stuck to his head, soaked with sea water. He was in wet rags of garments. Sadao stooped, Hana at his side, and turned the man's head. They saw the face.

"A white man!" Hana whispered.

Yes, it was a white man. The wet cap fell away, and there was his wet yellow hair, long, as though for many weeks it had not been cut, and upon his young and tortured face was a rough yellow beard. He was unconscious and knew nothing that they did to him.

Now Sadao remembered the wound, and with his expert fingers he began to search for it. Blood flowed freshly at his touch. On the right side of his lower back Sadao saw that a gun wound had been reopened. The flesh was blackened with powder. Sometime, not many days ago, the man had been shot and had not been tended. It was bad chance that the rock had struck the wound.

"Oh, how he is bleeding!" Hana whispered again in a solemn voice. The mists screened them now completely, and at this time of day no one came by. The fishermen had gone home, and even the chance beachcombers would have considered the day at an end.

"What shall we do with this man?" Sadao muttered. But his trained hands seemed of their own will to be doing what they could to stanch the fearful bleeding. He packed the wound with the sea moss that strewed the beach. The man moaned with pain in his stupor, but he did not awaken.

"The best thing that we could do would be to put him back in the sea," Sadao said, answering himself.

Now that the bleeding was stopped for the moment, he stood up and dusted the sand from his hands.

"Yes, undoubtedly that would be best," Hana said steadily. But she continued to stare down at the motionless man.

"If we sheltered a white man in our house, we should be arrested, and if we turned him over as a prisoner, he would certainly die," Sadao said.

"The kindest thing would be to put him back into the sea," Hana said. But neither of them moved. They were staring with a curious repulsion upon the inert figure.

"What is he?" Hana whispered.

"There is something about him that looks American," Sadao said. He took up the battered cap. Yes, there, almost gone, was the faint lettering. "A sailor," he said, "from an American warship." He spelled it out: "U.S. Navy." The man was a prisoner of war!

"He has escaped," Hana cried softly, "and that is why he is wounded."

"In the back," Sadao agreed.

They hesitated, looked at each other. Then Hana said with resolution:

"Come, are we able to put him back into the sea?"

"If I am able, are you?" Sadao asked.

"No," Hana said. "But if you can do it alone. . . ."

Sadao hesitated again. "The strange thing is," he said, "that if the man were whole, I could turn him over to the police without difficulty. I care nothing for him. He is my enemy. All Americans are my enemy. And he is only a common fellow. You see how foolish his face is. But since he is wounded. . . ."

"You also cannot throw him back to the sea," Hana said. "Then there is only one thing to do. We must carry him into the house."

"But the servants?" Sadao inquired.

"We must simply tell them that we intend to give him to the police — as indeed we must, Sadao. We must think of the children and your position. It would endanger all of us if we did not give this man over as a prisoner of war."

"Certainly," Sadao agreed. "I would not think of doing anything else."

Thus agreed, together they lifted the man. He was very light, like a fowl that has been half starved for a long time until it is only feathers and skeleton. So, his arms hanging, they carried him up the steps and into the side door of the house. This door opened into a passage, and down the passage they carried the man toward an empty bedroom. It had been the bedroom of Sadao's father, and since his death it had not been used. They laid the man on the deeply matted floor. Everything here had been Japanese, to please the old man, who would never in his own home sit on a chair or sleep in a foreign bed. Hana went to the wall cupboards and slid back a door and took out a soft quilt. She hesitated. The quilt was covered with flowered silk and the lining was pure white silk.

"He is so dirty," she murmured in distress.

"Yes, he had better be washed," Sadao agreed. "If you will fetch hot water, I will wash him."

"I cannot bear for you to touch him," she said. "We shall have to tell the servants he is here. I will tell Yumi now. She can leave the children for a few minutes and she can wash him."

Sadao considered a moment. "Let it be so," he agreed. "You tell Yumi and I will tell the others."

But the utter pallor of the man's unconscious face moved him first to stoop and feel his pulse. It was faint but it was there. He put his hand against the man's cold breast. The heart too was yet alive.

"He will die unless he is operated on," Sadao said, considering. "The question is whether he will not die anyway."

Hana cried out in fear. "Don't try to save him! What if he should live?"

"What if he should die?" Sadao replied. He stood gazing down on the motionless man. This man must have extraordinary vitality or he would have been dead by now. But then, he was very young — perhaps not yet twenty-five.

"You mean die from the operation?" Hana asked.

"Yes," Sadao said.

Hana considered this doubtfully, and when she did not answer, Sadao turned away. "At any rate something must be done with him," he said, "and first he must be washed." He went quickly out of the room and Hana came behind him. She did not wish to be left alone with the white man. He was the first she had seen since she left America, and now he seemed to have nothing to do with those whom she had known there. Here he was her enemy, a menace, living or dead.

She turned to the nursery and called, "Yumi!"

But the children heard her voice, and she had to go in for a moment and smile at them and play with the baby boy, now nearly three months old.

Over the baby's soft black hair she motioned with her mouth, "Yumi — come with me!"

"I will put the baby to bed," Yumi replied. "He is ready."

She went with Yumi into the bedroom next to the nursery and stood with the boy in her arms while Yumi spread the sleeping quilts on the floor and laid the baby between them.

Then Hana led the way quickly and softly to the kitchen. The two servants were frightened at what their master had just told them. The old gardener, who was also a house servant, pulled the few hairs on his upper lip.

"The master ought not to heal the wound of this white man," he said bluntly to Hana. "The white man ought to die. First he was shot. Then the sea caught him and wounded him with her rocks. If the master heals what the gun did and what the sea did, they will take revenge on us."

"I will tell him what you say," Hana replied courteously. But she herself was also frightened, although she was not superstitious as the old man was. Could it ever be well to help an enemy? Nevertheless, she told Yumi to fetch the hot water and bring it to the room where the white man was.

She went ahead and slid back the partitions. Sadao was not yet there. Yumi, following, put down her wooden bucket. Then she went over to the white man. When she saw him, her thick lips folded themselves into stubbornness. "I have never washed a white man," she said, "and I will not wash so dirty a one now."

Hana cried at her severely, "You will do what your master commands you!"

"My master ought not to command me to wash the enemy," Yumi said stubbornly.

There was so fierce a look of resistance upon Yumi's round dull face that Hana felt unreasonably afraid. After all, if the servants should report something that was not as it happened?

"Very well," she said with dignity. "You understand we only want to bring him to his senses so that we can turn him over as a prisoner?"

"I will have nothing to do with it," Yumi said. "I am a poor person and it is not my business."

"Then please," Hana said gently, "return to your own work."

At once Yumi left the room. But this left Hana with the white man alone. She might have been too afraid to stay had not her anger at Yumi's stubbornness now sustained her.

"Stupid Yumi," she muttered fiercely. "Is this anything but a man? And a wounded, helpless man!"

In the conviction of her own superiority she bent impulsively and untied the knotted rags that kept the white man covered. When she had his breast bare she dipped the small clean towel that Yumi had brought into the steaming hot water and washed his face carefully. The man's skin, though rough with exposure, was of a fine texture and must have been very blond when he was a child.

While she was thinking these thoughts, though not really liking the man better now that he was no longer a child, she kept on washing him until his upper body was quite clean. But she dared not turn him over. Where was Sadao? Now her anger was ebbing, and she was anxious again and she rose, wiping her hands on the wrung towel. Then, lest the man be chilled, she put the quilt over him.

"Sadao!" she called softly.

He had been about to come in when she called. His hand had been on the door and now he opened it. She saw that he had brought his surgeon's emergency bag and that he wore his surgeon's coat.

"You have decided to operate!" she cried.

"Yes," he said shortly. He turned his back to her and unfolded a sterilized towel upon the floor of the *tokonoma* [1] alcove, and put his instruments out upon it.

"Fetch towels," he said.

She went obediently, but how anxious now, to the linen shelves and took out the towels. There ought also to be old pieces of matting, so that the blood would not ruin the fine floor covering. She went out to the back veranda where the gardener kept strips of mat-

---

[1] *tokonoma* (tō·kō·nō′mə): a sacred alcove where pictures and flowers are placed in memory of the dead.

ting with which to protect delicate shrubs on cold nights and took an armful of them.

But when she went back into the room, she saw this was useless. The blood had already soaked through the packing in the man's wound and had ruined the mat under him.

"Oh, the mat!" she cried.

"Yes, it is ruined," Sadao replied, as though he did not care. "Help me to turn him," he commanded her.

She obeyed him without a word, and he began to wash the man's back carefully.

"Yumi would not wash him," she said.

"Did you wash him then?" Sadao asked, not stopping for a moment his swift, concise movements.

"Yes," she said.

He did not seem to hear her. But she was used to his absorption when he was at work. She wondered for a moment if it mattered to him what was the body upon which he worked, so long as it was for the work he did so excellently.

"You will have to give the anesthetic if he needs it," he said.

"I?" she repeated blankly. "But never have I!"

"It is easy enough," he said impatiently.

He was taking out the packing now, and the blood began to flow more quickly. He peered into the wound with the bright surgeon's light fastened on his forehead. "The bullet is still there," he said with cool interest. "Now I wonder how deep this rock wound is. If it is not too deep, it may be that I can get the bullet. But the bleeding is not superficial. He has lost much blood."

At this moment Hana choked. He looked up and saw her face the color of sulfur.

"Don't faint," he said sharply. He did not put down his exploring instrument. "If I stop now, the man will surely die." She clapped her hands to her mouth and leaped up and ran out of the room. Outside in the garden he heard her retching. But he went on with his work.

"It will be better for her to empty her stomach," he thought. He had forgotten that, of course, she had never seen an operation. But her distress, and his inability to go to her at once, made him impatient and irritable with this man who lay like dead under his knife.

"This man," he thought, "there is no reason under heaven why he should live."

Unconsciously, this thought made him ruthless, and he proceeded swiftly. In his dream the man moaned, but Sadao paid no heed except to mutter at him.

"Groan," he muttered, "groan if you like. I am not doing this for my own pleasure. In fact, I do not know why I am doing it."

The door opened and there was Hana again. She had not stopped even to smooth back her hair.

"Where is the anesthetic?" she asked in a clear voice.

Sadao motioned with his chin. "It is as well that you came back," he said. "This fellow is beginning to stir."

She had the bottle and some cotton in her hand.

"But how shall I do it?" she asked.

"Simply saturate the cotton and hold it near his nostrils," Sadao replied, without delaying for one moment the intricate detail of his work. "When he breathes badly, move it away a little."

She crouched close to the sleeping face of the young American. It was a piteously thin face, she thought, and the lips were twisted. The man was suffering, whether he knew it or not. Watching him, she wondered if the stories they heard sometimes of the sufferings of prisoners were true. They came like flickers of rumor, told by word of mouth and always contradicted. In the newspapers the reports were always that wherever the Japanese armies went the people received them gladly, with cries of joy at their liberation. But sometimes she remembered such men as General Takima, who at home beat his wife cruelly, though no one mentioned it now that he had fought so victorious a battle in Manchuria. If a man like that could be so cruel to a woman in his power, would he not be cruel to one like this, for instance?

She hoped anxiously that this young man had not been tortured. It was at this moment that she observed deep red scars on his neck, just under the ear. "Those scars," she murmured, lifting her eyes to Sadao.

But he did not answer. At this moment he felt the tip of his instrument strike against something hard, dangerously near the kidney. All thought left him. He felt only the purest pleasure. He probed with his fingers, delicately, familiar with every atom of this human body. His old American professor of anatomy had seen to that knowledge. "Ignorance of the human body is the surgeon's cardinal sin, sirs!" he had thundered at his classes year after year. "To operate without as complete knowledge of the body as if you had made it — anything less than that is murder."

"It is not quite at the kidney, my friend," Sadao murmured. It was his habit to murmur to the patient when he forgot himself in an operation. "My friend," he always called his patients, and so now he did, forgetting that this was his enemy.

Then quickly, with the cleanest and most precise of incisions, the bullet was out. The man quivered, but he was still unconscious. Nevertheless, he muttered a few English words.

"Guts," he muttered, choking. "They got . . . my guts. . . ."

"Sadao!" Hana cried sharply.

"Hush," Sadao said.

The man sank again into silence so profound that Sadao took up his wrist, hating the touch of it. Yes, there was still a pulse, so faint, so feeble, but enough, if he wanted the man to live, to give hope.

"But certainly I do not want this man to live," he thought.

"No more anesthetic," he told Hana.

He turned as swiftly as though he had never paused, and from his medicines he chose a small vial and from it filled a hypodermic and thrust it into the patient's left arm. Then, putting down the needle, he took the man's wrist again. The pulse under his fingers fluttered once or twice and then grew stronger.

"This man will live in spite of all," he said to Hana and sighed.

The young man woke, so weak, his blue eyes so terrified when he perceived where he was, that Hana felt compelled to apologize. She served him herself, for none of the servants would enter the room.

When she came in the first time, she saw him summon his small strength to be prepared for some fearful thing.

"Don't be afraid," she begged him softly.

"How come . . . you speak English . . . ?" he gasped.

"I was a long time in America," she replied.

She saw that he wanted to reply to that, but he could not, and so she knelt and fed him gently from the porcelain spoon. He ate unwillingly, but still he ate.

"Now you will soon be strong," she said, not liking him and yet moved to comfort him.

He did not answer.

When Sadao came in the third day after the operation, he found the young man sitting up, his face bloodless with the effort.

"Lie down," Sadao cried. "Do you want to die?"

He forced the man down gently and strongly and examined the wound. "You may kill yourself if you do this sort of thing," he scolded.

"What are you going to do with me?" the boy muttered. He looked just now barely seventeen. "Are you going to hand me over?"

For a moment Sadao did not answer. He finished his examination and then pulled the silk quilt over the man.

"I do not know myself what I shall do with you," he said. "I ought of course to give you to the police. You are a prisoner of war — no, do not tell me anything." He put up his hand as he saw the young man about to speak. "Do not even tell me your name unless I ask it."

They looked at each other for a moment, and then the young man closed his eyes and turned his face to the wall.

"O.K.," he whispered, his mouth a bitter line.

Outside the door Hana was waiting for Sadao. He saw at once that she was in trouble.

"Sadao, Yumi tells me the servants feel they cannot stay if we hide this man here any more," she said. "She tells me that they are saying that you and I were so long in America that we have forgotten to think of our country first. They think we like Americans."

"It is not true," Sadao said harshly, "Americans are our enemies. But I have been trained not to let a man die if I can help it."

"The servants cannot understand that," she said anxiously.

"No," he agreed.

Neither seemed able to say more, and somehow the household dragged on. The servants grew daily more watchful. Their courtesy was as careful as ever, but their eyes were cold upon the pair to whom they were hired.

"It is clear what our master ought to do," the old gardener said one morning. He had worked with flowers all his life, and had been a specialist too in moss. For Sadao's father he had made one of the finest moss gardens in Japan, sweeping the bright green carpets constantly so that not a leaf or a pine needle marred the velvet of its surface. "My old master's son knows very well what he ought to do," he now said, pinching a bud from a bush as he spoke. "When the man was so near death, why did he not let him bleed?"

"That young master is so proud of his skill to save life that he saves any life," the cook said contemptuously. She split a fowl's neck skillfully and held the fluttering bird and let its blood flow into the roots of a wisteria vine. Blood is the best of fertilizers, and the old gardener would not let her waste a drop of it.

"It is the children of whom we must think," Yumi said sadly. "What will be their fate if their father is condemned as a traitor?"

They did not try to hide what they said from the ears of Hana as she stood arranging the day's flowers on the veranda near by, and she knew they spoke on purpose that she might hear. That they were right she knew, too, in most of her being. But there was another part of her which she herself could not understand. It was not sentimental liking of the prisoner. She had come to think of him as a prisoner. She had not liked him even yesterday when he said in his impulsive way, "Anyway, let me tell you that my name is Tom." She had only bowed her little distant bow. She saw hurt in his eyes but she did not wish to assuage it. Indeed, he was a great trouble in this house.

As for Sadao, every day he examined the wound carefully. The last stitches had been pulled out this morning, and the young man would in a fortnight be nearly as well as ever. Sadao went back to his office and carefully typed a letter to the chief of police reporting the whole matter. "On the twenty-first day of February an escaped prisoner was washed up on the shore in front of my house." So far he typed, and then he opened a secret drawer of his desk and put the unfinished report into it.

On the seventh day after that two things happened. In the morning the servants left together, their belongings tied in large square cotton kerchiefs. When Hana got up in the morning nothing was done, the house not cleaned and the food not prepared, and she knew what it meant. She was dismayed and even terrified, but her pride as a mistress would not allow her to show it. Instead, she inclined her head gracefully when they appeared before her in the kitchen, and she paid them off and thanked them for all that they had done for her. They were crying, but she did not cry. The cook and the gardener had served Sadao since he was a little boy in his father's house, and Yumi cried because of the children. She was so grieving that after she had gone, she ran back to Hana.

"If the baby misses me too much tonight, send for me. I am going to my own house and you know where it is."

"Thank you," Hana said, smiling. But she told herself she would not send for Yumi however the baby cried.

She made breakfast and Sadao helped with the children. Neither of them spoke of the servants beyond the fact that they were gone. But after Hana had taken morning food to the prisoner, she came back to Sadao.

"Why is it we cannot see clearly what we ought to do?" she asked him. "Even the servants see more clearly than we do. Why are we different from other Japanese?"

Sadao did not answer. But a little later he went into the room where the prisoner was and said brusquely, "Today you may get up on your feet. I want you to stay up only five minutes at a time. Tomorrow you may try it twice as long. It would be well that you get back your strength as quickly as possible."

He saw the flicker of terror on the young face that was still very pale.

"O.K.," the boy murmured. Evidently he was determined to say more. "I feel I ought to thank you, doctor, for having saved my life."

"Don't thank me too early," Sadao said coldly. He saw the flicker of terror again in the boy's eyes — terror as unmistakable as an animal's. The scars on his neck were crimson for a moment. Those scars! What were they? Sadao did not ask.

In the afternoon the second thing happened. Hana, working hard at unaccustomed labor, saw a messenger come to the door in official uniform. Her hands went weak and she could not draw her breath. The servants must have told already. She ran to Sadao, gasping, unable to utter a word. But by then the messenger had simply followed her through the garden, and there he stood. She pointed at him helplessly.

Sadao looked up from his book. He was in his office, the outer partition of which was thrown open to the garden for the southern sunshine.

"What is it?" he asked the messenger, and then he rose, seeing the man's uniform.

"You are to come to the palace," the man said, "the old General is in pain again."

"Oh," Hana breathed, "is that all?"

"All?" the messenger exclaimed. "Is it not enough?"

"Indeed it is," she replied. "I am very sorry."

When Sadao came to say good-by, she was in the kitchen, but doing nothing. The children were asleep and she sat merely resting for a moment, more exhausted from her fright than from work.

"I thought they had come to arrest you," she said.

He gazed down into her anxious eyes. "I must get rid of this man for your sake," he said in distress. "Somehow I must get rid of him."

"Of course," the General said weakly, "I understand fully. But that is because I once took a degree in Princeton.[2] So few Japanese have."

"I care nothing for the man, Excellency," Sadao said, "but having operated on him with such success. . . ."

"Yes, yes," the General said. "It only makes me feel you more indispensable to me. Evidently you can save anyone — you are so skilled. You say you think I can stand one more such attack as I have had today?"

"Not more than one," Sadao said.

"Then certainly I can allow nothing to happen to you," the General said with anxiety. His long pale Japanese face became expressionless, which meant that he was in deep thought. "You cannot be arrested," the General said, closing his eyes. "Suppose you were condemned to death and the next day I had to have my operation?"

"There are other surgeons, Excellency," Sadao suggested.

"None I trust," the General replied. "The best ones have been trained by Germans and would consider the operation successful even if I died. I do not care for their point of view." He sighed. "It seems a pity that we cannot better combine the German ruthlessness with the American sentimentality. Then you could turn your prisoner over to execution and yet I could be sure you would not murder me while I was unconscious." The General laughed. He had an unusual sense of humor. "As a Japanese, could you not combine these two foreign elements?" he asked.

---

[2] *Princeton:* Princeton University, in New Jersey.

Sadao smiled. "I am not quite sure," he said, "but for your sake I would be willing to try, Excellency."

The General shook his head. "I had rather not be the test case," he said. He felt suddenly weak and overwhelmed with the cares of his life as an official in times such as these, when repeated victory brought great responsibilities all over the South Pacific. "It is very unfortunate that this man should have washed up on your doorstep," he said irritably.

"I feel it so myself," Sadao said gently.

"It would be best if he could be quietly killed," the General said. "Not by you, but by someone who does not know him. I have my own private assassins. Suppose I send two of them to your house tonight — or better, any night. You need know nothing about it. It is now warm — what would be more natural than that you should leave the outer partition of the white man's room open to the garden while he sleeps?"

"Certainly it would be very natural," Sadao agreed. "In fact, it is so left open every night."

"Good," the General said, yawning. "They are very capable assassins — they make no noise and they know the trick of inward bleeding. If you like I can even have them remove the body."

Sadao considered. "That perhaps would be best, Excellency," he agreed, thinking of Hana.

He left the General's presence then and went home, thinking over the plan. In this way the whole thing would be taken out of his hands. He would tell Hana nothing, since she would be timid at the idea of assassins in the house, and yet certainly such persons were essential in an absolute state such as Japan was. How else could rulers deal with those who opposed them?

He refused to allow anything but reason to be the atmosphere of his mind as he went into the room where the American was in bed. But as he opened the door, to his surprise he found the young man out of bed, and preparing to go into the garden.

"What is this!" he exclaimed. "Who gave you permission to leave your room?"

"I'm not used to waiting for permission," Tom said gaily. "Gosh, I feel pretty good again! But will the muscles on this side always feel stiff?"

"Is it so?" Sadao inquired, surprised. He forgot all else. "Now I thought I had provided against that," he murmured. He lifted the edge of the man's shirt and gazed at the healing scar. "Massage may do it," he said, "if exercise does not."

"It won't bother me much," the young man said. His young face was gaunt under the stubbly blond beard. "Say, doctor, I've got something I want to say to you. If I hadn't met a Jap like you — well, I wouldn't be alive today. I know that."

Sadao bowed but he could not speak.

"Sure, I know that," Tom went on warmly. His big thin hands gripping a chair were white at the knuckles. "I guess if all the Japs were like you there wouldn't have been a war."

"Perhaps," Sadao said with difficulty. "And now I think you had better go back to bed."

He helped the boy back into bed and then bowed. "Good night," he said.

Sadao slept badly that night. Time and time again he woke, thinking he heard the rustling of footsteps, the sound of a twig broken or a stone displaced in the garden — a noise such as men might make who carried a burden.

The next morning he made the excuse to go first into the guest room. If the American were gone, he then could simply tell Hana that so the General had directed. But when he opened the door he saw at once that it was not last night. There on the pillow was the shaggy blond head. He could hear the peaceful breathing of sleep and he closed the door again quietly.

"He is asleep," he told Hana. "He is almost well to sleep like that."

"What shall we do with him?" Hana whispered her old refrain.

Sadao shook his head. "I must decide in a day or two," he promised.

But certainly, he thought, the second night must be the night. There rose a wind that night, and he listened to the sounds of bending boughs and whistling partitions.

Hana woke too. "Ought we not to go and close the sick man's partition?" she asked.

"No," Sadao said. "He is able now to do it for himself."

But the next morning the American was still there.

Then the third night of course must be the night. The wind changed to quiet rain, and the garden was full of the sound of dripping eaves and running springs. Sadao slept a little better, but he woke at the sound of a crash and leaped to his feet.

"What was that?" Hana cried. The baby woke at her voice and began to wail. "I must go and see."

But he held her and would not let her move.

"Sadao," she cried, "what is the matter with you?"

"Don't go," he muttered, "don't go!"

His terror infected her and she stood breathless, waiting. There was only silence. Together they crept back into the bed, the baby between them.

Yet, when he opened the door of the guest room in the morning, there was the young man. He was very gay and had already washed and was now on his feet. He had asked for a razor yesterday and had shaved himself, and today there was a faint color in his cheeks.

"I am well," he said joyously.

Sadao drew his kimono around his weary body. He could not, he decided suddenly, go through another night. It was not that he cared for this young man's life. No, simply it was not worth the strain.

"You are well," Sadao agreed. He lowered his voice. "You are so well that I think if I put my boat on the shore tonight, with food and extra clothing in it, you might be able to row to that little island not far from the coast. It is so near the coast that it has not been worth fortifying. Nobody lives on it because in storm it is submerged. But this is not the season of storm. You could live there until you saw a Korean fishing boat pass by. They pass quite near the island because the water is many fathoms deep there."

The young man stared at him, slowly comprehending. "Do I have to?" he asked.

"I think so," Sadao said gently. "You understand — it is not hidden that you are here."

The young man nodded in perfect comprehension. "O.K.," he said simply.

Sadao did not see him again until evening. As soon as it was dark he had dragged the stout boat down to the shore and in it put food and bottled water that he had bought secretly during the day, as well as two quilts he had bought at a pawnshop. The boat he tied to a post in the water, for the tide was high. There was no moon and he worked without a flashlight.

When he came to the house he entered as though he were just back from his work, and so Hana knew nothing. "Yumi was here today," she said as she served his supper. Though she was so modern, still she did not eat with him. "Yumi cried over the baby," she went on with a sigh. "She misses him so."

"The servants will come back as soon as the foreigner is gone," Sadao said.

He went into the guest room that night before he went to bed and himself checked carefully the American's temperature, the state of the wound, and his heart and pulse. The pulse was irregular, but that was perhaps because of excitement. The young man's pale lips were pressed together and his eyes burned. Only the scars on his neck were red.

"I realize you are saving my life again," he told Sadao.

"Not at all," Sadao said. "It is only inconvenient to have you here any longer."

He had hesitated a good deal about giving the man a flashlight. But he had decided to give it to him after all. It was a small one, his own, which he used at night when he was called.

"If your food runs out before you catch a boat," he said, "signal me two flashes at the same instant the sun drops over the horizon. Do not signal in darkness, for it will be seen. If you are all right but still there, signal me once. You will find fish easy to catch, but you must eat them raw. A fire would be seen."

"O.K.," the young man breathed.

He was dressed now in the Japanese clothes which Sadao had given him, and at the last moment Sadao wrapped a black cloth about his blond head.

"Now," Sadao said.

The young American without a word shook Sadao's hand warmly, and then walked quite well across the floor and down the step into the darkness of the garden. Once — twice — Sadao saw his light flash to find his way. But that would not be suspected. He waited until from the shore there was one more flash. Then he closed the partition. That night he slept.

"You say the man escaped?" the General asked faintly. He had been operated upon a week before, an emergency operation to which Sadao had been called in the night. For twelve hours Sadao had not been sure the General would live. The gall bladder was much involved. Then the old man had begun to breathe deeply again and to demand food. Sadao had not been able to ask about the assassins. So far as he knew they had never come. The servants had returned, and Yumi had cleaned the guest room thoroughly and had burned sulfur in it to get the white man's smell out of it. Nobody said anything. Only the gardener was cross because he had got behind with his chrysanthemums.

But after a week Sadao felt the General was well enough to be spoken to about the prisoner.

"Yes, Excellency, he escaped," Sadao now said. He coughed, signifying that he had not said all he might have said, but was unwilling to disturb the General further. But the old man opened his eyes suddenly.

"That prisoner," he said with some energy, "did I not promise you I would kill him for you?"

"You did, Excellency," Sadao said.

"Well, well!" the old man said in a tone of amazement, "so I did! But you see, I was suffering a good deal. The truth is, I thought of nothing but myself. In short, I forgot my promise to you."

"I wondered, Your Excellency," Sadao murmured.

"It was certainly very careless of me," the General said, "but you understand it was not lack of patriotism or dereliction of duty." He looked anxiously at his doctor. "If the matter should come out, you would understand that, wouldn't you?"

"Certainly, Your Excellency," Sadao said. He suddenly comprehended that the General was in the palm of his hand, and that as a consequence he himself was perfectly safe. "I can swear to your loyalty, Excellency," he said to the old General, "and to your zeal against the enemy."

"You are a good man," the General murmured and closed his eyes. "You will be rewarded."

But Sadao, searching the spot of black in the twilighted sea that night, had his reward. There was no prick of light in the dusk. No one was on the island. His prisoner was gone — safe, doubtless, for he had warned him to wait only for a Korean fishing boat.

He stood for a moment on the veranda, gazing out to the sea from where the young man had come that other night. And into his mind, although without reason, there came other white faces he had known — the professor at whose house he had met Hana, a dull man, and his wife had been a silly, talkative woman, in spite of her wish to be kind. He remembered his old teacher of anatomy, who had been so insistent on mercy with the knife, and then he remembered the face of his fat and slatternly landlady. He had had great difficulty in finding a place to live in America because he was a Japanese. The Americans were full of prejudice, and it had been bitter to live in it, knowing himself their superior. How he had despised the ignorant and dirty old woman who had at last consented to house him in her miserable home! He had once tried to be grateful to her because she had in his last year nursed him through influenza, but it was difficult, for she was no less repulsive to him in her kindness. But then, white people were repulsive, of course. It was a relief to be openly at war with them at last. Now he remembered the youthful, haggard face of his prisoner — white and repulsive.

"Strange," he thought, "I wonder why I could not kill him?"

Annie Sullivan and Dr. Sadao Hoki had time to consider their commitments carefully. Louis Slotin was a young scientist who had to make his decision in an instant.

The Strange Death of Louis Slotin

STEWART ALSOP AND RALPH E. LAPP

Dr. Louis Slotin, a young and brilliant atomic scientist, began to die at precisely twenty minutes past three o'clock on the afternoon of May 21, 1946. The story of how he began to die, and of what happened afterward — which can only now be fully told — is in some ways a rather horrible story. Yet, if only because it helps strip the mystery from the most terrifying effect of atomic weapons — the invisible killer, nuclear radiation — Louis Slotin's story is worth telling all the same.

The place where Louis Slotin began to die was a laboratory in a canyon near Los Alamos, the war-built town in New Mexico where the world's first atomic bomb was made. A few minutes after he began to die, Doctor Slotin, with the precision of a trained scientist, drew a careful chart of this laboratory, showing the exact location of its occupants at the time. From this chart, and from the accounts of those who were present and survived, it is possible to reconstruct the scene accurately.

Visualize, then, a large, oblong, white-painted room, unfurnished except for a metal desk near the center and a table against one wall, bearing the complicated equipment of the atom-bomb-maker's trade. The spring sunshine floods obliquely through the single large window. There are eight people in the room. Their silence is broken only by the staccato clicking of a Geiger counter, as all attention is focused on a short figure standing over the metal desk.

This is Louis Slotin, thirty-four years old, five feet six inches in height, slender, wiry, his face heavily bronzed by the New Mexico sun, his black hair already graying a little at the temples. He is wearing an open sports shirt, a rather gaudy Mexican belt, and khaki trousers tucked into cowboy boots. Through thick, horn-rimmed spectacles — which betray the scientist and the intellectual, despite the cowboy boots — he is peering intently at certain objects on the desk.

These are two hollow, silvery-gray half globes of metal, which Slotin is deliberately manipulating closer to each other, using an ordinary screw driver as a lever. These hunks of metal are the guts of an atomic bomb.

Standing behind Slotin is a fellow scientist — Scientist X, we shall call him — a quiet-mannered, pleasant-faced man, also thirty-four years old. Scientist X has his hand resting casually on Slotin's shoulder, and he is leaning forward with intense interest — he has never seen this experiment before.

The six other people in the room are laboratory assistants, technicians, and others gathered more or less by chance to watch the experiment. Two are standing in front of the desk, at a distance of about six feet. The four others are grouped behind the desk, at a distance of eight feet or more. The scene is a casual one. Like Slotin, the others are dressed informally, in open shirts or sweaters. Slotin himself appears confident, almost gay. He loves this experiment — "tickling the dragon's tail," he calls it — and he has already performed it at least forty times. Even so, there is a certain tension in the room. Those present are aware that manipulating the guts of an atomic bomb is no child's play.

Slotin has his ear cocked to the click of the Geiger counter, and he also glances frequently at an instrument called a "neutron monitor," which is recording on a roll of paper, in a thin, wavy line of red ink, the radiation emitted by the lumps of metal. As Slotin slowly moves the lumps, the red line staggers upward and the Geiger counter clicks erratically, always a little faster, like a deranged clock.

Suddenly the Geiger counter begins to click insanely, and then stops dead. All in a moment, the people in the room sense rather than see a strange blue glow, stronger than the spring sunlight. Instantly Slotin throws himself forward, thrusting the half globes of deadly metal apart with his naked hands. Then he stands up, his face a chalky white beneath the tan.

In a concerted, instinctive, almost somnambulistic movement, the eight people file quickly from the room, without speaking. Some of them are aware of a dry, prickly, sour sensation on their tongues — a sign of excessive radiation. Some of them are no doubt also aware of a little flicker of fear in their hearts. Yet aside from the sour taste, they feel nothing else at all — not even Louis Slotin, who has already begun to die.

To understand what happened, and why, and what it means, it is necessary to know something about Louis Slotin, and the reason he tickled the dragon's tail. The bare facts of Slotin's thirty-four years can be quickly recited.

He was born, Louis Alexander Slotin, in 1912, of prosperous Jewish parents in Winnipeg, Canada. At the tender age of fifteen, he entered Winnipeg's University of Manitoba, and received his Master of Science degree at the equally tender age of twenty-one. He studied physics for four years at the University of London, and got his Ph.D. in 1936.

In 1937 he was in Chicago, apparently on his way home to Winnipeg, when he ran into Professor William D. Harkins, pioneer atomic chemist of the University of Chicago. Harkins remarked that he badly needed an assistant for cyclotron [1] work but that he had no money to pay an assistant. Slotin immediately went to work for nothing a week — a salary for which he worked for almost two years.

His work at Chicago University led him directly into the Manhattan District, the super-secret wartime atomic project. He worked for a time in Chicago, then at Indiana University, and later at Oak Ridge. In late 1943, when the job of actually putting the atomic bomb together was started, Slotin came to Los Alamos, and there he began to tickle the dragon's tail.

So much for the bare facts. The bare facts, of course, do not answer the question: What kind of man was Louis Alexander Slotin?

---

[1] *cyclotron* (sī'klə·tron): an apparatus that whirls charged particles through a strong magnetic field to such high speeds that they can enter and change the nuclei of certain atoms.

"No man," John Donne [2] wrote, "is an island unto himself." Yet Louis Slotin was more nearly an island unto himself than most men. He was extraordinarily reserved. "Louis was a sweet kind of guy," one of his former colleagues has remarked, "but no one ever got to know him really well."

Even so, certain well-marked characteristics of the man emerge through the mists of time. In the first place, Slotin was a brave man — but brave in an odd sort of way. "Slotin had a positive hankering for danger," another of those who knew him says. "He seemed to be suffering from some sort of inner tension, and he was always very quiet. But he was downright gay when he was doing something dangerous."

This hankering for danger led Slotin to pester the Manhattan District authorities to allow him to accompany the first atomic bombs to their Japanese targets, as a scientific observer. When the authorities refused, Slotin was deeply depressed for weeks. And the same strange hankering no doubt also led Slotin to become the Manhattan District's chief practitioner of the art of tickling the dragon's tail.

This experiment, it must be understood, was not a kind of scientific Russian roulette which Slotin and the other young physicists at Los Alamos thought up to relieve their boredom. It was a vitally important experiment, absolutely essential to the bomb-making process — and, indeed, it is still essential today.

Fissionable material — uranium-238 and plutonium — is queer stuff. Below a certain size and weight, a lump of this very heavy, greasy-gray metal is no more dangerous than a lump of lead. But it has one special characteristic which may one day destroy civilization as we know it. For if a certain amount of this metal is brought together all in one place, a chain reaction starts within the mass of metal. It is the chain reaction, of course, which lends to the atomic bomb the power to blast and sear a whole city. The amount of the metal required for the chain reaction to start is called a "critical mass" — a "crit," to use the physicists' shorthand.

But how much is a crit? There were and are ways of calculating theoretically the amount of fissionable material required to form a critical mass. But such calculations can never be wholly precise. Moreover, in order to achieve "optimum efficiency" — for which

---

[2] *John Donne*: English poet and clergyman (1573–1631).

read killing power — in an atomic bomb, the size of the crit had to be determined — and still must — under various conditions.

Even today, for reasons of security, it is necessary to be a little imprecise about the experiment which Louis Slotin performed that May day in 1946 — and which his successors are still performing under very different conditions. But it can be said, accurately though unscientifically, that the idea was to shove together lumps of fissionable material in such quantities, and in such a geometric relationship to each other, that the whole amount *just* went critical. In other words, a chain reaction was permitted to begin — thus establishing the crit — but it was stopped before the material became dangerously overcritical. The problem, of course, was to know when to stop.

No one at Los Alamos had any illusions about the danger involved. There was, to be sure, no danger that Los Alamos might be blown off the face of the map if something went wrong. In order to generate true explosive power, the critical mass must somehow be held together by an outside force — this is called "maintaining assembly." Otherwise, the power of the chain reaction automatically "disassembles the crit." In the meantime, however, if a true chain reaction is permitted really to get under way, the critical mass of fissionable material becomes briefly but intensely radioactive. It sends out precisely the same lethal radioactive rays as an atomic bomb does when it explodes over a city.

Slotin in particular had good reason to be aware of this danger. Before the day when Slotin tickled the dragon's tail for the last time, at least three people at Los Alamos had fallen victim to the invisible killer. One of these was Slotin's friend and laboratory assistant, Harry Daglian. Slotin spent many hours at his assistant's bedside during the month that it took Daglian to die.

Particularly after Daglian died, those in authority at Los Alamos worried about the radiation danger. One Nobel Prize winner told Slotin, "I predict you won't last a year if you keep on doing that experiment." But Slotin happily carried on.

"Sure, it's dangerous," Slotin remarked to one colleague, "but it has to be that way." One suspects that Slotin, perhaps unconsciously, wanted it to be that way.

Ironically, on May 21, 1946, Slotin was performing his beloved experiment for what he knew to be the last time. For more than two years he had performed the experiment again and again in different ways and under various conditions. He was particularly proud of the fact that he had been chosen to test the criticality of the world's first atomic bomb — he cherished the receipt which he got for this bomb when he returned it to be exploded at Alamogordo, after having tickled its tail. Now he had been ordered to Bikini, to participate in the bomb tests there. He was eager to be off — when final orders came to perform the experiment just once more, for the benefit of Scientist X. So Slotin tickled the dragon's tail just once more — and the dragon lashed back to destroy him.

What went wrong? Part of the answer may no doubt be found in Slotin's hankering for danger — such a man may always be tempted to go too far. But part of the answer is also certainly found in the fact that Slotin, at the age of thirty-four, was already an old-fashioned scientist.

Slotin received his whole training as a physicist in the thirties, before the time when national survival depended on the special skills of his kind. It was quite typical of those days that a brilliantly qualified physicist like Slotin should work for nothing a year. In the thirties, physicists led a hand-to-mouth existence, dependent for their equipment, their experiments, and their livelihood, not on an anxious and munificent Government but on the sometimes capricious generosity of a few great universities.

In those years physicists learned to perform their experiments with whatever came to hand — even an ordinary screwdriver. This cavalier attitude carried over into the well-financed period of the Manhattan District, and men like Slotin had a certain pride in their own casual approach to the great and mysterious forces locked up in matter. After Daglian died, for example, a rather simple spring-actuated safety device was designed to push the lumps of fissionable material apart as soon as they threatened to become dangerously radioactive.

Slotin would have none of it. He had, he said proudly, "a feeling for the experiment," and besides, he argued, such devices would cause accidents rather than prevent them — the experimenter would come to rely on the safety devices rather than on his own judgment.

Certain photographs which the Atomic Energy Commission recently released provide a striking contrast between present and past.

These pictures show two insanely complicated "critical assembly machines" — one is rather coyly called "Topsy" and the other "Godiva" because the assembly is allowed to become only "barely" critical. There is another photograph, of the remote-control panel used to work these machines. It is straight out of George Orwell's *Nineteen Eighty-Four* [3] — complete with levers, knobs, three television screens, and a blonde lady in an aseptic white blouse. The blonde lady is, according to the AEC release, "controlling the assembly of Godiva" — at a distance of a quarter of a mile.

In other words, the blonde lady is manipulating the guts of an atomic bomb, just as Louis Slotin was doing that day in May when the nuclear age was still young. But in his case, the deadly stuff was right under his nose, and he had no levers, no knobs, no television screens, no remote-control panels. He had his Geiger counter, his neutron monitor, his skill and experience — and his screwdriver.

There is no doubt about what happened that day in May or about when it happened. The record of the neutron monitor which Slotin used has been preserved. A thin red-ink line mounts gradually across the paper, showing the amount of radiation emitted by the lumps of metal at each given moment. At precisely 3:20 P.M., the line simply disappears. At this precise point the radiation became so intense that the instrument was forced right off scale.

As for why it happened, no one, not even Slotin himself, was entirely sure. The experiment was almost finished — it was a matter of manipulating one last piece of metal an eighth of an inch from the rest of the assembly. "When the point of criticality was almost reached," one of those present writes, "the piece somehow slipped and the gap was closed." The "somehow" is still unexplained. But the best explanation combines the overconfidence of an overbrave man with Slotin's casual use of an ordinary screwdriver to lever the deadly hunks of metal. In a word, the screwdriver slipped.

At any rate, Slotin knew instantly what had happened, and his reaction was instantaneous. When he lunged forward and pulled the chunks of metal apart, he "disassembled the critical mass." If he had not done so, if he had instantly ducked away from the ta-

---

[3] *Nineteen Eighty-Four:* a novel that depicts the horrors of a police state, where "Big Brother" watches every move the citizens make.

ble, he might conceivably have saved himself. It is far more probable that he would have condemned others in the room to death.

"It is unquestionably true," Scientist X has written, "that I and perhaps others of those present owe our lives to his action. I do not know whether this is heroism or not. I suspect that Louis would have objected to such a term."

To understand the meaning of Slotin's action, it is necessary to understand something of the nature of the invisible killer. The gamma rays emitted by a chain reaction penetrate into the body of anyone sufficiently exposed and kill individual cells deep within the body. A grim peculiarity of radiation injury is that there is a latent period before this killing of the cells becomes apparent. This is because the cells do not die until the periodic cell division — a process which is going on all the time in everyone's body — takes place. Thus, in a sense, radiation injury is the opposite of cancer. Cancer kills when the cells divide and reproduce themselves too rapidly. Nuclear radiation kills when the cells fail to divide and do not reproduce themselves at all.

But, even more than in the case of cancer, it is important for all of us who live in the age of nuclear war to understand that nuclear radiation need not be fatal. Everything depends on the size of the "dose." The "dose" is measured in r's, or roentgens,[4] of radiation. When a person receives a radiation injury, the first thing the doctors want to know is whether he has received "LD/50." This is medical shorthand for a "median lethal dose," which causes a 50 percent average death rate.

LD/50 has never been precisely determined, simply because there have not been many human guinea pigs on whom to test the human body's resistance to radiation injury. At the time of the accident, it was thought that LD/50 was in the neighborhood of 400 roentgens. The best estimates now place LD/50 at 525 roentgens, plus or minus 75.

The number of roentgens of radiation a person receives depends principally on the power of the radiation source and the time of exposure. When Slotin lunged forward to disperse the critical assembly and break the chain reaction, he sharply reduced the danger to

---

[4] *roentgen* (rent'gən): a unit for measuring X-rays, gamma rays, etc., on the basis of their ionizing effect.

the other people in the room, by reducing both the power of the radiation and the time of exposure of the others. He also, of course, exposed himself to actual physical contact with the lumps of fissionable material at the very moment the chain reaction was taking place.

Within an hour of the accident, all the eight people in the laboratory were taken to the Los Alamos hospital — a temporary, wartime, shacklike wooden structure — and placed under close observation. Other than Scientist X, the man who had been closest to Slotin was an unmarried fifty-four-year-old technician, who was standing about six feet in front of the metal desk. He was kept in the hospital for two weeks, and he showed certain symptoms of radiation injury, including measurable radiosodium and radiophosphorus in his urine. But he felt well — and six weeks later this man, who was something of an athlete, was happily hiking six miles in one day without ill effect.

Others who were standing somewhat farther away had even less reason to complain, although everyone in the room had taken a dose of radiation. So much nonsense has been spread abroad about the silent nuclear killer that many people have come to feel that it is absolutely lethal at almost any range. Actually, the athletic technician took a dose of about 100 roentgens, according to later calculations — the same dose he would have taken if he had been wholly exposed to the radiation effect of a modern, 100-kiloton atom bomb exploding at a distance of 6,500 feet.

Despite the technician's rapid and complete recovery, a dose of 100 roentgens is no laughing matter. If he had been exposed a little longer — if Slotin had not reacted so quickly — the technician would certainly have suffered as Scientist X suffered — and he might well have died.

Scientist X, remember, was standing with his hand on Louis Slotin's shoulder, watching intently the experiment which he himself would have to perform later, when the accident happened. According to later calculations, he took a dose of about 180 roentgens. This is still well under LD/50, but it is nevertheless in the danger area. It is the same dose he would have taken if he had been about 6,000 feet from a modern atomic bomb, only a few hundred feet less than the athletic technician. Where nuclear radiation is concerned, short distances can make an enormous difference.

A courageous and unexcitable man by nature, Scientist X was calm and made no complaints when he was admitted to the hospital. Shortly after being admitted, he vomited once. The feeling of nausea passed away in about ten hours, leaving Scientist X feeling weak and tired, with little appetite, but otherwise well enough. He continued thus for about five days. On the fifth day, the delayed effect of the gamma rays on his cell tissue began to make itself felt. His temperature climbed close to 103 degrees, and two blood transfusions were required. For some time he felt terribly drowsy and highly irritable, but his temperature fell gradually, and after the fifteenth day he was well enough to be sent home to rest.

But the gamma rays were not yet through with him. He had lost ten pounds, and for some weeks he tired very easily and spent upward of sixteen hours in bed each day. On the seventeenth day after the accident, an unpleasant experience, which Scientist X had known enough to expect, began. On that day the skin on his left temple and on the left side of his head — which had been most exposed — began to feel sensitive. In the two following days this sensitive feeling increased to the point of acute pain. On the twentieth day Scientist X was combing his hair and found large tufts coming out in the comb.

Thereafter, his hair came out easily by the handful. He lost almost all the hair on the left side of his head, and his beard also stopped growing over most of his left cheek. But the point to emphasize is that such symptoms were wholly temporary.

The only permanent aftereffect which Scientist X has suffered is a moderate radiation cataract in the left eye, which reduces his vision from 20/20 to 20/40. The fact that he has suffered no other ill effect is underscored by his brilliant subsequent contributions to our atomic-energy program, notably in the development of that most terrible of weapons, the hydrogen bomb.

In short, a man can survive even a vicious attack by the silent radiation killer on his living cell tissue. But Scientist X unquestionably had a close brush with death. Of Louis Slotin, to whom, as he says, he owes his life, Scientist X has written:

"I can perhaps tell you as much about his personality and character as I could in very many words if I merely quote to you his first statement to me when we were alone together in a hospital room. He said, 'I'm sorry I got you into this. I am afraid I have less than a fifty-fifty chance of living. I hope you have better than that.' My own estimate of our chances coincided pretty well with his. I felt I had a pretty good chance. I only hoped he had."

For some days there seemed reason for hope. Slotin vomited twice before he got to the hospital, and in the first twelve hours thereafter he continued to vomit repeatedly. But he, too, like Scientist X, recovered from his initial nausea, and his only other immediate general symptoms were a slight temperature and feeling of tiredness.

His hands, of course, had taken a terrible dose, since he had used them to shove the metal apart and break the chain reaction. Within three hours Slotin's left hand became very red, swollen, and bluish under the nails. Twenty-eight hours after the accident this hand began to blister painfully, and the symptoms spread to his right hand and both arms. From this time on, both arms were packed in ice, to reduce the swelling and the pain. His lower abdomen also became red and tender, and this spread gradually and became more intense.

Yet aside from these local symptoms, Slotin's general condition seemed greatly to improve after the first twenty-four hours. What had happened quickly became known throughout the Manhattan District, and everything possible was done to help him. No fewer than ten doctors were called in to consult on his case. Major General Leslie Groves wrote to him: "I have nothing but admiration for your heroic action. . . . Your quick reaction and disregard for the danger to yourself undoubtedly prevented a much more serious accident."

Groves's letter cheered Slotin, and he was cheered more when Groves ordered a special Army plane to bring his mother and father from Winnipeg to his bedside. When they arrived, they found their son normal, composed, and even downright cheerful, despite the pain in his arms. When friends and colleagues came to visit him, he would introduce them to his parents, and then ask, half jokingly, the crucial question: "Well, what's the dose?"

For five days no one knew. But on the fifth day, the answer became tragically obvious — the dose was more than LD/50. That morning Slotin had a new complaint — his tongue was sore opposite a tooth which had a gold inlay. The doctors found a small whitish ulceration on his tongue and immediately suspected the cause. The gold in his tooth was heavily radioactive. The inlay was capped with gold foil and the pain eased. But this was a bad sign.

There was a worse sign on the same day, when Anna May Dickey, then a nurse in the Los Alamos hospital, took Slotin's blood count. When she looked at the results, she began to weep. She knew the meaning of the sudden, precipitous fall in the leucocyte,[5] or white blood cell, count. The silent killer was at work on Louis Slotin's blood: the lifesaving white cells were failing to reproduce themselves.

On this same day Slotin's pulse rate rose very rapidly. Thereafter he could eat nothing and visibly lost weight. On the seventh day, his mind began to fail, and he had long periods of mental confusion, in which he could not recognize his parents or colleagues. Gradually, he sank into a coma. Early in the morning of the ninth day, May 30, 1946, Louis Slotin quietly died.

That is about the end of Louis Slotin's story. His parents flew back to Winnipeg with his corpse, and scientists and others from all over the United States and Canada attended his funeral. His parents offered a last sacrifice to the cause of science, when they permitted an autopsy to be performed on his body, although this was against the tenets of their religion. It was later estimated, according to the Atomic Energy Commission's recently declassified report on his case, that Slotin had taken about 880 roentgens of nuclear radiation. This was as though he had been fully exposed to the explosion of a modern atomic bomb at a distance of 4,800 feet. Nothing could have saved him.

Louis Slotin was not a great or famous man, and he has been in his grave now for years. Yet his story has seemed worth telling, and not only because nuclear radiation, which kills without being seen or felt, is more terrifying than need be, just because it is so mysterious. It has seemed worth telling also because it is a story of human bravery and sacrifice, qualities which may yet save a civilization threatened by the very weapons Louis Slotin helped to make.

---

[5] *leucocyte* (loo'kə·sīt).

A parable is a short fictional narrative, often told by a sage or religious leader, which clearly teaches a moral lesson or states a universal truth. This biblical parable fits its moral so well that the term "Good Samaritan" is still applied to someone who unselfishly helps another.

The Good Samaritan

And, behold, a certain lawyer stood up, and tempted him, saying Master, what shall I do to inherit eternal life?

He said unto him, What is written in the law? How readest thou?

And he answering said, Thou shalt love the Lord thy God with all thy heart, and with all thy soul, and with all thy strength, and with all thy mind; and thy neighbor as thyself.

And he said unto him, Thou hast answered right: this do, and thou shalt live.

But he, willing to justify himself, said unto Jesus, And who is my neighbor? And Jesus answering said:

A certain man went down from Jerusalem to Jericho, and fell among thieves, who stripped him of his raiment, and wounded him, and departed, leaving him half dead.

And by chance there came down a certain priest that way: and when he saw him, he passed by on the other side.

And likewise a Levite, when he was at the place, came and looked on him, and passed by on the other side.

But a certain Samaritan, as he journeyed, came where he was: and when he saw him, he had compassion on him; and went to him, and bound up his wounds, pouring in oil and wine, and set him on his own beast, and brought him to an inn, and took care of him.

And on the morrow when he departed, he took out two pence, and gave them to the host, and said unto him, Take care of him; and whatsoever thou spendest more, when I come again, I will repay thee.

Which now of these three, thinkest thou, was neighbor unto him that fell among the thieves?

And he said, He that showed mercy on him.

Then Jesus said unto him, Go and do thou likewise.

The following story — almost, but not quite, a fable — is by a Norwegian writer who won the Nobel Prize for Literature. Björnson looks at the theme of commitment to others in a harsher, more tragic light than do the other writers in this section.

A Father

BJÖRNSTERNE BJÖRNSON

The man whose story is here to be told was the wealthiest and most influential person in his parish; his name was Thord Overaas. He appeared in the priest's study one day, tall and earnest.

"I have a new son," said he, "and I wish to present him for baptism."

"What shall his name be?"

"Finn — after my father."

"And the sponsors?"

They were mentioned and proved to be the richest men and women of Thord's relations in the parish.

"Is there anything else?" inquired the priest, and looked up.

The peasant hesitated a little.

"I should like very much to have him baptized by himself," said he, finally, "and not with other children."

"That is to say on a weekday?" [1]

"Next Saturday at twelve o'clock noon."

"Is there anything else?" inquired the priest.

"There is nothing else." And the peasant twirled his cap as though he were about to go.

Then the priest rose. "There is yet this, however," said he, and walking toward Thord, he took him by the hand and looked gravely into his eyes: "God grant that the child may become a blessing to you!"

---

[1] *weekday*: that is, not on a Sunday, when the children of other families would be baptized.

One day sixteen years later, Thord stood once more in the priest's study.

"Really, you carry your age astonishingly well, Thord," said the priest; for he saw no change whatever in the man.

"That is because I have no troubles," replied Thord.

To this the priest said nothing, but after a while he asked: "What is your pleasure this evening?"

"I have come this evening about that son of mine who is to be confirmed tomorrow."

"He is a bright boy."

"I did not wish to pay the priest until I heard what number the boy would have when he takes his place in church tomorrow."

"He will stand number one — in front of all the others."

"Now I have heard; and here are ten dollars for the priest."

"Is there anything else I can do for you?" inquired the priest, fixing his eyes on Thord.

"There is nothing else."

Thord went out.

Eight years more rolled by, and then one day a noise was heard outside the priest's study, for many men were approaching, and at their head was Thord, who entered first.

The priest looked up and recognized him.

"You come well attended this evening, Thord," said he.

"I am here to request that the banns may be published for my son; he is about to marry Karen Storliden, daughter of Gudmund, who stands here beside me."

"Why, that is the richest girl in the parish."

"So they say," replied the peasant, stroking back his hair with one hand.

The priest sat a while as if in deep thought, then entered the names in his book, without making any comments, and the men wrote their signatures underneath. Thord laid three dollars on the table.

"One is all I am to have," said the priest.

"I know that very well, but he is my only child. I want to do it handsomely."

The priest took the money.

"This is now the third time, Thord, that you have come here on your son's account."

"But now I am through with him," said Thord, and, folding up his pocketbook, he said farewell and walked away.

The men slowly followed him.

Two weeks later, the father and son were rowing across the lake, one calm, still day, to Storliden to make arrangements for the wedding.

"This board is not secure," said the son, and stood up to straighten the seat on which he was sitting.

At the same moment the board he was standing on slipped from under him; he threw out his arms, uttered a shriek, and fell overboard.

"Take hold of the oar!" shouted the father, springing to his feet and holding out the oar.

But when the son had made a couple of efforts, he grew stiff.

"Wait a moment!" cried the father, and began to row toward his son. Then the son rolled over on his back, gave his father one long look, and sank.

Thord could scarcely believe it; he held the boat still, and stared at the spot where his son had gone down, as though he must surely come to the surface again. There rose some bubbles, then some more, and finally one large one that burst; and the lake lay there as smooth and bright as a mirror again.

For three days and three nights people saw the father rowing around and around the spot, without taking either food or sleep; he was dragging the lake for the body of his son. And toward the morning of the third day he found it, and carried it in his arms up over the hills to his farm.

It might have been about a year from that day, when the priest, late one autumn evening, heard someone in the passage outside the door, carefully trying to find the latch. The priest opened the door, and in walked a tall, thin man, with bowed form and white hair. The priest looked long at him before he recognized him. It was Thord.

"Are you out walking so late?" said the priest, and stood still in front of him.

"Ah, yes! it is late," said Thord, and took a seat.

The priest sat down also, as though waiting. A long, long silence followed. At last Thord said: "I have something with me that I should like to give to the poor; I want it to be invested as a legacy in my son's name."

He rose, laid some money on the table, and sat down again. The priest counted it.

"It is a great deal of money," said he.

"It is half the price of my farm. I sold it today."

The priest sat long in silence. At last he said, but gently: "What do you propose to do now, Thord?"

"Something better."

They sat there for a while, Thord with downcast eyes, the priest with his eyes fixed on Thord. Presently the priest said slowly and softly: "I think your son has at last brought you a true blessing."

"Yes, I think so myself," said Thord, looking up, while two big tears coursed slowly down his cheeks.

Thank You, M'am

LANGSTON HUGHES

She was a large woman with a large purse that had everything in it but a hammer and nails. It had a long strap, and she carried it slung across her shoulder. It was about eleven o'clock at night, dark, and she was walking alone, when a boy ran up behind her and tried to snatch her purse. The strap broke with the sudden single tug the boy gave it from behind. But the boy's weight and the weight of the purse combined caused him to lose his balance. Instead of taking off full blast as he had hoped, the boy fell on his back on the sidewalk and his legs flew up. The large woman simply turned around and kicked him right square in his blue-jeaned sitter. Then she reached down, picked the boy up by his shirt front, and shook him until his teeth rattled.

After that the woman said, "Pick up my pocketbook, boy, and give it here."

She still held him tightly. But she bent down enough to permit him to stoop and pick up her purse. Then she said, "Now ain't you ashamed of yourself?"

Firmly gripped by his shirt front, the boy said, "Yes'm."

The woman said, "What did you want to do it for?"

The boy said, "I didn't aim to."

She said, "You a lie!"

By that time two or three people passed, stopped, turned to look, and some stood watching.

"If I turn you loose, will you run?" asked the woman.

"Yes'm," said the boy.

"Then I won't turn you loose," said the woman. She did not release him.

"Lady, I'm sorry," whispered the boy.

"Um-hum! Your face is dirty. I got a great mind to wash your face for you. Ain't you got nobody home to tell you to wash your face?"

"No'm," said the boy.

"Then it will get washed this evening," said the large woman, starting up the street, dragging the frightened boy behind her.

He looked as if he were fourteen or fifteen, frail and willow-wild, in tennis shoes and blue jeans.

The woman said, "You ought to be my son. I would teach you right from wrong. Least I can do right now is to wash your face. Are you hungry?"

"No'm," said the being-dragged boy. "I just want you to turn me loose."

"Was I bothering *you* when I turned that corner?" asked the woman.

"No'm."

"But you put yourself in contact with *me*," said the woman. "If you think that that contact is not going to last awhile, you got another thought coming. When I get through with you, sir, you are going to remember Mrs. Luella Bates Washington Jones."

Sweat popped out on the boy's face and he began to struggle. Mrs. Jones stopped, jerked him around in front of her, put a half nelson about his neck, and continued to drag him up the street. When she got to her door, she dragged the boy inside, down a hall, and into a large kitchenette-furnished room at the rear of the house. She switched on the light and left the door open. The boy could hear other roomers laughing and talking in the large house. Some of their doors were open, too, so he knew he and the woman were not alone. The woman still had him by the neck in the middle of her room.

She said, "What is your name?"

"Roger," answered the boy.

"Then, Roger, you go to that sink and wash your face," said the woman, whereupon she turned him loose — at last. Roger looked at the door — looked at the woman — looked at the door — *and went to the sink.*

"Let the water run until it gets warm," she said. "Here's a clean towel."

"You gonna take me to jail?" asked the boy, bending over the sink.

"Not with that face, I would not take you nowhere," said the woman. "Here I am trying to get home to cook me a bite to eat, and you snatch my pocketbook! Maybe you ain't been to your supper either, late as it be. Have you?"

"There's nobody home at my house," said the boy.

"Then we'll eat," said the woman. "I believe you're hungry — or been hungry — to try to snatch my pocketbook!"

"I want a pair of blue suede shoes," said the boy.

"Well, you didn't have to snatch *my* pocketbook to get some suede shoes," said Mrs. Luella Bates Washington Jones. "You could've asked me."

"M'am?"

The water dripping from his face, the boy looked at her. There was a long pause. A very long pause. After he had dried his face, and not knowing what else to do, dried it again, the boy turned around, wondering what next. The door was open. He could make a dash for it down the hall. He could run, run, run, *run!*

The woman was sitting on the daybed. After a while she said, "I were young once and I wanted things I could not get."

There was another long pause. The boy's mouth opened. Then he frowned, not knowing he frowned.

The woman said, "Um-hum! You thought I was going to say *but,* didn't you? You thought I was going to say, *but I didn't snatch people's pocketbooks.* Well, I wasn't going to say that." Pause. Silence. "I have done things, too, which I would not tell you, son — neither tell God, if he didn't already know. Everybody's got something in common. So you set down while I fix us something to eat. You might run that comb through your hair so you will look presentable."

In another corner of the room, behind a screen, was a gas plate and an icebox. Mrs. Jones got up and went behind the screen. The woman did not watch the boy to see if he was going to run now, nor did she watch her purse, which she left behind her on the daybed. But the boy took care to sit on the far side of the room, away from the purse, where he thought she could easily see him out of the corner of her eye if she wanted to. He did not trust the woman *not* to trust him. And he did not want to be mistrusted now.

"Do you need somebody to go to the store," asked the boy, "maybe to get some milk or something?"

"Don't believe I do," said the woman, "unless you just want sweet milk yourself. I was going to make cocoa out of this canned milk I got here."

"That will be fine," said the boy.

She heated some lima beans and ham she had in the icebox, made the cocoa, and set the table. The woman did not ask the boy anything about where he lived, or his folks, or anything else that would embarrass him. Instead, as they ate, she told him about her job in a hotel beauty shop that stayed open late, what the work was like, and how all kinds of women came in and out, blondes, redheads, and Spanish. Then she cut him a half of her ten-cent cake.

"Eat some more, son," she said.

When they were finished eating, she got up and said, "Now here, take this ten dollars and buy yourself some blue suede shoes. And next time, do not make the mistake of latching onto *my* pocketbook *nor nobody else's* — because shoes got by devilish ways will burn your feet. I got to get my rest now. But from here on in, son, I hope you will behave yourself."

She led him down the hall to the front door and opened it. "Good night! Behave yourself, boy!" she said, looking out into the street as he went down the steps.

The boy wanted to say something other than, "Thank you, m'am," to Mrs. Luella Bates Washington Jones, but although his lips moved, he couldn't even say that as he turned at the foot of the barren stoop and looked up at the large woman in the door. Then she shut the door.

Playwright Arthur Miller (seated) and members of the cast watch actor Jason Robards, Jr. and director Elia Kazan rehearse a scene from Miller's play After the Fall.

BOOK TWO | PART 3

THE PLAYWRIGHT AT WORK

The theater partakes of the nature of festival. Life imitated is life raised to a higher power.
            Thornton Wilder

In the introduction to The Miracle Worker, you were asked to create a theater in your imagination, to see the actors as they moved around on the stage, to hear the sounds of their voices. This section, The Playwright at Work, looks at the problems that face a writer for the theater. Here, you will be asked to think about some of the things that go into the making of a play.

TWO KINDS OF INVOLVEMENT

There is no drama if you — as reader or member of an audience — do not become involved with the action. As you watch a play or a movie or a television drama, two things happen at once: you respond to the action of the play itself, and you respond to the play as a work of art. For example, imagine that the hero of a melodrama is about to be pushed out of a window. There is double involvement on the part of the audience: They become tense as they share the hero's danger; at the same time they know that they are only watching an actor who — even if he does fall from the window — will reappear for a curtain call at the end of the play.

This is a crude example of drama, but it serves to make a point. At this moment of danger, the members of the audience are at once afraid and not afraid for the hero-actor. The reason is that the play itself is not an action but a representation of an action. The theater — like all forms of literature — is a kind of illusion to which we willingly submit. We may know from the newspapers that a certain actress is bad-tempered, but in the theater we are willing to believe for a while that she is beautiful, noble, and kind. One of the leading modern directors, Tyrone Guthrie, has written:

> Action on the stage is a stylized re-enactment of real action, which is then imagined by the audience. The re-enactment is not merely an imitation but a symbol of the real thing.

The drama had its beginnings in primitive rituals in which there was no clear distinction between the actors and the audience. Later, when men began to write plays to be performed by trained actors, the audience merely sat back and watched. In recent years some playwrights have tried to re-establish a close contact between the actors and the audience. They have used such devices as having the actors speak directly to the audience and even having the audience participate in the action. The modern theater tends to emphasize the fact that a play is not a segment of real life, but the illusion of life.

The Miracle Worker *has its comic moments and a happy ending, but it is not a comedy. It is a serious drama with a serious theme. The following short play by the Russian playwright Anton Chekhov, however, is pure comedy through and through. Though you may not laugh out loud as you read it, you probably would if you saw a good production of it in a theater.* The Marriage Proposal *is a comedy because of the attitude Chekhov takes toward his characters. He wants to amuse the audience by exaggerating certain human foibles. No life-or-death issue hangs in the balance: the characters take themselves* seriously *and get into battles, but all the time the reader knows that no harm is going to come to anyone.*

The Marriage Proposal *is a kind of light comedy called* farce. *The situations are exaggerated, the characters are one-dimensional, and their motivations are not always realistic. This play is not typical of the more serious comedies for which Chekhov is famous, such as* The Cherry Orchard *and* The Three Sisters. *Chekhov himself called his short plays, like* The Marriage Proposal, *"jokes."*

The Marriage Proposal

ANTON CHEKHOV

CHARACTERS

CHUBUKOV (choo′boo′kof), a landowner
NATALIA (nə·täl′yə), his daughter, twenty-five years old
LOMOV (lom′of), a young man, their neighbor

The action takes place in a room in Chubukov's country house.

[CHUBUKOV *greets* LOMOV, *who enters wearing a formal suit and white gloves.*]

CHUBUKOV (*going toward him*) Well, look who's here! My dear Lomov! I'm so glad! (*They shake hands.*) This is a real surprise. How are you?
LOMOV Very well, thank you. How are you?
CHUBUKOV Getting by, my dear boy, getting by. Such a long time

since we've seen you. One shouldn't neglect one's neighbors. But, dear friend, why all this ceremony? You come here wearing a formal suit and gloves. Are you on your way to visit someone?

LOMOV No, I have come to visit you.

CHUBUKOV Then why the formal clothes? As if this were a New Year's visit.

LOMOV Well, I'll tell you. (*Takes* CHUBUKOV *by the hand.*) I have come to ask you a favor. Many times in the past I have asked you for help, and you have always . . . Excuse me, I'm nervous. May I have a drink of water? (*He takes a drink of water.*)

CHUBUKOV (*aside*) He wants to borrow money. I won't give him any! (*to* LOMOV) Well, my friend, what's the matter?

LOMOV I'm so nervous . . . you can see how nervous I am. . . . Let me get to the point: You are the only person who can help me. Of course I don't deserve your help. I have no reason to count on your help. . . .

CHUBUKOV Please don't beat around the bush! Go ahead, tell me.

LOMOV Immediately. In a minute. (*Suddenly*) I have come to ask for the hand in marriage of your daughter, Natalia.

CHUBUKOV (*delighted*) My dear Ivan! Say it again! I'm not sure I heard you. . . .

LOMOV I have come to ask for the hand. . . .

CHUBUKOV (*interrupting him*) My dear boy! I am so happy — and all that. (*Hugs him.*) I have been waiting for this for a long time. (*He begins to cry a bit.*) I have always loved you like a son. May God give you both love and blessings and all that. Yes, I have always wanted this to happen. . . . But why am I standing here like an idiot? I'm so happy I can't talk. Oh, from the depths of my soul . . . Well, I had better go and call Natalia.

LOMOV (*touched*) My friend, what do you think? Will she accept me?

CHUBUKOV Such a handsome boy and you wonder if she'll accept you? Why, she's probably in love with you like a little cat. I'll be right back. (*He goes out.*)

LOMOV (*to himself*) It's cold in here. I'm shaking just as if I were going to take an examination in school. The important thing is to make up your mind. If you wait forever to find an ideal true love — well, you'll never get married. Brr! It's cold in here. Natalia is an excellent housekeeper, not bad-looking, well-educated

— what else do I need? Oh, I'm so excited that my ears are roaring. (*Takes a drink of water.*) And I really have to get married. In the first place, I'm already thirty-five years old. You might call it a critical age. In the second place, I must have a nice, orderly life. I have a heart condition, constant palpitations. And I have a quick temper and am extremely nervous. Look at me! Right now my lips are trembling and my right eyelid is twitching. But worst of all is my sleep. As soon as I go to bed, and I'm just about to fall asleep, something begins to twitch in my left side. Then it goes into my shoulder and up into my head. I jump out of bed like a crazy man. I walk around for a while and then go back to bed. But as soon as I begin to fall asleep there it is again — twitch! And sometimes this happens twenty times a night. . . .

NATALIA (*entering*) Ah, it's you! And Father told me there was a man here trying to sell something. Good afternoon.

LOMOV Good afternoon, Natalia.

NATALIA Excuse me for wearing this apron and this old house dress . . . we've been shelling peas in the kitchen. Have you been here long? Please sit down. (*They sit down.*) Would you like something to eat?

LOMOV No, thank you. I have eaten.

NATALIA Smoke if you wish . . . here are some matches. The weather is so nice today; yesterday it rained so much that the farmhands could do nothing all day long. How many haystacks have you cut over at your place? Imagine! I was so greedy that I had them cut a whole field of hay, and now I'm afraid it may rot. I should have waited. But what's going on? Why are you all dressed up? I've never seen you like this. Are you going to a dance? My, you look so much better. . . . Really, why are you all dressed up?

LOMOV (*nervous*) You see, my dear Natalia . . . what I mean is that I have decided to ask you to listen to me. . . . Of course you will be surprised. You may even be angry, but I . . . (*Aside*) It's so cold!

NATALIA Yes, what is it? (*Pause*) Well?

LOMOV I will try to be short. Natalia Stepanovna, you are aware that I have for a long time — in fact since I was a little boy — that I have had the honor of knowing your family. My late aunt and her husband, from whom I have inherited my land, always respected your father and your late mother. The Lomovs and the Chubukovs have always been on friendly terms. You might even say they have been close. In addition, as you know, my farm is right next to yours. You know that my meadows go right up to your woods.

NATALIA I'm sorry, but I have to interrupt you. You said *my meadows*, but *are* they your meadows?

LOMOV Of course they are mine.

NATALIA Come now! The meadows are ours, not yours.

LOMOV No, they are mine, Natalia.

NATALIA This is news to me. How can they be yours?

LOMOV What do you mean how can they be mine? I am talking about the meadows that run between your woods and my swamp.

NATALIA That's right, that's right. Those meadows are ours.

LOMOV No, you are mistaken, Natalia, they are mine.

NATALIA Please don't get excited! How long have the meadows been yours?

LOMOV How long? As long as I can remember. They have always been ours.

NATALIA I'm sorry, I have to disagree with you there.

LOMOV It's all very clear if you just look into the records, Natalia. It is true that a long time ago there was some disagreement about who owned the meadows. But now everyone knows they are mine. There is no room for argument. What happened was that for a while my aunt's grandmother gave these meadows rent-free to some peasants who worked for your father's grandfather. They were making bricks for her. Now these peasants, who worked for your father's grandfather, used these meadows without paying rent on them for about forty years. And so they came to think that the meadows were theirs. But later on . . .

NATALIA That is not what happened! Both my grandfather and my great-grandfather always claimed that their land ran right up to the swamp. So the meadows are ours. What is there to argue about? I don't understand. This is annoying!

LOMOV I will show you the papers, Natalia. . . .

NATALIA No, you are joking or trying to make me angry. Well, what a surprise! We own a piece of land for three hundred years and suddenly someone comes in and says it is not ours. I can't believe my ears. I don't really care about these meadows at all. They don't amount to five acres and they aren't worth anything. But the injustice! Say whatever you want to, but there's one thing I cannot tolerate, and that is injustice.

LOMOV Listen to me, please! Your father's grandfather's peasants were making bricks for my aunt's grandmother. My aunt's grandmother wanted to be nice to them. . . .

NATALIA Grandmother! Grandfather! Aunt! I don't know what you're talking about. The meadows are ours and that's all there is to it!

LOMOV No, they are mine!

NATALIA They are ours! You can deny it forever. You can come in here wearing two dress suits. But the meadows are ours, ours, ours! That's all!

LOMOV My dear Natalia, I do not need the meadows. Yes, there is a question of principle involved, but if you wish I will *give* you the meadows!

NATALIA I am the one who can give them to *you!* They are mine! All this is very strange. Until now we have always thought of you as a good neighbor, a friend. Last year we let you borrow our threshing machine, and so we had to wait to thresh our own fields until November. Now you treat us as if we were gypsies. You have the nerve to give me my own land! I beg your pardon, but this is not proper behavior for a neighbor. In fact, it is very rude. Speaking frankly . . .

LOMOV Do you mean that I am some sort of thief? My dear lady, I have never taken other people's property, and I will not allow anyone to accuse me of such a thing. . . . (*Walks quickly over to the pitcher and takes a drink of water.*) The meadows are mine!

NATALIA Not true! They are ours!

LOMOV They are mine!

NATALIA A lie! I'll prove it to you! I'll send my farmhands over to the meadows today!

LOMOV What?

NATALIA I said I'll send my farmhands into the meadows today to start mowing.

LOMOV I shall chase them out!

NATALIA You won't dare to!

LOMOV (*putting his hand to his left side*) The meadows are mine!

Do you understand? Mine!

NATALIA Please don't shout. You may scream and shout in your own house, but when you are here please behave yourself.

LOMOV My dear lady, if my heart weren't hammering on my side, if the arteries in my head weren't about to burst, believe me I would speak to you in a very different way! (*He shouts.*) The meadows are mine!

NATALIA Ours!

LOMOV Mine!

CHUBUKOV (*entering*) What's going on here? Why are you shouting?

NATALIA Father, please explain to this gentleman who owns the meadows. Are they ours or his?

CHUBUKOV (*to* LOMOV) My friend, the meadows are ours.

LOMOV Good heavens, how can they be yours? I would have thought that you at least would be reasonable. My aunt's grandmother allowed your grandfather's peasants to use the meadows for a while free of cost. The peasants used the land for forty years as if it were theirs. They got used to it, but when . . .

CHUBUKOV Allow me to speak, my dear boy. You forget that the very reason why the peasants paid nothing to your grandmother and blah! blah! blah! is precisely because there was a question about who owned the land. But today, even dogs know that the meadows are ours. I gather that you have not seen the maps.

LOMOV I will prove to you that they are mine!

CHUBUKOV But you can't prove it, my friend.

LOMOV Yes, I'll prove it!

CHUBUKOV My friend, why are you shouting? You can't prove anything by shouting. I don't want anything that belongs to you, but at the same time I have no intention of giving up what is mine! Why should I? If it comes to this, my friend, I would rather give those meadows to the peasants than to you. That's how I feel.

LOMOV I don't see how you have the right to give away anything that does not belong to you.

CHUBUKOV Let me decide what rights I have and do not have! To be blunt, young man, I am not used to being spoken to this way. In fact, I am old enough to be your father, and I expect to be spoken to with respect, and all that.

LOMOV You must really think I am a fool. You are trying to make

fun of me! You call my land yours, and you want me to be calm and to speak to you with respect! This is not the way a good neighbor behaves! You are not a neighbor, you are a thief!
CHUBUKOV What? What did you say?
NATALIA Father, send our mowers into the meadows this minute!
CHUBUKOV (*to* LOMOV) What? What did you say, sir?
NATALIA The meadows are ours and I won't, won't, won't give them up.
CHUBUKOV Go to court! Sue me if you wish, sir! You have my permission! I know your kind, just waiting for an excuse to sue me. A cheap trickster! Your family has always been like this!
LOMOV I refuse to let you insult my family! All the Lomovs have been honest. None of them were dragged into court for stealing the way your uncle was!
CHUBUKOV The whole Lomov family was insane.
NATALIA All of them, all of them, all of them!
CHUBUKOV (*to* LOMOV) Your grandfather was a drunk. Your aunt — listen to this, Natalia — your aunt ran away with an architect, and so on. . . .
LOMOV And your mother was ugly. (*Puts his hand over his heart.*) Oh, I have a pain in my side . . . I have a headache . . . water!
CHUBUKOV Your father was a fat gambler.
NATALIA And your aunt gossiped about people.
LOMOV My left leg is numb. . . . You are . . . you are . . . oh, my heart! . . . And everyone knows that before the elections you . . . Oh, I can't see . . . where is my hat?
NATALIA You are low. You are dishonest. You are ugly.
CHUBUKOV You are a false, mean person. You really are.
LOMOV My hat . . . here it is. Oh, my heart. How can I get out? Where is the door? Oh, I think I'm dying. I can hardly walk. . . . (*He heads toward the door.*)
CHUBUKOV I don't want you ever to come to my house again!
NATALIA Sue us! Go ahead! We'll see who is right.

[LOMOV *staggers out the door.*]

CHUBUKOV Let him go. (*He walks around the room in excitement.*)
NATALIA He's good for nothing. You can't even trust your neighbors.
CHUBUKOV The man is a scoundrel.
NATALIA A monster. Took a piece of property that doesn't belong to

him and then has the nerve to argue about it.

CHUBUKOV And this good-for-nothing, this fool, dares to come here with a proposal. Imagine! A proposal!

NATALIA What kind of proposal?

CHUBUKOV Why, a marriage proposal. He came here to ask you to marry him.

NATALIA Me? To propose marriage? Why didn't you tell me sooner?

CHUBUKOV That's why he was all dressed up. The fool!

NATALIA Me? He wanted to marry me? Oh! (*She falls back into a chair and begins to moan.*) Bring him back! Bring him back! Oh, bring him back!

CHUBUKOV Bring who back?

NATALIA Hurry! Hurry! I'm going to faint. Bring him back! (*She is getting hysterical.*)

CHUBUKOV What is this? What's the matter with you? (*Puts his hand to his head.*) Lord, what luck! I'll shoot myself. You're driving me crazy!

NATALIA I am dying. Bring him back!

CHUBUKOV Yes, yes, in a minute. Stop crying. (*He runs out.*)

NATALIA (*alone*) What have we done? Bring him back!

CHUBUKOV (*runs back in*) He'll be back in a minute. Really, what nonsense. You'll have to speak to him yourself. I can't.

NATALIA Where is he?

CHUBUKOV (*shouting*) I told you he's coming! Good Lord, what a job being the father of a grown-up daughter! I will cut my throat. We've screamed at this man, insulted him, thrown him out of the house. It is your fault!

NATALIA No, it is your fault.

CHUBUKOV (*ironically*) Oh yes, it has to be my fault, doesn't it?

[LOMOV *enters.*]

CHUBUKOV (*to* NATALIA) All right, talk to him. (*He leaves.*)

LOMOV (*exhausted*) My heart is fluttering . . . my leg is numb . . . I have a twitch in my side. . . .

NATALIA You must forgive us, Ivan. We let ourselves get excited. But I remember now, the meadows are yours.

LOMOV My heart is just thumping away! My meadows . . . my eyelids are twitching. . . .

NATALIA The meadows are yours, they are yours. Please sit down. (LOMOV *sits*) We were wrong.

LOMOV It was the principle that was at stake. . . . I don't care about the land, it was a matter of principle.
NATALIA You're right, the principle! But let's talk about something else.
LOMOV Especially since I have the proof. My aunt's grandmother gave your father's grandfather's peasants . . .
NATALIA Oh, that's enough about the meadows. (*Aside*) I don't know where to begin. (*To* LOMOV) Are you going hunting soon?
LOMOV Yes, hunting for birds. I'll go as soon as the harvest is over. And did you hear what happened? Such bad luck! My dog, Uggy, is lame!
NATALIA Oh, what a pity! How did that happen?
LOMOV I don't know. He must have twisted it, or another dog may have bit him. (*Sighs.*) He's the best dog in the world, to say nothing of the money he's worth. I paid a hundred and twenty-five rubles for that dog.
NATALIA You paid too much, Ivan!
LOMOV Oh, no, it was very cheap. He's a wonderful dog.
NATALIA Father paid only eighty-five for his Okky, and Okky is, after all, a better dog than your Uggy.
LOMOV Okky better than Uggy? Impossible! (*He laughs.*) Okky is better than Uggy!
NATALIA Of course he's better. It's true that Okky is still just a puppy. But out on the hunt there isn't a better dog.
LOMOV Excuse me, Natalia. You forget that Okky has a short lower jaw, and a dog with a short lower jaw cannot snap.
NATALIA A short lower jaw? This is the first time I've heard it!
LOMOV I assure you: his lower jaw is shorter than his upper jaw.
NATALIA Have you measured it?
LOMOV As a matter of fact, I have. Of course he runs well. . . .
NATALIA First of all, our Okky is a thoroughbred. He has blue blood. Your dog is a mongrel. No one knows who his parents were . . . and he is old and ugly.
LOMOV He is old, but I wouldn't take five of your Okkys for him. How could I? Uggy is a dog, and your Okky . . . Well, it's silly to argue about it. Dogs like yours can be found by the dozen in any pet shop.
NATALIA You seem to insist on contradicting everything today, don't you? First you invented a story about the meadows being yours. Now you say that Uggy is better than Okky. I don't like it when

a man says something that he doesn't mean. You know very well that Okky is better than your . . . silly old Uggy. Why do you deny it?

LOMOV Why are you shouting, my dear lady?

NATALIA Why are you talking nonsense? Your dog is about ready to be shot and put out of his misery, and you compare him with Okky!

LOMOV I can't go on with this discussion. I have a bad heart.

NATALIA I have noticed that the worst hunters argue the most.

LOMOV My dear lady, I beg you to be quiet. . . . My heart is going to burst. . . . (*Shouting*) Be quiet!

NATALIA I will not be quiet until you admit that Okky is a hundred times better than Uggy.

LOMOV A hundred times worse! I wish your Okky were dead. . . . Oh, my head . . . my eye . . . my shoulder . . .

NATALIA Your stupid Uggy cannot die because he is dead already.

LOMOV (*shouts*) Quiet! I am having a heart attack!

NATALIA I will not be quiet!

CHUBUKOV (*enters*) What, you're still at it?

NATALIA Father, tell us frankly, on your honor, which dog is better? Our Okky or his Uggy?

LOMOV (*to* CHUBUKOV) Just tell me one thing. Does your dog have a short jaw or doesn't he? Yes or no.

CHUBUKOV What does it matter, my friend? After all . . . your Uggy has some good points . . . he is well-bred, he is strong, and all that. But if you ask me to be honest, I must say that your dog has two faults: he is too old and he has a short lower jaw.

LOMOV Oh, oh, my heart is thumping! . . . Let us look at the facts. The last time we went hunting my dog was way out in front and yours was behind.

CHUBUKOV He was behind because someone hit him with a whip.

LOMOV Yes, and they hit him for a good reason. Instead of chasing the fox he was chasing a sheep.

CHUBUKOV That is not true. My dear friend, I have a very bad temper and I ask you to stop this argument. The man hit him because he was jealous of my dog. . . . Yes, that's what happened. They are all jealous. And you, sir, you are not without blame. The minute you see that my dog is better than your Uggy you begin . . . to go on like this . . . and all that. . . . I remember what happened that day!

LOMOV So do I!

CHUBUKOV (*imitating him*) So do I! . . . And what do you remember?

LOMOV Heart palpitations . . . my leg is numb . . . I can't stand this!

NATALIA (*making fun of him*) Heart palpitations! What kind of hunter are you, anyway? You should stay in the kitchen with the cockroaches rather than go out hunting.

CHUBUKOV Yes, what kind of hunter are you? If you have a bad heart you should stay home and not go out bouncing on a horse. You don't really hunt. You just go out to get in the way of other people's dogs and to argue. I have a bad temper. Let's stop this discussion. You are not a hunter!

LOMOV And you? You only ride around to get in good with the Count, and to make trouble . . . oh, my heart! . . . Troublemaker!

CHUBUKOV I am a troublemaker? (*Shouting*) Quiet!

LOMOV Troublemaker!

CHUBUKOV You are a silly little boy! A puppy!

LOMOV And you are an old rat! A schemer!

CHUBUKOV Be quiet or I will get my gun and shoot you like a bird! You are a nincompoop!

LOMOV Everyone knows that . . . oh, my heart! . . . that your wife used to beat you . . . my leg! . . . my head! . . . I see sparks! . . . I'm falling, falling!

CHUBUKOV And in your house your servants order you around!

LOMOV Here, here . . . my heart has burst . . . my shoulder is torn apart . . . where is my shoulder? . . . I'm dying! (*Falls into the chair.*) Get the doctor! (*He faints.*)

CHUBUKOV (*to* LOMOV) Silly boy! Child! (*Making fun of him*) I'm fainting! I'm fainting! (*He drinks some water.*)

NATALIA (*shouting at* LOMOV) Yes, what kind of hunter are you? You don't even know how to sit on a horse. (*To* CHUBUKOV) Father! What's the matter with him? (*Screams.*) He's dead!

CHUBUKOV I'm going to faint! I can't breathe! Air!

NATALIA He's dead! (*She pulls* LOMOV's *arm.*) He's dead. What did we do? (*She falls into a chair.*) Get a doctor! (*She goes into hysterics.*)

CHUBUKOV What do you want?

NATALIA (*moaning*) He's dead . . . dead!

CHUBUKOV Who's dead? (*Looks at* LOMOV.) You're right, he's dead! Oh, Lord! Water! A doctor! (*Puts a glass of water to* LOMOV's *mouth.*) Drink! No, he doesn't drink . . . that means he's dead and all that. What kind of luck do I have? Why don't I shoot myself? Why don't I just cut my throat? What am I waiting for? Get me a knife or a gun!

[LOMOV *moves a bit.*]

CHUBUKOV He's coming back to life, I think. . . . Here, drink some water . . . ah, that's the way. . . .

LOMOV I see sparks. There is a great fog all around me. Where am I?

CHUBUKOV Get married as fast as you can. She has accepted! (*He joins* LOMOV's *hand and his daughter's.*) She has accepted. I give you my blessing. Now don't bother me anymore.

LOMOV (*getting up*) What? Who?

CHUBUKOV She has accepted. Well . . . go ahead and kiss each other . . . and let me alone.

NATALIA He's alive! Yes, yes! I accept.

CHUBUKOV Kiss each other.

LOMOV What? Who? (*He kisses* NATALIA.) Ah, very nice . . . but what's happening? . . . Oh, I understand . . . ah, sparks . . . my heart . . . I am so happy, Natalia . . . my leg is numb.

NATALIA I . . . I'm happy too.

CHUBUKOV I feel as if a mountain has fallen from my shoulders. . . .

NATALIA But still, come on now, agree, Okky is better than Uggy!

LOMOV He is worse!

NATALIA Better!

CHUBUKOV Ah, a happy family life begins! (*Calling to the servants*) Champagne!

LOMOV Worse!

NATALIA Better! Better! Better!

CHUBUKOV (*trying to shout louder than the others*) Champagne! Champagne!

CURTAIN

The following television play is based on a grimly comic story by English writer Evelyn Waugh. Following the play is the last part of Waugh's story. Compare the two versions to see how the playwright changed the story for television.

The Man Who Liked Dickens

EVELYN WAUGH

Television version by ROBERT TALLMAN

ACT 1

SCENE: *A clearing in the Amazonian jungle. We see a settlement of thatched huts dominated by a bungalow of the same native materials but having several rooms and a veranda. This is* MR. MCMASTER'S *house. On three sides the settlement is bounded by dense vegetation: on the fourth, by the river and one boat landing. The constant clamor of jungle birds and monkeys is heard.*

MR. MCMASTER, *seated on the steps of his veranda, has just finished cleaning his shotgun and is reassembling it. At the sound of the crackling of dry sticks underfoot,* MR. MCMASTER *lowers the gun and turns in the direction from which the sound seems to come. It becomes louder, and the hoarse gasping breath of a man is heard. Then the branches of two palmettos part and* JOHN HENTY *stumbles into the clearing and falls at full length.* MR. MCMASTER *goes forward to help him to his feet, supports him.*

MCMASTER Steady there . . . my poor man, you're ill. Very ill.
HENTY (*gasping, half sobbing, clinging to* MCMASTER) Tired. Can't go on any further. Too tired.
MCMASTER (*turning toward the house and pointing*) My house is just over there. Think you can make it?

375

HENTY Don't know. . . .

MCMASTER It is a very short way. When we get there, I will give you something to make you better.

HENTY (*as they cross the veranda*) You speak English.

MCMASTER As Mrs. Gamp [1] might say, I speaks enough.

HENTY Mrs. Gamp? Your wife?

MCMASTER Oh, dear no. I live quite alone. (*They are on the veranda.* MCMASTER *helps* HENTY *toward a hammock.*) How long have you been lost in the jungle?

HENTY Don't know . . . days . . . several days . . . expedition down the river . . . boat capsized . . . all the others drowned.

MCMASTER I see. You had better be quiet now. There will be much time for talking when you are better.

HENTY You're . . . (*swallows*) kind.

MCMASTER My name is McMaster. You may have heard my name in Manaos?

HENTY No. My name is Henty.

MCMASTER (*nods*) Mr. Henty. Now if you will rest here for a moment, I will fetch something for you.

[HENTY *manages a faint smile of gratitude.* MCMASTER *enters the house, takes down an earthen crock, and from a row of apothecary bottles on the same shelf shakes out dried leaves and bits of bark, crumbles them into the crock.*]

MCMASTER (*calling*) Traddles!

[*An Indian,* TRADDLES, *appears in the doorway.*]

Is the water hot?

TRADDLES Yes, master.

MCMASTER Bring it here. Hurry. (MCMASTER *rubs his hands and looks up at an attic platform at the end of the room. Several straw-wrapped bundles are seen at the top of the ladder. Then he turns briskly toward the doorway through which* TRADDLES *has disappeared.*) Step lively there! Hurry up, I say! (*The Indian trots in with an ordinary old-fashioned teakettle.*)

TRADDLES Water not boil yet, master. Fire burn too slow.

MCMASTER (*taking teakettle and lifting lid; it steams*) Hot enough.

---

[1] *Mrs. Gamp:* a character in Dickens's novel *Martin Chuzzlewit.*

(*Pours the water on top of the herbs and bark and stirs with a stick. To* TRADDLES) Mr. Henty — the gentleman out there — is to be my guest. He will stay here in the house with me, as Mr. Barnabas did. Do you understand? (TRADDLES *nods.*) Fetch down that calabash.[2] I believe this stuff is ready. (TRADDLES *hands him a calabash hanging on a wall peg.* MR. MCMASTER *dips out some of the brew, tastes it, and spits it out.*) Ah. Exactly right. Put those things away. (*Going out to* HENTY) Mr. Henty . . . (HENTY *opens his eyes.*) I want you to drink this, Mr. Henty.

[*He puts one arm under* HENTY'S *shoulders and lifts him up, holds the calabash under* HENTY'S *nose.* HENTY *winces.*]

HENTY What is it?

MCMASTER Medicine. In the forest, there is medicine for everything. There is medicine to make you well and to make you ill. Plants to cure you and to give you fever; to kill you and to send you mad. My mother was an Indian; she taught me many of them. (*Walks to the edge of veranda and looks toward edge of clearing, where two graves are marked with heavy crosses.*) They say there is a medicine that can bring dead people to life, but I have not seen it done. (*Back to* HENTY *with a smile.*) Perhaps I will live to see that, too. (*Arranges the pillow under* HENTY'S *head.*) Go to sleep, Mr. Henty.

[HENTY *closes his eyes, smiling gratefully.* MCMASTER *bends down over him.*]

MCMASTER Can you read, Mr. Henty? (*Whispering*) You can read, of course?

HENTY (*drowsily*) Of course.

[MCMASTER *straightens up. He smiles contentedly. Fade out.*

Fade in. Shortly before sunrise. TRADDLES *is blowing out a little lamp which burns on the veranda. He looks down, to see* HENTY *lying in the hammock staring up at him through insect netting.* HENTY *parts the net, looks about, slips his legs out, and gets to his feet a little unsteadily. He runs his hand over his stubble of beard and the Indian makes shaving motions on his own face and points.*

---

[2] *calabash:* a dipper made from the gourdlike fruit of the calabash tree.

Following the direction, HENTY *walks to a mirror that hangs over a washstand. He eyes his stubble, sees shaving things laid out, picks up shaving mug and starts to lather. There is a thud off as* MCMASTER *throws down one of the straw bundles from the attic platform.* HENTY *peers around the door.*]

HENTY Need some help there?

MCMASTER No, thank you, I can manage. (*He throws another bundle down, comes down the ladder, unwraps the bundles while* HENTY *shaves. They contain books.*) I hope that razor is satisfactory?

HENTY Splendid.

MCMASTER It belonged to poor Barnabas.

HENTY Barnabas?

MCMASTER He wandered into my village as you did — lost in the jungle and in the grip of a fever. He was a native, well educated in Georgetown.[3] (*Putting books lovingly on shelf*) I buried him only a week before you arrived.

HENTY (*with razor poised*) Poor chap. (*Resumes shaving.*) How long have you lived here?

MCMASTER All my life (*Proudly*) My father was English. He came to British Guiana as a missionary and took a Shiriana woman as his wife. The Shiriana are ugly but very devoted. Most of the men and women living in this savanna [4] are my children. That is why they obey me . . . (*picking up the shotgun*) . . . for that reason . . . and because I have the gun. My father was a man of education, Mr. Henty. I suppose you, too, can read?

HENTY Yes, of course.

MCMASTER It is not everyone who is so fortunate. I cannot.

HENTY (*an apologetic laugh, looking at the books*) You're joking, Mr. McMaster. I mean, all the books —

MCMASTER Oh, I have a great many books — a great many, Mr. Henty. (*To* TRADDLES) Put those shaving things away. Lock up the razor. (*As* TRADDLES *gathers up things and* HENTY *looks curious*) Metal tools are a rarity among these Indians, you know. Have to keep the cutlery under lock and key.

---

[3] *Georgetown:* a city in British Guiana.
[4] *savanna:* grassy plain.

HENTY How long was I sick? I've lost all track of time.
MCMASTER Time is our most plentiful commodity here in the jungle. It is two weeks since you arrived. You were very ill, Mr. Henty. Very. Come, I want to show you something.

[MCMASTER *leads him down the stairs of the veranda.* HENTY *is dizzy and has to lean on post for a moment.*]

HENTY Sorry.
MCMASTER You are still far from completely recovered, Mr. Henty.
HENTY It's all right now. What is it you wanted to show me?
MCMASTER Out here. (*Leads him to a carpenter's bench and takes a cross from vise.*) I started this the day you came . . . to commemorate your arrival. It is very hard mahogany, like the others.
HENTY (*looking toward grave area; two crosses are visible*) Is that — ?
MCMASTER Yes, that is where I buried poor Barnabas. The other is a man who died of snakebite many years ago. I never knew his name . . . he did not read as well as Barnabas.
HENTY Then you must have intended this for — you must have expected me to die.
MCMASTER I sincerely hoped not. Do you believe in God, Mr. Henty?
HENTY (*embarrassed*) Why. . . .
MCMASTER Dickens did.
HENTY Dickens?
MCMASTER Yes. Charles Dickens. It is apparent in all his books. (*They start into the house.*) I just unpacked them again today. I had to put them away to preserve them after Barnabas died. I was not expecting another visitor quite so soon. (HENTY *gives him an uneasy look.*) Here they all are. It has been hard to keep out the worms and ants. (*Picks up two tattered volumes.*) These two were practically destroyed. But there is an oil the Indians make that is useful.

[HENTY *runs a finger along the row of titles:* Bleak House, Nicholas Nickleby, Oliver Twist, Martin Chuzzlewit, Pickwick Papers, David Copperfield, Barnaby Rudge, Little Dorrit, Great Expectations, Old Curiosity Shop, Christmas Books, Hard Times, Dombey and Son.[5]]

---

[5] *Bleak . . . Son:* all of these novels were written by Dickens.

HENTY You're very fond of Dickens, I see.

MCMASTER More than fond, Mr. Henty. Far more. You see, they are the only books I have ever heard. My father used to read them and then later poor Barnabas. He was very kind to me. Every afternoon until he died, he read to me. Do you enjoy reading aloud?

HENTY Well, I think — yes.

MCMASTER I have heard all these books many times now and I never get tired. So many characters . . . so many changes of scene . . . so many words. Each time I think I find more to enjoy and admire.

HENTY Would you like me to read to you a bit now?

MCMASTER (*heartfelt gratitude*) I had hardly dared to hope. Oh, *yes!*

HENTY (*taking down* A Tale of Two Cities *and leafing through*) Well, which one shall we begin with?

MCMASTER It does not matter. I find them all equally delightful.

HENTY A *Tale of Two Cities* —

MCMASTER Splendid! That is the one in which Sydney Carton goes to the guillotine.

HENTY French Revolution, yes.

MCMASTER A distressing story, but it has a lofty and noble ending, I recall. I believe there is just time for a chapter before teatime.

HENTY Very well . . . (HENTY *sits down and opens the book.* MCMASTER *crouches on a low stool, hugging his knees like a child.* HENTY *reads.*) "Book the first. 'Recalled to Life' . . . It was the best of times, it was the worst of times; it was the age of wisdom, it was the age of foolishness; it was the season of light, it was the season of darkness; it was the spring of hope, it was the winter of despair . . ."

[*Camera moves in on* MCMASTER's *absorbed, rapt face.*

Slow dissolve to: The boat landing. Part of a large native canoe in drydock. Indians are repairing it. All activity ceases as HENTY *approaches.*]

HENTY Good morning. (*Indians do not reply.*) Uh — me guest — Mr. McMaster. (*They echo* "MCMASTER" *like an incantation.*

HENTY *is encouraged.*) You speak some English, don't you? (*No response*) Mr. McMaster says most of you are his children.

[MCMASTER *routine again.*]

Look — I'll be leaving here soon, and I'll be wanting a boat and a guide to take me up the river.

[*No response.*]

Boat . . . (*Slaps hull of canoe.*) Canoe . . . (*Rowing motion*) You — take — me — river. (*Takes wallet from pocket.*) Look — money. Me pay much money guide. (HENTY *shows money, extends banknote. One man takes it, passes it around to the others. They jabber, hand it back to him.*) How — surely one of you speaks a little English. (*They jabber some more and run off the scene.*)

MCMASTER (*voice over*) Ah, here you are, Mr. Henty.

[HENTY *turns.* MCMASTER *comes on.*]

HENTY I've been trying to get acquainted with some of your villagers. Without much success, I'm afraid.

MCMASTER They're a shy lot, the Shiriana. What is it you want of them, Mr. Henty?

HENTY I was trying to find out about getting a boat and a guide to take me upriver.

MCMASTER Oh, Mr. Henty, you cannot reach the main channel of the river by boat until the *rainy* season.

HENTY How far off is that?

MCMASTER A month or so. (*He looks up at the sun.*) Two o'clock, Mr. Henty. (*He takes* HENTY *by the arm and they walk.*) I'm most anxious to get on with Dr. Manette's manuscript. What unendurable sufferings he experienced. You read beautifully, with a far better accent than Barnabas had. It is almost as though my father were here again.

[*They walk out of the picture. The Indians look after them, shrug, return to work on the boat. Dissolve to: Book. Close-up of page in* A Tale of Two Cities. *Very slow pan up to close-up of* HENTY's *face.*]

HENTY (*voice over*) ". . . after having been long in danger at the hands of the villagers, I have been seized with great violence and indignity and brought a great journey on foot. And now, held here against my will, I suffer beyond hope. For the love of heaven, of justice, of generosity, I supplicate you to succor and release me from this prison of horror, where I find every hour nearer to destruction."

[HENTY *looks up for a moment, thoughtfully, then sighs and returns to the book. Move in on volume* — A Tale of Two Cities — *dissolve to copy of* Oliver Twist, Chapter Five. HENTY's *voice, reading* —]

"He was alone in a strange place; and the boy had no friends to care for him. And he wished, as he crept into his narrow bed, that it were his coffin."

[*Cut to* MCMASTER *listening as* HENTY *reads.*]

MCMASTER Poor lad, poor little Oliver Twist. (*He weeps.*)
HENTY Perhaps we'd better skip over this part.
MCMASTER (*weeping*) No, no. Every word. I must hear every word.

[HENTY *sighs and picks up the book again. There is the rumble of thunder.*]

HENTY Thunder! It's going to rain!
MCMASTER I believe you are right, Mr. Henty. We should be grateful for a roof over our heads, should we not?

[*Torrent of rain starts to fall. Lightning flashes.* HENTY *drops the book and rushes to the window.*]

HENTY It's started! The rainy season!
MCMASTER Is that such a cause for rejoicing?
HENTY I can get back home again! Back to civilization!
MCMASTER I'm afraid that will not be possible — not for a while, Mr. Henty. Not until the rain stops, most certainly.
HENTY But you said the rainy season was the only time. . . .
MCMASTER That is quite true, but the native canoes are not sturdy enough for upriver travel.
HENTY But they can build a stronger boat!
MCMASTER Yes. They are expert boat builders.
HENTY Well, then?
MCMASTER But they, unfortunately, are superstitious. It is absolutely

taboo to build a boat during the rainy season.
HENTY I don't believe it.
MCMASTER It is a fact that you can easily find out for yourself.
HENTY You might have told me.
MCMASTER Did I not mention it? I forgot.
HENTY I must know when I can get a boat! I can't stand it! I've been thinking of nothing but getting away!
MCMASTER Poor Barnabas was like that. He thought of it all the time. But he died here. . . .

[*The full horrible realization comes to* HENTY. *He turns away from* MCMASTER'S *stare and clutches the window sill. A series of lightning flashes show the crosses, now three in number, casting long, eerie shadows across the rain-swept earth. Music swells to big climax. Fade out.*]

ACT 2

SCENE: *Jungle village. The sun is breaking through. The leaves are dripping a little. It is the end of the rainy season.* THOMPSON, *a prospector with a heavy pack on his back and a pickax at his belt, approaches the bungalow.*

THOMPSON Hallo! Anyone at home?

[HENTY *appears at the door. Haggard and untidy, he tries to speak, but cannot.*]

Well, didn't know the old man had company.

[HENTY *looks up and down agitatedly, leaps forward, grasps* THOMPSON's *arm.*]

THOMPSON What's the trouble, friend? Touch of the fever?
HENTY (*pulling* THOMPSON *away from the doorway*) Listen to me — I don't know who you are, but you found your way here and you don't seem to be lost — you have a boat?
THOMPSON I beached it ten miles upriver. Heading north on foot. Stopped here for supplies.
HENTY Take me with you!
THOMPSON Prospecting for gold?

HENTY No. Back to the boat. Back upriver. I'll pay you. I'll pay you well.

THOMPSON Couldn't take you nohow. Got a one-man canoe, just room for my own supplies.

HENTY You've got to help. I'm being held prisoner here.

THOMPSON Huh? What would he be holding you prisoner for?

HENTY To read to him.

THOMPSON What!

HENTY He's buried two men out here — one supposedly died of snakebite, the other he held prisoner here for more than fifteen years.

THOMPSON Barnabas. You mean Barnabas Washington?

HENTY Yes. He died just before I arrived.

THOMPSON Sorry to hear that. But you're wrong about Barnabas. He was devoted to McMaster.

HENTY He was afraid to say anything. Wait. I'll prove it to you. He wrote down . . . (*Crosses to bookshelf, takes torn piece of notepaper from the leaves of book and hands it to* THOMPSON.) Here. Read this.

THOMPSON (*reads*) "June second, 1939. I, James McMaster of Brazil, do swear to Barnabas Washington of Georgetown that if he finish this book, in fact Martin Chuh-chuz — "

HENTY Chuzzlewit. Martin Chuzzlewit.

THOMPSON Who's he?

HENTY It's the title of a book by Dickens.

THOMPSON " — if he finish this book, I will let him go away back home as soon as finished. Mr. McMaster made this mark, signed Barnabas Washington." Well, I'll be — Who are you, anyway?

HENTY John Henty.

THOMPSON Henty. I heard that name in Manaos. Your wife's looking for you. But they're pretty sure you're dead.

HENTY Well, I pretty nearly am! There's my grave — right out there.

[THOMPSON *looks out at the crosses.*]

THOMPSON I don't get it.

HENTY The cross on the right. You'll see it has my name on it.

THOMPSON McMaster can't write.

HENTY I made the inscription. He said it was to commemorate my arrival.

THOMPSON I *see*. Well! A rescue expedition here costs a lot of money. I doubt if they'd do it on the word of a crazy old prospector like me.
HENTY (*takes watch from pocket*) Take this watch with you. My wife will identify it.
THOMPSON Okay. (*Reaches for it.*)
HENTY Wait, I'd better write a note.
THOMPSON (*looking out door*) Better hurry. Here comes McMaster now.
HENTY (*rummaging desperately*) Paper . . . paper. . . .
THOMPSON I'll talk to him outside. Slip it in my pocket later on.
HENTY Don't leave without it. Promise?
THOMPSON I promise.

[THOMPSON *goes out and meets* MCMASTER *on the steps*. HENTY *moves desperately around the room looking for pencil and paper*.]

HENTY (*breathing hard, talking under breath*) No paper, no pencil. He thought of everything. Paper . . . (*Suddenly*) The books . . . ! (*Takes down* A Tale of Two Cities, *turns pages feverishly, comes to one. Reads*) "After having been long in danger . . ." It's got to work! It's got to work. . . . (*He tears out page. Folds it. Puts it in back of watch.* MCMASTER *comes in.*)
MCMASTER (*over shoulder*) Go on over to the smokehouse, Mr. Thompson. I'll send a man over with the keys.
THOMPSON (*offstage*) Okay, pop.

[MCMASTER *goes into the back room*. HENTY *runs after* THOMPSON.]

HENTY Put it in your pocket.
THOMPSON Where's the note?
HENTY In the back of the watch. I couldn't find pencil and paper, but there's a page of a book. My wife — I hope she'll understand.

[MCMASTER *comes out after the two men part. There is no indication that he has seen anything*.]

MCMASTER Ah, Mr. Henty — I was just about to go have a look at my cocoa plantation. Care to go along?
HENTY (*a little anxious to please*) No, thank you, Mr. McMaster.

MCMASTER Excellent . . . excellent. I won't be long. (MCMASTER *checks the cartridge magazine in his gun and goes out.*)

[TRADDLES *enters, puts down an empty plate.*]

HENTY (*looking at it*) What's this supposed to be?
TRADDLES Master say you eat.
HENTY What are you talking about? There's nothing . . .
TRADDLES Master say you eat — this.

[*There is an offstage shot.*]

HENTY What was that?
TRADDLES Master out hunting.
HENTY He said he was going to the cocoa plantation.
TRADDLES Master is a great hunter.
HENTY (*bored*) Yes, yes; I'm sure. Well, take this and put some food on it. (*He lifts up the empty plate.*)

[MCMASTER *enters, sits at table. The shotgun is pointed at* HENTY.]

MCMASTER Did you have an interesting day, Mr. Henty?
HENTY Why do you ask?
MCMASTER I did. Most interesting. (*He peers outside.*) Goodness. It must be well past our usual hour. May I trouble you for the time, Mr. Henty?
HENTY (*pretending to fish in pockets for watch*) That's strange. I don't seem to have it on me.
MCMASTER (*rising and dangling* HENTY's *watch before him*) Is this it, Mr. Henty?
HENTY Where did you get that?
MCMASTER (*peers outside*) A prospector stopped here this afternoon for supplies. He met with an accident a short distance from here. Apparently he was light-fingered as well as careless, for this was found on his person.
HENTY You murdered him!
MCMASTER Murder a man for stealing a watch? I do not believe there is an instance for that, even in Dickens.
HENTY (*breaking*) Let me go — !
MCMASTER I have told you repeatedly you are free to go. You are under no restraint.
HENTY You know that I can't get to Manaos without help.

MCMASTER In that case, you must humor an old man. Read me another chapter.

[TRADDLES *enters with plate heaped high with food — roast duck, etc.*]

Ah! Roast duck with wild rice — delicious. I am sorry there is not another portion, Mr. Henty. But perhaps this will be a lesson for you. I felt in your reading of *Oliver Twist* that you were not sufficiently sympathetic with the plight of that unfortunate lad. Let us hope you do better by *David Copperfield*. (*He begins to eat.* HENTY *watches him, broken. He reaches automatically for the book, opens it.*)

[*Dissolve to: Exterior. Day.* TRADDLES *runs into clearing.* MCMASTER *comes out of the bungalow to greet him.*]

TRADDLES Master, big party, many boats, come this way.
MCMASTER Where did they land?
TRADDLES North of PyeWye village, one-two-day journey.
MCMASTER Send an escort of our men to meet them and bring them here.
TRADDLES They look for white man, lost in jungle. Henty.
MCMASTER Exactly.
TRADDLES There is a woman with them.
MCMASTER A woman? English?
TRADDLES They say she is wife of man who reads for master, Henty.
MCMASTER That is good. See that they are brought here, dear boy. I want the whole village to welcome them. There will be *piwari* and dancing — a feast day. (MCMASTER *goes up to the veranda where* HENTY *lies sleeping in the hammock.*) Mr. Henty, wake up.
HENTY No. No, please, I feel too ill to read today.
MCMASTER Today is a holiday, Mr. Henty.
HENTY Holiday?
MCMASTER One of the native feast days. We are invited to the chief's enclosure to drink *piwari*.
HENTY (*ironical*) You don't say.
MCMASTER *Piwari* is a ceremonial drink of the Shiriana. The effects are quite pleasant. I believe it will cheer you up.
HENTY If I thought it would cheer me up, I'd drink arsenic.

MCMASTER Then you accept the chief's invitation?
HENTY (*sits up, yawning*) By all means, Mr. McMaster. Tell him I'll be there.

[*Dissolve to compound at night. Torches. Indian dance in progress. Indians drinking out of skin flagons. Suddenly* TRADDLES *taps* MCMASTER'S *shoulder and points off. Cut to* MRS. HENTY *and two pith-helmeted white men,* WILLIAMS *and* SMYTHE, *approaching the scene.* MCMASTER *comes to greet them.*]

MCMASTER My dear lady, my dear, dear lady. I regret that my welcome must be tempered with bad news.
MRS. HENTY Bad news?
MCMASTER You are Mrs. Henty, are you not?
MRS. HENTY Yes. You have news of my husband?
MCMASTER He found his way here six months ago — ill and delirious. He spoke a few words and lapsed into a coma. The next morning he was dead.
MRS. HENTY (*dry sob*) Poor John. Where — ? Where is — ?
MCMASTER Just over there. He shares a plot with two others whose journey ended here.

[*He leads them to the graves. Camera pans slowly to: Lean-to enclosure near the dancers.* HENTY *and fat* CHIEF. CHIEF *drinks and hands calabash to* HENTY.]

HENTY Wonderful. Wonderful party. Wonderful drinks. What you say this was called?
CHIEF (*mumbling native word*) Piwari.
HENTY Piwari. (*Giggles.*) Remind me to buy a case — take back to England. (*Lifts calabash.*) God save the Queen! (*Drinks, then suddenly looks toward group at grave.*) There's my Wife! Brenda! (*He rises and takes a few steps forward, reels, drops calabash. Collapses.* CHIEF *helps* HENTY *to a straw mat where he passes out. Cut to grave.*)
MRS. HENTY But I tell you it sounded exactly like John's voice, calling my name. Didn't you hear anything?
WILLIAMS Nothing but the infernal howling of those savages.
MCMASTER Won't you come into the house? It will be quieter there.
MRS. HENTY Thank you. You're very kind.

[*They go ahead of* MCMASTER, *enter bungalow.*]

MCMASTER (*opens a cupboard and takes out* HENTY's *watch*) I saved this out of your husband's effects. I thought you might want a memento of him.

MRS. HENTY His watch . . . thank you, Mr. McMaster, you are very kind. . . .

MCMASTER You may well be proud of him, Mrs. Henty. He died trying to find help for his friends. His epitaph might well have said, like Sydney Carton: "It is a far, far better thing I do than I have ever done. It is a far better rest that I go to than I have ever known."

[MRS. HENTY *breaks up. Sobs on* WILLIAMS's *shoulder. She drops the watch. It falls open.* SMYTHE *picks it up.*]

SMYTHE (*unfolding the book page that was in the back of the watch*) This is peculiar . . .

MRS. HENTY (*stops weeping*) The watch —

SMYTHE I picked it up. But look — This was in it.

MRS. HENTY A page out of a book.

MCMASTER (*outraged*) My book. He defaced my book! (*Tries to grab page.*)

SMYTHE (*holds it away*) Wait a moment. (*Reads bits.*) "After having been long in danger . . . at the hands of the villagers . . . seized with great violence . . . held here against my will . . . for the love of heaven, of justice, of generosity, I supplicate you to succor and release me from this prison of horror. . . ."

MRS. HENTY Did you say my husband tore this from one of your books?

MCMASTER By accident, I'm sure. While he was reading to me.

MRS. HENTY Reading to you? But you said he spoke only a few words and lapsed into a coma.

MCMASTER I — I have had a most fatiguing day. I — I am not myself. We are so retired here as a rule. I must ask you to be tolerant of an old man's failing memory. (*Goes to door and shouts.*) Quiet! Stop that infernal howling and go to bed. (*Noise stops.*) My guides will see you back to your camp.

WILLIAMS You seem to be in a great hurry to be rid of us.

HENTY'S VOICE (*off — very faintly*) Brenda . . . Brenda. . . .

MRS. HENTY There it is again . . . his voice. (*Frantic*) I know it was his voice. I know. He's alive, and that thing in the watch was meant as a message —

[MCMASTER *is frozen to the spot.*]

WILLIAMS There's one simple way to make sure.
MRS. HENTY What?
WILLIAMS Dig up that grave.
MCMASTER No!

[*They turn. He raises the rifle.*]

MRS. HENTY Why are you keeping my husband?
WILLIAMS Three graves? Two occupied and one in readiness. Just what *is* your game, Mr. McMaster?

[HENTY *staggers into doorway.*]

HENTY I'll tell you. . . .

[MCMASTER *wheels around, is seized.*]

MRS. HENTY John!
HENTY Here's his game . . . and (*wildly*) here's the finish of it. (*Grabs a book.*) Bleak House! (*Throws it on the cooking fire in the hearth.*) Little Dorrit! (*Throws.*) Hard Times! (*Takes armload. Throws all at once.*)
MCMASTER My books. No! No! Don't! All my beautiful friends. . . .

[*Drops on his knees before the fire, grasping at singed pages of his books . . . as the curtain falls.*]

Television producers are sometimes accused of catering to the worst tastes of their audiences and of making palatable what they think is too serious or too depressing for these audiences. The original story of "The Man Who Liked Dickens" by Evelyn Waugh ended in quite a different way from the television adaptation. Other details of the story were also changed. Read the original ending of the story. Note the details that differ from the television play.

Waugh's Original Ending

"Mr. McMaster," said Henty, "I must speak frankly. You saved my life, and when I get back to civilization I will reward you to the best of my ability. But at present you are keeping me here against my will. I demand to be released."

"But, my friend, what is keeping you? Go when you like."

"You know very well that I can't get away without your help."

"In that case you must humor an old man. Read me another chapter."

"Mr. McMaster, I have read for the last time."

"I hope not," said Mr. McMaster politely.

That evening at supper only one plate of dried meat and farine was brought in, and Mr. McMaster ate alone. Henty lay without speaking, staring at the thatch.

Next day at noon a single plate was put before Mr. McMaster, but with it lay his gun, cocked, on his knee, as he ate. Henty resumed the reading of *Martin Chuzzlewit* where it had been interrupted.

Weeks passed hopelessly. They read *Nicholas Nickleby* and *Little Dorrit* and *Oliver Twist*. Then a stranger arrived, a half-caste prospector, one of that lonely order of men who wander for a lifetime through the forests, tracing the little streams, sifting the gravel and, ounce by ounce, filling the little leather sack of gold dust. Mr. McMaster was vexed at his arrival and sent him on his journey within an hour of his arrival, but in that hour Henty had time to scribble his name on a slip of paper and put it into the man's hand.

391

From now on there was hope. The days followed their unvarying routine; but Henty lived in quiet confidence and expectation.

The weeks passed; there was no sign of rescue, but Henty endured the day for hope of what might happen on the morrow; he even felt a slight stirring of cordiality toward his jailer, and was therefore quite willing to join him when, one evening after a long conference with an Indian, he proposed a celebration.

"It is one of the local feast days," he explained, "and they have been making *piwari*. You may not like it, but you should try some."

Accordingly, after supper they joined a party of Indians that were assembled around the fire in one of the huts at the other side of the savanna. They were singing in an apathetic, monotonous manner and passing a large calabash of liquid from mouth to mouth.

Henty gulped the dark liquid, trying not to taste it. He leaned back in the hammock feeling unusually contented. Then he shut his eyes and thought of England and his wife and fell asleep.

He awoke, still in the Indian hut, with the impression that he had outslept his usual hour. By the position of the sun he knew it was late afternoon. No one else was about. He looked for his watch and found to his surprise that it was not on his wrist. He had left it in the house, he supposed.

He found when he set his feet to the ground that he stood with difficulty; his walk was unsteady and his mind confused. When he reached the house he found Mr. McMaster sitting there.

"Ah, my friend, you are late for the reading this afternoon. There is scarcely another half-hour of light. How do you feel?"

"Rotten. That drink doesn't seem to agree with me."

"I will give you something to make you better. The forest has remedies for everything; to make you awake and to make you sleep."

"You haven't seen my watch?"

"You have missed it?"

"Yes. I thought I was wearing it. I say, I've never slept so long."

"Do you know how long? Two days."

"Nonsense. I can't have."

"Yes, indeed. It is a long time. It is a pity, because you missed our guests."

"Guests?"

"Why, yes. I have been quite gay while you were asleep. Three men from outside. Englishmen. It is a pity you missed them. A pity for them, too, as they particularly wished to see you. But what could I do? You were so sound asleep. They had come all the way to find you, so — I thought you would not mind — as you could not greet them yourself I gave them a little souvenir, your watch. They wanted something to take home to your wife, who is offering a great reward for news of you. They were very pleased with it.

"And they took some photographs of the little cross I put up to commemorate your coming. They were pleased with that, too. They were very easily pleased. But I do not suppose they will visit us again, our life here is so retired . . . no pleasures except reading. . . . I do not suppose we shall ever have visitors again . . . well, well, I will get you some medicine to make you feel better. Your head aches, does it not? . . . We will not have any Dickens today . . . but tomorrow, and the day after that, and the day after that. Let us read *Little Dorrit* again. There are passages in that book I can never hear without the temptation to weep."

Egyptian hieroglyphics
carved on limestone in
Thebes about 2100 B.C. *(Detail)*

The Metropolitan Museum of Art, Rogers Fund, 1913.

BOOK TWO | PART 4

LANGUAGE AND COMMUNICATION

*Now all I have to teach you is —
one word. Everything.*
    THE MIRACLE WORKER, Act 2

    Communication is the major function of language. In fact, human thought would be of little consequence without language to express and preserve it. Early men believed that words had a magical force that gave them power over the physical world and over other human beings. Words were essential to the practice of white magic and black magic. Remnants of these beliefs linger on still in incantations, children's games and sayings, and the commonly held idea that certain words are to be avoided and "nicer" words used in their place.
    Because this book is a study of literature, it is also a study of language. Since language is the raw material of literature, we cannot fully understand and enjoy what we read until we sharpen our awareness of how language itself works. Every five-year-old child uses the complicated code we call language. After mastering its elements, he has only to extend his vocabulary to become more sensitive to imaginative writing. Although certain literary works seem difficult because the writers use language in unfamiliar ways, written language is based upon spoken language. The source from which the writer draws — the language itself — is your possession as much as it is his.

One of the major themes of The Miracle Worker is the nature of language and communication. All the characters in the play were preoccupied with one thing: teaching Helen to communicate. But because they did not understand the nature of language itself, they were unable to break through to Helen's mind, until at last Annie Sullivan found the key.

The following section contains four essays on the nature of language. To study language itself is, in a sense, to study literature, too, because language is the raw material with which all writers work.

The first mention of language in the Bible occurs just after the Creation, when the Lord "formed every beast of the field, and every fowl of the air; and brought them unto Adam to see what he would call them: and whatsoever Adam called every living creature, that was the name thereof." Name-giving may properly be considered as the origin of language. A great leap forward was made when men invented ways of preserving their utterances. Although much of importance can be preserved by oral communication (the Odyssey is a good example), modern civilization depends upon the preservation of speech in permanent form.

According to the following essay, the first glimmerings of recorded language were also concerned with the "beasts of the field" — with early man's attempts to control his environment by showing in pictures his power over the animals that provided him with food and clothing. From these pictures evolved man's first attempts to preserve his speech in writing.

Words Began with Pictures

FRANCES ROGERS

1

Our story begins with a handful of pebbles. Not just any pebbles, such as you might find in the bed of a stream. On the contrary, these particular bits of water-worn stones are so valuable, historically, that they are treasured museum pieces.

For many thousands of centuries, these very pebbles and a great many more like them lay buried under layers of debris in a cave in southern France, a famous cave known as Mas d'Azil. Then one day about seventy-five years ago, they were unearthed by the shovel of an archeologist. And what caught his eye, what made him realize that he had come upon something extraordinary was this: all the little stones bore painted markings!

Now the finding of river pebbles decorated with lines and dots of red ocher [1] was not in itself too surprising. Prehistoric man was known to be clever with the paint brush. What was so amazing was that many of the designs looked exactly like a form of writing!

Compare them, if you will, with certain markings in use now, at this very time.

Odd as it may seem, the painted designs of more than ten thousand years ago appear more readable than the cattle brandings of our day. Especially that letter E — or what looks like a capital letter.

Yet we know full well that the Azilians (the name comes from the cave where the pebbles were found), knew nothing whatever about either letters or branding irons. They had no farms, no cattle, no buildings of any kind. In fact, a mark of ownership would have counted for less than nothing in a day when a man's home cave, his cherished harpoon painstakingly carved from a red deer's antler — even his wife and children — were his only so long as he could prevent others from taking possession of them by force.

So we find ourselves puzzling over an unsolved mystery. Why were those ancient pebbles decorated with dots and lines? Could they have been intended to endow the little stones with magic powers?

There is good reason to think that was indeed the case.

Talismans . . . good-luck charms . . . amulets that protect against misfortune . . . people the world over still believe them capable of working magic.

---

[1] *ocher* (ō'kər): an earthy material containing iron and used as a pigment.

Actually, belief in magic is as old as the hills, for it began in the minds of our cave-dwelling ancestors, and the human race has hardly had time, as yet, to outgrow its deep-rooted superstitions. We knock on wood, we cross our fingers, we search for four-leafed clovers, we avoid walking under ladders — all more or less in a spirit of fun.

When the first cave men discovered (or thought they did) that they could cast a spell over creatures they intended to hunt, by scratching pictures on the rock walls of a cave, they started a custom that would be followed for thousands of years.

As it happened, certain of their offspring were more talented than others. They were the artists of the tribe, the ones expected to work magic with a paint brush — or what passed for one. And the wild beasts they drew could be recognized at first glance because the pictures looked so much like the creatures.

Then as time went on, the descendants of the gifted cave men used their inherited skill to tell stories with pictures, stories about tribal doings. These artists might be called the first scribes, for they were the first to record ideas in picture form. And that is the way all writing actually began — as a series of recognizable pictures of people, things, and happenings.

Fortunately, we do not have to wonder what the ancient rock paintings were like, because a great many of them still exist, and in surprisingly good condition, too. Oldest of all are the murals in a certain cave at Altamira in northern Spain. Their estimated age is thirty thousand years.

But how could they possibly last that long?

Indeed, not a trace of them would remain today except for a lucky accident. Nature sealed the mouth of the cave with a landslide.

This occurred in the dim, far-off period known as the Ice Age, when most of Europe was buried under huge glaciers and thin sheets of ice. And from the time the entrance was blocked until the boulders were removed, a little less than a hundred years ago, no one had so much as set foot in the long dark cavern.

The men who discovered the stone-filled opening in the gently sloping field did so quite by chance. No effort was made to clear away the boulders, because nobody suspected at the time that the cave might contain anything of importance. Then one day a number of years later, a local nobleman, the Marquis de Sautuola, began poking about in the rubble between the big rocks. His interest in archeology had been aroused during a recent visit to Paris, where he had seen an exhibition of prehistoric findings. And now he was out to do a little exploring on his own.

From almost the first luck was with him. While digging, he came upon evidence of an ancient camping place — stone tools and flint spear tips. And because the stone ax-heads he found were so much like those he had seen in the French exhibition, he felt certain that they had been made by men of the Ice Age!

Here was reason enough to clear the entrance and search the cave.

It was necessary to remove a number of boulders before the Marquis could crawl on hands and knees through the low opening. But once inside he found that he could stand upright. The interior was inky-dark. His eyes were slow to adjust to the feeble light of the small open-wick lamp he carried, but he managed to grope his way cautiously along what appeared to be a tunnel.

Then all at once he caught sight of them — the red and black paintings strewn hit or miss across the rock walls.

They were amazing pictures unlike any he had ever seen before. There were deer with huge antlers, bison, wild horses, and strange prehistoric creatures. Some were very large, others quite small, and many of the pictures overlapped.

So intent was the Marquis on his startling discovery that he investigated the tunnel only, completely overlooking a large alcove filled with the finest murals of all. But the day that his little daughter, Maria, accompanied him to the cave she ventured, candle in hand, into the vaultlike room not far from the entrance.

The child could scarcely believe her eyes. Overhead and all along the walls were huge pictures of animals painted in a range of colors — yellow, red, brown, black. Some of them were astonishingly true to life. One bison had been placed in such a way that a great bulge in the rock fitted his shoulder, adding to the realism.

It was like a fairy tale. Here in this sealed-off cave time had been standing still for thousands upon thousands of years. A landslide had stopped the hands of the clock, and what had started it ticking again was a small girl with a lighted candle.

There are no story-telling pictures in the cave at Altamira. Such pictures belong to a much later period. Nevertheless, here and there among paintings of animals are a few silhouettes of human hands with outstretched fingers, framed in red paint. There are also two or three masked figures that look like men with animal skins draped over their heads — sorcerers, probably. Close by are some mysterious symbols which may, like the markings on the painted pebbles, have been intended to work magic.

During the past century other caves containing wall pictures of one kind or another have been discovered, not only in Spain but in other European countries as well. Recently, a team of archeologists exploring the Italian Alps came upon hundreds of remarkable rock murals. And these are of particular interest because they show what life was like in the mountains *after* men had learned to build huts, plow, and sow, but *before* they discovered how to write rather than draw what they wanted to record.

We know, of course, that prehistoric man wrote on all sorts of things less hard than stone. He engraved little pictures and symbols on bleached shoulder blades and thighbones, on tusks and antlers, with flint chipped to a sharp point. They have endured to this day. But his other writing materials, such as chips of wood, strips of hide, shells and the like, were bound to disintegrate in a fairly short time.

The wonder is that his paints, made from colored earths, have lasted so well. He first ground the earths to a powder in a stone mortar, and then added a binder, such as bird's eggs or melted fat. This thickish mixture could be applied to the rock with the hand.

The real puzzler is: how did he manage to *see* in those very dark caves? A torch of any kind would have filled the place with smoke. As for his stone lamps — blazing bowls of oil — think how they must have sputtered and burned in fits and starts.

Yet, handicapped as he was, the cave artist painted remarkable pictures — pictures that tell us much about the customs of men who roamed the earth thousands of years before the dawn of civilization.

2

Paper and pencil, pen and ink. Year in and year out we use tons of paper, carloads of pencils and pens, gallons of ink. And if for a single day we were deprived (by some trick of fate) of our familiar writing materials and in their place had to use a nail and hand-patted cakes of clay, we would be hard put to carry on at all.

Yet for centuries on end, clay was the only "paper" known to the people of the Land Between the Rivers — Mesopotamia.

Today this particular strip of country, the wide plain between the Tigris and Euphrates rivers, is called Iraq, and Baghdad is its capital. But some five thousand years ago it was the homeland of a sturdy, black-haired race known as the Sumerians.

These dwellers on the fertile river banks were unique. They had advanced far beyond any of their primitive neighbors. Why? Because their well-thought-out method of writing had swept them right across the threshold of civilization.

It was a very different kind of writing from the story-telling pictures found in the Italian Alps, for in order to read it, you had to use your ears as well as your eyes. In other words, each picture or symbol stood for a *sound* in the Sumerian language.

We know this form of picture-sound writing as a game called a "rebus." Take, for example, the word *belief*. It is impossible, of course, to draw anything so intangible. But the two syllables — *be* and *lief* — could be written, rebus fashion, like this:

And it's no trick at all for the ear to translate the sound of *bee–leaf* back to *belief*.

This, then, was the principle the Sumerians followed when they built up a lengthy vocabulary of sound-picture symbols.

But what exactly *is* a symbol? A symbol is something which stands for something else. Roman numerals do not "spell" the names of the numbers. They actually picture them, for they represent fingers held up while counting. At the same time, however, the numerals themselves do not look like fingers — they merely suggest them. They are symbols.

It is not difficult to see why the Sumerians used a bent line as the symbol for *to bend*, a couple of wavy lines for *water* (they do remind one of ripples on a pool), and a triangle for *wedge*. But for the most part, their sign-pictures mean nothing whatever to our eyes. Yet we may be sure they were not invented arbitrarily; nor were they invented all at once.

Sumerian scribes of very early days used almost as many curved lines as straight ones. As time went on, though, curves gave way to angles. You have only to compare the symbols on this ancient tablet with those in the accompanying table to see the way in which the writing changed.

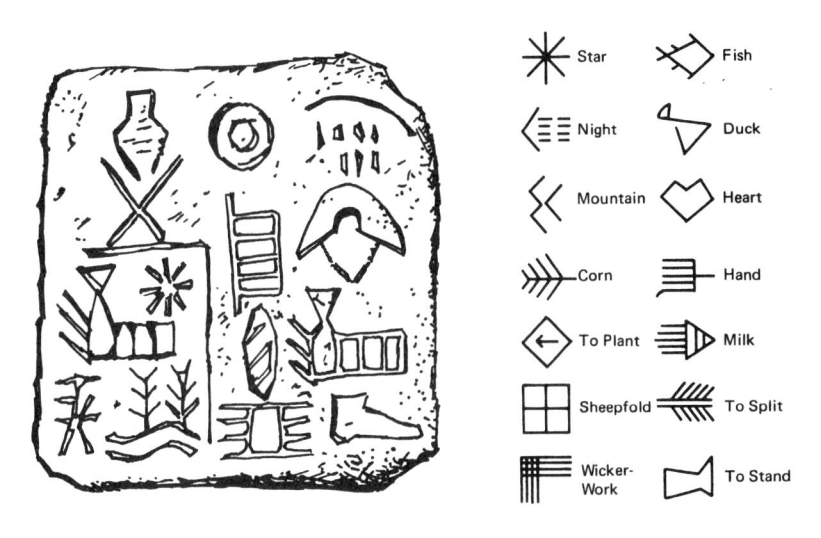

✴	Star	⟡	Fish
⟨≡≡	Night	⟁	Duck
⟪	Mountain	♡	Heart
⟫	Corn	⧉	Hand
⟨←	To Plant	⧊	Milk
⊞	Sheepfold	⋙	To Split
⫴	Wicker-Work	⋈	To Stand

One thing did remain the same throughout the centuries. From the very beginning the Sumerians wrote on clay.

But why, of all things, *clay?* For the good and simple reason that clay was plentiful, while cloth and dressed leather were not. In fact, there was an almost inexhaustible supply of clay. Their houses and huts, their towering temples and high city walls were built of sun-baked bricks. Writing tablets, too, were baked in the hot sun, but not until after the scribe had finished with them. He wrote on the clay while it was still damp and quite soft. Each scribe made his own tablets. Squatting on his heels, he patted the clay into shape with his hands, being careful to leave no fingerprints in the smooth surface. Even so, many an ancient tablet unearthed by archeologists does show thumbprints that had been baked along with the script. In size, the tablets might vary considerably. Some were fairly small, others were nearly a foot square. They looked rather like fat cushions with rounded corners.

As for pens, since the writing was a matter of scratching lines in the clay, any sharp object could be used — a splinter of bone, perhaps, or a pointed reed, even a copper nail. To be sure, reeds were far more plentiful than nails. Nevertheless, small copper spikes could be purchased from the local wheelwright. He used them to nail leather "tires" to the rims of the big wooden disks he made for war chariots. Wheels, no less! Another Sumerian invention.

What was it that started these clever people on the road to a practical form of writing?

Probably it was their need to keep track of everyday affairs such as who owned which plot of land, who had paid his taxes, and so on.

And since it was the temple that had charge of all such matters, the first scribes were those who did the temple bookkeeping. It was up to them to set down in readable symbols a careful record made up of numbers, names, and things, for example, how many baskets of seed grain had been issued to Nebu in exchange for five sheep.

Industrious and inventive, the Sumerians had solved one problem after another. Theirs was a land of little rain, but they dealt with this by digging a vast network of irrigation ditches that carried river water to their truck gardens, fields, and flourishing groves of date palms. And to make up for their lack of metals and other raw materials, they built up a lively barter trade with the peoples of other countries.

This in itself was enough to keep whole staffs of bookkeeping scribes busy. Think how those clumsy clay "books" must have piled up! Only one side of the tablet was used, yet it was necessary to list in detail all the pairs of sandals, yards of woolen cloth, jewelry, painted jars, and other things made by Sumerian craftsmen, that were exchanged for imported copper and gold in ingot form.

It was no easy matter to become a scribe in a day when it was necessary to memorize hundreds of symbols. Nor would it do to draw them so crudely that they could not be read by others. So the chances are that competent scribes were few and far between. In any case, as the work piled up scribes sought ways to speed up their writing.

It was easier, they found, to make incised marks — to press down on the pen — than it was to draw across the surface of the clay. So they began to cut the tips of their reed pens in a new way, in order to give direction to the incised line. Slightly triangular in shape, the tip made an impression somewhat wider at one end than at the other.

Picture symbols took on a new look.

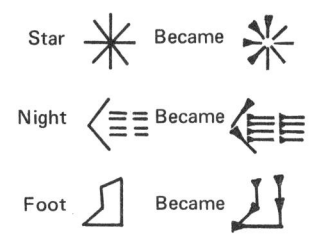

"If language had been the creation, not of poetry, but of logic, we should have only one." Every living language continues to create itself anew, and among the forces that change it are slang and its relatives. As Paul Roberts says, "Slang is essentially not respectable. There is always a more elegant way of saying the thing, but one chooses the slang term for reasons." What those reasons are, he describes in this essay.

Slang and Its Relatives

PAUL ROBERTS

1

Slang is one of those things that everybody can recognize and nobody can define. Not only is it hard to wrap slang in a definition; it is also hard to distinguish it from such similar things as colloquialisms, provincialisms, jargon, trade talk. As we shall see, these areas blend into one another, and it is often a waste of time to look for the boundary.

One characteristic of a slang term is that it exists side by side with another, more general term for the same thing. Take, for example, the word *chick*, which has been used by some speakers in the meaning *girl* or *young woman*. The difference between *chick* and *girl* can be stated only in reference to the people who use the words: some say, "This chick is my sister"; others, "This girl is my sister." *Chick* is slang and *girl* is not, because *chick* is used by a limited part of the population, mostly young people, whereas *girl* is used by everybody, including those who use *chick*.

It is often said that a slang term ceases to be slang when it is "accepted by the dictionary." This is not really the test. You will find many slang terms duly registered in dictionaries and still slang terms.

The term ceases to be slang when it drives out of use its respectable synonym, or when it acquires a meaning that cannot be expressed otherwise. If, for instance, people ceased to use the word *girl* and all used *chick* instead, then *chick* could no longer be called a slang term.

Such things have happened. The term *hot dog* was once a slang term, but it couldn't be considered so now. No one in America would go up to a counter and order a "sausage sandwich." Similarly *varsity*, originally a slang contraction of *university*, has acquired special meanings which only it expresses and is no longer slang. *Jazz*, when it means a particular kind of music, is scarcely a slang term, since there is no more respectable word meaning that kind of music.

Certainly respectability must enter into any discussion of slang. Slang is essentially not respectable. There is always a more elegant way of saying the thing, but one chooses the slang term for reasons. The reason may be a desire to be thought witty or clever or up to date. More often, it is a desire to show, by a particular use of language, that one is a member in good standing of a particular group of people.

Much of the slang in common use today comes ultimately from characters on the other side of the law. This will be recognizable, for example, in words relating to American money. For "money" in general we have such terms as *dough, lettuce,* the *green* or the *big green, folding stuff,* and various others. The different denominations all have their slang terms: *singles* or *fish* for one dollar bills; *fin* for a five; *sawbuck* for a ten and *double sawbuck* for a twenty; *C-note* or *century* for a hundred; *grand* for a thousand. All of these are old, well-weathered terms and are familiar to many people who wouldn't dream of holding up a drugstore. But it is clear that they have their highest frequency in those districts where policemen would prefer to go in pairs.

Musicians are another fertile source of slang terms. Again the element of more or less respectability enters: symphony orchestras are less prolific of slang terms than are purveyors of more popular music — jazz, swing, bebop, rock 'n' roll bands. Many of the slang terms in this area, as in others, have only the briefest existence, but a few linger. Even the youngest readers will be acquainted with *dig* (understand or appreciate), *cool* (excellent or moving), *crazy* (inspired), *cat* (talented musician or knowledgeable music lover), *real* (exceptionally moving).

High school and college slang probably derives as much from music language as from any other source. More than one college professor in the 1950's had to learn that the expression "dig that crazy course," coming from one of his earnest young disciples, was not a criticism but a high tribute. But colleges fill out their slang with terms that apply particularly to college activities. Many of these terms are simple abbreviations: *math, prof, exam, poly sci, econ, phys ed*. Others are names, varying from year to year and from campus to campus, for hard or easy courses, hard or easy teachers, passing and failing, studying, cheating, flattering the teacher (*apple-polishing* is an old term that persists). There are slang terms for those who raise class averages and for those who don't, for campus politicians, for campus reporters, for deans and college presidents, for football players, for serious students, for frivolous students, for fraternity and sorority men and women, for nonfraternity and nonsorority men and women, for pretty girls, for other girls, and for girls in general. Everyone and everything connected with college life can be referred to by a slang term as well as by a more general one.

It is sometimes said that the trouble with slang is that it is constantly changing, that a term becomes old-fashioned almost at birth. It is certainly true that some terms, particularly those that get quick and heavy use, wither faster than the rose. One has only to consider how obsolete terms like *zorch, George, hot* (hot music), *skirt* (girl), *flame* (girl or boy friend), *squire* (escort), sound today.

However, a short but merry life is by no means the rule for slang terms. Some linger on decade after decade, century after century indeed, never becoming quite respectable and never dying out either. The word *dough* for money is just as hardy as it ever was, though no more reputable. Others which seem likely to outlive the century are *cop* (policeman), *nuts* (insane), *limey* (Englishman), *jalopy* (automobile), *cram* (study hard). There are thousands of such — well below the salt but also well established at the table.

Teachers of English are often libeled to the effect that they are dedicated to a relentless pursuit of slang and are never so happy as when they are stamping out a slang term. This is part of the larger charge that teachers of English aren't people. Everybody uses slang as a natural result of speaking a language, though it is presumably true that the young and effervescent like to play with language more than their elders do. It is also true that what sounds gay and cute and clever to the young may sound merely banal to older ears.

The effect of slang is closely bound with the personality of the user. It is not simply a question of whether the slang is new or not or clever or not or incisive or not. It is a question of the total effect of the speaker. The writer can remember a friend who used a rather small selection of slang, none of it particularly witty, and used it rather constantly, with no infusion of new terms; yet his conversation always seemed to have a pleasant sparkle to it, presumably because he himself sparkled pleasantly. On the other hand, there was another character who always — *always* — greeted one with the salutation, "Dig that crazy cat." He usually prefaced this with the expression "Hey, hey!" This grew tiresome.

Slang spreads fast sometimes, but it doesn't transfer very easily. A person who moves into a new group and brings with him an old group's slang *may* find his language admired and imitated. More likely, people will consider him boring or affected or unpleasantly foreign. If he persists with his old talk and doesn't adopt that of the new group, he will find that people begin saying, "Here comes that type;[1] let's get out of here."

2

Slang — and much trade talk, too — merges imperceptibly with that of broad area of language that we call *colloquialism*. "Colloquial" is a rather vague word with different meanings for different people, but it would seem most generally to mean words and constructions that occur more commonly in speech than in writing. As such, it would include slang, but would not be limited to slang. It would include all the forms that people — educated as well as uneducated — use in conversation but tend to avoid in writing. A fur-

---

[1] *type:* To show how fast slang changes: the term "that type" was probably current when Paul Roberts wrote this essay in 1958. Already it sounds out of date. As this book goes to press we would more likely say "that square" or "that creep" but by the time you read this those expressions may have given way to new ones.

ther distinction is that *slang* usually denotes words rather than phrases, whereas *colloquialism* can mean a word, a phrase, a sentence — indeed can apply to the whole tone of the utterance.

Compare the sentences "He better take it easy" and "He should proceed carefully." Both might be uttered by people of impeccable breeding, and both might occur in writing as well as in speech. The difference is simply one of frequency and likelihood. "He better take it easy" is what you are likely to say if you are chatting casually with someone about the activity of a mutual friend. "He should proceed carefully" is what you are likely to write in a letter to the newspaper.

Colloquialisms are not hard to find, since they make up the bulk of our daily conversation. At random we can compare such colloquial and literary expressions as "do your darndest" (strive), "put something over on someone" (fool), "lend a hand" (assist), "kept his mouth shut" (refused to divulge something), "hit the books pretty hard" (studied diligently), "an awfully cute kid" (a strikingly handsome young man), "who you trying to fool" (whom are you seeking to mislead).

At some periods of history people have had the idea that writing is better the farther it is from speech and that colloquialisms should therefore regularly be avoided. But this is scarcely the mood of the present day. Naturally, if you want to sound dignified — and one *does* want to sound dignified sometimes — you choose dignified language and eschew terms that smack of shirtsleeves and ginger ale. If you're seeking a position with a corporation, you might damage your chances by writing, "I sure hope you'll let me take a crack at the job. I got a notion I'd do real well at it. Sure would try anyhow." It would normally be better sense to say, "I am hoping that you will find it possible to try me in the position. I feel that I would be able to do the work successfully. Certainly I would try very hard."

However, it is undeniable that the trend of much modern writing is toward a more colloquial tone. Not only in advertising, which is ever pally, but also in more or less serious books, magazine articles, newspaper accounts, the tendency is to reflect more and more the words and rhythms of ordinary speech. One finds, for example, a greater use than formerly of contracted forms: *don't, shouldn't, he'll,* in place of *do not, should not, he will.* Plain or folksy or even slang words are often preferred to elegant ones, and writers pay less attention than their predecessors did to the niceties of schoolbook grammar.

The explanation of this trend is no doubt to be sought in sociological developments. The educated class, formerly a pretty exclusive group, is now the great mass of the population. Reading and writing, even a hundred years ago, was the accomplishment of relatively few; now everybody does it. Today's writer is talking not to the country club set but to everybody in town, and he tries to talk everybody's language.

But he shouldn't try too hard. Writing should above all be consistent and natural and honest, and the writer who labors the "jus' us plain folks" approach is spotted as a phony by the plain folks as well as the fancy ones. Here, from a cereal box, is an example of nobody's language:

> Often, when I'm out ridin' the range, I find myself thinkin' about all the daredevil deeds the Indian Chiefs did in days gone by, and of the unforgettable adventures of the gallant scouts and frontiersmen who met them in battle. I reckon all you young pardners of mine would like to hear all about them, too!

Even the youngest pardners may have an inkling that this cowboy rides the range on his portable typewriter.

3

One of the troubles of colorful language, slang or other, is that its color rubs off. The first time you hear and understand an expression like "Dig that crazy cat," you may find it exceptionally expressive, piquant, and moving. The second time you hear it, it isn't quite so exciting. The tenth time it has no effect at all. The fiftieth time it grates a little. The five-hundredth time it may make you want to brain the speaker with a trombone.

If language isn't colorful to begin with, it doesn't pale. You can hear the sentence "Listen to that musician" five hundred times with no more pain the last time than the first. Clichés, or trite expressions, are simply dried up metaphors, figures of speech. They were racy ways of saying things, but they have slowed down.

The first person who said "It was like walking on eggs" thought up a pretty clever comparison. When you read this for the first time, you get not only the information that the situation was delicate but a picture that reinforces and impresses the message. But this happens the first time only. After that you get only the information that the situation was delicate plus the fact that the writer is not very inventive. So also with "He fought like a tiger," "He behaved like a lamb," "He ran like a deer," "He ate like a pig," "He took a powder," "He pulled the wool over my eyes," "He's all wool and a yard wide," "She's pretty as a picture," "He spelled out the government's policy," "We'd better shake a leg," "An ocean of faces looked up at him," "A forest of masts filled the harbor," "She led him a merry chase," "It slid off him like water off a duck's back," "You can't fly on one wing," "He was as drunk as a lord, but his brother was as sober as a judge." All of these were more or less effective once.

Some groups of people seem to run more to clichés than others. Politicians are notorious, and some of their clichés, like "point with pride" and "view with alarm," have been laughed out of use. Sports writers and announcers also have difficulty avoiding trite phrases. One thinks of such expressions as "the fourth and final quarter" (one knows that the fourth quarter of a football game is the final one, but announcers seldom fail to point it out), "the bags are bulging," "circus catch," "smart little field general." All quarterbacks are smart little field generals, though some of them are also magicians. Line drives, proceeding toward the outfield, always scream, unless they go past something, like first, in which case they whistle. Pitchers are mostly big right-handers or little southpaws. Successful players come through in the clutch.

In fairness we should realize that sports writers and sports announcers deserve sympathy as much as criticism. They have to report, day after day and year after year, activities in which the same features are endlessly repeated. Moreover, they must always report these activities feverishly. The announcer is scarcely at liberty to say that today's football game is a pretty routine affair and the performers of no more than average competence. He must, every Saturday, bubble about how this is the most exciting grid spectacle that he and his colleagues have been privileged to see in a long time and how he wishes all us fans could be out there in the stadium with him to see these two great teams fighting their hearts out.

The cliché is every writer's enemy. Good writers fight cliché all the time, but few, even among the very best, win all the time. The triter the phrase, the more readily it comes to the mind, the more likely it is to slip into the sentence. You want to describe a mob, and you don't want to just say it was a big mob. You want to impress the reader with its size. "Sea of faces," you think, and you write it down. The trouble is that so many other writers have also written it down that it's lost all its blood. It no longer means anything more than "big mob," so you might as well have written "big mob" and been done with it.

The cliché is a difficulty for the young writer particularly, because he may not recognize the cliché when he sees it. "Sea of faces" may strike him as a bright new figure, not only expressive but original. One solution to this problem is experience. As we mature as readers, we become better equipped to recognize the stock phrases of the language as stock phrases. But the principal solution is to learn to distrust the pleasing phrase that comes too readily. It is only reasonable to suppose that the metaphor that jumps at you will have jumped at thousands of others before you.

It is very easy to write, to speak, to think in clichés. That's what most people do. They don't think for themselves but let the popular mind think for them. Their language is not personal but general, composed of public sentences with a few names changed to fit private conditions. There is nothing sinful about talking in clichés, and nobody can avoid it altogether. But those who don't avoid it at all betray laziness and mediocrity.

Human communication can be difficult. Language is our chief medium for communication — but even people who speak the same language do not always mean the same things by it. Alice found this out in her discussion with the famous egg, Humpty Dumpty.

Alice in Wonderland and Through the Looking Glass are often thought of as children's books — as indeed they are. But they are a great deal more than that. They raise some of the same questions that philosophers and linguists continually puzzle over. As you will see in the following passage from Through the Looking Glass, *what seemed merely fun when you were a child has in fact some surprising implications about the nature of language.*

Humpty Dumpty on the Meaning of Words

LEWIS CARROLL

"This conversation is going on a little too fast: let's go back to the last remark but one."

"I'm afraid I can't quite remember it," Alice said, very politely.

"In that case we start afresh," said Humpty Dumpty, "and it's my turn to choose a subject — " ("He talks about it just as if it was a game!" thought Alice.) "So here's a question for you. How old did you say you were?"

Alice made a short calculation, and said, "Seven years and six months."

"Wrong!" Humpty Dumpty exclaimed triumphantly. "You never said a word like it!"

"I thought you meant 'How old *are* you?'" Alice explained.

"If I'd meant that, I'd have said it," said Humpty Dumpty.

Alice didn't want to begin another argument, so she said nothing.

"Seven years and six months!" Humpty Dumpty repeated thoughtfully. "An uncomfortable sort of age. Now if you'd asked *my* advice, I'd have said, 'Leave off at seven' — but it's too late now."

"I never ask advice about growing," Alice said indignantly.

"Too proud?" the other inquired.

Alice felt even more indignant at this suggestion. "I mean," she said, "that one can't help growing older."

"*One* can't, perhaps," said Humpty Dumpty; "but *two* can. With proper assistance, you might have left off at seven."

"What a beautiful belt you've got on!" Alice suddenly remarked. (They had had quite enough of the subject of age, she thought: and, if they really were to take turns in choosing subjects, it was *her* turn now.) "At least," she corrected herself on second thought, "a beautiful cravat, I should have said — no, a belt, I mean — I beg your pardon!" she added in dismay, for Humpty Dumpty looked thoroughly offended, and she began to wish she hadn't chosen that subject. "If only I knew," she thought to herself, "which was neck and which was waist!"

Evidently Humpty Dumpty was very angry, though he said nothing for a minute or two. When he *did* speak again, it was in a deep growl.

"It is a — most — provoking — thing," he said at last, "when a person doesn't know a cravat from a belt!"

"I know it's very ignorant of me," Alice said, in so humble a tone that Humpty Dumpty relented.

"It's a cravat, child, and a beautiful one, as you say. It's a present from the White King and Queen. There now!"

"Is it really?" said Alice, quite pleased to find that she *had* chosen a good subject after all.

"They gave it me," Humpty Dumpty continued thoughtfully as he crossed one knee over the other and clasped his hands around it, "They gave it me — for an un-birthday present."

"I beg your pardon?" Alice said with a puzzled air.

"I'm not offended," said Humpty Dumpty.

"I mean, what *is* an un-birthday present?"

"A present given when it isn't your birthday, of course."

Alice considered a little. "I like birthday presents best," she said at last.

"You don't know what you're talking about!" cried Humpty Dumpty. "How many days are there in a year?"

"Three hundred and sixty-five," said Alice.

"And how many birthdays have you?"

"One."

"And if you take one from three hundred and sixty-five what remains?"

"Three hundred and sixty-four, of course."

Humpty Dumpty looked doubtful. "I'd rather see that done on paper," he said.

Alice couldn't help smiling as she took out her memorandum-book, and worked the sum for him:

$$\begin{array}{r} 365 \\ -1 \\ \hline 364 \end{array}$$

Humpty Dumpty took the book and looked at it carefully. "That seems to be done right — " he began.

"You're holding it upside down!" Alice interrupted.

"To be sure I was!" Humpty Dumpty said gaily as she turned it around for him. "I thought it looked a little queer. As I was saying, that *seems* to be done right — though I haven't time to look it over thoroughly just now — and that shows that there are three hundred and sixty-four days when you might get un-birthday presents — "

"Certainly," said Alice.

"And only *one* for birthday presents, you know. There's glory for you!"

"I don't know what you mean by 'glory,'" Alice said.

Humpty Dumpty smiled contemptuously. "Of course you don't — till I tell you. I meant 'there's a nice knockdown argument for you!'"

"But 'glory' doesn't mean 'a nice knockdown argument,'" Alice objected.

"When *I* use a word," Humpty Dumpty said, in rather a scornful tone, "it means just what I choose it to mean — neither more nor less."

"The question is," said Alice, "whether you *can* make words mean so many different things."

"The question is," said Humpty Dumpty, "which is to be master — that's all."

Alice was too much puzzled to say anything; so after a minute Humpty Dumpty began again. "They've a temper, some of them — particularly verbs: they're the proudest — adjectives you can do anything with, but not verbs — however, *I* can manage the whole lot of them! Impenetrability! That's what *I* say!"

"Would you tell me please," said Alice, "what that means?"

"Now you talk like a reasonable child," said Humpty Dumpty, looking very much pleased. "I meant by 'impenetrability' that we've had enough of that subject, and it would be just as well if you'd mention what you mean to do next, as I suppose you don't mean to stop here all the rest of your life."

"That's a great deal to make one word mean," Alice said in a thoughtful tone.

"When I make a word do a lot of work like that," said Humpty Dumpty, "I always pay it extra."

"Oh!" said Alice. She was too much puzzled to make any other remark.

"Ah, you should see 'em come around me of a Saturday night," Humpty Dumpty went on, wagging his head gravely from side to side, "for to get their wages, you know."

Annie Sullivan's own letters are one of the sources William Gibson drew upon in writing The Miracle Worker. *It should be interesting to compare the "real" Annie of these letters with the portrait Gibson drew of her for the stage. Here, we see her to be not only a devoted teacher but a serious student of language as well. The first letter describes the scene at the water pump, the climax of the play. But that moment of understanding was only the beginning for Helen and Annie. The later letters tell of the long hard work that remained to be done after the key had been discovered.*

Everything Has a Name

ANNE SULLIVAN MACY

April 5, 1887.

I must write you a line this morning because something very important has happened. Helen has taken the second great step in her education. She has learned that *everything has a name, and that the manual alphabet is the key to everything she wants to know.*

In a previous letter I think I wrote you that "mug" and "milk" had given Helen more trouble than all the rest. She confused the nouns with the verb "drink." She didn't know the word for "drink," but went through the pantomime of drinking whenever she spelled "mug" or "milk." This morning, while she was washing, she wanted to know the name for "water." When she wants to know the name of anything, she points to it and pats my hand. I spelled "w-a-t-e-r" and thought no more about it until after breakfast. Then it occurred to me that with the help of this new word I might succeed in straightening out the "mug-milk" difficulty. We went out to the pump house, and I made Helen hold her mug under the spout while I pumped. As the cold water gushed forth, filling the mug, I spelled "w-a-t-e-r" in Helen's free hand. The word coming so close upon the sensation of cold water rushing over her hand seemed to startle her. She dropped the mug and stood as one transfixed. A new light came into her face. She spelled "water" several times. Then she dropped on the ground and asked for its name and pointed to the pump and the trellis, and suddenly turning around she asked for my name. I spelled "Teacher." Just then the nurse brought Helen's little sister into the pump house, and Helen spelled "baby" and pointed to the nurse. All the way back to the house she was highly excited, and learned the name of every object she touched, so that in a few hours she had added thirty new words to her vocabulary. Here are some of them: *Door, open, shut, give, go, come,* and a great many more.

April 10, 1887.

I see an improvement in Helen from day to day, almost from hour to hour. Everything must have a name now. Wherever we go, she asks eagerly for the names of things she has not learned at home. She is anxious for her friends to spell, and eager to teach the letters to every one she meets. She drops the signs and pantomime she used before, as soon as she has words to supply their place, and the acquirement of a new word affords her the liveliest pleasure. And we notice that her face grows more expressive each day.

I have decided not to try to have regular lessons for the present. I am going to treat Helen exactly like a two-year-old child. It occurred to me the other day that it is absurd to require a child to come to a certain place at a certain time and recite certain lessons, when he has not yet acquired a working vocabulary. I sent Helen away and sat down to think. I asked myself, "How does a normal child learn language?" The answer was simple: "By imitation." The child comes into the world with the ability to learn, and he learns of himself, provided he is supplied with sufficient outward stimulus. He sees people do things, and he tries to do them. He hears others speak, and he tries to speak. *But long before he utters his first word, he understands what is said to him.* I have been observing Helen's little cousin lately. She is about fifteen months old, and already understands a great deal. In response to questions she points out prettily her nose, mouth, eye, chin, cheek, ear. If I say, "Where is baby's other ear?" she points it out correctly. If I hand her a flower, and say, "Give it to mamma," she takes it to her mother. If I say, "Where is the little rogue?" she hides behind her mother's chair, or covers her face with her hands and peeps out at me with an expression of genuine roguishness. She obeys many commands like these: "Come," "Kiss," "Go to papa," "Shut the door," "Give me the biscuit." But I have not heard her try to say any of these words, although they have been repeated hundreds of times in her hearing, and it is perfectly evident that she understands them. These observations have given me a clue to the method to be followed in teaching Helen language. *I shall talk into her hand as we talk into the baby's ears.* I shall assume that she has the normal child's capacity of assimilation and imitation. *I shall use complete sentences in talking to her*, and fill out the meaning with gestures and her descriptive signs when necessity requires it; but I shall not try to keep her mind fixed on any one thing. I shall do all I can to interest and stimulate it, and wait for results.

April 24, 1887.

The new scheme works splendidly. Helen knows the meaning of more than a hundred words now, and learns new ones daily, without the slightest suspicion that she is performing a most difficult feat. She learns because she can't help it, just as the bird learns to fly. But don't imagine that she "talks fluently." Like her baby cousin, she expresses whole sentences by single words. "Milk," with a gesture means, "Give me more milk." "Mother," accompanied by an inquiring look, means, "Where is mother?" "Go" means, "I want to go out." But when I spell into her hand, "Give me some bread," she hands me the bread, or if I say, "Get your hat and we will go to walk," she obeys instantly. The two words, "hat" and "walk" would have the same effect; *but the whole sentence, repeated many times during the day, must in time impress itself upon the brain, and by and by she will use it herself.*

May 8, 1887.

Helen is learning adjectives and adverbs as easily as she learned nouns. The idea always precedes the word. She had signs for *small* and *large* long before I came to her. If she wanted a small object and was given a large one, she would shake her head and take up a tiny bit of the skin of one hand between the thumb and finger of the other. If she wanted to indicate something large, she spread the fingers of both hands as wide as she could, and brought them together, as if to clasp a big ball. The other day I substituted the words *small* and *large* for these signs, and she at once adopted the words and discarded the signs. I can now tell her to bring me a large book or a small plate, to go upstairs slowly, to run fast and to walk quickly. This morning she used the conjunction *and* for the first time. I told her to shut the door, and she added, "and lock."

May 22, 1887.

My work grows more absorbing and interesting every day. Helen is a wonderful child, so spontaneous and eager to learn. She knows about 300 words now and *a great many common idioms*, and it is not three months yet since she learned her first word. It is a rare privilege to watch the birth, growth, and first feeble struggles of a living mind; this privilege is mine; and moreover, it is given me to rouse and guide this bright intelligence.

We have reading lessons every day. Usually we take one of the little "Readers" up in a big tree near the house and spend an hour or two finding the words Helen already knows. *We make a sort of game of it* and try to see who can find the words most quickly, Helen with her fingers, or I with my eyes, and she learns as many new words as I can explain with the help of those she knows. When her fingers light upon words she knows, she fairly screams with pleasure and hugs and kisses me for joy, especially if she thinks she has me beaten. It would astonish you to see how many words she learns in an hour in this pleasant manner. Afterward I put the new words into little sentences in the frame, and sometimes it is possible to tell a little story about a bee or a cat or a little boy in this way. I can now tell her to go upstairs or down, out of doors or into the house, lock or unlock a door, take or bring objects, sit, stand, walk, run, lie, creep, roll, or climb. She is delighted with action-words; so it is no trouble at all to teach her verbs. She is always ready for a lesson, and the eagerness with which she absorbs ideas is very delightful. She is as triumphant over the conquest of a sentence as a general who has captured the enemy's stronghold.

June 2, 1887.

The weather is scorching. We need rain badly. We are all troubled about Helen. She is very nervous and excitable. She is restless at night and has no appetite. It is hard to know what to do with her. The doctor says her mind is too active; but how are we to keep her from thinking? She begins to spell the minute she wakes up in the morning, and continues all day long. If I refuse to talk to her, she spells into her own hand, and apparently carries on the liveliest conversation with herself.

I gave her my braille slate to play with, thinking that the mechanical pricking of holes in the paper would amuse her and rest her mind. But what was my astonishment when I found that the little witch was writing letters! I had no idea she knew what a letter was. She has often gone with me to the post office to mail letters, and I suppose I have repeated to her things I wrote to you. She knew, too, that I sometimes write "letters to blind girls" on the slate; but I didn't suppose that she had any clear idea what a letter was. One day she brought me a sheet that she had punched full of holes, and wanted to put it in an envelope and take it to the post office. She said, "Frank — letter." I asked her what she had written to Frank. She replied, "Much words. Puppy motherdog — five. Baby — cry. Hot. Helen walk — no. Sunfire — bad. Frank — come. Helen — kiss Frank. Strawberries — very good."

Helen is almost as eager to read as she is to talk. I find she grasps the import of whole sentences, catching from the context the meaning of words she doesn't know; and her eager questions indicate the outward reaching of her mind and its unusual powers.

The other night when I went to bed, I found Helen sound asleep with a big book clasped tightly in her arms. She had evidently been reading, and fallen asleep. When I asked her about it in the morning, she said, "Book — cry," and completed her meaning by shaking and other signs of fear. I taught her the word *afraid*, and she said: "Helen is not afraid. Book is afraid. Book will sleep with girl." I told her that the book wasn't afraid, and must sleep in its case, and that "girl" mustn't read in bed. She looked very roguish, and apparently understood that I saw through her ruse.

June 19, 1887.

During our walks she keeps up a continual spelling, and delights to accompany it with actions such as skipping, hopping, jumping, running, walking fast, walking slow, and the like. When she drops stitches she says, "Helen wrong, teacher will cry." If she wants water she says, "Give Helen drink water." She knows four hundred words besides numerous proper nouns. In one lesson I taught her these words: *bedstead, mattress, sheet, blanket, comforter, spread, pillow*. The next day I found that she remembered all but *spread*. The same day she had learned, at different times, the words: *house, weed, dust, swing, molasses, fast, slow, maple sugar*, and *counter*, and she had not forgotten one of these last. This will give you an idea of the retentive memory she possesses. She can count to thirty very quickly, and can write seven of the square-hand letters and the words which can be made with them. She seems to understand about writing letters, and is impatient to "write Frank letter." She enjoys punching holes in paper with the stiletto, and I supposed it was because she could examine the result of her work; but we watched her one day, and I was much surprised to find that she imagined she was writing a letter. She would spell "Eva" (a cousin of whom she is very fond) with one hand, then make believe to write it; then spell, "sick in bed," and write that. She kept this up for nearly an hour. She was (or imagined she was) putting on paper the things which had interested her. When she had finished the letter she carried it to her mother and spelled, "Frank letter," and gave it to her brother to take to the post office. She had been with me to take letters to the post office.

July 31, 1887.

Helen's pencil-writing is excellent, as you will see from the enclosed letter, which she wrote for her own amusement. I am teaching her the braille alphabet, and she is delighted to be able to make words herself that she can feel.

She has now reached the question stage of her development. It is "what?" "why?" "when?" — especially "why?" — all day long, and as her intelligence grows her inquiries become more insistent. I remember how unbearable I used to find the inquisitiveness of my friends' children; but I know now that these questions indicate the child's growing interest in the cause of things. The "why?" is the *door through which he enters the world of reason and reflection.* "How does carpenter know to build house?" "Who put chickens in eggs?" "Flies bite — why?" "Can flies know not to bite?" "Why did Father kill sheep?" Of course she asks many questions that are not as intelligent as these. Her mind isn't more logical than the minds of ordinary children. On the whole, her questions are analogous to those that a bright three-year-old child asks; but her desire for knowledge is so earnest, the questions are never tedious, though they draw heavily upon my meager store of information, and tax my ingenuity to the utmost.

"The Jockey," by the French artist Toulouse-Lautrec.

Sterling and Francine Clark Institute, Williamstown, Mass.

BOOK TWO | PART 5

SIGHTS AND SOUNDS

I have often thought it would be a blessing if each human being were stricken blind and deaf for a few days. . . . Darkness would make him more appreciative of sight; silence would teach him the joys of sound.

Helen Keller

Helen Keller grew up to be one of the most remarkable women of this century. She traveled all over the world and spoke with most of the famous people of her time. She wrote many books and lectured to hundreds of audiences. But the sights and sounds of the world were shut off from her except through the messages tapped into the palm of her hand by her friend and teacher, Annie Sullivan. Annie had to be a remarkable person, too — something of a poet — in order to bring the whole world back to Helen. Years after the incidents dramatized in The Miracle Worker, Helen Keller wrote:

> Now and then I have tested my seeing friends to discover what they see. Recently I was visited by a very good friend who had just returned from a long walk in the woods, and I asked her what she had observed. "Nothing in particular," she replied. I might have been incredulous had I not been accustomed to such responses, for long ago I became convinced that the seeing see little.

How was it possible, I asked myself, to walk for an hour through the woods and see nothing worthy of note? I, who cannot see, find hundreds of things to interest me through mere touch. I feel the delicate symmetry of a leaf. I pass my hands lovingly about the smooth skin of a silver birch, or the rough, shaggy bark of a pine. In spring I touch the branches of trees hopefully in search of a bud, the first sign of awakening Nature after her winter's sleep. I feel the delightful, velvety texture of a flower, and discover its remarkable convolutions; and something of the miracle of Nature is revealed to me. Occasionally, if I am very fortunate, I place my hand gently on a small tree and feel the happy quiver of a bird in full song. I am delighted to have the cool waters of a brook rush through my open fingers. To me a lush carpet of pine needles or spongy grass is more welcome than the most luxurious Persian rug. To me the pageant of seasons is a thrilling and unending drama, the action of which streams through my finger tips.

Though most of us are not blind and deaf like Helen Keller — and most of us are not as intelligent as Helen Keller, either! — we do not really appreciate the wonders around us. A good writer has the gift of seeing things sharply and freshly and of communicating what he sees through language. Joseph Conrad, the English novelist, stated his aim as a writer: "by the power of the written word to make you hear, to make you feel — before all, to make you see."

THE LANGUAGE OF POETRY

Poetry is the most controlled use of language. One of the things it can do is present to the reader vivid impressions of sights and sounds. When poetry is well written, it brings the reader a sense of delight in seeing something in a new way.

The following lyric poems are selected for the sharp sense impressions they convey. Before you read the poems, consider these statements about poetry:

1. Poetry is a natural way for human beings to express themselves. One of poetry's chief devices is metaphor. It suggests that something is like something else. It makes comparisons in order to startle the reader into seeing from a fresh viewpoint. Look at the following comparisons from two poems in this section. In the first, the planes are compared to horses: the sound of the planes in the air is like the thunder of horses' hoofs racing over the ground:

> Above the roofs three jet planes
> leave their hoofs of violence on naive ground.

In the second, a machine is compared to a human being.

> The juke box has a big square face.

Metaphors are something all of us use in our everyday speech. Our impulse is the same as the poet's, except that we tend to use stale metaphors where the poet uses new ones. If someone has been cheated, we say, "He got burned." If someone doesn't eat very much, we may say that he "eats like a bird." "As big as a house," "white as snow" — people use these expressions (which have become clichés) hardly aware that they are using metaphors.

2. Poetry is a compressed use of language. A good poem has nothing extra in it. Every word must contribute something to the imagery, to the sound pattern, to the meaning. The Japanese haiku at the end of this section are classic examples of a form that compresses a great deal of meaning into just seventeen syllables. A prose writer could use a paragraph — perhaps several pages — to describe a snake moving through the grass. The writer of the haiku says:

> A snake! though it passes,
> eyes that had glared at me
> stay in the grasses.

The force of poetry comes from packing a great deal of meaning into a short space. In this way poetry is not like our everyday speech, in which we tend to make false starts and to repeat ourselves.

3. A poem has patterns. In a poem, the way the words are arranged is as important as its ideas. As you read the following poems you will see many ways in which poets set up patterns of language. One way of establishing a pattern is to divide the poem into lines and to arrange them in a certain way on the page. Another way of setting up a pattern is through rhyme and other kinds of repeated sounds. Look back at the quotation from "Three Jet Planes" and notice the repetition of sound in the words roofs and hoofs. Finally, an important kind of pattern in poetry is rhythm.

The Sea

The first three poems are vivid pictures of the sea and its sounds. It is a slightly different sea that is presented in each poem, for each poet uses the sea as a reflection of a different mood.

All Day I Hear

JAMES JOYCE

All day I hear the noise of waters
    Making moan,
Sad as the sea-bird is when, going
    Forth alone,
He hears the winds cry to the waters'
    Monotone.

The gray winds, the cold winds are blowing
    Where I go.
I hear the noise of many waters
    Far below.
All day, all night, I hear them flowing
    To and fro.

Break, Break, Break

ALFRED, LORD TENNYSON

Break, break, break,
    On thy cold gray stones, O Sea!
And I would that my tongue could utter
    The thoughts that arise in me.

Oh, well for the fisherman's boy,
   That he shouts with his sister at play!
Oh, well for the sailor lad,
   That he sings in his boat on the bay!

And the stately ships go on
   To their haven under the hill;
But oh, for the touch of a vanished hand,
   And the sound of a voice that is still!

Break, break, break,
   At the foot of thy crags, O Sea!
But the tender grace of a day that is dead
   Will never come back to me.

The Tide Rises, the Tide Falls

HENRY WADSWORTH LONGFELLOW

The tide rises, the tide falls,
The twilight darkens, the curlew° calls;
Along the sea-sands damp and brown
The traveler hastens toward the town,
   And the tide rises, the tide falls.

Darkness settles on roofs and walls,
But the sea, the sea in the darkness calls;
The little waves, with their soft, white hands,
Efface the footprints in the sands,
   And the tide rises, the tide falls.

The morning breaks; the steeds in their stalls
Stamp and neigh, as the hostler° calls;
The day returns, but nevermore
Returns the traveler to the shore,
   And the tide rises, the tide falls.

---
2. *curlew:* a shore bird with a long bill and long legs.
12. *hostler* (hos′lər): a man who cares for horses in a stable.

The Sky

The next four poems are descriptions of events that happen in the skies.

Tornado Threat

ROQUA WASSAM

Suddenly, the wind
blows cold;
a high wind —
gusty, dusty,
cold.

Metallic,
brooding clouds
hang low.
Thunder mutters
wordless threats;

beware beware — beware?

The westway sun,
finding a crevice
in the clouds
casts golden light
serene.

Against the menace
of the wind,
the thunder threat,
the lowering clouds,

this false kindness
of the sun
is somehow frightful —
frightful, and obscene.

New Moon

TU FU

The bright, thin, new moon appears,
Tipped askew in the heavens.
It no sooner shines over
The ruined fortress than the
Evening clouds overwhelm it.
The Milky Way shines unchanging
Over the freezing mountains
Of the border. White frost covers
The garden. The chrysanthemums
Clot and freeze in the night.

Three Jet Planes

MAY SWENSON

Three jet planes skip above the roofs
   through a tri-square of blue
   tattooed by TV crossbars
   that lean in cryptic concert in their wake.

Like skaters on a lake
   combined into a perfect arrowhead up there
   they sever space with bloodless speed
   and are gone without a clue
   but a tiny bead the eye can scarcely find
   leaving behind
   where they first burst into blue
   the invisible boiling wind of sound

As horsemen used to do
As horsemen used to gallop through
   a hamlet on hunting morn

and heads and arms were thrust
through windows
leaving behind them the torn
shriek of the hound
and their wrestling dust 20

Above the roofs three jet planes
leave their hoofs of violence on naive ground.

Wind Song

CARL SANDBURG

Long ago I learned how to sleep,
In an old apple orchard where the wind swept by counting its money and throwing it away,
In a wind-gaunt orchard where the limbs forked out and listened or never listened at all,
In a passel° of trees where the branches trapped the wind into whistling, "Who, who are you?"
I slept with my head in an elbow on a summer afternoon and there I took a sleep lesson.
There I went away saying: I know why they sleep, I know how they trap the tricky winds.
Long ago I learned how to listen to the singing wind and how to forget and how to hear the deep whine,
Slapping and lapsing under the day blue and the night stars:
   Who, who are you?

   Who can ever forget
   listening to the wind go by
   counting its money
   and throwing it away?

---

4. *passel*: dialect for a group or a large number.

The World Around Us

The idea some people hold that poetry is only about "sweet" and "soft" things is contradicted by the following group of poems. Here you will find much conventional "poetic" language, such as jewels, woods by moonlight, and golden horns. But you will also find many words and phrases that you may not expect to see in poetry: onions fried, skunk, watertanks, and flies. Remember, however, the statement in the introduction: Poetry is a natural way for human beings to express themselves. If this is so, then everything in the world around us can be the stuff of poetry — watertanks as well as roses.

Crystal Moment

ROBERT P. TRISTRAM COFFIN

Once or twice this side of death
Things can make one hold his breath.

From my boyhood I remember
A crystal moment of September.

A wooded island rang with sounds
Of church bells in the throats of hounds.

A buck leaped out and took the tide
With jewels flowing past each side.

With his high head like a tree
He swam within a yard of me.   10

I saw the golden drop of light
In his eyes turned dark with fright.

I saw the forest's holiness
On him like a fierce caress.

Fear made him lovely past belief,
My heart was trembling like a leaf.

He leaned toward the land and life
With need upon him like a knife.

In his wake the hot hounds churned,
They stretched their muzzles out and yearned.　　20

They bayed no more, but swam and throbbed,
Hunger drove them till they sobbed.

Pursued, pursuers reached the shore
And vanished. I saw nothing more.

So they passed, a pageant such
As only gods could witness much,

Life and death upon one tether
And running beautiful together.

Claude McKay was born in Jamaica in the West Indies but spent most of his life in the United States. The title of his autobiography, A Long Way From Home, *reflects some of the same feeling as the following poem.*

The Tropics in New York

CLAUDE MCKAY

Bananas ripe and green, and gingerroot,
　　Cocoa in pods and alligator pears,
And tangerines and mangoes and grapefruit,
　　Fit for the highest prize at parish fairs,

Set in the window, bringing memories
　　Of fruit trees laden by low-singing rills,
And dewy dawns, and mystical blue skies
　　In benediction over nunlike hills.

My eyes grew dim, and I could no more gaze;
　　A wave of longing through my body swept,
And, hungry for the old, familiar ways,
　　I turned aside and bowed my head and wept.

Landscape as Metal and Flowers

WINFIELD TOWNLEY SCOTT

All over America railroads ride through roses.

I should explain this is thoroughly a matter of fact.
Wherever sandy earth is piled to make a road for train tracks
The banks on either side are covered with wild, sweet
Pink rambler roses: not because roses are pretty
But because ramblers grow in cheap soil and will hold
The banks firm against rain — therefore the railroad roses.

All over America the steel-supporting flowers,
Sometimes at village depots covering the shingled station,
Sometimes embracing watertanks, but mostly endless tendrils
Out of which locomotives and pullmans flash the morning —
And tunnels the other way into whose firm, sweet evening
The whistle fades, dragging freight cars, day coaches, and the caboose.

The Dark Hills

EDWIN ARLINGTON ROBINSON

Dark hills at evening in the west,
Where sunset hovers like a sound
Of golden horns that sang to rest
Old bones of warriors under ground,
Far now from all the bannered ways
Where flash the legions of the sun,
You fade — as if the last of days
Were fading, and all wars were done.

The Runaway

ROBERT FROST

Once when the snow of the year was beginning to fall,
We stopped by a mountain pasture to say, "Whose colt?"
A little Morgan had one forefoot on the wall,
The other curled at his breast. He dipped his head
And snorted at us. And then he had to bolt.
We heard the miniature thunder where he fled,
And we saw him, or thought we saw him, dim and gray,
Like a shadow against the curtain of falling flakes.
"I think the little fellow's afraid of the snow.
He isn't winter-broken. It isn't play
With the little fellow at all. He's running away.
I doubt if even his mother could tell him, 'Sakes,
It's only weather.' He'd think she didn't know!
Where is his mother? He can't be out alone."
And now he comes again with clatter of stone,
And mounts the wall again with whited eyes
And all his tail that isn't hair up straight.
He shudders his coat as if to throw off flies.
"Whoever it is that leaves him out so late,
When other creatures have gone to stall and bin,
Ought to be told to come and take him in."

Sounds

Two of the following poems are about the sounds of the modern world. The other poem is more about silence.

King Juke

KENNETH FEARING

The juke box has a big square face,
A majestic face, softly glowing with red and green and purple lights.
Have you got a face as bright as that?
BUT IT'S A PROVEN FACT, THAT A JUKE BOX HAS NO EARS.

With its throat of brass, the juke box eats live nickels raw;
It can turn itself on or shut itself off;
It has no hangovers, knows no regrets, and it never feels the need for sleep.
Can you do that?
What can you do that a juke box can't, and do it ten times better than you?

And it hammers at your nerves, and stabs you through the heart, and beats upon your soul —
But can you do that to the box?

Its resourceful mind, filled with thoughts that range from love to grief, from the gutter to the stars, from pole to pole,
Can seize its thoughts between fingers of steel,
Begin them at the start and follow them through in an orderly fashion to the very end.
Can you do that?
And what can you say that a juke box can't, and say it in a clearer, louder voice than yours?
What have you got, a juke box hasn't got?

Well, a juke box has no ears, they say.
The box, it is believed, cannot even hear itself.
IT SIMPLY HAS NO EARS AT ALL.

Juke Box Love Song

LANGSTON HUGHES

I could take the Harlem night
And wrap around you,
Take the neon lights and make a crown,
Take the Lenox Avenue buses,
Taxis, subways,
And for your love song tone their rumble down.
Take Harlem's heartbeat,
Make a drumbeat,
Put it on a record, let it whirl,
And while we listen to it play,
Dance with you till day —
Dance with you, my sweet brown Harlem girl.

The Listeners

WALTER DE LA MARE

"Is there anybody there?" said the Traveler,
   Knocking on the moonlit door;
And his horse in the silence champed the grasses
   Of the forest's ferny floor;
And a bird flew up out of the turret,
   Above the Traveler's head;
And he smote upon the door again a second time;
   "Is there anybody there?" he said.
But no one descended to the Traveler;
   No head from the leaf-fringed sill   10
Leaned over and looked into his gray eyes,
   Where he stood perplexed and still.
But only a host of phantom listeners
   That dwelt in the lone house then

Stood listening in the quiet of the moonlight
    To that voice from the world of men;
Stood thronging the faint moonbeams on the dark stair,
    That goes down to the empty hall,
Hearkening in an air stirred and shaken
    By the lonely Traveler's call.
And he felt in his heart their strangeness,
    Their stillness answering his cry,
While his horse moved, cropping the dark turf,
    'Neath the starred and leafy sky;
For he suddenly smote on the door, even
    Louder, and lifted his head —
"Tell them I came, and no one answered,
    That I kept my word," he said.
Never the least stir made the listeners,
    Though every word he spake
Fell echoing through the shadowiness of the still house
    From the one man left awake.
Ay, they heard his foot upon the stirrup,
    And the sound of iron on stone,
And how the silence surged softly backward,
    When the plunging hoofs were gone.

Haiku

The haiku (hī′kōō) is a very old form of Japanese poetry. Most haiku are impressions of Nature, though modern haiku can be about anything the poet sees. In Japanese, it is a very strict form, and its strictness is part of its appeal. The Japanese haiku has exactly seventeen syllables. They are arranged as follows:

> First line: five syllables
> Second line: seven syllables
> Third line: five syllables

The translator of the following haiku is a leading American authority on this form of poetry. He believes that it is impossible to insist on the strict seventeen syllables in English — for the simple reason that Japanese and English word-forms are so different from each other. In these translations, you will find as few as fourteen or as many as twenty syllables.

More important than the number of syllables is the spirit of the haiku. It is a sharp impression of nature, and it usually contains a contrast of opposites: hot and cold, dark and light, large and small, new and old, and so forth.

Eight Haiku

The Monkey's Raincoat

BASHŌ

The first cold showers pour.
  Even the monkey seems to want
    a little coat of straw.

The Seasons

SANPŪ

Cherry-bloom, cuckoo,
  moon, snow — and already
    the year is through!

Spring Concert

SHIKI

On how to sing
 the frog school and the skylark school
  are arguing.

The New and the Old

SHIKI

Railroad tracks; a flight
 of wild geese close above them
  in the moonlit night.

The Snake

KYOSHI

A snake! Though it passes,
 eyes that had glared at me
  stay in the grasses.

Loneliness

HASHIN

No sky at all,
 no earth at all — and still
  the snowflakes fall. . . .

Autumn

BASHŌ

On a withered branch
 a crow has settled
  autumn nightfall.

The New Moon

ISSA

Just three days old,
  the moon, and it's all warped and bent!
  How keen the cold!

translated by HAROLD G. HENDERSON

The haiku *above are classics of Japanese literature dating back to the seventeenth century. But the* haiku *is a form which appeals to poets of our own time as well. Although he is better known for his novels than for his poetry, Richard Wright, an American, reveals real understanding of this Japanese form.*

Four Haiku

RICHARD WRIGHT

1

Make up your mind snail!
You are half inside your house
And halfway out!

2

In the falling snow
A laughing boy holds out his palms
Until they are white

3

Keep straight down this block
Then turn right where you will find
A peach tree blooming

4

The crow flew so fast
That he left his lonely caw
Behind in the fields

Lincoln in 1857: "A short time before my nomination, I was in Chicago.... A photographer of that city asked me to sit for a picture, and I did so. This coarse, rough hair of mine was in a particularly bad tousle at the time, and the picture presented me in all its fright. After my nomination, this being about the only picture of me there was, copies were struck to show those who had never seen me how I looked. One newsboy carried them around to sell, and had for his cry: 'Here's your likeness of Old Abe! Will look a good deal better when he gets his hair combed!'"

BOOK THREE | PART 1

ABRAHAM LINCOLN
Carl Sandburg

Abraham Lincoln is one of the major heroes of modern times, not only to America but to the entire world. There is a sharp contrast between the qualities that make Lincoln a hero and the qualities we have seen in that hero of the ancient world, Odysseus. Two of Odysseus' outstanding qualities were:
1. His cleverness in outwitting his enemies, even if it meant resorting to lies.
2. His almost superhuman strength: for example, no other man could string his giant bow.

Now it is true that Lincoln is also remembered for his wit and youthful skill in logsplitting and wrestling. But it is most of all for his moral quality that Lincoln is remembered. In modern times heroism is no longer a question of noble birth and physical strength.

Another important difference between the two heroes is that in the case of Odysseus we are reading a legend — that is, fiction, while

Lincoln's story is true, a part of history. We know a great number of facts about Lincoln: there were people living when Sandburg began his book who knew Lincoln personally; there are letters, documents, photographs, which reveal a great deal about the man.

BIOGRAPHY

Legends have grown up about Lincoln, but the biographer's task is to separate the facts of his life from the myths about him. The desire to know the facts, the "truth," about a person or period is the reason for writing and reading history. The introduction to the Odyssey (p. 1) said that "an epic tells men about the past of their nation or race [and] attempts to give meaning to history." You saw how an epic focuses on the deeds of an individual hero. A biography does the same; it attempts to find meaning in history by concentrating on a particular person. But an epic is a work of fiction in which facts are unimportant. A biography is a work of nonfiction that relies on correct information.

When a biography is well written, it shares some of the qualities of fiction. It, too, is a story. Like fiction, a good biography brings its subject alive and depicts his life and times. It is more than a list of dates and events.

A biographer collects a vast amount of information, but he cannot include it all in his book. He must select, and in doing so he must use imagination and sensitivity. In choosing which information to put in and which to leave out, the biographer shapes both the material and our image of the person he is writing about. In the biography you are about to read, it is Sandburg's Lincoln you will come to know. Other biographies will give a different picture of the man.

ABRAHAM LINCOLN: THE COMMON MAN AS HERO

Odysseus was a king protected by gods; Lincoln was a man of humble origin, who had to rely on his own strength and courage to face difficult circumstances. He prevailed, and some of his achievements changed the course of American history.

Lincoln's accomplishments and character lend themselves to the creation of a new kind of mythic hero — the Common Man. The simplest fact of his life, that he went from log cabin to White House, typifies the American idea of success and has heroic proportions. Moreover, Lincoln was homely, ungainly, kind, and humorous, a man of the people who looked and acted the part. He certainly did not have any of the mannerisms we think of as aristocratic. Instead, he was a commoner who, leading the American people to greater freedom, symbolized in his life and death the tragic ordeal by which that freedom was gained. With very little effort, the details of Lincoln's life were converted into legend and myth.

Lincoln stands as a symbol of plain talk, common sense, the love of freedom, and of the hope of common people the world over. As such, he is, in the words of the American poet Mark Van Doren, "the most interesting man who ever lived." More than five thousand books have been written about Lincoln, but the most famous by far is the biography by Carl Sandburg.

CARL SANDBURG (1878–1967)

The son of Swedish immigrants, Sandburg was born in 1878 in Galesburg, Illinois, near where Lincoln lived before his presidency. Born only thirteen years after Lincoln's death, Sandburg grew up among people who had known and remembered Abraham Lincoln. Just as the young Lincoln tried many occupations, so too did Sandburg: he was a wagon driver, wheat harvester, dishwasher, and coal shoveler, as well as newspaper writer and editor, poet, lecturer, and singer of folk songs. He wrote more than thirty books.

For thirty years, Sandburg planned to write a book about Lincoln's life which would cover the years before he became President. The two-volume Abraham Lincoln: The Prairie Years was published in 1929. The four-volume Abraham Lincoln: The War Years was published in 1939 and won the Pulitzer Prize.

Together, The Prairie Years and The War Years took fifteen years to write and total one and a half million words. Sandburg's research for the biography involved his traveling all over the country. He interviewed people and examined many collections of Lincoln material, including letters, diaries, handbills, pictures, and cartoons. In 1954, Sandburg condensed his mammoth biography into one volume, adding newly discovered material to the new work. A selection from the one-volume edition appears on the following pages.

Abraham Lincoln

from
A Lincoln Preface

In the time of the April lilacs in the year 1865, a man in the city of Washington, D.C., trusted a guard to watch at a door, and the guard was careless, left the door, and the man was shot, lingered a night, passed away, was laid in a box, and carried north and west a thousand miles; bells sobbed; cities wore crepe; people stood with hats off as the railroad burial car came past at midnight, dawn, or noon.

During the four years of time before he gave up the ghost, this man was clothed with despotic power, commanding the most powerful armies till then assembled in modern warfare, enforcing drafts of soldiers, abolishing the right of habeas corpus, directing politically and spiritually the wild, massive forces loosed in civil war.

Four billion dollars' worth of property was taken from those who had been legal owners of it, confiscated, wiped out as by fire, at his instigation and executive direction; a class of chattel property recognized as lawful for two hundred years went to the scrap pile.

When the woman [1] who wrote *Uncle Tom's Cabin* came to see him in the White House, he greeted her, "So you're the little woman who wrote the book that made this great war," and as they seated themselves at a fireplace, "I do love an open fire; I always had one to home." As they were finishing their talk of the days of blood, he said, "I shan't last long after it's over."

An Illinois Congressman looked in on him as he had his face lathered for a shave in the White House, and remarked, "If anybody

---
[1] *woman:* Harriet Beecher Stowe.

had told me that in a great crisis like this the people were going out to a little one-horse town and pick out a one-horse lawyer for President, I wouldn't have believed it." The answer was, "Neither would I. But it was a time when a man with a policy would have been fatal to the country. I never had a policy. I have simply tried to do what seemed best each day, as each day came."

"I don't intend precisely to throw the Constitution overboard, but I will stick it in a hole if I can," he told a Cabinet officer. The enemy was violating the Constitution to destroy the Union, he argued, and therefore, "I will violate the Constitution, if necessary, to save the Union." He instructed a messenger to the Secretary of the Treasury, "Tell him not to bother himself about the Constitution. Say that I have that sacred instrument here at the White House, and I am guarding it with great care."

His life, mind, and heart ran in contrasts. When his white kid gloves broke into tatters while shaking hands at a White House reception, he remarked, "This looks like a general bustification." When he talked with an Ohio friend one day during the 1864 campaign, he mentioned one public man, and murmured, "He's a thistle! I don't see why God lets him live." Of a devious Senator, he said, "He's too crooked to lie still!" And of a New York editor, "In early life in the West, we used to make our shoes last a great while with much mending, and sometimes, when far gone, we found the leather so rotten the stitches would not hold. Greeley is so rotten that nothing can be done with him. He is not truthful; the stitches all tear out."

While the luck of war wavered and broke and came again, as generals failed and campaigns were lost, he held enough forces of the Union together to raise new armies and supply them, until generals were found who made war as victorious war has always been made, with terror, frightfulness, destruction, and valor and sacrifice past words of man to tell.

His own speeches, letters, telegrams, and official messages during that war form the most significant and enduring document from any one man on why the war began, why it went on, and the dangers beyond its end. As the platoons filed before him at a review of an army corps, he asked, "What is to become of these boys when the war is over?"

He was a chosen spokesman; yet there were times he was silent;

nothing but silence could at those times have fitted a chosen spokesman; in the mixed shame and blame of the immense wrongs of two crashing civilizations, with nothing to say, he said nothing, slept not at all, and wept at those times in a way that made weeping appropriate, decent, majestic.

His hat was shot off as he rode alone one night in Washington; a son he loved died as he watched at the bed; his wife was accused of betraying information to the enemy, until denials from him were necessary; his best companion was a fine-hearted and brilliant son with a deformed palate and an impediment of speech; when a Pennsylvania Congressman told him the enemy had declared they would break into the city and hang him to a lamppost, he said he had considered "the violent preliminaries" to such a scene; on his left thumb was a scar where an ax had nearly chopped the thumb off when he was a boy; over one eye was a scar where he had been hit with a club in the hands of a man trying to steal the cargo off a Mississippi River flatboat; he threw a cashiered [2] officer out of his room in the White House, crying, "I can bear censure, but not insult. I never wish to see your face again."

He rebuked with anger a woman who got on her knees to thank him for a pardon that saved her son from being shot at sunrise; and when an Iowa woman said she had journeyed out of her way to Washington just for a look at him, he grinned, "Well, in the matter of looking at one another, I have altogether the advantage."

He sent hundreds of telegrams, "Suspend death sentence" or "Suspend execution" of so-and-so, who was to be shot at sunrise. The telegrams varied oddly at times, as in one, "If Thomas Samplogh, of the First Delaware Regiment, has been sentenced to death, and is not yet executed, suspend and report the case to me." And another, "Is it Lieutenant Samuel B. Davis whose death sentence is commuted? If not done, let it be done."

While the war drums beat, he liked best, of all the stories told of him, one about two Quakeresses heard talking in a railway car. "I think that Jefferson [3] will succeed." "Why does thee think so?" "Because Jefferson is a praying man." "And so is Abraham a praying man." "Yes, but the Lord will think Abraham is joking."

---

[2] *cashiered*: dismissed in disgrace, as a military officer.
[3] *Jefferson*: Jefferson Davis, U.S. statesman and president of the Confederacy.

An Indiana man at the White House heard him say, "Voorhees, don't it seem strange to you that I, who could never so much as cut off the head of a chicken, should be elected, or selected, into the midst of all this blood?"

Of men taking too fat profits out of the war, he said, "Where the carcass is there will the eagles be gathered together."

An enemy general, Longstreet, after the war, declared him to have been "the one matchless man in forty millions of people," while one of his private secretaries, Hay, declared his life to have been the most perfect in its relationships and adjustments since that of Christ.

Between the days in which he crawled as a baby on the dirt floor of a Kentucky cabin, and the time when he gave his final breath in Washington, he packed a rich life with work, thought, laughter, tears, hate, love.

With vast reservoirs of the comic and the droll, and notwithstanding a mastery of mirth and nonsense, he delivered a volume of addresses and letters of terrible and serious appeal, with import beyond his own day, shot through here and there with far, thin ironies, with paragraphs having raillery of the quality of the Book of Job, and echoes as subtle as the whispers of wind in prairie grass.

Perhaps no human clay pot has held more laughter and tears.

The facts and myths of his life are to be an American possession, shared widely over the world, for thousands of years, as the traditions of Knute or Alfred, Lao-tse or Diogenes, Pericles or Caesar,[4] are kept. This because he was not only a genius in the science of neighborly human relationships and an artist in the personal handling of life from day to day, but a Strange Friend and a Friendly Stranger to all forms of life that he met.

He lived fifty-six years, of which fifty-two were lived in the West — the prairie years.

---

[4] *Knute . . . Caesar:* kings, philosophers, statesmen, and generals.

from
The Prairie Years

1

WILDERNESS BEGINNINGS

In May and the blossom-time of 1808, Tom and Nancy Lincoln with the baby Sarah moved from Elizabethtown in Kentucky to the farm of George Brownfield, where Tom did carpenter and farm work. Near their cabin wild crab apple trees stood thick and flourishing with riots of bloom and odor. And the smell of wild crab apple blossoms, and the low crying of all wild things, came keen that summer to Nancy Hanks Lincoln. The summer stars that year shook out pain and warning, strange and bittersweet laughters, for Nancy Hanks.

The same year saw Tom Lincoln's family moved to his land on the South Fork of Nolin Creek, about two and a half miles from Hodgenville. He was trying to farm stubborn ground and make a home in a cabin of logs he cut from timber nearby. The floor was packed-down dirt. One door, swung on leather hinges, let them in and out. One small window gave a lookout on the weather, the rain or snow, sun and trees, and the play of the rolling prairie and low hills. A stick-clay chimney carried the fire smoke up and away.

One morning in February 1809, Tom Lincoln came out of his cabin to the road, stopped a neighbor, and asked him to tell "the granny woman," Aunt Peggy Walters, that Nancy would need help soon. On the morning of February 12, a Sunday, the granny woman was at the cabin. And she and Tom Lincoln and the moaning Nancy Hanks welcomed into a world of battle and blood, of whispering dreams and wistful dust, a new child, a boy.

A little later that morning Tom Lincoln threw extra wood on the fire, an extra bearskin over the mother, and walked two miles up the road to where the Sparrows, Tom and Betsy, lived. Dennis Hanks, the nine-year-old boy adopted by the Sparrows, met Tom at the door. In his slow way of talking Tom Lincoln told them, "Nancy's got a boy baby." A half-sheepish look was in his eyes, as though maybe more babies were not wanted in Kentucky just then.

Dennis Hanks took to his feet down the road to the Lincoln cabin. There he saw Nancy Hanks on a bed of poles cleated to a corner of the cabin, under warm bearskins. She turned to look at Dennis and threw him a tired, white smile. He stood watching the even, quiet breaths of this fresh, soft red baby. "What you goin' to name him, Nancy?" the boy asked. "Abraham," was the answer, "after his grandfather."

He asked if he could hold the baby. Nancy, as she passed the little one into Dennis's arms, said, "Be keerful, Dennis, fur you air the fust boy he's ever seen." Dennis swung the baby back and forth, keeping up a chatter about how tickled he was to have a new cousin to play with. The baby screwed up its face and began crying with no letup. Dennis turned to Betsy Sparrow, handed her the baby, and said, "Aunt, take him! He'll never come to much."

Thus the birthday scene reported years later by Dennis Hanks, whose nimble mind sometimes invented more than he saw or heard. Peggy Walters, too, years later, gave the scene as her memory served: "The baby was born just about sunup, on Sunday morning. Nancy's two aunts took the baby and washed him and dressed him, and I looked after Nancy. And I remember after the baby was born, Tom came and stood beside the bed and looked down at Nancy lying there, so pale and so tired, and he stood there with that sort of hang dog look that a man has, sort of guilty like, but mighty proud, and he says to me, 'Are you sure she's all right, Mis' Walters?' And Nancy kind of stuck out her hand and reached for his, and said, 'Yes, Tom, I'm all right.' And then she said, 'You're glad it's a boy, Tom, aren't you? So am I.'"

Whatever the exact particulars, the definite event on that twelfth of February, 1809, was the birth of a boy they named Abraham after his grandfather who had been killed by Indians — born in silence and pain from a wilderness mother on a bed of perhaps cornhusks and perhaps hen feathers — with perhaps a laughing child prophecy later that he would "never come to much."

In the spring of 1811 Tom Lincoln moved his family ten miles northeast, to a 230-acre farm he had bought on Knob Creek, where the soil was a little richer and there were more neighbors. The famous Cumberland Trail, the main pike from Louisville to Nashville, ran nearby the new log cabin Tom built, and they could see covered wagons with settlers heading south, west, north; peddlers with tinware and notions; gangs of slaves or "kaffles" moving on foot ahead of an overseer or slave trader on horseback; and sometimes, in dandy carriages, Congressmen or legislative members going to sessions at Louisville.

Here little Abe grew out of one shirt into another, learned to walk and talk and, as he grew bigger, how to be a chore boy, to run errands, carry water, fill the woodbox, clean ashes from the fireplace. He learned the feel of blisters on his hands from using a hoe handle on rows of beans, onions, corn, potatoes. He ducked out of the way of the heels of the stallion and two brood mares his father kept and paid taxes on. That Knob Creek farm in their valley set round by high hills and deep gorges was the first home Abe Lincoln remembered.

Again there were quiet and anxious days in 1812 when another baby was on the way; again came neighbor helpers, and Nancy gave birth to her third child. They named him Thomas but he died a few days after, and Sarah and Abe saw, in a coffin their father made, the little cold still face and made their first acquaintance with the look of death in a personal grief in their own one-room cabin.

Four miles a day Sarah and Abe walked when school kept and they were not needed at home. In a log schoolhouse with a dirt floor and one door, seated on puncheon benches [1] with no backs, they learned the alphabet A to Z and numbers one to ten. It was called a "blab school"; the pupils before reciting read their lessons out loud to themselves to show they were busy studying. Young Abe learned to write and to like forming letters and shaping words. He said later that "anywhere and everywhere that lines could be drawn, there he improved his capacity for writing." He scrawled words with charcoal, he shaped them in the dust, in sand, in snow. Writing had a fascination for him.

In December 1816, Tom Lincoln with Nancy, Sarah, Abe, four horses, and their most needed household goods, made their breakaway from Kentucky, moving north and crossing the Ohio River into land then Perry County, later Spencer County, Indiana. They traveled a wild raw country, rolling land with trees everywhere, tall

---

[1] *puncheon* (pun'chən) *benches:* backless benches made from split logs.

oaks and elms, maples, birches, dogwood, underbrush tied down by ever-winding grapevines, thin mist and winter damp rising from the ground as Tom, with Abe perhaps helping, sometimes went ahead with an ax and hacked out a trail. "It was a wild region, with many bears and other wild animals still in the woods," Abe wrote later, where "the panther's scream filled night with fear" and "bears preyed on the swine." A lonesome country, settlers few, "about one human being to each square mile," families two and three miles apart.

They toiled and hacked their way through wilderness until, about sixteen miles from the Ohio River, they came to a rise of ground somewhat open near Little Pigeon Creek. Here the whole family pitched in and threw together a pole shed or "half-faced camp"; at the open side a log fire kept burning night and day. In the next weeks of that winter Tom Lincoln, with help from neighbors and young Abe, now nearly eight, erected a cabin 18 by 20 feet, with a loft. Abe later wrote that he "though very young, was large of his age, and had an ax put into his hands at once; and was almost constantly handling that most useful instrument." The chinking of wet clay and grass ("wattle and daub") between the logs in the new cabin had not been finished in early February when something happened that a boy remembers after he is a grown man. Years later Abe wrote, "At this place A.[braham] took an early start as a hunter, which was never much improved afterwards. A few days before the completion of his eighth year, in the absence of his father, a flock of wild turkeys approached the new log cabin, and A.[braham] with a rifle gun, standing inside, shot through a crack and killed one of them." Then came another sentence, "He has never since pulled a trigger on any larger game," making it clear that when they had deer or bear meat or other food from "larger game," it was not from his shooting. He didn't like shooting to kill and didn't care for a reputation as a hunter.

It was a hard year, "pretty pinching times," as Abe put it later. They had to chop down trees, clear away underbrush, on what few acres they planted after plowing the hard, unbroken sod. Their food was mostly game shot in the woods nearby — deer, bear, wild turkeys, ducks, geese. Wild pigeons in flocks sometimes darkened the sky. Their cabin lighting at night was from fire logs, pine knots, or hog fat. Sarah and Abe went barefoot from late spring till autumn frosts, brought home nuts and wild fruits, watched sometimes the excitement of their father smoking out a bee tree for the honey. One drawback was their water supply. Abe or Sarah had to walk nearly a mile to fetch spring water. Tom dug several wells but they all went dry.

A wagon one day late in 1817 brought into the Lincoln clearing their good Kentucky neighbors Tom and Betsy Sparrow and the odd, quizzical seventeen-year-old Dennis Friend Hanks. The Sparrows were to live in the Lincoln pole shed till they could locate land and settle. Hardly a year had passed, however, when Tom and Betsy Sparrow were taken down with the "milk sick," beginning with a whitish coat on the tongue, resulting, it was supposed, from cows eating white snakeroot or other growths that poisoned their milk. Tom and Betsy Sparrow died and were buried in September on a little hill in a clearing in the timbers nearby.

Soon after, there came to Nancy Hanks Lincoln that white coating of the tongue; her vitals burned; her tongue turned brownish; her feet and hands grew cold and colder, her pulse slow and slower. She knew she was dying, called for her children, and spoke to them her last dim choking words. Death came October 5, 1818, the banners of autumn flaming their crimsons over tall oaks and quiet maples. On a bed of poles cleated to a corner of the cabin, the body of Nancy Hanks Lincoln lay in peace and silence, the eyelids closed down in unbroken rest. To the children who tiptoed in, stood still, cried their tears of want and longing, whispered and heard only their own whispers answering, she looked as though new secrets had come to her in place of the old secrets given up with the breath of life.

Tom Lincoln took a log left over from the building of the cabin, and he and Dennis Hanks whipsawed it into planks, planed the planks smooth, and made them of a measure for a box to bury the dead wife and mother in. Little Abe, with a jackknife, whittled pine-wood pegs. And while Dennis and Abe held the planks, Tom bored holes and stuck the whittled pegs through the holes. This was the coffin they carried next day to the little timber clearing nearby, where a few weeks before they had buried Tom and Betsy Sparrow.

So Nancy Hanks Lincoln died, thirty-four years old, a pioneer sacrifice, with memories of monotonous, endless everyday chores, of mystic Bible verses read over and over for their promises, of blue wistful hills and a summer when the crab apple blossoms flamed white and she carried a boy child into the world.

A hard year followed, with twelve-year-old Sarah as housekeeper and cook, and Tom Lincoln, with the help of Dennis and Abe, trying to clear more land, plant it, and make the farm a go.

Lonesome days came for Abe and Sarah in November, when their father went away, promising to come back. He headed for Elizabethtown, Kentucky, through woods and across the Ohio River, to the house of the widow Sarah Bush Johnston. They said he argued straight-out: "I have no wife and you no husband. I came a-purpose to marry you. I knowed you from a gal and you knowed me from a boy. I've no time to lose; and if you're willin' let it be done straight off." She answered, "I got a few little debts," gave him a list and he paid them; and they were married December 2, 1819.

Abe and Sarah had a nice surprise one morning when four horses and a wagon came into their clearing, and their father jumped off, then Sarah Bush Lincoln, the new wife and mother, then her three children by her first husband, Sarah Elizabeth (13), Matilda (10), and John D. Johnston (9 years old). Next off the wagon came a feather mattress and pillows, a black walnut bureau, a large clothes chest, a table, chairs, pots and skillets, knives, forks, spoons.

"Here's your new mammy," his father told Abe as the boy looked up at a strong, large-boned, rosy woman, with a kindly face and eyes, a steady voice, steady ways. From the first she was warm and friendly for Abe's hands to touch. And his hands roved with curiosity over a feather pillow and a feather mattress.

The one-room cabin now sheltered eight people to feed and clothe. Dennis and Abe climbed on pegs to the loft for their sleep and liked it when later the logs were chinked against the rain or snow coming in on them. Dennis said "Aunt Sairy," the new mother, "had faculty and didn't 'pear to be hurried or worried none," that she got Tom to put in a floor and make "some good beds and cheers." Abe, like Dennis, said "cheers"; if he said "chairs," he would be taken as "uppety" and "too fine-haired."

In the earlier years he wore buckskin breeches and moccasins, a tow linen shirt and coonskin cap, "the way we all dressed them days," said Dennis Hanks. For winter snow and slush they had "birch bark, with hickory bark soles, stropped on over yarn socks."

And later, "when it got so we could keep chickens, an' have salt pork an' corn dodgers,[2] an' gyardin saas an' molasses, an' have jeans pants an' cowhide boots to wear, we felt as if we was gittin' along in the world."

Eleven-year-old Abe went to school again. Years later he wrote of where he grew up, "There were some schools, so called; but no qualification was ever required of a teacher, beyond *'readin', writin', and cipherin' '* to the Rule of Three. If a straggler supposed to understand Latin, happened to sojourn in the neighborhood, he was looked upon as a wizard." School kept at Pigeon Creek when a schoolmaster happened to drift in, usually in winter, and school was out when he drifted away. The schoolmasters were paid by the parents in venison, hams, corn, animal skins, and other produce. Four miles from home to school and four miles to home again Abe walked for his learning, saying later that "all his schooling did not amount to one year."

Abe kept his school sum book sheets as though they might be worth reading again with such rhymes as:

> Abraham Lincoln is my name
> And with my pen I wrote the same
> I wrote in both hast and speed
> and left it here for fools to read
>
> Abraham Lincoln his hand and pen
> he will be good but god knows When

Having learned to read, Abe read all the books he could lay his hands on. Dennis, years later, tried to remember his cousin's reading habits. "I never seen Abe after he was twelve 'at he didn't have a book some'ers 'round. He'd put a book inside his shirt an' fill his pants pockets with corn dodgers, an' go off to plow or hoe. When noon come he'd set down under a tree, an' read an' eat. In the house at night, he'd tilt a cheer by the chimbly, an' set on his backbone an' read. I've seen a feller come in an' look at him, Abe not knowin' anybody was 'round, an' sneak out agin like a cat, an' say, 'Well, I'll be darned.' It didn't seem natural, nohow, to see a feller read like that. Aunt Sairy'd never let the children pester him. She always said Abe was goin' to be a great man some day. An' she wasn't goin' to have him hendered."

---

[2] *corn dodgers:* cooked cakes of Indian meal.

They heard Abe saying, "The things I want to know are in books; my best friend is the man who'll git me a book I ain't read." One fall afternoon he walked to see John Pitcher, a lawyer at Rockport, nearly twenty miles away, and borrowed a book he heard Pitcher had. A few days later, with his father and Dennis and John Hanks, he shucked corn from early daylight till sundown. Then after supper he read the book till midnight and next day at noon hardly knew the taste of his corn bread because of the book in front of him. So they told it.

He read many hours in the family Bible, the only book in their cabin. He borrowed and read *Aesop's Fables, Pilgrim's Progress, Robinson Crusoe*, Grimshaw's *History of the United States*, and Weems's *The Life of George Washington, with Curious Anecdotes, Equally Honorable to Himself and Exemplary to His Young Countrymen*. Books lighted lamps in the dark rooms of his gloomy hours.

When John Hanks, a cousin of Nancy Hanks, came to live with them about 1823, there were nine persons sleeping, eating, washing, mending, dressing, and undressing in the one-room cabin, gathered close to the fireplace in zero weather. John Hanks and Dennis, with some neighbors, seemed to agree that while Abe wasn't "lazy," his mind was often on books to the neglect of work. A neighbor woman sized him up: "He could work when he wanted to, but he was no hand to pitch in like killing snakes." John Romine remarked, "Abe Lincoln worked for me . . . didn't love work half as much as his pay. He said to me one day that his father taught him to work, but he never taught him to love it."

When rain soaked Weems's *Life of Washington* that Josiah Crawford had loaned him, he confessed he had been careless and pulled fodder three days to pay for the book, making such a clean sweep that there wasn't an ear on a cornstalk in the field of Josiah Crawford.

Farm boys in evenings at the store in Gentryville, a mile and a half from the Lincoln cabin, talked about how Abe Lincoln was always digging into books, picking a piece of charcoal to write on the fire shovel, shaving off what he wrote, and then writing more. Dennis Hanks said, "There's suthin' peculiarsome about Abe." It seemed that Abe made books tell him more than they told other people. When he read in a book about a boat that came near a magnetic rock and how the magnets in the rock pulled all the nails out of the boat so it went to pieces and the people in the boat found themselves floundering in water, Abe thought it was interesting and told it to others. When he sat with the girl, Kate Roby, with their bare feet in the creek, and she spoke of the moon rising, he explained to her it was the earth moving and not the moon — the moon only seemed to rise. Kate was surprised at such knowledge.

The years passed and Abe Lincoln grew up, at seventeen standing six feet, nearly four inches, long-armed, with rare strength in his muscles. At eighteen he could take an ax at the end of the handle and hold it out from his shoulders in a straight horizontal line, easy and steady. He could make his ax flash and bite into a sugar maple or a sycamore, one neighbor saying, "He can sink an ax deeper into wood than any man I ever saw." He learned how suddenly life can spring a surprise. One day in the woods, as he was sharpening a wedge on a log, the ax glanced, nearly took his thumb off, and the cut after healing left a white scar for life. "You never cuss a good ax," was a saying then.

Sleep came deep to him after work outdoors, clearing timberland for crops, cutting brush and burning it, splitting rails, pulling crosscut saw and whipsaw, driving the shovel plow, harrowing, spading, planting, hoeing, cradling grain, milking cows, helping neighbors at house-raisings, logrollings, cornhuskings, hog killings. He found he was fast and strong against other boys in sports. He earned board, clothes, and lodgings, sometimes, working for a neighbor farmer.

Often Abe worked alone in the timbers, daylong with only the sound of his own ax, or his own voice speaking to himself, or the crackling and swaying of branches in the wind, or the cries and whirrs of animals, of brown and silver-gray squirrels, of partridges, hawks, crows, turkeys, grouse, sparrows, and an occasional wildcat. In wilderness loneliness he companioned with trees, with the faces of open sky and weather in changing seasons, with that individual one-man instrument, the ax. Silence found him for her own. In the making of him, the element of silence was immense.

On a misunderstanding one time between Lincoln and William Grigsby, Grigsby flared so mad he challenged Abe to a fight. Abe looked at Grigsby, smiled, and said the fight ought to be with John D. Johnston, Abe's stepbrother. The day was set, each man with his seconds. The two fighters, stripped to the waist, mauled at each other with bare knuckles. A crowd formed a ring and stood cheering, yelling, hissing, and after a while saw Johnston getting the worst of it. The ring of the crowd was broken when Abe shouldered his way through, stepped out, took hold of Grigsby, and threw him out of the center of the fight ring. Then, so they said, Abe Lincoln called out, "I'm the big buck of this lick," and his eyes sweeping the circle of the crowd he challenged, "If any of you want to try it, come on and whet your horns." Wild fist-fighting came, and for months around the store in Gentryville they argued about which gang whipped the other.

Asked by farmer James Taylor if he could kill a hog, Abe answered, "If you will risk the hog I'll risk myself." He put barefoot boys to wading in a mud puddle near the horse trough, picked them up one by one, carried them to the house upside down, and walked their muddy feet across the ceiling. The stepmother came in, laughed at the foot tracks, told Abe he ought to be spanked — and he cleaned the ceiling so it looked new.

Education came to the youth Abe by many ways outside of schools and books. As he said later, he "picked up" education. He was the letter writer for the family and for neighbors. As he wrote, he read the words out loud. He asked questions, "What do you want to say in the letter? How do you want to say it? Are you sure that's the best way to say it? Or do you think we can fix up a better way to say it?" This was a kind of training in grammar and English composition.

He walked thirty miles to a courthouse to hear lawyers speak and to see how they argued and acted. He heard roaring and ranting political speakers — and mimicked them. He listened to wandering evangelists who flung their arms and tore the air with their voices — and mimicked them. He told droll stories with his face screwed up in different ways. He tried to read people as keenly as he read books. He drank enough drams of whisky to learn he didn't like the taste and it wasn't good for his mind or body. He smoked enough tobacco to learn he wouldn't care for it. He heard rollicking verses and songs and kept some of them for their earthy flavor and sometimes meaningful intentions.

His stepmother was a rich silent force in his life. The family and the neighbors spoke of her sagacity and gumption, her sewing and mending, how spick-and-span she kept her house, her pots, pans, and kettles. Her faith in God shone in works more than words, and, hard as life was, she was thankful to be alive. She understood Abe's gloomy spells better than anyone else, and he named her as a deep influence in him. "Abe never spoke a cross word to me," she said and she found him truthful. Matilda in a wild prank hid and leaped out onto Abe's back to give him a scare in a lonely timber. Pulling her hands against his shoulders and pressing her knees against his back, she brought him down to the ground. His ax blade cut her ankle and strips from his shirt and her dress had to be torn to stop the bleeding. By then she was sobbing over what to tell her mother; on Abe's advice she told her mother the whole truth.

A mile across the fields from the Lincoln home was the Pigeon Creek Baptist Church, a log meetinghouse put up in 1822. Most of the church people could read only the shortest words in the Bible, or none at all. They sat in the log meetinghouse on the split-log benches their own axes had shaped, listening to the preacher reading from the Bible. They met understanding from the solemn young Lincoln, who had refused to join his schoolmates in putting fire on a live mud turtle and had written a paper arguing against cruelty to animals, who would bother to lug on his shoulders and save from freezing a man overloaded with whisky.

At the Pigeon Creek settlement, while the structure of his bones, the build and hang of his torso and limbs, took shape, other elements, invisible yet permanent, traced their lines in the tissues of his head and heart.

Young Abraham had worked as a farm hand and ferry helper for James Taylor, who lived at the mouth of Anderson Creek and operated a ferry across the Ohio River. Here Abe saw steamboats, strings of flatboats loaded with farm produce, other boats with cargoes from manufacturing centers. Houseboats, arks, sleds, flatboats with small cabins in which families lived and kept house, floated toward their new homesteads; on some were women washing, children playing. Here was the life flow of a main artery of American civilization, at a vivid time of growth. Here at eighteen Abe built a scow and was taking passengers from Bates Landing to steamboats in midstream. Two travelers anxious to get on a steamer came one day, and he sculled them out and lifted their trunks on board. Each threw him a silver half-dollar. It gave him a new feeling; the most he had ever earned was thirty-one cents a day. And when one of the half-dollars slipped from him and sank in the river, that too gave him a new feeling.

James Gentry, with the largest farms in the Pigeon Creek clearings and a landing on the Ohio River, had looked Lincoln over. He believed Abe could take a cargo of produce down the Mississippi to New Orleans. Abe built a flatboat, cut oaks for a double bottom of stout planks, and a deck shelter, two pairs of long oars at bow and stern, a check post, and a setting pole for steering. In charge of the boat Mr. Gentry had placed his son Allen and the nineteen-year-old Lincoln, "a hired hand," as he called himself. They loaded the boat and pushed off for a thousand-mile trip on the wide, winding waterway.

At New Orleans they sold their cargo and flatboat and lingered a few days. For the first time young Lincoln saw a city of 40,000 people, a metropolis, a world port, with seagoing ships taking on cotton, sugar, tobacco, and foodstuffs for Europe, a levee and wharves thick with planters, clerks, longshoremen, and roustabouts [3] loading and unloading cargoes. Sailors and deck hands from many nations and great world ports walked and straggled along, talking, shouting, roistering, their languages a fascinating jabber to the youths from Indiana. British, Yankee, and French faces, Spanish, Mexican, Creole, the occasional free Negro, and the frequent slave were on the streets. Gangs of chained slaves passed, headed for cotton plantations of a thousand and more acres. Here was a great and famous cathedral, here mansions of extravagant cost and upkeep, narrow streets with quaint iron grillwork fronting the second stories, live oaks drooping with Spanish moss, and many blocks of huts and hovels. The city had a feel of old times and customs, of mossy traditions, none of the raw and new as seen in Indiana.

Lincoln and Allen Gentry, heading for home after three months, rode an elegant steamboat up the Mississippi, the fare paid by James Gentry. Abe's wages at $8.00 a month, or what he hadn't spent out of $24, he paid over to his father, according to law and custom.

---

[3] *roustabouts:* laborers on the waterfront.

After a thousand miles of excitement and new sights every day, he worked a while in James Gentry's store in 1829. Then came a new excitement — Tom Lincoln was moving his family and kinfolk to Illinois, where John Hanks had gone. A new outbreak of the milk sick had brought a neighborhood scare. Tom's farm wasn't paying well, and John Hanks was writing letters about rich land and better crops.

They made wagons that winter, of wood all through, pegs, cleats, hickory withes, knots of bark holding some parts together, though the wheel rims were iron. They loaded bedclothes, skillets, ovens, furniture, on three wagons, ready to go early morning of March 1, 1830. Abraham Lincoln had been for some days a citizen who "had reached his majority"; he could vote at elections, was lawfully free from paying his wages to his father; he could come and go now; he was footloose.

After traveling over 200 miles to Macon County, Illinois, they found John Hanks, who showed them the location he had picked for them on the north bank of the Sangamon River, about ten miles southwest of Decatur, land joining timber and prairie. John Hanks had already cut the logs for their cabin, which soon was finished. They built a smokehouse and barn, cleared some fifteen acres, split rails to fence it, planted corn, after which Abraham with John Hanks split 3,000 rails for two neighbors and as "sodbusters" broke thirty acres of virgin prairie for John Hanks's brother Charles.

It was a change from the monotony of hard farm work in that summer of 1830 for Abraham to make his first political speech in Illinois. He had been delivering speeches to trees, stumps, rows of corn and potatoes, just practicing, by himself. But when two legislative candidates spoke at a campaign meeting in front of Renshaw's store in Decatur, Abraham stepped up and advocated improvement of the Sangamon River for better navigation.

Fall came, and most of the Lincoln family went down with chills, fever, and ague, Tom and Sarah using many doses of a quinine-and-whisky tonic mixture from a Decatur store. Then in December a blizzard filled the sky and piled snow two and a half feet on the ground. Soon another drive of snow made a four-foot depth of it on the level, with high drifts here and there. Rain followed, froze, and more snow covered the icy crust. For nine weeks that snow cover held the ground. Spring thaws came and sheets of water spread in wide miles on the prairies.

As the roads became passable, the Lincoln family and kin moved southeast a hundred miles to Coles County. Abraham had other plans and didn't go with them. He had "come of age."

2

NEW SALEM DAYS

In February 1831, John Hanks had made an agreement with a man named Denton Offutt, a frontier hustler big with promises and a hard drinker, that he, Abe Lincoln, and John D. Johnston would take a flatboat of cargo to New Orleans. They floated down the Mississippi River, meeting strings of flatboats and other river craft. Hanks, away from home longer than expected, left them at St. Louis. Stepping off the flatboat at New Orleans, Lincoln walked nearly a mile, on flatboats, to reach shore.

Again Abraham could see the narrow cobblestoned streets, a dazzling parade of the humanly ugly and lovely in a mingling — what his eyes met again in the old strange city had him thoughtful and brooding. After a month or so, with Johnston, he took a steamboat north.

From New Orleans up the Mississippi on the steamboat, and from St. Louis walking overland, Lincoln must have wondered about New Salem village, the people there, his new job, the new life he was moving into. Offutt had rented the gristmill at the Sangamon River dam below the hilltop village, and in St. Louis was buying a stock of goods for a new store. Lincoln was to be clerk in charge of store and mill at $15 a month and back room to sleep in. Arriving in late July, Lincoln walked the village street, looked over its dozen or more cabins, searched faces he expected to see many times for many months.

On August 1, 1831, he cast his first ballot. The polls were in the home of John Camron, where Lincoln was boarding and getting acquainted with Camron's eleven daughters, who teased him about his long legs and arms and heard him admit he "wasn't much to look at." Voting by word of mouth, each voter spoke to the election judges his candidates' names. A judge then called out the voter's name and his candidates, clerks recording the names on "poll sheets." Lincoln voted for a Henry Clay Whig for Congress — and against Joseph Duncan, then a Jackson man serving in Congress. He stayed around the polls most of the day, talking cheerily, telling stories, making friends, and getting acquainted with the names and faces of nearly all the men in the New Salem neighborhood.

A young and growing country, and no one more sure and proud of New Salem's future than Denton Offutt, promoter, booster, and boomer. He saw Lincoln as honest and able, picked him as a manager, told people, "He knows more than any man in the United States." Somehow at this particular time Offutt had an influence on Lincoln for good, perhaps made Lincoln feel more sure of himself.

On a lot Offutt bought for ten dollars, he and Lincoln built a cabin of logs for the new store. Offutt's goods arrived and Lincoln stacked shelves and corners. Soon stories got going about Lincoln's honesty, how he walked six miles to pay back a few cents a woman had overpaid for dry goods, and finding he had used a four-ounce weight instead of an eight, he walked miles to deliver to a woman the full order of tea she had paid for.

Offutt talked big about Lincoln as a wrestler, and Bill Clary, who ran a saloon thirty steps north of the Offutt store, bet Offutt ten dollars that Lincoln couldn't throw Jack Armstrong, the Clary's Grove champion. Sports from miles around came to a level square next to Offutt's store to see the match; bets of money, knives, trinkets, tobacco, drinks, were put up. Armstrong, short and powerful, aimed from the first to get in close to his man and use his thick muscular strength. Lincoln held him off with long arms, wore down his strength, got him out of breath, surprised and "rattled." They pawed and clutched in many holds and twists till Lincoln threw Armstrong and had both shoulders to the grass. Armstrong's gang started toward Lincoln with cries and threats. Lincoln stepped to the Offutt store wall, braced himself, and told the gang he would fight, race, or wrestle any who wanted to try him. Then Jack Armstrong broke through the gang, shook Lincoln's hand, told them Lincoln was "fair" and "the best feller that ever broke into this settlement."

The Clary's Grove boys called on Lincoln sometimes to judge

their horse races and cockfights, umpire their matches, and settle disputes. One story ran that Lincoln was on hand one day when an old man had agreed, for a gallon jug of whisky, to be rolled down a hill in a barrel. And Lincoln talked and laughed them out of doing it.

In spare hours Lincoln had sessions with Mentor Graham, the local schoolmaster, who told him of a grammar at John C. Vance's, six miles off; he walked the six miles, brought back the book, burned pine shavings at night in the Onstot cooper shop to light Samuel Kirkham's *English Grammar*. As he went further, he had Bill Greene hold the book and ask him questions. In the New Salem Debating Society, Lincoln in his first speech opened in a tone of apology, as though he wasn't sure of himself. He surprised both himself and those hearing him. James Rutledge, president of the society, was saying there was "more than wit and fun" in Abe's head.

Young Mr. Lincoln in late 1831 and early 1832 studied a book of legal forms, signed as a witness to four deeds, wrote in his own hand several legal documents, a bill of sale, and a bond, each beginning "Know all men by these presents." With the help of his good friend Bowling Green, the justice of the peace, he was edging into law and learning how to write the simpler documents.

On March 9, 1832, came the boldest and most important paper he had ever written, telling the public he was stepping into politics as a candidate for the legislature of the State of Illinois. The *Sangamo Journal* at Springfield printed it, and it was issued as a handbill. There was in it the tone of a young man a little bashful about what he was doing — and yet unafraid of his ideas and his platform, ready to debate them with any comer. For the benefit of any who might have heard otherwise, the young politician showed himself as favoring books, schools, churches, the Scriptures, religion, morality. He closed in a manner having the gray glint of his eyes and the loose hang of his long arms: "If the good people in their wisdom shall see fit to keep me in the background, I have been too familiar with disappointments to be very much chagrined."[1] That was all. He had made his first real start in politics.

Lincoln said later, "Offutt's business was failing — had almost

---

[1] *chagrined* (shə·grind'): distressed because of disappointment, failure, etc.

failed — when the Black-Hawk war of 1832 broke out." For months it seemed the store was run by Lincoln alone, while Offutt gave his time and funds to big and risky speculations in buying and shipping produce, leaving New Salem quietly in the spring of 1832 and not being heard of for years.

Lincoln borrowed a horse and rode nine miles to Richland Creek to join a company of friends and neighbors, mostly Clary's Grove boys. Voting for a captain, each man of the company stepped out and stood by either Lincoln or one William Kirkpatrick. Three fourths of the men at once went to Lincoln — and then one by one those standing by Kirkpatrick left him till he was almost alone. Lincoln was to write, years later, that he was "surprized" at this election and had "not since had any success in life which gave him so much satisfaction." He re-enlisted for twenty days and was mustered as a private into a company of mounted Independent Rangers under Captain Elijah Iles, a pioneer trader, land dealer, and one of the founders of Springfield. Lincoln on June 16 enlisted for the third time, becoming a thirty-day private in the Independent Spy Corps of Captain Jacob M. Early, a Springfield physician and Methodist preacher who had been a private in the companies of Lincoln and Iles. Six months after his discharge, an army paymaster in Springfield paid Lincoln some ninety-five dollars for his eighty days in the war. In those days Lincoln had seen deep into the heart of the American volunteer soldier, why men go to war, march in mud, sleep in rain on cold ground, eat pork raw when it can't be boiled, and kill when the killing is good. On a later day an observer was to say he saw Lincoln's eyes misty in his mention of the American volunteer soldier.

Election was eighteen days off on August 6, and Lincoln traveled over Sangamon County, gave the arguments in his long address issued in the spring. At Pappsville, where a crowd had come to a sale, as he stepped on a box for his speech he saw fellow citizens on the edge of the crowd in a fist fight. He noticed his friend Rowan Herndon getting the worst of it, stepped off the box, shouldered his way to the fight, picked a man up by the scruff of the neck and the seat of the breeches, and threw him. Back on his box, he swept the crowd with his eyes in a cool way, as though what had happened sort of happened every day, and then made a speech. Campaigning among farmers, he pitched hay and cradled wheat in the fields and showed the farmers he was one of them; at crossroads he threw the crowbar and let the local wrestlers try to get the "crotch hoist" on him. He closed his campaign with a speech in the county courthouse at Springfield. On Election Day Lincoln lost, running eighth in a field of thirteen candidates. But in his own New Salem precinct, he polled 277 of the 300 votes cast.

Later Lincoln wrote of himself after this August election, "He was now without means and out of business, but was anxious to remain with his friends who had treated him with so much generosity, especially as he had nothing elsewhere to go to. He studied what he should do — thought of learning the blacksmith trade — thought of trying to study law — rather thought he could not succeed at that without a better education."

He bought Rowan Herndon's interest in the partnership of Herndon and William F. Berry, merchants, giving Herndon his promissory note. Across later months there was more financing, several lawsuits and court judgments. They did nothing, as Lincoln said later, "but get deeper and deeper in debt" and "the store winked out."

During the fall and winter of 1832, business didn't pick up much. Lincoln could sit with uninterrupted thoughts, free day after day to turn and look into himself. He was growing as inevitably as summer corn in Illinois loam. Leaning against the doorpost of a store to which few customers came, he was growing, in silence, as corn grows. He had bought at an auction in Springfield a copy of Blackstone, the first of the law books to read. One morning he sat barefoot on a woodpile, with a book. "What are you reading?" asked Squire Godbey. "I ain't reading; I'm studying." "Studying what?" "Law." "Good God Almighty!"

Lincoln later came across an account of "the peculiar manner" of his law studies: "His favorite place of study was a wooded knoll near New Salem, where he threw himself under a wide-spreading oak and expansively made a reading desk of the hillside. Here he would pore over Blackstone day after day, shifting his position as the sun rose and sank, so as to keep in the shade, and utterly unconscious of everything but the principles of common law. People went by, and he took no account of them; the salutations of acquaintances were returned with silence, or a vacant stare; and altogether the manner of the absorbed student was not unlike that of one distraught." This picture of himself as a law student he accepted.

On May 7, 1833, as Lincoln told it, he "was appointed Postmaster at New Salem — the office being too insignificant, to make his politics an objection." The pay would run about fifty dollars a year, in commissions on receipts. He had to be in the office at Hill's store only long enough to receive and receipt for the mail, which came twice a week by postrider at first, and later by stage. It seemed he wasn't strict about regulations. At times the post office was left unlocked for hours while citizens who called for mail helped themselves.

For earning a living, jobs at common labor were plenty; Lincoln worked as rail splitter, mill hand, farm hand, helped out at the Hill store. Meanwhile he read or dipped into Volney's *The Ruins of Empire*, Gibbon's *Decline and Fall of the Roman Empire*, Paine's *The Age of Reason*. And his debts haunted him. They were little rats, a rat for every dollar, and he could hear them in the night when he wanted to sleep.

Squire Bowling Green, the justice of the peace, proved a friend and counselor, explained to Lincoln what he knew of the Illinois statutes, allowed Lincoln without fee to try small cases, examine witnesses, and make arguments.

In the fall of 1833 came Lincoln's entry into the most highly technical and responsible work he had known. There were farm sections, roads, and towns needing their boundary lines marked clear and beyond doubt on maps — more than the county surveyor, John Calhoun, could handle.

For six weeks, daytime and often all of nighttime, Lincoln had his head deep in Gibson's *Theory and Practice of Surveying* and Flint's *Treatise on Geometry, Trigonometry and Rectangular Surveying*. Many nights, said Mentor Graham's daughter, she woke at midnight to see Lincoln and her father by the fire, figuring and explaining, her mother sometimes bringing fresh firewood for better lighting. On some nights he worked alone till daylight, and it wore him down.

In six weeks, however, he had mastered his books, and Calhoun put him to work on the north end of Sangamon County. His surveys became known for care and accuracy, and he was called on to settle boundary disputes. In Petersburg, however, he laid out one street crooked. Running it straight and regular would have put the house of Jemima Elmore and her family into the street. Lincoln knew her to be working a small farm with her children, and she was the widow of Private Travice Elmore, honorable in service in Lincoln's company in the Black Hawk War.

Lincoln worked at occasional odd jobs when there was no surveying, but he made it a point to find time to keep up his political connections.

In those New Salem days some were saying Lincoln would be a great man, maybe governor or Senator, anyhow a great lawyer, what with his studying of law. Others saw him as an awkward, gangly giant, a homely joker who could go gloomy and show it. It was noticed he had two shifting moods, one of the rollicking, droll story, one when he lapsed silent and solemn beyond any bystander to penetrate.

In late summer or early fall of 1834 many people in New Salem, Lincoln included, wondered what had become of John McNeil. It was two years since he had left New Salem. Before leaving he had sold his interest in the Hill-McNeil store to Hill, but at thirty-two he was the owner of farms steadily rising in value and was rated one of the shrewdest and richest traders in New Salem. In money and looks he was considered by girls "a good catch." On December 9, 1831, Lincoln with Charles Maltby witnessed two deeds given by John Camron to John McNamar, and it was then, if not earlier, that Lincoln learned John McNeil's real name was John McNamar.

The one person most anxious about him when he went away from New Salem in 1832 was, in all probability, nineteen-year-old Ann Rutledge. They were engaged to marry, and it was understood he would straighten out affairs of his family in New York State and in not too long a time would come back to her for the marriage. But for nearly two years no one in New Salem had heard from the man.

And Lincoln, who called McNamar "Mack," who had surveyed the land McNamar owned, and who had lived under the same roof with Ann during the months "Mack" was a boarder at the Rutledge tavern, could hardly have been unaware of what she was going through. Did she talk over with Lincoln the questions, bitter and haunting, that harassed her? Had death taken her betrothed? Or was he alive and any day would see him riding into New Salem to claim her? And again, possibly, she kept a silence and so did Lincoln, and there was some kind of understanding beneath their joined silence.

Lincoln was to go away and stay away for months on important duties, writing her no letters that she kept and saved, she writing him no letters that he laid by as keepsakes. During the six weeks he mastered the surveying books, he could have seen her for only brief moments, if at all. And his surveying, as he said, "procured bread, and kept body and soul together." So definitely he was no man of property who, like McNamar, could offer her land and money, the creature comforts of life. He had arrived in New Salem "a piece of floating driftwood," as he later wrote, and was haunted by debts that had crept high on him.

Did he tell Ann of any dream, daydream, or reverie that came to him about love in general or a particular love for her? Or did he shrink from such talk because she might be clinging to some last desperate hope that her betrothed would return? Or did she lean to a belief that McNamar was gone for all time, then, shifting to another awful possibility, that he would surely come back to his land and properties, perhaps bringing a wife with him? Two years of silence could be heavy and wearing. She was twenty-one and Lincoln twenty-five, and in the few visits he had time for in this year when surveying and politics pressed him hard, he may have gone no further than to be a comforter. He may have touched and stroked her auburn hair once or more as he looked deep into her blue eyes and said no slightest word as to what hopes lay deep in his heart. Both were figures of fate — he caught with debts, with surveying "to keep body and soul together" while flinging himself into intense political activities, she the victim of a betrothal that had become a mysterious scandal. They were both young, with hope endless, and it could have been he had moments when the sky was to him a sheaf of blue dreams and the rise of the blood-gold red of a full moon in the evening was almost too much to live, see, and remember.

3
THE YOUNG LEGISLATOR

On April 19, 1834, Lincoln's name ran again in the *Sangamo Journal* as a candidate for the state legislature. Before that and after, he attended all sorts of political powwows, large and small, and those for whom he surveyed, and those he delivered letters to, did not fail to hear he was in the running. He had become a regular wheel horse of the Whig party, backed by John T. Stuart, a Springfield lawyer and county Whig leader.

In the election for members of the Ninth General Assembly, August 4, 1834, Lincoln ran second among thirteen Sangamon County candidates. Now, at twenty-five, Lincoln had won his first important political office, with better pay than ever before in his life, where he would train in the tangled and, to him, fascinating games of lawmaking and parliamentary management amid political labyrinths. After election he ran the post office, made surveys and appraisals, clerked in an October election, made court appearances in connection with his debts, and November 22 was elected a delegate to the State Education Convention to be held in Vandalia December 5. Lincoln paid a small pressing debt or two, bought cloth for a suit to be made at sixty dollars, and other apparel. With other members of the legislature, in the last week of November, he made the two-day, seventy-five-mile trip to Vandalia, the state capital, by stage. When later he saw a printed statement that he had walked to Vandalia, he wrote on the same page, "No harm, if true; but, in fact, not true."

He roomed with Stuart, whose leadership made their room a Whig center. Here and in the legislature Lincoln was to meet men, most of them young, who would become governors, Congressmen, U.S. Senators, men of influence and portent. Here he would meet a short and almost dwarfish man, a little giant, thick of body, with a massive head, twenty-one years old and absolutely confident of himself — Stephen A. Douglas, lobbying for his selection as state's attorney of the First Circuit. Many members had their wives and daughters along, and there was a social life new to Lincoln — parties, cotillions, music and flowers, elegant food and liquor, a brilliance of silk gowns, and talk that ranged from idle gabble to profound conversation about the state and nation.

On December 1, in a two-story ramshackle brick building facing the public square, meeting on the lower floor, the House was called to order. Of the eleven standing committees, Lincoln was appointed to the Committee on Public Accounts and Expenditures, and he was to serve on several special committees. His votes generally ran with those of Stuart and the Whig minority. Several times members put in bills that were in Lincoln's handwriting and it seemed his hand was in more affairs than he openly showed. One lobbyist noted Lincoln in this legislature as "raw-boned, angular, features deeply furrowed, ungraceful, almost uncouth . . . and yet there was a magnetism and dash about the man that made him a universal favorite."

Before midnight of February 13 the last batch of hacked and amended bills was passed, and Lincoln in two days of below-zero weather rode the stage to New Salem.

After the fixed program and schedules of Vandalia, the smoke-filled rooms and hullabaloo, Lincoln now rode lonely country roads and walked in open winter air over fields he was surveying. He had seen lawmaking and politics at a vortex,[1] and vague resolves deepened him. As he wrote later, he "still mixed in the surveying to pay board and clothing bills"; his law books, "dropped" when a legislature met, "were taken up again at the end of the session."

Before March was over he had completed several surveys. After March he seemed to have little surveying work over the rest of 1835. During that year, of whatever letters he wrote only three were kept and saved, and they were scant and perfunctory, shedding no light on his personal life or love or growth. It was certain that Ann Rutledge and Lincoln knew each other and he took an interest in her; probably they formed some mutual attachment not made clear to the community; possibly they loved each other and her hand went into his long fingers whose bones told her of refuge and security. They were the only two persons who could tell what secret they shared, if any. It seemed definite that she had had letters from Mc-

---

[1] *vortex:* whirlwind or whirlpool, hence a state of affairs that is similar to a vortex.

Namar and probable that after a time she had once written him that she expected release from her pledge. Summer of 1835 came, and in September it would be three years since McNamar had gone, more than two years since any letter had come from him.

Lincoln was reading law, hoping and expecting the next year to be admitted for practice. Later he advised a young student, "Get the books, and read and study them till you understand them in their principal features; and that is the main thing. . . . Your own resolution to succeed is more important than any other one thing." His resolution to study law drove him hard; friends worried about his health; he couldn't call on Ann often or for long. It was a seven-mile ride or walk when he called on her and her folks or at the nearby farm of "Uncle Jimmy" Short where Ann worked for a time.

There seemed to have been an understanding between Ann and Lincoln, with no pledges, that they would take what luck might hand them in whatever was to happen, while they advanced their education. Lincoln had his debts, his law studies, his driving political ambitions, while she had her quandaries related to John McNamar. They would see what time might bring. August came, and corn and grass stood stunted for lack of rain. Settlers came down with chills, fever, malaria, Lincoln for his aches taking spoonfuls of Peruvian bark, boneset tea, jalap, and calomel.[2]

Soon New Salem heard that Ann Rutledge lay fever-burned, her malady baffling the doctors. Many went out to the Rutledge place. Days passed. Her cousin, McGrady Rutledge, a year younger than Ann, rode to New Salem and told Lincoln of her sickness growing worse. Lincoln rode out, and they let him in for what might be his last hour with her. He saw her pale face and wasted body, the blue eyes and auburn hair perhaps the same as always. Few words were spoken, probably, and he might have gone only so far as to let his bony right hand and gnarled fingers lie softly on a small white hand while he tried for a few monosyllables of bright hope.

A few days later, on August 25, 1835, death came to Ann Rutledge, and burial was in nearby Concord cemetery. Whether Lincoln went to her funeral, whether he wept in grief with others at the sight of her face in the burial box, no one later seemed to know.

---

[2] *boneset . . . . calomel:* herbs, roots, and a white compound, formerly used as medicines.

Her cousin, McGrady Rutledge, wrote far later, "Lincoln took her death verry hard."

It was to come to pass that thirty years later New Salem villagers soberly spoke and wrote that Lincoln went out of his mind, wandered in the woods mumbling and crazy, and had to be locked up, all of which was exaggeration and reckless expansion of his taking Ann's death "verry hard." Woven with the recollections of his "insanity" were also the testimonies of what a deep flaming of lyric love there had been between him and Ann. A legend of a shining, deathless, holy, and pure passion arose, spread, grew by some inherent vital sheen of its own or the need of those who wanted it, of Ann Rutledge, as a poet [3] wrote, "beloved in life of Abraham Lincoln/wedded to him,/not through union,/but through separation."

To this young, raw country John McNamar returned three weeks after Ann died, bringing with him his aged mother, and reported that his father had died and he had straightened out what there was of the estate. What he said of Ann's passing and whether he visited the grave of his once-betrothed, of this there is no record. He lived to be seventy-eight, unaware that in chronicles to come he would figure as an enigmatic lover.

In a snowfall over hills and rolling prairie Lincoln rode a stage, arriving to see Vandalia blanketed white. A special session of the legislature opened December 7, 1835. The senators on the upper floor were not feeling good about fresh large cracks down the walls, the north wall bulging out, and snow sifting down on the floor, which at its center had sunk half a foot. Over the next six weeks 139 bills came up in the House. Lincoln collected $262 as his pay for the session and after adjournment January 18 rode the stage homeward in that occasional fair and warmer Illinois winter weather that whispers of spring on the way.

Again Lincoln worked away as surveyor, law student, politician. He wrote wills, located roads, settled boundary disputes, and on March 26 advertised a reward for return of his horse, "a large bay horse, star in his forehead, eight years old, shod all round, and trots and paces." On March 24 the Sangamon Circuit Court recorded him as a person of good moral character, his first step toward admission

---

[3] *poet:* Edgar Lee Masters, "Ann Rutledge."

to the bar and law practice. He advertised that sixty-four persons had uncalled-for letters which unless called for would be sent to the dead-letter office. On May 30 he handed out mail as postmaster for the last time and told his New Salem public that their post office was moved to Petersburg.

The convention system not yet operating, he put himself in the running in June as a candidate for the legislature. He stumped the county, often speaking as one of a string of Whig candidates. In the election of August 1, the county gave Lincoln the highest vote of seventeen candidates for the legislature. Sangamon County was taken by the Whigs, having now seven representatives and two senators.

Soon after this sweeping victory, Lincoln in stride took his bar examination before two justices of the Supreme Court, passed, gave a dinner to his examiners, and on September 9, 1836, held in his hands a license to practice law in all the courts of Illinois. On October 5 he was in a Springfield court, appearing in a case for John T. Stuart, the beginning of their partnership as a law firm.

In October and November he made three more known surveys and said goodbye to surveying.

The tall Whigs from Sangamon County averaged six feet in height, Lincoln the longest, and were nicknamed the "Long Nine." Robert L. Wilson of the village of Athens, one of the Long Nine, wrote of Lincoln as having "a quaint and peculiar way" and "he frequently startled us." He seemed a "born" politician. "We followed his lead; but he followed nobody's lead. It may almost be said that he did our thinking for us. He inspired respect, although he was careless and negligent. . . . He was poverty itself, but independent." They had seen much of each other in the legislature and campaigning together, Wilson writing, "He sought company, and indulged in fun without stint . . . still when by himself, he told me that he was so overcome by mental depression, that he never dared carry a knife in his pocket; and as long as I was intimately acquainted with him, he never carried a pocketknife." At a banquet in Athens, Wilson gave the toast: "Abraham Lincoln; one of Nature's Noblemen."

In Springfield, Lincoln read lavish compliments to himself in the press, and sat with the Long Nine and sixty guests at a game supper where one toast ran: "Abraham Lincoln: he has fulfilled the expectations of his friends, and disappointed the hopes of his enemies."

In April he packed his saddlebags to leave New Salem, where six years before he had arrived, as he said, "a piece of floating driftwood," being now a licensed lawyer, a member of the state legislature, and floor leader of the Whig party. The hilltop village, now fading to become a ghost town, had been to him a nourishing mother, a neighborhood of many names and faces that would always be dear and cherished with him, a friendly place with a peculiar equality between man and man, where Bill Greene was nearly correct in saying, "In New Salem every man is a principal citizen." Bitter hours, but more sweet than bitter, he had had. Here he had groped in darkness and grown toward light. Here newspapers, books, mathematics, law, the ways of people and life had taken on new and subtle meanings for him.

4

LAWYER IN SPRINGFIELD

It was no wilderness that Abraham Lincoln, twenty-eight years old, saw as he rode into Springfield April 15, 1837. Many of its people had come from Kentucky by horse, wagon, and boat, across country not yet cleared of wolves, wildcats, and horse thieves.

Lincoln pulled in his horse at the general store of Joshua Speed. He asked the price of bedclothes for a single bedstead, which Speed figured at seventeen dollars. "Cheap as it is, I have not the money to pay," he told Speed. "But if you will credit me until Christmas, and my experiment here as a lawyer is a success, I will pay you then. If I fail in that I will probably never pay you at all." Speed said afterward: "The tone of his voice was so melancholy that I felt for him. . . . I thought I never saw so gloomy and melancholy a face in my life." Speed offered to share his own big double bed upstairs over the store. Lincoln took his saddlebags upstairs, came down with his face lit up, and said, "Well, Speed, I'm moved." A friendship, to last long, began, as with William Butler, clerk of the Sangamon Circuit Court, who told Lincoln he could take his meals at the Butler home and there would be no mention of board bills.

The circuit courtroom was in a two-story building in Hoffman's Row, and upstairs over the courtroom was the law office of the new firm of Stuart and Lincoln: a little room with a few loose boards for bookshelves, an old wood stove, a table, a chair, a bench, a buffalo robe, and a small bed. Stuart was running for Congress, so Lincoln most of the time handled all of their law practice in range of his ability. Between law cases he kept up his political fences, writing many letters.

   In law office routine Lincoln took depositions, drew deeds, filed declarations, bills of complaint, praecipes,[1] perhaps taking an afternoon off when the famous Whig, Daniel Webster, made an hour-and-a-half speech at a barbecue in a grove west of town. An official of the Post Office Department came one day to Springfield and asked about a certain amount of dollars and cents that had come into the hands of Lincoln as postmaster at New Salem. Lincoln brought out a sack and counted the money in it, the exact amount asked for by the inspector, who took the money, gave a receipt, and went away satisfied. People in trouble over land or money or love, witnesses, murderers, scandalmongers, and slanderers came to pour out their stories within the walls of the Stuart and Lincoln law office. In one of his first murder cases, Lincoln failed to save William Fraim, a twenty-year-old, who in a drunken brawl killed a fellow laborer; he was convicted and hanged.

   Ninian W. Edwards of the Long Nine, a polished aristocrat and son of a former governor of Illinois, was the same age as Lincoln, and they had campaigned together and joined in Whig conferences. The Edwards's house, built of brick, stood two stories high and could have held a dozen prairie-farmer cabins. To this house in 1839 came a young woman from Lexington, Kentucky. She had been there two years before on a short visit. Now she had come to stay, Miss Mary Todd, a younger sister of Elizabeth, the wife of Ninian W. Edwards.

   Miss Mary Todd was twenty-one, plump, swift, beaming. For Lincoln, as he came to know her, she was lighted with magnets, the first aggressively brilliant feminine creature who had crossed his path, so that he lost his head. He saw in Mary Todd, with her pink-rose smooth soft skin, light brown hair hinting of bronze, ample

---

[1] *deeds . . . praecipes*: terms for legal documents.

bosom, flying glimpses of slippers, a triumph of some kind; she had finished schools where "the accomplishments" were taught; she spoke and read French. She was impetuous. A shaft of wanted happiness could strike deep in her. Mary Todd was read, informed, and versed in apparel and appearance.

In 1840 Lincoln and Mary Todd were engaged to be married. Ninian W. Edwards and his wife had argued she was throwing herself away, it wasn't a match, she and Lincoln came from different classes of society. Her stubborn blood rose; she knew her own mind and spoke it. Lincoln had a future; he was her man more than any other she had met.

The months passed. Lincoln, the solitary, the melancholy, was busy, lost, abstracted; he couldn't go to all the parties, dances, concerts Mary Todd was going to. She flared with jealousy and went with other men; she accused him, tears, misunderstandings. They made up, fell out, made up again. The wedding was set for New Year's Day, 1841.

And then something happened. The bride or the groom, or both, broke the engagement. Lincoln was a haunted man. Was he sure he didn't love her? He walked the streets of Springfield; he brooded. He wrote his partner, Stuart: "I am now the most miserable man living. If what I feel were equally distributed to the whole human family, there would not be one cheerful face on the earth."

The legislature adjourned. Josh Speed was selling his store and going back to his folks in Kentucky. Lincoln, in a struggle to come back, traveled to Louisville in August and, staying with Speed some three weeks, shared talk and counsel with that rare friend. Speed recalled Lincoln saying he had done nothing to make any human being remember that he had lived; he wished to live to connect his name with events of his day and generation and to the interest of his fellow men. Slowly, he came back.

In mid-September he was in Illinois again, writing to Speed's sister Mary about his tooth that failed of extraction when he was in Kentucky, "Well, that same old tooth got to paining me so much, that about a week since I had it torn out, bringing with it a bit of the jawbone . . . my mouth is now so sore that I can neither talk, nor eat."

5

"I AM GOING TO BE MARRIED"

Joshua Speed, deep-chested, broad between the ears, had spots soft as May violets. And he and Abraham Lincoln told each other their secrets about women. "I do not feel my own sorrows much more keenly than I do yours," Lincoln wrote Speed in one letter. And again: "You know my desire to befriend you is everlasting."

The wedding day of Speed and Fanny Henning had been set, and Speed was afraid he didn't love her. It was wearing him down; the date of the wedding loomed as the hour for a sickly affair. He wrote Lincoln he was sick. And Lincoln wrote what was wrong with Speed's physical and mental system, a letter tender as loving hands swathing a feverish forehead yet direct in its facing of immediate facts. It was a letter showing that Lincoln in unlucky endings of love affairs must have known deep-rooted, tangled, and baffling misery.

Speed's wedding day came; the knot was tied. A few days after the wedding, the newly married man wrote to Lincoln that he was still haunted by "something indescribably horrible and alarming." Lincoln's reply February 25, 1842, gave light on his own experience and methods of overcoming melancholy, "hypo," [1] torment of mind and nerves. He believed he could see that since Speed's last letter, Speed had grown *"less miserable"* and not worse, writing: "You say that 'something indescribably horrible and alarming' still haunts you. You will not say *that* three months from now, I will venture. When your nerves once get steady now, the whole trouble will be over forever. Nor should you become impatient at their being very slow, in becoming steady."

A month passed, and Lincoln had news from Speed that the marriage was a complete success and bells rang merrily, Speed far happier than he ever expected to be. To which Lincoln replied: "I know you too well to suppose your expectations were not, at least sometimes, extravagant; and if the reality exceeds them all, I say,

---

[1] *"hypo"*: hypochondria; anxiety about one's health.

enough, dear Lord. I am not going beyond the truth, when I tell you, that the short space it took me to read your last letter, gave me more pleasure, than the total sum of all I have enjoyed since that fatal first of Jany. '41."

He referred to Mary Todd for the first time in his letters to Speed. ". . . it seems to me, I should have been entirely happy, but for the never-absent idea, that there is *one* still unhappy whom I have contributed to make so. That still kills my soul. I can not but reproach myself, for even wishing to be happy while she is otherwise. She accompanied a large party on the Rail Road cars, to Jacksonville last Monday; and on her return, spoke, so that I heard of it, of having enjoyed the trip exceedingly. God be praised for that."

Mrs. Simeon Francis, wife of the editor of the *Sangamo Journal*, invited Lincoln to a party in her parlor, brought Lincoln and Miss Todd together, and said, "Be friends again." Whatever of fate or woman-wit was at work, and whatever hesitations and broodings went on in Lincoln's heart, they were friends again. But they didn't tell the world so.

At the meetings of Lincoln and Mary Todd in the Francis home, Miss Todd made it clear to him that if another date should be fixed for a wedding, it should not be set so far in the future as it was the time before. Lincoln agreed, and early in October wrote to Speed: "You have now been the husband of a lovely woman nearly eight months. That you are happier now than you were the day you married her I well know . . . and the returning elasticity of spirits which is manifested in your letters. But I want to ask a closer question — 'Are you now, in *feeling* as well as *judgment,* glad you are married as you are?' From anybody but me, this would be an impudent question not to be tolerated; but I know you will pardon it in me. Please answer it quickly as I am impatient to know." Speed answered yes and yes, his marriage had brought happiness. A few weeks later, Lincoln came to the room of James Matheny, before Matheny was out of bed, telling his friend, "I am going to be married today."

On the street Lincoln met Ninian W. Edwards and told Edwards that he and Mary were to be married that evening. Edwards gave notice, "Mary is my ward, and she must be married at my house." When Edwards asked Mary Todd if what he had heard was true, she told him it was true and they made the big Edwards house ready.

Lincoln took all care of a plain gold ring, the inside engraved: "Love is eternal." At the Edwards house on the evening of November 4, 1842, the Reverend Charles Dresser in canonical robes performed the ring ceremony of the Episcopal church for the groom, thirty-three, and the bride, soon to be twenty-four.

Afterward, in talk about the wedding, Jim Matheny said Lincoln had "looked as if he was going to slaughter." Gossip at the Butler house, where Lincoln roomed, had it that, as he was dressing, Bill Butler's boy came in and asked, "Where are you going?" Lincoln answering, "To hell, I suppose." However dubious such gossip, Lincoln, seven days after his wedding, wrote to Sam Marshall at Shawneetown, discussed two law cases, and ended the letter: "Nothing new here, except my marrying, which to me, is matter of profound wonder."

The Lincoln couple boarded and roomed at four dollars per week in the plain Globe Tavern, where their first baby came August 1, 1843, and was named Robert Todd. Soon after, they moved into their own home, bought for fifteen hundred dollars, a story-and-a-half frame house a few blocks from the city center. Three blocks east the cornfields began and farms mile after mile.

[Riding the circuit throughout the fifteen counties of east-central Illinois, Lincoln argued cases in many frontier towns. He formed a law partnership with William H. Herndon which was to last the rest of his life. In 1847 Lincoln was elected to Congress. After one term he returned to Springfield, took up his law practice, and continued his political activity. In 1854 he was defeated for the United States Senate. Two years later Lincoln ran second in the nomination for Vice-President at the first Republican convention in Philadelphia. In 1858, he was again nominated for the Senate. By this time Lincoln had formed his views on the preservation of the Union. His speech accepting the nomination included the famous lines, " 'A house divided against itself cannot stand.' I believe this government cannot endure permanently half slave and half free." Lincoln and his opponent, Stephen A. Douglas, conducted seven major debates, known as the "Great Debate." When Lincoln lost the election, he spoke of his defeat as "a slip and not a fall." During these years,

Lincoln and Mary had four sons, Robert, Edward, who lived for only four years, William, and Thomas, or "Tad."]

6

STRANGE FRIEND AND FRIENDLY STRANGER

Lincoln was fifty-one years old. With each year since he had become a grown man, his name and ways, and stories about him, had been spreading among plain people and their children. So tall and so bony, with so peculiar a slouch and so easy a saunter, so sad and so haunted-looking, so quizzical and comic, as if hiding a lantern that lighted and went out and that he lighted again — he was the Strange Friend and the Friendly Stranger. Like something out of a picture book for children — he was. His form of slumping arches and his face of gaunt sockets were a shape a Great Artist had scrawled from careless clay.

He didn't wear clothes. Rather, clothes hung upon him as if on a rack to dry, or on a loose ladder up a windswept chimney. His clothes, to keep the chill or the sun off, seemed to whisper, "He put us on when he was thinking about something else."

He dressed any which way at times, in broadcloth, a silk hat, a silk choker, and a flaming red silk handkerchief, so that one court clerk said Lincoln was "fashionably dressed, as neatly attired as any lawyer at court, except Ward Lamon." Or again, people said Lincoln looked like a huge skeleton with skin over the bones, and clothes covering the skin.

The stovepipe hat he wore sort of whistled softly: "I am not a hat at all; I am the little garret roof where he tucks in little thoughts he writes on pieces of paper." And people tried to guess what was going on under that hat. Written in pencil on the imitation satin paper that formed part of the lining was the signature "A. Lincoln, Springfield, Ill.," so that any forgetful person who might take the hat by mistake would know where to bring it back.

The umbrella with the name "Abraham Lincoln" stitched in, faded and drab from many rains and regular travels, looked sleepy and murmuring. "Sometime we shall have all the sleep we want; we shall turn the law office over to the spiders and the cobwebs; and we shall quit politics for keeps."

There could have been times when children and dreamers looked at Abraham Lincoln and lazily drew their eyelids half shut and let their hearts roam about him — and they half-believed him to be a tall horse chestnut tree or a rangy horse or a big wagon or a log barn full of newmown hay — something else or more than a man, a lawyer, a Republican candidate with principles, a prominent citizen — something spreading, elusive, and mysterious — the Strange Friend and the Friendly Stranger.

The year of the big debates a boy had called out, "There goes old Mr. Lincoln," and Lincoln, hearing it, remarked to a friend, "They commenced it when I was scarcely thirty years old." Often when people called him "Old Abe," they meant he had the texture and quaint friendliness of old handmade Bibles, old calfskin law books, weather-beaten oak and walnut planks, or wagon axles always willing in storm or stars.

A neighbor boy, Fred Dubois, joined with a gang who tied a string to knock off Lincoln's hat. "Letters and papers fell out of the hat and scattered over the sidewalk," said Dubois. "He stooped to pick them up and us boys climbed all over him." As a young man he played marbles with boys; as an older man he spun tops with his own boys, Tad and Willie.

When Tad was late bringing home the milk, he hunted the boy and came home with Tad on his shoulders and carrying the milk pail himself. Once he chased Tad and brought the little one home, holding him at arm's length; the father chuckled at his son's struggle to kick him in the face. Once, as he lugged the howling Willie and Tad, a neighbor asked, "Why, Mr. Lincoln, what's the matter?" The answer: "Just what's the matter with the whole world. I've got three walnuts and each wants two."

Germans and Irishmen had greetings from him. "I know enough German to know that Kaufman means merchant, and Schneider means tailor — am I not a good German scholar?" Or, "That reminds me of what the Irishman said, 'In this country one man is as good as another; and for the matter of that, very often a great deal better.'"

He told of a Kentucky horse sale where a small boy was riding a fine horse to show off points. A man whispered, "Look here, boy, hain't that horse got the splints?" and the boy, "Mister, I don't know what the splints is, but if it's good for him, he has got it; if it ain't good for him, he ain't got it."

Riding to Lewistown, an old acquaintance, a weather-beaten farmer, spoke of going to law with his next neighbor. "Been a neighbor of yours for long?" "Nigh onto fifteen year." "Part of the time you get along all right, don't you?" "I reckon we do." "Well, see this horse of mine? I sometimes get out of patience with him. But I know his faults; he does fairly well as horses go; it might take me a long time to get used to some other horse's faults, for all horses have faults."

He could write an angry letter, with hard names and hot epithets — and then throw it in the stove. He advised it was a help sometimes to write a hot letter and then burn it. On being told of a certain man saying, "I can't understand those speeches of Lincoln," he laughed, "There are always some fleas a dog can't reach."

The name of the man had come to stand for what he was, plus beliefs, conjectures, and guesses. He was spoken of as a "politician" in the sense that politics is a trade of cunning, ambitious, devious men. He chose a few issues on which to explain his mind fully. Some of his reticences were not evasions but retirements to cloisters of silence. Questions of life and destiny shook him close to prayers and tears in his own hidden corners and byways; the depths of the issues were too dark, too pitiless, inexorable, for a man to open his mouth and try to tell what he knew.

There was a word: democracy. Tongues of politics played with it. Lincoln had his slant at it. "As I would not be a *slave*, so I would not be a *master*. This expresses my idea of democracy. Whatever differs from this, to the extent of the difference, is no democracy."

He had faced men who had yelled, "I'll fight any man that's goin' to vote for that miserable skunk, Abe Lincoln." And he knew homes where solemn men declared, "I've seen Abe Lincoln when he played mournin' tunes on their heartstrings till they mourned with the mourners." He was taken, in some log cabins, as a helper of men. "When I went over to hear him at Alton," said one, "things looked onsartin. 'Peared like I had more'n I could stand up under. But he hadn't spoken more'n ten minutes afore I felt like I never had no load. I begin to feel ashamed o' bein' weary en complainin'."

Somewhere in this period Milton Hay of Springfield heard Lincoln speak offhand a rule or maxim in politics. Hay later passed it on to Joseph Fifer of Bloomington, who found it so simple and so nicely singsong that he couldn't forget it: "You can fool some of the people all of the time, and all of the people some of the time, but you can't fool all of the people all of the time."

At a remark in Mayor Sanderson's house in Galesburg that he was "afraid of women," Lincoln laughed, "A woman is the only thing I am afraid of that I know can't hurt me." After a tea party at the home of Mayor Boyden of Urbana, the mayor and Henry C. Whitney, a lawyer friend of Lincoln from Urbana, excused themselves for an hour and left Lincoln alone with Mrs. Boyden, Mrs. Whitney, and her mother. Whitney, on returning, found Lincoln "ill at ease as a bashful country boy," eyes shifting from floor to ceiling and back, arms behind and then in front, then tangled as though he tried to hide them, and his long legs tying and untying themselves. Whitney couldn't understand it, unless it was because he was alone in a room with three women.

A woman wrote her admiration of his course in politics, and he thanked her in a letter. "I have never corresponded much with ladies; and hence I postpone writing letters to them, as a business which I do not understand."

Herndon told of his partner coming to the office sometimes at seven in the morning when his usual hour to arrive was nine. Or of Lincoln at noon, having brought to the office a package of crackers and cheese, sitting alone eating. Mrs. Lincoln and Herndon hated each other. While Herndon was careless as to where he spat, she was not merely scrupulously neat and immaculate as to linen and baths, she was among the most ambitious women in Springfield in the matter of style and fashion. She knew of such affairs as Herndon getting drunk with two other men and breaking a windowpane that her husband had to hustle the money for so that the sheriff wouldn't lock up his law partner. She didn't like it that her husband had a drinking partner reckless with money, occasionally touching Lincoln for loans. She carried suspicions and nursed misgivings as to this swaggering upstart, radical in politics, transcendentalist[1] in philosophy, antichurch.

At parties, balls, social gatherings, she moved, vital, sparkling, often needlessly insinuating or directly and swiftly insolent. If the mu-

---

[1] *transcendentalist:* believer in inner feeling, rather than reasoning, as a guide to truth.

sic was bad, what was the need of her making unkind remarks about the orchestra? Chills, headaches, creepers of fear came; misunderstandings rose in waves so often around her; she was alone, so all alone, so like a child thrust into the wrong room.

At parties, balls, social gatherings, she trod the mazy waltzes in crinoline gowns, the curves of the hoop skirts shading down the plump curves of her figure. Once, when talk turned to Lincoln and Douglas, she had said, "Mr. Lincoln may not be as handsome a figure, but people are perhaps not aware that his heart is as large as his arms are long."

How often good times shone for them, only they two could tell. They were intense individuals, he having come through hypochondria and she moving by swirls toward a day when she would cry out that hammers were knocking nails into her head, that hot wires were being drawn through her eyes. Between flare-ups and regrets, his was most often the spirit of accommodation. He was ten years older than she, with a talent for conciliation and adjustment.

A lawyer was talking business to Lincoln once at home and suddenly the door opened. Mrs. Lincoln put her head in and snapped the question whether he had done an errand she told him to do. He looked up quietly, said he had been busy but would attend to it as soon as he could. The woman wailed; she was neglected, abused, insulted. The door slammed; she was gone. The visiting lawyer, open-eyed, muttered his surprise. Lincoln laughed, "Why, if you knew how much good that little eruption did, what a relief it was to her, and if you knew her as well as I do, you would be glad she had had an opportunity to explode."

She was often anxious about her boys, had mistaken fears about their safety or health, exaggerated evils that might befall them. She gave parties for them and wrote with her own pen, in a smooth and even script, gracious invitations.

Mary Todd had married a genius who made demands; when he wanted to work, it was no time for interruptions or errands. For this brooding and often somber man, she was wife, housekeeper, and counselor in personal and political affairs in so far as he permitted. She watched his "browsing" in the pantry and tried to bring him to regular meals. She had kept house years ago, too poor for a hired girl; they burned wood then; now they had a coal cookstove with four lids and a reservoir to warm rain water. She had chosen the beautiful, strong black-walnut cradle into which she had put, one after the other, four boy babies.

She knew of the money cost in 1858 when he dropped nearly all law cases for months and paid his way at hotels and in 4,200 miles of travel, writing in one letter after the campaign closed, "I am absolutely without money now for even household purposes." At times he did the shopping, Herndon saying that of a winter's morning he might be seen around the market house, a basket on his arm, "his old gray shawl wrapped around his neck."

With their rising income and his taking place as the outstanding leader of his party, Mary Lincoln in the late 1850's enjoyed giving parties occasionally for two or three hundred people. Isaac N. Arnold noted of these evenings "everything orderly and refined" and "every guest perfectly at ease," with a table "famed for the excellence of many rare Kentucky dishes, and in season, loaded with venison, wild turkeys, prairie chickens, quail, and other game." She had moved with him from lean years to the comforts of the well-to-do middle class. With ownership of his house and lot, with farm lands and collectible bills he had out, Lincoln in 1859 had property worth perhaps $15,000 or more.

[As a result of the Great Debate, Lincoln's name as a speaker and thinker spread far. In February 1860, he spoke at Cooper Union in New York City, ending with the words "Let us have faith that right makes might, and in that faith, let us, to the end, dare to do our duty as we understand it." This speech, and others Lincoln made throughout New England, greatly impressed Republican party leaders and made him a prime candidate for the presidential nomination. His chief rival was Senator William H. Seward of New York.]

7

"MARY, WE'RE ELECTED"

Into the state Republican convention at Decatur on May 9 came John Hanks carrying two fence rails tied with flags and streamers, with the inscription, "Abraham Lincoln, the Rail Candidate for

President in 1860: Two rails from a lot of 3,000 made in 1830 by Thos. Hanks and Abe Lincoln — whose father was the first pioneer of Macon County." Shouts followed: "Lincoln! Lincoln! Speech!" He thanked them with a sober face. Cheers: "Three times three for Honest Abe, our next President." Shouts from the convention: "Identify your work!" "It may be that I split these rails," and scrutinizing further, "Well, boys, I can only say that I have split a great many better-looking ones."

Thus the Rail Candidate was brought forth and the nickname of Rail Splitter. The idea came from Richard Oglesby, a Decatur lawyer, Kentucky-raised, a plain and witty man, who shared Lincoln's belief in the people. Far more important was it that the convention instructed its delegates to the Chicago convention to vote as a unit for Lincoln.

Illinois delegates were outfitting with silk hats and broadcloth suits for the Chicago Republican convention May 16. Lincoln was saying, "I am a little too much a candidate to stay home and not quite enough a candidate to go." Norman B. Judd and others had made a special point of getting the convention for Chicago. They told the national committee that holding the convention in an eastern city would "run a big chance of losing the West." At the corner of Lake and Market Streets, the Sauganash Hotel had been torn down, and a huge rambling lumber structure, to hold 10,000 people, had been put up and named the Wigwam.

Judge David Davis had adjourned the Eighth Circuit courts, took over the entire third floor of Chicago's finest hotel, the Tremont House, paying a rental of $300 for spacious Lincoln headquarters and rooms for his staff of Lincoln hustlers, evangelists, salesmen, pleaders, exhorters, schemers. In the parlor of the Lincoln headquarters were cigars and wine, porter, brandy, whisky, for any delegate or important guest.

Seward victory was in the air; champagne fizzed at the Richmond House. Straw votes on all incoming railroad trains had given William H. Seward of New York overwhelming majorities. Lincoln workers were saying with clenched fists and blazing eyes that the Republicans were beaten at the start if Seward headed the ticket.

Ward Lamon had been to the printers of seat tickets. Young men worked nearly a whole night signing names of convention officers to counterfeit seat tickets so that next day Lincoln men could jam the hall and leave no seats for the Seward shouters. On the first two days of the convention's routine business, the Seward men were allowed by the Chicago managers to have free run of the floor. But on May 18, when sunrise saw thousands milling about the Wigwam doors, the Lincoln shouters were shoved through the doors till they filled all seats and standing room; hundreds of New York hurrah boys couldn't squeeze in. Lamon and Jesse Fell got a thousand men recruited for their lung power. They watched their leaders, two men located on opposite sides of the Wigwam. These two Leather Lungs watched Cook on the platform; when he took out his handkerchief, they cut loose with all they had and kept it up till Cook put his handkerchief back. They were joined by the thousand recruits picked for voice noise.

On May 18 Lincoln was talking with two law students when his office door burst open and the *Journal* editor, Baker, told him of the first ballot in Chicago. They walked to the telegraph office, found no later news, and at the *Journal* office met a crowd shouting good news would be coming. Lincoln slouched in a chair but straightened up at the next news of his big gains on the second ballot. And when the wires sang that his nomination had been made unanimous, he knew that a great somber moment had come to him, and the firing of one hundred jubilant guns made a shadowed music. He read a flurry of gay telegrams, shook hands all round, then went home to tell the news and see his wife's face beam and glow.

Bonfires of boxes, barrels, and brushwood lighted up the Sangamon River country that Friday night. A brass band and a cheering crowd at the Lincoln house surged to the front porch and called for a speech. He saw the honor of the nomination not for him personally but as the representative of a cause; he wished his house big enough so he could ask them all inside. Shouts and yells of hurrah parties broke on the night till the gray dawn of the morning after.

The man in Springfield picked to carry the banner stood at moments as a shy and furtive figure. He wanted the place — and he didn't. His was precisely the clairvoyance that knew terrible days were ahead. He had his hesitations. And he was in the end the dark horse on whom the saddle was put. He could contemplate an old proverb: "The horse thinks one thing, he that saddles him another."

The notification committee at his house formally told Lincoln he was nominated for President. He formally replied, and later, after reading the platform, sent a letter of acceptance. He would cooperate, "imploring the assistance of Divine Providence."

In June the adjourned Democratic national convention met in Baltimore and, after bitter and furious debates, nominated Stephen Douglas of Illinois for President. Douglas stumped the country in what seemed for him a losing fight; he went on tireless, men amazed at the way he wore out, went to bed, and came back fighting.

Lincoln saw the powerful young political party shaping his figure into heroic stature, coloring his personality beyond reality. From hundreds of stump orators and newspapers came praise and outcry for "Abe," "Old Abe," "the Rail Candidate," "the Backwoodsman," "Honest Abe," "the Man of the People," the sagacious, eloquent Man of the Hour, one who, starting from a dirt-floor cabin, was to move on into the Executive Mansion in Washington.

Letters kept coming to Lincoln — what would he do with slavery if elected? Would he interfere? Would it not be wise now to say plainly he wouldn't interfere? One he had answered, "Those who will not read, or heed, what I have already publicly said, would not read, or heed, a repetition of it."

The campaign came to its last week. As the summer and fall drew on, Lincoln was to those who met him the same friendly neighbor as always — but with more to think about. He shook hands with Henry C. Whitney in a big crowd, and a half-hour later, seeing Whitney again, he shook hands and called him by name. "He didn't know me the first time," said Whitney.

Millions of people had by this time read his words of two years ago in the House Divided speech. They struck the soft, weird keynote of the hour. "If we could first know *where* we are, and *whither* we are tending, we could then better judge *what* to do, and *how* to do it."

Twice, since he had first so spoken, the corn had grown from seed to the full stalk and been harvested. In a book he had carried, it was told, "All rising to power is by a winding stair." As he went higher, it was colder and lonelier. The last leaves were blowing off the trees and the final geese honking south. Winter would come and go before seed corn went into the ground again.

From nine o'clock on election evening Lincoln sat in the Springfield telegraph office. With friends he stepped across the street to where the Republican Ladies' Club had fixed a supper. Hardly were the men seated when a messenger rushed in waving a telegram. New York had gone Republican. Lincoln's election was clinched.

In the streets, and around the Statehouse, crowds surged, shouting themselves hoarse. The jubilee was still going as Lincoln walked home to say to a happy woman, "Mary, we're elected."

8

THE HOUSE DIVIDING

Lincoln's election was a signal. The Atlanta newspaper *Confederacy* spoke for those who had visions of violence: "Let the consequences be what they may — whether the Potomac is crimsoned in human gore, and Pennsylvania Avenue is paved ten fathoms deep with mangled bodies, or whether the last vestige of liberty is swept from the face of the American continent, the South will never submit to such humiliation and degradation as the inauguration of Abraham Lincoln." This was in part bravado and blowoff, and in part hope and determination.

In the day's mail for Lincoln came letters cursing him for an ape and a baboon who had brought the country evil. He was buffoon and monster, an idiot; they prayed he would be flogged, burned, hanged, tortured. Pen sketches of gallows and daggers arrived from "oath-bound brotherhoods." Mrs. Lincoln saw unwrapped a painting on canvas, her husband with a rope around his neck, his feet chained, his body tarred and feathered.

The trains into Springfield on a single day would unload hundreds of passengers, arriving to see the President-elect. Some carried shining faces; they just wanted to look at him and tell him they hoped to God he'd live and have good luck. Others, too, carried shining faces, singing, "Ain't we glad we joined the Republicans?" They said they nominated and elected him President and inquired about post offices, revenue collectorships, clerkships, secretaryships. They wore him. Behind their smiles some had snouts like buzzards, pigs, rats.

Henry Villard earlier had written of Lincoln: "More than once I heard him 'with malice aforethought' get off purposely some repulsive fiction in order to rid himself of an uncomfortable caller. Again and again I felt disgust and humiliation that such a person should have been called upon to direct the destinies of a great nation." Villard later still, reporting for the New York *Herald,* judged the President-elect "a man of good heart and good intentions" but "not firm." Weeks passed, and he definitely saw Lincoln as "a man of immense power and force of character and natural talent . . . a man to act and decide for himself . . . tremendously rough and tremendously honest and earnest." Thus judgments, in favor and against, shifted as the winds shift.

"Resistance to Lincoln is Obedience to God" flared a banner at an Alabama mass meeting. Against Southern advice that South Carolina wait till President Buchanan's term ended, Robert Barnwell Rhett and his forces had manipulated the precise dramatic event of secession. Rhett wrote the ordinance of disunion, and in secret session the convention's 169 delegates in St. Andrew's Hall at Charleston, December 16, 1860, passed it without debate in forty-five minutes. One by one, the six other cotton states of the lower South joined South Carolina in leaving the Union.

Senators and representatives from the South spoke sad and bitter farewells to Congress; U.S. postmasters, judges, district attorneys, customs collectors by the hundreds sent their resignations to Washington. Of the 1,108 officers of the U.S. Regular Army, 387 were preparing resignations, many having already joined the Confederate armed forces. The U.S. mint at New Orleans and two smaller mints were taken over by the Confederate states, as were post offices and customhouses. Governors of seceded states marched in troops and took over U.S. forts that had cost six million dollars.

Newly organized artillery companies were drilling in Chicago. A thousand Negro slaves were throwing up fortifications in Charleston, South Carolina. Governor Yates notified the legislature, "Illinois counts among her citizens 400,000 who can bear arms." Five million dollars and a hundred thousand troops would be offered by their state, Pennsylvania legislators were saying.

If Lincoln should try to retake the seized forts, he would have to kill in sickening numbers, said John Y. Brown of Kentucky. Lincoln delivered remarks such as, "Please excuse me . . . from making a speech," and, "Let us at all times remember that all American citizens are brothers of a common country." Lincoln told friends privately that the forts seized by the seceded states would have to be retaken. But as to public declarations of policy on this and that, he was waiting.

Delegates at Montgomery, Alabama, on February 4 organized a provisional government named the Confederate States of America, electing Jefferson Davis of Mississippi as President and Alexander Stephens of Georgia as Vice-President.

Conventions in North Carolina and Arkansas deliberated and joined the Confederacy. In Tennessee the voters balloted 105,000 to 47,000 in favor of secession, Union votes coming heavy from the mountaineers. In Virginia, three to one of 130,000 voters were in favor of "the Mother of Presidents" going into the Confederacy, the mountaineers chiefly being Unionist. In Texas, Governor Sam Houston refused to call the legislature and tried to stop secession, but was bowled over.

Henry Adams of Massachusetts was writing a brother, "No man is fit to take hold now who is not as cool as death." It was sunset and dawn, moonrise and noon, dying time and birthing hour, dry leaves of the last of autumn and springtime blossom roots.

9
"I BID YOU AN AFFECTIONATE FAREWELL"

When a Brooklyn hatter one day in January presented Lincoln with a black silk hat, he turned to say, "Well, wife, if nothing else comes out of this scrape, we are going to have some new clothes." Such attentions pleased Mrs. Lincoln. She had a sprightly manner of saying, "We are pleased with our advancement."

Pressure came on her to give her husband the names of men he should appoint to offices, with reasons why. She spoke of fears about her health, would mention "my racked frame" to other women, and say she hoped the chills she had suffered from in earlier years would not return in Washington. She might find Washington a city of tears and shadows. She would go there with new clothes, fresh ribbons, and see. She made a trip in January to New York City, there meeting Robert, who came down from Harvard. She had as good a time as possible for her, choosing and buying gowns, hats, footwear, and adornments becoming to one to be called "the First Lady of the Land."

Henry Villard wrote for the New York *Herald* January 26 of the President-elect "delighted" at the return of Mrs. Lincoln and Bob from the east. "Dutiful husband and father that he is, he had proceeded to the railroad depot for three successive nights in his anxiety to receive them, and that in spite of snow and cold. Mrs. Lincoln returned in good health and excellent spirits; whether she got a good scolding from Abraham for unexpectedly prolonging her absence, I am unable to say; but I know she found it rather difficult to part with the winter gaieties of New York." Villard noted, too, that Robert, fresh from Harvard, dressed in an elegance in "striking contrast to the loose, careless, awkward rigging of his Presidential father."

Lincoln rode to Mattoon, missed connections with a passenger train, and took the caboose of a freight train to Charleston. With a shawl over his shoulders and his boots in slush, mud, and ice, he picked his way in the late evening dusk alongside the tracks the length of the freight train to the station, where a buggy was ready. Friends took him to the house where he stayed overnight. Next day he drove eight miles out to an old farm. Sarah Bush Lincoln and he put their arms around each other and listened to each other's heartbeats. They held hands and talked, they talked without holding hands. Each looked into eyes thrust back in deep sockets. She was all of a mother to him. He was her boy more than any born to her. He gave her a photograph of her boy, a hungry picture of him standing and wanting, wanting. He stroked her face a last time, kissed goodbye, and went away. She knew his heart would go roaming back often, that even when he rode in an open carriage in New York or Washington, with soldiers, flags, and cheering thousands along the streets, he might just as like be thinking of her in the old log farmhouse out in Coles County, Illinois.

Lincoln cleaned out files, threw away useless odds and ends. Manuscripts he wished to preserve and didn't want to be encumbered with in Washington, he put into a carpetbag and gave to Elizabeth Todd Grimsley, whom he called "Cousin Lizzie." His "literary bureau," he termed it, and told Mrs. Grimsley to watch it with care, but if he should not return to Springfield, she might dispose of the manuscripts as she pleased.

Between seven and twelve o'clock on the night of February 6, there came to the Lincoln home several hundred "ladies and gentlemen," wrote one correspondent, "the political élite of this State, and the beauty and fashion of this vicinity." It was the Lincolns' goodbye house party. The President-elect stood near the front door shaking hands, and nearby were Bob and Mrs. Lincoln and four of her sisters.

"Lincoln is letting his whiskers grow," men were saying in January, when his upper lip and cheeks were shaved but a stubble left on the chin. Then in February hair had grown over jaws, chin, and throat, the upper lip shaven. This facial design was wrought by William Florville, a Haitian-born Negro, known as "Billy the Barber" whose shop in Springfield dated back to 1831. For more than twenty years he had shaved and done the haircuts of Lincoln while Lincoln handled several real estate title cases for Billy, who owned town lots and a farm. In his house was celebrated, it was said, the first Catholic mass in Springfield. He wrote for the Springfield *Journal* droll and charming praise of his razor skill, had keen humor, and Lincoln while being shaved undoubtedly picked up new funny stories. Why Lincoln took to whiskers at this time nobody seemed to know.

At sunset the evening before the day set for starting to Washington, Lincoln and Herndon sat in their office for a long talk about their sixteen years as partners. As Lincoln gathered a bundle of papers and stood ready to leave, he told Herndon their partnership would go on, their "shingle" stay up. As they walked down the stairs Lincoln said he was "sick of office-holding already" and "I shudder when I think of the tasks that are still ahead."

In a dusty third-story locked room over the store of his brother-in-law, C. M. Smith, Lincoln, with a few books and documents he consulted, had hidden away from all callers while he worked on his inaugural address for March 4, in Washington. Two printers, sworn to secrecy, had in January set up and run off twenty copies of the address. Weeks had gone by. Nobody had told or been careless. The inaugural text was still a well-kept secret.

Lincoln took walks alone. Whitney ran across him in a section of Springfield where he had no business, unless to be walking alone. His arms were full of papers and bundles of mail. Where was he going? "Nowhere in particular," he told Whitney.

Clothes, furniture, books, the household goods were packed in boxes and trunks. The family took rooms a few days in the Chenery House; the old home was leased, horse, buggy, and cow sold off.

At the hotel Lincoln had roped his trunks himself and had written, "A. Lincoln, The White House, Washington, D.C." on cards he fastened on the trunks.

A cold drizzle of rain was falling February 11 when Lincoln and his party of fifteen were to leave Springfield on the eight o'clock at the Great Western Railway station. Chilly gray mist hung the circle of the prairie horizon. A short locomotive with a flat-topped smokestack stood puffing with a baggage car and special passenger car coupled on; a railroad president and superintendent were on board. A thousand people crowded in and around the brick station, inside of which Lincoln was standing, and one by one came hundreds of old friends, shaking hands, wishing him luck and Godspeed, all faces solemn. Even the huge Judge Davis, wearing a new white silk hat, was a somber figure.

A path was made for Lincoln from the station to his car; hands stretched out for one last handshake. He hadn't intended to make a speech; but on the platform of the car, as he turned and saw his home people, he took off his hat, stood perfectly still, and raised a hand for silence. They stood, with hats off.

Then he spoke slowly, amid the soft gray drizzle from the sky. Later, on the train he wrote with a pencil about half of his speech, dictating to his secretary, John Nicolay, the remainder of his good-bye words to Springfield: "My friends — No one, not in my situation, can appreciate my feeling of sadness at this parting. To this place, and the kindness of these people, I owe everything. Here I have lived a quarter of a century, and have passed from a young to an old man. Here my children have been born, and one is buried. I now leave, not knowing when, or whether ever, I may return, with a task before me greater than that which rested upon Washington. Without the assistance of that Divine Being, who ever attended him, I cannot succeed. With that assistance I cannot fail. Trusting in Him, who can go with me, and remain with you and be everywhere for good, let us confidently hope that all will yet be well. To His care commending you, as I hope in your prayers you will commend me, I bid you an affectionate farewell."

Bells rang, there was a grinding of wheels, the train moved and carried Lincoln away from his home town and folks. The tears were not yet dry on some faces when the train had faded into the gray to the east.

[Lincoln was inaugurated on March 4, 1861. Less than six weeks later, Confederate artillery fired on Fort Sumter, and the Civil War began. "A Lincoln Preface" (pages 448–51) gave a sketch of Lincoln's life during the terrible war years. In spite of fierce opposition, he was elected for a second term in November 1864 and inaugurated on March 4, 1865. His short inaugural address closed with the moving words: "With malice toward none, with charity for all, with firmness in the right as God gives us to see the right, let us finish the work we are in, to bind up the nation's wounds, to care for him who shall have borne the battle, and for his widow and orphans, to do all which may achieve and cherish a just and lasting peace among ourselves and with all nations." A month later, on Palm Sunday, the Confederate army surrendered, and the war was over. Lincoln was to live only five days more. In the following chapters, Sandburg recounts Lincoln's assassination and funeral.]

from
The War Years

10

BLOOD ON THE MOON

On the calendar it was Holy Week, and April 14 was Good Friday. Some were to say they had never before this week seen such a shine of beneficence, such a kindling glow, on Lincoln's face. He was down to lean flesh and bone, thirty pounds underweight, his cheeks haggard, yet the inside of him moved to a music of peace on earth and good will to men. He let it come out in the photograph Gardner made this Holy Week.

The schedule for this Good Friday as outlined beforehand was: office business till eight; breakfast, and then interviews till the Cabinet meeting at eleven, luncheon, more interviews, a later afternoon drive with Mrs. Lincoln, an informal meeting with old Illinois friends, during the day and evening one or more trips to the War

Department, another interview, then to the theater with Mrs. Lincoln and a small party.

The party walked into the theater at about nine o'clock. An usher led them to their box. The audience in their one thousand seats saw or heard that the President had arrived. They applauded; many rose from their seats; some cheered. The President paused and nodded his acknowledgment of their welcome to him.

On the stage proceeds *Our American Cousin*, a play written fourteen years before by the English dramatist Tom Taylor. The play is not unpleasant, often stupid, sprinkled with silly puns, forced humor. The laughter says the audience is having a good time.

From the upholstered rocking armchair in which Lincoln sits, he can see only the persons in the box with him, the players on the stage, and any persons off stage on the left. The box has two doors. The door forward is locked. The President's party has the roominess and convenience of double space, extra armchairs, side chairs, a small sofa. In the privacy achieved, he is in sight only of his chosen companions, the actors he has come to see render a play, and the few people who may be off stage to the left.

This privacy, however, is not as complete as it seems. A few feet behind the President is the box door, the only entry to the box unless by a climb from the stage. In this door is a small hole, bored that afternoon to serve as a peephole — from the outside. Through this peephole it is the intention of the Outsider who made it with a gimlet to stand and watch the President, then at a chosen moment to enter the box. This door opens from the box on a narrow hallway that leads to another door opening on the balcony of the theater.

Through these two doors the Outsider must pass in order to enter the President's box. Close to the door connecting with the balcony, two inches of plaster have been cut from the brick wall of the narrow hallway. The intention of the Outsider is that a bar placed in this cut-away wall niche and then braced against the panel of the door will hold that door against intruders, will serve to stop anyone from interference with the Outsider while making his observations of the President through the gimleted hole in the box door.

At either of these doors, the one to the box or the one from the balcony to the hallway, it is the assigned duty and expected responsibility of John F. Parker to stand or sit constantly, with unfailing vigil. The custom was for a chair to be placed in the narrow hallway for the guard to sit in. The doorkeeper Buckingham told the guard Crook that such a chair was provided this evening. "Whether Parker occupied it at all, I do not know," wrote Crook. "Mr. Buckingham is of the impression that he did. If he did, he left it almost immediately, for he confessed to me the next day that he went to a seat, so that he could see the play." The door to the President's box is shut. It is not kept open so that the box occupants can see the guard on duty.

Either between acts, or at some time when the play was not lively enough to suit him, or because of an urge for a pony of whisky under his belt, John F. Parker leaves his seat in the balcony and goes down to the street and joins companions in a little whiff of liquor — this on the basis of a statement of the coachman Burns, who declared he stayed outside on the street with his carriage and horses, except for one interlude when "the special police officer [meaning John F. Parker] and the footman of the President [Forbes] came up to him and asked him to take a drink with them, which he did." Thus circumstances favor the lurking and vigilant Outsider.

The play goes on. Out in a main-floor seat is one Julia Adelaide Shephard, writing a letter to her father about this Good Friday evening at the theater. "Cousin Julia has just told me," she reports, "that the President is in yonder upper right-hand private box so handsomely decked with silken flags festooned over a picture of George Washington. The young and lovely daughter of Senator Harris is the only one of his party we see, as the flags hide the rest. But we know Father Abraham is there like a Father watching what interests his children. The American cousin has just been making love to a young lady who says she'll never marry but for love, but when her mother and herself find out that he has lost his property, they retreat in disgust at the left hand of the stage while the American cousin goes out at the right. We are waiting for the next scene."

And the next scene? The next scene is to crash and blare and flare as one of the wildest, one of the most inconceivable, fateful, and chaotic that ever stunned and shocked a world.

The moment of high fate is not seen by the theater audience. Only one man sees that moment. He is the Outsider, the one who waited and lurked and made his preparations. He comes through the outer door into the little hallway, fastens the strong though slender bar into the two-inch niche in the brick wall, and braces it against the door panel. He moves softly to the box door and through the little hole studies the box occupants and his Human Target seated in an upholstered rocking armchair. Softly he opens the door and steps toward his prey, in his right hand a one-shot brass derringer [1] pistol, a little eight-ounce vest-pocket weapon winged for death, in his left hand a steel dagger. He is cool and precise and times his every move. He raises the derringer, lengthens his right arm, runs his eye along the barrel in a line with the head of his victim less than five feet away — and pulls the trigger.

A lead ball somewhat less than a half-inch in diameter crashes into the left side of the head of the Human Target, into the back of the head, in a line with and three inches from the left ear. For Abraham Lincoln it is lights out, good night, farewell — and a long farewell to the good earth and its trees, its enjoyable companions, and the Union of States and the world Family of Man he has loved. He is not dead yet. He is to linger in dying. But the living man can never again speak, see, hear, or awaken into conscious being.

The last breath is drawn at twenty-one minutes and fifty-five seconds past 7 A.M., and the last heart beat flickers at twenty-two minutes and ten seconds past the hour on Saturday, April 15, 1865.

The Pale Horse had come. To a deep river, to a far country, to a by-and-by whence no man returns, had gone the child of Nancy Hanks and Tom Lincoln, the wilderness boy who found far lights and tall rainbows to live by, whose name even before he died had become a legend inwoven with men's struggle for freedom the world over.

The widow was told. She came in and threw herself with uncontrollable moaning on the body. When later she went away the cry broke from her, "O my God, and I have given my husband to die!"

Out on the Illinois prairie of Coles County, they went to a farmhouse and told the news to an old woman who answered: "I knowed when he went away he'd never come back alive." This was Sarah Bush Lincoln, prepared for her sorrow which came that day.

---

[1] *derringer* (der'in·jər): a pistol having a short barrel (invented by Henry Derringer).

11

VAST PAGEANT, THEN GREAT QUIET

In the East Room of the White House lay the body of a man, embalmed and prepared for a journey. On a platform, under a canopy of folds and loops of black silk and crepe, rested the coffin. Tassels, shamrock leaves, silver stars, and silver cords could be seen on facings and edges. A shield with a silver plate had the inscription:

Abraham Lincoln
Sixteenth President of the United States
Born Feb. 12, 1809
Died April 15, 1865

It was Tuesday, April 18, and outside surged the largest mass of people that had ever thronged the White House lawn, the estimate 25,000. In two columns they filed through the East Room, moving along the two sides of the coffin, many pale and limping soldiers out of the convalescent wards of the hospitals, many women and children sobbing and weeping aloud as they passed, pausing only the slightest moment for a look.

On Wednesday, April 19, arrived sixty clergymen, the Cabinet members, the Supreme Court Justices, important officials, foreign Ministers, General Grant with white sash across his breast, the new President Andrew Johnson — six hundred dignitaries in all. Mrs. Lincoln was still too distracted to be present, but Robert Lincoln came.

Bishop Matthew Simpson of the Methodist Episcopal church offered prayer that smitten hearts might endure, might not be called upon for further sacrifices. A bitter cup from the hand of a chastening Divine Father had been given the mourning nation, the Reverend Dr. Phineas D. Gurley, of Washington's New York Avenue Presbyterian Church, said in the funeral address.

The closing invocation was spoken by a Baptist clergyman, chaplain of the U.S. Senate, the Reverend Dr. E. H. Gray.

The services were over. The pallbearers took the silver handles. The bong of big bells on cathedrals struck, and the little bells of lesser steeples chimed in, as across the spring sunshine came the tolling of all the church bells of Washington and Georgetown, and Alexandria across the river. Counting the minutes with their salutes came the hoarse boom of fort guns encircling the national capital and several batteries sent into the city.

Out of the great front door of the Executive Mansion for the last time went the mortal shape of Abraham Lincoln, sixteenth President of the United States. On the one-mile route to the Capitol, pavements and curbs were packed with onlookers, who also filled every roof, window, doorway, balcony, and stairway. Sixty thousand spectators watched a parade of forty thousand mourners. From his sickbed, sore with his dagger wounds, Secretary Seward gazed from the window with mingled grief and thanks.

In the rotunda of the Capitol, under the great white dome that had come to its finished construction while the war raged, twelve sergeants of the Veteran Reserve Corps carried the coffin to a huge catafalque.

In silence during night watches, the body of Lincoln lay with eyes never opening to see far above him the arches of the great dome that for him symbolized the Union. In the night watches, while the guard mount changed, whispering, quiet on soft feet, into midnight and past into daybreak, midway between House and Senate chambers, midway between those seats and aisles of heartbreak and passion, he lay, a horizontal clay tabernacle.

In the morning at ten o'clock, the doors opened in special consideration for wounded soldiers from the hospitals, weak and battered men, some with empty sleeves, others on crutches, to file by. Afterward came the public, at times three thousand to the hour, before midnight twenty-five thousand persons.

Friday morning, April 21, saw the coffin placed aboard a special burial car at the Washington depot. Railroad-yard engine bells tolled, and a far-stretching crowd stood with uncovered heads as the train of seven cars moved out of Washington for Baltimore.

This was the start of a funeral journey that was to take the lifeless body on a 1,700-mile route which included practically the same points and stops that the living form had made four years and two months before on the way to the first inauguration.

Baltimore wore mourning everywhere and paid reverence; the human outpouring was unmistakable. As the funeral train moved slowly over Pennsylvania soil, at lonely country crossroads were people and faces, horsemen, farmers with their wives and children, standing where they had stood for hours before, waiting, performing the last little possible act of ceremony and attention and love — with solemn faces and uncovered heads standing and gazing as the funeral car passed. In villages and small towns stood waiting crowds, sometimes with a little silver cornet band, often with flowers, in hope the train might stop and they could leave camellias, roses, lilies-of-the-valley, wreaths of color and perfume.

Through heavy rains at Harrisburg came thirty thousand in the night and morning to see the coffin in circles of white flowering almond. At noon on Saturday, April 22, in Philadelphia, a half-million people were on hand for the funeral train. In Independence Hall stood the coffin. Outside the line of mourners ran three miles.

At Newark, New Jersey, on the morning of April 24, the train moved slowly amid acres of people, a square mile of them. At Jersey City was a like scene. The Empire State formally received the body from Governor Parker of New Jersey.

Never before, so everyone agreed, had New York put on such garb and completely changed its look so that it seemed another city. On the marble and brownstone fronts, in the ramshackle tenements of "those who live from hand to mouth," came out crape or black folds or drapery or black muslin, rosettes, sable emblems, what the news reporters termed "the habiliments of mourning."

From near noon Monday, April 24, to noon the next day, the remains of Abraham Lincoln, horizontal amid white satin, lay in the City Hall. A vast outpouring of people hour by hour passed by to see this effigy and remembrance of his face and form.

At noon on Tuesday, April 25, a procession moved from the City Hall to Ninth Avenue and the Hudson River Railroad depot. Nearly every race, nationality, religion, political faith was represented among those who marched, near a hundred thousand. The sidewalk, street, curb, and window spectators ran perhaps to a million. At the Union Square exercises following the parade, the Roman Catholic Archbishop John McCloskey pronounced the benediction, Rabbi Samuel M. Isaacs of the Jewish Synagogue read the scriptures, the Reverend Stephen H. Syng of St. George's Church offered a prayer, the Reverend J. P. Thompson intoned Lincoln's second inaugural. Evening had come.

Up the Hudson River east bank the night of April 25 chugged the train of seven cars. On every mile of the route to Albany, those on the train could see bonfires and torches, could hear bells and cannon and guns, could see forms of people and white sorry faces. Past midnight of April 25 into the morning hours of April 26, the columns of mourners passed the coffin in Albany.

On this morning of April 26, hunted like a wild beast and cornered like a rat, his broken shinbone betraying him, assassin J. Wilkes Booth met his end. Near Bowling Green, Virginia, in a burning barn set afire from the outside, a bullet drove through his neck bone "perforating both sides of the collar," and he was dragged away from reaching flames and laid under a tree. Water was given him. He revived, to murmur from parched lips, "Tell my mother — I died — for my country." He was carried to a house veranda, there muttering, "I thought I did for the best." He lingered for a time. A doctor came. Wilkes Booth asked that his hands might be raised so that he could look at them. So it was told. And as he looked on his hands, he mumbled hoarsely, "Useless! useless!" And those were his last words.

Across the Empire State that day and night it was a mural monotone of mourning, the Erie Canal zone in sober grief with evergreens, flowers, sable emblems. The endless multitudinous effect became colossal.

At Cleveland it was said that more than a million pilgrims from northern Ohio had paid their homage. A lashing wind drove torrents of rain as the night procession moved on, escorting the hearse through crowded streets to the depot.

From Cleveland to Crestline the rain kept on in torrents. Nevertheless, at all towns and crossroads were the mourners, with uncovered heads, with torches and flags crossed with black. Five miles out from Columbus stood an old woman alone as the slow train came by, tears coursing down her furrowed cheeks.

In the rotunda of Ohio's capitol, on a mound of green moss dotted with white flowers, rested the coffin on April 28, while eight thousand persons passed by each hour from nine-thirty in the morning till four in the afternoon. On the slow night run to Chicago, it was as in Ohio, thousands in Lafayette standing mute and daybreak not yet, thousands more at Michigan City.

Then at last home to Springfield. In the state capitol where he had spoken his prophet warnings of the House Divided, stood the casket. Now passed those who had known him long, part of the seventy-five thousand who came. They were awed, subdued, shaken, stony, strange. They came from Salem, Petersburg, Clary's Grove, Alton, Charleston, Mattoon, the old Eighth Circuit towns and villages. There were clients for whom he had won or lost, lawyers who had tried cases with him and against, neighbors who had seen him milk a cow and curry his horse, friends who had heard his stories around a hot stove and listened to his surmises on politics and religion. All day long and through the night, the unbroken line moved, the home town having its farewell.

On May 4 of this year 1865 anno Domini, a procession moved with its hearse from the state capitol to Oak Ridge Cemetery. There, on green banks and hillsides flowing away from a burial vault, the crowded thousands of listeners and watchers heard prayers and hymns, heard the second inaugural read aloud. Bishop Matthew Simpson in a moving oration spoke as an interpreter and foreteller: "There are moments which involve in themselves eternities. There are instants which seem to contain germs which shall develop and bloom forever. Such a moment came in the tide of time to our land when a question must be settled, affecting all the powers of the earth. The contest was for human freedom. Not for this republic merely, not for the Union simply, but to decide whether the people, as a people, in their entire majesty, were destined to be the Governments, or whether they were to be subject to tyrants or aristocrats, or to class rule of any kind. This is the great question for which we have been fighting, and its decision is at hand, and the result of this contest will affect the ages to come. If successful, republics will spread in spite of monarchs all over this earth." Came then from the people, noted the *Illinois State Journal*, exclamations of "Amen! thank God!"

Evergreen carpeted the stone floor of the vault. On the coffin set in a receptacle of black walnut, they arranged flowers carefully and precisely, they poured flowers as symbols, they lavished heaps of fresh flowers as though there could never be enough to tell either their hearts or his.

And the night came with great quiet.

And there was rest.

The prairie years, the war years, were over.

Dignity and experience are seen in this portrait
of Willard Snowden by Andrew Wyeth.

Mrs. Andrew Wyeth

BOOK THREE | PART 2

THE BIOGRAPHER'S ART

*Supposing all could be told, it
would take a far longer time
to tell it than was taken to enact
it in life.*

                Carl Sandburg

    A biography is the story of a real person's life. Sandburg's Lincoln is based on fact, not on imagination, and yet without imagination Sandburg could not have produced a great biography. The biographer is both historian and artist. He must conduct research to find out everything there is to know about his subject. He must scrutinize all the information and test it for accuracy. Then he must put all the pieces together and look for the connections between them. Biography is more than a list of dates and events. Once the "facts" are assembled and put in order, the work of the artist begins.

    The biographer, like all writers, uses his imagination and his skill with language. But he is "an artist who is on oath." He is sworn to tell the truth about his subject. He cannot invent details. He is limited by the truth, and if he is a good biographer, he will tell all the truth — the good and the bad, the faults as well as the virtues. It was

Oliver Cromwell who, when he ruled over England, told a portrait artist to paint him "warts and all."

Within these limits of "fact" and "truth," however, the biographer is still an artist. He must recreate the subject's character and personality. He must bring to life the world his subject lived in. He draws upon everything he knows about human beings in order to find in one unique life something which is common to all lives.

Many readers prefer biography to fiction because they are impatient with reading about things which "did not really happen." Considered as literature, however, biography and fiction are not altogether different in their aims. Neither of them is "real" in the sense that our daily lives are real. Both are imaginative reconstructions of reality. And the biographer, like the storyteller, has a point of view — he can't help but have one.

In autobiography the subject writes about himself. His job is both easier and harder than that of the biographer. To begin with, he doesn't have to do much research because — presumably — he knows what has happened to him. But does he know who he is? The task of being objective about oneself is a difficult one. Usually the autobiographer knows more but tells less than the biographer.

Biographies are no more, and no less, than the varied records of other lives.

Seventeen years before he became President of the United States, John F. Kennedy proved himself to be a strong and courageous leader. As the young commander of a PT boat off the Solomon Islands in the South Pacific, he saved himself and his crew from capture and death. John Hersey, a Pulitzer-Prize-winning author, tells about Kennedy's exploits in this biographical narrative.

Survival

JOHN HERSEY

It seems that Kennedy's PT, the 109, was out one night with a squadron patrolling Blackett Strait, in mid-Solomons. Blackett Strait is a patch of water bounded on the northeast by the volcano called Kolombangara, on the west by the island of Vella Lavella, on the south by the island of Gizo and a string of coral-fringed islets, and on the east by the bulk of New Georgia. The boats were working about forty miles away from their base on the island of Rendova, on the south side of New Georgia. They had entered Blackett Strait, as was their habit, through Ferguson Passage, between the coral islets and New Georgia.

The night was a starless black and Japanese destroyers were around. It was about two-thirty. The 109, with three officers and ten enlisted men aboard, was leading three boats on a sweep for a target. An officer named George Ross was up on the bow, magnifying the void with binoculars. Kennedy was at the wheel and he saw Ross turn and point into the darkness. The man in the forward machine-gun turret shouted, "Ship at two o'clock!" Kennedy saw a shape and spun the wheel to turn for an attack, but the 109 answered sluggishly. She was running slowly on only one of her three engines, so as to make a minimum wake and avoid detection from the air. The shape became a Japanese destroyer, cutting through the night at forty knots and heading straight for the 109. The thirteen men on the PT hardly had time to brace themselves. Those who saw the Japanese ship coming were paralyzed by fear in a curious way: they could move their hands but not their feet. Kennedy whirled the wheel to the left, but again the 109 did not respond. Ross went through the gallant but futile motions of slamming a shell into the breech of the 37-millimeter antitank gun which had been temporarily mounted that very day, wheels and all, on the foredeck. The urge to bolt and dive over the side was terribly strong, but still no one was able to move; all hands froze to their battle stations. Then the Japanese crashed into the 109 and cut her right in two. The sharp enemy forefoot struck the PT on the starboard side about fifteen feet from the bow and crunched diagonally across with a racking noise. The PT's wooden hull hardly even delayed the destroyer. Kennedy was thrown hard to the left in the cockpit, and he thought, "This is how it feels to be killed." In a moment he found himself on his back on the deck, looking up at the destroyer as it passed through his boat. There was another loud noise and a huge flash of yellow-red light, and the destroyer glowed. Its peculiar, raked, inverted-Y stack stood out in the brilliant light and, later, in Kennedy's memory.

There was only one man below decks at the moment of collision. That was McMahon, engineer. He had no idea what was up. He was just reaching forward to wrench the starboard engine into gear when a ship came into his engine room. He was lifted from the narrow passage between two of the engines and thrown painfully against the starboard bulkhead aft of the boat's auxiliary generator. He landed in a sitting position. A tremendous burst of flame came back at him from the day room, where some of the gas tanks were. He put his hands over his face, drew his legs up tight, and waited to die. But he felt water hit him after the fire, and he was sucked far downward as his half of the PT sank. He began to struggle upward through the water. He had held his breath since the impact, so his lungs were tight and they hurt. He looked up through the water. Over his head he saw a yellow glow — gasoline burning on the water. He broke the surface and was in fire again. He splashed hard to keep a little island of water around him.

Johnston, another engineer, had been asleep on deck when the collision came. It lifted him and dropped him overboard. He saw the flame and the destroyer for a moment. Then a huge propeller pounded by near him and the awful turbulence of the destroyer's wake took him down, turned him over and over, held him down, shook him, and drubbed on his ribs. He hung on and came up in water that was like a river rapids. The next day his body turned black and blue from the beating.

Kennedy's half of the PT stayed afloat. The bulkheads were sealed, so the undamaged watertight compartments up forward kept the half hull floating. The destroyer rushed off into the dark. There was an awful quiet: only the sound of gasoline burning.

Kennedy shouted, "Who's aboard?"

Feeble answers came from three of the enlisted men, McGuire, Mauer, and Albert; and from one of the officers, Thom.

Kennedy saw the fire only ten feet from the boat. He thought it might reach her and explode the remaining gas tanks, so he shouted, "Over the side!"

The five men slid into the water. But the wake of the destroyer swept the fire away from the PT, so after a few minutes Kennedy and the others crawled back aboard. Kennedy shouted for survivors in the water. One by one they answered: Ross, the third officer; Harris, McMahon, Johnston, Zinsser, Starkey, enlisted men. Two did not answer: Kirksey and Marney, enlisted men. Since the last bombing at base, Kirksey had been sure he would die. He had huddled at his battle station by the fantail gun, with his kapok life jacket tied tight up to his cheeks. No one knows what happened to him or to Marney.

Harris shouted from the darkness, "Mr. Kennedy! Mr. Kennedy! McMahon is badly hurt." Kennedy took his shoes, his shirt, and his sidearms off, told Mauer to blink a light so that the men in the water would know where the half hull was, then dived in and swam toward the voice. The survivors were widely scattered. McMahon and Harris were a hundred yards away.

When Kennedy reached McMahon, he asked, "How are you, Mac?"

McMahon said, "I'm all right. I'm kind of burnt."

Kennedy shouted out, "How are the others?"

Harris said softly, "I hurt my leg."

Kennedy, who had been on the Harvard swimming team five years before, took McMahon in tow and headed for the PT. A gentle breeze kept blowing the boat away from the swimmers. It took forty-five minutes to make what had been an easy hundred yards.

On the way in, Harris said, "I can't go any farther." Kennedy, of the Boston Kennedys, said to Harris, of the same home town, "For a guy from Boston, you're certainly putting up a great exhibition out here, Harris." Harris made it all right and didn't complain any more. Then Kennedy swam from man to man, to see how they were doing. All who had survived the crash were able to stay afloat, since they were wearing life preservers — kapok jackets shaped like overstuffed vests, aviators' yellow Mae Wests,[1] or air-filled belts like small inner tubes. But those who couldn't swim had to be towed back to the wreckage by those who could. One of the men screamed for help. When Ross reached him, he found that the screaming man had two life jackets on. Johnston was treading water in a film of gasoline which did not catch fire. The fumes filled his lungs and he fainted. Thom towed him in. The others got in under their own power. It was now after 5:00 A.M., but still dark. It had taken nearly three hours to get everyone aboard.

The men stretched out on the tilted deck of the PT. Johnston, McMahon, and Ross collapsed into sleep. The men talked about how wonderful it was to be alive and speculated on when the other PT's would come back to rescue them. Mauer kept blinking the light to point their way. But the other boats had no idea of coming back. They had seen a collision, a sheet of flame, and a slow burning on the water. When the skipper of one of the boats saw the sight, he put his hands over his face and sobbed, "My God! My God!" He and the others turned away. Back at the base, after a couple of days, the squadron held services for the souls of the thirteen men, and one of the officers wrote his mother, "George Ross lost his life for a cause that he believed in stronger than any one of us, because he was an idealist in the purest sense. Jack Kennedy, the Ambassador's[2] son, was on the same boat and also lost his life. The man that said the cream of a nation is lost in war can never be accused of making an overstatement of a very cruel fact. . . ."

When day broke, the men on the remains of the 109 stirred and looked around. To the northeast, three miles off, they saw the monumental cone of Kolombangara; there, the men knew, ten thou-

---

[1] *Mae Wests:* inflatable life preservers named for the movie queen of the 1930's.
[2] *Ambassador:* Joseph P. Kennedy, Ambassador to Britain, 1937–40.

sand Japanese swarmed. To the west, five miles away, they saw Vella Lavella; more Japanese. To the south, only a mile or so away, they actually could see a Japanese camp on Gizo. Kennedy ordered his men to keep as low as possible, so that no moving silhouettes would show against the sky. The listing hulk was gurgling and gradually settling. Kennedy said, "What do you want to do if they come out? Fight or surrender?" One said, "Fight with what?" So they took an inventory of their armament. The 37-millimeter gun had flopped over the side and was hanging there by a chain. They had one Tommy gun, six 45-caliber automatics, and one .38. Not much.

"Well," Kennedy said, "what do you want to do?"

One said, "Anything you say, Mr. Kennedy. You're the boss."

Kennedy said, "There's nothing in the book about a situation like this. Seems to me we're not a military organization any more. Let's just talk this over."

They talked it over, and pretty soon they argued, and Kennedy could see that they would never survive in anarchy. So he took command again.

It was vital that McMahon and Johnston should have room to lie down. McMahon's face, neck, hands, wrists, and feet were horribly burned. Johnston was pale and he coughed continually. There was scarcely space for everyone, so Kennedy ordered the other men into the water to make room, and went in himself. All morning they clung to the hulk and talked about how incredible it was that no one had come to rescue them. All morning they watched for the plane which they thought would be looking for them. They cursed war in general and PT's in particular. At about ten o'clock the hulk heaved a moist sigh and turned turtle. McMahon and Johnston had to hang on as best they could. It was clear that the remains of the 109 would soon sink. When the sun had passed the meridian, Kennedy said, "We will swim to that small island," pointing to one of a group three miles to the southeast. "We have less chance of making it than some of these other islands here, but there'll be less chance of Japanese, too." Those who could not swim well grouped themselves around a long two-by-six timber with which carpenters had braced the 37-millimeter cannon on deck and which had been knocked overboard by the force of the collision. They tied several pairs of shoes to the timber, as well as the ship's lantern, wrapped in a life jacket to keep it afloat. Thom took charge of this unwieldy group. Kennedy took McMahon in tow again. He cut loose one end of a long strap on McMahon's Mae West and took the end in his teeth. He swam breast stroke, pulling the helpless McMahon along on his back. It took over five hours to reach the island. Water lapped into Kennedy's mouth through his clenched teeth, and he swallowed a lot. The salt water cut into McMahon's awful burns, but he did not complain. Every few minutes, when Kennedy stopped to rest, taking the strap out of his mouth and holding it in his hand, McMahon would simply say, "How far do we have to go?"

Kennedy would reply, "We're going good." Then he would ask, "How do you feel, Mac?"

McMahon always answered, "I'm O.K., Mr. Kennedy. How about you?"

In spite of his burden, Kennedy beat the other men to the reef that surrounded the island. He left McMahon on the reef and told him to keep low, so as not to be spotted by Japanese. Kennedy went ahead and explored the island. It was only a hundred yards in diameter; coconuts on the trees but none on the ground; no enemy visible. Just as the others reached the island, one of them spotted a Japanese barge chugging along close to shore. They all lay low. The barge went on. Johnston, who was very pale and weak and who was still coughing a lot, said, "They wouldn't come here. What'd they be walking around here for? It's too small." Kennedy lay in some bushes, exhausted by his effort, his stomach heavy with the water he had swallowed. He had been in the sea, except for short intervals on the hulk, for fifteen and a half hours. Now he started thinking. Every night for several nights the PT's had cut through Ferguson Passage on their way to action. Ferguson Passage was just beyond the next little island. Maybe . . .

He stood up. He took one of the pairs of shoes. He put one of the rubber life belts around his waist. He hung the .38 around his neck on a lanyard. He took his pants off. He picked up the ship's lantern, a heavy battery affair ten inches by ten inches, still wrapped in the kapok jacket. He said, "If I find a boat, I'll flash the lantern twice. The password will be 'Roger,' the answer will be 'Willco.'" He walked toward the water. After fifteen paces he was dizzy, but in the water he felt all right.

It was early evening. It took half an hour to swim to the reef around the next island. Just as he planted his feet on the reef, which lay about four feet under the surface, he saw the shape of a very big fish in the clear water. He flashed the light at it and splashed hard. The fish went away.

Now it was dark. Kennedy blundered along the uneven reef in water up to his waist. Sometimes he would reach forward with his leg and cut one of his shins or ankles on sharp coral. Other times he would step forward onto emptiness. He made his way like a slow-motion drunk, hugging the lantern. At about nine o'clock he came to the end of the reef, alongside Ferguson Passage. He took his shoes off and tied them to the life jacket, then struck out into open water. He swam about an hour, until he felt he was far enough out to intercept the PT's. Treading water, he listened for the muffled roar of motors, getting chilled, waiting, holding the lamp. Once he looked west and saw flares and the false gaiety of an action. The lights were far beyond the little islands, even beyond Gizo, ten miles away. Kennedy realized that the PT boats had chosen, for the first night in many, to go around Gizo instead of through Ferguson Passage. There was no hope. He started back. He made the same painful promenade of the reef and struck out for the tiny island where his friends were. But this swim was different. He was very tired and now the current was running fast, carrying him to the right. He saw that he could not make the island, so he flashed the light once and shouted "Roger! Roger!" to identify himself.

On the beach the men were hopefully vigilant. They saw the light and heard the shouts. They were very happy, because they thought that Kennedy had found a PT. They walked out onto the reef, sometimes up to their waists in water, and waited. It was very painful for those who had no shoes. The men shouted, but not much, because they were afraid of Japanese.

One said, "There's another flash."

A few minutes later a second said, "There's a light over there."

A third said, "We're seeing things in this dark."

They waited a long time, but they saw nothing except phosphorescence and heard nothing but the sound of waves. They went back, very discouraged.

One said despairingly, "We're going to die."

Johnston said, "Aw shut up. You can't die. Only the good die young."

Kennedy had drifted right by the little island. He thought he had never known such deep trouble, but something he did shows that unconsciously he had not given up hope. He dropped his shoes, but he héld onto the heavy lantern, his symbol of contact with his fellows. He stopped trying to swim. He seemed to stop caring. His body drifted through the wet hours, and he was very cold. His mind was a jumble. A few hours before he had wanted desperately to get to the base at Rendova. Now he only wanted to get back to the little island he had left that night, but he didn't try to get there; he just wanted to. His mind seemed to float away from his body. Darkness and time took the place of a mind in his skull. For a long time he slept, or was crazy, or floated in a chill trance.

The currents of the Solomon Islands are queer. The tide shoves and sucks through the islands and makes the currents curl in odd patterns. It was a fateful pattern into which Jack Kennedy drifted. He drifted in it all night. His mind was blank, but his fist was tightly clenched on the kapok around the lantern. The current moved in a huge circle — west past Gizo, then north and east past Kolombangara, then south into Ferguson Passage. Early in the morning the sky turned from black to gray, and so did Kennedy's mind. Light came to both at about six. Kennedy looked around and saw that he was exactly where he had been the night before when he saw the flares beyond Gizo. For a second time, he started home. He thought for a while that he had lost his mind and that he only imagined that he was repeating his attempt to reach the island. But the chill of the water was real enough, the lantern was real, his progress was measurable. He made the reef, crossed the lagoon, and got to the first island. He lay on the beach awhile. He found that his lantern did not work any more, so he left it and started back to the next island, where his men were. This time the trip along the reef was awful. He had discarded his shoes, and every step on the coral was painful. This time the swim across the gap where the current had caught him the night before seemed endless. But the current had changed; he made the island. He crawled up on the beach. He was vomiting when his men came up to him. He said, "Ross, you try it tonight." Then he passed out.

Ross, seeing Kennedy so sick, did not look forward to the execution of the order. He distracted himself by complaining about his hunger. There were a few coconuts on the trees, but the men were too weak to climb up for them. One of the men thought of sea food, stirred his tired body, and found a snail on the beach. He said, "If we were desperate, we could eat these." Ross said, "Desperate! Give me that. I'll eat that." He took it in his hand and looked at it. The snail put its head out and looked at him. Ross was startled, but he shelled the snail and ate it, making faces because it was bitter.

In the afternoon, Ross swam across to the next island. He took a pistol to signal with, and he spent the night watching Ferguson Passage from the reef around the island. Nothing came through. Kennedy slept badly that night; he was cold and sick.

The next morning everyone felt wretched. Planes which the men were unable to identify flew overhead and there were dogfights. That meant the enemy as well as friends, so the men dragged themselves into the bushes and lay low. Some prayed. Johnston said, "You guys make me sore. You didn't spend ten cents in church in ten years, then all of a sudden you're in trouble and you see the light." Kennedy felt a little better now. When Ross came back, Kennedy decided that the group should move to another, larger island to the southeast, where there seemed to be more coconut trees and where the party would be nearer Ferguson Passage. Again Kennedy took McMahon in tow with the strap in his teeth, and the nine others grouped themselves around the timber.

This swim took three hours. The nine around the timber were caught by the current and barely made the far tip of the island. Kennedy found walking the quarter mile across to them much harder than the three-hour swim. The cuts on his bare feet were festered and looked like small balloons. The men were suffering most from thirst, and they broke open some coconuts lying on the ground and avidly drank the milk. Kennedy and McMahon, the first to drink, were sickened, and Thom told the others to drink sparingly. In the middle of the night it rained, and someone suggested moving into the underbrush and licking water off the leaves. Ross and McMahon kept contact at first by touching feet as they licked. Somehow they got separated, and, being uncertain whether there were any Japanese on the island, they became frightened. McMahon, trying to make his way back to the beach, bumped into someone and froze. It turned out to be Johnston, licking leaves on his own. In the morning the group saw that all the leaves were covered with droppings. Bitterly, they named the place Bird Island.

On this fourth day, the men were low. Even Johnston was low. He had changed his mind about praying. McGuire had a rosary around his neck, and Johnston said, "McGuire, give that necklace a working over." McGuire said quietly, "Yes, I'll take care of all you fellows." Kennedy was still unwilling to admit that things were hopeless. He asked Ross if he would swim with him to an island called Naru, to the southeast and even nearer Ferguson Passage. They were very weak indeed by now, but after an hour's swim they made it.

They walked painfully across Naru to the Ferguson Passage side, where they saw a Japanese barge aground on the reef. There were two men by the barge — possibly Japanese. They apparently spotted Kennedy and Ross, for they got into a dugout canoe and hurriedly paddled to the other side of the island. Kennedy and Ross moved up the beach. They came upon an unopened rope-bound box and, back in the trees, a little shelter containing a keg of water, a Japanese gas mask, and a crude wooden fetish shaped like a fish. There were Japanese hardtack and candy in the box and the two had a wary feast. Down by the water they found a one-man canoe. They hid from imagined Japanese all day. When night fell, Kennedy left Ross and took the canoe, with some hardtack and a can of water from the keg, out into Ferguson Passage. But no PTs came, so he paddled to Bird Island. The men there told him that the two men he had spotted by the barge that morning were natives, who had paddled to Bird Island. The natives had said that there were Japanese on Naru and the men had given Kennedy and Ross up for lost. Then the natives had gone away. Kennedy gave out small rations of crackers and water, and the men went to sleep. During the night, one man, who kept himself awake until the rest were asleep, drank all the water in the can Kennedy had brought back. In the morning the others figured out which was the guilty one. They swore at him and found it hard to forgive him.

Before dawn, Kennedy started out in the canoe to rejoin Ross on Naru, but when day broke a wind arose and the canoe was swamped. Some natives appeared from nowhere in a canoe, rescued Kennedy, and took him to Naru. There they showed him where a two-man canoe was cached. Kennedy picked up a coconut [3] with a smooth shell and scratched a message on it with a jackknife: "ELEVEN ALIVE NATIVE KNOWS POSIT AND REEFS NAURO ISLAND KENNEDY." Then he said to the natives, "Rendova, Rendova."

One of the natives seemed to understand. They took the coconut and paddled off.

Ross and Kennedy lay in a sickly daze all day. Toward evening it rained and they crawled under a bush. When it got dark, conscience took hold of Kennedy and he persuaded Ross to go out into Ferguson Passage with him in the two-man canoe. Ross argued against it. Kennedy insisted. The two started out in the canoe. They had shaped paddles from the boards of the Japanese box, and they took a coconut shell to bail with. As they got out into the Passage, the wind rose again and the water became choppy. The canoe began to fill. Ross bailed and Kennedy kept the bow into the wind. The waves grew until they were five or six feet high. Kennedy shouted, "Better turn around and go back!" As soon as the canoe was broadside to the waves, the water poured in and the dugout was swamped. The two clung to it, Kennedy at the bow, Ross at the stern. The tide carried them southward toward the open sea, so they kicked and tugged the canoe, aiming northwest. They struggled that way for two hours, not knowing whether they would hit the small island or drift into the endless open.

The weather got worse; rain poured down and they couldn't see more than ten feet. Kennedy shouted, "Sorry I got you out here, Barney!" Ross shouted back, "This would be a great time to say I told you so, but I won't!"

Soon the two could see a white line ahead and could hear a frightening roar — waves crashing on a reef. They had got out of the tidal current and were approaching the island all right, but now they realized that the wind and the waves were carrying them toward the reef. But it was too late to do anything, now that their canoe was swamped, except hang on and wait.

When they were near the reef, a wave broke Kennedy's hold, ripped him away from the canoe, turned him head over heels, and spun him in a violent rush. His ears roared and his eyes pinwheeled,

---

[3] *coconut:* when John F. Kennedy was in office as President, he kept the coconut on his desk in the White House.

and for the third time since the collision he thought he was dying. Somehow he was not thrown against the coral but floated into a kind of eddy. Suddenly he felt the reef under his feet. Steadying himself so that he would not be swept off it, he shouted, "Barney!" There was no reply. Kennedy thought of how he had insisted on going out in the canoe, and he screamed, "Barney!" This time Ross answered. He, too, had been thrown on the reef. He had not been as lucky as Kennedy; his right arm and shoulder had been cruelly lacerated by the coral, and his feet, which were already infected from earlier wounds, were cut some more.

The procession of Kennedy and Ross from reef to beach was a crazy one. Ross's feet hurt so much that Kennedy would hold one paddle on the bottom while Ross put a foot on it, then the other paddle forward for another step, then the first paddle forward again, until they reached sand. They fell on the beach and slept.

Kennedy and Ross were wakened early in the morning by a noise. They looked up and saw four husky natives. One walked up to them and said in an excellent English accent, "I have a letter for you, sir." Kennedy tore the note open. It said, "On His Majesty's Service. To the Senior Officer, Naru Island. I have just learned of your presence on Naru Is. I am in command of a New Zealand infantry patrol operating in conjunction with U.S. Army troops on New Georgia. I strongly advise that you come with these natives to me. Meanwhile I shall be in radio communication with your authorities at Rendova, and we can finalize plans to collect balance of your party. Lt. Wincote. P. S. Will warn aviation of your crossing Ferguson Passage." [4]

Everyone shook hands and the four natives took Ross and Kennedy in their war canoe across to Bird Island to tell the others the good news. There the natives broke out a spirit stove and cooked a feast of yams and C ration. Then they built a lean-to for McMahon, whose burns had begun to rot and stink, and for Ross, whose arm had swelled to the size of a thigh because of the coral cuts. The natives put Kennedy in the bottom of their canoe and covered him

---

[4] The wording and signature of this message are as Kennedy gave them to me in Boston in 1944. The message was in fact slightly, though not substantially, different; and many years later, after Kennedy had become President, the identity of the actual signer was uncovered — A. Reginald Evans. Wherever the name Wincote appears in the rest of this story, the reader will understand that that of Lieutenant Evans should be substituted. [Author]

with sacking and palm fronds, in case Japanese planes should buzz them. The long trip was fun for the natives. They stopped once to try to grab a turtle, and laughed at the sport they were having. Thirty Japanese planes went over low toward Rendova, and the natives waved and shouted gaily. They rowed with a strange rhythm, pounding paddles on the gunwales between strokes. At last they reached a guarded place. Lieutenant Wincote came to the water's edge and said formally, "How do you do. Leftenant [5] Wincote."

Kennedy said, "Hello. I'm Kennedy."

Wincote said, "Come up to my tent and have a cup of tea."

In the middle of the night, after several radio conversations between Wincote's outfit and the PT base, Kennedy sat in the war canoe waiting at an arranged rendezvous for a PT. The moon went down at eleven-twenty. Shortly afterward Kennedy heard the signal he was waiting for — four shots. Kennedy fired four answering shots.

A voice shouted to him, "Hey, Jack!"

Kennedy said, "Where've you been?"

The voice said, "We got some food for you."

Kennedy said bitterly, "No, thanks, I just had a coconut."

A moment later a PT came alongside. Kennedy jumped onto it and hugged the men aboard — his friends. In the American tradition, Kennedy held under his arm a couple of souvenirs: one of the improvised paddles and the Japanese gas mask.

With the help of the natives, the PT made its way to Bird Island. A skiff went in and picked up the men. In the deep of the night, the PT and its happy cargo roared back toward base. The squadron medic had sent some brandy along to revive the weakened men. Johnston felt the need of a little revival. In fact, he felt he needed quite a bit of revival. After taking care of that, he retired topside and sat with his arms around a couple of roly-poly, mission-trained natives. And in the fresh breeze on the way home they sang together a hymn all three happened to know:

> Jesus loves me, this I know,
> For the Bible tells me so;
> Little ones to him belong,
> They are weak, but He is strong.
> Yes, Jesus loves me; yes, Jesus loves me . . .

---

[5] *Leftenant:* British for "lieutenant."

Sandburg's biography of Lincoln is an elaborately researched voyage into the past. He worked from thousands of documents, letters, photographs, and books. No one who had known Lincoln well was still alive for Sandburg to talk with.

John Hersey's account of John Kennedy's PT 109 is based on an entirely different type of research. Those who had survived the adventure were still alive (Hersey was writing only a few months after the event), and most of Hersey's information came from personal interviews with them. The biographer's task was to weigh conflicting accounts and put them into a smooth, clean narrative.

The next selection is autobiography. No research was involved in the writing. The author had only to look objectively at her own memories. Margaret Bourke-White is a famous Life photographer who as a war correspondent during World War II had lived through a ship torpedoing and many combat missions. Suddenly, at the height of her career, she was stricken by a mysterious illness, which she met with another kind of heroism.

My Mysterious Malady

MARGARET BOURKE-WHITE

My mysterious malady began so quietly I could hardly believe there was anything wrong. Nothing to see or feel except a slight dull ache in my left leg, which I noticed when I walked upstairs. This was not strong enough to dignify by the name of pain. Just strong enough to make me aware that my left leg was not properly sharing the duty of carrying around one photographer on shank's mare. I had the uneasy feeling that this was different from any ache I had ever had. Little did I dream this was the stealthy beginning of a lifetime siege during which I would have to add a new word to my vocabulary — "incurable."

For a half a year there were no further developments except that the dull ache moved about in a will-o'-the-wisp fashion to other parts of my leg and even to my arm. But it confined its wanderings to my left side. Then something small but very peculiar crept into my life. I discovered that after sitting for perhaps an hour, as at lunch, on rising from the table my first three steps were grotesque staggers. On the fourth step, my ability to walk returned. I first noticed these difficulties at the luncheon table in the Tokyo Press Club. I had already been in and out of Korea several times.

I was highly embarrassed by these staggers, and thought up little concealing devices such as dropping my gloves and retrieving them; with the smallest delaying action, I could walk. I consulted with doctors I ran across, but my wisp of a symptom meant as little to them as it did to me.

When it refused to disappear after I got back to the States, I started the weary, time-consuming round of specialists. I learned the long list of diseases I did not have. I did not have cancer, heart trouble, infantile paralysis, or arthritis. I was amazed that I could have contracted anything when I thought of the near misses of two wars. I had always been arrogantly proud of my health and durability. Strong men might fall by the wayside, but I was "Maggie the Indestructible."

A discerning friend suggested that I talk to Dr. Howard Rusk. Through our common interest in Korea, I already knew Dr. Rusk, a greathearted man who had done much with rehabilitation of polio victims, but it was a shock to think of myself in the same breath with a polio victim, with all the crippling that term implied. (Later I was to find that severe crippling was a frequent conclusion to the malady I had.)

Dr. Rusk took me to the staff neurologist,[1] Dr. Morton Marks, to whom my malady was no mystery.

"I am not going to give it a name," he said, "because someday you may see a very advanced case and that might discourage you. You can do a great deal to control your disease by therapeutic physical exercises. From now on, exercise is more important to you than rest. If you skip one day, you'll fall back two. If you skip three days, you'll lose six."

He called in the head physical therapist, Mr. Jack Hofkosh, to draw up a program of exercises "to help her save what she's got."

---

[1] *neurologist* (noo·rol'ə·jist): a doctor who deals with the nervous system and its disorders.

Save what I've got! He must be thinking of ten other girls, I said to myself.

Mr. Hofkosh was a short, powerful man, and his unusually large head was completely bald. Before long he became a kind of archangel to me, and during all the years of fighting against the creeping rigidity which was afflicting me so strangely, I came to revere each feather of his invisible wings, but on that day of our first meeting I treated him as crossly as though I were a petulant child.

"Crumpling pages of newspaper into a ball, using all four fingers and the thumb in proper juxtaposition, would be excellent to strengthen the fingers of that left hand," he said. "And for the wrist, nothing could be better than mixing up a cake batter. Soon you will be able to mix a cake with your left hand."

"I don't make cake," I snapped.

He carried the idea further by explaining the benefit to the wrists which would come if I would twist and squeeze out wet clothes under the warm tap.

"I don't wash my own clothes," I scolded him foolishly.

And then a few weeks later something happened that frightened me out of all that nonsense. I found I was losing my ability to write on the typewriter, even my own electric typewriter with its featherlight touch. My fingers were becoming far too stiff to reach the keys properly. The letter "C," for instance, seemed to have removed itself by miles from any position that I could reach. I was working on this book.[2] Dictating is no good to me. When it comes to writing, my flow of thoughts always comes best on the typewriter. Maybe I won't even be able to finish my book, I thought with alarm. Maybe I should be less haughty about the benefits to be gained from squeezing wet clothes. Maybe I had better get back to that little man with his high-polished dome and master whatever exercises he wants to teach me.

From then on everything became an exercise. A *Life* assignment to the Colorado Dust Bowl, which included airplane photographs, meant that instead of setting the clock for 4:00 A.M. so as to meet the pilot on the airstrip just before sunrise, I set the alarm for 3:30 A.M. so that I would have time to crumple newspapers. When

---

[2] *this book:* her autobiography, *Portrait of Myself*, of which this selection is an excerpt.

MY MYSTERIOUS MALADY

I left the tourist room or the motel where I had spent the night, the floor would be nearly hidden in the rising piles of crumpled newspapers squeezed into popcorn-ball size. If I traveled by myself on an airplane, train, or bus, when I disembarked, the space under the seat overflowed with popcorn balls. Any well-appointed hotel bathroom was a clear invitation from the management to wring out all the beautiful turkish towels under the warm water tap. The bath mat was last. When my camera cases were all packed and my hastily assembled suitcases were bulging, I called for the bellhop, squeezed out the mat, plopped it into the bathub, and out I went.

At home, a session of watching television was an opportunity to practice precision movements with the left hand. I used colored crayons to fill in patterns in children's outline drawings.

Those child's colored crayons certainly earned their way. Soon a fair amount of control came back to the fingers of my left hand. No longer was the letter "C" unreachable. I took special pride in that left hand. I felt as though I had made it myself, and I was able to go on writing. The feeling of continuity this gave me helped to sustain me during the difficult years that lay just ahead.

Of greatest help to my strength of spirit was the fact that I could continue to work to some extent. Work to me is a sacred thing, and while writing the book was important to me, photography is my profession. My great dread in connection with my illness was that people would try to spare me too much. My editors were wonderfully understanding of this. When I told them I was under doctor's orders to walk four miles a day, they shuddered at the thought but gave me assignments where I could walk, run, climb, fly.

Not knowing the name of my ailment, I dramatized it, told myself I had something very rare. My doctors need not have been so cautious about naming it. When I did learn that I had Parkinson's disease, the name could not frighten me because I did not know what in the world it was. Then, slowly, an old memory came back: of a dinner meeting of photographers perhaps eight or ten years earlier. Captain Steichen [3] spoke with tears on his cheeks of the illness of the "dean of photographers," the great Edward Weston, who had Parkinson's disease. I can still hear the break in Steichen's voice. "A

---

[3] *Captain Steichen:* Edward Steichen, a great photographer, whose sister was married to Carl Sandburg.

terrible disease . . . you can't work because you can't hold things . . . you grow stiffer and stiffer each year until you are a walking prison . . . no known cure. . . ."

Was this a photographer's occupational disease? Then I learned that Eugene O'Neill had it. So, it was an author's malady! Soon I was to discover there were many illustrious members of the club in many fields: Justice Burton, who had to resign from the Supreme Court because of the progression of his case; Alexander Ruthven, retired president of the University of Michigan. Sister Kenny was a severe sufferer, and I think it highly likely that her experience with her own illness, and the benefits physical therapy had brought her, had a lot to do with her approach to polio. The thing that interested me most was not the fame and eminence of some Parkinsonians, but that they are "struck down," in many cases, when they are at a peak in their productive life — people who are creative and active, people who do not baby themselves, the never-had-a-sick-day-in-my-life type.

But the discovery that astonished me most was to learn that, far from being a rare malady, it could hardly be less exclusive. We don't know how many people have it, but they are in the hundreds of thousands. Its existence has been known for more than four thousand years (Parkinsonism is the shaking palsy of the Bible), and it has been named and documented for more than a century.

The disease's odd name comes from Dr. James Parkinson, a paleontologist [4] as well as a practicing physician. In 1817, he published his observations of six victims of the disease, noting each weird and ugly symptom. This chronicle has become a medical classic, and yet in the one hundred and twenty-eight years from Dr. Parkinson's death to the onset of my own siege, little more had been learned.

Parkinsonism does not affect the thinking part of the brain but the brain's motor centers, which coordinate voluntary movements. It is Hydra-headed. Push it down in one spot and it rears up in another. It is easy to list its two main symptoms: rigidity and tremor. But to know what Parkinsonism is you must know the surprise of finding yourself standing in a sloping position as though you were trying to impersonate the leaning tower of Pisa. You must know the bewilderment of finding yourself a prisoner in your own clothes closet, unable to back out of it. You must experience the awkward-

---
[4] *paleontologist* (pā'lē·on·tol'ə·jist) : one who studies ancient forms of life.

ness of trying to turn around in your own kitchen — eleven cautious little steps when one swift pivot used to do the job. You must live with the near panic which you face when you have to walk into a roomful of people, and the uneasiness of the questions you ask yourself: Do I just imagine that I can't seem to turn over in bed any more? How will I get my feet moving when they want to stay glued to the floor? How will I disengage myself from a group of people and step away if they're all around me? How will I keep from knocking them down? What can I do with my hands when I'm only standing still? How will I get my meat cut up? What a waste of good steak! You feel so clumsy if you cut it yourself and so conspicuous if you have someone do it for you. How did I look this time? Did I get through it all right? Did people notice anything wrong?

Did people notice anything wrong? Of course they did. I don't know why with Parkinsonism there is this overwhelming compulsion toward secrecy. A wise woman doctor who had known me for many years said to me, "Your friends won't stop loving you if they learn you are ill. Perhaps it will have the opposite effect and they will understand and love you more. I think you are adding greatly to your difficulties in your efforts for concealment."

I knew this was good advice, and I wish I had been able to take it. But that was for others. I was the exception. Nobody must know I was anything but a paragon of health.

If I could give only one message after sifting down this experience, it would be to urge others to banish the secrecy. I see now how futile are the obsessive efforts to keep the illness hidden. In most cases it isn't secret anyway, and it is the most harmful possible course to follow, because it robs you of the release of talking it over. I found that many of my friends knew all about it — in some cases they knew more than I. They were distressed most by not knowing how to help me. I was surrounded by a wall of loving silence which no one dared to break through.

Parkinsonism is a strange malady. It works its way into all paths of life, into all that is graceful and human and outgoing in our lives, and poisons it all.

I often thought with thankfulness that if I had to be saddled with some kind of ailment, I was fortunate that it was something where my own efforts could help. I was amazed to see what the human body will do for you if you insist. Having to plug away at some exercise and finding I could make small advances gave me the feeling I was still captain of my ship — an attitude which is very important to me.

I never would have believed there could be such towering difficulties in relearning to walk — something we have all done so easily from childhood. I had not realized that I was trying to compress into a few years something it took the human race millions of years to learn.

"Why is it so difficult?" I asked the doctor.

He gave me an interesting answer. "It is the newest skill, along with speech, that man acquired in the evolutionary process. It is also one of the most complex."

To keep your balance, your arms must swing. Mine had grown so rigid they refused to do so naturally. I had to *learn* to pick up my feet instead of shuffling along like an ill-shod ice skater, as Parkinson victims tend to do. I had to try to keep a straight back. Otherwise that chest, which seemed to be permanently bound in bands of steel, would contract even more and make me grotesquely round-shouldered, further destroying my precarious balance. I had to learn to toe out and step with my feet somewhat apart. This Mr. Hofkosh insisted on above everything else.

"You will need that broad base for balance; otherwise you will stumble and fall."

Mr. Hofkosh said, "Walk four miles every day. Walk *at least* four. Walk all day if you can. And remember all these things, and follow an imaginary line down the road, making sure you are putting your feet on opposite sides of it."

And so I walked. Every day, in snow or rain or sun, I walked and walked, and point by point I tried to embed all the separate items deep in my mind. I said to myself, see that little bush ahead? I am going to swing my left arm until we reach it. I am going to think only about straightening my back until we come to the first mailbox. I am going to concentrate on heel-toe, heel-toe till we get around the next bend in the road. I am going to step wide over that imaginary line and acquire the Hofkoshian pace.

Only intellectually could I recall that walking can be a pleasure. In the all-absorbing effort of trying to perform these interlacing movements, all rhythm and joy of motion were blotted out. But very occasionally, at the end of one well-walked mile, and at a certain spot on a gently sloping wooded road, where there were lichen-covered rocks, cool ferns, and the strong base of a tall tree, the awkwardness faded away and I seemed to glide into that interlocking mesh in which most people walk naturally, and for a short time — as though it had been out on loan — the consciousness of joy in movement was restored to me. During this brief respite walking again became a happy thing.

Strangely, as I look back, this was not an unhappy period. The discovery that I could do so much by my own will and concentration was part of a deepened awareness that was making its own new pattern, and the fact that I could continue to work on my book was a great assurance to me and helped give me a sense of purpose in my life.

I managed to avoid the great crashing falls which are the curse of most Parkinsonians (although I had some close calls), and I am sure that the steadiness I acquired in all my walking was responsible. The terrifying falls come about when a Parkinsonian, unbalanced as he is and unable to walk with control, finds himself running forward, taking shorter and shorter steps, caught in an acceleration pattern which he cannot escape. He is thrown helplessly forward, and often the unhappy sufferer completely lacks the muscle control to pick himself up again. He may lie where he has fallen until someone finds him.

Nor was I afflicted with the terrible tremor which plagues so many, and I believe my determination not to have it helped me fend it off. I was resolved not to let even the feeling of it get into my mind, and when I noticed even the slightest trembling, I stopped whatever I was doing and took exercises immediately to loosen the fingers and the shoulders. I knew I could not banish it forever, because I realized only too well I was on an escalator which was moving down while I was trying to run up.

Balance is a mysterious and highly personal thing. If my cat unexpectedly brushed the back of my legs with his feathery tail, it was enough to send me soaring off to the left side or to the right, whichever way my internal tower of Pisa was leaning that day. Because of the benefits of the therapy, I could usually recover my balance. Even in an emergency, such as tripping badly, where I had to save myself quickly, I found if I could just raise one arm — throw it over my head as casually as though calling "Hi" to a passerby — I could stop that particular fall. Immediately I would turn my attention to a few balancing exercises to reinforce myself against the next threat of falling. As I walked into a room, I surveyed it much as a pilot in a single-engine plane surveys the ground beneath to spot a little landing strip just in case of emergency. I picked something that would break my fall, in case I did fall.

Through all this I was writing on water, and well I knew it. I could not shout down the fact that Parkinsonism is a progressive disease. In spite of everything Mr. Hofkosh taught me, and everything I tried to do for myself, time moved on and Parkinsonism took its toll. When the relentless, unearthly pull which erases all control of balance — "forward compulsion" — started in earnest, this was something that could not be dismissed by a wave of the hand. This was the face of the enemy.

In the early spring of 1958 I went South to give a lecture in Asheville, North Carolina, and decided to go to the nearby beautiful Pisgah National Forest to write and walk. I had expected to find the whole mountaintop riotous with rhododendrons, but I was too early for this. The charming inn was lost in the rain clouds, and I was the only guest. Everybody else knew better than to come at this time of the year. The weather never changed. It was uniformly drizzly, soggy, damp, and dark. One thing kept me there.

There was a road winding its tortuous way through the mountain peaks. Down the middle of that road ran a white line stretching from me to infinity. The empty road was an elongated, fog-bound gymnasium in which to practice the Hofkosh pace. Every day I did my four miles or more, straddling that white line. It was hard to believe there were great precipices plunging downward just beyond the shoulders of the road, or that one of America's proudest views, a sweeping panorama of the Great Smokies, lay beyond, blotted from sight by the impenetrable mist. At any time I wished, I could stop to bend over to touch my toes or do deep knee bends, in total privacy. At the end of my morning stint a great fire would be blazing away in my cozy room at the inn. After lunch I would add a few pages to my book and go outside again to follow the white line.

"Keep your knees up," I could all but hear Mr. Hofkosh saying. This was so arduous that to keep myself at it, I chanted a syllable at a time: Hof-kosh, Hof-kosh, with each rising knee.

If anyone had asked me, and frequently I asked myself, why I did all this, I would have been hard put to find an answer. I suppose in part it was a carry-over from my professional work, where the highest praise my editors could give me was "Maggie won't take no for an answer."

Well-meaning people frequently advise that you must learn to accept your illness. My conviction was just the opposite. Try to take a realistic approach, yes. But accept an illness, never. Laying down my weapons in the middle of the fight was unthinkable. And there was, too, another reason, which went much deeper. Somehow I had the unshakable faith that if I could just manage to hang on and keep myself in good shape, somewhere a door would open.

And that door did indeed open.

Gift of Science

The door was opened by a very young and very gifted surgeon who quite by chance discovered the key to a cure for Parkinsonism. Dr. Irving S. Cooper was performing a brain operation on a patient who had Parkinsonism. He accidentally tore a small artery which nourished the rebellious nerves whose malfunctioning controlled Parkinsonism. After the operation, to his astonishment, the patient's terrible tremor and rigidity dramatically ceased. He had an important clue, and fortunately he had the imagination to build on what he had found, and the skill and inventiveness to use it.

That he looked a little like a Greek god, with the evenly sculptured waves in his blond hair and his impressive height, made him no less of a surgeon. He was still under thirty in 1952 when he began experimenting with a radically, magically new operating procedure. Like all great things, his procedure was simple. He drilled a hole in the skull the size of a dime. Checking everything on X-rays as he worked, he probed for precisely that spot which was responsible for the patient's difficulties. The more conservative members of the medical world were skeptical. Gaining recognition was an uphill road for him.

Getting to him was an uphill climb, also, for many of his patients, as I discovered when I tried to get some precise information about him and about the operation. I found it difficult to get a dispassionate or objective answer. Also, I was bucking the old school of thought about Parkinson's: You might as well wait for surgery until you are old, because then the disease will be so advanced anything will be an improvement. That, to me, was almost immoral. My idea was just the opposite. Don't wait passively on the sidelines for a shambling old age. Go into it as young as possible. Bring all the assets you have, and play to win!

When I received my prized appointment for the operation, I discovered there was an eight-week waiting list, with some candidates coming from the Netherlands and other parts of Europe, but I did not mind the wait. I went right back to my exercises and redoubled my efforts. I was determined to bring to the operation the strongest body I could make.

This was the first operation of my life. That is, the first in which I was the patient. Of course, I had photographed operations during the war, but being the patient is quite different from being the photographer.

It had never occurred to me that I would not go to my own operation under my own steam, and I was rather startled on that great morning to find I was flat on my back, flat on something with wheels, and could see only the ceiling which was rushing over me, or so it seemed, at breakneck speed. Here, as the long, narrow, cream-colored corridor ceiling swept on relentlessly, I had a childish urge to stretch out my arms and catch something that would slow me down so I could have a minute to breathe and think. And then I said to myself, There is nothing more to think about. I've thought it through and made the decision. This is the most important step toward my goal. I'm in it now. This is it.

The ceilings had stopped in their race. As I lay there quietly waiting, the X-ray technician came and stood at my side. He was interested in my travels, and asked, as so many people do, "To what distant part of the globe are you going next?"

I was thinking of another "globe," much smaller, and of the very personal and remarkable journey that was about to be conducted inside it. This would be the shortest journey of my life — it could be measured in inches; its importance was without measure. I realized this was an assignment, the greatest in my life, and to accomplish it successfully I must be willing to travel anywhere and must try to learn everything. As long as I thought of it in the context of my work, it held no fears for me.

There would be no pain; only an occasional feeling of pressure. I was very glad that as part of the technique I would be kept conscious during the operation. This was to help the doctors find the precise trouble spot. The doctors kept questioning me and asked me repeatedly to do special things.

"Maggie, raise your arm. Clench your fist. Stretch out your fingers."

Another doctor said, "Peggy, squeeze my hand as hard as you can. Squeeze my hand *tight*."

I never dreamed so much hand holding could go on during an operation.

It was reassuring that the doctors had learned my various nicknames, and a comfort as the operation progressed to hear them speaking to me. At one point, Dr. Cooper said, "Maggie, can you hear me?" When I said yes, he said, "We'll be right here, but we're taking a few minutes out to take pictures." And I thought, *take pictures!* What am I doing in here? I should be out there helping them!

I do not know what phase the operation had reached when I was conscious of a remarkable feeling. I *knew* the doctors were doing precisely the right thing. I could tell by the kind of inner harmony and almost ecstasy I felt. In my mind I was saying, "Keep at it; keep at it. Go right at it. Keep on digging. Get out all the Parkinsonism. Get it all out!"

My instinct must have been right, because within a very short time Dr. Cooper was saying, "Maggie, everything is fine. It turned out beautifully."

It was about this time that I wanted terribly to take a deep breath. I remember no point in my life when I had felt the need for such a deep breath and felt it so positively. I was floating in a kind of half dreamworld. I was so lightly suspended there, I hesitated to move in the tiniest degree, and in the meantime the breath seemed to hover close like a wind-filled sail, like a bird's wing. Now I knew it was meant for me. I accepted the gift of breath and inhaled deeply, much, I suppose, as a baby does who needs just such a breath to be launched into the outside world.

The next few weeks were a continuous Christmas. Every second or third day brought its own magic gift. First came that long-awaited arm swing. My left arm swung and swung and swung from the socket as though it was about to take off on its own, like an animated baseball bat. I would have found its new independence alarming had I not been sure I could teach it that it belonged to me. Next, my back began to straighten up bit by bit as the chest began to free itself from the iron-stiff muscle bands that had been forcing me to stoop for so long. Then came a morning when I was given, as usual, a fresh hospital gown to put on, and I discovered that without even thinking I had tied the little laces at the back of my neck. A friend came to pick me up at the hospital and parked her station wagon near the entrance. Before I realized what I was doing, I found myself sitting in the front seat, surrounded by the glass and metal of the car. I had jumped in myself. In the old days it used to take a couple of strong-armed friends, no doubt wishing fervently for a derrick.

The most blesssed gift of all was a modest, inconspicuous one which arrived just two days after the operation. I was talking with someone and my hands were under a light blanket in my lap. The left hand began thrashing about as though it were trying to scrabble upward to the light. What on earth is going on here? I thought. I threw off the blanket and realized I was making a gesture as I talked, *with my left hand!* A gesture! A gesture is not something you will yourself to make. It comes from the heart. To me, it was a bridge from myself to that warm living world I had wanted so deeply to reenter. Now the way was open.

Not all the gifts were pleasant ones. Some were unwanted, puzzling, and had to be disciplined away. First, there was the invisible magnet which seemed to be dragging my hands and wrists down to earth. My foot had somehow picked up the iron lid of a manhole which could not be shaken loose. A floating chunk of fog the size of a small suitcase seemed to be blocking my arms in any movement I wanted to make. My hands were out of focus somehow, so that if I reached for the bed rail, I missed and fell back in bed, and I could feel my fingers getting sucked into the field of the invisible magnet with its powerful downward pull. I remember lying there in my criblike hospital bed, trying to fight off my grief and fright.

My long training in physical therapy saved me from giving in to despair and helped me to approach the problem. I tried to analyze the errors. I was undershooting the mark by two inches. I practiced raising my arm — trying to reach the bed rail, a towel rack, any handy target — making allowance for the out-of-focus two inches, and each time I succeeded, I tried to get the feeling of the reach into my memory. As always, the accomplishment of something on your own is a source of confidence and strength. And so it was now, when correcting the faulty arm reach.

Much later, when the dreamlike state of the operation was dispelled and I was trying to recapture whatever I could of evanescent memories of the operation itself, I realized that they always appeared against the same shadowy background: the edge of a wood with lichen-covered rocks and dark ferns, and the strong base of a tall tree which grew out of an island in the middle of the road. Against this all the images floated. Why, I wondered, did I see everything against this particular background? Then I remembered the little roadside things I had noticed in the weary months of the long walks. And I recalled the reward I sometimes received if I managed to struggle through that first hardest mile with any small semblance of coordination — that fleeting interlude with its soft reminder that walking is not always an obstacle race but can be a bright and light-footed thing. I feel sure it was no accident that during the peak of the operation, when I was being set free, my release came against this background.

After a few weeks of therapy, Dr. Cooper sent me to Dr. Howard Rusk's Rehabilitation Institute, my old training ground, to continue my physical therapy. My return to the Institute was like a welcoming parade up Broadway. As I walked along the corridor, swift and sure, with easy balance, heel-toe, heel-toe, and those arms swinging like a metronome, people began to run after me: the therapists, the doctors, patients who knew me, the elevator boys. They could hardly believe I was the same person. A doctor walking in back of me said, "How does it feel now?"

"Delicious," I said. "As though I had strawberry ice cream on the top of my head, melting and pouring down!"

Outside my window was a field of rubble left after the demolition of a building. That's my kind of terrain, I said to myself. Just the kind of shifting ground a photographer must be able to keep balance on with ease. Then other skills the photographer requires came crowding back into my mind. I began to practice loading cameras and working to improve the small precision movements. Just being able to walk down a corridor wasn't enough.

So next I worked on "ambulation." I practiced running and stopping short, and making quick turns on shouted commands. Then I went outside with a therapist and walked through crowds in the street to be sure my new-gained balance was firm enough to stand up against the jostling of other people. It was. Then I ran up the rubble pile in a strong wind.

This had been a long road from the place where I lost my balance from the touch of my cat's tail. I had learned to walk again; I had learned to run again. What was going on inside me during the recuperation was more than a healing. It is hard to describe. It was a kind of drawing together of loose strands in my own life, and feeling closer to the lives of others, probing perhaps a little deeper than before, noticing more, caring more.

In this experience of mine, there was one continuing marvel: the precision timing running through it all. The ailment which was draining all the good out of my life is one of the world's oldest diseases. Against the somber background of this venerable malady, with its span of four millenniums or more, by great good fortune, I am born in the right century, in the right decade, and even in the right group of months, to profit from the swift-running advance of modern medical science. My greatest need comes at that pinpoint in time when I can reap the benefits of science and be made whole. By some special graciousness of fate I am deposited — as all good photographers like to be — in the right place at the right time.

Postscript

This book has been my constant companion for the last ten years, through sickness, surgery, and health. I did not go so far as to carry it to the operating table, but it was a comfort to have it under the same roof. It gave me a sense of continuity in my life to know the manuscript was there in its unfinished roughness, and as soon as I was able, I would be back to it — adding a few words a day, a few sentences a week, more as I grew stronger.

"What happens next?" is a natural question. A Parkinsonian would add another: "Did you go back for a second operation?" The answer is yes. The first operation treated only my left side. Two years later, I went back to have the untreated side taken care of. The second operation was a triumph of surgery. It did all the right things, and it has held well.

Keeping up my daily exercises faithfully has helped greatly. The neighborhood children have also helped greatly by teaching me games — everything from jacks to badminton. Learning a game mastered so easily in childhood was for me the very symbol of returning health.

Vacationtime I spend at Martha's Vineyard at a lovely summer school in a pine grove on a bluff overlooking the Sound. The School of Creative Arts was organized by a dancer, Kathleen Hinni, who has great gifts for inspiring creativity in children. One of the arts is dance, and its special value for me is that the basic exercises for body control in dancing are similar to those of physical therapy — and much more fun. And when I find myself charging down the studio with several dozen small girls, I have to coordinate and balance — or else!

A few months after the second operation, I went back to the hospital for a checkup. In the midst of the routine tests for coordination, I applied a test of my own that was not entirely routine. I whipped my jumping rope out of my handbag and gave a little demonstration. Through the sphere of the moving rope, I could hear the surprised exclamations of my delighted doctors. This gave me special pleasure, as there was a time, not so far back, when mastery of a jumping rope seemed more impossible of attainment than a trip to the moon.

Not long ago, I did have moon plans. When the possibilities of space travel were more problematic than today, I asked for and received the *Life* assignment to the moon, as soon as we could get transportation. My dearest hope was that the science of space travel would advance enough in our lifetimes to enable me to carry out the assignment. Perhaps knowing how to skip rope does not qualify me for the moon, but short of that . . . at the present gallop of science . . . who knows?

The following selection is only a sketch — a short, vivid impression instead of a full-length portrait. Its subject is a great composer. Deems Taylor was himself a composer and music critic.

This kind of writing is sometimes called "popular biography" because it speaks to a very wide audience of readers. The author assumes very little scientific or historical background on the part of the reader, and tries to make his style as lively and amusing as possible.

The Monster

DEEMS TAYLOR

He was an undersized little man, with a head too big for his body — a sickly little man. His nerves were bad. He had skin trouble. It was agony for him to wear anything next to his skin coarser than silk. And he had delusions of grandeur.

He was a monster of conceit. Never for one minute did he look at the world or at people, except in relation to himself. He was not only the most important person in the world, to himself; in his own eyes he was the only person who existed. He believed himself to be one of the greatest dramatists in the world, one of the greatest thinkers, and one of the greatest composers. To hear him talk, he was Shakespeare, and Beethoven, and Plato, rolled into one. And you would have no difficulty in hearing him talk. He was one of the most exhaustive conversationalists that ever lived. An evening with him was an evening spent in listening to a monologue. Sometimes he was brilliant; sometimes he was maddeningly tiresome. But whether he was being brilliant or dull, he had one sole topic of conversation: himself. What *he* thought and what *he* did.

He had a mania for being in the right. The slightest hint of disagreement, from anyone, on the most trivial point, was enough to set him off on a harangue that might last for hours, in which he proved himself right in so many ways that in the end his hearer, stunned and deafened, would agree with him, for the sake of peace.

It never occurred to him that he and his doings were not of the most intense and fascinating interest to anyone with whom he came in contact. He had theories about almost any subject under the sun, including vegetarianism, the drama, politics, and music; and in support of these theories he wrote pamphlets, letters, books . . . thousands upon thousands of words, hundreds and hundreds of pages. He not only wrote these things, and published them — usually at somebody else's expense — but he would sit and read them aloud, for hours, to his friends and his family.

He wrote operas; and no sooner did he have the synopsis of a story, or poem, but he would invite — or rather summon — a crowd of his friends to his house and read it aloud to them. Not for criticism. For applause. When the complete poem was written, the friends had to come again, and hear *that* read aloud. Then he would publish the poem, sometimes years before the music that went with it was written. He played the piano like a composer, in the worst sense of what that implies, and he would sit down at the piano before parties that included some of the finest pianists of his time, and play for them by the hour — his own music, needless to say. He had a composer's voice. And he would invite eminent vocalists to his house, and sing them his operas, taking all the parts.

He had the emotional stability of a six-year-old child. When he felt out of sorts, he would rave and stamp, or sink into suicidal gloom and talk darkly of going to the East to end his days as a Buddhist monk. Ten minutes later, when something pleased him, he would rush out of doors and run around the garden, or jump up and down on the sofa, or stand on his head. He could be grief-stricken over the death of a pet dog, and he could be callous and heartless to a degree that would have made a Roman emperor shudder.

He was almost innocent of any sense of responsibility. Not only did he seem incapable of supporting himself, but it never occurred to him that he was under any obligation to do so. He was convinced that the world owed him a living. In support of this belief, he borrowed money from everybody who was good for a loan — men, women, friends, or strangers. He wrote begging letters by the score, sometimes groveling without shame, at others loftily offering his intended benefactor the privilege of contributing to his support, and being mortally offended if the recipient declined the honor. I have found no record of his ever paying or repaying money to anyone who did not have a legal claim upon it.

What money he could lay his hands on he spent like an Indian rajah. The mere prospect of a performance of one of his operas was enough to set him to running up bills amounting to ten times the amount of his prospective royalties. On an income that would reduce a more scrupulous man to doing his own laundry, he would keep two servants. Without enough money in his pocket to pay his rent, he would have the walls and ceiling of his study lined with pink silk. No one will ever know — certainly he never knew — how much money he owed. We do know that his greatest benefactor gave him six thousand dollars to pay the most pressing of his debts in one city, and a year later had to give him sixteen thousand more to enable him to live in another city without being thrown into jail for debt. . . .

He was completely selfish in his personal relationships. His liking for his friends was measured solely by the completeness of their devotion to him, or by their usefulness to him, whether financial or artistic. The minute they failed him — even by so much as refusing a dinner invitation — or began to lessen in usefulness, he cast them off without a second thought. At the end of his life he had exactly one friend left whom he had known even in middle age.

He had a genius for making enemies. He would insult a man who disagreed with him about the weather. He would pull endless wires in order to meet some man who admired his work and was able and anxious to be of use to him — and would proceed to make a mortal enemy of him with some idiotic and wholly uncalled-for exhibition of arrogance and bad manners. A character in one of his operas was a caricature of one of the most powerful music critics of his day. Not content with burlesquing him, he invited the critic to his house and read him the libretto aloud in front of his friends.

The name of this monster was Richard Wagner. Everything that I have said about him you can find on record — in newspapers, in police reports, in the testimony of people who knew him, in his own letters, between the lines of his autobiography. And the curious thing about this record is that it doesn't matter in the least.

Because this undersized, sickly, disagreeable, fascinating little man was right all the time. The joke was on us. He *was* one of the world's great dramatists; he *was* a great thinker; he *was* one of the most stupendous musical geniuses that, up to now, the world has ever seen. The world did owe him a living. People couldn't know those things at the time, I suppose; and yet to us, who know his music, it does seem as though they should have known. What if he did talk about himself all the time? If he had talked about himself for twenty-four hours every day for the span of his life, he would not have uttered half the number of words that other men have spoken and written about him since his death.

When you consider what he wrote — thirteen operas and music dramas, eleven of them still holding the stage, eight of them unquestionably worth ranking among the world's great musico-dramatic masterpieces — when you listen to what he wrote, the debts and heartaches that people had to endure from him don't seem much of a price. Eduard Hanslick, the critic whom he caricatured in *Die Meistersinger* [1] and who hated him ever after, now lives only because he was caricatured in *Die Meistersinger*. The women whose hearts he broke are long since dead; and the man who could never love anyone but himself has made them deathless atonement, I think, with *Tristan und Isolde*. Think of the luxury with which, for a time, at least, fate rewarded Napoleon, the man who ruined France and looted Europe; and then perhaps you will agree that a few thousand dollars' worth of debts were not too heavy a price to pay for the *Ring*.[2]

What if he was faithless to his friends and to his wives? He had one mistress to whom he was faithful to the day of his death: Music. Not for a single moment did he ever compromise with what he believed, with what he dreamed. There is not a line of his music that could have been conceived by a little mind. Even when he is dull, or downright bad, he is dull in the grand manner. There is greatness about his worst mistakes. Listening to his music, one does not forgive him for what he may or may not have been. It is not a matter of forgiveness. It is a matter of being dumb with wonder that his poor brain and body didn't burst under the torment of the demon of creative energy that lived inside him, struggling, clawing, scratching to be released; tearing, shrieking at him to write the music that was in him. The miracle is that what he did in the little space of seventy years could have been done at all, even by a great genius. Is it any wonder that he had no time to be a man?

---

[1] *Die Meistersinger* (dē mīs′tər-sing′ər): Wagner's only comic opera.
[2] *Ring*: *Ring of the Nibelung*, four related operas based on Germanic legends.

Moss Hart, who was to become one of America's most successful playwrights and directors, grew up in New York City in, as he once said, "an atmosphere of unrelieved poverty." He was stage-struck at an early age and at twelve wrote his first play. Later he worked as an office boy in a theater, had a brief "fling" as an actor, and directed amateur plays and resort shows. In 1930, when he was twenty-six, Hart wrote a comedy called Once in a Lifetime. The play showed such great promise that George S. Kaufman, one of the most popular playwrights of the day, agreed to collaborate with Hart on it. Once in a Lifetime became a hit. The morning after the opening night on Broadway, Hart, having stayed up late with his friends waiting for the reviews in the morning newspapers, hailed a taxi for his "first ride to Brooklyn above ground." What happened next is described in the following selection from Hart's autobiography. In it we see a young man's reaction to success, the kind of success every young man — especially one who has known poverty — supposedly dreams of. Unlike the other selections in this unit, this one covers only a few hours in its subject's life.

from Act One

MOSS HART

No one has ever seen the skyline of the city from Brooklyn Bridge as I saw it that morning with three hit notices under my arm. The face of the city is always invested with grandeur, but grandeur can be chilling. The overpowering symmetry of that skyline can crush the spirit and make the city seem forbidding and impenetrable, but today it seemed to emerge from cold anonymity and grant its acknowledgment and acceptance. There was no sunlight — it was a gray day and the buildings were half shrouded in mist — but it was a city that would know my name today, a city that had not turned me aside, and a city that I loved. Unexpectedly and without warning a great wave of feeling for this proud and beautiful city swept over me. We were off the bridge now and driving through the sprawling, ugly area of tenements that stretch interminably over the approaches to each of its boroughs. They are the first in the city to awake, and the long, unending rows of drab, identical houses were already stirring with life. Laundry was being strung out to dry along roof tops and fire escapes, men with lunch boxes were coming out of the houses, and children returning from the corner grocery with bottles of milk and loaves of bread were hurrying up the steps and into the doorways.

I stared through the taxi window at a pinch-faced ten-year-old hurrying down the steps on some morning errand before school, and I thought of myself hurrying down the street on so many gray mornings out of a doorway and a house much the same as this one. My mind jumped backward in time and then whirled forward, like a many-faceted prism — flashing our old neighborhood in front of me, the house, the steps, the candy store — and then shifted to the skyline I had just passed by, the opening last night, and the notices I still hugged tightly under my arm. It was possible in this wonderful city for that nameless little boy — for any of its millions — to have a decent chance to scale the walls and achieve what they wished. Wealth, rank, or an imposing name counted for nothing. The only credential the city asked was the boldness to dream. For those who did, it unlocked its gates and its treasures, not caring who they were or where they came from. I watched the boy disappear into a tailor shop, and a surge of shamefaced patriotism overwhelmed me. I might have been watching a victory parade on a flag-draped Fifth Avenue instead of the mean streets of a city slum. A feeling of patriotism, however, is not always limited to the feverish emotions called forth by war. It can sometimes be felt as profoundly and perhaps more truly at a moment such as this.

It had suddenly begun to rain very hard, and in a few minutes I could no longer see much of anything through the windows. All too quickly I made that swift turnabout from patriotism to enlightened self-interest. I closed my eyes and thought about how I would spend the money that would soon start to pour in. To my surprise, affluence did not seem nearly as easy to settle into as I had always imagined it would be. Try as I would, I could not think of how to begin or in what ways I wanted to spend the large sums that would now be mine to command. I could think of little ways to spend it — new suits, new shirts, new ties, new overcoats — but after that my mind went disappointingly blank. In some ways sudden riches are no easier to live with than poverty. Both demand artistry of a kind, if one or the other is not to leave the mark of a sour and lingering cynicism, and opulence in many ways is harder to manage than penury. It is, however, one of the pleasantest problems with which to drift off to sleep. It is a problem that apparently also induces the deepest and most refreshing kind of sleep. I cheated myself out of the major portion of that first taxi ride by sleeping soundly through the rest of it. The driver had to leave his seat and shake me awake to collect his fare.

I was wide awake again, thoroughly wide awake, and disappointed to find the shades still drawn and the family fast asleep, when I unlocked the door and stepped into the apartment. It was, of course, only a little after seven o'clock in the morning, but today was too memorable a day to waste on anything so commonplace as sleep. I was tempted to wake them up at once and show them the notices, but I went into the kitchen instead and fixed a pot of coffee. I wanted a little more time alone to think about something.

I stood in the doorway of the kitchen while I waited for the water to boil and gazed at the sleeping figure of my brother on the daybed in the dining room, and beyond it at the closed door of the one bedroom, where my parents slept. The frayed carpet on the floor was the carpet I had crawled over before I could walk. Each flower in the badly faded and worn design was sharply etched in my mind. Each piece of furniture in the cramped, dim room seemed mildewed with a thousand double-edged memories. The ghosts of a thousand leaden meals hovered over the dining-room table. The dust of countless black-hearted days clung to every crevice of the squalid, ugly furniture I had known since childhood. To walk out of it forever — not piecemeal, but completely — would give meaning to the wonder of what had happened to me, make success tangible, decisive.

The goal behind the struggle for success is not always one goal, but many — some real, some hidden; some impossible to achieve, even with success piled upon success. The goal differs with each of us in the mysterious and wonderful way each human being is different from any other, in the way each of us is the sum total of the unexpressed longings and desires that strew the seas of childhood and are glimpsed long afterward from a safe distance — a submerged iceberg, only the tip of which is seen.

Whatever dominant force in my nature shaped the blind demands that made it imperative to me to make the theater my goal, had taken possession of me early and I was still possessed by it. What fulfillment it held I would know only when I walked resolutely out of one world and into another. I poured myself a cup of coffee, and by the time I had finished it, my mind was made up.

It is always best if one is about to embark on a wild or reckless venture not to discuss it with anybody beforehand. Talk will rob the scheme of its fire and make what seemed mettlesome and daring merely foolhardy. It is easier on everyone concerned to present it as an accomplishd fact, turn a deaf ear to argument, and go ahead with it.

I awakened my brother by dumping the papers on the bed for him to read, and then called through the bedroom door to my mother and father to get up right away. I gave them barely enough time to read the notices, and then plunged. "We're moving into New York today — as soon as you have a cup of coffee — and we're not taking anything with us. We're walking out of here with just the clothes on our backs and nothing else. The coffee's on the stove, so hurry up and get dressed."

My mother stared at me and then spoke quietly, as if a raised voice at this moment might send me further out of my senses. "Where are we going?" she asked, logically enough.

"To a hotel," I said, "until we find an apartment and furnish it." There was a stunned silence, and before anyone else could speak, I spoke again, not impatiently, but as if what I was saying was inarguable. "There's nothing to pack; we just walk out of the door. No," I added in answer to my mother's mute startled look around the room, "not a thing. We leave it all here just as it stands, and close the door. We don't take anything — not even a toothbrush, a bathrobe, pajamas, or nightgown. We buy it all new in New York. We're walking out of here and starting fresh."

My mother walked to the window and pulled up the shades as though she might hear or understand what I was saying better with more light, and then turned helplessly toward my father.

He was the first to recover his breath and his wits. "We just paid two months' rent in advance," he said, as though that solid fact would help me recover my own.

"That gives us the right to let this stuff sit here and rot, or you can give it to the janitor," I replied. "We're walking out of here with just what clothes you put on, and tomorrow we'll get rid of those, too."

This second bit of information created an even more astonished silence than the first. "Don't you understand?" I heard myself shouting. "All I'm asking you to do *now* is — "

"I'm not walking out of here without the pictures," my mother said with great firmness.

It was my turn to be astonished. "What pictures?" I asked.

"*All* the pictures," she replied. "The baby pictures of you and Bernie and the pictures of my father and my sister, and Bernie's diploma and your letters, and all the other pictures and things I've got in the closet in that big box."

I threw my arms around her and kissed her. I had won. It was being accepted as a fact — incomprehensible but settled.

"One suitcase," I ordered. "Put it all into one suitcase, but one suitcase — that's all."

I looked at my brother, who had remained silent through all of this. He handed the papers back to me with a flourish and winked. "Don't you have to give *some* of the money to George Kaufman?" he asked.

"Half," I replied. "But my share will be over a thousand dollars a week."

"That'll buy a lot of toothbrushes," he said. "I'm going to get ready." And he climbed out of bed.

My mother and father stared at us as if to make sure we were not indulging in some elaborate joke for their benefit.

"It's true," I said soberly. "It's not a salary. I get a percentage of every dollar that comes into the box office. Don't you understand how it works?"

Obviously, they did not, and I realized somewhat belatedly that it had never occurred to either of them to translate good fortune in the theater into anything more than what my mother's friends defined as "making a good living." No wonder my proposal had sounded lunatic, but now, as the belief came to them that what I had just said might be the literal truth, they were suddenly seized with some of my own excitement. My mother's reaction was a curious one. She burst into a peal of laughter. She had a merry and ringing laugh, and it was contagious. My father and I joined in her laughter, though we would have been hard put to tell exactly what we were laughing at.

We were all ready to leave in less than an hour, despite the fact that there were more things of heaven and earth in that box in the closet than could be contained in one suitcase. I carried the box, my father and brother each carried a suitcase, and my mother, her victory complete, hugged a brown paper parcel of last-minute treasures that had turned up in an old tin box. We walked out of the door and waited in the lobby while my brother hurried out in the rain to try to get a taxi. The rain was pouring down in a great solid sheet now, and gusts of wind were slashing it against the building. I watched it burst savagely against the glass doors of the lobby and was seized by a sudden and irresistible impulse.

"I forgot something," I said shortly. "I'll be right back."

I unlocked the door of the empty apartment and closed and locked it again carefully behind me. I took one quick look around to keep the memory of that room forever verdant, and then walked to each window and threw it wide open. The rain whipped in through the windows like a broadside of artillery fire. I watched a large puddle form on the floor and spread darkly over the carpet. The rain streamed across the top and down the legs of the dining-room table and splashed over the sideboard and the china closet. It soaked the armchair and cascaded down the sofa. It peppered the wallpaper with large wet blotches, and the wind sent two lamps crashing to the floor. I kicked them out of my way and walked over to the daybed, which was still dry, and pulled it out into the middle of the room, where a fresh onset of wind and rain immediately drenched it. I looked around me with satisfaction, feeling neither guilty nor foolish. More reasonable gestures have seldom succeeded in giving me half the pleasure this meaningless one did. It was the hallmark, the final signature, of defiance and liberation. Short of arson, I could do no more.

I slammed the door behind me without looking back.

Although an autobiography is based on events that really happened, it is still an act of the imagination, like all literature. The fact that a man is writing about himself does not guarantee that what he says is true. He may omit aspects of his life that show him in a bad light; he may even invent to make his life more interesting. Most of all, he sees his own life in terms of some struggle or drama. He gives it a meaning and a shape. An autobiography is not important because of "what happened" but because of "how it is remembered."

As Piri Thomas looks back on his childhood, he remembers a warm family life surrounded by big city poverty. His family — like thousands of other Americans from Puerto Rico — had come to New York seeking a better life.

Puerto Rican Paradise

PIRI THOMAS

Poppa didn't talk to me the next day. Soon he didn't talk much to anyone. He lost his night job — I forget why, and probably it was worth forgetting — and went back on home relief. It was 1941, and the Great Hunger called Depression was still down on Harlem.

But there was still the good old WPA. If a man was poor enough, he could dig a ditch for the government. Now Poppa was poor enough again.

The weather turned cold one more time, and so did our apartment. In the summer the cooped-up apartments in Harlem seem to catch all the heat and improve on it. It's the same in the winter. The cold, plastered walls embrace that cold from outside and make it a part of the apartment, till you don't know whether it's better to freeze out in the snow or by the stove, where four jets, wide open, spout futile, blue-yellow flames. It's hard on the rats, too.

Snow was falling. "My *Cristo*," Momma said, "*qué frío*.[1] Doesn't

---

[1] *qué frío* (kā frē'ō): how cold.

that landlord have any *corazón*? [2] Why don't he give more heat?" I wondered how Pops was making out working a pick and shovel in that falling snow.

Momma picked up a hammer and began to beat the beat-up radiator that's copped a plea from so many beatings. Poor steam radiator, how could it give out heat when it was freezing itself? The hollow sounds Momma beat out of it brought echoes from other freezing people in the building. Everybody picked up the beat and it seemed a crazy, good idea. If everybody took turns beating on the radiators, everybody could keep warm from the exercise.

We drank hot cocoa and talked about summertime. Momma talked about Puerto Rico and how great it was, and how she'd like to go back one day, and how it was warm all the time there, and no matter how poor you were over there, you could always live on green bananas, *bacalao*,[3] and rice and beans. "*Dios mío*," she said, "I don't think I'll ever see my island again."

"Sure you will, Mommie," said Miriam, my kid sister. She was eleven. "Tell us, tell us all about Porto Rico."

"It's not Porto Rico, it's Puerto Rico," said Momma.

"Tell us, Moms," said nine-year-old James, "about Puerto Rico."

"Yeah, Mommie," said six-year-old José.

Even the baby, Paulie, smiled.

Moms copped that wet-eyed look and began to dream-talk about her *isla verde*,[4] Moses' land of milk and honey.

"When I was a little girl," she said, "I remember the getting up in the morning and getting the water from the river and getting the wood for the fire and the quiet of the greenlands and the golden color of the morning sky, the grass wet from the *lluvia*[5] . . . Ai, Dios, the *coquís*[6] and the *pajaritos*[7] making all the *música*. . . ."

"Mommie, were you poor?" asked Miriam.

"*Sí, muy pobre*, but very happy. I remember the hard work and the very little bit we had, but it was a good little bit. It counted very much. Sometimes when you have too much, the good gets lost

---

[2] *corazón* (kōr·ä·sōn) : heart.
[3] *bacalao* (bä·kä·lä′ō) : codfish.
[4] *isla verde*: green island.
[5] *lluvia* (lyū′vē·ä) : rain.
[6] *coquís* (kō·kēs′) : small chirping frogs.
[7] *pajaritos* (pä·hä·rē′tōs) : little birds.

within and you have to look very hard. But when you have a little, then the good does not have to be looked for so hard."

"Moms," I asked, "did everybody love each other — I mean, like if everybody was worth something, not like if some weren't important because they were poor — you know what I mean?"

"*Bueno hijo*,[8] you have people everywhere who, because they have more, don't remember those who have very little. But in Puerto Rico those around you share *la pobreza*[9] with you and they love you, because only poor people can understand poor people. I like *los Estados Unidos*, but it's sometimes a cold place to live — not because of the winter and the landlord not giving heat, but because of the snow in the hearts of the people."

"Moms, didn't our people have any money or land?" I leaned forward, hoping to hear that my ancestors were noble princes born in Spain.

"Your grandmother and grandfather had a lot of land, but they lost that."

"How come, Moms?"

"Well, in those days there was nothing of what you call *contratos*, and when you bought or sold something, it was on your word and a handshake, and that's the way your *abuelos*[10] bought their land and then lost it."

"Is that why we ain't got nuttin' now?" James asked pointedly.

"Oh, it — "

The door opened and put an end to the kitchen yak. It was Poppa coming home from work. He came into the kitchen and brought all the cold with him. Poor Poppa, he looked so lost in the clothes he had on. A jacket and coat, sweaters on top of sweaters, two pairs of long johns, two pairs of pants, two pairs of socks, and a woolen cap. And under all that he was cold. His eyes were cold; his ears were red with pain. He took off his gloves and his fingers were stiff with cold.

"*Cómo está?*"[11] said Momma. "I will make you coffee."

Poppa said nothing. His eyes were running hot frozen tears. He

---

[8] *Bueno hijo* (bwā′nō ē′hō): Well, my child (in this context).
[9] *la pobreza* (lä pō·brä′sä): poverty.
[10] *abuelos* (ä·bwā′lōs): grandparents.
[11] *Cómo está* (cō′mō ës·tä′): How are you?

worked his fingers and rubbed his ears, and the pain made him make faces. "Get me some snow, Piri," he said finally.

I ran to the window, opened it, and scraped all the snow on the sill into one big snowball and brought it to him. We all watched in frozen wonder as Poppa took that snow and rubbed it on his ears and hands.

"Gee, Pops, don't it hurt?" I asked.

"Sí, but it's good for it. It hurts a little first, but it's good for the frozen parts."

I wondered why.

"How was it today?" Momma asked.

"Cold. Ice cold."

Gee, I thought, I'm sorry for you, Pops. You gotta suffer like this.

"It was not always like this," my father said to the cold walls. "It's all the fault of the damn Depression."

"Don't say 'damn,'" Momma said.

"Lola, I say 'damn' because that's what it is — *damn.*"

And Momma kept quiet. She knew it was "damn."

My father kept talking to the walls. Some of the words came out loud, others stayed inside. I caught the inside ones — the damn WPA, the damn Depression, the damn home relief, the damn poorness, the damn cold, the damn crummy apartments, the damn look on his damn kids, living so damn damned and his not being able to do a damn thing about it.

And Momma looked at Poppa and at us and thought about her Puerto Rico and maybe being there where you didn't have to wear a lot of extra clothes and feel so full of damns, and how when she was a little girl all the green was wet from the *lluvias*.

And Poppa looked at Momma and us, thinking how did he get trapped and why did he love us so much that he dug in damn snow to give us a piece of chance? And why couldn't he make it from home, maybe, and keep running?

And Miriam, James, José, Paulie, and me just looking and thinking about snowballs and Puerto Rico and summertime in the street and whether we were gonna live like this forever and not know enough to be sorry for ourselves.

Paul Revere, a Boston silversmith who became a hero of the American Revolution. Portrait by John Singleton Copley.

Museum of Fine Arts, Boston.

BOOK THREE | PART 3

THE COMMON MAN AS HERO

Between the days in which he crawled as a baby on the dirt floor of a Kentucky cabin, and the time when he gave his final breath in Washington, he packed a rich life with work, thought, laughter, tears, hate, love.
                    A LINCOLN PREFACE

The stories in the first part of this book told of the exploits of heroes from the worlds of myth and legend. Sometimes these heroes were divine or semi-divine beings like Zeus, Apollo, or Theseus. If they were human, like Odysseus, they were presented as larger than life-size. Odysseus was aided by gods and goddesses in his struggles; he was stronger, cleverer, nobler than his competitors.

Such a hero in the older myths and epics was often a king or the son of a king. He went on quests into far-off kingdoms, where he conquered his enemies and slaughtered dragons and giants. Perhaps in time he married a princess. His royal nature set him apart from other men as he performed his heroic deeds. Because his victories liberated or protected his people, he often became a national symbol: Arthur and the knights of the Round Table, Beowulf, Roland, and El Cid.

The following section turns to another kind of hero: the common man. The modern world no longer places faith in the special glory of high birth and royal blood. The heroes in modern literature are often men and women whose backgrounds are much like our own. They are not marked from birth for a heroic destiny. Sandburg's biography of Lincoln presented a towering example of an ordinary man who became a great hero. His heroism, however, sprang from his own mental and moral qualities.

The writers in the following section examine heroism in a non-heroic age. They ask: what forms can heroism take? Does every man carry within him the potential for heroic action? What are the circumstances that release this heroism in the common man?

The men and women you will meet in these stories, essays, and poems include a wandering laborer, a young schoolteacher who became a national symbol, a brother and sister caught up in the crisis of war, and an immigrant in a hostile neighborhood. None of them were very different from ourselves; most of their lives were lived in ordinary ways. But, on at least one occasion, each stepped out of the ordinary and onto a heroic stage.

The section on Greek myths showed how many of the ancient myths had their beginnings in actual events. This process of mythmaking continues in our own time. The short novel The Lilies of the Field *is the story of an ordinary man who became a myth or legend.*

Our study of The Common Man as Hero began with Sandburg's biography of Lincoln. Lincoln was common in that he was a man of the people, but he was not ordinary. Sandburg shows that Lincoln was a genius, whose powerful mind and self-discipline raised him out of his humble background. The hero of The Lilies of the Field *is like Lincoln in that he comes from a poor background and has little formal schooling. But he is a much more ordinary person than Lincoln; we would not be surprised to find him living or working in any American city or town.*

The Lilies of the Field

WILLIAM E. BARRETT

CHAPTER 1

There is a young legend developing on the west side of the mountains. It will, inevitably, grow with the years. Like all legends, it is composed of falsehood and fact. In this case, the truth is more compelling than the trappings of imagination with which it has been invested. The man who has become a legendary figure was, perhaps, of greater stature in simple reality than he ever will be in the oft-repeated, and expanded, tales which commemorate his deeds. Here, before the whole matter gets out of hand, is how it was. . . .

His name was Homer Smith. He was twenty-four. He stood six foot two, and his skin was a deep, warm black. He had large, strong features and widely spaced eyes. A sculptor would have interpreted the features in terms of character, but Homer Smith's mother had once said of him that he was two parts amiable and one part plain devil. It was a verdict that he accepted, as he accepted the days that came to him. He lived his life one day at a time. There was laughter in him.

He was a buck sergeant when he received his army discharge at Fort Lewis. The army years had been good to him, and he had accumulated a sum of money through some slight thrift, much moonlighting, and occasional gambling luck. He bought a secondhand station wagon in Seattle, equipped it for sleeping, and started out to see the West. He had not believed much of what he heard in the army, and he did not believe the tales that Westerners told about their country; he was, however, a curious man.

On a morning in May, Homer Smith drove into a valley west of the Rocky Mountain Range. Spring, which had stood aloof from him on the higher levels, moved down the valley to meet him. Blue, yellow, and pink flowers twinkled in the tawny expanse of buffalo and grama grass. He had grown up in South Carolina, a far different land from this. On his left, as he drove south, blue- and purple-tinted mountains tipped with snow formed a seemingly unbroken barrier against the East, and everything that the East represented. In this country, he had discovered, there was no South; "south" was merely an adjective prefixed to the noun "west."

Where the road curved away from the mountains to parallel a narrow, sluggish stream, he saw the women. One of them was working in an area of cultivated land, and three more were building a fence behind a dilapidated farmhouse. There were no men visible and that was curious. The women wore bulky-looking garments and they had white cloths tied, scarf fashion, around their heads. Homer appraised the house and the outbuildings with one glance.

"Place needs a lot of work," he said.

He hadn't worked for a week. It wasn't necessary that he work unless he felt the urge. In that fact lay a new concept of freedom. He was a man of many skills, and when he became restless with idle traveling, he had no difficulty in finding work to do; when work became onerous,[1] or the road called to him, he moved on. Impulse turned the wheel, and he drove into the badly rutted road which led to the farmhouse.

The woman in the field paused briefly to look toward the station

---

[1] *onerous* (on'ər·əs) : hard to bear.

wagon, and so did the three women who were building a fence; a mere turning of heads, a brief pause, before resuming the tasks which occupied them. The short, squat, older woman who walked into the sunlight from the direction of the chicken run stood and watched Homer as he braked to a stop and slid from under the wheel. He chuckled in recognition of a familiar type. This was the sergeant, the top, the boss of these other women. No doubt about it.

"If you need a day's work done," he said cheerfully, "I'm for hire."

The woman had a hard, weather-beaten look. There were many deep lines on the broad surface of her face. Her eyes were small and sharply intent. She measured Homer before she spoke. She had a deep, guttural voice.

"*Gott ist gut,*" she said. "He hass sent to me a big, stronk man."

Homer was intrigued by the heavy German accent, the careful spacing of words. He was amused, too, at the idea which the words conveyed.

"I dunno," he said. "He didn't say anything to me about sending me some place. I was just passing by."

"*Ja.* You did not pass."

There was aggressiveness in this old woman, an air of certainty which is the mark of bosses. Homer felt antagonism stir in him, but it was a fine day and he was carrying the day in his spirit. He had no quarrel with anyone. He waved one hand.

"I can build that fence better than those girls you've got," he said.

All of the lines in the woman's face seemed to draw together. He could see the effort that she was making to translate what he said in her own mind. He smiled reassuringly and strode away from her.

The three women had their fence half built, a high fence enclosing an area behind the house. Someone had dug postholes and spotted the posts in place. The women had fresh, unpainted planks, and their method was for one woman to brace herself against the post, another to steady the plank, and the third to drive nails. All things considered, they were not doing badly. They stopped work, startled, when Homer's tall figure loomed over them. He gripped the post and shook it. It was a more solid job than he anticipated. The older woman was right behind him.

"*Nein!*" she said.

Her voice sputtered through three emphatic German sentences, and he did not have to understand the words. She did not want him meddling with the fence. She had other work for him to do. He turned, and the woman tapped herself on the chest. He caught the words, "Mutter Maria Marthe" which registered as a name. She indicated each of the three women in turn with a jabbing forefinger.

"Sister Elisabeth, Sister Gertrud, Sister Agnes."

"Religious folk," Homer thought. He nodded his head to each of them. "I'm real happy to meet you," he said. "I'm Homer Smith."

Mother Maria Marthe formed his name silently with her lips, then uttered it as it translated in her mind: "Homerus Schmidt."

"Oh, *ja!* Schmidt!"

Broad smiles broke across the faces of the three women. This was something that they could understand, a stranger named Schmidt. Their smiles made him welcome, and Homer felt immediately at ease with them. They did not have any color line; he was just people to them. He made another attempt to do something about the fence, but the harsh voice of the older woman stopped him at the first gesture.

"*Nein*, Schmidt," she said.

She pointed to the roof and delivered herself of another series of inexplicable sentences. Homer understood her without difficulty. This old woman was a natural boss, and bosses always got their ideas across. She wanted the roof fixed.

"That's not something you do with Scotch tape and chewing gum," he said. "I'd need a good ladder and shingles, and the right kind of nails."

She made no effort to understand him; she merely anticipated him. With a purposeful stride, she led the way to the barn. There was a large room given over to tools and equipment. She had shingles, not enough to reshingle a roof, but enough to repair one that was not too far gone. She had nails of several sizes, including 3d flatheads. She had roofing cement. She had a ladder. Homer looked at her with respect. Here was a woman who knew what had to be done and what was needed to do it.

"Okay," he said. "I'll fix it good."

He was happy when he climbed the ladder and looked out over the valley. There was a chill in the wind, but the sun was warm. He could see the three women working doggedly on their fence, and from his point of vantage, he could see what the fence enclosed.

There was nothing in that little patch except a small statue and a privy.

"How about that?" he said softly. "All that work for just privacy. Away out here where there's nobody."

There was another privy north of the barn, behind the foundation which marked the site of a house that had, obviously, burned down. This, he decided, was where the hired man had lived once, in a smaller house. It was curious that a fire would burn a man's house down and leave his privy standing. It hardly seemed sensible.

He surveyed the roof carefully, aware from the markings that someone had surveyed it before him, indicating the places where it would have to be repaired. He was glad of that, because a man couldn't tell from the outside where a wood-shingle roof leaked, and he had not been invited inside. He wondered if the women would have done this job if he hadn't come along. Probably so. He looked down on the woman who was beating away at the fence planks with a hammer. It would be comical, he thought, to watch them on this roof beating on the shingles.

He worked while he amused himself thinking, rocking the broken and warped shingles to break them away from the hidden nails, sliding new shingles into place and nailing them, covering the nails with roofing cement. He worked swiftly, easily, finding the rhythm best suited to the job and maintaining it. He didn't count time, and he was startled when a deep, heavy, carrying voice called: "Schmidt!"

Mother Maria Marthe was gesturing him down. The other women had already entered the house. The sun was directly overhead. Lunchtime. He scrambled down the ladder and slowed his pace as he approached the door of the house. There was a crucifix above the door, not a rugged Protestant cross but a crucifix. The word, "Catholic" came into his mind, and with it the strange, awesome word, "nun." It had not occurred to him that these women were nuns. He found the idea incredible. What were they doing out here building fences?

They were standing in their places at a rough pine rectangular table that lacked a tablecloth, two on each side, Mother Maria Marthe at the head, and a place for him facing her. When he stood in his place, the older woman made the sign of the cross and the others followed her example. There was no doubt now. This was a

Catholic place, and these were nuns. Homer didn't join in the prayer and couldn't have done so if his Baptist conscience had permitted it. They prayed in German. It was a long prayer, and at a certain point, the rhythm changed as though something new had been added, something that wasn't in the memorized pattern. Homer was sensitive to rhythm. He was sensitive, too, to attitudes toward himself, a sensitivity born of race and skin color that set a man apart. He had delicate, invisible antennae which told him when he was noticed or discussed. He knew at the change in the prayer that these women were praying about him. The knowledge made him vaguely uncomfortable. Nobody was going to pray about getting a roof fixed, particularly a roof that wasn't in very bad shape. There had to be more to it than that.

"Amen" was the signal to be seated. Lunch consisted of thick cheese slices and coarse bread from a homemade loaf that was like a big, swollen pancake but solid. There was a glass of milk at each place; no coffee. Nobody talked, and Homer studied the faces without staring at anybody. These were not young women, but two of them had a young look in spite of weather-roughened skin and tight dishtowel turbans that concealed their hair; Sister Gertrud, who was the shortest nun, the one with the longest nose, and Sister Albertine, who was frail-looking with large eyes, very blue. The other two, Sister Elisabeth and Sister Agnes, were sturdier and had broad faces. The eyes of Sister Elisabeth were brown.

Mother Maria Marthe presided grimly, and it was obvious that no one was going to dawdle over lunch. All hands were going to eat in a hurry and go back to work. The sisters, seemingly, paid no attention to Homer Smith, but he was aware of occasional hurried glances in his direction, and, more important to him, he felt friendliness. When he went back to his roof, he was humming, and the hum grew to full song as he fell into the rhythm of the work. This was an interesting experience. The pay probably wouldn't be much. He didn't care. Maybe he wouldn't take any pay. He didn't know. Come night, he'd roll again.

In the pink of the evening, as he was cleaning the roof gutters, he saw Sister Agnes bringing in a cow, one cow in a country of herds. A few minutes later, as he gathered up his tools, he saw Mother Maria Marthe emerge from the house, followed by Sisters Elisabeth and Gertrud, who were carrying an army cot. The older woman carried a bucket. He watched them, momentarily baffled, but when the toolroom in the barn became their obvious destination, he put all of the pieces of the puzzle together.

"They are doing that for me," he said. "Room and bath."

The idea touched him. A cot to sleep on and a bucket in which to wash! It was what they had. He swung down the ladder and followed them with long strides. They turned, startled, when they heard him. The two sisters held firmly to the cot. It was not army, merely army-type, the kind that is sold in surplus stores, collapsible and cheaply made.

"I didn't figure to stay," he said, "but I've got me a bed in the car."

Mother Maria Marthe did not understand him, so he gestured to the car and turned toward it. She followed him. The two sisters, after a moment of hesitation and lacking definite instructions, joined the procession, still carrying the cot. He opened the station wagon from the rear and showed them the bed on which he slept. He had equipped that vehicle for living. He had his own bucket, too, a foot locker, a tool chest, and a guitar. The older nun nodded, then spoke to the other two in rapid-fire German. They started back to the house with the cot.

"*Das ist gut*, Schmidt," she said. "For zupper I rink a bell."

She walked away, and Homer filled his bucket at the well, hauling it behind the barn for his wash-up. Supper was preceded by an even longer prayer than the one at lunch, and was only slightly more substantial as a meal. Sister Albertine served omelet with the coarse bread and a glass of milk. This was it; a houseful of people living on the efforts of one cow and a few chickens. When another prayer had been said, two of the nuns made deft work of clearing away the dishes. There was a general air of relaxation. Sister Albertine, with badly concealed excitement, departed on a mysterious errand. Mother Maria Marthe sat less stiffly in her chair.

"Ve are Cherman," she said, "mit two from Hungary. Ve learn der Englisch."

Sister Albertine returned with a small, tinny, wind-up-model phonograph, the type that is bought for very young children. She placed a record on the turntable when the dishwashing nuns returned. A harsh, badly distorted voice squawked something in German from the speaker, followed by the English equivalent. The five voices repeated the English, including in the pronunciation all of the phonograph noises.

"Please send the valet up to my room," they said.
"I have something to be pressed."
"Do not starch the collars of the shirts."
"Here is my laundry list."
"Four shirts."
"Five pairs of socks."
"One blouse."
"Two pajamas."

Homer listened, fascinated and repelled. He had never been exposed to the problem of learning another language. He resented the voice on the record which wasted the time of these people by teaching them to say stupid things. These nuns weren't ever going to see a valet, and they weren't going to have anything pressed. He had an expressive face, and Mother Maria Marthe read it when the pause at the end of the record occurred. She halted Sister Albertine, who was about to turn the record over.

"Vait!" she said. "Schmidt! He spiks der Englisch."

Homer sat suspended in the sudden hush, aware of the eyes. He was, suddenly, elevated above his status as a big, strong man, above the disembodied voice on the record. Sister Albertine was so carried away that she spoke without waiting for permission. She pointed to the phonograph.

"Vot iss named this?" she said.
"A phonograph."

Homer's reply broke down discipline. If Sister Albertine could ask a question so could anyone else. Each nun was indicating some object in the room. He named them as rapidly as he could, trying to speak the words distinctly. He could tell from their delighted expressions that they already knew the words "table," "chair," "window," "door," and the words for the other familiar objects. His identification pleased them by confirming what they knew. Mother Maria Marthe put a stop to the obvious. She went through the pantomime of shaking hands with one of the nuns and he told her what she was doing, pointing out the "you" and the "her." He became self-conscious about the South Carolina in his voice.

"If you learn English from me," he said apologetically, "you're sure enough going to get yourselves segregated some places."

They looked at him uncomprehendingly, and he let the subject drop. That was something that he could not explain even to himself. Sister Albertine was drawing a sketch on a piece of paper. She showed it to him. It was a very good sketch of his station wagon. "Automobile? No?" she said. "Auto bus, no?"

She knew that it had a special name, and she did better with English than did the others. They were all interested, but when he told them that it was a station wagon, he drew blank looks. With a few deft strokes, the nun drew a depot, then a wagon. This was a station, and this, a wagon. How could you put them together and obtain something that resembled an automobile?

He did not explain that very well, but he tried. He was sorry when Mother Maria Marthe clapped her hands as a signal that class was over. He walked to his home on wheels in the cool darkness, with a thousand stars swung low above him and his brain filled with strange rhythms; German words and English words flavored with German. He did not ask himself why he was spending the night; he was here and it happened. He wondered which of the nuns would have slept on the floor and managed without a bucket if he hadn't had his own equipment.

These nuns are nice people, he thought, and that old lady's got a shrewd mind, loose and easy.

CHAPTER 2

One of the privileges of freedom was that a man slept until he felt like rising, with no bugles blowing. Homer Smith was not a late sleeper, but he did not believe in stumbling around in half light, waking up birds. The morning was nicely lighted in the sky when he rose, filled his bucket at the well, and hauled it beyond the barn. There was a hammer hammering, and from the corners of his eyes, he could see Mother Maria Marthe watching him while he was filling his bucket. She did not bother him until he came back to the station wagon; then she descended angrily.

"Schmidt!" Her words tumbled out and they were so German, or so German-English, that they were incomprehensible. She did not, however, need words to convey meaning; she needed only gestures and emphasis. The gist of the message was plain. He was a lazy loafer who had no business sacking out when there was work to be done. Homer drew himself up, looking at her from his commanding height, as angry as she was.

"Look!" he said. "I ain't no nun and I ain't no hired hand, neither. I get up when I feel like getting up. If I don't want to work, I don't work."

He did not awe her. She stamped her foot, pointing emphatically at the house. "*Geh!*" she said. "*Mach schnell!*"

Being commanded to go to the house meant that he was expected to eat breakfast. That was an idea that made sense. He turned away, still angry. Sister Albertine greeted him shyly in the communal dining room. She had, obviously, been forced to waste her time preparing a late breakfast for him, and she was nervous about it. She set two fried eggs before him, following them with two slabs of coarse bread, toasted. There was no coffee, only the inevitable milk.

"Old Mother sure sets a poor table," Homer said. "How come she can afford all that lumber outside and no money for chow?"

Sister Albertine stared at him, her large eyes seeming larger still as she tried to understand him. Homer didn't expect her to understand him. It was a comfort to him to express his feelings in words with a human audience to listen to him; he did not require a response.

"There's a mean streak in that old woman," he said. "I don't know why you girls put up with her. People got to sleep. People got to eat. People got to have a little joy in living. She don't go for that. All this milk all the time and no coffee! And no milk of human kindness, neither. That woman just hasn't got it."

Sister Albertine gestured helplessly. "I do not understand," she said. "Speak slowly please."

Her English sounded like English, or more like English than Mother Maria Marthe's, even if she did speak one word at a time.

"I'm going to give you some soup," he said. "Got some soup in the car. Emergency rations. Got a can of peaches, too. You wait right here! I'll bring them right in."

Sister Albertine looked frightened, but there was one note in the human voice that she understood, the note of command. She nodded her head weakly and started clearing the dishes from the table. Homer strode out to the station wagon.

"I hope Old Mother tries to stop me," he said. "Just let her ask me what I'm doing."

He was in a high, exalted mood, flying the flags of rebellion against authority. No one attempted to stop him, and he took five cans of soup out of his locker, a can of peaches, a can opener. He saw Mother Maria Marthe bearing down on him as he started back to the house, and his flags drooped on the flagstaff. He pretended that he did not see her and lengthened his stride. He piled his cans on the table, resisting the impulse to look over his shoulder. He went through the pantomime of opening the cans for the benefit of Sister Albertine.

"Soup," he said.

"*Ja*. Thank you."

She looked interested, but she also looked fearful. She did not have the authority to accept gifts, but she lacked the vocabulary necessary to refuse acceptance or to explain her dilemma. Homer sensed it.

"Old Mother will like that soup," he said. "Save a little wear and tear on that cow and those chickens."

He went out to face the dragon and the dragon was waiting for him. "Schmidt," Mother Maria Marthe said, "Ve build a shapel. I show you."

She led the way with firm tread to the old foundation over which a house had burned. Coarse grasses had grown around it, and the foundation itself was a pit into which ash and brick and partially consumed timbers had fallen. She reached into her pocket and produced a sketch on a piece of coarse wrapping paper. It was a good sketch of a small church, a frame church that looked like many Baptist churches in the South, except that it did not have a steeple. There was a cross on the first roof truss above the door.

"Who builds it?" he said.

Her eyes drilled into him. She was patient, and she could wait upon the perception of a dull-witted male. Homer looked from the unsightly foundation to the sketch and back again. There was a pile of new lumber behind the barn.

"If you think that I'm building that, you're out of your mind," he said. "I'm one man. I ain't no contractor with a crew. I don't need all that work, neither." He handed the sketch back to her. "No."

There was hard-eyed contempt in the old woman's face. She

folded the sketch into a hidden pocket. "Ve are vimmen," she said. "Ve build it."

"All right. You build it."

Anger boiled and bubbled in Homer Smith. He could feel the steam from it rising into his brain. He looked away from Mother Maria Marthe, and it helped to bring his anger down to a simmer, not looking at her. She was a mean-minded, overriding, unreasonable old woman. He was going to get in his station wagon and drive. The warmth of the day touched his skin, and he was looking toward the debris in the foundation. He had had his breakfast. He felt strongly about people passing judgment on him, and he did not want this woman justified in thinking ill of him.

"I'll clean that old foundation for you before I go," he said.

He walked away from her, tall in his pride. There was a scoop shovel in the toolhouse, and, surprisingly, a crowbar. He had a spade in his car. He came back and surveyed the ruin of a house. The builder had put down a solid foundation of granite. Not many farmhouses in this section of country were built like this. It made sense. A man had to have a cool place for his perishable stuff. The big house where the nuns lived was probably built the same way. The chimney stood above the foundation, tall and built of brick, a lonely thing without a house to keep it company.

"Strange how it burned the man's house and left his privy."

Homer shook his head over the familiar thought as he surveyed the ruin. The years had fallen on the grave of that house; snows and rains and blowing sand. The debris was packed into the pit and it looked like a town dump set in cement. A bulldozer would churn it up fast. He knew how to handle a bulldozer, but this was a place of hungry labor where a man was lucky because he had a shovel and a crowbar. Resentment against Mother Maria Marthe moved hotly in him again. He paced off the dimensions of the foundation, confirming what his eye told him. It was 18 × 26.

He dropped down into the pit and started probing. It had been a hot fire, and the house had probably gone fast. Some of the lumber had survived, charred but not burned through. Someone had started the cleaning-out process long ago and quit. It was impossible to tell how that fire had gone. It probably smothered out some way. Maybe it happened in the winter and the snow came. There weren't any clues left to show what had happened to the room. He did not believe that it had been reduced to ash.

"Old farmer took him some salvage," he said. "Hauled away what would haul."

He was encouraged when he discovered that the burned lumber moved against his pry. It had partially roofed the excavation. This hole wasn't as solidly packed as it looked. Fire-eaten though they were, the lumbers were heavy, and he strained his muscles against them, heaving them out. His body absorbed thought and emotion, condensing them into sweat. When he heard a bell ringing in the distance, he did not immediately translate it into meaning.

"Old Mother going to feed the slaves," he said.

Resentment returned. He was filthy. Clouds of black ash rose from his work clothes when he slapped them. He went to the station wagon for his bucket and washed in cold water from the well, accepting the icy touch of it gratefully. The nuns were standing in their places at the table, waiting for him before starting their prayers. He didn't say Catholic prayers with them, but he had to be there. It was some idea in Old Mother's mind. He bowed his head. He had a prayer in his own heart when he accepted food. Nobody took food for granted when he was a child. It wasn't always easy to get, and a person learned to be thankful when it was there.

He sat down at the table, and there were soup plates at each place. Sister Albertine came in with a pot and a ladle. She looked happy. All the nuns looked happy. Mother Maria Marthe didn't look exactly happy, but she didn't look as stern as usual. Homer's mood lifted. They were serving his soup.

Nobody talked. That seemed to be the rule at lunchtime. Still, without talking, it was a pleasant meal. Nice atmosphere. These girls, Homer thought, need better food. He wished that he had more cans in his car. He didn't feel full-fed when he rose, but his stomach was friendly to him. When a man felt welcome at a table, the food tasted better.

He was whistling when he returned to the excavation. He stood with his hands in his pockets looking at it. Old Mother, he repeated to himself, was out of her mind. Nobody could build a church like her drawing unless he was a contractor with people working for him, people skilled in doing different things. Women weren't ever going to build it, especially not women that built a fence so clumsy. All of which made cleaning out all of this mess ridiculous. He had told her that he'd clean it out before he left, however, and he'd do it.

He was a strong man, and the work went fast when he didn't think about it. He got all of the odds and ends of wood and metal out of the hole, then worked them into a trench about a dozen yards away. He cleaned the stone steps that had led into the cellar from the outside, but the cellar was deep. A man could walk around in it with the top of his head under ground. Getting out the ash and the sand was not mere shoveling; it was hauling. He did not want to use his own pail, so he rummaged around in the barn until he found a bucket that had seen hard service. After that, monotony claimed him; shoveling, filling, carrying out, and dumping.

He created a refuse pile that would have to be leveled off some day, but he had no alternative and it did not worry him. Blue dusk came down on an uncompleted job and his muscles ached. The distant bell rang again.

They were back to eggs for the evening meal. The eggs irritated him. He was tired and hungry, and he'd spent his day doing a job that didn't add up to anything. There wasn't enough food to satisfy him, and Mother Maria Marthe sat stiffly at the head of the table keeping everything on a low key. She never said a word of thanks to anybody for anything.

"I'm going to get me my pay and leave."

The resolve sustained him, even when he was swept into an English lesson after dinner. The nuns, he discovered, had been studying English, not merely trying to learn it from a phonograph record. They brought their books with them, and they knew many English words. Their problem was that they never heard anyone speak those words, and they had no practice in speaking them. Homer was not in a mood for teaching anybody anything, and he gave their problem only half his mind. He could feel the disappointment of the nuns, but he was concentrating on the boss nun, and he couldn't give any thought to the others. When Mother Maria Marthe clapped her hands at the conclusion of the lesson, he braced himself.

"I want to talk to you," he said. "I've been doing work for you. Good work. I want pay for what I do."

She sat silent, with her hands clasped in front of her. Her small eyes looked at him out of the wrinkled mask of her face, but there was no light in them. He did not know whether she understood him or not; if she did, she would not admit it. She could make a person feel wrong, like a miserable sinner, by just looking at him. If she refused to cross over into English, he couldn't talk to her. He looked past her to the little table under the statue of the Mother of Jesus in the corner of the room. There was a book on the table, a big book, and it talked to him. The Bible! He crossed the room and looked at it, turning a few pages. The type was outlandish and did not look like words,[1] but no other book was organized like this one.

"You wait right here," he said. "I'm coming back."

He was afraid that she would not wait, that she would close the door on him, but she waited. He brought his own Bible from the station wagon. It was the one he had got in the army. He had a passage in his mind, and he turned pages rapidly. He tore half of the wrapping from a package of cigarettes and wrote on the white side, *Luke* 10:7.

Mother Maria Marthe rose heavily and crossed the room to her big Bible. She turned the pages, and he knew what she was reading when the page-turning stopped:

"And in the same house remain, eating and drinking such things as they give: for the laborer is worthy of his hire."

It wasn't exactly what he wanted to say, but he hoped that she would get the idea about the laborer. She walked slowly back and reached for his pencil. In bold letters, she wrote, *Proverbs* 1:14.

He spun his own pages and read: "Cast in thy lot among us: let us all have one purse."

"No," he said. "I'm a poor man. I have to work for wages."

Mother Maria Marthe did not change expression. Without returning to consult her Bible, she wrote again on the fragment of cigarette package, *Matthew* 6:28, 29.

"And why take ye thought for raiment? Consider the lilies of the field, how they grow; they toil not, neither do they spin.

"And yet I say unto you that even Solomon in all his glory was not arrayed like one of these."

Homer read, baffled. This old woman had answers out of the Book, which surprised him. They did not come to grips with the

---

[1] *words:* Mother Maria Marthe's Bible was printed in German.

situation, they did not deal directly with his right to be paid, but they slowed down a man in argument. Before he went into the army, he had had a head filled with Bible words and figures, but they would not march straight for him now as they did once. It wouldn't make any difference. This old woman wasn't going to pay him. She'd never had any intention of paying him. She sat straight with her unblinking eyes fixed on his face.

"Schmidt," she said. "Tomorrow Sunday ist. Der Mass in Piedras iss nine by der clock."

"I don't go to Mass."

"Ve do."

She sat immovable, letting the statement stand in all finality until his comprehension caught up with it. She expected him to drive the nuns to Mass.

"How did you get there before I came?" he said.

"Ve valked."

That, too, had finality in it, completeness. Piedras was a little town. Homer had driven through it before he stopped here. It was over two miles away. He thought about those nuns, working hard all day on thin rations, walking miles along the road on Sunday. He liked those nuns. It wasn't fair to them.

"I'll drive you in," he said.

He walked out, then; not expecting thanks and not wanting any. A man was free when he could say "yes" or say "no." Old Mother had her ways, and she was a tricky woman, but she hadn't asked him to take her to Mass. He had to be honest about it; she hadn't asked him that. That wasn't her way. She put a problem up to a man. She knew how to set a problem up for him so there wasn't anything he could do but take it from her.

CHAPTER 3

The morning was still, with no movement in the wide and lonely land. Homer Smith rose early. He dressed in a pair of army slacks, a button-down gray shirt, a blue necktie, a gray jacket. A man had to look sharp on Sunday if no other time. He wandered around aimlessly, missing the sense of life, movement, and activity that he associated with this strange place in which he found himself. As time passed, with no bell sounding, it became apparent that there would be no breakfast. He remembered vaguely from the army that Catholics, or some Catholics, did not have breakfast before Mass. His own hunger was the captive of Catholic custom, and he was uncomfortable. He removed his bed from the station wagon, providing space if not comfort for his passengers. At eight-thirty they emerged.

Mother Maria Marthe and her four nuns wore long black robes with white starched bibs, and white bands across their foreheads under black hoods. They looked now like his idea of nuns, but he was astonished at them.

"You girls sure look nice," he said.

Whether they understood his English or not, they recognized a compliment by its tone. They looked pleased. Mother Maria Marthe wasted no time on looking pleased. She sized up the station wagon, ordered the nuns into the back, and elected to ride with the driver. There were no seats in the back, so the passengers sat on the floor. There was something pleasant and companionable about that, and Homer had an impulse to sing as he drove out onto the road. He didn't sing. The stiff, no-nonsense woman beside him wouldn't put in with singing. He was certain of that.

Piedras was a shabby little town, and the church was a flat-roofed structure of adobe. Homer let his passengers out and stood beside the station wagon, ignoring the hard stare of Old Mother. This close was as close as he intended to go to a Catholic Mass. He waited until the nuns entered the church, then crossed the street. There were signs in Spanish all over the windows of a small café, and he did not have to understand Spanish to recognize a place that sold beer and miscellaneous food. He wasn't certain that it would be open, but it was. A thin man with sad brown eyes rose from a stool and moved behind the counter.

"I want a man's breakfast," Homer said. "Ham and eggs, with lots of ham, and pancakes, and anything else you've got, and coffee. I want lots of coffee, and I start with it."

"Sí. I can do it. You are the man who does the work for those nuns?"

"They do a lot of work themselves."

"Sí. This I know. It is a great folly. They cannot make the living in this country. It is not possible."

A steaming cup of coffee appeared on the counter in front of Homer, and he inhaled the fragrance of it. The sad man had a grill behind the counter, and he broke eggs onto it. Ham sizzled and Homer's nostrils twitched. He hadn't ever thought about nuns making a living. New thoughts interested him.

"They are Germans. They speak the good Spanish, but nobody listens. There is no reason for it."

The little man talked on. He knew all about the nuns, or claimed that he did. They were from the wrong Germany, "the one that is Communist," and they escaped, which was a great embarrassment to their Order. But yes. There was some politics about it which no one could understand. "It is Church politics and politics of Europe, and who can understand the politics even when it is of his own country?" The nuns could not stay in Germany, and the Order owned this land. It came to them in the will of Gus Ritter. Did the customer know Gus Ritter?

Everybody in this place knew him; *todo el mundo*.[1] He was a hard, mean man who worked his family night and day to make money for him. His son and his son's wife burned to death in the house next to his. A lamp of kerosene caused it. He was too mean, Gus Ritter, to have electricity, although poor people in this country had it. After his son burned up, he did not live long. He left his land to this Order of nuns because his sister in Germany belonged to it. For a long time the land was idle. Gus Ritter made good money from it growing the potato. These nuns came, and they had nothing. They knew nothing except to teach. There was no school, and they did not know the English. How could they teach? They sold some land to buy tools and furniture and lumber. For what purpose? What could they do? Would the customer have some more of the eggs?

The customer wasn't interested in eggs, but he would have more ham. Homer Smith was enjoying this experience. He was catching up on his victuals after two lean days. The steady flow of talk from behind the counter fascinated him. He had always had a weakness for good talkers. He liked the cadences which Spanish brought to English, and the occasional Spanish words or phrases, meaning

---

[1] *todo el mundo*: everybody.

nothing, delighted him because they so obviously belonged to what the man was trying to say.

"The Mass is finish," the man said.

There were a few people coming out of the church across the street. Homer rose and stretched. It had been a noble breakfast. As he was paying for it, he thought about those hungry nuns. He hesitated. Working only occasionally and traveling much, he had learned thrift. He shrugged and purchased five slices of ham which he carried to the car in a paper sack.

The main body of worshipers moved slowly out of the church; Spanish, all of them. Poor people. Homer towered above them as he stood beside his station wagon, and he was aware of his physical superiority as he was aware of the curious glances that he attracted. Nobody spoke to him.

The nuns did not come out until after everyone else had gone. The priest came with them, a short, thin man in a brown robe with a white cord around his waist. Mother Maria Marthe was talking to him in Spanish. Her Spanish did not have a lot of German in it like her English did. She introduced Homer to the priest and he did not understand what she said about him, but he caught his own name. She called him "Señor Schmidt." Señor means "mister" in Spanish. He knew that. She never called him mister in English. The priest was Father Gomez. These Catholics were a comical people. They called themselves "Father" and "Mother" when they weren't and when they didn't aim to be.

The priest shook hands with him. He was a quiet man, half sad, like all these Spanish, with a low voice. He wouldn't be likely to get a call from a Baptist church. He wasn't an exhorting type. He said something nice about Homer being good to the nuns.

"Mother Superior tells me that you are going to build her a chapel," he said.

"That is just an idea she's got in her head. One man can't do that."

Homer felt embarrassed when he read disappointment in the priest's eyes. He had no reason to feel embarrassed, but he did. He spoke hurriedly to cover what he felt.

"I been studying your church. Never saw one like it before. Not close up."

"It is not impressive, but I would like to show it to you."

The priest brightened. He led Homer to the wall of the church and showed him where the outside coating of adobe had cracked. There were adobe bricks underneath. "They are simple bricks," he said. "They are made out of adobe clay and a little straw, sometimes the manure of the horse, then dried in the sun."

The door was of rough board. Homer hesitated when the priest opened it. He had never been inside a Catholic church. There were vague memories in his mind about tales he had heard of weird Catholic spells and of idol worship, but he was curious about the construction of the building, so he followed the priest in. There was an altar, and there were rows of rough benches, strange-looking images that wore clothes, murals of Biblical scenes painted on the walls. The walls were whitewashed adobe, concealing the brickwork. There was a poverty about it that attracted Homer Smith. He understood poverty.

The priest was telling him that he had three other churches like this one in which he said Mass on Sundays, that his home parish was in the larger town of North Fork. Homer nodded. This was a busy man, a circuit-riding preacher. He respected him.

"I'm glad I saw your church," he said.

"It is a poor church, but God comes down to it." The priest's eyes were intent upon Homer's face. "Mother Superior says that she prayed for someone to help her and that you came. What do you think about that?"

Homer laughed. He did not mean to laugh, but this was a disturbing subject. "I think that she figures that she owns me. She figures that the Lord gave me to her as a present because she did all that praying."

"Not that!" the priest said. "I am certain, not that. But she has a need and she trusted in prayer. It is not a fault in her if she believes that God sent you."

"He didn't send a black Baptist to a Catholic nun. He didn't do anything like that."

"It would be odd, wouldn't it?"

"I don't see much sense in what she's doing."

"She does what she must at the present. These nuns have to live. She wants a place here ultimately for poor boys from the city; Spanish-speaking boys who get into trouble. No one is interested in them. They could work and learn and be happier in the country than in the city. No one will believe that until she proves it. She knows what she wants to do, and she is strong of will."

"Yes," Homer said. "I know that. She's a strong-minded woman. But God didn't give me to her, and she doesn't own me. She's got to get that out of her head."

He was thoughtful driving home, and he declined the breakfast invitation, abrupt in his presentation of the paper sack to Mother Maria Marthe. "Just a little ham," he said. "Maybe you girls might like it."

He gave her no opportunity to say thanks or not to say thanks. He turned away hurriedly and climbed into the station wagon. He drove to a parking place close to the excavation and changed into his working clothes. He had an innate respect for the Sabbath, and a disinclination to profane it with servile work, but the army had relaxed the rigid rules of his boyhood. In the army a job that had to be done on Sunday was done on Sunday. It was like the ass or the ox falling into a pit and having to be hauled out. The nuns, however, seemed to be abiding by the old rules, so he restrained his urge to plunge in and finish the clearing of the excavation.

He walked around the excavation and measured it again. He returned to the station wagon and obtained a small pad from his locker. He covered the pad with figures. He had worked for many people and he had done many things. He had varied skills. Always he had worked with someone telling him what to do. Nobody, in all of his life before this, had told him to build a church. Nobody had ever said to him: "Here is the ground and here I want a church and it is your job to build it." It was like a call. It elevated him. He was all alone, one man, with a hole in the ground and a church to be built, and no one to tell him how.

He took his black pipe from his locker and packed it. He smoked cigarettes during the week, but on Sunday he smoked a pipe. It was his father's habit. His father could not afford to smoke tobacco seven days a week, so he settled for Sunday. Homer had been smoking a black pipe like his father's on Sunday ever since his father died. In his mind it was sort of a memorial, and he drew satisfaction from it.

He sat on the small pile of partly consumed lumber that he had stacked a few yards away from the foundation. He puffed on his pipe, and there was a sheen over his eyes. He was seeing something before him that wasn't there, and the world around him did not exist. He was unaware of Mother Maria Marthe until she spread the wide skirts of her black robe and sat beside him on the lumber. It was the most companionable thing that she had ever done.

"Schmidt," she said, "ve can do it?"

It wasn't a statement; it was a question. That, too, was unusual, but Homer's mind was away out where the unusual is usual and nothing ordinary matters.

"It would take a powerful lot of work," he said, "and a lot of those 'dobe bricks."

"How much?"

"About the work, I don't know. Nearly four thousand bricks."

They sat silent, contemplating the foundation where once a house had stood and where a man and woman had burned to death. Mother Maria Marthe rose.

"Tomorrow ve go to North Fork," she said.

Homer didn't answer. North Fork was the big town of this section. He hadn't seen it yet. If she wanted to go, he'd take her. She wouldn't do anything about the gasoline. Gasoline was like the lilies of the field to her; somehow it would be provided.

The noon heat pressed down, and he moved into the shade of the station wagon. The land was big, and there was loneliness all around him. He thought about going back to Piedras and listening to the Spanish man at the eating place, but that was too much trouble. The day, without work or travel, seemed as big and as empty as the country. He took his guitar out of the station wagon. He traveled with everything that he liked in that old vehicle because it was his home while he rambled. He had bought the guitar in a pawnshop in Tacoma, a better instrument than the one he had owned back in South Carolina. He tuned it and played softly, feeling his way into a mood. In a little while he was singing, keeping his voice down, not putting out anything, singing to his own soul.

He sang "Wade in the Water" and "Deep River," "Blind Barnabas" and "Old Time Religion." He let his voice swell out a little on "Shenandoah" because, suddenly, the mood was right and the song was saying what he felt inside of him. Mother Maria Marthe returned then, and he felt her presence without seeing her. His mood was stronger than her presence, and his voice made its last crossing of the wide Missouri before he looked up. The old face, with its deeply graven wrinkles, was forbidding, but the small eyes seemed less hard than usual.

"Schmidt," she said. "Come! Brink der music."

He rose reluctantly to follow her. He had been doing all right alone. His resentment melted when he saw the four nuns waiting expectantly in the dining room. The table had been pushed back, and his chair was placed so that he would face them. They were women without music in a great, flat, lonely place that was intolerable without it. He looked at them and his heart lifted. These were people who needed something that he had to give.

He started softly, offering religion to religious people. "Swing Low, Sweet Chariot" and "Didn't My Lord Deliver Daniel." He warmed to them, then, and worked to lift them, swinging into: "Ezekiel Saw the Wheel" and "Dry Bones." Their feet moved, and their eyes were alive. Old Mother, sitting stiffly, didn't seem to mind, so he did "Water Boy" and "John Henry." He had no particular awareness of his voice except as an instrument, like his guitar. It was deep, a bass-baritone, and he could do with a song whatever he felt like doing at the moment, but he did not try to make his voice obey any rules. When he finished "John Henry," Mother Maria Marthe clapped her hands. It wasn't applause; it was the end of his solo.

"Ve sing," she said.

He nodded, accepting the role of accompanist. "Give me the key," he said, "and let us hear how it goes."

The old nun nodded to Sister Albertine, who had a moment of shyness. She wet her lips, and her thin fingers tightened, making fists out of her hands. Her large blue eyes met Homer's, and she leaned forward. She sang, and her voice was true, a sweet voice, not strong but perfectly pitched. A man could follow it. Homer watched her and listened to her, tuning the guitar. What she was doing was chant, a simple thing. He drew deep organ sounds from the guitar, and it was right. Everything was right; the voice, the music, the accompaniment. Sister Albertine felt him with her and she signaled to the others. They came in and they knew what they were doing. None of the voices was as good as Sister Albertine's, but this chant did not call for good voices. Sister Gertrud's voice was harsh.

Sisters Agnes and Elisabeth sounded like just anybody out of a Baptist choir, and the old Mother's voice was cracked; but, together, they made a strange, solemn sense.

This was Latin. It was Homer's first experience with sung Latin, and he approved the sound of it. It belonged to this music. As they changed from one hymn to another, Sister Albertine led him into the sense of the new chant, and the others joined in as he picked it up. Loneliness had long since dropped away from him, and he felt exultation. He wanted to mingle his voice with these others, but the words eluded him so long as he regarded them as words; when he thought of them merely as sounds, they made a pattern in his mind. He signaled to Sister Albertine for a repeat at one point and when he heard the sounds a second time they clung to his mind. The voices of the nuns came in again, and his voice joined them.

> Ave maris stella
> Dei mater alma
> Atque semper virgo
> Felix coeli porta.[2]

It was that easy. They stopped when Mother Maria Marthe clapped her hands. It was suppertime, but Homer paid no attention to his food. He ate it, but it made no impression on him. When he walked to the station wagon, he was empty of thought but filled with throbbing sound, a happy feeling of reverence. He stood for a long time looking at the shadowed shape of the excavation.

CHAPTER 4

North Fork had a population of 7,094 people, which made it the metropolis of the west slope, where towns were small and widely spaced. It was a spread-out town, and the Livingston Construction Company was on the northern outskirts. Mother Maria Marthe was accompanied by Sister Gertrud. The two nuns left Homer Smith beside the station wagon while they entered the Livingston office.

---

[2] *Ave . . . porta:* "Hail, Star of the Sea," a well-known Catholic hymn (in Latin).

Homer lighted a cigarette and looked at the construction company property with interest. He had no idea why Old Mother was visiting this place, but it had a prosperous look.

Politician, this man Livingston, he decided.

There were several earth-moving machines standing in a row, and spaces indicating that there were others out on a job. There were four good-sized buildings and an adjoining lumberyard. All of which, on this side of the mountains, added up to road-building contracts and government work. A man didn't employ such equipment out in the wide open spaces by merely hanging out a sign or putting an ad in the paper.

Rolling in it, Homer thought. This man is doing all right.

He was idly curious about Mother Maria Marthe's mission, but speculation never engaged his mind for long. He either knew something or he didn't know, found out ultimately or never found out. He walked around, admiring the equipment. He had resumed his post beside the station wagon when a short, firm-jawed, gray-haired man exited briskly from the office door. The man seemed angry, either temporarily or permanently so. He looked at Homer challengingly, looked past him, then met his eyes.

"Are you Schmidt?" he said incredulously.

"That's a German idea," Homer said softly. "My folks figured that it was Smith. Named me Homer."

"You're the man who is going to build a chapel for those nuns?"

Homer was about to say that that was another German idea, one of Old Mother's ideas, but he didn't like the man's attitude. The man didn't seek information in a polite and orderly way.

"Yes," he said.

"I expected a different type. Hell! You'll never do it."

Homer kept his eyes on the other man's face, not answering, merely waiting. This was an attitude that he understood, although he had not encountered it lately. This man expected to meet somebody white; when he discovered that he was dealing with a Negro, he "knew" that the job wouldn't be done. A voice inside Homer said: "The man's right. You know he's right. You won't do it." He closed the voice out, refusing to listen.

"I'm Orville Livingston," the man said. "I don't know how you got mixed up in this, but I told this nun when she first came here that she'd better go back again. I was Gus Ritter's friend and the executor of his estate. I turned his property over to this religious Order, which was what he wanted. I sold land for those nuns after they came here, without taking a commission. I had a man plow for them when they insisted on working the land that they kept, and I paid him personally. Now they want bricks. I've got to stop somewhere. I'm a Methodist."

"I'm a Baptist myself."

"You are? Then why are you working for them? If you are?"

"I haven't figured that out yet."

"You'll figure it out. Then you'll quit. Those nuns will figure it out, too; figure out that what people told them was right. Then they'll quit. They must. Women can't work that land, and if their Church was interested in them, it wouldn't leave them out here. They'll quit, and anything that they start will fall to ruin."

"Old Mother has a strong idea in her mind," Homer said softly. "She's going to do what she feels she must."

"Certainly. If somebody else supplies the bricks! Well, I won't. I wanted to see you before I told her."

Orville Livingston did not seem to realize that he had made Homer Smith the last toppling weight in the scales of decision against the nuns, and that he was telling him so.

"You've got that right," Homer said. "I can't talk against you on that. I'm still doing that job for them. I'm going to need two days' work a week to keep it going. I can handle a bulldozer, almost any machinery you've got. Learned how in the army."

"All right. I can use you Thursday and Friday if you can only work two days. I'll pay the going rate on whatever job you're assigned. Seven Thursday morning. I'll try you out."

Orville Livingston turned away. "Another thing," Homer said, "I'll need two sacks of cement. For them I'll pay cash."

"Three dollars. I'll have a man wheel them out."

Homer lighted another cigarette. Something had happened to him. He didn't plan any part of it. He had taken a job that he didn't want, under a man whom he didn't like, and he'd told the man that he was going to build a church. It didn't make sense. He stared across the big lot of the Livingston Construction Company, seeing none of it, seeking in his mind for a way out of a worrisome situation. A sentence kept repeating itself like an outside voice speaking to him: "*I expected a different type.*" Then another sentence: "*I wanted to see you before I told her.*" He'd let Old Mother down merely by being black.

A man wheeled out two sacks of cement and Homer paid for them. They weighed ninety-four pounds a sack, and he heaved them into the back of the station wagon. His muscles felt good doing it.

The two nuns emerged from the office, and any sentimental feeling that he had developed for Mother Maria Marthe vanished immediately. She was in bad humor.

"Schmidt," she said curtly, "ve go back."

"No, we don't. I've got things to do."

His pride stood tall, contradicting her and not explaining anything. The two nuns were riding in the front with him because there was no sensible alternative. He could hear the old nun breathing heavily.

"Ve haff no time," she said.

He ignored her and drove downtown. North Fork had a variety of stores concentrated on two streets. He found the town interesting after a period of isolation. He bought a spirit level and a couple of good saws, a heavy hammer, a chisel, and a hoe with a ventilated blade. The expenditure dismayed him, but he assured himself that he would pay the money back to his fund out of his pay on Friday. He couldn't afford a big investment in something that probably wasn't going to get done.

"Schmidt," Mother Maria Marthe said when they were halfway home, "ve haff no bricks."

"We'll get some."

He didn't know where or how, but that was a problem of the future, and the future was never quite real to him. A man couldn't calculate on time that hadn't arrived, happenings that hadn't happened; he had all that he could do in coping with what was already here. The here and the now of this afternoon was the finishing of the foundation clean-out. It took his afternoon and part of the next day. He built a mortar box, got a level on the foundation, chiseled off the rough spots, and mixed cement. He started on the task of smoothing the top of the foundation with cement, and he worked carefully, missing the direction of a boss while savoring the joy of being his own man, with a job that was his to plan and to execute. On Thursday and Friday he worked in one of the Livingston road gangs, and on Friday night he drew his pay.

"I owe myself more money than I earned."

The flat statement admitted of no argument. It was a fact. He weighed the fact thoughtfully for as long as it took him to walk to the North Fork supermarket. That market had been beckoning to him since he first saw it. He entered and selected a wheeled basket, pushing it before him. He passed all of the products which needed refrigeration, but he selected an accumulation of canned goods and two cans of coffee. He hesitated for a long two minutes before buying a whole ham.

"We've got to eat better than we've been eating," he said defensively.

When he presented the two sacks of groceries to Mother Maria Marthe, her face tightened like one of her hands folding into a fist, more bone and skin than flesh, more contraction than expression. He had a startled impression that there were tears in her eyes, but he could not be certain because she turned away so abruptly, the groceries in her arms.

"*Ach*, Schmidt!" she said.

The next day she was more annoying than ever, yelling "Schmidt!" at him when he was counseling with himself over his work, bothering his life with orders and suggestions and just plain interference. He decided that she was a natural henpecker and that he'd been foolish in his idea that she had softness in her.

"Hard as a hammer," he muttered. "Always beating on something."

He had, however, established a new pattern without thinking about it. Buying groceries seemed the natural thing to do when he had his second payday a week later, and he engaged in no hesitations or arguments with himself.

"Mouths to feed," he said.

He rather liked the idea, liked the nuns, and responded warmly to their obvious liking for himself. He enjoyed the English lessons and the Sunday music. Everything in his life seemed to fall into line, work and more work, music, a little visiting, a little pondering, regular things to do at regular hours, and no time to think about doing anything else.

The nuns worked all day in the fields as the weather grew warmer. He neither tried to understand their work nor to interfere with it. They were irrigating the land from a stream which fed into another puny stream that Westerners called a river. All that he knew about the irrigating process was that it was hard work. He had grown up in Columbia, South Carolina, and he was strictly city.

The idea of building a church obsessed him. He had no bricks, but he laid floor when he had the foundation topped with cement. He used common lumber for his subfloor and the best of his planks from the lumber pile for the surface. Some day, he thought, we'll maybe have money for linoleum or something. These planks won't take no polish.

He studied the church in Piedras every Sunday. There was not much to learn from it, but one feature of his own dream church baffled him. The brick chimney which had survived the fire stood high against the sky, higher than his projected roof. The fireplace and part of the stone mantel had survived, too, and that fireplace would be halfway down the right-hand side aisle of his church. He had never seen a church with a fireplace, nor one with a chimney; that is, not a big chimney that called attention to itself.

Old Mother will probably have someone lay a log and sit herself in that warm spot come cold weather, he thought.

He tried to take it lightly, but the chimney wasn't right. The church in Piedras had only a small hole near the altar side where a stovepipe would fit in winter, and it was a larger structure than his church. He could wreck the chimney, of course, but that old German, Gus Ritter, had built things to last. It would be difficult to get that chimney out of there with the equipment that he had. He did not like destroying something that had survived a disaster. That didn't seem right, either.

On a Tuesday in late July, the sad-faced man who ran the café in Piedras drove a beer truck up the road and parked behind the station wagon. He had another man with him, and neither man was friendly.

"The padre says to the people that you must have brick."

There were about five hundred adobe bricks in the truck, and the two men made only a pretense of helping to unload it. Homer unloaded five bricks to their one.

"It is of no use," the sad-faced man said, "but we have brought it."

"Thanks."

Homer did not waste time talking to people who did not want to talk to him. He understood dimly the attitude of these people. It was the attitude of Orville Livingston. They saw no future for the nuns, and they did not want to encourage what they did not approve. They did not want to be involved or called upon for a succession of services, either.

Brick gave Homer a new impetus. He puddled adobe to use as mortar, and he set his guide lines. He had done a little bricklaying but not much of it. This adobe brick was tricky. The bricks were uneven in size and crude. He had to socket his floor joists, and he built a temporary wooden bracing for his wall. He experimented and he worked slowly, but, with the brick, the thing that he was creating became a reality.

He was leading three lives; the life of work in North Fork, the communal life of eating and singing with the nuns, the highly personal life of building a church. Mother Maria Marthe was a grimly irritating figure with her eternal "Schmidt!" and her interference, but most of the time he could block her out of his mind. When she annoyed him to the point where he could not block her out, he had spells of dark brooding during which he wondered why he was working harder than he had ever worked in his life, and for no pay; why he was staying here on this sun-baked prairie with so much world yet to see. It was a dull wonder, requiring no answer from him. The answer was before him. He was building a church.

He ran out of brick, and, on a Monday night of full moon, life caught up with him.

It had been blazing, relentlessly hot for days, and there was no moisture. Everything that he touched was hot, and his clothing clung to his skin; yet this was not a sweating heat like the heat of the South, it was a frying heat that skilleted a man, making his skin itch. There was a restlessness in his blood and in his nerves, a vague unhappiness clouding his thought. He sat with his back against the left rear wheel of his station wagon and picked listlessly on his guitar. In the distance a coyote howled.

The cry was a high-pitched keening, a sound that climbed to a peak and broke. Homer lifted his head. The silver-white of the moon lay over everything like snow. He felt along the strings for that coyote cry. He knew that he wouldn't find it, but he understood it.

He had heard coyotes before, almost every night. He was sensitive to animal tongue. He knew when a coyote was seeking a woman of his own kind. This coyote was not seeking that. He was finding the night unbearable because it was so big and so bright. He was lonely in it, feeling small and lost.

The cry rose again, and another coyote answered. The other coyote was lonely, too, but the coyotes were not lonely for each other. It was bigger than that. Homer fingered the string on his guitar, then laid it down. He couldn't say what they were saying; he could only feel it. He straightened his body and stood, looking to the west where the coyotes were. There was nothing out there, nothing but wide, flat land and miserable little places like Piedras. He turned his body slowly so that he was facing east.

The mountains were a deep violet color slashed with silver. Everything was still. The hush had swallowed the last cry of the coyote and frightened him into joining the silence. Homer stretched his arms wide.

"Time to go," he said.

He returned his guitar to its case and climbed into the front seat of the station wagon. The noisy roar of the engine responding to the starter shattered the night, but there was an urgency in Homer Smith that ignored sound and silence now. He drove down the rutted road to the main highway, and as the car picked up speed, he relaxed under the wheel.

Over the pass, beyond the mountains, lay the big city of the state. It had been a long time, too long a time! He could not tolerate nights so vast as this; he needed a city where people huddled together and kept one another warm. He sang softly as he drove, and his car was a spinning reel on which the road wound up.

CHAPTER 5

The city was traffic-choked and noisy, and its lights were bright. The heat of summer rested on it like a cloud without rain, but a man could wet his throat with cold beer in the daytime and mingle with his own kind at night, eating and drinking whatever he found. He could listen to loud, rhythmic sound from juke boxes and dance with women and laugh at jokes. He could look into the eyes of women and see himself there, feeling pride in his manhood. He could stand big in his body with gray fog in his mind and hear his own blood running in his veins. He could go to the Baptist church on Sunday and sing hymns that his mother and his father sang before he was born, weeping a little because he had been a sinner all week. He could leave the church with all the sin washed out of him, feeling clean.

Homer Smith loved all of it, the standing tall and the falling down. Most of all, he liked the speech of men and women like himself, and the humor of them. A man heard no funny stories from people of another language who could not speak English well, and he could tell no funny stories. Humor belonged to the language that a man knew. He liked companionship and his room in the boardinghouse and the bathroom down the hall where he could bathe in a tub instead of showering himself from a bucket. He liked the hard feel of pavement under his feet, the odor of cooking food that floated out of strange windows and doorways, the children who were in constant motion around him. He liked the sirens of police, fire, and hospital vehicles, the bright exteriors of taverns and the twilight dimness within. This was the city.

The nuns and a town named Piedras and the Livingston Construction Company belonged to a hazy dream, as unreal as incidents in the life of another man. He never sat down deliberately to think about them, and such stray memories as floated in and out of his mind did not disturb him. His life in the army was gone, too, to be recalled only through conscious effort and not worth that. He lived in what he had, and with what he had, finding life good.

His money ran low in ten days and he went to work for a wrecking company. His first job was with a crew that was wrecking a car-barn no longer used by the tramway company. It was heavy, dirty, dangerous work, with much steel to handle and grime over everything. The next job, by comparison, was easy. A half-block of houses had to come down to create a blank which could be converted into a parking lot. They were small and old, low-rent houses, known in the South as row houses but in the West as terraces; houses all alike, built together wall to wall. Everything that could be stripped by hand was stripped, then a crane, with a big metal ball, knocked the walls down. The job took three days.

On the third day, Homer was sorting through the salvage, stacking the theoretically usable doors, window frames, and fixtures. There were sinks, basins, eight bathtubs. He piled the bathtubs, then stood looking at them, hearing in his mind a high, clear call as compelling as a coyote's cry to the moon.

"Those girls need a bathtub," he said.

It was the first time he had consciously thought about the nuns, and they were suddenly alive in his mind. He had seen them hauling buckets of water from the well in the evening, many buckets, and he had seen how crude everything was about the house. Gus Ritter, that old German farmer, had been a tight-fisted man. He didn't improve a place except where it paid him.

The foreman was a big man, almost as big as Homer was. Homer sought him out. "How's to buy one of those tubs?" he said.

"Sure enough? You want your own personal tub, boy?"

"How much?"

"You could steal it and nobody would care. That kind is no good. You got some way to haul it?"

"Yes."

"Okay. Give me two bucks to keep it honest."

Homer gave him the two dollars. He saw the bills go into the foreman's pocket, and he knew that the company would never see those bills. That didn't matter. He'd bought what he wanted at the price asked. The bathtubs were high and narrow, standing on dragon feet. He picked the best one of them. It wouldn't go into the station wagon, so he upended it on the top, the feet pointing skyward, lashing it in place with rope. The bathroom windows had been removed intact, small windows of red, yellow, and green glass in diamond pattern. He bought two of them from the foreman for a dollar each, and with the purchase a vision returned, haunting him.

He drew his pay at the end of the day and headed for the hills.

It was afternoon on Friday when he drove into familiar territory. He stayed on the highway when it looped around North Fork. The crops were prospering under a bright sun; potatoes, wheat, barley, lettuce, cauliflower. The hazy blue mountains were on his right. Within a few miles the fields on his left became bleak, sage and greasewood sprinkled with a few indomitable flowers of blue, yellow, and pink. A hawk floated low, gliding on motionless wings, and a rabbit scurried across the road.

Homer drove over a small bridge, and the stream below it was a thin trickle. He turned to his right on a rutted road, and the nuns were in the field, working on their variegated crop, fighting for their growing stuff against weeds and voracious insects and the parched dryness of the soil. It was good to see them again, but he did not slow down nor look in their direction. He was not certain of his reception, and he was willing to defer it. He parked in his accustomed spot and sat looking at his unfinished church.

Nobody had disturbed it, and no one had brought bricks with which to complete it. It had a desolate look; one wall built as high as a man's shoulder, the others low; the chimney pointing upward like the skeleton finger of a giant. There was an untidy scattering of rubble on the ground. Homer got the scoop shovel from the barn toolroom and started shoveling. He cleared the area and dug a hole with his spade into which he tumbled the debris.

The bell rang, and he straightened. Old Mother never rang the bell for the nuns, because they knew when to come for meals. That bell was for him. He laid the spade aside, carried his bucket to the well, washed his hands, and walked into the house. They were waiting for him, standing in their places at the table, just as if he had never been away. He bowed his head while they prayed. When he looked up after the "Amen," they were all looking at him happily. Nobody said anything, but they were glad that he was home. A man felt a thing like that. Nobody had to say anything.

There was an omelet and coarse bread, but there were vegetables, too, fresh vegetables. The farm was starting to pay off.

They resumed the English lessons after supper, and Homer's ear was sharper because he had been away. They were doing better with the language, but he could hear the soft echo of South Carolina coming back to him when they spoke.

Better than a phonograph accent, he thought. Used to be you could hear the turntable going around when they spoke anything in English.

He did not unveil the bathtub until after breakfast the next day. He drove the station wagon close to the house and eased the tub down from the top. He called Old Mother out to see it. Sisters

Gertrud and Albertine came with her. He made an awkward gesture toward the tub, not naming it. After all, these were girls who built a high fence around the privy.

"A present," he said.

He was facing Mother Maria Marthe. Her eyes squinted as though she found the sun too bright. *"Das ist gut,* Schmidt," she said, *"Das ist gut."*

She said something in German to the two nuns and went hurriedly into the house. Homer did not have to explain to her that he needed a place in which to install the tub. When she returned, she led him to a pantry off the kitchen. This was the deepest penetration that he had made into the nuns' quarters. He had not even known that the pantry existed.

"Here," she said.

It was a small room, but that was her problem. He hauled the tub in and set it on its feet. He had taken some pipe as a necessary accessory to the tub, and he had bought a secondhand blowtorch in the city. He cut a hole in the floor where it met the wall and angled the pipe through it, attaching it to the drain pipe of the tub and soldering it in place. He put the rubber plug in the drain and the tub was in business. He dug a trench outside the house to run the water off. They would still have to haul water, because he couldn't give them a pump and a plumbing job, but this was something. He felt good about it.

He still lacked bricks, so he settled down to carpentry, making pews and kneelers like those in the church at Piedras. He lacked a lathe, and he had to work with what he had, so the pews were mere benches without polish or curlicues, but he built them solidly and the day passed swiftly.

"Old Mother's got to pray me some bricks," he said softly. "If she doesn't, she's wasting my time."

He sat at the counter in Piedras while the nuns were at Mass on Sunday. He ordered his big breakfast. The sad-looking man broke eggs into the skillet and surrounded them with bacon.

"It is not reasonable that you have come back," he said.

"It makes sense to me."

"It could not. Everybody says that you are gone and this is how it had to be. They laugh at the nuns because the nuns say that you will return."

Homer's body stiffened. "I don't want to see nobody laughing at those nuns."

"This they know." The man cast a wary eye at his big customer. "Now nobody will laugh."

"No. That's right. Nobody's going to laugh."

"The padre says to them that you will return."

"How did he know?"

"That Mother Superior, she told him."

"How did she know?"

"She knew."

Homer drank his coffee, savoring the fine aroma of bacon. He had not known, himself, that he would ever come back. He had not given it a thought. How could Old Mother know? He had a dark suspicion that it had something to do with her praying. She had never got it out of her head that God had given Homer Smith to her. If that was a fact, she'd be certain that he couldn't wander off. He belonged to her. That was something Homer had never liked. The idea of belonging to someone stirred a racial antagonism in him. No Negro was ever going to belong to anybody again. Not ever! He was free.

The breakfast was good and he ate it. The idea of freedom moved around in his mind while he ate, not moving in a worrisome way, merely in a curious manner. It was a strange thing, freedom. He had been free in the city. Nobody told him to do anything. He kept his own hours, ate when he wanted to eat, slept as late as he liked. Here, Old Mother was always ringing bells or yelling "Schmidt" or telling him to do something. She exploded inside of herself if he didn't get up at bird-waking time. She was so certain about owning him that she never said "thank you" for anything. Not one time had she said "thank you."

"The padre, that Father Gomez, he will be very happy that you have come back to those nuns," the man behind the counter said.

"Why should he be happy?"

"He will say that it proves a religious thing."

"What religious thing?"

"Faith. It is a word for what is unreasonable. If a man believes in an unreasonable thing, that is faith. It is not reasonable that you should come back to this place and work for nothing. Nobody believed it. You have come back."

Homer ate contentedly. That was an interesting idea. He liked interesting ideas. Faith was what Old Mother had. She believed that he would come back. She believed that he could build a church all by himself, maybe even without bricks. That wasn't a reasonable idea. He hadn't ever built anything all by himself. He was free, building that church, just as free as he was in the city, even more so. There wasn't anybody else to build it. He didn't need any wages. He had a full life. He had many things. He was free like the lilies of the field. It was a strange thing. As this Spanish man said, it wasn't reasonable.

"Me," the man said. "I have no faith. I do not believe in the Church. I do not go to Mass."

Homer looked at him with interest. "I don't know what that does for you," he said. "All those other Spanish are in there sitting on those benches or doing whatever they do at Mass, not working. You're over here, working, fixing my breakfast."

"It is reasonable. You pay me. I make money."

"I never saw another customer in here during the Mass. Unless you get a hungry Baptist in your place, you don't make money."

"So, I sit here and do nothing. It is a reasonable thing. No priest tells me what to do."

The first stragglers were coming out of the church. Homer rose and paid for his breakfast. The man behind the counter baffled him in a mild way, but he was not interested in him. The man could stay just as he was, where he was, being reasonable. If the man ever got faith, Sunday was going to be a hungry day in Piedras.

The nuns, as usual, were the last ones out of the church. Homer amused himself, looking big and dangerous beside the station wagon, frowning at all of these people who had laughed at his nuns, seeing them turn quickly away from him. He did not frown at Father Gomez, who came out with Old Mother. The priest was smiling and he extended his hand.

"It is nice to see you again," he said. "I believe that you will have a surprise or two this week, Señor Smith." He turned his head. "Don't you agree, Mother Superior?"

Mother Maria Marthe either understood, or sensed, what he was saying. She nodded, and amazingly, for the first time since Homer Smith had known her, she smiled.

"Ja," she said.

The surprise was not long in developing. Early Monday morning, vehicles of various types and ages arrived at Homer's working area. Each vehicle brought adobe bricks, and each driver had approximately the same speech.

"I am happy to bring these bricks for the chapel. I have had in my heart a doubt of you, and I am sorry."

After his astonishment at the first two versions of the speech, Homer adjusted cheerfully to the situation. Old Padre must have preached hell to these Spanish, he thought. Wish I could have heard it.

The bricks piled up, and he went to work again. The day climaxed with the beer truck and the largest donation of the day, five hundred bricks. The driver, a wide-shouldered, husky, embarrassed man, made the set approach. His companion, the sad man from the café, spat at a grasshopper, missing him.

"I have come only to see this thing," he said. "I have brought no bricks."

Homer shrugged. It made no difference. This man probably did not believe in bricks. It was not reasonable that all of these bricks should be here, so they were not. The broad-shouldered man laughed. Now that he had made his speech, he was no longer embarrassed. He slapped his companion on the back and walked around the partially built chapel, shaking his head.

"You do not know well the adobe," he said.

"I'm learning."

"You should have help."

Homer resented him, and he was glad to see him go. A shadow had fallen on his church, which everyone else called a chapel. Now that these Spanish were bringing bricks, they were going to tell him what to do and how to do it. That could not be. He had to finish it as he had begun it. It was his church. For the first time since he started work on the project, he worried. Mother Maria Marthe added to his worry. She walked around his bricks, making clucking noises like a hen that has just laid something, owning his bricks as she owned him, acting like she'd prayed them into existence.

If I hadn't come back, there wouldn't be no bricks, he thought sullenly.

Old Mother was oblivious. "Schmidt," she said. "Dese people

vill help you. All iss vell."

"I don't want any help."

His mind was set on that point, and when helpful neighbors came to watch and make suggestions, he was curtly hostile. They brought no brick on Tuesday or on Wednesday, but men with time to spare from whatever they did normally came in person. Some of them wanted to lay bricks, and all of them were mouth experts, telling him what he should do. They were very friendly about it. When he wouldn't let them work, they sat and smoked, watching him and sometimes shaking their heads, making remarks to one another in Spanish.

They ain't commenting on how good I'm doing neither, he thought.

Thursday bothered him. He did not know whether he would still have a job with Livingston Construction Company, and he was reluctant to leave his own job unguarded. There wasn't any sense in telling Old Mother to chase these Spanish, because she liked the idea of having them do some of the work. She didn't understand how he felt about it. All that she cared about was getting her chapel-church built. She didn't care who built it.

Homer made two signs and placed them conspicuously on his walls. One read KEEP OFF! and the other was equally uncompromising: DON'T TOUCH ANYTHING! He drove off then to North Fork.

Orville Livingston's eyebrows moved upward and his jaw moved forward when he saw Homer Smith. "Where have you been?" he said.

"Vacation."

"Yeah? Why did you come back?"

"Had to finish my church."

"Are you going to finish it?"

"I'll finish it. Right now I'm gaining on my brick."

"Humph. Well, they ought to read you out of the Baptist Church, but I'm glad you're back. I'm short-handed."

Homer went out on a road gang, and Livingston had not exaggerated his short-handedness. The work was heavy. Thursday night Homer checked his church, and no one had disturbed it. Friday night, with his two days' pay, he loaded up on groceries, enjoying the adventure of pushing his cart through the supermarket again and selecting what he wanted. When he reached home and presented his sacks to Old Mother, she shook her head at him.

"*Nein*, Schmidt," she said. "No more."

She showed him vegetables in jars which the nuns had canned for winter eating, fresh vegetables ready for the table, an entire new generation of chickens in the fowl run ready to be thinned out. He had been blind to all that. He experienced an odd twinge of disappointment.

"That's fine," he said. "That's just fine."

He had never been vitally interested in what the nuns did, or how. He knew that they worked hard, and that was all that he cared to know. Now they had something to show for their work. They didn't need his groceries any more. He walked across the clearing to his church. The Spanish had been interfering in his absence. They had built a big mortar box with some of his old lumber. He sat and smoked, taking counsel with himself.

There was a way of spreading adobe on the outside of the brick and smoothing it out, a little like stone. He had studied the church in Piedras, and he believed that he knew how it was done, but he had never seen anyone do it. These Spanish planned to do it for his church. That's why they built that box to do their puddling. He resented any and every hand laid on that church other than his own, but he told himself that this was a practical matter and that the Spanish knew how to do this work.

"No sense in me getting sore," he said.

Some intangible thing, some joyful spirit, had gone out of his life, and he tried to call it back. He sang as he laid brick on Saturday, and he was friendly to the Spanish people who came out to watch him, so friendly that he surprised them. They got in his way, trying to help him. No one attempted to mix adobe clay; everyone wanted to help lay brick.

"No!" he said. "I got my ideas. I got to do it my way."

"*Como?* There is only one way to lay the brick."

They did not understand his attitude, and he had taken a positive stand at an awkward time. He had reached the point in one wall that called for the installation of a window, high up and placed, as in the church at Piedras, so that light would fall on the altar. He had the window intact in its frame, a small window that need never be opened. It was not easy to set it properly in place with the bricks holding it firm. He had measured his space carefully, but he had difficulty when he tried to set it. A short, thin man named Juan Archuleta joined him on his working platform.

"It is a matter of aggravation, this," Juan Archuleta said. "I have done it."

He broke a brick deftly, scarcely seeming to glance at it, but breaking it to the exact size that he wanted. He wedged pieces into place, and he spread his adobe mortar. He knew how to set a window, and Homer grudgingly admitted it. The little man took no credit for what he did and made no point of it. He talked as he worked.

"I like how you sing," he said.

"A man works better singing."

"*Si*. Singing is good. You like guitar?"

"Got one of my own."

"*Bueno*. You come to my house tonight for the dinner. Drink a little, sing a little, play the guitar."

"Sounds good."

A man couldn't stay hostile to another man who helped him work and who invited him to dinner. "I have worked much with adobe," Juan Archuleta said. "It is the stuff of this country."

He helped Homer with the twin window on the other wall, and he backed him up in telling the other men that two workers on the bricks were enough. Without making a point of it, he worked over a couple of trouble spots where the wall met the chimney and enclosed the fireplace.

"You work smooth," Homer said grudgingly.

"A little work. *De nada*.[1] You have worked much. I could not do so much. I am not a strong man."

Homer shook his head. This Juan Archuleta was easy to like, a man with honey on his tongue. He met Juan's wife and his children and his neighbors. He drank white liquor that he could feel in the roots of his hair like electricity, and he sang songs for his new friends. He ate food that was hotter than the liquor but strangely satisfying, and he listened to songs that he had never heard before in a language that he did not understand.

---

[1] *De nada*: It's nothing.

> "Adios, Mariquita linda,
> Yo me voy
> Porque tú ya no me quieres
> Como yo to quiero a ti." [2]

He admired it. It had sadness but no misery. He could pick it up on the guitar and play along with it, but he could not sing it as he sang Latin with the nuns. This language did not break down to sounds that he could carry in his head or shape with his mouth. On the faster, more cheerful music, it was easier. He could make a lot of *ya-ya-ya* sounds that were almost Spanish, even if they didn't mean anything.

Homer did not know when the party ended; it tapered off slowly. He rode home in Juan Archuleta's old car, singing. There was a silvery whiteness over the land, a chill in the air. He chuckled foolishly as he stood beside his station wagon watching Juan drive away. A dozen impressions of the evening whirled around in his mind, but the one that rose to the surface was inconsequential.

"Those Spanish have a way with beans," he said. "Make them taste like food."

CHAPTER 6

A Livingston Construction Company truck delivered a thousand bricks on Monday morning. There was no message, no explanation offered. There did not have to be.

"Old man lost a bet with himself," Homer said. "He bet I wouldn't ever do this work. He bet I would be long gone by now."

The new bricks were far superior to any that Homer had laid; regular brickyard adobe, uniform in size and quality. It did not seem right to lay them on the upper levels with the inferior bricks below. The adobe coating, of course, would hide them, but Homer considered tearing out the front of the church and using the new bricks there. He didn't mind the work, but he decided against it. The people who had brought him bricks when he needed them had a right to have their bricks in the church where they were put.

---

[2] *Adios . . . ti:* Goodbye, my pretty butterfly/I'm leaving/Because you no longer love me/The way that I love you.

He had more bricks now than he had hoped for, and he decided to build his church higher. That would change the proportions, but it would be more impressive. He had a driving urgency in him, a sense of time that he had not had earlier. Time had not mattered; now it did. He did not try to reason why.

The helpful Spanish brought him logs for his roof beams, and they were more of a problem than ever. They were his friends, and they were all over the place. Whatever they should be doing to make a living was obviously being neglected, but his blunt query — "Shouldn't you be doing something else somewhere?" — brought only shrugs and grins. They had developed a religious fervor, and the finishing of the church had become important to them. They refused to accept the idea that it was his church.

"Look!" he said. "You fellows build an altar. I don't know about such things. If this chapel-church has got to have statues in it, you fix it about them. You let these bricks alone!"

They built an altar within his church while he was laying the long beams across the walls with two feet of log projecting on either side, as in the Piedras church. He laid board across the beams, and at this point Juan Archuleta insisted upon helping him again. Together they coated the boards thickly with adobe mud. Juan helped, too, with the adobe plaster on the inside walls of the church itself.

The approach of Thursday posed a problem. If he went to work for Orville Livingston, there would be no one to control the Spanish. There was no longer any purpose in his work for Livingston. The nuns didn't need groceries any more.

The man sent you all those bricks, his conscience said.

"No. He didn't. He didn't send me anything. I gave him work for wages. He sent those bricks to Old Mother. Ashamed of how he said 'no' to her."

With that settled, he continued to work on the church. On Thursday afternoon, Father Gomez came out to see it. He walked all around it, making pleasant comments, then went to see Mother Maria Marthe. She came to where Homer was working after the priest left. He was whitewashing the interior and he did not want to stop.

"Schmidt," she said. "I talk to you."

"*Ja*," he said.

It was his way of kidding her when she annoyed him. She sat on one of his pews and motioned for him to sit beside her.

"It is finish — nearly — der shapel," she said.

"Almost."

She nodded, her eyes momentarily closed. "*Ja. Gott ist gutt*, Schmidt. Sunday, Father Gomez say Mass in dis shapel, der first Mass. You vill sit dere. Der front pew."

She pointed to the space before the altar where the pew had not yet been placed. She seemed very happy, very proud. She was, Homer knew, trying to do something for him, give him an honor; but his Baptist soul recoiled at the thought of sitting up front, in the first pew or any pew, at a Catholic Mass. He looked at her and he couldn't take her happiness away or do anything to hurt her.

"That will be nice," he said.

He resumed his work with even greater urgency when she left him, understanding more clearly the sense of time that drove him. He joked with the Spanish, he ate with the nuns, he continued the English lessons after supper; but only half of him did these things. The other half listened always to the ticking of an invisible clock.

On Saturday, not even the Spanish could find much to do. Homer used them in the clean-up, the removal and stacking of lumber that had been used for scaffolding, the break-up of mortar boxes, the leveling of ground. This was not very interesting, so by early afternoon the Spanish had all left. Homer finished the policing himself, cleaning and leveling and removing trash.

He sat, then, smoking a cigarette and looking at his church. He had done it. Old Mother had said; "Build me a chapel-church." He had built it. He had not known how to do it, he had had no plans, adobe was a new stuff in his life — but there it was! His church stood strong with blue sky behind it, a church with angles that would be stiff and harsh in wood, soft in adobe. It had a pediment that he had made in place above the door, with a crucifix at the peak. He rose and walked inside, glad to be alone.

The sunlight flowed through two windows that had come out of row-house bathrooms. The light took color from the diamonds in the panes and spilled that color on the whitewashed walls. The church in Piedras lacked this cathedral touch; it had only plain glass. His pews were in place, and he walked down the aisle. He stood with his back to the altar and looked at the places where the five nuns would sit. His throat felt tight, and he had no thoughts at all. He walked hurriedly down the aisle and out into the sunlight.

A flight of birds flew overhead. They were flying high and heading south. It was September, and his spring was gone, and his summer. Another flight of birds passed over, and he watched them out of sight.

Those birds got a message, he thought. A man ought to have as much sense as a bird.

The bell summoned him to supper, and Old Mother was feeling festive tonight. She had put a couple of her chickens in the pot, and there was chicken stew. All the nuns seemed excited and happy. They had a chapel-church of their own and a priest coming to say Mass in the morning. It didn't seem like a night for English lessons. Homer brought his guitar in and played for them. He played some of the Spanish music that he remembered, not trying to sing it.

"*Adios, Mariquita linda.* . . ."

He played some of his own music, too, and he sang that: "Water Boy" and "Shenandoah" and "Deep River." He started playing the Latin music, and Sister Albertine sang, bringing the others in. He sang Latin sounds with them, and it was a happy evening, better than the night with the Spanish.

He sat for a long time beside the station wagon after the nuns had retired. He told himself that he should have said goodbye to Old Mother, but it wasn't his way to put his feelings into words. Old Mother looked into a man's heart, and she had an understanding mind. When he was gone, nobody would have to tell her anything; she would just know.

He'd like to say a word to Sister Albertine, too. He'd like to tell her that he liked her singing. She wasn't so strong as the other nuns, Sister Albertine, but she did delicate things that a man liked. She was the one who drew the picture of the wooden church that he couldn't ever build. She had made pictures of him, too. Somebody sent her a package from Germany with pencils and brushes and paper and paint. He hadn't seen her paint anything, but she'd made a lot of pictures of him with her pencils when he was singing or talking English at the nuns or working on the church. Better than a camera, she was. He had one of the pictures of himself that she gave him. It was signed with her name. Saying goodbye to her wasn't something that he could do, either.

He looked long at his church, then he went inside. It was filled with silent shadow except where starlight filtered through his small windows. He walked down the aisle, and he knew that there was something that he wanted to say to God about this church. He knelt in one of the pews, and he lifted up his heart, but no words came. It wasn't something that he could talk about, not even to God.

A rabbit bounded across the clearing when he came out of the church. It vanished, and no other night creature moved or spoke. It was deep night, a late hour, and that was the best time.

The starter awakened the engine of the station wagon to noisy life, and a touch of the switch sent a flow of light down the rutted road. Homer Smith drove that road to the highway, and he knew that he was never coming back. A man couldn't roam forever, nor pleasure himself in strange cities indefinitely. There was a settling-down time at the end of all that. The road was lonely and he sang softly to himself as he drove.

CHAPTER 7

The legend of Homer Smith came into being within twenty-four hours of his disappearance from the scene of his labors. Father Gomez spoke feelingly of him, and a Methodist named Orville Livingston came to see the chapel that he had not believed would be built. The newspaper in North Fork ran a story with a photograph of the chapel. Because that chapel is unique in appearance and history, a reporter from the state's largest newspaper made the trip to Piedras and interviewed many people who were eager to talk of its building. Every Spanish-American in the region claimed to have known Homer Smith well, and they are a people who like tales of saints who walk the earth and of angels that take men unaware.

A man named Juan Archuleta swore that he had laid bricks beside Homer Smith and that often the bricks flew into place with no one touching them. Another man named José Gonzalez, who owned a café in Piedras, claimed that he was the intimate and the closest confidant of the chapel builder, that often a white light shone around the man and that on one occasion Homer Smith said to him: "God sent me to this place to build a church and to make these nuns famous. When I have done this thing you will see me no more."

Mother Maria Marthe and her nuns were reticent, reluctant to speak for publication about Homer Smith. That very reticence drew them into the legend and created curiosity. People wrote to them and sent them money, soliciting prayers. Orville Livingston, a Rotarian, was invited to speak to the Capital City Rotarians about his experience with Homer Smith and the nuns after he had spoken to his own group in North Fork. Publicity created more publicity, and tourists journeyed to a section of the state which they had never seen because they were told that an unusual experience awaited them, that here was a modern shrine.

No one can explain these things. The aim of Mother Maria Marthe was publicized with the rest of the story, and substantial sums of money were contributed to help her realize her aim.

Today there are several fine buildings and four new nuns under the direction of the aging Mother Superior. The buildings have electricity and modern plumbing. There are boys from broken homes, and boys who have been in difficulty with the law, studying in the classrooms, working in the fields and in the workshops. They have made their school a noted institution by their loyalty to it. The school is growing in public esteem and in facilities for service to Spanish-American young people, who are easy to neglect because they are difficult to understand.

The chapel occupies the key position, with the other buildings grouped in an arc around it. It is a favorite subject of photographers, and one may buy postcards of its exterior and interior in Piedras or in North Fork. Three prominent artists have painted it, and one of the paintings hangs in the State Museum of Art. There is no chapel like it anywhere. It is of conventional adobe, but some trick of proportion makes it memorable. There is strength in its lines and an indefinable grace. A voluble and oft-quoted sculptress has described it as "a true primitive," whatever that means. The chimney, of course, is its really distinctive feature; a brick chimney designed for a two-story house, rising above the flat-roofed adobe chapel like a steeple.

There is a fireplace halfway down the right-hand aisle of the chapel. It is a tradition with the nuns to burn logs in the fireplace on Sundays during the cold weather. The hardier tourists of the fall and winter season consider this a charming touch.

Mother Maria Marthe has grown older. Her English has improved, but she still struggles with the "w" and the "th," although the struggle is scarcely apparent in the speeches that she has memorized. She is at her best when she performs her favorite task, the guiding of tourists through the buildings, climaxing always with the chapel. There is, as in the speech of several other nuns, a touch of the South in her voice, a soft slurring, an odd emphasis on certain syllables.

She directs attention first to the oil painting on the wall in the rear of the chapel. It is the painting of a powerful Negro with large features and widely spaced eyes. His head is thrown back in an attitude of exhortation, or, perhaps, of song, his lips parted to reveal two perfect rows of teeth. There is a nimbus [1] of light around the man's head.

"This is the chapel of Saint Benedict the Moor," Mother Maria Marthe says. "That painting of the saint is the work of Sister Albertine. The model was a man named Schmidt, who came to us under the direction of God. He built this chapel with his two hands under great difficulties. It is all from him."

She pauses then and her voice drops. "He was not of our faith, nor of our skin," she says, "but he was a man of greatness, of an utter devotion."

---

[1] *nimbus:* halo.

The deeds of Theseus ("How Much Is True?," pp. 101–06), Abraham Lincoln, and Homer Smith in The Lilies of the Field *became the material from which myths and legends sprang. Nathan Hale's contribution to the American Revolution was not a great one. It was his spirit rather than his deeds which captured the imagination of a young nation. Nancy Hale writes that the War of Independence "seemed to me almost a family affair; when I was six, we were asked one day at school to tell what our ancestors had done in the American Revolution, and I reported with pride 'I had a great-uncle who was hanged.' "*

Nathan Hale

NANCY HALE

"The boy was only a couple of years out of New Haven [1] when he joined up. He'd hardly got started. He'd been teaching school, you know, up at East Haddam and then down in New London, and it looked as if he was shaping up into a fine teacher. He'd made a lot of friends everywhere he went, and the girls always liked him. They say he was a good-looking boy.

"Then the war came. Things had looked bad to us Americans for a long time, but when the first gun was fired on that April day [2] it seemed to light a sudden strong fire in everyone's heart. It seemed to call out — 'Americans!' The boy's brothers, John and Joseph, volunteered first off. It was a patriotic family — the father'd been a deputy in the old Connecticut Assembly. The boy himself had signed up with the school for a year. He wasn't the kind to let people down, but he did write and ask to be released from his contract two weeks early. He joined up in July, as a lieutenant in Webb's Seventh Connecticut.

"Well, you know how things went after that. The boy was in

---

[1] *New Haven:* where Yale University is located. Hale had been an outstanding scholar and athlete.
[2] *April day:* April 19, 1775, in Lexington, Massachusetts.

605

camp up near Boston all winter. It wasn't an exciting siege. But there was a lot to do getting the men to re-enlist. Most of their terms of enlistment ran out in December. The General was worried about it. Our boy offered the men in his company his own pay for a month if they'd stay that much longer. Anyway the siege was maintained.

"He got a leave in the winter and went home. Maybe that was when he got engaged. Alicia Adams. A lovely girl; they would have made a handsome couple. When spring came the enemy evacuated Boston and our army went down to New York, where real trouble was threatening. The boy'd been made a captain by that time. He was twenty-one years old.

"Our Long Island campaign was just this side of disastrous. Morale was none too good, afterwards. I don't suppose the General was in a worse spot in the whole war than he was for those three weeks right after the Battle of Long Island. There we lay, facing the enemy across the East River, and no way of knowing what they had up their sleeve. Surprise was what we feared. The answer to that was companies of rangers, to scout around and find out what was up. Knowlton's Rangers was organized, and our boy switched over to it. He wanted action, you see.

"But the rangers weren't enough. The General wanted to know two things: when the enemy was planning to attack, and where. Nobody could tell him. The General let it be known that he'd welcome volunteers to spy.

"Now, people didn't take kindly to the word *spy* around these parts. It didn't mean excitement or glamour or any of those things. It meant something degrading. It was a job they gave to bums, who didn't care. But the General said he wanted a spy. Well, our boy volunteered. His friends tried to talk him out of it. They spoke of the indignity; they also told him he'd make a terrible spy — frank, open boy like him.

"But his idea was, the job was necessary. That was the great thing. Its being necessary seemed to him to make it honorable. He was sent through the enemy lines dressed up like a Dutch schoolmaster.

"He didn't make such a bad spy, after all. He got what he went after, and hid the drawings in his shoes. He was on his way back, crossing their lines, when they caught him. They found the information on him. He admitted he was over there to spy. You know what a spy gets. They hanged him in the morning. He wrote some letters to the family at home, but they were destroyed before his eyes, they say. But in his last moment they let him say what he wanted to. And later one of their officers told one of our officers what he'd said.

"There he was, with the noose around his neck. He hadn't got much done. He'd got caught on the first big job of his life. He wasn't going to marry Alicia Adams, nor to have any children, nor to do any more teaching, nor to finish fighting this war. He stood there in the morning air, and he spoke and said who he was, his commission and all. And then he added, 'I only regret that I have but one life to lose for my country.'"

You could tell the story like that, simply, because it is a simple story, and when you'd finished you'd have told about all there is to tell about Nathan Hale. There isn't even a contemporary picture of him. Most of the friends to whom he wrote didn't keep his letters. He was just a young American who'd gone to war, who'd lived for twenty-one ordinary enough years before — in the day's work — he died for his country.

One of his brothers, Enoch, was my great-great-grandfather.

When I was a child there was a small bronze statue, about four feet high, that stood in the corner of the living room at home. It was just about my height, but it wasn't another child. It was a young man, with his wrists tied behind him and his ankles bound. I passed it several times a day, every day of my childhood. Sometimes I used to touch the bronze face. It was a small-scale replica of the Nathan Hale statue at Yale.

I must have been told his story, because I always knew it. But my father never went on about it, if you know what I mean. There his story was, for what it might mean to you. Some of my other ancestors were the kind of characters that have a whole legend of anecdotes surrounding them, pointed, stirring, or uproarious. But the young man with his hands bound had died at twenty-one, a patriot, as stark and all alone and anecdoteless as young men of twenty-one must be.

Once I was set upon the knees of an old gentleman whose grandmother had been Alicia Adams. She had married and had children, and lived to be eighty-eight, a pretty, sparkling old lady. And when she died she said, "Where is Nathan?" But about the young man himself there were no family reminiscences, no odd little jokes, no tales beyond the short, plain story of his life and death. He had had no time to do anything memorable but die.

Nevertheless.... It was my job as a child to fill the kitchen scuttle with coal from the cellar. I was not a brave child, and to me the long corners of the cellar seemed menacing and full of queer, moving shadows — wolves? robbers? I cannot remember when I first started taking the thought of Nathan Hale down cellar with me, for a shield and a buckler.[3] I thought, "If he could be hanged, I can go down cellar." The thing was, he was no impossible hero; he was a member of the family, and he was young too. He was a hero you could take along with you into the cellar of a New England farmhouse. You felt he'd be likely to say, "Aren't any wolves or robbers back there that I can see."

Well, I am grown up now, and I know very little more about Nathan Hale than I did then. There are, of course, a mass of details about his short life. A devoted scholar named George Dudley Seymour has spent years in collecting all that can be collected about him. There's a wartime diary. They know his friends. He played football and checkers at camp. He drank wine at Brown's Tavern and cider at Stone's. But when you add all these little things, you only affirm the peculiar simplicity of the story.

Hale is a symbol of all the young American men who fight and who die for us. Partly he is a symbol because he was the first of our heroes in the first of our own wars. He was the first to show the world what Americans are made of. The reason they destroyed his letters home at the time of his death was, they said, so that "the rebels should not know they have a man who can die so firmly." He showed them.

He is no Washington or Jefferson, although he ranks with the heroes. Washington was a great general and Jefferson was a genius. All of our nation's heroes are great men who are great by their minds and by their deeds and by their careers. All except Hale. His special gift to his country, and to us who love that country, was the manner of his death.

He is the young American. He is the patron of all the young

---

[3] *buckler:* small, round shield.

Americans who have grown up as he did in quiet, self-respecting families; who have gone to college and done well, and had fun too; who have started out along their life's careers, well spoke of, promising; and then broken off to join their country's forces in time of war without an instant's hesitation, knowing what must be done and who must do it. He was no different than they. He was an American boy. Everything that can be said of them can be said of him. In the letters of his friends written about him after his death, certain words keep cropping up. They sound oddly familiar. "Promising . . . patriotic . . . generous . . . modest . . . high-spirited . . . devoted . . ." His friends fitted the words to Hale. They fit Americans.

Nothing was more American in Hale than his taking on the duties that led to his death. It was a dirty job, spying. Nobody wanted it. He took it. There's something about that, taking on a dirty job that's got to be done, that rings a bell. It's an American custom of American heroes. He wasn't a remarkably articulate boy. His letters are nothing special. He just jotted things in his diary. But he became the spokesman for young American fighting men who have to die for their country. He chanced to say the thing they think; the thing they mean, when there's not even a split second to think. He stood there at Turtle Bay on Manhattan Island. Don't think he declaimed. He wasn't that kind. He had those few moments, and he was thinking about all the different things that were ending for him. He said, and I think it was more like a remark:

"I only regret . . ."

Enemy Territory

WILLIAM MELVIN KELLEY

I peered over a rotting tree stump and saw him moving, without a helmet, in the bushes. I got his forehead in my sights, squeezed the trigger, and imagined I saw the bullet puncture his head and blood trickle out. "I got you, Jerome. I got you!"

"Awh, you did not."

"I got you; you're dead."

I must have sounded very definite, because he compromised. "You only wounded me."

"Tommy? Tommy! Come here." Her voice came from high above me.

I scrambled to my knees. "What, Ma?" She was on the porch of our house, next to the vacant lot where we were playing.

"Come here a minute, dear. I want you to do something for me." She was wearing a yellow dress. The porch was red brick.

I hopped up and ran to the foot of our steps. She came to the top. "Mister Bixby left his hat."

As I had waited in ambush for Jerome, I had seen Mister Bixby climb and, an hour later, chug down the steps. He was one of my father's poker-playing friends. It was only after she mentioned it that I remembered Mister Bixby had been wearing, when he arrived, a white, wide-brimmed panama hat with a black band.

Entering my parents' room on the second floor, I saw it on their bed. My mother picked it up. "Walk it around to his house. Now walk, I say. Don't run, because you'll probably drop it and ruin it." It was so white a speck of dirt would have shone like a black star in a white sky. "So walk! Let me see your hands."

I extended them palms up and she immediately sent me to the bathroom to wash. Then she gave me the hat. I did not really grip it; rather, with my finger in the crown, I balanced it, as if about to twirl it.

When I stepped onto the porch again, I saw them playing on their corner — Valentine's Gang. Well, in this day of street gangs organized like armies, I cannot rightly call Joey Valentine, who was eight, and his acquaintances, who ranged in age from five to seven, a gang. It was simply that they lived on the next block, and since my friends and I were just at the age when we were allowed to cross the street, but were not yet used to this new freedom, we still stood on opposite sides of the asphalt strip that divided us and called each other names. It was not until I got onto the porch that I realized, with a sense of dread that only a six-year-old can conjure up, that Mister Bixby lived one block beyond Valentine's Territory.

Still, with faith that the adult nature of my mission would give me unmolested passage, I approached the corner, which was guarded by a red fire alarm box, looked both ways for the cars that seldom came, and, swallowing, began to cross over.

They were playing with toy soldiers and tin tanks in the border of dry yellow dirt that separated the flagstones from the gutter. I was in the middle of the street when they first realized I was invading; they were shocked. At the time, I can remember thinking they must have been awed that I should have the unequaled courage to cross into their territory. But looking back, I realize it probably had little to do with me. It was the hat, a white panama hat. A more natural target for abuse has never existed.

I was two steps from the curb when Joey Valentine moved into my path. "Hey, what you got?"

Since he was obviously asking the question to show off, I bit my lips and did not answer. I saw myself as one of my radio heroes resisting Japanese interrogation. I was aloof. However, the white panama hat was not at all aloof. Before I knew it, Joey Valentine reached out a mud-caked hand and knocked the hat off my finger to a resounding chorus of cheers and laughter.

I scooped up the hat before any of them, retreated at a run across the street, and stopped beside the red alarm box. Wanting to save some small amount of my dignity, I screamed at them: "I'll get you guys! I'll get you. I'm not really an American. I'm an African and Africans are friends of the Japs and I'll get them to *bomb your house!*"

But even as I ranted at them, I could see I was doing so in vain. Across the way, Valentine's Gang lounged with the calm of movie Marines listening to Japanese propaganda on the radio. I turned toward my house, inspecting the hat for smudges. There were none; it was as blinding white as ever. Already I felt tears inching down my cheeks.

Not until I was halfway up the porch steps did I see my grandmother sitting in her red iron chair. But before I could say anything, before I could appeal for understanding and comfort, she lifted herself out of the chair and disappeared into the house. She had seen it all — I knew that — and she was too ashamed of me to face me.

Suddenly, she was coming back, holding a broom handle. She had never before lifted a hand to me, but in my state, I felt sure that many things would change. I closed my eyes and waited.

Instead of the crunch of hard wood on bone, I heard her chair creak. I opened my eyes and found the end of the broom handle under my nose.

"You know if you don't go back and deliver that hat, you'll feel pretty bad tonight."

I nodded.

"Well, take this. We don't like you fighting. But sometimes you have to. So now you march down there and tell those boys if they don't let you alone, you'll have to hit them with this. Here." She pushed the broom handle at me.

I took it, but was not very happy about it. I studied her; she looked the same, her white hair bunned at her neck, her blue eyes large behind glasses, her skin the color of unvarnished wood. But something inside must have changed for her actually to tell me to hit someone. I had been in fights, fits and starts of temper that burned out in a second. But to walk deliberately down to the corner, threaten someone, and hit him if he did not move aside, this was completely different, and, as my parents and grandmother had raised me, downright evil. She must have realized what I was thinking.

"You know who Teddy Roosevelt was?"

I nodded.

"Well, he once said: *Speak softly and carry a big stick; you will go far.*"

I understood her, but to do something like this was still alien to my nature. I held back.

"Come on." She stood abruptly and took my hand. We went into the house, down the hall, and into her bedroom. "I have to see to the brown rice. You sit on my bed and look at the picture on the wall." She went on to the kitchen. I was still holding the broom handle, and now put it down across the bed, and climbed up beside it, surrounded by her room, an old woman's room, with its fifty years of perfume, powder, and sweet soap. I felt a long way from the corner and Valentine's Gang.

There were three pictures on the wall and I was not certain which she wanted me to study. The smallest was of my granduncle Wilfred, who lived on Long Island and came to Thanksgiving dinner. The largest was of Jesus, the fingers of his right hand crossed and held up, his left hand baring his chest, in the middle of which was his heart, red and dripping blood. In the cool darkness of the room, he looked at me with gentle eyes, a slight smile on his lips. The third was my grandmother's husband, who had died so long before that I had never known him and had no feeling for him as my grandfather. He was light, like my grandmother, but more like some of the short, sallow Italian men who lived on the block. His black hair was parted in the middle. He wore a big mustache which hid his mouth. His jaw was square and dimpled. With black eyes, he seemed to look at something just above my head.

"Well, all right now." My grandmother came in, sweating from standing over the stove, and sat in a small arm chair beside the bed. "Did you look at the picture?"

"I didn't know which one." I looked at Jesus again.

"No, not him this time. This one." She indicated her husband. "I meant him."

Now Pablo Cortés, your grandfather — she started — was just like you, as gentle as a milkweed flower settling into honey, and as friendly as ninety-seven puppy dogs. He was from Cuba, which is an island in the Atlantic Ocean.

He was so kind that he'd meet every boat coming in from Cuba and talk to all of the people getting off, and if he found that one of them didn't have a place to stay, and no money for food, he'd bring him home. He'd lead his new friend into the kitchen and say: "Jennie, this is a countryman. He's got no place to sleep, and he's hungry." And I'd sigh and say: "All right. Dinner'll be ready in ten minutes." They'd go into the living room and sing and roll cigars.

That's what he did for a living, roll cigars, working at home. The leaves were spread out all over the floor like a rug, and I never did like cigars because I know somebody's been walking all over the leaves, sometimes in bare feet, like your mother did when she was a little girl.

Pablo was so friendly he gave a party every day while I was at work. I'd come home and open the door and the cigar smoke would tumble out, and through the haze I would see twenty Cubans, most with guitars, others rolling cigars, and all of them howling songs.

So now fifty years ago, I'd come from down South to stay with my brother Wilfred, and I was so dumb that the first time I saw snow I thought somebody upstairs'd broken open a pillow out the window. So my brother Wilfred had to explain a lot of things to me. And the first thing was about the neighborhoods. In those days, New York was all split up into neighborhoods. The Italians lived in one neighborhood, and the Polish in another, and the Negroes and Cubans someplace else. After Pablo and I got married, we lived with the Negroes. And if you walked two blocks one way, you'd come to the Irish neighborhood, and if you were smart, you'd turn around and come back, because if the Irish caught you, they'd do something terrible to you.

I don't know if Pablo knew this or not, or if he just thought he was so friendly that everybody would just naturally be friendly right back. But one day he went for a walk. He got over into the Irish neighborhood and got a little thirsty — which he did pretty often — so he went into an Irish bar and asked for a drink. I guess they thought he was new in this country, because the bartender gave him his drink. So Pablo, smiling all the time, and waiting for them to smile back, stood there in that Irish bar and drank slow. When he was finished, the bartender took the glass and instead of washing it, he smashed it down on the floor and stepped on it and crushed the pieces under his heel. What he meant was that it was pretty bad to be a Cuban and no Irishman would want to touch a glass a Cuban had drunk from.

I don't know if Pablo knew that either. He asked for another drink. And he got it. And after he finished this one, the bartender smashed it in the sink and glared at him.

Pablo was still thirsty and ordered again.

The bartender came and stood in front of him. He was a big man, with a face as red as watermelon. "Say, buddy, can't you take a hint?"

Pablo smiled. "What hint?"

The bartender was getting pretty mad. "Why you think I'm breaking them glasses?"

"I thought you like to break glasses. You must got a high bill on glasses."

The bartender got an axhandle from under the bar. "Get out of here, Cuban!"

So now Pablo knew the bartender didn't want him in the bar. "Now, let me get this straight. If I ask you for drink, and you give me drink, you would break that glass too?"

"That's right. But you better not order again."

Pablo sighed. He was sad. "Well, then we will pretend I got drunk in this bar." And the next thing anybody knew Pablo was behind the bar, breaking all the glasses he could reach.

"And we will pretend that I look at myself in your mirror." He picked up a bottle and cracked the big mirror they had.

By now there was a regular riot going on, with all the men in the bar trying to catch and hold him, and Pablo running around, breaking chairs and tables. Finally, just before they caught and tied him up, he tipped over their piano. "We will pretend I played a Cuban song on this piano!"

They called the police and held him until the wagon came. And the next time I saw him was in court the next morning, where the judge kept looking at Pablo like he really didn't believe that a man who seemed so kind and gentle could do such things. But it was plain Pablo had wrecked the Irishman's bar. The judged sentenced him to thirty days in the city jail and fifty dollars damages, which Pablo couldn't pay. So the judge gave him thirty extra days.

I didn't see Pablo for the next two months. When he came home, he was changed. He wasn't smiling at all, and you remember that he used to smile all the time. As soon as he came in the house, he told me he was going out again. I knew where, and I got mad. "Do you want to spend another two months in jail? Is that what you want?"

He didn't understand me. "Why you ask me that?"

"Why! You're going over there to that white man's bar and get into a fight and go on back to jail. Did you like it that much? Did jail change you so much?"

"Jennie, don't you see? I try not to change." He picked up five boxes of cigars he'd made before he went to jail and put them into a brown paper bag and tucked the bag under his arm.

I watched him go out the door and then started to cry. I loved him, you see, and didn't want him back in jail. And I cried because I didn't understand him now and was afraid of that.

When the Irishmen saw him coming into their bar, they were stunned. Their mouths dropped open, and they all got very quiet. Pablo didn't pay them any mind, just walked up to the bar and put his foot on the brass rail.

The bartender picked up his axhandle. "What you want here, Cuban? Ain't you had enough?"

"No." Pablo didn't smile. He took the brown paper bag and put it gently on the counter. Cigars, he said, are delicate and shouldn't be tossed around.

The bartender looked at the bag. "What you got there?"

"Maybe you find out." He touched the bag with his fingers. "I like a drink."

The bartender stared at him for a second and then at the paper bag for a long time. He started to sweat. "All right." He set the drink down in front of Pablo.

For a minute, Pablo just looked at it. Then he lifted it to his lips and drank it down and pushed it across the bar to the bartender.

The bartender picked it up and studied it. Finally, he looked at Pablo again. "I had to close up for a week after you was here the first time." He took the glass to the sink, washed it with soap and water, and put it with the other clean glasses. Then he looked at Pablo again. "Satisfied?"

"Not yet." Pablo grabbed the paper bag and started to open it.

"Watch out, fellows!" The bartender yelled in his ear. When Pablo looked up, all the men in the bar were lying on their stomachs covering their heads. The bartender was behind the bar on his knees, his hands over his ears.

Pablo took a cigar box out of the bag, opened it, pulled himself up and across the bar, and reached the box down to the bartender. "Hey, you want fine, handmade Havana cigar?" He was smiling.

"Are you going back down to that corner?" My grandmother took my hand.

I looked into her face and then at the picture of her husband. He was still studying something just above my head. "I guess so." I did not really want to do it.

"You may not even have to use that." She pointed at the broom handle. "But you should know you can."

I knew this was true and climbed off the bed and picked up the white hat and the broom handle. "Okay."

"I'll be waiting on the porch for you." She smiled, got up, and, sighing, went out to the kitchen.

For a while, I listened to pots knocking and being filled with water. Then I stood in her room and practiced what I would say to Valentine's Gang: "If you guys don't let me go by, I'll have to hit you with this." There was a quake in my voice the first time I said it out loud, but, if I had to, I thought I would actually be able to say it and then use the stick. I went down the hall, onto the porch, and looked down toward the corner.

It was empty. The mothers of the members of Valentine's Gang had summoned them home to supper.

Early in World War II a large British force fighting on the Continent was almost surrounded by the German army at Dunkirk, a French town on the English Channel. There were not enough military vessels to evacuate the besieged troops. A major disaster seemed likely, but Britons of all ages and occupations manned hundreds of little boats and rescued their army. A participant in the evacuation wrote:

> "The whole thing from first to last was covered with that same strange feeling of something supernatural. We muddled, we quarreled, everybody swore and was bad-tempered and made the wildest accusations of inefficiency and worse in high places. Boats were badly handled and broke down, arrangements went wrong.
>
> "And yet, out of all that mess we beat the experts, we defied the law and the prophets, and where the Government and the Board of Admiralty had hoped to bring away 30,000 men, we brought away 335,000. If that was not a miracle, there are no miracles left."

In this narrative poem, Robert Nathan tells the Dunkirk story in terms of what a young brother and sister did.

Dunkirk

ROBERT NATHAN

Will came back from school that day,
And he had little to say.
But he stood a long time looking down
To where the gray-green Channel water
Slapped at the foot of the little town,
And to where his boat, the *Sarah P*,
Bobbed at the tide on an even keel.
With her one old sail, patched at the leech,°
Furled like a slattern down at heel.

He stood for a while above the beach; 10
He saw how the wind and current caught her.

---

8. *leech:* edge.

He looked a long time out to sea.
There was steady wind and the sky was pale
And a haze in the east that looked like smoke.

Will went back to the house to dress.
He was halfway through when his sister Bess,
Who was near fourteen and younger than he
By just two years, came home from play.
She asked him, "Where are you going, Will?"
He said, "For a good long sail." 20
"Can I come along?"
                "No, Bess," he spoke.
"I may be gone for a night and a day."
Bess looked at him. She kept very still.
She had heard the news of the Flanders rout,
How the English were trapped above Dunkirk,
And the fleet had gone to get them out —
But everyone thought that it wouldn't work.
There was too much fear, there was too much doubt.
She looked at him, and he looked at her.
They were English children, born and bred. 30
He frowned her down, but she wouldn't stir.
She shook her proud young head.
"You'll need a crew," she said.

They raised the sail on the *Sarah P*,
Like a pennoncel° on a young knight's lance,
And headed the *Sarah* out to sea,
To bring their soldiers home from France.

There was no command, there was no set plan,
But six hundred boats went out with them
On the gray-green waters, sailing fast, 40
River excursion and fisherman,
Tug and schooner and racing M,°
And the little boats came following last.

From every harbor and town they went

---

35. *pennoncel* (pen'ən·sel): a small, pointed flag, or pennant.
42. M: a class of small boat.

Who had sailed their craft in the sun and rain,
From the South Downs, from the cliffs of Kent,
From the village street, from the country lane.
There are twenty miles of rolling sea
From coast to coast, by the sea gull's flight,
But the tides were fair and the wind was free, 50
And they raised° Dunkirk by the fall of night.

They raised Dunkirk with its harbor torn
By the blasted stern and the sunken prow;
They had raced for fun on an English tide,
They were English children bred and born,
And whether they lived or whether they died,
They raced for England now.

Bess was as white as the *Sarah*'s sail,
She set her teeth and smiled at Will.
He held his course for the smoky veil 60
Where the harbor narrowed thin and long.
The British ships were firing strong.

He took the *Sarah* into his hands,
He drove her in through fire and death
To the wet men waiting on the sands.
He got his load and he got his breath,
And she came about, and the wind fought her.
He shut his eyes and he tried to pray.
He saw his England where she lay.
The wind's green home, the sea's proud daughter, 70
Still in the moonlight, dreaming deep,
The English cliffs and the English loam —
He had fourteen men to get away.
And the moon was clear and the night like day
For planes to see where the white sails creep
Over the black water.

He closed his eyes and he prayed for her;
He prayed to the men who had made her great,
Who had built her land of forest and park,

---

51. *raised*: sailed toward, thus causing it to appear above the horizon.

Who had made the seas an English lake; 80
He prayed for a fog to bring the dark;
He prayed to get home for England's sake.
And the fog came down on the rolling sea,
And covered the ships with English mist.
The diving planes were baffled and blind.
For Nelson was there in the *Victory*,
With his one good eye, and his sullen twist,
And the guns were out on *The Golden Hind*,°
Their shot flashed over the *Sarah P.*
He could hear them cheer as he came about. 90

By burning wharves, by battered slips,
Galleon, frigate, and brigantine,
The old dead captains fought their ships,
And the great dead admirals led the line.
It was England's night, it was England's sea.

The fog rolled over the harbor key.
Bess held to the stays and conned° him out.
And all through the dark, while the *Sarah*'s wake
Hissed behind him, and vanished in foam,
There at his side sat Francis Drake, 100
And held him true and steered him home.

---

88. *Golden Hind*: Sir Francis Drake's ship, in which he sailed around the world (1577–80).
97. *conned*: gave directions for steering the ship.

Zapata, a hero of the Mexican Revolution, from a mural by Diego Rivera.

BOOK FOUR | PART 1

THE PEARL

John Steinbeck

What one thing do you want most in all the world? If you had it, would it bring you happiness? In The Pearl a young fisherman finds "the greatest pearl in the world," one as large as a sea gull's egg. Suddenly a simple world becomes a complicated one. The young fisherman (and with him the reader) is forced to ask himself: What are the real values I wish to live by? Who or what determines my destiny — society? fate? or myself alone?

Although The Pearl is a modern novel, John Steinbeck gives it the simplicity of a folk legend, a story "told so often it has taken root in every man's mind." The Pearl, like a fable or parable, is meant to tell a good story at the same time that it teaches a lesson. Following

The Pearl are more fables and legends (pages 693–701). You will see that the traditional fable or legend is shorter and less complex than Steinbeck's novel, which has several layers of meaning.

As in all fables and legends, the story itself is uncomplicated. The characters are simply described. Perhaps Steinbeck does this in order to make his story a universal one: Kino comes to represent all men, and Juana to represent all wives and mothers. The problem they face is one we all face — especially those of us who live in a rich and powerful nation.

Steinbeck has made the pearl the central symbol in his story because it is a traditional symbol of beauty and value. The reader may also be reminded of the parable in the Bible (Matthew 13:45–46) which tells that:

> The kingdom of heaven is like unto a merchant man, seeking goodly pearls:
> Who, when he had found one pearl of great price, went and sold all that he had, and bought it.

Although John Steinbeck suggests that The Pearl can be read as a fable, it is longer and more complex than a traditional fable. In spite of the fact that the preface states that everything in it is either good or bad, black or white, this is not quite so. The hero, Kino, has several sides to his character. His motives change from time to time. Kino changes, too, from a simple fisherman to a man facing a difficult problem and finally to a man who carries a tragic burden of guilt. The Pearl is, in fact, a modern novel which is like a fable in many ways.

The Pearl

In the town they tell the story of the great pearl — how it was found and how it was lost again. They tell of Kino,[1] the fisherman, and of his wife, Juana,[2] and of the baby, Coyotito.[3] And because the story has been told so often, it has taken root in every man's mind. And, as with all retold tales that are in people's hearts, there are only good and bad things and black and white things and good and evil things and no in-between anywhere.

If this story is a parable, perhaps everyone takes his own meaning from it and reads his own life into it. In any case, they say in the town that . . .

CHAPTER 1

Kino awakened in the near dark. The stars still shone, and the day had drawn only a pale wash of light in the lower sky to the east. The roosters had been crowing for some time, and the early pigs were already beginning their ceaseless turning of twigs and bits of wood to see whether anything to eat had been overlooked. Outside the brush house in the tuna clump, a covey of little birds chittered and flurried with their wings.

Kino's eyes opened, and he looked first at the lightening square which was the door, and then he looked at the hanging box where Coyotito slept. And last he turned his head to Juana, his wife, who lay beside him on the mat, her blue head shawl over her nose and over her breasts and around the small of her back. Juana's eyes were

---

[1] *Kino* (kē′nō).
[2] *Juana:* (hwä′nə).
[3] *Coyotito* (koi·ō·tē′tō).

open too. Kino could never remember seeing them closed when he awakened. Her dark eyes made little reflected stars. She was looking at him as she was always looking at him when he awakened.

Kino heard the little splash of morning waves on the beach. It was very good — Kino closed his eyes again to listen to his music. Perhaps he alone did this, and perhaps all of his people did it. His people had once been great makers of songs, so that everything they saw or thought or did or heard became a song. That was very long ago. The songs remained; Kino knew them, but no new songs were added. That does not mean that there were no personal songs. In Kino's head there was a song now, clear and soft; and if he had been able to speak it, he would have called it the Song of the Family.

His blanket was over his nose to protect him from the dank air. His eyes flicked to a rustle beside him. It was Juana arising, almost soundlessly. On her hard bare feet she went to the hanging box where Coyotito slept, and she leaned over and said a little reassuring word. Coyotito looked up for a moment and closed his eyes and slept again. Juana went to the fire pit and uncovered a coal and fanned it alive while she broke little pieces of brush over it.

Now Kino got up and wrapped his blanket about his head and nose and shoulders. He slipped his feet into his sandals and went outside to watch the dawn.

Outside the door he squatted down and gathered the blanket ends about his knees. He saw the specks of Gulf clouds flame high in the air. And a goat came near and sniffed at him and stared with its cold, yellow eyes. Behind him Juana's fire leaped into flame and threw spears of light through the chinks of the brush house wall and threw a wavering square of light out the door. A late moth blustered in to find the fire. The Song of the Family came now from behind Kino. And the rhythm of the family song was the grinding stone where Juana worked the corn for the morning cakes.

The dawn came quickly now, a wash, a glow, a lightness, and then an explosion of fire as the sun arose out of the Gulf. Kino looked down to cover his eyes from the glare. He could hear the pat of the corncakes in the house and the rich smell of them on the cooking plate. The ants were busy on the ground, big black ones with shiny bodies, and little, dusty, quick ants. Kino watched with the detachment of God while a dusty ant frantically tried to escape the sand trap an ant lion had dug for him. A thin, timid dog came close and, at a soft word from Kino, curled up, arranged its tail neatly over its feet, and laid its chin delicately on the pile. It was a black dog, with yellow-gold spots where its eyebrows should have been. It was a morning like other mornings and yet perfect among mornings.

Kino heard the creak of the rope when Juana took Coyotito out of his hanging box and cleaned him and hammocked him in her shawl, in a loop that placed him close to her breast. Kino could see these things without looking at them. Juana sang softly an ancient song that had only three notes and yet endless variety of interval. And this was part of the family song too. It was all part. Sometimes it rose to an aching chord that caught the throat, saying this is safety, this is warmth, this is the *Whole*.

Across the brush fence were other brush houses, and the smoke came from them too, and the sound of breakfast; but those were other songs, their pigs were other pigs, their wives were not Juana. Kino was young and strong, and his black hair hung over his brown forehead. His eyes were warm and fierce and bright, and his mustache was thin and coarse. He lowered his blanket from his nose now, for the dark poisonous air was gone, and the yellow sunlight fell on the house. Near the brush fence, two roosters bowed and feinted at each other with squared wings and neck feathers ruffed out. It would be a clumsy fight. They were not game chickens. Kino watched them for a moment, and then his eyes went up to a flight of wild doves twinkling inland to the hills. The world was awake now, and Kino arose and went into his brush house.

As he came through the door, Juana stood up from the glowing fire pit. She put Coyotito back in his hanging box, and then she combed her black hair and braided it in two braids and tied the ends with thin green ribbon. Kino squatted by the fire pit and rolled a hot corncake and dipped it in sauce and ate it. And he drank a little pulque,[4] and that was breakfast. That was the only breakfast he had ever known, outside of feast days and one incredible fiesta on cookies that had nearly killed him. When Kino had finished, Juana came back to the fire and ate her breakfast. They had spoken once, but there is not need for speech if it is only a

---

[4] *pulque* (pul′kē): a drink made from a plant grown mainly in Mexico.

habit anyway. Kino sighed with satisfaction — and that was conversation.

The sun was warming the brush house, breaking through its crevices in long streaks. And one of the streaks fell on the hanging box where Coyotito lay, and on the ropes that held it.

It was a tiny movement that drew their eyes to the hanging box. Kino and Juana froze in their positions. Down the rope that hung the baby's box from the roof support, a scorpion moved slowly. His stinging tail was straight out behind him, but he could whip it up in a flash of time.

Kino's breath whistled in his nostrils, and he opened his mouth to stop it. And then the startled look was gone from him and the rigidity from his body. In his mind a new song had come, the Song of Evil, the music of the enemy, of any foe of the family, a savage, secret, dangerous melody; and underneath, the Song of the Family cried plaintively.

The scorpion moved delicately down the rope toward the box. Under her breath Juana repeated an ancient magic to guard against such evil, and on top of that she muttered a Hail Mary between clenched teeth. But Kino was in motion. His body glided quietly across the room, noiselessly and smoothly. His hands were in front of him, palms down; and his eyes were on the scorpion. Beneath it, in the hanging box, Coyotito laughed and reached up his hand toward it. It sensed danger when Kino was almost within reach of it. It stopped; its tail rose up over its back in little jerks, and the curved thorn on the tail's end glistened.

Kino stood perfectly still. He could hear Juana whispering the old magic again, and he could hear the evil music of the enemy. He could not move until the scorpion moved, and it felt for the source of the death that was coming to it. Kino's hand went forward very slowly, very smoothly. The thorned tail jerked upright. And at that moment the laughing Coyotito shook the rope, and the scorpion fell.

Kino's hand leaped to catch it; but it fell past his fingers, fell on the baby's shoulder, landed and struck. Then, snarling, Kino had it, had it in his fingers, rubbing it to a paste in his hands. He threw it down and beat it into the earth floor with his fist, and Coyotito screamed with pain in his box. But Kino beat and stamped the enemy until it was only a fragment and a moist place in the dirt. His teeth were bared, and fury flared in his eyes, and the Song of the Enemy roared in his ears.

But Juana had the baby in her arms now. She found the puncture, with redness starting from it already. She put her lips down over the puncture and sucked hard and spat and sucked again, while Coyotito screamed.

Kino hovered; he was helpless; he was in the way.

The screams of the baby brought the neighbors. Out of their brush houses they poured — Kino's brother Juan Tomás and his fat wife Apolonia and their four children crowded in the door and blocked the entrance, while behind them others tried to look in, and one small boy crawled among legs to have a look. And those in front passed the word back to those behind — "Scorpion. The baby has been stung."

Juana stopped sucking the puncture for a moment. The little hole was slightly enlarged and its edges whitened from the sucking, but the red swelling extended farther around it in a hard lymphatic mound. And all of these people knew about the scorpion. An adult might be very ill from the sting, but a baby could easily die from the poison. First, they knew, would come swelling and fever and tightened throat, and then cramps in the stomach, and then Coyotito might die if enough of the poison had gone in. But the stinging pain of the bite was going away. Coyotito's screams turned to moans.

Kino had wondered often at the iron in his patient, fragile wife. She, who was obedient and respectful and cheerful and patient, she could stand fatigue and hunger almost better than Kino himself. In the canoe she was like a strong man. And now she did a most surprising thing.

"The doctor," she said. "Go to get the doctor."

The word was passed out among the neighbors where they stood close-packed in the little yard behind the brush fence. And they repeated among themselves, "Juana wants the doctor." A wonderful thing, a memorable thing, to want the doctor. To get him would be a remarkable thing. The doctor never came to the cluster of brush houses. Why should he, when he had more than he could do to take care of the rich people who lived in the stone and plaster houses of the town.

"He would not come," the people in the yard said.

"He would not come," the people in the door said, and the thought got into Kino.

"The doctor would not come," Kino said to Juana.

She looked up at him, her eyes as cold as the eyes of a lioness. This was Juana's first baby — this was nearly everything there was in Juana's world. And Kino saw her determination, and the music of the family sounded in his head with a steely tone.

"Then we will go to him," Juana said, and with one hand she arranged her dark blue shawl over her head, and made of one end of it a sling to hold the moaning baby, and made of the other end of it a shade over his eyes to protect him from the light. The people in the door pushed against those behind to let her through. Kino followed her. They went out of the gate to the rutted path and the neighbors followed them.

The thing had become a neighborhood affair. They made a quick, soft-footed procession into the center of the town, first Juana and Kino, and behind them Juan Tomás and Apolonia, her big stomach jiggling with the strenuous pace, then all the neighbors, with the children trotting on the flanks. And the yellow sun threw their black shadows ahead of them so that they walked on their own shadows.

They came to the place where the brush houses stopped and the city of stone and plaster began, the city of harsh outer walls and inner cool gardens, where a little water played and the bougainvillea [5] crusted the walls with purple and brick-red and white. They heard from the secret gardens the singing of caged birds, and heard the splash of cooling water on hot flagstones. The procession crossed the blinding plaza and passed in front of the church. It had grown now, and on the outskirts the hurrying newcomers were being softly informed how the baby had been stung by a scorpion, how the father and mother were taking it to the doctor.

And the newcomers, particularly the beggars from the front of the church, who were great experts in financial analysis, looked quickly at Juana's old blue skirt, saw the tears in her shawl, appraised the green ribbon on her braids, read the age of Kino's blanket and the thousand washings of his clothes, and set them down as poverty people and went along to see what kind of drama might

---

[5] *bougainvillea* (bōō'gən·vil'ē·ə): flowering vines.

develop. The four beggars in front of the church knew everything in the town. They were students of the expressions of young women as they went into confession, and they saw them as they came out and read the nature of the sin. They knew every little scandal and some very big crimes. They slept at their posts in the shadow of the church so that no one crept in for consolation without their knowledge. And they knew the doctor. They knew his ignorance, his cruelty, his avarice, his appetites, his sins. They knew his clumsy operations and the little brown pennies he gave sparingly for alms. They had seen his corpses go into the church. And, since early Mass was over and business was slow, they followed the procession, these endless searchers after perfect knowledge of their fellow men, to see what the fat, lazy doctor would do about an indigent[6] baby with a scorpion bite.

The scurrying procession came at last to the big gate in the wall of the doctor's house. They could hear the splashing water and the singing of caged birds and the sweep of the long brooms on the flagstones. And they could smell the frying of good bacon from the doctor's house.

Kino hesitated a moment. This doctor was not of his people. This doctor was of a race which for nearly four hundred years had beaten and starved and robbed and despised Kino's race, and frightened it, too, so that the indigene[7] came humbly to the door. And, as always when he came near to one of this race, Kino felt weak and afraid and angry at the same time. Rage and terror went together. He could kill the doctor more easily than he could talk to him, for all of the doctor's race spoke to all of Kino's race as though they were simple animals. And as Kino raised his right hand to the iron ring knocker in the gate, rage swelled in him, and the pounding music of the enemy beat in his ears, and his lips drew tight against his teeth — but with his left hand he reached to take off his hat. The iron ring pounded against the gate. Kino took off his hat and stood waiting. Coyotito moaned a little in Juana's arms, and she spoke softly to him. The procession crowded close, the better to see and hear.

After a moment the big gate opened a few inches. Kino could see

---

[6] *indigent* (in'də·jənt): needy, poor.
[7] *indigene* (in'də·jēn): native.

the green coolness of the garden and little splashing fountains through the opening. The man who looked out at him was one of his own race. Kino spoke to him in the old language. "The little one — the first born — has been poisoned by the scorpion," Kino said. "He requires the skill of a healer."

The gate closed a little, and the servant refused to speak in the old language. "A little moment," he said. "I go to inform myself," and he closed the gate and slid the bolt home. The glaring sun threw the bunched shadows of the people blackly on the white wall.

In his chamber the doctor sat up in his high bed. He had on his dressing gown of red watered silk that had come from Paris, a little tight over the chest now if it was buttoned. On his lap was a silver tray with a silver chocolate pot and a tiny cup of eggshell china, so delicate that it looked silly when he lifted it with his big hand, lifted it with the tips of thumb and forefinger and spread the other three fingers wide to get them out of the way. His eyes rested in puffy little hammocks of flesh, and his mouth drooped with discontent. He was growing very stout, and his voice was hoarse with the fat that pressed on his throat. Beside him on a table were a small Oriental gong and a bowl of cigarettes. The furnishings of the room were heavy and dark and gloomy. The pictures were religious, even the large tinted photograph of his dead wife, who, if Masses willed and paid for out of her own estate could do it, was in Heaven. The doctor had once for a short time been a part of the great world, and his whole subsequent life was memory and longing for France. "That," he said, "was civilized living." He poured his second cup of chocolate and crumbled a sweet biscuit in his fingers. The servant from the gate came to the open door and stood waiting to be noticed.

"Yes?" the doctor asked.

"It is a little Indian with a baby. He says a scorpion stung it."

The doctor put his cup down gently before he let his anger rise.

"Have I nothing better to do than cure insect bites for 'little Indians'? I am a doctor, not a veterinary."

"Yes, patron," said the servant.

"Has he any money?" the doctor demanded. "No, they never have any money. I, I alone in the world am supposed to work for nothing — and I am tired of it. See if he has any money!"

At the gate the servant opened the door a trifle and looked out at the waiting people. And this time he spoke in the old language.

"Have you money to pay for the treatment?"

Now Kino reached into a secret place somewhere under his blanket. He brought out a paper folded many times. Crease by crease he unfolded it, until at last there came to view eight small, misshapen seed pearls, as ugly and gray as little ulcers, flattened and almost valueless. The servant took the paper and closed the gate again, but this time he was not gone long. He opened the gate just wide enough to pass the paper back.

"The doctor has gone out," he said. "He was called to a serious case." And he shut the gate quickly out of shame.

And now a wave of shame went over the whole procession. They melted away. The beggars went back to the church steps, the stragglers moved off, and the neighbors departed, so that the public shaming of Kino would not be in their eyes.

For a long time Kino stood in front of the gate with Juana beside him. Slowly he put his suppliant hat on his head. Then, without warning, he struck the gate a crushing blow with his fist. He looked down in wonder at his split knuckles and at the blood that flowed down between his fingers.

CHAPTER 2

The town lay on a broad estuary, its old yellow plastered buildings hugging the beach. And on the beach the white and blue canoes that came from Nayarit [1] were drawn up, canoes preserved for generations by a hard, shell-like waterproof plaster whose making was a secret of the fishing people. They were high and graceful canoes, with curving bow and stern and a braced section midships where a mast could be stepped to carry a small lateen sail.

The beach was yellow sand, but at the water's edge a rubble of shell and algae [2] took its place. Fiddler crabs bubbled and sputtered in their holes in the sand, and in the shallows little lobsters popped in and out of their tiny homes in the rubble and sand. The

---

[1] *Nayarit* (nä′yä·rēt′): a state in western Mexico.
[2] *algae* (al′jē): seaweeds.

sea bottom was rich with crawling and swimming and growing things. The brown algae waved in the gentle currents, and the green eelgrass swayed, and little sea horses clung to its stems. Spotted botete, the poison fish, lay on the bottom in the eelgrass beds; and the bright-colored swimming crabs scampered over them.

On the beach, the hungry dogs and the hungry pigs of the town searched endlessly for any dead fish or sea bird that might have floated in on a rising tide.

Although the morning was young, the hazy mirage was up. The uncertain air that magnified some things and blotted out others hung over the whole Gulf, so that all sights were unreal and vision could not be trusted; so that sea and land had the sharp clarities and the vagueness of a dream. Thus it might be that the people of the Gulf trust things of the spirit and things of the imagination, but they do not trust their eyes to show them distance or clear outline or any optical exactness. Across the estuary from the town, one section of mangroves stood clear and telescopically defined, while another mangrove clump was a hazy, black-green blob. Part of the far shore disappeared into a shimmer that looked like water. There was no certainty in seeing, no proof that what you saw was there or was not there. And the people of the Gulf expected all places were that way, and it was not strange to them. A copper haze hung over the water, and the hot morning sun beat on it and made it vibrate blindingly.

The brush houses of the fishing people were back from the beach on the right-hand side of the town, and the canoes were drawn up in front of this area.

Kino and Juana came slowly down to the beach and to Kino's canoe, which was the one thing of value he owned in the world. It was very old. Kino's grandfather had brought it from Nayarit, and he had given it to Kino's father, and so it had come to Kino. It was at once property and source of food, for a man with a boat can guarantee a woman that she will eat something. It is the bulwark against starvation. And every year Kino refinished his canoe with the hard, shell-like plaster by the secret method that had also come to him from his father. Now he came to the canoe and touched the bow tenderly as he always did. He laid his diving rock and his basket and the two ropes in the sand by the canoe. And he folded his blanket and laid it in the bow.

Juana laid Coyotito on the blanket, and she placed her shawl over him so that the hot sun could not shine on him. He was quiet now, but the swelling on his shoulder had continued up his neck and under his ear, and his face was puffed and feverish. Juana went to the water and waded in. She gathered some brown seaweed and made a flat, damp poultice of it; this she applied to the baby's swollen shoulder, which was as good a remedy as any, and probably better than the doctor could have done. But the remedy lacked his authority because it was simple and didn't cost anything. The stomach cramps had not come to Coyotito. Perhaps Juana had sucked out the poison in time, but she had not sucked out her worry over her first-born. She had not prayed directly for the recovery of the baby — she had prayed that they might find a pearl with which to hire the doctor to cure the baby, for the minds of people are as unsubstantial as the mirage of the Gulf.

Now Kino and Juana slid the canoe down the beach to the water; and when the bow floated, Juana climbed in, while Kino pushed the stern in and waded beside it until it floated lightly and trembled on the little breaking waves. Then, in coordination, Juana and Kino drove their double-bladed paddles into the sea; and the canoe creased the water and hissed with speed. The other pearlers were gone out long since. In a few moments Kino could see them clustered in the haze, riding over the oyster bed.

Light filtered down through the water to the bed where the frilly pearl oysters lay fastened to the rubbly bottom, a bottom strewn with shells of broken, opened oysters. This was the bed that had raised the King of Spain to be a great power in Europe in past years, had helped to pay for his wars, and had decorated the churches for his soul's sake. The gray oysters with ruffles like skirts on the shells, the barnacle-crusted oysters with little bits of weed clinging to the skirts and small crabs climbing over them. An accident could happen to these oysters; a grain of sand could lie in the folds of muscle and irritate the flesh until, in self-protection, the flesh coated the grain with a layer of smooth cement. But once started, the flesh continued to coat the foreign body until it fell free in some tidal flurry or until the oyster was destroyed. For centuries men had dived down and torn the oysters from the beds and ripped them open, looking for the coated grains of sand. Swarms of fish lived near the bed to live near the oysters thrown back by the searching men and to nibble at the shining inner shells. But the pearls were accidents; and the finding of one was luck, a little pat on the back by God or the gods or both.

Kino had two ropes, one tied to a heavy stone and one to a basket. He stripped off his shirt and trousers and laid his hat in the bottom of the canoe. The water was oily smooth. He took his rock in one hand and his basket in the other, and he slipped feet first over the side, and the rock carried him to the bottom. The bubbles rose behind him until the water cleared and he could see. Above, the surface of the water was an undulating mirror of brightness, and he could see the bottoms of the canoes sticking through it.

Kino moved cautiously so that the water would not be obscured with mud or sand. He hooked his foot in the loop on his rock; and his hands worked quickly, tearing the oysters loose, some singly, others in clusters. He laid them in his basket. In some places the oysters clung to one another so that they came free in lumps.

Now, Kino's people had sung of everything that happened or existed. They had made songs to the fishes, to the sea in anger and to the sea in calm, to the light and the dark and the sun and the moon; and the songs were all in Kino and in his people — every song that had ever been made, even the ones forgotten. And as he filled his basket, the song was in Kino; and the beat of the song was his pounding heart as it ate the oxygen from his held breath; and the melody of the song was the gray-green water and the little scuttling animals and the clouds of fish that flitted by and were gone. But in the song there was a secret little inner song, hardly perceptible, but always there, sweet and secret and clinging, almost hiding in the counter-melody; and this was the Song of the Pearl That Might Be, for every shell thrown in the basket might contain a pearl. Chance was against it, but luck and the gods might be for it. And in the canoe above him, Kino knew that Juana was making the magic of prayer, her face set rigid and her muscles hard to force the luck, to tear the luck out of the god's hands, for she needed the luck for the swollen shoulder of Coyotito. And because the need was great and the desire was great, the little secret melody of the pearl that might be was stronger this morning. Whole phrases of it came clearly and softly into the Song of the Undersea.

Kino, in his pride and youth and strength, could remain down over two minutes without strain, so that he worked deliberately, selecting the largest shells. Because they were disturbed, the oyster shells were tightly closed. A little to his right a hummock of rubbly rock stuck up, covered with young oysters not ready to take. Kino moved next to the hummock; and then, beside it, under a little overhang, he saw a very large oyster lying by itself, not covered with its clinging brothers. The shell was partly open, for the overhang protected this ancient oyster, and in the liplike muscle Kino saw a ghostly gleam, and then the shell closed down. His heart beat out a heavy rhythm, and the melody of the maybe pearl shrilled in his ears. Slowly he forced the oyster loose and held it tightly against his breast. He kicked his foot free from the rock loop, and his body rose to the surface, and his black hair gleamed in the sunlight. He reached over the side of the canoe and laid the oyster in the bottom.

Then Juana steadied the boat while he climbed in. His eyes were shining with excitement, but in decency he pulled up his rock, and then he pulled up his basket of oysters and lifted them in. Juana sensed his excitement, and she pretended to look away. It is not good to want a thing too much. It sometimes drives the luck away. You must want it just enough, and you must be very tactful with God or the gods. But Juana stopped breathing. Very deliberately Kino opened his short, strong knife. He looked speculatively at the basket. Perhaps it would be better to open *the* oyster last. He took a small oyster from the basket, cut the muscle, searched the folds of flesh, and threw it in the water. Then he seemed to see the great oyster for the first time. He squatted in the bottom of the canoe, picked up the shell, and examined it. The flutes were shining black to brown, and only a few small barnacles adhered to the shell. Now Kino was reluctant to open it. What he had seen, he knew, might be a reflection, a piece of flat shell accidentally drifted in, or a complete illusion. In this Gulf of uncertain light there were more illusions than realities.

But Juana's eyes were on him, and she could not wait. She put her hand on Coyotito's covered head. "Open it," she said softly.

Kino deftly slipped his knife into the edge of the shell. Through the knife he could feel the muscle tighten hard. He worked the blade leverwise, and the closing muscle parted, and the shell fell apart. The liplike flesh writhed up and then subsided. Kino lifted the flesh; and there it lay, the great pearl, perfect as the moon. It captured the light and refined it and gave it back in silver incandescence. It was as large as a sea gull's egg. It was the greatest pearl in the world.

Juana caught her breath and moaned a little. And to Kino the secret melody of the maybe pearl broke clear and beautiful, rich and warm and lovely, glowing and gloating and triumphant. In the surface of the great pearl he could see dream forms. He picked the pearl from the dying flesh and held it in his palm, and he turned it over and saw that its curve was perfect. Juana came near to stare at it in his hand, and it was the hand he had smashed against the doctor's gate, and the torn flesh of the knuckles was turned grayish-white by the sea water.

Instinctively Juana went to Coyotito where he lay on his father's blanket. She lifted the poultice of seaweed and looked at the shoulder. "Kino," she cried shrilly.

He looked past his pearl, and he saw that the swelling was going out of the baby's shoulder, the poison was receding from its body. Then Kino's fist closed over the pearl, and his emotion broke over him. He put back his head and howled. His eyes rolled up, and he screamed, and his body was rigid. The men in the other canoes looked up, startled; and then they dug their paddles into the sea and raced toward Kino's canoe.

CHAPTER 3

A town is a thing like a colonial animal. A town has a nervous system and a head and shoulders and feet. A town is a thing separate from all other towns, so that there are no two towns alike. And a town has a whole emotion. How news travels through a town is a mystery not easily to be solved. News seems to move faster than small boys can scramble and dart to tell it, faster than women can call it over the fences.

Before Kino and Juana and the other fishers had come to Kino's brush house, the nerves of the town were pulsing and vibrating with the news — Kino found the Pearl of the World. Before panting little boys could strangle out the words, their mothers knew it. The news swept on past the brush houses, and it washed in a foaming wave into the town of stone and plaster. It came to the priest walking in his garden, and it put a thoughtful look in his eyes, and a memory of certain repairs necessary to the church. He wondered what the pearl would be worth. And he wondered whether he had baptized Kino's baby, or married him for that matter. The news came to the shopkeepers, and they looked at men's clothes that had not sold so well.

The news came to the doctor where he sat with a woman whose illness was age, though neither she nor the doctor would admit it. And when it was made plain who Kino was, the doctor grew stern and judicious at the same time. "He is a client of mine," the doctor said. "I'm treating his child for a scorpion sting." And the doctor's eyes rolled up a little in their fat hammocks, and he thought of Paris. He remembered the room he had lived in there as a great and luxurious place; and he remembered the hard-faced woman who had lived with him as a beautiful and kind girl, although she had been none of these three. The doctor looked past his aged patient and saw himself sitting in a restaurant in Paris and a waiter was just opening a bottle of wine.

The news came early to the beggars in front of the church, and it made them giggle a little with pleasure, for they knew that there is no almsgiver in the world like a poor man who is suddenly lucky.

Kino had found the Pearl of the World. In the town, in little offices, sat the men who bought pearls from the fishers. They waited in their chairs until the pearls came in, and then they cackled and fought and shouted and threatened until they reached the lowest price the fisherman would stand. But there was a price below which they dared not go, for it had happened that a fisherman in despair had given his pearls to the church. And when the buying was over, these buyers sat alone; and their fingers played restlessly with the pearls; and they wished they owned the pearls. For there were not many buyers really — there was only one, and he kept these agents in separate offices to give a semblance of competition. The news came to these men, and their eyes squinted and their fingertips burned a little, and each one thought how the patron could not live forever and someone had to take his place. And each one thought how with some capital he could get a new start.

All manner of people grew interested in Kino — people with things to sell and people with favors to ask. Kino had found the Pearl of the World. The essence of pearl mixed with essence of men, and a curious, dark residue was precipitated.[1] Every man suddenly became related to Kino's pearl; and Kino's pearl went into the dreams, the speculations, the schemes, the plans, the futures, the wishes, the needs, the lusts, the hungers, of everyone; and only one person stood in the way, and that was Kino; so that he became curiously every man's enemy. The news stirred up something infinitely black and evil in the town; the black distillate [2] was like the scorpion, or like hunger in the smell of food, or like loneliness when love is withheld. The poison sacs of the town began to manufacture venom, and the town swelled and puffed with the pressure of it.

But Kino and Juana did not know these things. Because they were happy and excited, they thought everyone shared their joy. Juan Tomás and Apolonia did, and they were the world too. In the afternoon, when the sun had gone over the mountains of the Peninsula to sink in the outward sea, Kino squatted in his house with Juana beside him. And the brush house was crowded with neighbors. Kino held the great pearl in his hand, and it was warm and alive in his hand. And the music of the pearl had merged with the music of the family, so that one beautified the other. The neighbors looked at the pearl in Kino's hand, and they wondered how such luck could come to any man.

And Juan Tomás, who squatted on Kino's right hand because he was his brother, asked, "What will you do now that you have become a rich man?"

Kino looked into his pearl, and Juana cast her eyelashes down and arranged her shawl to cover her face so that her excitement could not be seen. And in the incandescence of the pearl, the pictures formed of the things Kino's mind had considered in the past and had given up as impossible. In the pearl he saw Juana and Coyotito and himself standing and kneeling at the high altar, and they were being married now that they could pay. He spoke softly, "We will be married — in the church." [3]

---

[1] *residue was precipitated:* surplus substance was thrown off.
[2] *distillate* (dis'ti·lit): essence.
[3] *church:* In Mexico, and many other places where people are poor, married couples often postpone a church wedding for many years until they can afford the new clothes and festivities that seem appropriate to a church wedding.

In the pearl he saw how they were dressed — Juana in a shawl stiff with newness, and a new skirt, and from under the long skirt Kino could see that she wore shoes. It was in the pearl — the picture glowing there. He himself was dressed in new white clothes, and he carried a new hat — not of straw but of fine black felt — and he too wore shoes — not sandals, but shoes that laced. But Coyotito — he was the one — he wore a blue sailor suit from the United States, and a little yachting cap such as Kino had seen once when a pleasure boat put into the estuary. All of these things Kino saw in the lucent pearl, and he said, "We will have new clothes."

And the music of the pearl rose like a chorus of trumpets in his ears.

Then to the lovely gray surface of the pearl came the little things Kino wanted: a harpoon to take the place of one lost a year ago, a new harpoon of iron with a ring in the end of the shaft; and — his mind could hardly make the leap — a rifle — but why not, since he was so rich. And Kino saw Kino in the pearl, Kino holding a Winchester carbine. It was the wildest daydreaming, and very pleasant. His lips moved hesitantly over this — "A rifle," he said. "Perhaps a rifle."

It was the rifle that broke down the barriers. This was an impossibility; and if he could think of having a rifle, whole horizons were burst, and he could rush on. For it is said that humans are never satisfied, that you give them one thing and they want something more. And this is said in disparagement, whereas it is one of the greatest talents the species has and one that has made it superior to animals that are satisfied with what they have.

The neighbors, close pressed and silent in the house, nodded their heads at his wild imaginings. And a man in the rear murmured, "A rifle. He will have a rifle."

But the music of the pearl was shrilling with triumph in Kino. Juana looked up, and her eyes were wide at Kino's courage and at his imagination. An electric strength had come to him now the horizons were kicked out. In the pearl he saw Coyotito sitting at a little desk in a school, just as Kino had once seen it through an open door. And Coyotito was dressed in a jacket, and he had on a white collar and a broad silken tie. Moreover, Coyotito was writing on a big piece of paper. Kino looked at his neighbors fiercely. "My son will go to school," he said, and the neighbors were hushed. Juana caught her breath sharply. Her eyes were bright as she watched him, and she looked quickly down at Coyotito in her arms to see whether this might be possible.

But Kino's face shone with prophecy. "My son will read and open the books, and my son will write and will know writing. And my son will make numbers, and these things will make us free because he will know — he will know, and through him we will know." And in the pearl Kino saw himself and Juana squatting by the little fire in the brush hut while Coyotito read from a great book. "This is what the pearl will do," said Kino. And he had never said so many words together in his life. And suddenly he was afraid of his talking. His hand closed down over the pearl and cut the light away from it. Kino was afraid as a man is afraid who says, "I will," without knowing.

Now the neighbors knew they had witnessed a great marvel. They knew that time would now date from Kino's pearl, and that they would discuss this moment for many years to come. If these things came to pass, they would recount how Kino looked and what he said and how his eyes shone; and they would say, "He was a man transfigured. Some power was given to him, and there it started. You see what a great man he has become, starting from that moment. And I myself saw it."

And if Kino's planning came to nothing, those same neighbors would say, "There it started. A foolish madness came over him so that he spoke foolish words. God keep us from such things. Yes, God punished Kino because he rebelled against the way things are. You see what has become of him. And I myself saw the moment when his reason left him."

Kino looked down at his closed hand, and the knuckles were scabbed over and tight where he had struck the gate.

Now the dusk was coming. And Juana looped her shawl under the baby so that he hung against her hip, and she went to the fire hole and dug a coal from the ashes and broke a few twigs over it and fanned a flame alive. The little flames danced on the faces of the neighbors. They knew they should go to their own dinners, but they were reluctant to leave.

The dark was almost in, and Juana's fire threw shadows on the brush walls when the whisper came in, passed from mouth to mouth. "The Father is coming — the priest is coming." The men uncovered their heads and stepped back from the door, and the women gathered their shawls about their faces and cast down their eyes. Kino and Juan Tomás, his brother, stood up. The priest came in — a graying, aging man with an old skin and a young, sharp eye. Children he considered these people, and he treated them like children.

"Kino," he said softly, "thou [4] art named after a great man — and a great Father of the Church." He made it sound like a benediction. "Thy namesake tamed the desert and sweetened the minds of thy people, didst thou know that? It is in the books."

Kino looked quickly down at Coyotito's head, where he hung on Juana's hip. Someday, his mind said, that boy would know what things were in the books and what things were not. The music had gone out of Kino's head; but now, thinly, slowly, the melody of the morning, the music of evil, of the enemy, sounded; but it was faint and weak. And Kino looked at his neighbors to see who might have brought this song in.

But the priest was speaking again. "It has come to me that thou hast a great fortune, a great pearl."

Kino opened his hand and held it out, and the priest gasped a little at the size and beauty of the pearl. And then he said, "I hope thou wilt remember to give thanks, my son, to him who has given thee this treasure, and to pray for guidance in the future."

Kino nodded dumbly, and it was Juana who spoke softly. "We will, Father. And we will be married now. Kino has said so." She looked at the neighbors for confirmation, and they nodded their heads solemnly.

The priest said, "It is pleasant to see that your first thoughts are good thoughts. God bless you, my children." He turned and left quietly, and the people let him through.

But Kino's hand had closed tightly on the pearl again, and he was glancing about suspiciously; for the evil song was in his ears, shrilling against the music of the pearl.

The neighbors slipped away to go to their houses, and Juana squatted by the fire and set her clay pot of boiled beans over the

---

[4] *thou:* In Spanish these are two ways of saying *you: tu* and *usted.* Steinbeck has the priest say *thou* and *thy* to show that he is using the familiar form *tu* which is used in speaking to children and servants.

little flame. Kino stepped to the doorway and looked out. As always, he could smell the smoke from many fires, and he could see the hazy stars and feel the damp of the night air, so that he covered his nose from it. The thin dog came to him and threshed itself in greeting like a wind-blown flag, and Kino looked down at it and didn't see it. He had broken through the horizons into a cold and lonely outside. He felt alone and unprotected, and scraping crickets and shrilling tree frogs and croaking toads seemed to be carrying the melody of evil. Kino shivered a little and drew his blanket more tightly against his nose. He carried the pearl still in his hand, tightly closed in his palm, and it was warm and smooth against his skin.

Behind him he heard Juana patting the cakes before she put them down on the clay cooking sheet. Kino felt all the warmth and security of his family behind him, and the Song of the Family came from behind him like the purring of a kitten. But now, by saying what his future was going to be like, he had created it. A plan is a real thing, and things projected are experienced. A plan, once made and visualized, becomes a reality along with other realities — never to be destroyed but easily to be attacked. Thus Kino's future was real; but having set it up, other forces were set up to destroy it; and this he knew, so that he had to prepare to meet the attack. And this Kino knew also — that the gods do not love men's plans, and the gods do not love success unless it comes by accident. He knew that the gods take their revenge on a man if he be successful through his own efforts. Consequently Kino was afraid of plans; but having made one, he could never destroy it. And to meet the attack, Kino was already making a hard skin for himself against the world. His eyes and his mind probed for danger before it appeared.

Standing in the door, he saw two men approach; and one of them carried a lantern which lighted the ground and the legs of the men. They turned in through the opening of Kino's brush fence and came to his door. And Kino saw that one was the doctor and the other the servant who had opened the gate in the morning. The split knuckles on Kino's right hand burned when he saw who they were.

The doctor said, "I was not in when you came this morning. But now, at the first chance, I have come to see the baby."

Kino stood in the door, filling it, and hatred raged and flamed in back of his eyes, and fear too; for the hundreds of years of subjugation [5] were cut deep in him.

"The baby is nearly well now," he said curtly.

The doctor smiled, but his eyes in their little lymph-lined hammocks did not smile.

He said, "Sometimes, my friend, the scorpion sting has a curious effect. There will be apparent improvement, and then without warning — pouf!" He pursed his lips and made a little explosion to show how quick it could be, and he shifted his small black doctor's bag about so that the light of the lamp fell upon it, for he knew that Kino's race love the tools of any craft and trust them. "Sometimes," the doctor went on in a liquid tone, "sometimes there will be a withered leg or a blind eye or a crumpled back. Oh, I know the sting of the scorpion, my friend; and I can cure it."

Kino felt the rage and hatred melting toward fear. He did not know, and perhaps this doctor did. And he could not take the chance of pitting his certain ignorance against this man's possible knowledge. He was trapped as his people were always trapped, and would be until, as he had said, they could be sure that the things in the books were really in the books. He could not take a chance — not with the life or with the straightness of Coyotito. He stood aside and let the doctor and his man enter the brush hut.

Juana stood up from the fire and backed away as he entered, and she covered the baby's face with the fringe of her shawl. And when the doctor went to her and held out his hand, she clutched the baby tight and looked at Kino where he stood with the fire shadows leaping on his face.

Kino nodded, and only then did she let the doctor take the baby.

"Hold the light," the doctor said, and when the servant held the lantern high, the doctor looked for a moment at the wound on the baby's shoulder. He was thoughtful for a moment, and then he rolled back the baby's eyelid and looked at the eyeball. He nodded his head while Coyotito struggled against him.

"It is as I thought," he said. "The poison has gone inward, and it will strike soon. Come look!" He held the eyelid down. "See — it is blue. And Kino, looking anxiously, saw that indeed it was a little

---

[5] *subjugation:* domination by a conqueror.

blue. And he didn't know whether or not it was always a little blue. But the trap was set. He couldn't take the chance.

The doctor's eyes watered in their little hammocks. "I will give him something to try to turn the poison aside," he said. And he handed the baby to Kino.

Then from his bag he took a little bottle of white powder and a capsule of gelatine. He filled the capsule with the powder and closed it, and then around the first capsule he fitted a second capsule and closed it. Then he worked very deftly. He took the baby and pinched its lower lip until it opened its mouth. His fat fingers placed the capsule far back on the baby's tongue, back of the point where he could spit it out, and then from the floor he picked up the little pitcher of pulque and gave Coyotito a drink, and it was done. He looked again at the baby's eyeball and he pursed his lips and seemed to think.

At last he handed the baby back to Juana, and he turned to Kino. "I think the poison will attack within the hour," he said. "The medicine may save the baby from hurt, but I will come back in an hour. Perhaps I am in time to save him." He took a deep breath and went out of the hut, and his servant followed him with the lantern.

Now Juana had the baby under her shawl, and she stared at it with anxiety and fear. Kino came to her, and he lifted the shawl and stared at the baby. He moved his hand to look under the eyelid, and only then saw that the pearl was still in his hand. Then he went to a box by the wall, and from it he brought a piece of rag. He wrapped the pearl in the rag, then went to the corner of the brush house and dug a little hole with his fingers in the dirt floor, and he put the pearl in the hole and covered it up and concealed the place. And then he went to the fire where Juana was squatting, watching the baby's face.

The doctor, back in his house, settled into his chair and looked at his watch. His people brought him a little supper of chocolate and sweet cakes and fruit, and he stared at the food discontentedly.

In the houses of the neighbors, the subject that would lead all conversations for a long time to come was aired for the first time to see how it would go. The neighbors showed one another with their thumbs how big the pearl was, and they made little caressing gestures to show how lovely it was. From now on they would watch

Kino and Juana very closely to see whether riches turned their heads, as riches turn all people's heads. Everyone knew why the doctor had come. He was not good at dissembling, and he was very well understood.

Out in the estuary a tight-woven school of small fishes glittered and broke water to escape a school of great fishes that drove in to eat them. And in the houses the people could hear the swish of the small ones and the bouncing splash of the great ones as the slaughter went on. The dampness arose out of the Gulf and was deposited on bushes and cacti and on little trees in salty drops. And the night mice crept about on the ground, and the little night hawks hunted them silently.

The skinny black puppy with flame spots over his eyes came to Kino's door and looked in. He nearly shook his hind quarters loose when Kino glanced up at him, and he subsided when Kino looked away. The puppy did not enter the house, but he watched with frantic interest while Kino ate his beans from the little pottery dish and wiped it clean with a corncake and ate the cake and washed the whole down with a drink of pulque.

Kino was finished and was rolling a cigarette when Juana spoke sharply. "Kino." He glanced at her and then got up and went quickly to her, for he saw fright in her eyes. He stood over her, looking down, but the light was very dim. He kicked a pile of twigs into the fire hole to make a blaze, and then he could see the face of Coyotito. The baby's face was flushed and his throat was working and a little thick drool of saliva issued from his lips. The spasm of the stomach muscles began, and the baby was very sick.

Kino knelt beside his wife. "So the doctor knew," he said; but he said it for himself as well as for his wife; for his mind was hard and suspicious, and he was remembering the white powder. Juana rocked from side to side and moaned out the little Song of the Family as though it could ward off the danger, and the baby vomited and writhed in her arms. Now uncertainty was in Kino, and the music of evil throbbed in his head and nearly drove out Juana's song.

The doctor finished his chocolate and nibbled the little fallen pieces of sweet cake. He brushed his fingers on a napkin, looked at his watch, arose, and took up his little bag.

The news of the baby's illness traveled quickly among the brush houses, for sickness is second only to hunger as the enemy of poor people. And some said softly, "Luck, you see, brings bitter friends." And they nodded and got up to go to Kino's house. The neighbors scuttled with covered noses through the dark until they crowded into Kino's house again. They stood and gazed, and they made little comments on the sadness that this should happen at a time of joy; and they said, "All things are in God's hands." The old women squatted down beside Juana to try to give her aid if they could and comfort if they could not.

Then the doctor hurried in, followed by his man. He scattered the old women like chickens. He took the baby and examined it and felt its head. "The poison it has worked," he said. "I think I can defeat it. I will try my best." He asked for water, and in the cup of it he put three drops of ammonia, and he pried open the baby's mouth and poured it down. The baby spluttered and screeched under the treatment, and Juana watched him with haunted eyes. The doctor spoke a little as he worked. "It is lucky that I know about the poison of the scorpion. Otherwise — " and he shrugged to show what could have happened.

But Kino was suspicious, and he could not take his eyes from the doctor's open bag and from the bottle of white powder there. Gradually the spasms subsided, and the baby relaxed under the doctor's hands. And then Coyotito sighed deeply and went to sleep, for he was very tired with vomiting.

The doctor put the baby in Juana's arms. "He will get well now," he said. "I have won the fight." And Juana looked at him with adoration.

The doctor was closing his bag now. He said, "When do you think you can pay this bill?" He said it even kindly.

"When I have sold my pearl, I will pay you," Kino said.

"You have a pearl? A good pearl?" the doctor asked with interest.

And then the chorus of the neighbors broke in. "He has found the Pearl of the World," they cried, and they joined forefinger with thumb to show how great the pearl was.

"Kino will be a rich man," they clamored. "It is a pearl such as one has never seen."

The doctor looked surprised. "I had not heard of it. Do you keep this pearl in a safe place? Perhaps you would like me to put it in my safe?"

Kino's eyes were hooded now, his cheeks were drawn taut. "I have it secure," he said. "Tomorrow I will sell it, and then I will pay you."

The doctor shrugged, and his wet eyes never left Kino's eyes. He knew the pearl would be buried in the house, and he thought Kino might look toward the place where it was buried. "It would be a shame to have it stolen before you could sell it," the doctor said, and he saw Kino's eyes flick involuntarily to the floor near the side post of the brush house.

When the doctor had gone and all the neighbors had reluctantly returned to their houses, Kino squatted beside the little glowing coals in the fire hole and listened to the night sounds: the soft sweep of the little waves on the shore and the distant barking of dogs; the creeping of the breeze through the brush house roof and the soft speech of his neighbors in their houses in the village. For these people do not sleep soundly all night; they awaken at intervals and talk a little and then go to sleep again. And after a while, Kino got up and went to the door of his house.

He smelled the breeze and he listened for any foreign sound of secrecy or creeping, and his eyes searched the darkness, for the music of evil was sounding in his head, and he was fierce and afraid. After he had probed the night with his senses, he went to the place by the side post where the pearl was buried; and he dug it up and brought it to his sleeping mat, and under his sleeping mat he dug another little hole in the dirt floor and buried his pearl and covered it up again.

And Juana, sitting by the fire hole, watched him with questioning eyes; and when he had buried his pearl, she asked, "Who do you fear?"

Kino searched for a true answer, and at last he said, "Everyone." And he could feel a shell of hardness drawing over him.

After a while they lay down together on the sleeping mat, and Juana did not put the baby in his box tonight, but cradled him on her arms and covered his face with her head shawl. And the last light went out of the embers in the fire hole.

But Kino's brain burned, even during his sleep, and he dreamed that Coyotito could read, that one of his own people could tell him the truth of things. And in his dream, Coyotito was reading from a book as large as a house with letters as big as dogs, and the words galloped and played on the book. And then darkness spread over the page, and with the darkness came the music of evil again, and Kino stirred in his sleep; and when he stirred, Juana's eyes opened in the darkness. And then Kino awakened with the evil music pulsing in him, and he lay in the darkness with his ears alert.

Then from the corner of the house came a sound so soft that it might have been simply a thought, a little furtive movement, a touch of a foot on earth, the almost inaudible purr of controlled breathing. Kino held his breath to listen, and he knew that whatever dark thing was in his house was holding its breath too, to listen. For a time no sound at all came from the corner of the brush house. Then Kino might have thought he had imagined the sound. But Juana's hand came creeping over to him in warning, and then the sound came again! the whisper of a foot on dry earth and the scratch of fingers in the soil.

And now a wild fear surged in Kino's breast, and on the fear came rage, as it always did. Kino's hand crept into his breast where his knife hung on a string, and then he sprang like an angry cat, leaped striking and spitting for the dark thing he knew was in the corner of the house. He felt cloth, struck at it with his knife and missed, and struck again and felt the knife go through cloth; and then his head crashed with lightning and exploded with pain. There was a soft scurry in the doorway and running steps for a moment, and then silence.

Kino could feel warm blood running down from his forehead, and he could hear Juana calling to him. "Kino! Kino!" And there was terror in her voice. Then coldness came over him as quickly as the rage had, and he said, "I am all right. The thing has gone."

He groped his way back to the sleeping mat. Already Juana was working at the fire. She uncovered an ember from the ashes and shredded little pieces of cornhusk over it and blew a little flame into the cornhusks so that a tiny light danced through the hut. And then from a secret place Juana brought a little piece of consecrated candle and lighted it at the flame and set it upright on a fireplace stone. She worked quickly, crooning as she moved about. She dipped the end of her head shawl in water and swabbed the blood from Kino's bruised forehead. "It is nothing," Kino said; but his eyes and his voice were hard and cold, and <u>a brooding hate was growing in him.</u>

Now the tension which had been growing in Juana boiled up to the surface, and her lips were thin. "This thing is evil," she cried harshly. "This pearl is like a sin! It will destroy us," and her voice rose shrilly. "Throw it away, Kino. Let us break it between stones. Let us bury it and forget the place. Let us throw it back into the sea. It has brought evil. Kino, my husband, it will destroy us." And in the firelight her lips and her eyes were alive with her fear.

But Kino's face was set, and his mind and his will were set. "This is our one chance," he said. "Our son must go to school. He must break out of the pot that holds us in."

"It will destroy us all," Juana cried. "Even our son."

"Hush," said Kino. "Do not speak any more. In the morning we will sell the pearl, and then the evil will be gone and only the good remain. Now hush, my wife." His dark eyes scowled into the little fire, and for the first time he knew that his knife was still in his hands, and he raised the blade and looked at it and saw a little line of blood on the steel. For a moment he seemed about to wipe the blade on his trousers, but then he plunged the knife into the earth and so cleansed it.

The distant roosters began to crow, and the air changed, and the dawn was coming. The wind of the morning ruffled the water of the estuary and whispered through the mangroves, and the little waves beat on the rubbly beach with an increased tempo. Kino raised the sleeping mat and dug up his pearl and put it in front of him and stared at it.

And the beauty of the pearl, winking and glimmering in the light of the little candle, cozened his brain with its beauty. So lovely it was, so soft; and its own music came from it — its music of promise and delight, its guarantee of the future, of comfort, of security. Its warm lucence promised a poultice against illness and a wall against insult. It closed a door on hunger. And as he stared at it, Kino's eyes softened and his face relaxed. He could see the little image of the consecrated candle reflected in the soft surface of the pearl, and he heard again in his ears the lovely music of the undersea, the tone of the diffused, green light of the sea bottom. Juana, glancing secretly at him, saw him smile. And because they were in some way one thing and one purpose, she smiled with him.

And they began this day with hope.

CHAPTER 4

It is wonderful the way a little town keeps track of itself and of all its units. If every single man and woman, child and baby, acts and conducts itself in a known pattern and breaks no walls and differs with no one and experiments in no way and is not sick and does not endanger the ease and peace of mind or steady unbroken flow of the town, then that unit can disappear and never be heard of. But let one man step out of the regular thought or the known and trusted pattern, and the nerves of the townspeople ring with nervousness, and communication travels over the nerve lines of the town. Then every unit communicates to the whole.

Thus, in La Paz, it was known in the early morning through the whole town that Kino was going to sell his pearl that day. It was known among the neighbors in the brush huts, among the pearl fishermen; it was known among the Chinese grocery store owners; it was known in the church, for the altar boys whispered about it. Word of it crept in among the nuns; the beggars in front of the church spoke of it, for they would be there to take the tithe [1] of the first fruits of the luck. The little boys knew about it with excitement, but most of all the pearl buyers knew about it; and when the day had come, in the offices of the pearl buyers, each man sat alone with his little black velvet tray; and each man rolled the pearls about with his fingertips and considered his part in the picture.

It was supposed that the pearl buyers were individuals acting alone, bidding against one another for the pearls the fishermen brought in. And once it had been so. But this was a wasteful method, for often, in the excitement of bidding for a fine pearl, too great a price had been paid to the fishermen. This was extravagant and not to be countenanced. Now there was only one pearl buyer with many hands; and the men who sat in their offices and waited for Kino knew what price they would offer, how high they would bid, and what method each one would use. And although these men would not profit beyond their salaries, there was excitement among the pearl buyers, for there was excitement in the hunt; and if it be

---

[1] *tithe* (tīth): one-tenth.

a man's function to break down a price, then he must take joy and satisfaction in breaking it as far down as possible. For every man in the world functions to the best of his ability, and no one does less than his best, no matter what he may think about it. Quite apart from any reward they might get, from any word of praise, from any promotion, a pearl buyer was a pearl buyer, and the best and happiest pearl buyer was he who bought for the lowest prices.

The sun was hot yellow that morning, and it drew the moisture from the estuary and from the Gulf and hung it in shimmering scarves in the air, so that the air vibrated and vision was insubstantial. A vision hung in the air to the north of the city — the vision of a mountain that was over two hundred miles away, and the high slopes of this mountain were swaddled with pines, and a great stone peak arose above the timber line.

And the morning of this day the canoes lay lined up on the beach; the fishermen did not go out to dive for pearls, for there would be too much happening, too many things to see, when Kino went to sell the great pearl.

In the brush houses by the shore, Kino's neighbors sat long over their breakfasts; and they spoke of what they would do if they had found the pearl. And one man said that he would give it as a present to the Holy Father in Rome. Another said that he would buy Masses for the souls of his family for a thousand years. Another thought he might take the money and distribute it among the poor of La Paz; and a fourth thought of all the good things one could do with the money from the pearl, of all the charities, benefits, of all the rescues one could perform if one had money. All of the neighbors hoped that sudden wealth would not turn Kino's head, would not make a rich man of him, would not graft onto him the evil limbs of greed and hatred and coldness. For Kino was a well-liked man; it would be a shame if the pearl destroyed him. "That good wife Juana," they said, "and the beautiful baby Coyotito, and the others to come. What a pity it would be if the pearl should destroy them all."

For Kino and Juana this was the morning of mornings of their lives, comparable only to the day when the baby was born. This was to be the day from which all other days would take their arrangement. Thus they would say, "It was two years before we sold the pearl," or, "It was six weeks after we sold the pearl." Juana, considering the matter, threw caution to the winds; and she dressed Coyotito in the clothes she had prepared for his baptism, when there would be money for his baptism. And Juana combed and braided her hair and tied the ends with two little bows of red ribbon, and she put on her marriage skirt and waist. The sun was quarter high when they were ready. Kino's ragged white clothes were clean at least, and this was the last day of his raggedness. For tomorrow, or even this afternoon, he would have new clothes.

The neighbors, watching Kino's door through the crevices in their brush houses, were dressed and ready too. There was no self-consciousness about their joining Kino and Juana to go pearl selling. It was expected, it was a historic moment, they would be crazy if they didn't go. It would be almost a sign of unfriendship.

Juana put on her head shawl carefully; and she draped one end under her right elbow and gathered it with her right hand so that a hammock hung under her arm; and in this little hammock she placed Coyotito, propped up against the head shawl so that he could see everything and perhaps remember. Kino put on his large straw hat and felt it with his hand to see that it was properly placed, not on the back or side of his head, like a rash, unmarried, irresponsible man, and not flat, as an elder would wear it, but tilted a little forward to show aggressiveness and seriousness and vigor. There is a great deal to be seen in the tilt of a hat on a man. Kino slipped his feet into his sandals and pulled the thongs up over his heels. The great pearl was wrapped in an old soft piece of deerskin and placed in a little leather bag, and the leather bag was in a pocket in Kino's shirt. He folded his blanket carefully and draped it in a narrow strip over his left shoulder, and now they were ready.

Kino stepped with dignity out of the house, and Juana followed him, carrying Coyotito. And as they marched up the freshet-washed alley toward the town, the neighbors joined them. The houses belched people; the doorways spewed out children. But because of the seriousness of the occasion, only one man walked with Kino, and that was his brother Juan Tomás.

Juan Tomás cautioned his brother. "You must be careful to see they do not cheat you," he said.

"Very careful," Kino agreed.

"We do not know what prices are paid in other places," said Juan Tomás. "How can we know what is a fair price, if we do not know what the pearl buyer gets for the pearl in another place?"

"That is true," said Kino, "but how can we know? We are here, we are not there."

As they walked up toward the city, the crowd grew behind them; and Juan Tomás, in pure nervousness, went on speaking.

"Before you were born, Kino," he said, "the old ones thought of a way to get more money for their pearls. They thought it would be better if they had an agent who took all the pearls to the capital and sold them there and kept only his share of the profit."

Kino nodded his head. "I know," he said. "It was a good thought."

"And so they got such a man," said Juan Tomás, "and they pooled the pearls, and they started him off. And he was never heard of again, and the pearls were lost. Then they got another man, and they started him off, and he was never heard of again. And so they gave the whole thing up and went back to the old way."

"I know," said Kino. "I have heard our father tell of it. It was a good idea, but it was against religion, and the Father made that very clear. The loss of the pearls was a punishment visited on those who tried to leave their station. And the Father made it clear that each man and woman is like a soldier sent by God to guard some part of the castle of the Universe. And some are in the ramparts and some far deep in the darkness of the walls. But each one must remain faithful to his post and must not go running about, else the castle is in danger from the assaults of Hell."

"I have heard him make that sermon," said Juan Tomás. "He makes it every year."

The brothers, as they walked along, squinted their eyes a little, as they and their grandfathers and their great-grandfathers had done for four hundred years, since first the strangers came with arguments and authority, and gunpowder to back up both. And in the four hundred years Kino's people had learned only one defense — a slight slitting of the eyes and a slight tightening of the lips and a retirement. Nothing could break down this wall, and they could remain whole within the wall.

The gathering procession was solemn, for they sensed the importance of this day, and any children who showed a tendency to scuffle, to scream, to cry out, to steal hats and rumple hair, were hissed to silence by their elders. So important was this day that an old man came to see, riding on the stalwart shoulders of his nephew. The procession left the brush huts and entered the stone and plaster city, where the streets were a little wider and there were narrow pavements beside the buildings. And as before, the beggars joined them as they passed the church; the grocers looked out at them as they went by; the little saloons lost their customers, and the owners closed up shop and went along. And the sun beat down on the streets of the city, and even tiny stones threw shadows on the ground.

The news of the approach of the procession ran ahead of it, and in their little dark offices the pearl buyers stiffened and grew alert. They got out papers so that they could be at work when Kino appeared, and they put their pearls in the desks, for it is not good to let an inferior pearl be seen beside a beauty. And word of the loveliness of Kino's pearl had come to them. The pearl buyers' offices were clustered together in one narrow street, and they were barred at the windows, and wooden slats cut out the light, so that only a soft gloom entered the offices.

A stout, slow man sat in an office waiting. His face was fatherly and benign, and his eyes twinkled with friendship. He was a caller of good mornings, a ceremonious shaker of hands, a jolly man who knew all jokes and yet who hovered close to sadness, for in the midst of a laugh he could remember the death of your aunt, and his eyes could become wet with sorrow for your loss. This morning he had placed a flower in a vase on his desk, a single scarlet hibiscus, and the vase sat beside the black, velvet-lined pearl tray in front of him. He was shaved close to the blue roots of his beard, and his hands were clean and his nails polished. His door stood open to the morning, and he hummed under his breath while his right hand practiced legerdemain.[2] He rolled a coin back and forth over his knuckles and made it appear and disappear, made it spin and sparkle. The coin winked into sight and as quickly slipped out of sight, and the man did not even watch his own performance. The fingers did it all mechanically, precisely, while the man hummed to himself and peered out the door. Then he heard the tramp of feet of the approaching crowd, and the fingers of his right hand worked faster and faster until, as the figure of Kino filled the doorway, the coin flashed and disappeared.

---

[2] *legerdemain* (lej'ər·də·mān') : sleight of hand or tricks of magic.

"Good morning, my friend," the stout man said. "What can I do for you?"

Kino stared into the dimness of the little office, for his eyes were squeezed from the outside glare. But the buyer's eyes had become as steady and cruel and unwinking as a hawk's eyes, while the rest of his face smiled in greeting. And secretly, behind his desk, his right hand practiced with the coin.

"I have a pearl," said Kino. And Juan Tomás stood beside him and snorted a little at the understatement. The neighbors peered around the doorway, and a line of little boys clambered on the window bars and looked through. Several little boys, on their hands and knees, watched the scene around Kino's legs.

"You have a pearl," the dealer said. "Sometimes a man brings in a dozen. Well, let us see your pearl. We will value it and give you the best price." And his fingers worked furiously with the coin.

Now Kino instinctively knew his own dramatic effects. Slowly he brought out the leather bag, slowly took from it the soft and dirty piece of deerskin; and then he let the great pearl roll into the black velvet tray, and instantly his eyes went to the buyer's face. But there was no sign, no movement; the face did not change, but the secret hand behind the desk missed in its precision. The coin stumbled over a knuckle and slipped silently into the dealer's lap. And the fingers behind the desk curled into a fist. When the right hand came out of hiding, the forefinger touched the great pearl, rolled it on the black velvet; thumb and forefinger picked it up and brought it near to the dealer's eyes and twirled it in the air.

Kino held his breath, and the neighbors held their breath, and the whispering went back through the crowd. "He is inspecting it — No price has been mentioned yet — They have not come to a price."

Now the dealer's hand had become a personality. The hand tossed the great pearl back to the tray, the forefinger poked and insulted it, and on the dealer's face there came a sad and contemptuous smile.

"I am sorry, my friend," he said, and his shoulders rose a little to indicate that the misfortune was no fault of his.

"It is a pearl of great value," Kino said.

The dealer's finger spurned the pearl, so that it bounced and rebounded softly from the sides of the velvet tray.

"You have heard of fool's gold," the dealer said. "This pearl is like fool's gold. It is too large. Who would buy it? There is no market for such things. It is a curiosity only. I am sorry. You thought it was a thing of value, and it is only a curiosity."

Now Kino's face was perplexed and worried. "It is the Pearl of the World," he cried. "No one has ever seen such a pearl."

"On the contrary," said the dealer, "it is large and clumsy. As a curiosity it has interest; some museum might perhaps take it to place in a collection of seashells. I can give you, say, a thousand pesos." [3]

Kino's face grew dark and dangerous. "It is worth fifty thousand," he said. "You know it. You want to cheat me."

And the dealer heard a little grumble go through the crowd as they heard his price. And the dealer felt a little tremor of fear.

"Do not blame me," he said quickly. "I am only an appraiser. Ask the others. Go to their offices and show your pearl — or, better, let them come here, so that you can see there is no collusion.[4] Boy," he called. And when his servant looked through the rear door, "Boy, go to such a one, and such another one, and such a third one. Ask them to step in here and do not tell them why. Just say that I will be pleased to see them." And his right hand went behind the desk and pulled another coin from his pocket, and the coin rolled back and forth over his knuckles.

Kino's neighbors whispered together. They had been afraid of something like this. The pearl was large, but it had a strange color. They had been suspicious of it from the first. And after all, a thousand pesos was not to be thrown away. It was comparative wealth to a man who was not wealthy. And suppose Kino took a thousand pesos. Only yesterday he had nothing.

But Kino had grown tight and hard. He felt the creeping of fate, the circling of wolves, the hover of vultures. He felt the evil coagulating about him, and he was helpless to protect himself. He heard in his ears the evil music. And on the black velvet the great pearl glistened, so that the dealer could not keep his eyes from it.

The crowd in the doorway wavered and broke and let the three pearl dealers through. The crowd was silent now, fearing to miss a

---

[3] *pesos* (pā′sōs): a Mexican peso is worth about eight U.S. cents.
[4] *collusion*: secret agreement for a wrongful purpose.

word, to fail to see a gesture or an expression. Kino was silent and watchful. He felt a little tugging at his back, and he turned and looked in Juana's eyes; and when he looked away, he had renewed strength.

The dealers did not glance at one another or at the pearl. The man behind the desk said, "I have put a value on this pearl. The owner here does not think it fair. I will ask you to examine this — this thing and make an offer. Notice," he said to Kino, "I have not mentioned what I have offered."

The first dealer, dry and stringy, seemed now to see the pearl for the first time. He took it up, rolled it quickly between thumb and forefinger, and then cast it contemptuously back into the tray.

"Do not include me in the discussion," he said dryly. "I will make no offer at all. I do not want it. This is not a pearl — it is a monstrosity." His thin lips curled.

Now the second dealer, a little man with a shy, soft voice, took up the pearl, and he examined it carefully. He took a glass from his pocket and inspected it under magnification. Then he laughed softly.

"Better pearls are made of paste," he said. "I know these things. This is soft and chalky; it will lose its color and die in a few months. Look — " He offered the glass to Kino, showed him how to use it; and Kino, who had never seen a pearl's surface magnified, was shocked at the strange-looking surface.

The third dealer took the pearl from Kino's hands. "One of my clients likes such things," he said. "I will offer five hundred pesos, and perhaps I can sell it to my client for six hundred."

Kino reached quickly and snatched the pearl from his hand. He wrapped it in the deerskin and thrust it inside his shirt.

The man behind the desk said, "I'm a fool, I know, but my first offer stands. I still offer one thousand. What are you doing?" he asked, as Kino thrust the pearl out of sight.

"I am cheated," Kino cried fiercely. "My pearl is not for sale here. I will go, perhaps, even to the capital."

Now the dealers glanced quickly at one another. They knew they had played too hard; they knew they would be disciplined for their failure; and the man at the desk said quickly, "I might go to fifteen hundred."

But Kino was pushing his way through the crowd. The hum of

talk came to him dimly, his rage blood pounded in his ears, and he burst through and strode away. Juana followed, trotting after him.

When the evening came, the neighbors in the brush houses sat eating their corncakes and beans, and they discussed the great theme of the morning. They did not know; it seemed a fine pearl to them, but they had never seen such a pearl before, and surely the dealers knew more about the value of pearls than they. "And mark this," they said. "Those dealers did not discuss these things. Each of the three knew the pearl was valueless."

"But suppose they had arranged it before?"

"If that is so, then all of us have been cheated all of our lives."

Perhaps, some argued, perhaps it would have been better if Kino took the one thousand five hundred pesos. That is a great deal of money, more than he has ever seen. Maybe Kino is being a pigheaded fool. Suppose he should really go to the capital and find no buyer for his pearl. He would never live that down.

And now, said other fearful ones, now that he has defied them, those buyers will not want to deal with him at all. Maybe Kino has cut off his own head and destroyed himself.

And others said, Kino is a brave man and a fierce man; he is right. From his courage we may all profit. These were proud of Kino.

In his house Kino squatted on his sleeping mat, brooding. He had buried his pearl under a stone of the fire hole in his house, and he stared at the woven tules[5] of his sleeping mat until the crossed design danced in his head. He had lost one world and had not gained another. And Kino was afraid. Never in his life had he been far from home. He was afraid of strangers and of strange places. He was terrified of that monster of strangeness they called the capital. It lay over the water and through the mountains, over a thousand miles; and every strange, terrible mile was frightening. But Kino had lost his old world, and he must clamber on to a new one. For his dream of the future was real and never to be destroyed; and he had said "I will go," and that made a real thing, too. To determine to go and to say it was to be halfway there.

Juana watched him while he buried his pearl, and she watched him while she cleaned Coyotito and nursed him, and while she

---

[5] *tules:* bulrushes.

made the corncakes for supper.

Juan Tomás came in and squatted down beside Kino and remained silent for a long time, until at last Kino demanded, "What else could I do? They are cheats."

Juan Tomás nodded gravely. He was the elder, and Kino looked to him for wisdom. "It is hard to know," he said. "We do know that we are cheated from birth to the overcharge on our coffins. But we survive. You have defied not the pearl buyers, but the whole structure, the whole way of life; and I am afraid for you."

"What have I to fear but starvation?" Kino asked.

But Juan Tomás shook his head slowly. "That we must all fear. But suppose you are correct — suppose your pearl is of great value — do you think then the game is over?"

"What do you mean?"

"I don't know," said Juan Tomás, "but I am afraid for you. It is new ground you are walking on; you do not know the way."

"I will go. I will go soon," said Kino.

"Yes," Juan Tomás agreed. "That you must do. But I wonder if you will find it any different in the capital. Here, you have friends and me, your brother. There, you will have no one."

"What can I do?" Kino cried. "Some deep outrage is here. My son must have a chance. That is what they are striking at. My friends will protect me."

"Only so long as they are not in danger or discomfort from it," said Juan Tomás. He arose, saying, "Go with God."

And Kino said, "Go with God," and did not even look up; for the words had a strange chill in them.

Long after Juan Tomás had gone, Kino sat brooding on his sleeping mat. A lethargy had settled on him, and a little gray hopelessness. Every road seemed blocked against him. In his head he heard only the dark music of the enemy. His senses were burningly alive; but his mind went back to the deep participation with all things, the gift he had from his people. He heard every little sound of the gathering night: the sleepy complaint of settling birds, the love agony of cats, the strike and withdrawal of little waves on the beach, and the simple hiss of distance. And he could smell the sharp odor of exposed kelp from the receding tide. The little flare of the twig fire made the design on his sleeping mat jump before his entranced eyes.

Juana watched him with worry, but she knew him, and she knew she could help him best by being silent and by being near. And, as though she too could hear the Song of Evil, she fought it, singing softly the melody of the family, of the safety and warmth and wholeness of the family. She held Coyotito in her arms and sang the song to him, to keep the evil out; and her voice was brave against the threat of the dark music.

Kino did not move nor ask for his supper. She knew he would ask when he wanted it. His eyes were entranced; and he could sense the wary, watchful evil outside the brush house; he could feel the dark, creeping things waiting for him to go out into the night. It was shadowy and dreadful, and yet it called to him and threatened him and challenged him. His right hand went into his shirt and felt his knife; his eyes were wide; he stood up and walked to the doorway.

Juana willed to stop him; she raised her hand to stop him, and her mouth opened with terror. For a long moment Kino looked out into the darkness, and then he stepped outside. Juana heard the little rush, the grunting struggle, the blow. She froze with terror for a moment, and then her lips drew back from her teeth like a cat's lips. She set Coyotito down on the ground. She seized a stone from the fireplace and rushed outside, but it was over then. Kino lay on the ground, struggling to rise; and there was no one near him. Only the shadows and the strike and rush of waves and the hiss of distance. But the evil was all about, hidden behind the brush fence, crouched beside the house in the shadow, hovering in the air.

Juana dropped her stone, and she put her arms around Kino and helped him to his feet and supported him into the house. Blood oozed down from his scalp, and there was a long, deep cut in his cheek from ear to chin, a deep, bleeding slash. And Kino was only half conscious. He shook his head from side to side. His shirt was torn open and his clothes half pulled off. Juana sat him down on his sleeping mat, and she wiped the thickening blood from his face with her skirt. She brought him pulque to drink in a little pitcher, and still he shook his head to clear out the darkness.

"Who?" Juana asked.

"I don't know," Kino said. "I didn't see."

Now Juana brought her clay pot of water, and she washed the cut on his face while he stared dazed ahead of him.

"Kino, my husband," she cried, and his eyes stared past her.

"Kino, can you hear me?"

"I hear you," he said dully.

"Kino, this pearl is evil. Let us destroy it before it destroys us. Let us crush it between two stones. Let us — let us throw it back in the sea where it belongs. Kino, it is evil; it is evil!"

And as she spoke, the light came back in Kino's eyes so that they glowed fiercely; and his muscles hardened, and his will hardened.

"No," he said. "I will fight this thing. I will win over it. We will have our chance." His fist pounded the sleeping mat. "No one shall take our good fortune from us," he said. His eyes softened then, and he raised a gentle hand to Juana's shoulder. "Believe me," he said. "I am a man." And his face grew crafty.

"In the morning we will take our canoe, and we will go over the sea and over the mountains to the capital, you and I. We will not be cheated. I am a man."

"Kino," she said huskily. "I am afraid. A man can be killed. Let us throw the pearl back into the sea."

"Hush," he said fiercely. "I am a man. Hush." And she was silent, for his voice was command. "Let us sleep a little," he said. "In the first light we will start. You are not afraid to go with me?"

"No, my husband."

His eyes were soft and warm on her then; his hand touched her cheek. "Let us sleep a little," he said.

CHAPTER 5

The late moon arose before the first rooster crowed. Kino opened his eyes in the darkness, for he sensed movement near him, but he did not move. Only his eyes searched the darkness; and in the pale light of the moon that crept through the holes in the brush house, Kino saw Juana arise silently from beside him. He saw her move toward the fireplace. So carefully did she work that he heard only the lightest sound when she moved the fireplace stone. And then like a shadow she glided toward the door. She paused for a moment beside the hanging box where Coyotito lay, then for a second she was back in the doorway, and then she was gone.

And rage surged in Kino. He rolled up to his feet and followed her as silently as she had gone, and he could hear her quick footsteps going toward the shore. Quietly he tracked her, and his brain was red with anger. She burst clear of the brush line and stumbled over the little boulders toward the water, and then she heard him coming, and she broke into a run. Her arm was up to throw when he leaped at her and caught her arm and wrenched the pearl from her. He struck her in the face with his clenched fist, and she fell among the boulders, and he kicked her in the side. In the pale light he could see the little waves break over her, and her skirt floated about and clung to her legs as the water receded.

Kino looked down at her, and his teeth were bared. He hissed at her like a snake; and Juana stared at him with wide, unfrightened eyes, like a sheep before the butcher. She knew there was murder in him, and it was all right, she had accepted it, and she would not resist or even protest. And then the rage left him, and a sick disgust took its place. He turned away from her and walked up the beach and through the brush line. His senses were dulled by his emotion.

He heard the rush, got his knife out and lunged at one dark figure and felt his knife go home; and then he was swept to his knees and swept again to the ground. Greedy fingers went through his clothes; frantic fingers searched him; and the pearl, knocked from his hand, lay winking behind a little stone in the pathway. It glinted in the soft moonlight.

Juana dragged herself up from the rocks on the edge of the water. Her face was a dull pain, and her side ached. She steadied herself on her knees for a while, and her wet skirt clung to her. There was no anger in her for Kino. He had said, "I am a man," and that meant certain things to Juana. It meant that he was half insane and half god. It meant that Kino would drive his strength against a mountain and plunge his strength against the sea. Juana, in her woman's soul, knew that the mountain would stand while the man broke himself, that the sea would surge while the man drowned in it. And yet it was the thing that made him a man, half insane and half god; and Juana had need of a man; she could not live without a man. Although she might be puzzled by these differences between man and woman, she knew them and accepted them and needed them. Of course she would follow him; there was no question of that. Sometimes the quality of woman, the reason, the caution, the sense of preservation, could cut through Kino's manness and save them all. She climbed painfully to her feet, and she dipped her cupped palms in the little waves and washed her bruised face with the stinging salt water, and then she went creeping up the beach after Kino.

A flight of herring clouds had moved over the sky from the south. The pale moon dipped in and out of the strands of clouds, so that Juana walked in darkness for a moment and in light the next. Her back was bent with pain and her head was low. She went through the line of brush when the moon was covered; and when it looked through, she saw the glimmer of the great pearl in the path behind the rock. She sank to her knees and picked it up, and the moon went into the darkness of the clouds again. Juana remained on her knees while she considered whether to go back to the sea and finish her job; and as she considered, the light came again; and she saw two dark figures lying in the path ahead of her. She leaped forward and saw that one was Kino and the other a stranger, with dark shiny fluid leaking from his throat.

Kino moved sluggishly; arms and legs stirred like those of a crushed bug; and a thick muttering came from his mouth. Now, in an instant, Juana knew that the old life was gone forever. A dead man in the path and Kino's knife, dark-bladed beside him, convinced her. All of the time Juana had been trying to rescue something of the old peace, of the time before the pearl. But now it was gone, and there was no retrieving it. And knowing this, she abandoned the past instantly. There was nothing to do but to save themselves.

Her pain was gone now, her slowness. Quickly she dragged the dead man from the pathway into the shelter of the brush. She went to Kino and sponged his face with her wet skirt. His senses were coming back, and he moaned.

"They have taken the pearl. I have lost it. Now it is over," he said. "The pearl is gone."

Juana quieted him as she would quiet a sick child. "Hush," she said. "Here is your pearl. I found it in the path. Can you hear me now? Here is your pearl. Can you understand? You have killed a man. We must go away. They will come for us; can you understand? We must be gone before the daylight comes."

"I was attacked," Kino said uneasily. "I struck to save my life."

"Do you remember yesterday?" Juana asked. "Do you think that will matter? Do you remember the men of the city? Do you think your explanation will help?"

Kino drew a great breath and fought off his weakness. "No," he said. "You are right." And his will hardened, and he was a man again.

"Go to our house and bring Coyotito," he said, "and bring all the corn we have. I will drag the canoe into the water, and we will go."

He took his knife and left her. He stumbled toward the beach, and he came to his canoe. And when the light broke through again, he saw that a great hole had been knocked in the bottom. And a searing rage came to him and gave him strength. Now the darkness was closing in on his family; now the evil music filled the night, hung over the mangroves, skirled in the wave beat. The canoe of his grandfather, plastered over and over, and a splintered hole broken in it. This was an evil beyond thinking. The killing of a man was not so evil as the killing of a boat. For a boat does not have sons, and a boat cannot protect itself, and a wounded boat does not heal. There was sorrow in Kino's rage, but this last thing had tightened him beyond breaking. He was an animal now, for hiding, for attacking; and he lived only to preserve himself and his family. He was not conscious of the pain in his head. He leaped up the beach, through the brush line toward his brush house; and it did not occur to him to take one of the canoes of his neighbors. Never once did the thought enter his head, any more than he could have conceived breaking a boat.

The roosters were crowing, and the dawn was not far off. Smoke of the first fires seeped out through the walls of the brush houses, and the first smell of cooking corncakes was in the air. Already the dawn birds were scampering in the bushes. The weak moon was losing its light, and the clouds thickened and curdled to the southward. The wind blew freshly into the estuary, a nervous, restless wind with the smell of storm on its breath; and there was change and uneasiness in the air.

Kino, hurrying toward his house, felt a surge of exhilaration. Now he was not confused, for there was only one thing to do, and Kino's hand went first to the great pearl in his shirt and then to his knife hanging under his shirt.

He saw a little glow ahead of him, and then without interval a tall flame leaped up in the dark with a crackling roar, and a tall edifice of fire lighted the pathway. Kino broke into a run; it was his brush house, he knew. And he knew that these houses could burn down in a very few moments. And as he ran, a scuttling figure ran toward him — Juana, with Coyotito in her arms and Kino's shoulder blanket clutched in her hand. The baby moaned with fright, and Juana's eyes were wide and terrified. Kino could see the house was gone, and he did not question Juana. He knew; but she said, "It was torn up and the floor dug — even the baby's box turned out; and as I looked, they put the fire to the outside."

The fierce light of the burning house lighted Kino's face strongly. "Who?" he demanded.

"I don't know," she said. "The dark ones."

The neighbors were tumbling from their houses now, and they watched the falling sparks and stamped them out to save their own houses. Suddenly Kino was afraid. The light made him afraid. He remembered the man lying dead in the brush beside the path, and he took Juana by the arm and drew her into the shadow of a house away from the light, for light was danger to him. For a moment he considered, and then he worked among the shadows until he came to the house of Juan Tomás, his brother; and he slipped into the doorway and drew Juana after him. Outside, he could hear the squeal of children and the shouts of the neighbors, for his friends thought he might be inside the burning house.

The house of Juan Tomás was almost exactly like Kino's house; nearly all the brush houses were alike, and all leaked light and air; so that Juana and Kino, sitting in the corner of the brother's house, could see the leaping flames through the wall. They saw the flames tall and furious; they saw the roof fall and watched the fire die down as quickly as a twig fire dies. They heard the cries of warning of their friends, and the shrill, keening cry of Apolonia, wife of Juan Tomás. She, being the nearest woman relative, raised a formal lament for the dead of the family.

Apolonia realized that she was wearing her second-best head shawl, and she rushed to her house to get her fine new one. As she rummaged in a box by the wall, Kino's voice said quietly, "Apolonia, do not cry out. We are not hurt."

"How do you come here?" she demanded.

"Do not question," he said. "Go now to Juan Tomás and bring him here and tell no one else. This is important to us, Apolonia."

She paused, her hands helpless in front of her; and then, "Yes, my brother-in-law," she said.

In a few moments Juan Tomás came back with her. He lighted a candle and came to them where they crouched in a corner, and he said, "Apolonia, see to the door, and do not let anyone enter." He was older, Juan Tomás, and he assumed the authority. "Now, my brother," he said.

"I was attacked in the dark," said Kino. "And in the fight I have killed a man."

"Who?" asked Juan Tomás quickly.

"I do not know. It is all darkness — all darkness and shape of darkness."

"It is the pearl," said Juan Tomás. "There is a devil in this pearl. You should have sold it and passed on the devil. Perhaps you can still sell it and buy peace for yourself."

And Kino said, "Oh, my brother, an insult has been put on me that is deeper than my life. For on the beach my canoe is broken, my house is burned, and in the brush a dead man lies. Every escape is cut off. You must hide us, my brother."

And Kino, looking closely, saw deep worry come into his brother's eyes; and he forestalled him in a possible refusal. "Not for long," he said quickly. "Only until a day has passed and the new night has come. Then we will go."

"I will hide you," said Juan Tomás.

"I do not want to bring danger to you," Kino said. "I know I am like a leprosy. I will go tonight, and then you will be safe."

"I will protect you," said Juan Tomás, and he called, "Apolonia, close up the door. Do not even whisper that Kino is here."

They sat silently all day in the darkness of the house, and they could hear the neighbors speaking of them. Through the walls of the house, they could watch their neighbors raking the ashes to find the bones. Crouching in the house of Juan Tomás, they heard the shock go into their neighbor's minds at the news of the broken boat. Juan Tomás went out among the neighbors to divert their suspicions, and he gave them theories and ideas of what had happened to Kino and to Juana and to the baby. To one he said, "I think they have gone south along the coast to escape the evil that was on them." And to another, "Kino would never leave the sea. Perhaps he found another boat." And he said, "Apolonia is ill with grief."

And in that day the wind rose up to beat the Gulf and tore the kelps and weeds that lined the shore, and the wind cried through the brush houses, and no boat was safe on the water. Then Juan Tomás told among the neighbors, "Kino is gone. If he went to the sea, he is drowned by now." And after each trip among the neighbors Juan Tomás came back with something borrowed. He brought a little woven straw bag of red beans and a gourd full of rice. He borrowed a cup of dried peppers and a block of salt, and he brought in a long working knife, eighteen inches long and heavy, as a small ax, a tool, and a weapon. And when Kino saw this knife, his eyes lighted up; and he fondled the blade, and his thumb tested the edge.

The wind screamed over the Gulf and turned the water white, and the mangroves plunged like frightened cattle, and a fine sandy dust arose from the land and hung in a stifling cloud over the sea. The wind drove off the clouds and skimmed the sky clean and drifted the sand of the country like snow.

Then Juan Tomás, when the evening approached, talked long with his brother. "Where will you go?"

"To the north," said Kino. "I have heard that there are cities in the north."

"Avoid the shore," said Juan Tomás. "They are making a party to search the shore. The men in the city will look for you. Do you still have the pearl?"

"I have it," said Kino. "And I will keep it. I might have given it as a gift, but now it is my misfortune and my life, and I will keep it." His eyes were hard and cruel and bitter.

Coyotito whimpered, and Juana muttered little magics over him to make him silent.

"The wind is good," said Juan Tomás. "There will be no tracks."

They left quietly in the dark before the moon had risen. The family stood formally in the house of Juan Tomás. Juana carried Coyotito on her back, covered and held in by her head shawl; and the baby slept, cheek turned sideways against her shoulder. The head shawl covered the baby, and one end of it came across Juana's nose to protect her from the evil night air. Juan Tomás embraced his brother with the double embrace and kissed him on both cheeks. "Go with God," he said, and it was like a death. "You will not give up the pearl?"

"This pearl has become my soul," said Kino. "If I give it up, I shall lose my soul. Go thou also with God."

CHAPTER 6

The wind blew fierce and strong; and it pelted them with bits of sticks, sand, and little rocks. Juana and Kino gathered their clothing tighter about them and covered their noses and went out into the world. The sky was brushed clean by the wind, and the stars were cold in a black sky. The two walked carefully, and they avoided the center of town, where some sleeper in a doorway might see them pass. For the town closed itself in against the night, and anyone who moved about in the darkness would be noticeable. Kino threaded his way around the edge of the city and turned north, north by the stars, and found the rutted sandy road that led through the brushy country toward Loreto, where the miraculous Virgin has her station.

Kino could feel the blown sand against his ankles, and he was glad, for he knew there would be no tracks. The little light from the stars made out for him the narrow road through the brushy country. And Kino could hear the pad of Juana's feet behind him. He went quickly and quietly, and Juana trotted behind him to keep up.

Some ancient thing stirred in Kino. Through his fear of dark and the devils that haunt the night, there came a rush of exhilaration; some animal thing was moving in him so that he was cautious and wary and dangerous; some ancient thing out of the past of his people was alive in him. The wind was at his back, and the stars guided him. The wind cried and whisked in the brush; and the family went on monotonously, hour after hour. They passed no one and saw no one. At last, to their right, the waning moon arose; and when it came up, the wind died down; and the land was still.

Now they could see the little road ahead of them, deep-cut with sand-drifted wheel tracks. With the wind gone there would be footprints, but they were a good distance from the town, and perhaps their tracks might not be noticed. Kino walked carefully in a wheel rut, and Juana followed in his path. One big cart, going to the town in the morning, could wipe out every trace of their passage.

All night they walked and never changed their pace. Once Coyotito awakened, and Juana shifted him in front of her and soothed him until he went to sleep again. And the evils of the night were about them. The coyotes cried and laughed in the brush, and the owls screeched and hissed over their heads. And once some large animal lumbered away, crackling the undergrowth as it went. And Kino gripped the handle of the big working knife and took a sense of protection from it.

The music of the pearl was triumphant in Kino's head, and the quiet melody of the family underlay it, and they wove themselves into the soft padding of sandaled feet in the dusk. All night they walked, and in the first dawn Kino searched the roadside for a covert to lie in during the day. He found his place near to the road, a little clearing where deer might have lain; and it was curtained thickly with the dry, brittle trees that lined the road. And when Juana had seated herself and had settled to nurse the baby, Kino went back to the road. He broke a branch and carefully swept the footprints where they had turned from the roadway. And then, in the first light, he heard the creak of a wagon; and he crouched beside the road and watched a heavy two-wheeled cart go by, drawn by slouching oxen. And when it had passed out of sight, he went back to the roadway and looked at the rut and found that the footprints were gone. And again he swept out his traces and went back to Juana.

She gave him the soft corncakes Apolonia had packed for them, and after a while she slept a little. But Kino sat on the ground and stared at the earth in front of him. He watched the ants moving, a little column of them near his foot, and he put his foot in their path. Then the column climbed over his instep and continued on its way, and Kino left his foot there and watched them move over it.

The sun arose hotly. They were not near the Gulf now; and the air was dry and hot, so that the brush cricked with heat, and a good resinous smell came from it. And when Juana awakened, when the sun was high, Kino told her things she knew already.

"Beware of that kind of tree there," he said, pointing. "Do not touch it, for if you do and then touch your eyes, it will blind you. And beware of the tree that bleeds. See, that one over there. For if you break it, the red blood will flow from it; and it is evil luck." And she nodded and smiled a little at him, for she knew these things.

"Will they follow us?" she asked. "Do you think they will try to find us?"

"They will try," said Kino. "Whoever finds us will take the pearl. Oh, they will try."

And Juana said, "Perhaps the dealers were right and the pearl has no value. Perhaps this has all been an illusion."

Kino reached into his clothes and brought out the pearl. He let the sun play on it until it burned in his eyes. "No," he said, "they would not have tried to steal it if it had been valueless."

"Do you know who attacked you? Was it the dealers?"

"I do not know," he said. "I didn't see them."

He looked into his pearl to find his vision.

"When we sell it at last, I will have a rifle," he said; and he looked into the shining surface for his rifle, but he saw only a huddled dark body on the ground with shining blood dripping from its throat. And he said quickly, "We will be married in a great church." And in the pearl he saw Juana with her beaten face, crawling home through the night. "Our son must learn to read," he said frantically. And there in the pearl was Coyotito's face, thick and feverish from the medicine.

And Kino thrust the pearl back into his clothing, and the music of the pearl had become sinister in his ears, and it was interwoven with the music of evil.

The hot sun beat on the earth, so that Kino and Juana moved into the lacy shade of the brush; and small gray birds scampered on the ground in the shade. In the heat of the day, Kino relaxed and covered his eyes with his hat and wrapped his blanket about his face to keep the flies off; and he slept.

But Juana did not sleep. She sat quiet as a stone, and her face was quiet. Her mouth was still swollen where Kino had struck her, and big flies buzzed around the cut on her chin. But she sat as still as a sentinel; and when Coyotito awakened, she placed him on the ground in front of her and watched him wave his arms and kick his feet; and he smiled and gurgled at her, until she smiled too. She picked up a little twig from the ground and tickled him, and she gave him water from the gourd she carried in her bundle.

Kino stirred in a dream, and he cried out in a guttural voice, and his hand moved in symbolic fighting. And then he moaned and sat up suddenly, his eyes wide and his nostrils flaring. He listened and heard only the cricking heat and the hiss of distance.

"What is it?" Juana asked.

"Hush," he said.

"You were dreaming."

"Perhaps." But he was restless; and when she gave him a corncake from her store, he paused in his chewing to listen. He was uneasy and nervous; he glanced over his shoulder; he lifted the big knife and felt its edge. When Coyotito gurgled on the ground, Kino said, "Keep him quiet."

"What is the matter?" Juana asked.

"I don't know."

He listened again, an animal light in his eyes. He stood up then, silently; and, crouched low, he threaded his way through the brush toward the road. But he did not step into the road; he crept into the cover of a thorny tree and peered out along the way he had come.

And then he saw them moving along. His body stiffened, and he drew down his head and peeked out from under a fallen branch. In the distance he could see three figures, two on foot and one on horseback. But he knew what they were, and a chill of fear went through him. Even in the distance he could see the two on foot moving slowly along, bent low to the ground. Here, one would pause and look at the earth, while the other joined him. They were the trackers; they could follow the trail of a bighorn sheep in the stone mountains. They were as sensitive as hounds. Here, he and Juana might have stepped out of the wheel rut; and these people from the inland, these hunters, could follow, could read a broken straw or a little tumbled pile of dust. Behind them, on a horse, was a dark man, his nose covered with a blanket; and across his saddle a rifle gleamed in the sun.

Kino lay as rigid as the tree limb. He barely breathed, and his eyes went to the place where he had swept out the track. Even the sweeping might be a message to the trackers. He knew these inland hunters. In a country where there is little game, they managed to live because of their ability to hunt; and they were hunting him. They scuttled over the ground like animals, and found a sign and crouched over it, while the horseman waited.

The trackers whined a little, like excited dogs on a warming trail. Kino slowly drew his big knife to his hand and made it ready. He knew what he must do. If the trackers found the swept place, he must leap for the horseman, kill him quickly, and take the rifle. That was his only chance in the world. And as the three drew nearer on the road, Kino dug little pits with his sandaled toes, so that he could leap without warning, so that his feet would not slip. He had only a little vision under the fallen limb.

Now Juana, back in her hidden place, heard the pad of the horse's hoofs; and Coyotito gurgled. She took him up quickly and put him under her shawl and gave him her breast, and he was silent.

When the trackers came near, Kino could see only their legs and only the legs of the horse from under the fallen branch. He saw the dark, horny feet of the men and their ragged white clothes, and he heard the creak of leather of the saddle, and the clink of spurs. The trackers stopped at the swept place and studied it, and the horseman stopped. The horse flung his head up against the bit, and the bit-roller clicked under his tongue, and the horse snorted. Then the dark trackers turned and studied the horse and watched his ears.

Kino was not breathing, but his back arched a little, and the muscles of his arms and legs stood out with tension, and a line of sweat formed on his upper lip. For a long moment the trackers bent over the road; and then they moved on slowly, studying the ground ahead of them; and the horseman moved after them. The trackers scuttled along, stopping, looking, and hurrying on. They would be back, Kino knew. They would be circling and searching, peeping, stooping; and they would come back sooner or later to his covered track.

He slid backward and did not bother to cover his tracks. He could not; too many little signs were there, too many broken twigs and scuffed places and displaced stones. And there was a panic in Kino now, a panic of flight. The trackers would find his trail; he knew it. There was no escape, except in flight. He edged away from the road and went quickly and silently to the hidden place where Juana was. She looked up at him in question.

"Trackers," he said. "Come!"

And then a helplessness and a hopelessness swept over him, and his face went black, and his eyes were sad. "Perhaps I should let them take me."

Instantly Juana was on her feet, and her hand lay on his arm. "You have the pearl," she cried hoarsely. "Do you think they would take you back alive to say they had stolen it?"

His hand strayed limply to the place where the pearl was hidden under his clothes. "They will find it," he said weakly.

"Come," she said. "Come!"

And when he did not respond, "Do you think they would let me live? Do you think they would let the little one here live?"

Her goading struck into his brain; his lips snarled and his eyes were fierce again. "Come," he said. "We will go into the mountains. Maybe we can lose them in the mountains."

Frantically he gathered the gourds and the little bags that were their property. Kino carried a bundle in his left hand, but the big knife swung free in his right hand. He parted the brush for Juana; and they hurried to the west, toward the high stone mountains. They trotted quickly through the tangle of the undergrowth. This was panic flight. Kino did not try to conceal his passage; he trotted, kicking the stones, knocking the telltale leaves from the little trees. The high sun streamed down on the dry, creaking earth, so that even vegetation ticked in protest. But ahead were the naked granite mountains, rising out of erosion rubble and standing monolithic against the sky. And Kino ran for the high place, as nearly all animals do when they are pursued.

This land was waterless, furred with the cacti, which could store water, and with the great-rooted brush, which could reach deep into the earth for a little moisture and get along on very little. And underfoot was not soil but broken rock, split into small cubes, great slabs, but none of it water-rounded. Little tufts of sad, dry grass grew between the stones, grass that had sprouted with one single rain and headed, dropped its seed, and died. Horned toads watched the family go by and turned their little pivoting dragon heads. And now and then a great jackrabbit, disturbed in his shade, bumped away and hid behind the nearest rock. The singing heat lay over this desert country, and ahead the stone mountains looked cool and welcoming.

And Kino fled. He knew what would happen. A little way along the road the trackers would become aware that they had missed the path, and they would come back, searching and judging; and in a little while they would find the place where Kino and Juana had rested. From there it would be easy for them — these little stones, the fallen leaves and the whipped branches, the scuffed places where a foot had slipped. Kino could see them in his mind, slipping along the track, whining a little with eagerness, and behind them, dark and half disinterested, the horseman with the rifle. His work would come last, for he would not take them back. Oh, the music of evil sang loud in Kino's head now; it sang with the whine of heat and with the dry ringing of snake rattles. It was not large and overwhelming now, but secret and poisonous; and the pounding of his heart gave it undertone and rhythm.

The way began to rise; and as it did, the rocks grew larger. But now Kino had put a little distance between his family and the trackers. Now, on the first rise, he rested. He climbed a great boulder and looked back over the shimmering country, but he could not see his enemies, not even the tall horseman riding through the brush. Juana had squatted in the shade of the boulder. She raised her bottle of water to Coyotito's lips; his little dried tongue sucked greedily at it. She looked up at Kino when he came back; she saw him examine her ankles, cut and scratched from the stones and brush; and she covered them quickly with her skirt. Then she handed the bottle to him, but he shook his head. Her eyes were bright in her tired face. Kino moistened his cracked lips with his tongue.

"Juana," he said, "I will go on, and you will hide. I will lead them into the mountains, and when they have gone past, you will go north to Loreto or to Santa Rosalia. Then, if I can escape them, I will come to you. It is the only safe way."

She looked full into his eyes for a moment. "No," she said. "We go with you."

"I can go faster alone," he said harshly. "You will put the little one in more danger if you go with me."

"No," said Juana.

"You must. It is the wise thing, and it is my wish," he said.

"No," said Juana.

He looked then for weakness in her face, for fear or irresolution; and there was none. Her eyes were very bright. He shrugged his shoulders helplessly then, but he had taken strength from her. When they moved on, it was no longer panic flight.

The country, as it rose toward the mountains, changed rapidly. Now there were long outcroppings of granite with deep crevices between, and Kino walked on bare unmarkable stone when he could, and leaped from ledge to ledge. He knew that wherever the trackers lost his path they must circle and lose time before they found it again. And so he did not go straight for the mountains any more; he moved in zigzags, and sometimes he cut back to the south and left a sign, and then went toward the mountains over bare stone again. And the path rose steeply now, so that he panted a little as he went.

The sun moved downward toward the bare stone teeth of the mountains, and Kino set his direction for a dark and shadowy cleft in the range. If there were any water at all, it would be there where he could see, even in the distance, a hint of foliage. And if there were any passage through the smooth stone range, it would be by this same deep cleft. It had its danger, for the trackers would think of it too, but the empty water bottle did not let that consideration enter. And as the sun lowered, Kino and Juana struggled wearily up the steep slope toward the cleft.

High in the gray stone mountains, under a frowning peak, a little spring bubbled out of a rupture in the stone. It was fed by shade-preserved snow in the summer, and now and then it died completely, and bare rocks and dry algae were on its bottom. But nearly always it gushed out, cold and clean and lovely. In the times when the quick rains fell, it might become a freshet and send its column of white water crashing down the mountain cleft, but nearly always it was a lean little spring. It bubbled out into a pool and then fell a hundred feet to another pool, and this one, overflowing, dropped again, so that it continued, down and down, until it came to the rubble of the upland, and there it disappeared altogether. There wasn't much left of it then anyway; for every time it fell over an escarpment, the thirsty air drank it; and it splashed from the pools to the dry vegetation. The animals from miles around came to drink from the little pools: the wild sheep and the deer, the pumas and raccoons, and the mice — all came to drink. And the birds which spent the day in the brushland came at night to the little pools, that were like steps in the mountain cleft. Beside this tiny stream, wherever enough earth collected for roothold, colonies of plants grew, wild grape and little palms, maidenhair fern, hibiscus, and tall pampas grass with feathery rods raised above the spike leaves. And in the pool lived frogs and waterskaters, and waterworms crawled on the bottom of the pool. Everything that loved water came to these few shallow places. The cats took their prey there and strewed feathers and lapped water through their bloody teeth. The little pools were places of life because of the water, and places of killing because of the water, too.

The lowest step, where the stream collected before it tumbled down a hundred feet and disappeared into the rubbly desert, was a little platform of stone and sand. Only a pencil of water fell into the pool, but it was enough to keep the pool full and to keep the ferns green in the underhang of the cliff, and wild grape climbed the stone mountain, and all manner of little plants found comfort here. The freshets had made a small sandy beach through which the pool flowed, and bright green watercress grew in the damp sand. The beach was cut and scarred and padded by the feet of animals that had come to drink and to hunt.

The sun had passed over the stone mountains when Kino and Juana struggled up the steep, broken slope and came at last to the water. From this step they could look out over the sunbeaten desert to the blue Gulf in the distance. They came utterly weary to the pool, and Juana slumped to her knees and first washed Coyotito's face and then filled her bottle and gave him a drink. And the baby was weary and petulant, and he cried softly until Juana gave him her breast, and then he gurgled and clucked against her. Kino drank long and thirstily at the pool. For a moment, then, he stretched out beside the water and relaxed all his muscles and watched Juana feeding the baby, and then he got to his feet and went to the edge of the step where the water slipped over, and he searched the distance carefully. His eyes set on a point and he became rigid. Far down the slope he could see the two trackers; they were little more than dots or scurrying ants, and behind them a larger ant.

Juana had turned to look at him, and she saw his back stiffen.

"How far?" she asked quietly.

"They will be here by evening," said Kino. He looked up the long, steep chimney of the cleft where the water came down. "We must go west," he said, and his eyes searched the stone shoulder behind the cleft. And thirty feet up on the gray shoulder he saw a series of little erosion caves. He slipped off his sandals and clambered up to them, gripping the bare stone with his toes, and he looked into the shallow caves. They were only a few feet deep, wind-hollowed scoops, but they sloped slightly downward and back. Kino crawled into the largest one and lay down and knew that he could not be seen from the outside. Quickly he went back to Juana.

"You must go up there. Perhaps they will not find us there," he said.

Without question she filled her water bottle to the top, and then

Kino helped her up to the shallow cave and brought up the packages of food and passed them to her. And Juana sat in the cave entrance and watched him. She saw that he did not try to erase their tracks in the sand. Instead, he climbed up the brush cliff beside the water, clawing and tearing at the ferns and wild grape as he went. And when he had climbed a hundred feet to the next bench, he came down again. He looked carefully at the smooth rock shoulder toward the cave to see that there was no trace of passage, and last he climbed up and crept into the cave beside Juana.

"When they go up," he said, "we will slip away, down to the lowlands again. I am afraid only that the baby may cry. You must see that he does not cry."

"He will not cry," she said, and she raised the baby's face to her own and looked into his eyes, and he stared solemnly back at her.

"He knows," said Juana.

Now Kino lay in the cave entrance, his chin braced on his crossed arms, and he watched the blue shadow of the mountain move out across the brushy desert below until it reached the Gulf, and the long twilight of the shadow was over the land.

The trackers were long in coming, as though they had trouble with the trail Kino had left. It was dusk when they came at last to the little pool. And all three were on foot now, for a horse could not climb the last steep slope. From above they were thin figures in the evening. The two trackers scurried about on the little beach, and they saw Kino's progress up the cliff before they drank. The man with the rifle sat down and rested himself, and the trackers squatted near him, and in the evening the points of their cigarettes glowed and receded. And then Kino could see that they were eating, and the soft murmur of their voices came to him.

Then darkness fell, deep and black in the mountain cleft. The animals that used the pool came near and smelled men there and drifted away again into the darkness.

He heard a murmur behind him. Juana was whispering, "Coyotito." She was begging him to be quiet. Kino heard the baby whimper, and he knew from the muffled sounds that Juana had covered his head with her shawl.

Down on the beach a match flared; and in its momentary light Kino saw that two of the men were sleeping, curled up like dogs, while the third watched; and he saw the glint of the rifle in the match light. And then the match died, but it left a picture on Kino's eyes. He could see it, just how each man was, two sleeping curled and the third squatting in the sand with the rifle between his knees.

Kino moved silently back into the cave. Juana's eyes were two sparks reflecting a low star. Kino crawled quietly close to her, and he put his lips near to her cheek.

"There is a way," he said.

"But they will kill you."

"If I get first to the one with the rifle," Kino said, "I must get to him first, then I will be all right. Two are sleeping."

Her hand crept out from under her shawl and gripped his arm. "They will see your white clothes in the starlight."

"No," he said. "And I must go before moonrise."

He searched for a soft word and then gave it up. "If they kill me," he said, "lie quietly. And when they are gone away, go to Loreto."

Her hand shook a little, holding his wrist.

"There is no choice," he said. "It is the only way. They will find us in the morning."

Her voice trembled a little. "Go with God," she said.

He peered closely at her, and he could see her large eyes. His hand fumbled out and found the baby, and for a moment his palm lay on Coyotito's head. And then Kino raised his hand and touched Juana's cheek, and she held her breath.

Against the sky in the cave entrance Juana could see that Kino was taking off his white clothes; for dirty and ragged though they were, they would show up against the dark night. His own brown skin was a better protection for him. And then she saw how he hooked his amulet [1] neck-string about the horn handle of his great knife, so that it hung down in front of him and left both hands free. He did not come back to her. For a moment his body was black in the cave entrance, crouched and silent; and then he was gone.

Juana moved to the entrance and looked out. She peered like an owl from the hole in the mountain; and the baby slept under the blanket on her back, his face turned sideways against her neck and

---

[1] *amulet* (am'yə·lit): a magic charm, which Kino wore on a string around his neck.

shoulder. She could feel his warm breath against her skin; and Juana whispered her combination of prayer and magic, her Hail Marys and her ancient intercession, against the black, unhuman things.

The night seemed a little less dark when she looked out; and to the east there was a lightening in the sky, down near the horizon where the moon would show. And, looking down, she could see the cigarette of the man on watch.

Kino edged like a slow lizard down the smooth rock shoulder. He had turned his neck-string so that the great knife hung down from his back and could not clash against the stone. His spread fingers gripped the mountain, and his bare toes found support through contact, and even his chest lay against the stone, so that he would not slip. For any sound, a rolling pebble or a sigh, a little slip of flesh on rock, would rouse the watchers below. Any sound that was not germane to the night would make them alert. But the night was not silent: the little tree frogs that lived near the stream twittered like birds, and the high metallic ringing of the cicadas filled the mountain cleft. And Kino's own music was in his head, the music of the enemy, low and pulsing, nearly asleep. But the Song of the Family had become as fierce and sharp and feline as the snarl of a female puma. The family song was alive now and driving him down on the dark enemy. The harsh cicada seemed to take up its melody, and the twittering tree frogs called little phrases of it.

And Kino crept silently as a shadow down the smooth mountain face. One bare foot moved a few inches, and the toes touched the stone and gripped, and the other foot a few inches, and then the palm of one hand a little downward, and then the other hand, until the whole body, without seeming to move, had moved. Kino's mouth was open so that even his breath would make no sound, for he knew that he was not invisible. If the watcher, sensing movement, looked at the dark place against the stone which was his body, he could see him. Kino must move so slowly he would not draw the watcher's eyes. It took him a long time to reach the bottom and to crouch behind a little dwarf palm. His heart thundered in his chest, and his hands and face were wet with sweat. He crouched and took slow long breaths to calm himself.

Only twenty feet separated him from the enemy now, and he tried to remember the ground between. Was there any stone which might trip him in his rush? He kneaded his legs against cramp and found that his muscles were jerking after their long tension. And then he looked apprehensively to the east. The moon would rise in a few moments now, and he must attack before it rose. He could see the outline of the watcher, but the sleeping men were below his vision. It was the watcher Kino must find — must find quickly and without hesitation. Silently he drew the amulet string over his shoulder and loosened the loop from the horn handle of his great knife.

He was too late; for as he rose from his crouch, the silver edge of the moon slipped above the eastern horizon; and Kino sank back behind his bush.

It was an old and ragged moon, but it threw hard light and hard shadow into the mountain cleft, and now Kino could see the seated figure of the watcher on the little beach beside the pool. The watcher gazed full at the moon, and then he lighted another cigarette, and the match illumined his dark face for a moment. There could be no waiting now; when the watcher turned his head, Kino must leap. His legs were as tight as wound springs.

And then from above came a little murmuring cry. The watcher turned his head to listen, and then he stood up, and one of the sleepers stirred on the ground and awakened and asked quietly, "What is it?"

"I don't know," said the watcher. "It sounded like a cry, almost like a human — like a baby."

The man who had been sleeping said, "You can't tell. Some coyote bitch with a litter. I've heard a coyote pup cry like a baby."

The sweat rolled in drops down Kino's forehead and fell into his eyes and burned them. The little cry came again, and the watcher looked up the side of the hill to the dark cave.

"Coyote maybe," he said, and Kino heard the harsh click as he cocked the rifle.

"If it's a coyote, this will stop it," the watcher said as he raised the gun.

Kino was in mid-leap when the gun crashed, and the barrel-flash made a picture on his eyes. The great knife swung and crunched hollowly. It bit through neck and deep into chest, and Kino was a terrible machine now. He grasped the rifle even as he wrenched free his knife. His strength and his movement and his speed were a machine. He whirled and struck the head of the seated man like a melon. The third man scrabbled away like a crab, slipped into the pool; and then he began to climb frantically, to climb up the cliff where the water penciled down. His hands and feet threshed in the tangle of the wild grapevine, and he whimpered and gibbered as he tried to get up. But Kino had become as cold and deadly as steel. Deliberately he threw the lever of the rifle, and then he raised the gun and aimed deliberately and fired. He saw his enemy tumble backward into the pool, and Kino strode to the water. In the moonlight he could see the frantic frightened eyes, and Kino aimed and fired between the eyes.

And then Kino stood uncertainly. Something was wrong; some signal was trying to get through to his brain. Tree frogs and cicadas were silent now. And then Kino's brain cleared from its red concentration, and he knew the sound — the keening, moaning, rising hysterical cry from the little cave in the side of the stone mountain, the cry of death.

Everyone in La Paz remembers the return of the family; there may be some old ones who saw it, but those whose fathers and whose grandfathers told it to them remember it nevertheless. It is an event that happened to everyone. *Universality*

It was late in the golden afternoon when the first little boys ran hysterically in the town and spread the word that Kino and Juana were coming back. And everyone hurried to see them. The sun was settling toward the western mountains, and the shadows on the ground were long. And perhaps that was what left the deep impression on those who saw them.

The two came from the rutted country road into the city, and they were not walking in single file, Kino ahead and Juana behind, as usual, but side by side. The sun was behind them, and their long shadows stalked ahead, and they seemed to carry two towers of darkness with them. Kino had a rifle across his arm, and Juana carried her shawl like a sack over her shoulder. And in it was a small, limp, heavy bundle. The shawl was crusted with dried blood, and the bundle swayed a little as she walked. Her face was hard and lined and leathery with fatigue and with the tightness with which she fought fatigue. And her wide eyes stared inward on herself. She was as remote and as removed as Heaven. Kino's lips were thin and his jaws tight, and the people say that he carried fear with him, that he was as dangerous as a rising storm. The people say that the two seemed to be removed from human experience, that they had gone through pain and had come out on the other side, that there was almost a magical protection about them. And those people who had rushed to see them crowded back and let them pass and did not speak to them.

Kino and Juana walked through the city as though it were not there. Their eyes glanced neither right nor left nor up nor down, but stared only straight ahead. Their legs moved a little jerkily, like well-made wooden dolls, and they carried pillars of black fear about them. And as they walked through the stone and plaster city, brokers peered at them from barred windows, and servants put one eye to a slitted gate, and mothers turned the faces of their youngest children inward against their skirts. Kino and Juana strode side by side through the stone and plaster city and down among the brush houses, and the neighbors stood back and let them pass. Juan Tomás raised his hand in greeting and did not say the greeting and left his hand in the air for a moment uncertainly.

In Kino's ears the Song of the Family was as fierce as a cry. He was immune and terrible, and his song had become a battle cry. They trudged past the burned square where their house had been without even looking at it. They cleared the brush that edged the beach and picked their way down the shore toward the water. And they did not look toward Kino's broken canoe.

And when they came to the water's edge, they stopped and stared out over the Gulf. And then Kino laid the rifle down, and he dug among his clothes, and then he held the great pearl in his hand. He looked into its surface, and it was gray and ulcerous. Evil faces peered from it into his eyes, and he saw the light of burning. And in the surface of the pearl he saw the frantic eyes of the man in the pool. And in the surface of the pearl he saw Coyotito lying in the little cave with the top of his head shot away. And the pearl was ugly; it was gray, like a malignant growth. And Kino heard the music of the pearl, distorted and insane. Kino's hand shook a little, and he turned slowly to Juana and held the pearl out to her. She stood beside him, still holding her dead bundle over her shoulder. She looked at the pearl in his hand for a moment, and then she looked into Kino's eyes and said softly, "No, you."

And Kino drew back his arm and flung the pearl with all his

might. Kino and Juana watched it go, winking and glimmering under the setting sun. They saw the little splash in the distance, and they stood side by side watching the place for a long time.

And the pearl settled into the lovely green water and dropped toward the bottom. The waving branches of the algae called to it and beckoned to it. The lights on its surface were green and lovely. It settled down to the sand bottom among the fernlike plants. Above, the surface of the water was a green mirror. And the pearl lay on the floor of the sea. A crab scampering over the bottom raised a little cloud of sand; and when it settled, the pearl was gone.

And the music of the pearl drifted to a whisper and disappeared.

"The Fox and the Crow,"
woodcut by Antonio Frasconi.

BOOK FOUR | PART 2

FABLES AND LEGENDS

If this story is a parable, perhaps everyone takes his own meaning from it and reads his own life into it.
THE PEARL

An Arabian proverb says that a fable is "a bridge that leads to truth." Like the myths, which are stories about gods, fables belong to the very beginnings of literature. Most fables are short, simple, often humorous tales. Many are about animals who resemble humans. The purpose of a fable is to teach a moral lesson. Sometimes the moral of a fable is so obvious that it does not have to be stated. But usually a fable includes a direct statement of its moral: Slow and steady wins the race. Kindness will get you more than force.

There is an important difference between a fable or a legend and most other forms of literature: Most literature is not intended to convey a moral to the reader. Many readers, however, being incurable "message-hunters," find this idea difficult to grasp. They think that if an author's ideas agree with theirs he is a good writer; if his ideas don't agree with theirs, there is something wrong with him.

Now literature, in some sense, must be "true" and "real." It is about life as the writer sees it or imagines it. It contains experience, and it examines values. It is about things that are important to us as human beings. But good writers are more interested in asking hard questions than in giving easy answers. As readers, we must try to approach a story or poem as an experience of the imagination. We do violence to it if we reduce it to a single simple "message."

Look, for example, at three of the longer works in this volume: the Odyssey, The Miracle Worker, and The Lilies of the Field. It would not be hard to think up morals or messages to go with them. For example:

The Odyssey: If you persist, in spite of hardships, you will be rewarded.

The Miracle Worker: We should help those who are less fortunate than we are.

The Lilies of the Field: The true reward in giving is the act of giving, itself.

However, if you have read any or all of these works, you will see at once that such statements do not come close to summing up these books. There are all kinds of themes and meanings in them which will not fit a simple formula. And, of course, the "message" completely leaves out the author's style and the imaginative world he constructed.

But the fables in the following section belong to another tradition, that of didactic (teaching) literature. They are intended to point up a moral or message. That is one reason that most of them are so short and the characters in them are not greatly developed. If they were to become more complicated, they would no longer be good examples for simple lessons.

The tradition of the fable or legend is not dead. It is still used by preachers, politicians, and writers who wish to make a point quickly and sharply. Also, many modern storytellers, like Steinbeck, reach back to the tradition of the fable in order to give their work a simplicity that carries with it a moral force. At the end of the section, you will find three modern short stories that in one way or another adopt the tone of the fable or simple legend.

Five Fables

The best known fables in Western literature have come down to us under the name of Aesop. Many of his fables can also be found in the literature of other peoples. It is not known whether Aesop invented any of his fables or merely gathered them together.

1: THE DOG IN THE MANGER

A Dog who wanted to take his afternoon nap jumped into the manger of an Ox and curled up on the straw. But soon the Ox returned from its afternoon's work. It came up to the manger to eat some of the straw. The Dog, awakened from his nap, grew very angry. He stood up and barked at the Ox, and whenever the Ox came near the manger, he tried to bite it. At last the Ox gave up and went away hungry. He muttered to himself: "Ah, people often begrudge others what they cannot enjoy themselves."

2: THE MICE AND THE CAT

Once upon a time, the Mice held a meeting to decide what they could do to outwit their common enemy, the Cat. Many ideas were put forth, but at last a Young Mouse got up to offer a new proposal. "You will agree," he said, "that our danger comes from the fact that our enemy is able to creep up on us silently, in a sly and treacherous manner. So, if we only knew that she was coming, we could escape from her. My suggestion, then, is that we get a small bell and attach it to the Cat's neck with a ribbon. That way we will always know when she is crawling about, and we can get out of her way."

The idea was received with enthusiasm, until an Old Mouse got up and said, "That is all very well. But who is going to put the bell around the Cat's neck?" The Mice had not thought about that. They all looked at each other, but had nothing to say.

Then the Old Mouse sat down, saying: "It is easy to come up with ideas, but hard to carry them out."

Here are two tales from Africa. Susan Feldman of Columbia University has published a collection, African Myths and Tales *(Dell), which you may wish to read. In her preface, Mrs. Feldman writes:*

> The Africans' attitude to their tradition is more flexible and complex than we would suppose. "We do not really mean, we do not really mean, that what we are going to say is true," is the traditional beginning of every Ashanti tale. The Sudanese regard their tales as lies in which not everything is false — lies containing a grain of truth, a form of wisdom, common sense, and a moral. Storytelling sessions usually begin with the following formula:
> "I'm going to tell a story," the narrator begins.
> "Right!" the audience rejoins.
> "It's a lie."
> "Right!"
> "But not everything in it is false."
> "Right!"

3: HOW THE ANIMALS GOT THEIR COLOR

The color of all the animals is said to have been painted on by the meercat. The meercat said to the animals, "If anyone will kill a buck and bring me the meat, I will paint color on him."

The hyena heard him, so he went and killed a buck; he ate all the meat himself and took the bones to the meercat.

The meercat said, "Lie down." The hyena knelt down, and the meercat painted ugly marks on him, saying, "If anyone cheats me, I do the same to him."

The leopard went out hunting and killed a buck and brought it to the meercat unskinned. The meercat told him to kneel down and painted him a beautiful color, saying, "If anyone keeps his word with me, I will do the same to him."

The story is finished.

4: HOW THE ANIMALS GOT THEIR TAILS

It is said that animals were created without tails by their Maker. The Maker one day called them to come and select what tails would suit them. The first group of animals appeared and selected the long and best tails. The second group came and received good tails. The

last group were the hares, who are very lazy, and they told the other animals to pick out tails for them. The other animals, having taken the best tails for themselves, brought the short and ugly tails for the hares. If you want a thing well done, do it yourself.
The story is finished.

La Fontaine took the fables of Aesop and turned them into witty, sophisticated verses. Frenchmen of the seventeenth century saw their own manners reflected in the speech and actions of La Fontaine's animals.

5: THE OLD CAT AND THE YOUNG MOUSE

A very young mouse one day was caught
By a wise, old cat. The poor mouse thought
(She lacked experience) that she could *reason* with a cat!
"Oh let me live!" she cried. "Let me live and get fat.
I'm so thin I'm not worth the trouble to eat.
Think of your children! What a marvelous treat
I'll be for them *some day*. A grain of wheat
Once in a while is all I need. I'd be immense
If I ate a walnut. Dear Cat, your common sense
Tells you my needs are no drain upon this house."   10

But the cat replied, "I'm afraid you are wrong.
Do you *really* think you can sell me a song
Like that? You expect to be pardoned by a cat?
An *old* cat? Things just don't work like that.
Die now, and tell your sad story to the Fates.
My children can find food for their own plates."

The cat had the last word. And now I'm able
To add this little moral to the fable:
*The young seem to think they should have the whole city
And everything in it. But the old don't have much pity.*   20

This legend is drawn from the Gulistan (*The Garden of Roses*), *a Persian classic. Saadi lived in the thirteenth century.*

The Legend of the King and the Peasant

SAADI

A king, attended by his courtiers, was out on a hunting expedition in the midst of winter. They had got far from the hunting lodge, and the night was falling fast, when they saw a peasant's house in the distance.

The king said, "Let us go there, where we may shelter ourselves for the night from this freezing wind."

One of the courtiers replied, "It would not become the dignity of a king to enter the cottage of a low peasant. Rather, let us pitch a tent here and light a fire."

The peasant saw what was happening. He came forth with all the refreshments he had on hand, and laid them at the king's feet. He kissed the ground and said, "Nothing can destroy the lofty dignity of Your Majesty, not even entering my poor house. These gentlemen must be unwilling to see the condition of a poor peasant exalted."

The king was pleased with this speech, and, in spite of the objections of his courtiers, he passed into the peasant's cottage, where he spent the night. In the morning he bestowed a handsome cloak and many fine gifts upon his host.

I have heard that the peasant accompanied the king for some distance along the road, walking by the side of his horse and touching the king's stirrups. The peasant said:

"*The state and pomp of the king suffered no degradation by being a guest in the house of a peasant. But the brim of the peasant's cap rose to a level with the sun when the shadow of such a monarch fell upon it.*"

La Fontaine made his animals speak with the accents of seventeenth-century Frenchmen. James Thurber makes his speak like modern Americans.

The Tiger Who Would Be King

JAMES THURBER

One morning the tiger woke up in the jungle and told his mate that he was king of beasts.

"Leo, the lion, is king of beasts," she said.

"We need a change," said the tiger. "The creatures are crying for a change."

The tigress listened but she could hear no crying, except that of her cubs.

"I'll be king of beasts by the time the moon rises," said the tiger. "It will be a yellow moon with black stripes, in my honor."

"Oh, sure," said the tigress as she went to look after her young, one of whom, a male, very like his father, had got an imaginary thorn in his paw.

The tiger prowled through the jungle till he came to the lion's den. "Come out," he roared, "and greet the king of beasts! The king is dead, long live the king!"

Inside the den, the lioness woke her mate. "The king is here to see you," she said.

"What king?" he inquired, sleepily.

"The king of beasts," she said.

"I am king of beasts," roared Leo, and he charged out of the den to defend his crown against the pretender.

It was a terrible fight, and it lasted until the setting of the sun. All the animals of the jungle joined in, some taking the side of the tiger and others the side of the lion. Every creature from the aardvark to the zebra took part in the struggle to overthrow the lion or

693

to repulse the tiger, and some did not know which they were fighting for, and some fought for both, and some fought whoever was nearest, and some fought for the sake of fighting.

"What are we fighting for?" someone asked the aardvark.

"The old order," said the aardvark.

"What are we dying for?" someone asked the zebra.

"The new order," said the zebra.

When the moon rose, fevered and gibbous,[1] it shone upon a jungle in which nothing stirred except a macaw and a cockatoo, screaming in horror. All the beasts were dead except the tiger, and his days were numbered and his time was ticking away. He was monarch of all he surveyed, but it didn't seem to mean anything.

MORAL: *You can't very well be king of beasts if there aren't any.*

---

[1] *gibbous* (gib′əs) : nearly circular, as the moon when it is more than half full but less than full.

The writer of the next story is an American of Armenian background. The story told by his grandmother shows how natural it is for simple people to express themselves through exemplary tales. Compare the grandmother's lesson with that given to Claude Brown by his father (p. 161).

The Shepherd's Daughter

WILLIAM SAROYAN

It is the opinion of my grandmother, God bless her, that all men should labor, and at the table, a moment ago, she said to me: You must learn to do some good work, the making of some item useful to man, something out of clay, or out of wood, or metal, or cloth. It is not proper for a young man to be ignorant of an honorable craft. Is there anything you can make? Can you make a simple table, a chair, a plain dish, a rug, a coffee pot? Is there anything you can do?

And my grandmother looked at me with anger.

I know, she said, you are supposed to be a writer, and I suppose you are. You certainly smoke enough cigarettes to be anything, and the whole house is full of the smoke, but you must learn to make solid things, things that can be used, that can be seen and touched.

There was a king of the Persians, said my grandmother, and he had a son, and this son fell in love with a shepherd's daughter. He went to his father and he said, My Lord, I love a shepherd's daughter, and I would have her for my wife. And the king said, I am king and you are my son, and when I die you shall be king; how can it be that you would marry the daughter of a shepherd? And the son said, My Lord, I do not know, but I know that I love this girl and would have her for my queen.

The king saw that his son's love for the girl was from God, and he said, I will send a message to her. And he called a messenger to him and he said, Go to the shepherd's daughter and say that my son loves her and would have her for his wife. And the messenger went to the girl and he said, The king's son loves you and would have you for his wife. And the girl said, What labor does he do? And the messenger said, Why, he is the son of the king; he does no labor. And the girl said, He must learn to do some labor. And the messenger returned to the king and spoke the words of the shepherd's daughter.

The king said to his son, The shepherd's daughter wishes you to learn some craft. Would you still have her for your wife? And the son said, Yes, I will learn to weave straw rugs. And the boy was taught to weave rugs of straw, in patterns and in colors and with ornamental designs, and at the end of three days he was making very fine straw rugs, and the messenger returned to the shepherd's daughter, and he said, These rugs of straw are the work of the king's son.

And the girl went with the messenger to the king's palace, and she became the wife of the king's son.

One day, said my grandmother, the king's son was walking through the streets of Baghdad, and he came upon an eating place which was so clean and cool that he entered it and sat at a table.

This place, said my grandmother, was a place of thieves and murderers, and they took the king's son and placed him in a large dungeon where many great men of the city were being held, and the thieves and murderers were killing the fattest of the men and feeding them to the leanest of them, and making sport of it. The king's son was of the leanest of the men, and it was not known that he was the son of the king of the Persians, so his life was spared, and he said to the thieves and murderers, I am a weaver of straw rugs and these rugs have great value. And they brought him straw and asked him to weave, and in three days he weaved three rugs, and he said, Carry these to the palace of the king of the Persians, and for each rug he will give you a hundred gold pieces of money. And the rugs were carried to the palace of the king, and when the king saw the rugs he saw that they were the work of his son, and he took the rugs to the shepherd's daughter and he said, These rugs were brought to the palace and they are the work of my son who is lost. And the shepherd's daughter took each rug and looked at it closely, and in the design of each rug she saw in the written language of the Persians a message from her husband, and she related this message to the king.

And the king, said my grandmother, sent many soldiers to the place of the thieves and murderers, and the soldiers rescued all the captives and killed all the thieves and murderers, and the king's son was returned safely to the palace of his father, and to the company of his wife, the little shepherd's daughter. And when the boy went into the palace and saw again his wife, he humbled himself before her and he embraced her feet, and he said, My love, it is because of you that I am alive, and the king was greatly pleased with the shepherd's daughter.

Now, said my grandmother, do you see why every man should learn an honorable craft?

I see very clearly, I said, and as soon as I earn enough money to buy a saw and a hammer and a piece of lumber I shall do my best to make a simple chair or a shelf for books.

"Leaving the Canyon" by Frederic Remington,
painter of the American West.
Federal troops rescue a wounded Indian.

BOOK FOUR | PART 3

TWISTS OF FATE

DEATH SPEAKS: *There was a merchant in Baghdad who sent his servant to market to buy provisions, and in a little while the servant came back, white and trembling, and said, Master, just now when I was in the marketplace I was jostled by a woman in the crowd, and when I turned I saw it was Death that jostled me. She looked at me and made a threatening gesture; now, lend me your horse, and I will ride away from this city and avoid my fate. I will go to Samarra, and there Death will not find me. The merchant lent him his horse, and the servant mounted it, and he dug his spurs in its flanks, and as fast as the horse could gallop he went. Then the merchant went down to the marketplace and he saw me standing in the crowd and he came to me and said, Why did you make a threatening gesture to my servant when you saw him this morning? That was not a threatening gesture, I said, it was only a start of surprise. I was astonished to see him in Baghdad, for I had an appointment with him tonight in Samarra.*

W. Somerset Maugham

In classical mythology, there were three goddesses called the Fates, who spun the thread of human life and cut it off as they pleased. Like most myths, the myth of the Fates is an expression of a deep human concern. Is each of us at birth allotted a fate or destiny which we must act out whether we wish to or not? Can we know this destiny? What can we do about it? To what extent are we free and responsible for our actions?

Clearly, this is one of the most puzzling questions that a human being may face. It is a question that has always fascinated writers and storytellers. In the Odyssey, for example, the question of fate forms one of the threads that makes the story interesting. At the very beginning of the story, we see the gods in council and hear Zeus declare that Odysseus will come safely through his trials. And yet Odysseus does not know this. He still has to rely on himself. At one point he tells his sailors: "Trust in Zeus, and row on with might and main." In Book Sixteen, he says to his son: "What you wonder at is the work of the goddess Athena, who does with me whatever she will, for she can do what she pleases. At one moment she makes me look like a beggar, and the next I am a young man with good clothes on my back; it is an easy matter for the gods who live in heaven to make any man look either rich or poor."

In The Pearl, too, there is a tension between the hero's own actions and the twists of fate that seem to be guiding his life. The climax of the novel comes when Kino's son, Coyotito, is killed just at the moment when he and his family seem about to escape from danger.

The writers of the stories that follow are all concerned with questions of fate. Is a man's fate controlled by some force beyond himself, or by his own actions? How much of life is sheer chance? Does a man's success or destruction lie within his own character?

For centuries, Ireland had been dominated by England. Finally, after years of rebellion, the British agreed to give Ireland a certain amount of independence. A new nation was formed, the Irish Free State, with a constitution which kept Ireland bound to England by an oath of allegiance to the king. In the following story (which takes place in 1922), the Free State forces are fighting to defend the new nation, while the Republicans are fighting for complete freedom.

The Sniper

LIAM O'FLAHERTY

The long June twilight faded into night. Dublin lay enveloped in darkness but for the dim light of the moon that shone through fleecy clouds, casting a pale light as of approaching dawn over the streets and the dark waters of the Liffey. Around the beleaguered Four Courts the heavy guns roared. Here and there through the city, machine guns and rifles broke the silence of the night, spasmodically, like dogs barking on lone farms. Republicans and Free Staters were waging civil war.

On a rooftop near O'Connell Bridge, a Republican sniper lay watching. Beside him lay his rifle and over his shoulders were slung a pair of field glasses. His face was the face of a student, thin and ascetic, but his eyes had the cold gleam of the fanatic. They were deep and thoughtful, the eyes of a man who is used to looking at death.

He was eating a sandwich hungrily. He had eaten nothing since morning. He had been too excited to eat. He finished the sandwich, and, taking a flask of whisky from his pocket, he took a short draft. Then he returned the flask to his pocket. He paused for a moment, considering whether he should risk a smoke. It was dangerous. The flash might be seen in the darkness and there were enemies watching. He decided to take the risk.

Placing a cigarette between his lips, he struck a match. There was a flash and a bullet whizzed over his head. He dropped immediately. He had seen the flash. It came from the opposite side of the street.

He rolled over the roof to a chimney stack in the rear, and slowly drew himself up behind it, until his eyes were level with the top of the parapet. There was nothing to be seen — just the dim outline of the opposite housetop against the blue sky. His enemy was under cover.

Just then an armored car came across the bridge and advanced slowly up the street. It stopped on the opposite side of the street, fifty yards ahead. The sniper could hear the dull panting of the motor. His heart beat faster. It was an enemy car. He wanted to fire, but knew it was useless. His bullets would never pierce the steel that covered the gray monster.

Then around the corner of a side street came an old woman, her head covered by a tattered shawl. She began to talk to the man in the turret of the car. She was pointing to the roof where the sniper lay. An informer.

The turret opened. A man's head and shoulders appeared, looking toward the sniper. The sniper raised his rifle and fired. The head fell heavily on the turret wall. The woman darted toward the side street. The sniper fired again. The woman whirled around and fell with a shriek into the gutter.

Suddenly from the opposite roof a shot rang out and the sniper dropped his rifle with a curse. The rifle clattered to the roof. The sniper thought the noise would wake the dead. He stooped to pick the rifle up. He couldn't lift it. His forearm was dead.

"I'm hit," he muttered.

Dropping flat onto the roof, he crawled back to the parapet. With his left hand he felt the injured right forearm. There was no pain — just a deadened sensation, as if the arm had been cut off.

Quickly he drew his knife from his pocket, opened it on the breastwork of the parapet, and ripped open the sleeve. There was a small hole where the bullet had entered. On the other side there was no hole. The bullet had lodged in the bone. It must have fractured it. He bent the arm below the wound. The arm bent back easily. He ground his teeth to overcome the pain.

Then taking out the field dressing, he ripped open the packet with his knife. He broke the neck of the iodine bottle and let the bitter fluid drip into the wound. A paroxysm of pain swept through him.

He placed the cotton wadding over the wound and wrapped the dressing over it. He tied the ends with his teeth.

Then he lay against the parapet, and, closing his eyes, he made an effort of will to overcome the pain.

In the street beneath all was still. The armored car had retired speedily over the bridge, with the machine gunner's head hanging lifelessly over the turret. The woman's corpse lay still in the gutter.

The sniper lay still for a long time nursing his wounded arm and planning escape. Morning must not find him wounded on the roof. The enemy on the opposite roof covered his escape. He must kill that enemy, and he could not use his rifle. He had only a revolver to do it. Then he thought of a plan.

Taking off his cap, he placed it over the muzzle of his rifle. Then he pushed the rifle slowly over the parapet, until the cap was visible from the opposite side of the street. Almost immediately there was a report, and a bullet pierced the center of the cap. The sniper slanted the rifle forward. The cap slipped down into the street. Then catching the rifle in the middle, the sniper dropped his left hand over the roof and let it hang lifelessly. After a few moments he let the rifle drop to the street. Then he sank to the roof, dragging his hand with him.

Crawling quickly to the left, he peered up at the corner of the roof. His ruse had succeeded. The other sniper, seeing the cap and rifle fall, thought he had killed his man. He was now standing before a row of chimney pots, looking across, with his head clearly silhouetted against the western sky.

The Republican sniper smiled and lifted his revolver above the edge of the parapet. The distance was about fifty yards — a hard shot in the dim light, and his right arm was paining him like a thousand devils. He took a steady aim. His hand trembled with eagerness. Pressing his lips together, he took a deep breath through his nostrils and fired. He was almost deafened with the report, and his arm shook with the recoil.

Then when the smoke cleared he peered across and uttered a cry of joy. His enemy had been hit. He was reeling over the parapet in his death agony. He struggled to keep his feet, but he was slowly falling forward, as if in a dream. The rifle fell from his grasp, hit the parapet, fell over, bounded off the pole of a barber's shop beneath, and then clattered on the pavement.

Then the dying man on the roof crumpled up and fell forward. The body turned over and over in space and hit the ground with a dull thud. Then it lay still.

The sniper looked at his enemy falling and he shuddered. The lust of battle died in him. He became bitten by remorse. The sweat stood out in beads on his forehead. Weakened by his wound and the long summer day of fasting and watching on the roof, he revolted from the sight of the shattered mass of his dead enemy. His teeth chattered, he began to gibber to himself, cursing the war, cursing himself, cursing everybody.

He looked at the smoking revolver in his hand, and with an oath he hurled it to the roof at his feet. The revolver went off with the concussion and the bullet whizzed past the sniper's head. He was frightened back to his senses by the shock. His nerves steadied. The cloud of fear scattered from his mind, and he laughed.

Taking the whisky flask from his pocket, he emptied it at a draft. He felt reckless under the influence of the spirit. He decided to leave the roof now and look for his company commander, to report. Everywhere around was quiet. There was not much danger in going through the streets. He picked up his revolver and put it in his pocket. Then he crawled down through the skylight to the house underneath.

When the sniper reached the laneway on the street level, he felt a sudden curiosity as to the identity of the enemy sniper whom he had killed. He decided that he was a good shot, whoever he was. He wondered did he know him. Perhaps he had been in his own company before the split in the army. He decided to risk going over to have a look at him. He peered around the corner into O'Connell Street. In the upper part of the street there was heavy firing, but around here all was quiet.

The sniper darted across the street. A machine gun tore up the ground around him with a hail of bullets, but he escaped. He threw himself face downward beside the corpse. The machine gun stopped.

Then the sniper turned over the dead body and looked into his brother's face.

Trifles

SUSAN GLASPELL

CHARACTERS

GEORGE HENDERSON   county attorney; a young man
HENRY PETERS   sheriff; middle-aged
LEWIS HALE   a neighboring farmer; middle-aged
MRS. PETERS   the sheriff's wife; slight, wiry, and nervous
MRS. HALE   the farmer's wife; a large, hearty woman

SCENE. *The kitchen in the now abandoned farmhouse of* JOHN WRIGHT, *a gloomy kitchen, and left without having been put in order — unwashed pans under the sink, a loaf of bread outside the breadbox, a dish towel on the table — other signs of incompleted work. At the rear the outer door opens and the* SHERIFF *comes in, followed by the* COUNTY ATTORNEY *and* HALE. *All are much bundled up and go at once to the stove. They are followed by the two women — the* SHERIFF'S *wife first.* MRS. HALE *is disturbed now and looks fearfully about as she enters. The women have come in slowly and stand close together near the door.*

COUNTY ATTORNEY (*rubbing his hands*). This feels good. Come up to the fire, ladies.
MRS. PETERS (*after taking a step forward*). I'm not — cold.
SHERIFF (*unbuttoning his overcoat and stepping away from the stove as if to mark the beginning of official business*). Now, Mr. Hale, before we move things about, you explain to Mr. Henderson just what you saw when you came here yesterday morning.
COUNTY ATTORNEY. By the way, has anything been moved? Are things just as you left them yesterday?

SHERIFF (*looking about*). It's just the same. When it dropped below zero last night I thought I'd better send Frank out this morning to make a fire for us — no use getting pneumonia with a big case on, but I told him not to touch anything except the stove — and you know Frank.

COUNTY ATTORNEY. Someone should have been left here yesterday.

SHERIFF. Oh — yesterday. When I had to send Frank to Morris Center for that man who went crazy — I want you to know I had my hands full yesterday. I knew you could get back from Omaha by today, and as long as I went over everything here myself —

COUNTY ATTORNEY. Well, Mr. Hale, tell just what happened when you came here yesterday morning.

HALE. Harry and I had started to town with a load of potatoes. We came along the road from my place, and as I got here I said, "I'm going to see if I can't get John Wright to go in with me on a party telephone." I spoke to Wright about it once before and he put me off, saying folks talked too much anyway, and all he asked was peace and quiet — I guess you know how much he talked himself; but I thought maybe if I went to the house and talked about it before his wife, though I said to Harry that I didn't know as what his wife wanted made much difference to John —

COUNTY ATTORNEY. Let's talk about that later, Mr. Hale. I do want to talk about that, but tell now just what happened when you got to the house.

HALE. I didn't hear or see anything; I knocked at the door, and still it was all quiet inside. I knew they must be up, it was past eight o'clock. So I knocked again, and I thought I heard somebody say, "Come in." I wasn't sure, I'm not sure yet, but I opened the door — this door (*indicating the door by which the two women are still standing*) and there in that rocker — (*pointing to it*) sat Mrs. Wright.

[*They all look at the rocker.*]

COUNTY ATTORNEY. What — was she doing?

HALE. She was rockin' back and forth. She had her apron in her hand and was kind of — pleating it.

COUNTY ATTORNEY. And how did she — look?

HALE. Well, she looked queer.

COUNTY ATTORNEY. How do you mean — queer?

HALE. Well, as if she didn't know what she was going to do next. And kind of done up.
COUNTY ATTORNEY. How did she seem to feel about your coming?
HALE. Why, I don't think she minded — one way or other. She didn't pay much attention. I said, "How do, Mrs. Wright, it's cold, ain't it?" And she said, "Is it" — and went on kind of pleating at her apron. Well, I was surprised; she didn't ask me to come up to the stove, or to sit down, but just sat there, not even looking at me, so I said, "I want to see John." And then she — laughed. I guess you would call it a laugh. I thought of Harry and the team outside, so I said a little sharp: "Can't I see John?" "No," she says, kind o' dull-like. "Ain't he home?" says I. "Yes," says she, "he's home." "Then why can't I see him?" I asked her, out of patience. " 'Cause he's dead," says she. "*Dead?*" says I. She just nodded her head, not getting a bit excited, but rockin' back and forth. "Why — where is he?" says I, not knowing what to say. She just pointed upstairs — like that (*himself pointing to the room above*). I got up, with the idea of going up there. I walked from there to here — then I says, "Why, what did he die of?" "He died of a rope around his neck," says she, and just went on pleatin' at her apron. Well, I went out and called Harry. I thought I might — need help. We went upstairs and there he was lyin' —
COUNTY ATTORNEY. I think I'd rather have you go into that upstairs, where you can point it all out. Just go on now with the rest of the story.
HALE. Well, my first thought was to get that rope off. It looked . . . (*stops, his face twitches*) . . . but Harry, he went up to him, and he said, "No, he's dead all right, and we'd better not touch anything." So we went back downstairs. She was still sitting that same way. "Has anybody been notified?" I asked. "No," says she, unconcerned. "Who did this, Mrs. Wright?" said Harry. He said it businesslike — and she stopped pleatin' her apron. "I don't know," she says. "You don't *know?*" says Harry. "No," says she. "Weren't you sleepin' in the bed with him?" says Harry. "Yes," says she, "but I was on the inside." "Somebody slipped a rope around his neck and strangled him and you didn't wake up?" says Harry. "I didn't wake up," she said after him. We must 'a' looked as if we didn't see how that could be, for after a minute she said,

"I sleep sound." Harry was going to ask her more questions, but I said maybe we ought to let her tell her story first to the coroner, or the sheriff, so Harry went fast as he could to Rivers' place, where there's a telephone.

COUNTY ATTORNEY. And what did Mrs. Wright do when she knew that you had gone for the coroner?

HALE. She moved from that chair to this one over here (*pointing to a small chair in corner*) and just sat there with her hands held together and looking down. I got a feeling that I ought to make some conversation, so I said I had come in to see if John wanted to put in a telephone, and at that she started to laugh, and then she stopped and looked at me — scared. (*The* COUNTY ATTORNEY, *who has had his notebook out, makes a note.*) I dunno, maybe it wasn't scared. I wouldn't like to say it was. Soon Harry got back, and then Dr. Lloyd came, and you, Mr. Peters, and so I guess that's all I know that you don't.

COUNTY ATTORNEY (*looking all around*). I guess we'll go upstairs first — and then out to the barn and around there. (*To the* SHERIFF) You're convinced that there was nothing important here — nothing that would point to any motive?

SHERIFF. Nothing here but kitchen things.

[*The* COUNTY ATTORNEY, *after again looking around the kitchen, opens the door of a cupboard closet. He gets up on a chair and looks on the shelf. Pulls his hand away, sticky.*]

COUNTY ATTORNEY. Here's a nice mess.

[*The women draw nearer.*]

MRS. PETERS (*to the other woman*). Oh, her fruit; it did freeze. (*To the* LAWYER) She worried about that when it turned so cold. She said the fire'd go out and her jars would break.

SHERIFF. Well, can you beat the woman! Held for murder and worryin' about her preserves.

COUNTY ATTORNEY. I guess before we're through she may have something more serious than preserves to worry about.

HALE. Well, women are used to worrying over trifles.

[*The two women move a little closer together.*]

COUNTY ATTORNEY (*with the gallantry of a young politician*). And yet, for all their worries, what would we do without the ladies? (*The women do not unbend. He goes to the sink, takes a dipperful of water from the pail, and pouring it into a basin, washes his hands. Starts to wipe them on the roller towel, turns it for a cleaner place.*) Dirty towels! (*Kicks his foot against the pans under the sink.*) Not much of a housekeeper, would you say, ladies?

MRS. HALE (*stiffly*). There's a great deal of work to be done on a farm.

COUNTY ATTORNEY. To be sure. And yet (*with a little bow to her*) I know there are some Dickson county farmhouses which do not have such roller towels. (*He gives it a pull to expose its full length again.*)

MRS. HALE. Those towels get dirty awful quick. Men's hands aren't always as clean as they might be.

COUNTY ATTORNEY. Ah, loyal to your sex, I see. But you and Mrs. Wright were neighbors. I suppose you were friends, too.

MRS. HALE (*shaking her head*). I've not seen much of her of late years. I've not been in this house — it's more than a year.

COUNTY ATTORNEY. And why was that? You didn't like her?

MRS. HALE. I liked her well enough. Farmers' wives have their hands full, Mr. Henderson. And then —

COUNTY ATTORNEY. Yes — ?

MRS. HALE (*looking about*). It never seemed a very cheerful place.

COUNTY ATTORNEY. No — it's not cheerful. I shouldn't say she had the home-making instinct.

MRS. HALE. Well, I don't know as Wright had, either.

COUNTY ATTORNEY. You mean that they didn't get on very well?

MRS. HALE. No, I don't mean anything. But I don't think a place'd be any cheerfuller for John Wright's being in it.

COUNTY ATTORNEY. I'd like to talk more of that a little later. I want to get the lay of things upstairs now. (*He goes to the left, where three steps lead to a stair door.*)

SHERIFF. I suppose anything Mrs. Peters does'll be all right. She was to take in some clothes for her, you know, and a few little things. We left in such a hurry yesterday.

COUNTY ATTORNEY. Yes, but I would like to see what you take, Mrs. Peters, and keep an eye out for anything that might be of use to us.

MRS. PETERS. Yes, Mr. Henderson.

[*The women listen to the men's steps on the stairs, then look about the kitchen.*]

MRS. HALE. I'd hate to have men coming into my kitchen, snooping around and criticizing. (*She arranges the pans under sink which the* LAWYER *had shoved out of place.*)

MRS. PETERS. Of course it's no more than their duty.

MRS. HALE. Duty's all right, but I guess that deputy sheriff that came out to make the fire might have got a little of this on. (*Gives the roller towel a pull.*) Wish I'd thought of that sooner. Seems mean to talk about her not having things slicked up when she had to come away in such a hurry.

MRS. PETERS (*who has gone to a small table in the left rear corner of the room, and lifted one end of a towel that covers a pan*). She had bread set. (*Stands still.*)

MRS. HALE (*eyes fixed on a loaf of bread beside the breadbox, which is on a low shelf at the other side of the room. Moves slowly toward it*). She was going to put this in there. (*Picks up loaf, then abruptly drops it. In a manner of returning to familiar things*) It's a shame about her fruit. I wonder if it's all gone. (*Gets up on the chair and looks.*) I think there's some here that's all right, Mrs. Peters. Yes — here; (*holding it toward the window*) this is cherries, too. (*Looking again*) I declare, I believe that's the only one. (*Gets down, bottle in her hand. Goes to the sink and wipes it off on the outside.*) She'll feel awful bad after all her hard work in the hot weather. I remember the afternoon I put up my cherries last summer.

[*She puts the bottle on the big kitchen table, center of the room. With a sigh, is about to sit down in the rocking chair. Before she is seated realizes what chair it is; with a slow look at it, steps back. The chair which she has touched rocks back and forth.*]

MRS. PETERS. Well, I must get those things from the front room closet. (*She goes to the door at the right, but after looking into the other room, steps back.*) You coming with me, Mrs. Hale? You could help me carry them.

[*They go into the other room; reappear,* MRS. PETERS *carrying a dress and skirt,* MRS. HALE *following with a pair of shoes.*]

MRS. PETERS. My, it's cold in there. (*She puts the clothes on the big table, and hurries to the stove.*)
MRS. HALE (*examining the skirt*). Wright was close. I think maybe that's why she kept so much to herself. She didn't even belong to the Ladies' Aid. I suppose she felt she couldn't do her part, and then you don't enjoy things when you feel shabby. She used to wear pretty clothes and be lively, when she was Minnie Foster, one of the town girls singing in the choir. But that — oh, that was thirty years ago. This all you was to take in?
MRS. PETERS. She said she wanted an apron. Funny thing to want, for there isn't much to get you dirty in jail, goodness knows. But I suppose just to make her feel more natural. She said they was in the top drawer in this cupboard. Yes, here. And then her little shawl that always hung behind the door. (*Opens stair door and looks.*) Yes, here it is. (*Quickly shuts door leading upstairs.*)
MRS. HALE (*abruptly moving toward her*). Mrs. Peters?
MRS. PETERS. Yes, Mrs. Hale?
MRS. HALE. Do you think she did it?
MRS. PETERS (*in a frightened voice*). Oh, I don't know.
MRS. HALE. Well, I don't think she did. Asking for an apron and her little shawl. Worrying about her fruit.
MRS. PETERS (*starts to speak, glances up, where footsteps are heard in the room above. In a low voice*). Mr. Peters says it looks bad for her. Mr. Henderson is awful sarcastic in a speech and he'll make fun of her sayin' she didn't wake up.
MRS. HALE. Well, I guess John Wright didn't wake when they was slipping that rope under his neck.
MRS. PETERS. No, it's strange. It must have been done awful crafty and still. They say it was such a — funny way to kill a man, rigging it all up like that.
MRS. HALE. That's just what Mr. Hale said. There was a gun in the house. He says that's what he can't understand.
MRS. PETERS. Mr. Henderson said coming out that what was needed for the case was a motive; something to show anger, or — sudden feeling.
MRS. HALE (*who is standing by the table*). Well, I don't see any signs of anger around here. (*She puts her hand on the dish towel which lies on the table, stands looking down at table, one half*

of which is clean, the other half messy.) It's wiped to here. (*Makes a move as if to finish work, then turns and looks at loaf of bread outside the breadbox. Drops towel. In that voice of coming back to familiar things*) Wonder how they are finding things upstairs. I hope she had it a little more redd-up [1] there. You know, it seems kind of *sneaking*. Locking her up in town and then coming out here and trying to get her own house to turn against her!

MRS. PETERS. But Mrs. Hale, the law is the law.

MRS. HALE. I s'pose 'tis. (*Unbuttoning her coat*) Better loosen up your things, Mrs. Peters. You won't feel them when you go out.

[MRS. PETERS *takes off her fur tippet, goes to hang it on hook at back of room, stands looking at the under part of the small corner table.*]

MRS. PETERS. She was piecing a quilt. (*She brings the large sewing basket and they look at the bright pieces.*)

MRS. HALE. It's a log-cabin pattern. Pretty, isn't it? I wonder if she was goin' to quilt it or just knot it?

[*Footsteps have been heard coming down the stairs. The* SHERIFF *enters, followed by* HALE *and the* COUNTY ATTORNEY.]

SHERIFF. They wonder if she was going to quilt it or just knot it!

[*The men laugh, the women look abashed.*]

COUNTY ATTORNEY (*rubbing his hands over the stove*). Frank's fire didn't do much up there, did it? Well, let's go out to the barn and get that cleared up.

[*The men go outside.*]

MRS. HALE (*resentfully*). I don't know as there's anything so strange, our takin' up our time with little things while we're waiting for them to get the evidence. (*She sits down at the big table, smoothing out a block with decision.*) I don't see as it's anything to laugh about.

MRS. PETERS (*apologetically*). Of course they've got awful important things on their minds. (*Pulls up a chair and joins* MRS. HALE *at the table.*)

---

[1] *redd-up:* straightened up.

MRS. HALE (*examining another block*). Mrs. Peters, look at this one. Here, this is the one she was working on, and look at the sewing! All the rest of it has been so nice and even. And look at this! It's all over the place! Why, it looks as if she didn't know what she was about!

[*After she has said this they look at each other, then start to glance back at the door. After an instant* MRS. HALE *has pulled at a knot and ripped the sewing.*]

MRS. PETERS. Oh, what are you doing, Mrs. Hale?

MRS. HALE (*mildly*). Just pulling out a stitch or two that's not sewed very good. (*Threading a needle*) Bad sewing always made me fidgety.

MRS. PETERS (*nervously*). I don't think we ought to touch things.

MRS. HALE. I'll just finish up this end. (*Suddenly stopping and leaning forward*) Mrs. Peters?

MRS. PETERS. Yes, Mrs. Hale?

MRS. HALE. What do you suppose she was so nervous about?

MRS. PETERS. Oh — I don't know. I don't know as she was nervous. I sometimes sew awful queer when I'm just tired. (MRS. HALE *starts to say something, looks at* MRS. PETERS, *then goes on sewing.*) Well, I must get these things wrapped up. They may be through sooner than we think. (*Putting apron and other things together*) I wonder where I can find a piece of paper, and string.

MRS. HALE. In that cupboard, maybe.

MRS. PETERS (*looking in cupboard*). Why, here's a bird cage. (*Holds it up.*) Did she have a bird, Mrs. Hale?

MRS. HALE. Why, I don't know whether she did or not — I've not been here for so long. There was a man around last year selling canaries cheap, but I don't know as she took one; maybe she did. She used to sing real pretty herself.

MRS. PETERS (*glancing around*). Seems funny to think of a bird here. But she must have had one, or why would she have a cage? I wonder what happened to it?

MRS. HALE. I s'pose maybe the cat got it.

MRS. PETERS. No, she didn't have a cat. She's got that feeling some people have about cats — being afraid of them. My cat got in her room and she was real upset and asked me to take it out.

MRS. HALE. My sister Bessie was like that. Queer, ain't it?

MRS. PETERS (*examining the cage*). Why, look at this door. It's broke. One hinge is pulled apart.

MRS. HALE (*looking too*). Looks as if someone must have been rough with it.

MRS. PETERS. Why, yes. (*She brings the cage forward and puts it on the table.*)

MRS. HALE. I wish if they're going to find any evidence they'd be about it. I don't like this place.

MRS. PETERS. But I'm awful glad you came with me, Mrs. Hale. It would be lonesome for me sitting here alone.

MRS. HALE. It would, wouldn't it? (*Dropping her sewing*) But I tell you what I do wish, Mrs. Peters. I wish I had come over sometimes when *she* was here. I — (*looking around the room*) — wish I had.

MRS. PETERS. But of course you were awful busy, Mrs. Hale — your house and your children.

MRS. HALE. I could've come. I stayed away because it weren't cheerful — and that's why I ought to have come. I — I've never liked this place. Maybe because it's down in a hollow and you don't see the road. I dunno what it is, but its a lonesome place and always was. I wish I had come over to see Minnie Foster sometimes. I can see now — (*Shakes her head.*)

MRS. PETERS. Well, you mustn't reproach yourself, Mrs. Hale. Somehow we just don't see how it is with other folks until — something turns up.

MRS. HALE. Not having children makes less work — but it makes a quiet house, and Wright out to work all day, and no company when he did come in. Did you know John Wright, Mrs. Peters?

MRS. PETERS. Not to know him; I've seen him in town. They say he was a good man.

MRS. HALE. Yes — good; he didn't drink, and kept his word as well as most, I guess, and paid his debts. But he was a hard man, Mrs. Peters. Just to pass the time of day with him — (*Shivers.*) Like a raw wind that gets to the bone. (*Pauses, her eye falling on the cage.*) I should think she would 'a' wanted a bird. But what do you suppose went with it?

MRS. PETERS. I don't know, unless it got sick and died.

[*She reaches over and swings the broken door, swings it again. Both women watch it.*]

MRS. HALE. You weren't raised around here, were you? (MRS. PETERS *shakes her head.*) You didn't know — her?

MRS. PETERS. Not till they brought her yesterday.

MRS. HALE. She — come to think of it, she was kind of like a bird herself — real sweet and pretty, but kind of timid and — fluttery. How — she — did — change. (*Silence; then as if struck by a happy thought and relieved to get back to everyday things.*) Tell you what, Mrs. Peters, why don't you take the quilt in with you? It might take up her mind.

MRS. PETERS. Why, I think that's a real nice idea, Mrs. Hale. There couldn't possibly be any objection to it, could there? Now, just what would I take? I wonder if her patches are in here — and her things.

[*They look in the sewing basket.*]

MRS. HALE. Here's some red. I expect this has got sewing things in it. (*Brings out a fancy box.*) What a pretty box. Looks like something somebody would give you. Maybe her scissors are in here. (*Opens box. Suddenly puts her hand to her nose.*) Why — (MRS. PETERS *bends nearer, then turns her face away.*) There's something wrapped up in this piece of silk.

MRS. PETERS. Why, this isn't her scissors.

MRS. HALE (*lifting the silk*). Oh, Mrs. Peters — it's —

[MRS. PETERS *bends closer.*]

MRS. PETERS. It's the bird.

MRS. HALE (*jumping up*). But, Mrs. Peters — look at it! Its neck! It's all — other side *to*.

MRS. PETERS. Somebody — wrung its — neck.

[*Their eyes meet. A look of growing comprehension, of horror. Steps are heard outside.* MRS. HALE *slips box under quilt pieces, and sinks into her chair. Enter* SHERIFF *and* COUNTY ATTORNEY. MRS. PETERS *rises.*]

COUNTY ATTORNEY (*as one turning from serious things to little pleasantries*). Well, ladies, have you decided whether she was going to quilt it or knot it?

MRS. PETERS. We think she was going to — knot it.

COUNTY ATTORNEY. Well, that's interesting, I'm sure. (*Seeing the bird cage*) Has the bird flown?

MRS. HALE (*putting more quilt pieces over the box*). We think the — cat got it.

COUNTY ATTORNEY (*preoccupied*). Is there a cat?

[MRS. HALE *glances in a quick covert way at* MRS. PETERS.]

MRS. PETERS. Well, not *now*. They're superstitious, you know. They leave.

COUNTY ATTORNEY (*to* SHERIFF PETERS, *continuing an interrupted conversation*). No sign at all of anyone having come from the outside. Their own rope. Now let's go up again and go over it piece by piece. (*They start upstairs.*) It would have to have been someone who knew just the —

[MRS. PETERS *sits down. The two women sit there, not looking at one another, but as if peering into something and at the same time holding back. When they talk now it is in the manner of feeling their way over strange ground, as if afraid of what they are saying, but as if they cannot help saying it.*]

MRS. HALE. She liked the bird. She was going to bury it in that pretty box.

MRS. PETERS (*in a whisper*). When I was a girl — my kitten — there was a boy took a hatchet, and before my eyes — and before I could get there — (*Covers her face an instant.*) If they hadn't held me back I would have — (*catches herself, looks upstairs where steps are heard, falters weakly*) — hurt him.

MRS. HALE (*with a slow look around her*). I wonder how it would seem never to have had any children around. (*Pause.*) No, Wright wouldn't like the bird — a thing that sang. She used to sing. He killed that, too.

MRS. PETERS (*moving uneasily*). We don't know who killed the bird.

MRS. HALE. I knew John Wright.

MRS. PETERS. It was an awful thing was done in this house that night, Mrs. Hale. Killing a man while he slept, slipping a rope around his neck that choked the life out of him.

MRS. HALE. His neck. Choked the life out of him. (*Her hand goes out and rests on the bird cage.*)

MRS. PETERS (*with rising voice*). We don't know who killed him. We don't *know*.

MRS. HALE (*her own feeling not interrupted*). If there'd been years

and years of nothing, then a bird to sing to you, it would be awful — still, after the bird was still.
MRS. PETERS (*something within her speaking*). I know what stillness is. When we homesteaded [2] in Dakota, and my first baby died — after he was two years old, and me with no other then —
MRS. HALE (*moving*). How soon do you suppose they'll be through looking for the evidence?
MRS. PETERS. I know what stillness is. (*Pulling herself back*) The law has got to punish crime, Mrs. Hale.
MRS. HALE (*not as if answering that*). I wish you'd seen Minnie Foster when she wore a white dress with blue ribbons and stood up in the choir and sang. (*A look around the room.*) Oh, I *wish* I'd come over here once in a while! That was a crime! That was a crime! Who's going to punish that?
MRS. PETERS (*looking upstairs*). We mustn't — take on.
MRS. HALE. I might have known she needed help! I know how things can be — for women. I tell you, it's queer, Mrs. Peters. We live close together and we live far apart. We all go through the same things — it's all just a different kind of the same thing. (*Brushes her eyes, noticing the bottle of fruit, reaches out for it.*) If I was you I wouldn't tell her her fruit was gone. Tell her it *ain't*. Tell her it's all right. Take this in to prove it to her. She — she may never know whether it was broke or not.
MRS. PETERS (*takes the bottle, looks about for something to wrap it in; takes petticoat from the clothes brought from the other room, very nervously begins winding this around the bottle. In a false voice*). My, it's a good thing the men couldn't hear us. Wouldn't they just laugh! Getting all stirred up over a little thing like a — dead canary. As if that could have anything to do with — with — wouldn't they *laugh*!

[*The men are heard coming downstairs.*]

MRS. HALE (*under her breath*). Maybe they would — maybe they wouldn't.
COUNTY ATTORNEY. No, Peters, it's all perfectly clear, except a reason for doing it. But you know juries when it comes to women. If there was some definite thing. Something to show — something

---

[2] *homesteaded*: settled on land granted by the government.

to make a story about — a thing that would connect up with this strange way of doing it —

[*The women's eyes meet for an instant. Enter* HALE *from outer door.*]

HALE. Well, I've got the team around. Pretty cold out there.

COUNTY ATTORNEY. I'm going to stay here awhile by myself. (*To the* SHERIFF) You can send Frank out for me, can't you? I want to go over everything. I'm not satisfied that we can't do better.

SHERIFF. Do you want to see what Mrs. Peters is going to take in?

[*The* LAWYER *goes to the table, picks up the apron, laughs.*]

COUNTY ATTORNEY. Oh, I guess they're not very dangerous things the ladies have picked out. (*Moves a few things about, disturbing the quilt pieces which cover the box. Steps back.*) No, Mrs. Peters doesn't need supervising. For that matter, a sheriff's wife is married to the law. Ever think of it that way, Mrs. Peters?

MRS. PETERS. Not — just that way.

SHERIFF (*chuckling*). Married to the law. (*Moves toward the other room.*) I just want you to come in here a minute, George. We ought to take a look at these windows.

COUNTY ATTORNEY (*scoffingly*). Oh, windows!

SHERIFF. We'll be right out, Mr. Hale.

[HALE *goes outside. The* SHERIFF *follows the* COUNTY ATTORNEY *into the other room. Then* MRS. HALE *rises, hands tight together, looking intensely at* MRS. PETERS, *whose eyes make a slow turn, finally meeting* MRS. HALE'S. *A moment* MRS. HALE *holds her, then her own eyes point the way to where the box is concealed. Suddenly* MRS. PETERS *throws back quilt pieces, stands there helpless. Sound of a knob turning in the other room.* MRS. HALE *snatches the box and puts it in the pocket of her big coat. Enter* COUNTY ATTORNEY *and* SHERIFF.]

COUNTY ATTORNEY (*facetiously*). Well, Henry, at least we found out that she was not going to quilt it. She was going to — what is it you call it, ladies?

MRS. HALE (*her hand against her pocket*). We call it — knot it, Mr. Henderson.

CURTAIN

A Ride on the Short Dog

JAMES STILL

We flagged the bus on a curve at the mouth of Lairds Creek by jumping and waving in the road, and Dee Buck Engle had to tread the brake the instant he saw us. He wouldn't have halted unless compelled. Mal Dowe and I leaped aside finally, but Godey Spurlock held his ground. The bus stopped a yard from Godey, and vexed faces pressed the windows and we heard Old Liz Hyden cry, "I'd not haul them jaspers." [1]

Dee Buck opened the door and blared, "You boys trying to get killed?"

We climbed on grinning and shoved fares to Roscoe into his hand, and for once we didn't sing out, To Knuckle Junction, and Pistol City, and Two Hoots. We even strode the aisle without raising elbows to knock off hats, having agreed among ourselves to sort of behave and make certain of a ride home. Yet Dee Buck was wary. He warned, "Bother my passengers, you fellers, and I'll fix you. I've put up with your mischief till I won't."

That set Godey and Mal laughing, for Dee Buck was a bluffer. We took the seat across from Liz Hyden, and on wedging into it my bruised arm started aching. Swapping licks was Godey's delight.

The bus wheezed and jolted in moving away, yet we spared Dee Buck our usual advice: Feed her a biscuit and see will she mend, and, Twist her tail and teach her a few manners. The vehicle was scarcely half the length of regular buses — "The Short Dog" everybody called it. It traveled from Thacker to Roscoe and back twice a day. Enos Webb occupied the seat in front, and Godey greeted, "Hey-o, chum. How's your fat?" Enos ducked his head, fearing a

---
[1] *jaspers:* slang for fellows or guys.

rabbit lick,[2] and he changed his seat. He knew how Godey served exposed necks. Godey could cause you to see forked lightning and hear thunder balls. Though others shunned us, Liz Hyden gazed in our direction. Her eyes were scornful, her lips puckered sour. She was as old as a hill.

Godey and Mal couldn't sit idle. They rubbed the dusty pane with their sleeves and looked abroad, and everything they saw they remarked on: hay doodles in Alonzo Tate's pasture, a crazy chimney leaning away from a house, long johns on clotheslines. They kept a count of the bridges. They pointed toward the mountain ahead, trying to fool, calling, "Gee-o looky yonder." But they couldn't trick a soul. My arm throbbed and I had no notion to prank, and after a while Godey muttered, "I want to know what's eating you."

"We'd better decide what we can do in town," I grouched. Roscoe folk looked alive at sight of us. And, except for our return fares, we hadn't a dime. The poolroom had us ousted. We'd have to steer clear of the courthouse where sheriffs were thick. And we dare not rouse the county prisoners again. On our last trip we'd bellowed in front of the jail, "Hey-o, you wife-beaters, how are you standing the times?" We'd jeered and mocked until they had begged the turnkey to fetch us inside, they'd notch our ears, they'd trim us. The turnkey had told them to be patient, we'd get in on our own hook.

Godey said, "We'll break loose in town, no two ways talking."

I gloomed. "The law will pen us for the least thing. We'll be thrown in among the meanest fellers that ever breathed."

Godey screwed his eyes narrow. "My opinion, the prisoners scared you plumb. You're ruint for trick-pulling." He knotted a fist and hit me squarely on my bruise.

My arm ached the fiercer. My eyes burned, and had I not glanced sideways they'd come to worse. "Now, no," I said; but Godey's charge was true.

"Well, act like it," he said. "And pay me."

I returned the blow.

Old Liz was watching and she blurted, "I swear to my gracious. A human being can't see a minute's peace."

Godey chuckled, "What's fretting you, old woman?"

"Knock and beat and battle is all you think on," she snorted.

---

[2] *rabbit lick*: a short, sharp blow to the back of the neck.

"Collar and drag 'em off," Old Liz taunted. "A coward, are ye?"

"Anybody spoiling to tussle," Godey challenged, "well, let 'em come humping."

Dee Buck flared, "Listen, you devils, I can put a quietus on you and not have to soil my hands. My opinion, you'll not want to be aboard when I pull into town. I can draw up at the courthouse and fetch the law in two minutes."

"Sick a sheriff on us," Godey said, "and you'll wish to your heart you hadn't. We paid to ride this dog."

"Walk off and I'll return your fares."

"Now, no."

"I won't wait all day."

"Dynamite couldn't budge us."

Dee Buck swept his cap onto his head. He changed gear, readying to leave. "I'm willing to spare you and you won't have it."

"Drive on, Big Buddy."

The bus started and Old Liz flounced angrily in her seat. She turned her back and didn't look around until we got to Roscoe.

We crossed two bridges. We passed Hilton and Chunk Jones's sawmill and Gayheart and Thorne. Beyond Thorne the highway began to rise. We climbed past the bloom of coal veins and tipples of mines hanging the slope; we mounted until we'd gained the saddle of the gap and could see Roscoe four miles distant. Godey and Mal cut up the whole way, no longer trying to behave. They hailed newcomers with, "Take a seat and sit like you were at home, where you ought to be," and sped the departers, "I'll see you later, when I can talk to you straighter." The twins left at Cowen and Godey shouted, "Good-by, Dirty Ears. Recollect I done you a favor." We rolled through the high gap and on down the mountain.

I nursed my hurt and sulked, and eventually Godey growled, "I want to know, did you come along just to pout?"

"You've fixed us," I accused bitterly, and I openly covered my crippled arm.

Godey scoffed, "Dee Buck can't panic me. You watch him turn good-feller by the time we reach town, watch him unload in the square the same as usual. Aye, he knows what suits his hide." He grabbed loose my arm and his fist shot out.

It was too much. My face tore up, my lips quivered, and tears smeared my cheeks. Godey stared in wonder. His mouth fell open.

"We're not so bad we try to hinder people from riding the bus," he countered. "Aye, we heard you squall back yonder."

Old Liz's lips quivered, her veiny hands trembled. "Did I have strength to reach," she croaked, "I'd pop your jaws. I'd addle you totally."

Godey thrust his head across the aisle and turned a cheek. He didn't mind a slap. "See your satisfaction," he invited.

"Out o' my face," she ordered, lifting her voice to alert Dee Buck. She laced her fingers to stay their shaking.

Dee Buck adjusted the rearview mirror and inquired, "What's the matter, Aunt Liz?"

"It's these boys tormenting me," she complained. "They'd drive a body to raving."

Dee Buck slowed. "I told you fellers — "

"What've we done now?" Godey asked injuredly.

"Didn't I say not to bother my passengers?"

"I never tipped the old hen."

"One more antic and off you three go."

Godey smirked. "Know what?" he said. "We've been treating you pretty but we've done no good."

"You heard me," Dee Buck said.

The twins got on at Lucus. They were about nine years old, as like as two peas, and had not a hair on their heads. Their polls were shaven clean. Godey chirruped, "Gee-o, look who's coming," and he beckoned them to the place quitted by Enos Webb. Dee Buck seated the two up front, and Godey vowed, "I'll trap the chubs, just you wait," and he made donkey ears with his hands and brayed. The twins stared, their mouths open.

Mal said, "Why don't we have our noggins peeled?"

"Say we do," laughed Godey, cocking a teasing eye on me. "They can't jail us for that shorely."

I replied, "We're broke as grasshoppers, keep in mind."

It didn't take Godey long to entice the twins. He picked nothings out of the air and chewed them — chewed to match a sheep eating ivy; he feigned to pull teeth, pitch them again into his mouth, to swallow. The twins stole a seat closer, the better to see, and then two more. Directly Godey had them where he wanted. He spoke: "Hey-o, Dirty Ears."

The twins nodded, too shy to answer.

"What's you little men's names?" he asked.

They swallowed timidly, their eyes meeting.

"Ah, tell."

"Woodrow," ventured one; "Jethro," said the other. They were solemn as fire pokers.

"Hustling to a store to spend a couple of nickels, I bet."

"Going to Cowen," said one. "To Grandpaw's," said his image.

"Well, who skinned you alive, I want to know?"

"Pap," they said.

Godey gazed at their skulls, mischief tingling him. He declared, "Us fellers aim to get cut bald in Roscoe. Too hot to wear hair nowadays."

I slipped a hand over my bruise and crabbed, "I reckon you know haircuts cost money in town." Plaguing Godey humored me.

"Witless," Godey said, annoyed, "we'll climb into the chairs, and when the barbers finish we'll say, 'Charge it on your short list.'"

"They'd summons the law in an eye-bat."

"Idjit," he snapped, "people can't be jailed for a debt." Yet he wouldn't pause to argue. He addressed the twins: "You little gents have me uneasy. There are swellings on your noggins and I'm worried on your behalf."

The twins rubbed their crowns. They were smooth as goose eggs.

"Godey's sharp on this head business," said Mal.

"Want me to examine you and find your ailment?" asked Godey.

The twins glanced one to the other. "We don't care," said one.

Godey tipped a finger to their polls. He squinted and frowned. And then he drew back and gasped, "Oh-oh." He punched Mal and blabbed, "Do you see what I see? Horns, if ever I saw them."

"The tom truth," Mal swore.

"Sprouting horns like bully-cows," Godey said. "Budding under the hide and ready to pip."

"You're in a bad way," Mal moaned.

"In the fix of a boy on Lotts Creek," Godey said. "He growed horns, and he turned into a brute and went hooking folks. Mean? Upon my word and honor, the bad man wouldn't claim him."

"A feller at Scuddy had the disease," Mal related. "Kept shut in a barn, he was, and they fed him hay and cornstalks, and he never tasted victuals. I saw him myself, I swear to my thumb. I saw him chewing a cud and heard him bawl a big bawl."

Godey sighed. "The only cure is to deaden the nubs before they break the skin."

"And, gee-o, you're lucky," Mal poured on. "Godey Spurlock's a horn-doctor. Cured a hundred, I reckon."

"Oh, I've treated a few," admitted Godey.

"Spare the little masters," pled Mal.

Dee Buck was trying to watch both road and mirror, his head bobbing like a chicken drinking water. Old Liz's eyes glinted darkly. I poked Godey, grumbling, "Didn't we promise to mind ourselves?" But he went on:

"They may enjoy old long hookers, may want to bellow and snort and hoof up dirt."

"We don't neither," a twin denied.

Godey brightened. "Want me to dehorn you?"

The boys nodded.

Though I prodded Godey's ribs, he ignored me. He told the twins, "The quicker the medicine the better the cure," and he made short work of it. Without more ado he clapped a hand on each of their heads, drew them wide apart, and bumped them together. The brakes began to screech and Old Liz to fill the bus with her groans. The twins sat blinking. Dee Buck halted in the middle of the roa and commanded: "All right, you scamps, pile off."

We didn't stir.

"You're not deaf. Trot."

"Deef in one ear, and can't hear out of the other'n," Godey jeste

Dee Buck slapped his knee with his cap. "I said Go."

Old Liz was in a fidget. "Shut of them," she rasped, her ar a-jiggle, her fingers dancing. "See that they walk. Make 'em foot

"Old Liz," Godey chided, "if you don't check yourself you'r able to fly to pieces."

"Rid the rascals," she shrilled to Dee Buck. "Are ye afraid? ye man enough?"

Godey scoffed, "He'll huff and he'll puff — all he ever does might as well feed the hound a sup of gas and travel."

Dee Buck blustered, "I've got a bait of you fellers. I'm off you a chance to leave of your own free will."

Mal took my part, rebuking him, "No use to injure people."

"I don't give knocks I can't take myself," Godey said; and he invited, "Pay me double. Hit me a rabbit lick, I don't care. Make me see lightning." He leaned forward and bared his neck.

I wiped the shameful tears, thinking to join no more in Godey's game.

"Whap him and even up," Mal said. "We're nearly to the bottom of the mountain."

"Level up with me," said Godey, "or you're no crony of mine. You'll not run with my bunch."

I shook my head.

"Hurry," said Mal. "I see town smoking."

I wouldn't.

Mal advised Godey, "Nettle him. Speak a thing he can't let pass. Make him mad."

Godey said, "Know what I'm in the opinion of? Hadn't it been for Mal and me you'd let Dee Buck bounce you off the bus and never lifted a finger. You'd have turned chicken."

"I'd not," I gulped.

"Jolt him," Mal urged. "What I'd do."

"You're a chicken leg," Godey said, "and everybody akin to you is a chicken leg, and if you're yellow enough to take that I'll call you 'Chicken Leg' hereinafter."

I couldn't get around Godey. Smite him I must, and I gripped a fist and struck as hard as I could at close quarters, mauling his chest.

"Is that your best?" he belittled. "Anyhow, didn't I call for a rabbit lick? Throw one and let me feel it; throw one, else you know your name." Again he leaned and exposed his neck.

"He's begging," Mal incited.

I'd satisfy him, I resolved, and I half rose to get elbowroom. I swung mightily, my fist striking the base of his skull. I made his head pitch upward and thump the seat board; I made his teeth grate. "That ought to do," I blurted.

Godey walled his eyes and clenched his jaws. He began to gasp and strain and flounder. His arms lifted, clawing the air. Tight as we were wedged the seat would hardly hold him. Mal was ready to back up a sham and he chortled, "Look, you people, if you want to see a feller perish." But none bothered to glance.

Then Mal and me noticed the odd twist of Godey's neck. We

saw his lips tingle, his ears turn tallow. His tongue waggled to speak and could not. And of a sudden we knew and we sat frozen. We sat like posts while he heaved and pitched and his soles rattled the floor and his knees banged the forward seat. He bucked like a spoiled nag. . . . He quieted presently. His arms fell, his hands crumpled. He slumped and his gullet rattled.

We rode on. The mountain fell aside and the curves straightened. The highway ran a beeline. We crossed the last bridge and drew into Roscoe, halting in the square. Dee Buck stood at the door while the passengers alighted, and all hastened except Old Liz and us. Old Liz ordered over her shoulder, "Go on ahead. I'll not trust a set o' jaspers coming behind me." We didn't move. She whirled and her eyes lit on Godey. She sputtered, "What's the matter with him?"

Mal opened his mouth numbly. "He's doing no good," he said.

All of the previous selections in this section were fiction. The authors could contrive the fates of their characters as they wished. This last selection, however, is a true story of how a single event changed the lives of two men.

The Real Message to Garciá

STEWART HOLBROOK

The forgotten hero of the Spanish-American War was Lieutenant Andrew Summers Rowan. Nearer the truth, perhaps, would be to say that Rowan is not only forgotten but was never known. He was the man who took the famous message to García,[1] and for obvious reasons any mention of García must bring up the name of Elbert Hubbard, the odd genius who immortalized the name of García, yet did nothing for the man who took that gentleman the celebrated Message.

Hubbard was the long-haired editor of *The Philistine*, a monthly magazine written wholly by himself in which he commented on life, literature and the arts. In February of 1899 Hubbard needed a piece to fill the March number of his magazine. He had just been reading an item which told, now that the war was over, how one Lieutenant Rowan had carried a message from Washington, D.C., to Cuban insurgents, just before the start of the war. Inspired, Hubbard sat down and within the hour had dashed off *A Message to García*. Hubbard was a facile writer, and one of the most inaccurate ever in practice, and in this instance he had President McKinley calling Lieutenant Rowan secretly to the White House, where he gave him a letter "sealed in an oilskin pouch" which Rowan "strapped over his heart." This letter was to be delivered to General García, the insurgent leader, who was "somewhere in the mountain fastnesses of

---
[1] *García* (gär·sē′ä).

727

Cuba," and a reply brought back as quickly as possible.

Characteristically, Hubbard got nearly all of the facts wrong; but it mattered little, anyway, for after a couple of paragraphs devoted to getting the Message delivered, the author dropped the matter entirely and went into an attack on slipshod office workers. The rest of the article was merely a preachment to careless employees, anybody's employees, admonishing them to snap out of it, to be alive, to work for the good of their employer, to take pride in their work and duties, no matter how lowly.

The "Message" was exactly what thousands of American employers had been waiting for. The March *Philistine* was a sudden sellout, and orders for reprints started to roll in, one for 100,000 copies from the New York Central Railroad, which distributed them to employees, then ordered half a million more copies. Industrial concerns, department stores, churches, schools, lodges, all kinds of societies except labor unions took up the demand. Hubbard's Roycrofter Press had to work nights to supply more "Messages." A decade after its appearance, John Wanamaker's stores asked for 200,000 copies, and in World War I millions more reprints were called for by do-good groups of various kinds, who inflicted them on soldiers, sailors, munitions workers, and school children. Not even the Roycrofters have been able to estimate with much accuracy the number of "Messages" that have been printed and distributed, but the total is thought to have reached at least 100,000,000 copies.

The booklet went abroad. The Russian railroads had the work translated and printed and a copy given to each employee. During the Russo-Japanese War, Japanese officers found copies of the "Message" on so many Russian prisoners that they thought it must be pretty important. So, typically enough, the Japanese translated it and had it printed for every employee of the government. It is said to have been printed in at least twenty languages.

Well, Lieutenant Rowan's name did appear once or twice early in the story, but Rowan was not the reason for the pamphlet; he was merely an allusion, vague, ghostly, a mere symbol for the "Message." García was no more than a bewhiskered foreigner in a Cuban jungle. Hubbard was a business man. The "Message" was for businessmen — and their employees. Few who read the "Message" could remember, an hour later, even the name of the courageous soldier who braved the jungle in an enemy land.

Andrew Summers Rowan was born in 1857, in Virginia. He was graduated from West Point twenty years later, then assigned to the Fifteenth and later to the Ninth Infantry. For some reason or other, he took an interest in Cuba and, although he never went there, wrote a book about the country. This book was probably the reason he was summoned by his chief, Colonel Arthur Wagner, twelve days before war was declared on Spain. It is questionable that President McKinley ever heard of Rowan until later. Wagner gave Rowan no "sealed oilskin pouch." He did not even give Rowan a letter. Orally he ordered the young officer to find General García in the Cuban interior, learn how many troops he had, observe their morale and equipment, discuss with García what plan of action he might have for cooperation with American troops. Rowan was also to learn, if possible, the number of Spanish forces on the island.

Rowan's mission was going to be just as perilous as Hubbard made it appear. Dressed in civilian clothes, he sailed to Jamaica and got in touch, secretly, with Cuban insurgents there. They put him in a closed carriage and drove him seventy miles to a remote spot on the coast, where the driver, also a sailor of sorts, uncovered a small boat. Into it went Rowan, the sailor-driver, and an interpreter. Cuba was better than a hundred miles distant, but the little craft made it in thirty-six hours, although not without a bad moment. The craft was hailed by a Spanish patrol boat, but Sabio — the cabby-sailor — made out that he was a lone fisherman having very bad luck. He was allowed to sail on.

On the day the United States declared war on Spain, the party landed in Oriente Bay, in Cuba. Here Rowan was met by Cubans who, mysteriously enough so far as Rowan could learn, knew of his coming. For the next six days they guided the American through the jungle. When food ran out the first two or three times, the guides would presently stop, look around a bit, concentrate on a spot, then dig up a fresh supply of edibles that obviously had been cached for this occasion. But finally the caches seemed to have petered out, and the rest of the journey was accomplished pretty much on a fare of sweet potatoes. "I thought of Marion [2] and his men in the American Revolution," Rowan said later in telling the story of

---

[2] *Marion:* Francis Marion (1732–1795), American Revolutionary general, called the Swamp Fox.

the trip. "They had fought their battles on a like diet, and through my mind flashed the idea that as Marion and his men had fought to victory, so also would these Cubans."

It was a rather frightful trip for Rowan. The heat was intense and damp. Bugs of all sorts were biting. One day the party fell in with several men who said they were Spanish deserters, and Rowan asked that they be carefully guarded. One, attempting to escape, was shot and killed. Another tried to get at Rowan with a long knife. He was decapitated by one of the Cubans.

On May 1 the tired party reached General García, who was found besieging the village of Bayamo. There ensued the business of scrutinizing Rowan's credentials, and he discovered that he had been described in a letter written by a Cuban not as a man of confidence but as a confidence man.[3] But García accepted the phrase as it was meant and not as it sounded to the amused Rowan. They discussed matters, and the Cuban told the American that he needed artillery and muskets and ammuntion for both. After a conference lasting most of one day, Rowan was guided to the north coast of Cuba, a five-day trip even worse than the trip in, and Rowan and party got into a tiny boat having gunnysack sails. Two days later they landed on Nassau in the Bahamas; and after telling monumental lies to the British authorities there, Rowan was permitted to sail to the United States.

On May 13, exactly one month from the day he left, Lieutenant Rowan reported back to Colonel Wagner in Washington. His courage, resourcefulness, and all-round ability gave him a captain's bars at once. But there was no public to-do, no heroism party, for the affair was kept secret till the war's end. Then, with authentic heroes already enshrined and immortal with the public, and with the excitement of war evaporated, there was no interest shown in Rowan or his brave achievement by the American public.

Nor did Hubbard's booklet create any interest in the man. He remained to his dying day a mere name in a pamphlet.

Rowan went on to serve with distinction in the Philippine Insurrection, and was cited for gallantry in the attack on Sudlón Mountain. He continued in the army until 1909, when he resigned on account of ill health. He was retired with the rank of major, and spent

---

[3] *confidence man:* a man who defrauds his victim after winning his confidence.

much of the remainder of his life in California. Only one flurry marked the obscurity of his retirement. That was in 1922, when, through the offices of Senator Samuel Shortridge of California, he was awarded the Distinguished Service Cross. A movie company, at last catching up on history, at once approached the old soldier with a demand that he appear in a film based on his exploit in Cuba, but when he learned that pretty Cuban girl dancers would be a feature of the drama, he declined savagely. Hollywood went ahead anyhow, and made a film about *A Message to Garcia*, in which the actor playing Rowan falls in love, and you may be certain, with a lush Cuban beauty. Rowan indignantly refused to see the movie.

The man who actually took the message to Garcia lived to be almost eighty-six years of age. He died January 11, 1943, in San Francisco, but not before he had let go one historic line. It was at a dinner. One of the gushing type of females was sitting next to the old soldier, and she brightly spoke up to ask him: "Colonel, what *was* this message to Garcia, anyway?" Said the gallant colonel: "It was, madam, an invitation from President McKinley to an old-fashioned New England boiled dinner at the White House."

As for General Garcia, he did not pan out very well. Most military students of the war appear to believe that it would have been much better had no message reached him. After the naval engagement of Santiago, Garcia's insurgents amused themselves by shooting at Spanish sailors who were clinging to the ghastly wreckage for their lives. Garcia refused to put a stop to the butchery until General Shafter sent word that if the amusement was not stopped at once, he would open up with his artillery on Garcia's camp.

Garcia gave little aid to the Americans. He also allowed some two thousand Spanish troops to march through his lines and join the defenders of Santiago city. General Garcia died while on an official visit to Washington in 1899, and, seemingly oddly enough, was buried with military honors in Arlington cemetery.

Hubbard, the man who made the "Message" famous and received an estimated $250,000 in royalties for his trouble, went down on the *Lusitania*, May 7, 1915.

A Japanese poet, from a scroll
painted about A.D. 1250.

BOOK FOUR | PART 4

THE POET'S SEARCH FOR VALUES

His people had once been great makers of songs, so that everything they saw or thought or did or heard became a song.

THE PEARL

Earlier sections of this book contained narrative poems ("The Storyteller") and poems which mainly attempt to convey sense impressions ("Sights and Sounds"). In addition to being a storyteller and a recorder of sights and sounds, a poet is also a thinker, a person who asks basic questions about man's place in the universe. The poet examines man's values and probes his motives; he is always a questioner. Sometimes, as the poet Walt Whitman pointed out, he is also "the answerer."

There is no major difference in the poet's method whether he is telling a story, appealing to our senses, or considering human values. The difference in the three types of poems is one of emphasis. In a sense, every poem tells a story, presents images, and comments on human behavior.

A good poet uses words efficiently. He selects and organizes his words for their sound and for their picture-producing power. He does not always make his point directly; he may adopt an ironic view. Metaphor and words that carry more than one meaning are among his favorite tools. Like any artist, he wants to make his work interesting and beautiful. He wants to find for it a shape and form that will give it a "life" of its own.

Carl Sandburg once said that a book of verse is not like an arithmetic book; there are no answers in the back. Poetry is an art of suggestiveness and of compression. This can sometimes cause problems for the reader. To deal with the compressed language of poetry, you must pay attention to each word. You must be willing to read and re-read. You must be aware, as one critic has put it, that "you haven't read the first line of a poem until you've read the last." You must be prepared to analyze, to make connections. To express the idea of a poem in your own words is often helpful.

But — and this is important — you must remember that your analysis and paraphrasing are not the poem. The poem itself is the poet's words, and the pattern he has given them. So, after taking a poem apart to look at it, you have to put it back together again. This is another way of saying that the question "What does a poem mean" is not so important as the question "What experience does the poem provide"? For, as the poet Archibald MacLeish has said:

> A poem should not mean
> But be.

The poems in this section have been organized into six groups. Within each group you will find poems with a variety of shapes and patterns, but all on one particular topic. These topics are: Life and Death, Man and Nature, Youth and Age, Success and Failure, Faith and Courage. These have been concerns of all men in all ages and cultures. One of the aims of this book is to show that literature is meaningful only if it is about things which are important to us all. These poems should give you much to think about and help you to see yourself more clearly. Thus "The Poet's Search for Values" becomes "The Reader's Search for Values," too.

Finally, the emphasis in the title should be on the word *search*. Literature deals with questions rather than with answers because the vital questions that men ask themselves in all ages are never answered once and for all.

Life and Death

These lines are from Richard II, *one of Shakespeare's plays about English history. The speaker is the King.*

The Hollow Crown
WILLIAM SHAKESPEARE

For God's sake, let us sit upon the ground
And tell sad stories of the death of kings —
How some have been deposed, some slain in war,
Some haunted by the ghosts they have deposed,
Some poisoned by their wives, some sleeping killed,
All murdered. For within the hollow crown
That rounds the mortal temples of a king
Keeps Death his Court, and there the antic sits,
Scoffing his state and grinning at his pomp,
Allowing him a breath, a little scene,
To monarchize, be feared, and kill with looks,
Infusing him with self and vain conceit,
As if this flesh which walls about our life
Were brass impregnable, and humored thus
Comes at the last and with a little pin
Bores through his castle wall, and farewell King!

Limited
CARL SANDBURG

I am riding on a limited express, one of the crack trains of the nation.
Hurtling across the prairie into blue haze and dark air go fifteen all-steel coaches holding a thousand people.
(All the coaches shall be scrap and rust and all the men and women laughing in the diners and sleepers shall pass to ashes.)
I ask a man in the smoker where he is going and he answers "Omaha."

The next poem comes from a book called archy and mehitabel. *Archy is a poet who has been reborn as a cockroach. He writes poems by jumping on the keys of a typewriter. To save his strength, he does not use capital letters or punctuation. In this poem, Archy tells about his meeting with a moth. But the poem is about much more than the meeting of a moth and a cockroach.*

the lesson of the moth

DON MARQUIS

i was talking to a moth
the other evening
he was trying to break into
an electric light bulb
and fry himself on the wires

why do you fellows
pull this stunt i asked him
because it is the conventional
things for moths or why
if that had been an uncovered
candle instead of an electric
light bulb you would
now be a small unsightly cinder
have you no sense

plenty of it he answered
but at times we get tired
of using it
we get bored with the routine
and crave beauty
and excitement
fire is beautiful
and we know that if we get
too close it will kill us
but what does that matter
it is better to be happy
for a moment

and be burned up with beauty
than to live a long time
and be bored all the while
so we wad all our life up
into one little roll
and then we shoot the roll
that is what life is for

it is better to be a part of beauty
for one instant and then cease to
exist than to exist forever
and never be a part of beauty
our attitude toward life
is come easy go easy
we are like human beings
used to be before they became
too civilized to enjoy themselves

and before i could argue him
out of his philosophy
he went and immolated himself
on a patent cigar lighter
i do not agree with him
myself i would rather have
half the happiness and twice
the longevity

but at the same time i wish
there was something i wanted
as badly as he wanted to fry himself
     archy

When an airplane travels at a speed greater than the speed of sound, the nose of the plane produces a shock wave in the air. When this shock wave reaches the ground it makes a noise like an explosion. Many citizens find this sound objectionable. A large manufacturer of high-speed planes, however, simply calls the noise "a twentieth-century sound."

Sonic boom, however, is more than annoying; it sometimes does damage. A recent news article stated that "Sonic booms from military planes in the past have collapsed the roof of a French farmhouse, killing three workers; demolished a prehistoric cliff dwelling in northwestern Arizona; and fouled up the dedication of the Ottawa Air Terminal, with $300,000 in damages."

Sonic Boom

JOHN UPDIKE

I'm sitting in the living room,
When, up above, the Thump of Doom
Resounds. Relax. It's sonic boom.

The ceiling shudders at the clap,
The mirrors tilt, the rafters snap,
And Baby wakens from his nap.

"Hush, babe. Some pilot we equip,
Giving the speed of sound the slip,
Has cracked the air like a penny whip."

Our world is far from frightening; I
No longer strain to read the sky
Where moving fingers (jet planes) fly.
Our world seems much too tame to die.

And if it does, with one more *pop*,
I shan't look up to see it drop.

Man and Nature

The next group of poems examines the relationship of man to the natural world. To what extent is man a part of the world of nature? What can man gain by opening his senses to the beauty of nature? Why are men sometimes blind and indifferent to what lies around them?

Loveliest of Trees

A. E. HOUSMAN

Loveliest of trees, the cherry now
Is hung with bloom along the bough,
And stands about the woodland ride
Wearing white for Eastertide.

Now, of my threescore years and ten,
Twenty will not come again,
And take from seventy springs a score,
It only leaves me fifty more.

And since to look at things in bloom
Fifty springs are little room,
About the woodlands I will go
To see the cherry hung with snow.

When I Heard the Learn'd Astronomer

WALT WHITMAN

When I heard the learn'd astronomer,
When the proofs, the figures, were ranged in columns before me,
When I was shown the charts and diagrams, to add, divide, and measure them,
When I, sitting, heard the astronomer where he lectured with much applause in the lecture room,
How soon unaccountable I became tired and sick,
Till rising and gliding out I wandered off by myself,
In the mystical moist night air, and from time to time,
Looked up in perfect silence at the stars.

Spring

EDNA ST. VINCENT MILLAY

To what purpose, April, do you return again?
Beauty is not enough.
You can no longer quiet me with the redness
Of little leaves opening stickily.
I know what I know.
The sun is hot on my neck as I observe
The spikes of the crocus.
The smell of the earth is good.
It is apparent that there is no death.
But what does that signify?
Not only under ground are the brains of men
Eaten by maggots.
Life in itself
Is nothing,
An empty cup, a flight of uncarpeted stairs.
It is not enough that yearly, down this hill,
April
Comes like an idiot, babbling and strewing flowers.

Eight-Cylinder Man
FLORENCE RIPLEY MASTIN

He grinds the clover at its root
with a creaking and enormous foot.
In his circumference vast and dim
no small life has a place for him.
The needlepoint of curious moss
where delicate footprints cross,
the brook composing mountain blues,
the bereaved and cynical yews,
columbines dancing on a wall —
these he has never seen at all.

Speed is the only register
within his mind, and in that blur
of gas and gleaming chromium
he adds the swiftly mounting sum
of miles, a purely abstract space,
and passes summer face to face.

At the Aquarium
MAX EASTMAN

Serene the silver fishes glide,
Stern-lipped, and pale, and wonder-eyed!
As, through the aged deeps of ocean,
They have no pathway where they go,
They flow like water to and fro,
They watch with never winking eyes,
They watch with staring, cold surprise,
The level people in the air,
The people peering, peering there:
Who wander also to and fro.
And know not why or where they go,
Yet have a wonder in their eyes,
Sometimes a pale and cold surprise.

Youth and Age

In the section on "Life and Death" you saw how a serious subject can be treated lightly. This light tone is characteristic of several of the following poems about youth and age and the differences between them.

Those Winter Sundays

ROBERT HAYDEN

Sundays too my father got up early
and put his clothes on in the blueblack cold,
then with cracked hands that ached
from labor in the weekday weather made
banked fires blaze. No one ever thanked him.

I'd wake and hear the cold splintering, breaking.
When the rooms were warm, he'd call,
and slowly I would rise and dress,
fearing the chronic angers of that house,

Speaking indifferently to him,
who had driven out the cold
and polished my good shoes as well.
What did I know, what did I know
of love's austere and lonely offices?

old age sticks

E. E. CUMMINGS

old age sticks
up Keep
Off
signs)&

youth yanks them
down(old
age
cries No

Tres)&(pas)
youth laughs
(sing
old age

scolds Forbid
den Stop
Must
n't Don't

&)youth goes
right on
gr
owing old

This speech from Shakespeare's play As You Like It *is delivered by a character named Jaques. In the context of the play Jaques enjoys his melancholy in such a self-conscious way that he appears comic.*

The Seven Ages of Man

WILLIAM SHAKESPEARE

           All the world's a stage,
And all the men and women merely players.
They have their exits and their entrances,
And one man in his time plays many parts,
His acts being seven ages. At first the infant,
Mewling and puking in the nurse's arms.
Then the whining schoolboy, with his satchel
And shining morning face, creeping like snail
Unwillingly to school. And then the lover,
Sighing like furnace, with a woeful ballad   10
Made to his mistress' eyebrow. Then a soldier,
Full of strange oaths and bearded like the pard,°
Jealous in honor, sudden and quick in quarrel,
Seeking the bubble reputation
Even in the cannon's mouth. And then the justice,
In fair round belly with good capon lined,
With eyes severe and beard of formal cut,
Full of wise saws and modern instances.
And so he plays his part. The sixth age shifts
Into the lean and slippered Pantaloon°   20
With spectacles on nose and pouch on side,
His youthful hose, well saved, a world too wide
For his shrunk shank and his big manly voice,
Turning again toward childish treble, pipes
And whistles in his sound. Last scene of all,
That ends this strange eventful history,
Is second childishness and mere oblivion,
Sans° teeth, sans eyes, sans taste, sans everything.

---

12. *pard:* leopard.
20. *Pantaloon:* a foolish old man (from Italian comedy).
28. *sans:* without

A *parody is a piece of writing that makes fun of another writer's work by imitating it. Often, as in the following poem, the parody applies the style of a famous passage in literature to a subject which is light or trivial. The inspiration for the following parody, of course, is the well-known speech that you have just read from Shakespeare's As You Like It.*

The Seven Ages of a Newspaper Subscriber

PHYLLIS MCGINLEY

From infancy, from childhood's earliest caper,
He loved the daily paper.

Propped on his grubby elbows, lying prone,
He took, at first, the Comics for his own.
Then, as he altered stature and his voice,
Sports were his single choice.

For a brief time, at twenty, Thought became
A desultory flame.
So with a critic eye he would peruse
The better Book Reviews.   10

Behold the bridegroom, then — the dazzled suitor
Turned grim commuter,
Learning without direction
To fold his paper to the Housing Section.

Forty enlarged his waistline with his wage.
The Business Page
Engrossed his mind. He liked to ponder well
The charted rise of Steel or Tel & Tel.

Choleric, pompous, and too often vext,
The fifties claimed him next.   20
The Editorials, then, were what he scanned.
(Even, at times, he took his pen in hand.)

But witness how the human viewpoint varies:
Of late he reads the day's Obituaries.

Success and Failure

One of man's traits is his drive for success. But what is success? Who is to measure a man's success or failure? Can a man appear to be a success and yet be a failure? Can he appear to be a failure and in fact be a success? As you read, weigh the ideas of success in the poems against your own.

Ozymandias

PERCY BYSSHE SHELLEY

I met a traveler from an antique land
Who said: "Two vast and trunkless legs of stone
Stand in the desert. . . . Near them, on the sand,
Half sunk, a shattered visage lies, whose frown,
And wrinkled lip, and sneer of cold command
Tell that its sculptor well those passions read
Which yet survive, stamped on these lifeless things,
The hand that mocked them, and the heart that fed;
And on the pedestal these words appear;
'My name is Ozymandias, king of kings;
Look on my works, ye Mighty, and despair!'
Nothing beside remains. 'Round the decay
Of that colossal wreck, boundless and bare
The lone and level sands stretch far away."

Homage

KENNETH FEARING

They said to him, "It is a very good thing that you have done, yes, both good and great, proving this other passage to the Indies. Marvelous," they said. "Very. But where, Señor, is the gold?"

They said: "We like it, we admire it very much, don't misunderstand us, in fact we think it's almost great. But isn't there, well, a little too much of this Prince of Denmark? After all, there is no one quite like you in your lighter vein."

"Astonishing," they said. "Who would have thought you had it in you, Orville?" They said, "Wilbur, this machine of yours is amazing, if it works, and perhaps some day we can use it to distribute eggs, or to advertise."

And they were good people, too. Decent people.
They did not beat their wives. They went to church. And they kept the law.

A Caution to Everybody

OGDEN NASH

Consider the auk;
Becoming extinct because he forgot how to fly, and could only walk.
Consider man, who may well become extinct
Because he forgot how to walk and learned how to fly before he thinked.

Richard Cory

EDWIN ARLINGTON ROBINSON

Whenever Richard Corey went down town,
   We people on the pavement looked at him:
He was a gentleman from sole to crown,
   Clean favored, and imperially slim.

And he was always quietly arrayed,
   And he was always human when he talked;
But still he fluttered pulses when he said,
   "Good morning," and he glittered when he walked.

And he was rich — yes, richer than a king,
   And admirably schooled in every grace:
In fine, we thought that he was everything
   To make us wish that we were in his place.

So on we worked, and waited, for the light,
   And went without the meat, and cursed the bread;
And Richard Cory, one calm summer night,
   Went home and put a bullet through his head.

Song

M. CARL HOLMAN

Dressed up in my melancholy
With no place to go,
Sick as sin of inwardness
And sick of being so

I walked out on the avenue,
Eager to give my hand
To any with the health to heal
Or heart to understand.

I had not walked a city block
And met with more than ten
Before I read the testament
Stark behind each grin:

Beneath the hat brims haunting me,
More faithful than a mirror,
The figuration of my grief,
The image of my error.

Faith and Courage

Many poems assert man's need to live by more than "bread alone," to believe in something larger than himself, in order to sustain his spirit and give his life meaning and purpose.

The Courage That My Mother Had

EDNA ST. VINCENT MILLAY

The courage that my mother had
Went with her, and is with her still:
Rock from New England quarried;
Now granite in a granite hill.

The golden brooch my mother wore
She left behind for me to wear;
I have no thing I treasure more:
Yet, it is something I could spare.

Oh, if instead she'd left to me
The thing she took into the grave! —
That courage like a rock, which she
Has no more need of, and I have.

This poem suggests that we often look down upon those who have the courage to be different — and even call them names.

The Crazy Woman

GWENDOLYN BROOKS

I shall not sing a May song.
A May song should be gay.
I'll wait until November
And sing a song of gray.

I'll wait until November.
That is the time for me.
I'll go out in the frosty dark
And sing most terribly.

And all the little people
Will stare at me and say,
"That is the Crazy Woman
Who would not sing in May."

I Never Saw a Moor

EMILY DICKINSON

I never saw a moor,
I never saw the sea;
Yet know I how the heather looks,
And what a wave must be.

I never spoke with God,
Nor visited in heaven;
Yet certain am I of the spot
As if the chart were given.

Index

Abraham Lincoln, 445
 Lincoln Preface, A, 448
 from *The Prairie Years*, 452
 from *The War Years*, 499
Act One, 544
Adventure of the Norwood Builder,
 The, 185
Aesop, 689
African Folk Tales, 690
All Day I Hear, 428
Alsop, Stewart, 339
Any Man's Advice to His Son, 163
Appointment in Samarra, 699
Asimov, Isaac, 107
At the Aquarium, 741

Ballad of Blasphemous Bill, The, 222
Barrett, William E., 557
Beachcroft, T. O., 144
Bible, The, 351
Björnson, Björnsterne, 352
Bourke-White, Margaret, 524
Bradbury, Ray, 178
Break, Break, Break, 428
Brooks, Gwendolyn, 751
Brown, Claude, 161
Buck, Pearl S., 319

Carroll, Lewis, 414
Cask of Amontillado, The, 171
Caution to Everybody, A, 747
Chekhov, Anton, 363
Christmas, 157
Coffin, Robert P. Tristram, 433
Conan Doyle, Sir Arthur, 185
Coolidge, Olivia, 89
Courage That My Mother Had, The,
 750
Crazy Woman, The, 751
Crystal Moment, 433
Cummings, E. E., 743

Dark Hills, The, 435
De la Mare, Walter, 438
Dell, Floyd, 157
Dickinson, Emily, 751
Dog in the Manger, The, 689
Dunkirk, 618

Early Marriage, 127
Eastman, Max, 741

Eight-Cylinder Man, 741
Enemy, The, 319
Enemy Territory, 610
Erne from the Coast, The, 144
Everything Has a Name, 418

Father, A, 352
Father Sees a Son Nearing Manhood,
 A, 164
Fearing, Kenneth, 163, 437, 747
Frost, Robert, 220, 436

Gibson, William, 227
Glaspell, Susan, 705
Good Samaritan, The, 351
Goodbye Speech, A, 161
Graves, Robert, 75

Haiku, 440–442
Hale, Nancy, 605
Hart, Moss, 544
Hayden, Robert, 742
Henderson, Harold G., 440
Hersey, John, 511
Highwayman, The, 216
Holbrook, Stewart, 721
Hollow Crown, The, 735
Holman, M. Carl, 749
Homage, 747
Homer, 1
Housman, A. E., 739
How Much Is True?, 101
How the Animals Got Their Color,
 690
How the Animals Got Their Tails, 690
Hughes, Langston, 356, 438
Humpty Dumpty on the Meaning of
 Words, 414

I Never Saw a Moor, 751

Joyce, James, 428
Juke Box Love Song, 438

Kelley, William Melvin, 610
King Juke, 437
Kingsley, Charles, 91

La Fontaine, Jean de, 691
Land of Our Enemies, 208
Landscape as Metal and Flowers, 435

INDEX

Lapp, Ralph E., 339
Laye, Camara, 115
Legend of the King and the Peasant, The, 692
Lesson of the Moth, The, 736
Lilies of the Field, The, 557
Limited, 735
Listeners, The, 438
Longfellow, Henry Wadsworth, 429
Loveliest of Trees, 739

Macpherson, Jay, 82
Macy, Anne Sullivan, 418
Man Who Liked Dickens, The, 375
Marquis, Don, 736
Marriage Proposal, The, 363
Mastin, Florence Ripley, 741
Maugham, W. Somerset, 699
McGinley, Phyllis, 745
McKay, Claude, 434
Mice and the Cat, The, 689
Millay, Edna St. Vincent, 740, 750
Miracle Worker, The, 227
Monster, The, 540
My Mysterious Malady, 524

Nash, Ogden, 747
Nathan Hale, 605
Nathan, Robert, 618
New Moon, 431
Night of Kondén Diara, The, 115
Noyes, Alfred, 216

Odyssey, The, 1
O'Flaherty, Liam, 701
old age sticks, 743
Old Cat and the Young Mouse, The, 691
Orpheus and Eurydice, 85
"Out, Out—," 220
Ozymandias, 746

Palace of Olympus, The, 75
Pearl, The, 623
Phaëthon, 82
Poe, Edgar Allan, 171
Puerto Rican Paradise, 550
Pygmalion and Galatea, 89

Real Message to Garcia, The, 721
Renault, Mary, 101
Richard Cory, 748
Richter, Conrad, 127
Ride on the Short Dog, A, 719
Roberts, Paul, 406
Robinson, Edwin Arlington, 435, 748

Rogers, Frances, 397
Rouse, W. H. D., 85
Runaway, The, 436

Saadi, 692
Sandburg, Carl, 164, 432, 445, 735
Saroyan, William, 695
Scott, Winfield Townley, 435
Service, Robert W., 222
Seven Ages of a Newspaper Subscriber, The, 745
Seven Ages of Man, The, 744
Shakespeare, William, 735, 744
Shelley, Percy Bysshe, 746
Shepherd's Daughter, The, 695
Slang and Its Relatives, 406
Sniper, The, 701
Song, 749
Sonic Boom, 738
Spring, 740
Steinbeck, John, 623
Still, James, 719
Strange Death of Louis Slotin, The, 339
Stuart, Jesse, 208
Survival, 511
Swenson, May, 431

Tallman, Robert, 375
Taylor, Deems, 540
Tennyson, Alfred, Lord, 428
Thank You, M'am, 356
There Will Come Soft Rains, 178
Theseus, 91
Thomas, Piri, 550
Those Winter Sundays, 742
Three Jet Planes, 431
Thurber, James, 693
Tide Rises, The Tide Falls, The, 429
Tiger Who Would Be King, The, 693
Tornado Threat, 430
Trifles, 705
Tropics in New York, The, 434
Tu Fu, 431

Updike, John, 738

Wassam, Roqua, 430
Waugh, Evelyn, 375
When I Heard the Learn'd Astronomer, 740
Whitman, Walt, 740
Wind Song, 432
Words Began with Pictures, 397
Words from the Myths, 107
Wright, Richard, 442